South Asia and Africa After Independence
Bernard Waites

Post-colonial South Asia and Africa invite comparison: along with their political boundaries, they inherited from colonial regimes administrative languages, a cluster of sovereign state institutions and modern economic nuclei. When they became independent, South Asian and African states were – for all their diversity – thrust into a common position in the international system, and embarked on a common history as 'emergent', 'non-aligned', 'developing' nations. This is the first book to offer a single-volume comparative history of post-colonial South Asia and sub-Saharan Africa in the first generation since independence.

South Asia and Africa After Independence draws together the political and economic history of these two regions, assessing the colonial impact, establishing breaks and continuities, and highlighting their diversity and interplay. Bernard Waites sets out a framework for analysing the first generation of post-colonial history, offering an interpretation of 'postcolonialism' as a historical phenomenon, and provocatively challenging us to re-think this term in relation to South Asian and African history. This book is an important reference for the study of global, world, African and South Asian history.

Bernard Waites is Visiting Senior Research Fellow at The Open University, UK. His publications include *A Class Society at War* and *Europe and the Third World* (also published by Palgrave Macmillan, 1999).

South Asia and Africa After Independence
Post-colonialism in Historical Perspective

Bernard Waites

First published 2012 by
PALGRAVE MACMILLAN

Palgrave Macmillan in the UK is an imprint of Macmillan Publishers Limited, registered in England, company number 785998, of Houndmills, Basingstoke, Hampshire RG21 6XS.

Palgrave Macmillan in the US is a division of St Martin's Press LLC, 175 Fifth Avenue, New York, NY 10010.

Palgrave Macmillan is the global academic imprint of the above companies and has companies and representatives throughout the world.

Palgrave® and Macmillan® are registered trademarks in the United States, the United Kingdom, Europe and other countries.

ISBN 978–0–230–23983–8   hardback
ISBN 978–0–230–23984–5   paperback

This book is printed on paper suitable for recycling and made from fully managed and sustained forest sources. Logging, pulping and manufacturing processes are expected to conform to the environmental regulations of the country of origin.

A catalogue record for this book is available from the British Library.

A catalog record for this book is available from the Library of Congress.

10 9 8 7 6 5 4 3 2 1
21 20 19 18 17 16 15 14 13 12

Printed in China

Contents

Acknowledgements   viii

List of Tables   ix

List of Maps   x

Abbreviations   xi

Introduction: Post-colonialism in Historical Perspective   1
Post-colonialism as history   1
'Postcolonialism' in theory   6
Postcolonial South Asia and Africa: a thumb-nail sketch   9
Modern colonialism   17
Post-colonialism   29
The post-colonial phase in outline   35

1 Post-colonial Trajectories in South Asia   42
Introduction   42
The trauma of partition and the fragility of Pakistan   43
The Kashmir conflict   47
Constructing Pakistan's political economy of defence   50
The economics of partition   52
Institutional continuities and discontinuities: India   54
Telangana: aborted agrarian revolution   59
The electoral bases of the Congress Raj   62
The Congress 'system' under Mrs Gandhi   65
Pakistan: the failure to establish democracy   71
Containing the Bengali autonomy movement: the dual
   crisis of 1954   72
Shutting down Pakistan's democracy   74
Congress and the linguistic reorganisation of the Indian states   78
The Ayub Khan regime: October 1958 to March 1969   83
The fall of the Ayub Khan regime   91
Things fall apart: the break-away of Bangladesh   93
Conclusions   98
Epilogue: the parallel elections of March 1977   101

2 **Democracy, Economic Planning and Economic Stagnation in India: 1947–c. 1975**   105
   Introduction: economic planning and post-colonial
      consciousness   105
   The origins and implementation of economic planning   107
   Realising 'a socialistic picture of society'   113
   The crisis of 1965–6 and the planning hiatus   119
   From radical turn to social crisis: 1969–74   121
   The Emergency of 1975   126
   The achievements and shortcomings of Nehruvian socialism   128
   Poverty and the land   134
   Conclusions   142

3 **Caste in Post-colonial India**   145
   Introduction: constitutional secularism and the ritual
      hierarchy   145
   The *jatis* in Indian villages   154
   Caste and political mobilisation in the Congress system   156
   'Non-Brahminism', Dravidian ideology and Dalit
      assertiveness in Tamil Nadu   162
   Bihar: the origins of the 'caste wars'   167
   'Mandalisation' and after   174

4 **Politics and Economics in Independent African States**   179
   Introduction   179
   Africa's five-phased trajectory since 1960   185
   Stagnant agriculture and the climacteric of the later 1970s   202
   De-regulating agriculture: winners and losers in the 1990s   208
   The business of politics and the patrimonial state   210
   Structural adjustment and after   216
   Conclusions: the end of post-colonialism in Africa   223

5 **Nigeria and Congo-Zaire, 1960–c. 1975: Decolonisation, Civil War and State Recovery**   226
   Introduction   226
   Contrasting colonial legacies   228
   The crisis of the first Congolese Republic   240
   The demand for a 'second independence'   247
   Mobutu's second coming   250
   Nigeria 1960–6: the crises of the First Republic and the road
      to civil war   255
   Conclusions   270

6 **Nigeria and Congo-Zaire from the 1970s to the Late 1990s:**
  Regional Giants, Giant Failures? 271
    African absolutism: Mobutu in his pomp 272
    Military rule and the Nigerian oil boom 276
    Indigenising the economy: Zairianisation and Nigerianisation
      compared 283
    The decay and persistence of the Mobutist state 289
    The Second Nigerian Republic and its aftermath (1979–85) 293
    Nigeria and Zaire in the 1980s and beyond: lame Leviathans? 303
    Zaire: attempted reform, hyperinflation and the
      dismemberment of the formal economy 304
    Structural adjustment and economic decline in Nigeria 307
    Heading off democracy in Zaire and Nigeria 309
    Conclusions 314
    Postscript 317

7 **Colonialism, Post-colonialism and Ethnic Violence: The**
  Examples of Rwanda and Burundi 321
    Introduction 321
    Rwanda and Burundi; Hutu and Tutsi 323
    Burundi: the emergence of a Tutsi dictatorship 333
    Rwanda: the first and second republics 339
    Convergent catastrophes: Burundi and Rwanda 1993–4 344
    Divergent paths to recuperating state and society in
      the 1990s 351
    Post-colonial Burundi and Rwanda in retrospect 355

8 **Angola and Mozambique** 359
    Introduction 359
    The colonial background and the wars of independence 361
    Acceding to power 368
    Nation-building in one-party Marxist states 372
    RENAMO and UNITA 377
    Towards the elections of 1992 and 1994, and after 385
    Angola and Mozambique in the 1990s 393

Summary and Conclusions 400

Bibliography 413

Index 439

Acknowledgements

This book was written while I was a member of the Open University (OU) History Department and I am grateful for the help, support and friendship my departmental colleagues gave me over many years. Working with the 'Empire' course team was a privilege and inspiration – they know who they are, so 'no names, no pack drill'! Dennis Walder, in the English Department, kindly read and commented on Chapter 1. The staff of the OU Library dealt with my innumerable inter-library requests with unfailing efficiency. My biggest debts are to the scholars on whose books and articles I have drawn in trying to compose analytic narratives of the post-colonial decades in South Asia and Africa. The mistakes are my own.

Many African and South Asian place names changed during the decades with which I deal. I have followed the convention of using the name current at the time about which I write: thus Léopoldville up to 1971, Kinshasa thereafter.

BERNARD WAITES

List of Tables

1.1 Annual percentage growth of GDP in India and Pakistan, 1950–70   86

1.2 Annual percentage growth in per capita GDP in Pakistan, 1960–73   87

1.3 Annual percentage growth in agriculture and manufacturing in Pakistan, 1960–73   88

2.1 Value added in manufacturing as a percentage of GDP in selected Asian states   133

2.2 Incidence of poverty in India: 1973–2000, percentage below the poverty line   136

5.1 Sectoral output as a share of Nigerian GDP, 1950–77   230

6.1 Per capita GDP in Nigeria and Congo-Zaire, 1970–2000   277

6.2 Life expectancy and infant mortality in Nigeria, Congo-Zaire and Bangladesh, 1960/5–2000/5   316

C.1 Selected economic and demographic data on South Asian and African states   411

List of Maps

I.1 South Asia in 1948   36
I.2 Africa, showing dates of independence   38
1.1 India after states reorganisation   81
5.1 Nigeria at independence   233
5.2 The Democratic Republic of the Congo at independence   239
5.3 Nigerian states, 1967–76   269

Abbreviations

Abako	Alliance des Bakongo
AERC	African Economic Research Consortium
AG	Action Group [Western Nigeria]
AIDMK	All India Anna Dravida Munnetra Kazagham [offshoot of the DMK, now dominant regional party in Tamil Nadu]
ANC	African National Congress
ANC	Armée Nationale Congolaise
CDR	Coalition pour la Défense de la République [Rwanda]
CFA	Communauté financière africaine
CFD	Congress for Democracy [India]
CFSA	Congress Forum for Socialist Action [India]
CNDD	Conseil national pour la défense de la démocratie [Burundi]
Conakat	Confédération des Associations Tribales de Katanga
CPI	Communist Party of India
CPM	Communist Party of India (Marxist)
CPP	Convention People's Party [Ghana]
CSK	Comité special du Katanga
DK	Dravida Kazagham (Dravidian Federation)
DMK	Dravida Munnetra Kazagham [Progressive Dravidian Federation]
DRC	Democratic Republic of the Congo
EEC	European Economic Community
FAOSTAT	Food and Agricultural Organisation of the United Nations Statistics
FDD	Forces pour la défense de la démocratie [Burundi]
FNLA	Front for the National Liberation of Angola
FRELIMO	Front for the Liberation of Mozambique
FRODEBU	Front Démocratique du Burundi
FROLINA	Front pour la libération nationale [Burundi]
FRUS	Foreign Relations of the United States
GATT	General Agreements on Tariffs and Trade
GDI	gross domestic investment
GDP	gross domestic product

GNPP	Great Nigeria People's Party
IAS	Indian Administrative Service
ICS	Indian Civil Service
IFFs	international financial institutions
IMF	International Monetary Fund
IRC	International Rescue Committee
MGR	M.G. Ramachandran [star of the Tamil film industry turned politician]
MLA	Member of Legislative Assembly [Indian States]
MNC	Mouvement National Congolais
MNC(L)	Mouvement National Congolais (Lumumba)
MNC(K)	Mouvement National Congolais (Kalonji)
MONUC	UN Mission in the Congo
MPLA	Popular Movement for the Liberation of Angola
MPR	Mouvement populaire de la révolution [Zaire]
MRND	Mouvement Révolutionnaire National pour le Développement [Rwanda]
NCNC	National Council of Nigeria and the Cameroons (after 1962 the National Council of Nigerian Citizens)
NEPU	Northern Elements Progressive Union [Northern Nigeria]
NGO	non-governmental organisation
NNDP	Nigerian National Democratic Party
NNPC	Nigerian National Petroleum Corporation
NPC	Northern People's Congress [Nigeria]
NPN	National Party of Nigeria
NPP	Nigerian People's Party
OAU	Organisation of African Unity
OBCs	Other Backward Classes [or sometimes 'Castes']
ODA	Overseas Development Assistance
OPEC	Organisation of Petroleum Exporting Countries
Palipehutu	Parti de la libération du peuple Hutu [Burundi]
PARMEHUTU	Parti du Mouvement de l'Emancipation Hutu [Rwanda]
PDC	Parti Démocratique Chrétien [Burundi]
PDR	Party for Democracy and Regeneration [Rwanda]
PML	Pakistan Muslim League
PNA	Pakistan National Alliance
PP	[British] Parliamentary Papers
PPP	Pakistan People's Party
PRP	People's Redemption Party [Nigeria]

PSA	Parti Solidaire Africain [DRC]
RENAMO	Mozambique National Resistance Movement
RPA	Rwandan Patriotic Army
RPF	Rwandan Patriotic Front
SADF	South African Defence Forces
SWAPO	South West Africa People's Organisation
TUC	Trades Union Congress
UDPS	Union pour la démocratie et le progrès social [Zaire]
UMHK	Union Minière du Haut Katanga
UNAVEM	United Nations Angola Verification Mission
UNITA	National Union for the Total Independence of Angola
UNR	Union Nationale du Rwanda
UPGA	United Progressive Grand Alliance [Nigeria]
UPN	Unity Party of Nigeria
UPRONA	Union pour le progrès national [Burundi]
ZANLA	Zimbabwean National Liberation Army
ZANU	Zimbabwe African National Union

Introduction: Post-colonialism in Historical Perspective

Post-colonialism as history

In 1945, roughly 30 per cent of humanity or over 700 million people lived under European colonial rule; 20 years later the only substantial colonial territories were Portuguese Africa and Rhodesia (now Zimbabwe) with a combined population of around 22 million – and their days were numbered. This great transformation reshaped the international order: in South Asia, which provides one geographic focus for this book, a sub-continental colonial empire was partitioned in 1947 into the sovereign states of India and Pakistan. In sub-Saharan Africa, my second geographic focus, individual colonies were reconstituted as sovereign states: seventeen became independent in 1960, and a further eight in 1961–4. (Henceforth, it will be referred to simply as 'Africa'.) Since power was transferred to politicians enjoying an electoral mandate, it was an extraordinary 'wave' of democratisation, though soon followed by a flurry of coups and constitutional revisions that installed one-party regimes or military governments. (Regrettably, South East Asia – the third great region of transformation – has been excluded from this study for want of space.) By transmitting the principle of territorial sovereignty into the contemporary world, the colonial experience left a lasting imprint, as is plainly evident from the political map of Africa where the correspondence between formerly colonial and now national territories is near perfect.

Two telling though not so obvious examples of this 'imprinting' are Bangladesh and Eritrea: Bangladesh's frontiers broadly correspond to the partition of East and West Bengal ordered for ostensibly administrative purposes by the Viceroy, Lord Curzon in 1905. The measure was vociferously denounced by nationalists as a 'divide and rule' tactic and rescinded in late 1911. If the ulterior purpose had been to alienate Hindus from Muslims (and vice versa), then it succeeded in ways Curzon could never have envisaged. In defiance of economic logic, and notwithstanding the common language and cultural heritage of all Bengalis, East Bengal became first the east 'wing' of Islamic Pakistan in 1947 and then the Bangladeshi nation-state when it seceded in 1971. As a framework for state cohesion, the (temporary) colonial administrative division has proved more effective and durable than either Bengali language and culture or Islam. The secession of Eritrea from Ethiopia in 1993 affords a striking instance of a colonial border being restored long after the Italian colony it demarcated disappeared from the map. Eritrea was federated with Ethiopia under United Nations auspices in 1951, and formally annexed in 1962, when it was incorporated into Haile Selassie's system of personal rule. The Eritrean nationalists who sought independence through armed struggle had no easy task convincing Eritreans they were a 'nation', for they are divided by ethnicity, language, religion and ways of living. As one scholar remarks, 'There was nothing which made Eritrea in any sense "natural", and as a political idea it arose out of Italian colonialism' (Nugent, 2004, p. 437). If – as seems virtually certain at the time of writing – Southern Sudan secedes, then it will be the first major breach of the principle adopted by the Organisation of African Unity in 1963 that Africa's inherited colonial borders are inviolable.

This book is not about decolonisation as such; rather it is a historical and comparative analysis of the first generation of independence in India and Pakistan and Africa. The secession of Bangladesh from Pakistan in 1971 (which occasioned a third war with India) and the state of emergency imposed by Mrs Gandhi in 1975–7 together formed a major caesura in South Asia's post-colonial history, and a vantage point from which one can look back to establish breaks and continuities with the colonial past, while picking out the political and economic forces shaping late twentieth-century South Asia. There is no such clear vantage point in Africa's post-colonial history but the onset of the sub-continental war in Central Africa, following the Rwandan genocide and the overthrow of the Mobutu regime in 1997, is a terminal point of sorts. These are not rigid chronological limits – which are as helpful to a historian as a straitjacket to a swimmer – and I often stray beyond them. My central concern is the interplay between economics and politics in these years, which can now be viewed as a reasonably well-defined post-colonial period. South Africa has been 'bracketed off' because it has been a post-colonial state from the formation of the Union in 1910, when the white minority was given a free hand by Britain to begin constructing a racially segregated state. It figures in this study primarily as a destructive external influence on independent Angola and Mozambique (Chapter 8). My endeavour has been to compose analytic narratives tracing the evolution of a selection of post-colonial states which do justice to their diversity, the unpredictability of events, human agency and the constraints on political and economic agency in South Asia and Africa. They were, very broadly, of two kinds: historical constraints arising from comparative economic 'backwardness' and a 'low' level of social development; and structural constraints arising from geography, factor endowments, natural resource wealth and resource penury, climate and disease ecology. ('Backwardness' and 'low' have pejorative undertones which I do not intend, and refer to measureable indices such as the prevalence of subsistence agriculture and high infant and maternal mortality.) Whether the historical constraints had been exacerbated or alleviated by colonialism is not a question which can be dogmatically answered one way or another; it is best addressed, in my view, by examining how South Asian and African political actors sought to overcome them. Structural constraints can be relaxed or tempered by human agency, but at a cost which only the state can incur. My treatment is inevitably selective, but the scope is, I trust, sufficiently wide to offer an interpretation of post-colonialism – as a historical phenomenon – 'in the round'.

Post-colonial South Asia and Africa invite comparison for obvious reasons: along with their political boundaries, they inherited from the colonial regimes administrative languages, a cluster of sovereign state institutions and modern economic nuclei. Their nationalist elites had an understanding of modern nationhood heavily influenced by the colonial experience and that of the European metropolitan power. Hence the distinctiveness (in Anglo-Saxon eyes!) of Francophone African nationalism: under the Fourth Republic's constitution adopted in late 1945, a two college franchise for 'Overseas France' meant that African subjects could vote in metropolitan elections – though their votes carried much less weight than those of full citizens – and this led to a dozen or so African deputies serving in the National Assembly. One, Félix Houphouët-Boigny (1905–1993), was a senior minister in the last four administrations of the Fourth Republic and responsible for the Loi cadre or 'Framework Law' of 1956, which devolved self-government to the African territories. In becoming so intimately acquainted with the French political system, Francophone African politicians imbibed French ideas of the 'nation' and the 'state', and the French outlook on politics. They also gained a realistic appreciation of how much the African territories gained by membership of the franc zone –

which brought privileged access to the metropolitan market for their primary exports – and from French overseas aid. So they were much more willing than their counterparts in Anglophone Africa to maintain close political and economic ties after independence.

When they became independent, South Asian and African states were – for all their diversity – thrust into a common position in the international system, and embarked on a common history as 'emergent', 'non-aligned', 'developing nations'. Political scientists and development economists have written many, many books and articles which illuminate parts of this common history, and historians have produced good accounts of Africa, India and Pakistan up to the millennium (Nugent, 2004; Cooper, 2002; Guha, 2007; Talbot, 1998). But, as far as I know, nobody else has been rash enough to essay a comparative analysis of the post-colonial phase in African and South Asian history. This book originated in an endeavour to answer two apparently simple, but actually dauntingly complex questions: to what extent did the colonial experience and its institutional residue determine the post-colonial trajectories of South Asian and African states and societies? Conversely, to what extent were these trajectories determined by indigenous social forces and institutions which either originated before the colonial conquests or evolved more or less autonomously under the political cover of colonialism? Both questions presuppose that similar causes in similar circumstances will have similar effects. I say this because a superficially puzzling feature of post-colonial history is that countries embarking on independence with much the same colonial legacy have followed different trajectories. India and Pakistan are the most notable instances: in Chapters 1 and 2, I seek to explain why the former managed to institutionalise democracy and a left-of-centre form of economic planning while the latter succumbed to military rule, combined with economic policies which tolerated greater economic inequality in the interests of maximising growth.

Before proceeding, it is worth asking whether the colonial imprint on popular political attitudes has been as long-lasting as its imprint on political geography. (My discussion is confined to Africa because I have no evidence for South Asia.) That is obviously difficult to answer: while maps are easy to consult, mentalities are fluid and hard to assess with any confidence. But the question is not entirely futile because it helps expose the historical distance between the recent past and the post-colonial era, which is not simply a matter of calendar years but includes the suppression and restoration of multi-party politics, economic decline and (not infrequently) political disorder. Kwame

Nkrumah famously declared that 'Without exception [the colonial powers] left us nothing but our resentment ... It was when they had gone, and we were faced with the stark realities ... that the destitution of the land after long years of colonial rule was brought home to us' (Nkrumah, 1963, p. xiii). Since his name carries even greater prestige in Africa than Nelson Mandela's, we might expect a 'folk memory' which accords with that rhetoric. What evidence we have suggests otherwise. A survey undertaken by GlobeScan for the UK government's Commission for Africa (which reported in 2005) found that 49 per cent of respondents deemed their own politicians and national governments responsible for their countries' problems, as compared with 16 per cent who blamed the former colonial powers, and 11 per cent the rich countries (Commission for Africa, 2005, p. 35). The details of the survey are unavailable, and sceptics may wonder whether the sample accurately represented a culturally diverse population of around 700 million spread over a huge land mass and more than 40 states. But the findings are scarcely surprising for the simple reason that African societies are very youthful and African lives comparatively short. Apart from Zimbabweans, for whom independence came in 1980, only a tiny proportion of Africans has any lived experience of colonialism. In 2006, the median age in sub-Saharan Africa was 18.2 years and life expectancy at birth was just under 50 years (48.4 for males, 50.3 for females). Fifty-four per cent of the sub-continent's population was born since 1986 and only one in ten were aged over 50 (Velkoff and Kowal, 2007; see also Tabutin and Schoumaker, 2004).[1] Assuming the GlobeScan survey accurately reflected the age structure, most respondents were born in countries that had been independent for the best part of a generation, and where long-serving 'founding fathers' were frequently held in contempt, charged by political opponents with having squandered a rich inheritance.

Zambia's first president, Kenneth Kaunda, is a not untypical example. When he assumed office in 1964, he was widely admired for his humanity, moral integrity and selfless dedication to the people's welfare. When his successor, Frederick Chiluba, was sworn in on 2 November 1991 – the first occasion a government was changed by the ballot box in independent Anglophone Africa – he eloquently denounced the post-colonial political record as a shameful fall from

---

1. The quality of African demographic statistics is poor and there are irresolvable discrepancies in the sources: Tabutin and Schoumaker put the population of sub-Saharan Africa at 626 million in 2001, with a 2.4 per cent annual growth rate, while Velkoff and Kowal make it 753 million in 2006, with a 2.2 per cent annual growth rate. The implied discrepancy is around 53 million!

grace: the ideals that inspired independence had withered in the stony ground of one-party rule, autocracy, corruption, 'tribalism' and elite self-enrichment. (His inauguration speech is quoted at length in Callaghy and Ravenhill, 1993, pp. 520–1.) Disinterested observers would have agreed that this denunciation was substantially true: against considerable opposition, Kaunda had imposed one-party authoritarianism and used government control of economic resources and public employment to secure a support base, while denying economic opportunity to regional groups considered hostile to the regime (Rakner, 2003, p. 52; Bates, 2008, pp. 68–9). The manifesto of Chiluba's Movement for Multiparty Democracy had included a programme of liberal economic reforms, so by voting for it in overwhelming numbers the electorate repudiated the statist economic policies Kaunda had championed. The humiliated 'father of the nation' was deprived of his citizenship in 1999, on the grounds that his parents were immigrants from Nyasaland (now Malawi), though it was later restored. The story does not end there: the ignominious end to Chiluba's own career illustrates why African publics no longer regard 'colonialism' as *the* explanation for their common woes. After relinquishing office in 2001, he was indicted on massive corruption charges. In May 2007, a London High Court convicted him in a civil case, brought on behalf of the Zambian Attorney General, of stealing $46 million of public money. This was not an isolated incident: in the early 2000s outrageously corrupt practices were routine at the very heart of government in Nigeria, Kenya and other major African countries (Ellis, 2006). National governments were widely seen as the greatest obstacle to reducing poverty: when asked unprompted by opinion pollsters in 2006, 46 per cent of Africans mentioned their government as impeding poverty reduction. Twenty-seven per cent specified government corruption, 13 per cent a lack of government administration and capacity, and 6 per cent a lack of political will within government (GlobeScan, 2011; there were nearly 12,000 respondents in ten African countries).

'Postcolonlalism' in theory

The core thesis of this book is that the post-colonial decades – when the authority and prestige of national leaders was bound up with their stewardship of economic modernisation and development – are not part of a continuous present but belong to a different historical era. Although not especially contentious, this thesis sets the book apart from what are normally considered academic 'postcolonial' studies, which take 'postcoloniality' to be part of the continuous global present and have given little attention to historical discontinuities since independence. 'Postcolonialism' – usually without the hyphen – has for some time been the focal term for a diffuse body of humane scholarship, mainly in literary and cultural studies. Being diffuse, it is hard to characterise, but what distinguished its first practitioners was their contention that European or western knowledge of the so-called Third World is profoundly ethnocentric, coupled with an affiliation, by birth or descent, with the object of that knowledge. The point is best clarified by illustration: the foundational text in postcolonial studies is Edward Said's *Orientalism*, an analysis of eighteenth- and nineteenth-century European (mainly British and French) writing on the Islamic world of the Middle East. Said's central claim was that the 'Orient' was a discursive and ideological construct which empowered Europeans in their dealings with Middle Eastern polities and cultures. Orientalism helped define and legitimise Europe as the actor in a history of territorial expansion and economic hegemony, while representing (or misrepresenting) the Orient as a passive object of that history (Said, 1978). As a Palestinian Christian who made a distinguished career in American academia as a literary scholar, Said was able to read and deconstruct Orientalist writing from both within the traditions of western scholarship and from without. That, I think, was the defining characteristic of postcolonial analysis on its first appearance: it was posited on the perspective afforded 'Third World' intellectuals when they relocated to Europe and North America and acquired a hybrid status as expatriate cultural critics working within western academic traditions, yet disclosing the historical conditions of extra-European exploitation that – arguably – made these traditions possible. (The most substantial synthesis of postcolonial thinking to date is Young, 2001, though it is marred by many factual errors; for a clear introduction to the field see Loomba, 1998.)

A body of rigorous historical scholarship closely associated with the postcolonial perspective has been produced under the rubric of 'Subaltern Studies', an annual collection of essays which began appearing in 1982. Most are empirical case studies investigating colonial India's history-from-below, whose authors drew on the ideas of the Italian Marxist, Antonio Gramsci, for a shared theoretical framework. Rather few are concerned with South Asian history after 1947, so the body of work has not been directly helpful in preparing this book. The 'Subaltern' project was an intellectual response to the crises of the

Indian state in the 1970s, which included a rash of peasant insurgencies and the moral eclipse of the Indian National Congress, and a repudiation of the nationalist narrative – with its 'top-down' historiography – that legitimised Congress's historic triumph over colonialism (Prakash, 1994, p. 1476). To put the matter simplistically: whereas Nehru wrote of the 'discovery of India' as the emotive force behind his political life, Subaltern scholars discerned the 'invention' of 'India' by early nationalists and the subsequent 'imagining' of an Indian nation by the Anglophone political elite. Excluded from this 'imaginary' entity were many demotic forms of political life (such as peasant insurgencies and religious 'fanaticism') repugnant to what became secular nationalism, as personified above all by Nehru (Kaviraj, 1992).

Of great pertinence to this book is the thesis advanced by the Subaltern political scientist, Partha Chatterjee, that 'the *general* form of the transition from colonial to post-colonial national states' was 'a passive revolution' (Chatterjee, 1986, p. 50). The term comes from Gramsci's writings on Italian reunification, when the Piedmontese monarchy and traditional ruling classes managed both to suppress popular radicalism and draw the industrial bourgeoisie into subordinate alliance. Chatterjee recognises the political diversity of post-colonial states and does not argue for close parallels between their formation and Italy's 'passive revolution'. But at a general level of analysis, there were homologies in the relations between the national movement, social forces and structures (such as the pattern of land ownership) and the political economy of development (the policies adopted to promote industrialisation and economic independence). With important exceptions, nationalist movements did not achieve independence by armed force: they had to negotiate the incremental transfer of power from a position of military-political weakness which required the broadest possible nationalist alliance, in which there were conflicting social interests. The nationalist movements' most potent weapon was mass civil disobedience, but they had to deploy it cautiously for fear of alienating elements in the alliance. Their generally 'moderate' stance entailed restraining social radicalism and, once in power, retaining the colonial regime's economic institutions and administrative and legal structures. The primary reason of state for the nationalists was economic modernisation, to which end they instituted a 'mixed' economy, with government having a 'planning' role and a large public sector coexisting with private enterprise protected from foreign competition. The state claimed to stand above narrow interest groups and classes and the governing party was an umbrella organisation, under which a broad social and ideological spectrum could coalesce. The post-colonial revolution was 'passive' because it preserved many of the colonial regime's' institutions, did not involve an assault on the traditional agrarian hierarchy, contained class conflicts within manageable dimensions and lacked a dimension of class agency (Chatterjee, 1986, pp. 43–9; Chatterjee, 1993).

This is an abstraction from the Indian historical experience and one may well ask how useful the concept of 'passive revolution' is in understanding post-colonial African states (leaving aside those which underwent 'active' revolutions). In fact, the French political scientist, Jean-François Bayart, found the concept extremely useful in providing an explanatory framework for his comparative study of African politics. African nationalist movements were either created or captured by western-educated elites who contained the radicalism of popular protest against colonialism. The 'educated' – who were known in Francophone Africa as *évolués* – seized state resources as power was devolved in the late colonial years. After independence, they monopolised administrative employment, while retaining European salary scales, and often invested wealth accumulated in public office in modern farms, thus 'straddling' the urban and rural worlds. The African 'passive revolution' also effected what Bayart calls the 'reciprocal assimilation of elites' or the coalescence of traditional or 'chiefly' political leaders and modern politicians, entrepreneurs and bureaucrats into the 'post-colonial historic bloc' (Bayart, 1993, pp. 180–3). Educated Africans and their social allies look to the state both to develop and indigenise the modern economy, while neutralising social forces (organised labour, messianic cults, ethnic dissidence) that threatened the emergence of market capitalism. The parallels with Chatterjee's South Asian paradigm of 'passive revolution' are not exact but they are sufficiently close to underline the usefulness of the concept for comparative analysis. This must begin, however, with those historical and structural constraints to which I referred earlier.

Post-colonial South Asia and Africa: a thumb-nail sketch

South Asia and Africa include about a third of the world's population and roughly the same proportion of its land surface, so any brief statements about them are inevitably tendentious. But there can be little argument that, at independence, their societies exhibited acute symptoms of 'underdevelopment': endemic poverty, unproductive agriculture, a low level of industrialisation, a life expectancy of about 32 years in South Asia in 1947, of 39 years in sub-Saharan Africa in 1960, with infant mortality rates exceeding 150 deaths per 1000 live births. In the poorest regions of South Asia and Africa, out of every 1000 children born nearly 400 did not reach the age of 15. The total fertility rate ranged from six in India to over seven in Pakistan and Africa. An African or South Asian woman could expect to spend well over a third of her adult life either carrying a child in her womb or breast-feeding. Maternal mortality was the largest single cause of death amongst women in their reproductive years (Kumar with Desai, 1983, Tables 5.11 and 5.12; Cooper, 2002, pp. 108–10; Dasgupta, 1993, p. 348). In both sub-continents, about 85 per cent of the population was illiterate, so there was a dearth of human capital and administrative skills in the new national states. Though there were substantial industrial nuclei in undivided India, they constituted a small part of the total economy: mining and manufacturing accounted for about 17 per cent of total output in 1947, and only 12 per cent of the labour force; most industrial workers worked in small-scale, unmechanised workshops (Tomlinson, 1993, pp. 92–5). In African countries in 1960, manufacturing typically contributed 4–6 per cent of output; its share of employment was even smaller. Regular wage-earning of any sort was still an unusual experience for Africans: there were probably no more than 10 million wage-earners during any part of the year, and most of them were migrants with families in the natal village and a customary right to land. In Ghana, a fifth of the labour force was in waged employment, and in Nigeria, one-twentieth. Only in white-dominated Southern Rhodesia did wage-earners constitute more than 10 per cent of the total population (and about one-third of the labour force) (Harwitz, 1964, p. 16; Munro, 1984, p. 52).

The overwhelming majority of South Asians and Africans were primarily engaged in subsistence agriculture, using techniques that had changed little over 50 or even 100 years and only intermittently involved in the modern monetised economy. As far as they were concerned, colonialism had not been a juggernaut of capitalist modernity. Up to the later 1960s, between three-quarters and two-thirds of Indian food grain output was not marketed for cash. Rice and jowar were grown largely for household consumption, and wheat primarily for the market, but a substantial proportion of all grain was bartered by producers, shared out amongst sharecroppers or paid as wages-in-kind (Chandavarkar, 1983, pp. 764–5; Tomlinson, 1988, p. 133). Around 1960, about 70 per cent of the cultivated land in Africa was devoted to subsistence crops while less than 10 per cent was planted for export. Where farmers had adopted new cash crops, they had often done so on their own initiative, just as they had continued the centuries-old process of colonising vacant land.

There is, of course, a gross political difference which greatly complicates comparison. Sub-Saharan Africa is the world's most politically segmented region: the combined population of its 48 states is roughly half that of the Indian Union. It is, nonetheless, misleading to imagine that the colonialists had 'Balkanised' Africa: estimates of the number of distinct polities before the late nineteenth-century 'scramble' range from 600 to 10,000 (Low, 1991a, p. 272). Colonialism had amalgamated culturally heterogeneous populations into political units of unprecedented size and territorial solidity by African standards. However, the median African state in the 1960s had a population no bigger than the average Indian district. Ghanaians numbered about 7 million in 1961, when India's population was 439 million. Obviously, it is as meaningful in the appropriate context to talk of the political economy of Ghana as it is to talk of the political economy of India, but we are not talking about comparable entities. The small size and specialist nature of Ghana's economy rendered it vulnerable to authoritarian manipulation by its new political masters, though they did not – alas – guarantee the success of that manipulation. India's sub-continental economy in 1947 was comparatively more diverse, with enclaves of modern development, but seemingly trapped in a low-level equilibrium by its huge subsistence sector. In the later-1970s, the American scholar Francine Frankel concluded that nearly 30 years of state-led development had failed to transform the economy's basic characteristics (Frankel, 2005).

Africa and South Asia differ not only at macro-political level but also in the basic structures of material and cultural life. Africa is both land-abundant and land-locked. Four out of five Africans live more than 100 kilometres from the sea or a navigable river; railways are few and far between, and designed to take minerals and export crops to the sea. Inland transport of bulk goods is difficult and expensive, which has discouraged regional economic specialisation, while low population densities have permitted exceptional cultural heterogeneity. Africans are the world's most ethnically and linguistically diverse people (Collier and Gunning, 1999a, p. 9). In recent memory, the sub-continent's tyrannous distances and poor communications isolated local societies, or more particularly their women folk, from the simplest products of a modern economy: in Southern Rhodesia, two or three days' travel from the Zambezi, there were many women in the late 1950s who had never struck a match, never held an electric torch or threaded a needle. Labour migration often entailed weeks of walking: to take one example amongst many, about 200,000 men left Sokoto Province in Nigeria every year in the early 1960s to cover hundreds of miles to the forest belt on foot (Hunter, 1962, pp. 66–72). In pre-colonial Africa, the vacant spaces between settlements meant that fixed political boundaries were virtually unknown; in post-colonial Africa, despite rapid demographic growth, states such as Angola – which is more than twice the size of France and has about one-fifth of its population – still have difficulty exercising physical control over all their territory (Herbst, 1996–7, 2000). The Indian sub-continent, by contrast, is more spatially and culturally integrated. It had the fourth largest railway system in the world in 1947; four out five Indians live within 50 kilometres of a railway. South Asia has many language groups but it is less diverse linguistically than Africa. At independence, Hindus and Muslims alike across northern India used Hindustani as a lingua franca (which is why Gandhi wanted it adopted as the national language); to this day ordinary language communication between Hindi and Urdu speakers is far easier than it is between the Igbo and Yoruba speakers of southern Nigeria and the Hausa speakers of the north.

For many centuries, Africa's surplus of land and scarcity of labour dictated extensive methods of cultivation and prevented the emergence of a land market (Austin, 2008). To concentrate on a specific example, which is reasonably representative of the sub-continent, less than 10 per cent of Tanganyika's land was cultivated in 1960, though a considerably larger proportion was grazed. But this must be seen in relation to the land's generally low productive potential: soils are poor and rainfall inadequate over large areas and nutriments easily leach out in tropical conditions. About 60 per cent of Tanganyika was infested with tsetse fly in 1960, which inhibited the use of draught animals. So there were localised land shortages amongst land abundance. Farmers still practised shifting cultivation: they cleared an area of forest or regenerated bush by fire, cultivated it for a number of years, and then moved elsewhere to repeat the process, leaving the land to recuperate under bush fallow. The initially high fertility of virgin forest was never fully replaced, because arable land was not manured and fertilisers were used in negligible quantities. A team of visiting economists concluded: 'The combination of shifting cultivation and fire has reduced huge areas of Africa, formerly under woodland, to mediocre scrub on soils of reduced fertility' (International Bank for Reconstruction and Development, 1960, p. 44). The introduction of cash crops had not fundamentally altered the cultivation system: farmers grew coffee, cotton and ground-nuts as a supplementary activity costing little in terms of either money outlay or alternative income forgone. Exports were a major source of money income for Tanganyikans, and the doubling of export volumes in the 1950s had led to rising living standards, but the great majority remained in an intermediate position between the subsistence and the monetised economy.

Historically, Africans have enjoyed easy access to land as lineage members and only exceptionally been dominated by a landed ruling class. 'The big men of pre-colonial Africa' – writes John Lonsdale – 'could do little to re-shape productive relations, and white colonial rulers were scarcely as revolutionary in this respect as they first intended' (Lonsdale, 1986, p. 127). At independence, very few Africans were landless; debt peonage was unknown, as was the mass destitution so evident in contemporary India, where around 40 per cent of the rural population and over half the urban population, were so poor as to be unable to afford an adequate diet (Dandekar and Rath, 1971). Around 1960, Africa was a food surplus region, while much of the world's food aid was going to India. American grain imports – subsidised by the US Federal Government – were essential for survival in northern India after the disastrous harvests of 1957 and 1965–6. African landholdings were remarkably egalitarian, outright sales of land were unusual, the idea of land alienation uncommon. The typical African farmer had 5 to 15 acres under cultivation in any one year and frequently as much or more land in fallow (Eicher, 1986, p. 151). Most rural households were only partly integrated into produce markets; however straitened their way of life, it was not dominated by economic compulsion. They worked to eat, to perform their social obligations and perhaps to earn prestige; they might get credit for being hard workers in some cultures, but in others they did not. In the cocoa-growing areas of western Nigeria in the early 1950s, men worked on average 209 days a year and women 242. They invested much of their time in social networks, which were essential for economic security and for the advancement of their sons, but when all is said and done they preferred more leisure to more income (Hailey, 1957, p. 1285). Not that the 'spirit' of agrarian capitalism was entirely absent: in southern Ghana, Côte d'Ivoire, Buganda and elsewhere, there were prosperous market-oriented farmers who employed migrant labour on a regular basis and were beginning to accumulate land (Hunter, 1962, pp. 98–9). But in many places there were socio-cultural obstacles impeding individualist economic behaviour: in 1955, the East Africa Royal Commission noted that, 'in whatever direction he turns, the African, whether he wishes to become a peasant farmer, a businessman, a permanent wage-earner in the towns or a modern tenant on the land, is hampered by the requirements of his tribal society with its obligations and restraints' (East Africa Royal Commission, 1955, p. 51).

The structure and ethos of Indian rural society were strikingly different: the frontier of cultivation was reached around 1900 in many regions, given existing techniques, and widespread land shortages were evident by the late 1930s. In the last four decades of British rule, per capita food grain availability declined by about 1 per cent per year, the reasons being that the extension of the cultivated area lagged behind population growth while there was virtually no investment in improved techniques and soil conservation. Agrarian social relations had tended to 'ossify' in colonial India because the legal protection given to tenants partially insulated the land from market forces. It has been convincingly shown that there was no marked tendency to 'landlessness' before 1900: a substantial class of landless serfs and communal slaves existed in the early nineteenth century, whose descendants made up the substantial class of agricultural wage-earners in the early twentieth century. A century or more of British rule had scarcely affected their abject status in the ritual hierarchy (Kumar, 1962). Land ownership was highly unequal at independence: more than half rural households either owned no land or their holdings were too small to support the average family; roughly two-thirds of the entire cultivated area was owned by the peasant elite with holdings of 10 acres or more (Frankel, 2005, p. 97). The great majority of rural households depended on the labour market for their survival, though waged work was rarely a simple cash nexus. With many regional variations, the pyramid of rural property interlaced with both the ritual hierarchy of endogamous *jatis* and the *jajmani* system which involved the exchange of services for grain across the pollution barrier. To what extent a religious culture of hereditary inequality explains the near stasis of the Indian rural economy is deeply contentious (see Lal, 1988; and for a critique, Tomlinson, 1993, pp. 26–7). That it was static is a matter of fact. Despite long exposure to world market forces and significant industrial growth, the process of structural economic change had been agonisingly slow. The proportion of the labour force engaged in agriculture actually rose slightly between 1911 and 1951. In an influential study published in 1968, Gunnar Myrdal was deeply pessimistic about the possibility of the Indian economy breaking out of the low-level equilibrium in which it appeared to be trapped by 'the inefficiency, rigidity and inequality of the established institutions and attitudes and the economic and social power relations embodied in this framework of institutions and attitudes' (Myrdal, 1968, p. 47). Western advisers to African governments were, by contrast, generally optimistic about African development prospects. In 1967, Andrew Kamarck, a World Bank economist, predicted that a cluster of countries (including Congo-Zaire, Ghana, Nigeria and Zambia) would soon reach or surpass a 7 per cent growth rate, which would enable them to 'take off' into self-sustained economic growth and dispense with foreign aid (Kamarck, 1967, p. 247).

These different agrarian structures have conditioned both economic development and political mobilisation. Paradoxically, Africa's economic growth has been constrained by its favourable land–labour ratios: its 'uncaptured' peasants retained considerable economic discretion and were an obstacle both to the spread of rural capitalism and to state-directed development, such as the village collectivisation attempted in Tanzania and Mozambique (Hyden, 1980). In India, modern politics and the state's programmes of agrarian development have intermeshed more successfully with the rural hierarchy. The rural elite were the transmission belt for the so-called Green Revolution that got under way in the mid-1960s in Punjab and Haryana – a revolution that has yet to be replicated in Africa. While increasing numbers of Africans have been confronted by food insecurity and famine, the Malthusian threat has been seen off in South Asia.

Even a thumb-nail sketch such as this would be inadequate without some indications of the sub-continent's great internal diversity. The key socio-economic indicators – life expectation, women's fertility, the incidence of infant mortality and poverty, the female literacy rate – demonstrate considerable variations in regional experiences in the Indian Union (Drèze and Sen, 1995, pp. 45–56). Some are of fairly recent origin and due to the interventions of state governments since the 1950s; communist-administered Kerala, though poor in terms of average incomes, has been notably successful in lowering infant mortality, improving women's literacy and giving them greater control over their own fertility. But other regional variations have a 'deeper' history; for example, in the late 1930s, per capita income in Bengal, Bihar and Orissa was probably less than half the income level in Bombay province (Heston, 1983, Table 4A.12, p. 455). Behind this difference lay more adverse land–labour ratios in eastern India, the morcellisation of holdings and declining per capita output, as well as calamitous impact of the collapse of world trade on Bengal's jute farmers. Around 1990, Bihar and Orissa remained India's poorest states, with roughly two-thirds of the rural population living in poverty as compared with between a fifth and a quarter in Punjab and Haryana (Drèze and Sen, 1995, Table A3).

The variations in material well-being in Africa have been just as striking: in 1959, annual per capita GDP in Uganda was reckoned to be £18, compared with £34 in Kenya, £71 in Ghana and £82 in Northern Rhodesia (now Zambia) (Hunter, 1962, Table 1, p. 49). We would be rash to assume that African household incomes in Northern Rhodesia were over four times greater than in Uganda, but the differences were nevertheless considerable. At independence in 1964, Zambia was a relatively urbanised society with a substantial stratum of well-paid wage-earners by African and South Asian standards. Fifty-three per cent of adult males were literate. Thanks to its copper earnings, which accounted for a per capita GDP about three times the African average in 1970, Zambia was considered a 'middle-income' country in the making. In the early 1990s, it was one of Africa's poorest countries.

One further economic contrast between South Asia and Africa on the eve of independence must be highlighted: by 1940, Indians had wrested control of much modern enterprise from expatriates; in Africa, in 1960, the indigenisation of the modern economy lay in the future. Indian businessmen had taken over a swathe of expatriate enterprise by acquiring major shareholdings in the Managing Agency Houses, while much new investment in industry was coming from native business communities, such as the Marwaris. From the early 1930s, foreign direct investment in manufacturing was mostly by Indian subsidiaries of British-based multinationals, which represented about half of British capital holdings at independence (Tomlinson, 1993, p. 143). Multinational corporations (MNCs) had been induced to create subsidiaries by the nationalist boycott of foreign imports and the trade barrier erected when tariff autonomy devolved to the Indian Government after 1919; it was one of several ways in which the transition to a new political economy pre-dated the transfer of sovereignty (Tomlinson, 1979).

In Africa, the ownership and management of manufacturing enterprise was the exclusive preserve of European expatriates and Asian and Lebanese immigrants, as was the provision of modern commercial and financial services. Asians (so-called, most were second- or third generation Africans of Asian descent) possessed a quasi-monopoly over the retail trade and urban crafts of British East Africa and were the main investors in urban real estate. From the early 1950s, the more enterprising of Kenya's Asian trading families had been investing in the local manufacturing of consumer products. By 1961, two-thirds of the locally owned industrial enterprises with 50 or more employees were

Asian-owned. Probably three-quarters of Kenya's private non-agricultural assets were owned by the 177,000-strong Asian community on the eve of independence (Leys, 1975, p. 45). Levantine traders played a not dissimilar role in the late colonial economy of British West Africa, though they were a far smaller community. In the Gold Coast, Levantine immigrants numbered only about 1370 but were responsible for two-fifths of the colony's imports by the mid-1950s. They had entirely displaced the giant European trading firms from retailing, and had invested considerable sums in houses and land. A few firms combined money-lending with commerce, thereby profiting from the habitual caution of the European banks when it came to advancing credit to African entrepreneurs (Hailey, 1957, p. 412).

Modern colonialism

By itself, post-colonialism is an empty historical term. To give it empirical substance, we need to define colonialism – more specifically modern colonialism – and say something about its economic and political legacies. It was both a fairly well-delineated phase in the overseas expansion of European states, when they seized tropical and sub-tropical territories with the set purpose of bringing economic benefit to their own nationals, *and* a doctrine that rationalised this policy. Its central drama was the European partition of Africa, which began in the late 1870s and was virtually complete by 1914, though this has tended to obscure the contemporaneous expansion of European power into South East Asia and the South Pacific. If we concentrate solely on the fact of conquest and ignore the doctrine, then dating the onset of colonialism to the 1870s, as historians conventionally do, appears decidedly arbitrary (Fieldhouse, 1981). After all, some spectacular instances of European overseas conquest predated the 'onset' by several centuries; why they should be construed as 'preceding' modern colonialism may seem a bit mysterious to non-historians.

The matter is less arcane if we attend to the new meanings attached to the word 'colony' by the late nineteenth century: this once referred solely to an overseas dependency in sparsely populated regions where European settlers exploited the land with their own or slave labour, replicated the political, legal and religious institutions of the 'mother country', and sooner or later invested their capital in production for local markets. Schemes for 'colonisation' usually revolved around state-promoted emigration by the early nineteenth century; their intellectual rationale derived from Malthusian wage-fund theory and the supposedly ineluctable tendency for the rate of profit to decline as the ratio of fixed to circulating capital rose. Significantly, India, the most important centre of British imperial power, was not considered part of the 'Colonial Empire' by John Seeley in his influential lectures on *The Expansion of England* (1883). Colonialism, for Seeley, was an expression of the expansion of nationality, and in India, the British 'State [had advanced] beyond the limits of the nationality'; in consequence, its power was 'precarious and artificial' (Seeley, 1900, p. 54).

To exclude India from an analysis of colonialism on the say-so of a long-dead Cambridge professor would be taking academic deference to extremes. Though never settled in significant numbers by Europeans, and never the formal responsibility of the Colonial Office, the British Empire in India was the most populous, and one of the 'most stable and subtly-managed' colonial polities of all times (Nandy, 1983, p. 30). It was by far the greatest market ever subordinated to an industrial empire and the classic instance of the colonial remoulding of a premodern economy. However, the dynamics of the British conquest (substantially achieved by 1820) were fundamentally different from those which drew the major powers into colonial competition after 1870. India was conquered when commercial relations between Europe and Asia were both 'pre-colonial' and pre-industrial. The first decades of Company rule more resembled previous Asiatic conquests than modern colonialism: it accommodated itself to Mughal political culture by using Persian in its courts and administration and excluding Christian missionaries from its territories until 1813.

There were, clearly, underlying continuities between the conquest of India and modern colonialism after 1870; at a rather abstract level, both can be related to the centuries-long expansion of the European capitalist 'world economy' (Wallerstein, 1974, 1979, 1988). Yet, not to recognise modern colonialism as a novel irruption in late nineteenth-century global politics would be to miss its historical significance. It was 'modern' in the non-trivial sense of expressing the widening material disparities between the world's industrialising and 'under-developed' regions, disparities which had been scarcely evident 50 years before. Relations of military, economic and administrative power between western and non-western states and societies were rendered vastly more asymmetrical from about 1850 by the industrialisation under way in Britain, Continental Europe and North East America (Headrick, 1981). By the 1890s, superior weaponry, western military discipline and quinine prophylaxis were bringing Europeans almost costless victories in Africa. Rarely have such huge territories been acquired with such paltry forces.

The intellectual rationale for modern colonialism discarded the Malthusian-inspired arguments for 'settler' colonisation; instead, it stressed the need for new markets for the manufactured products of industrialising economies prone to over-production; the political control of sources of indispensable raw materials; and the investment abroad of surplus capital at a higher rate of profit than could be obtained domestically. This rationale was not any less potent for resting on shaky premises: as we now know, African and Asian colonies were too poor to absorb more than a narrow range of European manufactures; they furnished a rather small proportion of Europe's industrial raw materials; and were never a major site of overseas investment. Before about 1950, the European capital in modern colonies (India aside) was either commercial or invested in production for metropolitan markets; local consumer demand was satisfied by importing from the metropolis or by indigenous handicraft production.

Despite its coincidence with the largest inter-continental migrations in history, modern colonialism was not a colonising process in the classical sense. The new colonies only exceptionally attracted white settlers, and the exceptions were usually small minorities. Southern Rhodesia, for example, though designated a 'white settler' colony, had only 136,000 European residents in 1951, or less than 7 per cent of the total population. Modern colonialism did not attempt to replicate metropolitan civil society: customary law was applied to native subjects, although in French and Portuguese Africa tiny elites of assimilated citizens were entitled to be judged by European law. A wafer-thin stratum of European bureaucrats normally ruled Asians and Africans indirectly, through native authorities, whom they suborned but also strengthened in their dealings with villagers and townspeople. Racial distinctions were built into modern colonial rule in a way that had not been the case in the early nineteenth century: in the Gold Coast Colony, for example, Africans and mulattoes had been regularly nominated to the magistracy and administration up to the 1850s, but were excluded in the openly racist climate of the later nineteenth century (Mair, 1971, p. 182).

A discursive definition of modern colonialism is one thing; assessing its historical *import* for the evolution of colonised societies is another. The spatial context of politics, trade and production was, of course, altered by the imposition of sharp territorial borders where they had not existed. This was particularly evident in Africa, where kings and chiefs had generally ruled by accumulating people, rather than land. Before the colonial conquest not all Africans lived within centralised political formations, but even these tended to be 'porous': they inter-meshed with lineages, religious and language communities and trading diasporas. Africa's colonial boundaries contained and identified their inhabitants much more firmly, and now delimit its national states. Traditional rulers may have 'owned' their subjects, but territorially bounded states require of their nationals a singular and in some ways more exclusive allegiance, and they discriminate rigorously against aliens when the so-called national interest requires. Within its 'hard' borders, colonialism's core residual legacy was the 'apparatus of the modern state'. But that rather portentous phrase can give an exagger-ated impression of the scale and permanence of colonial government. Before 1919, the number of colonial political officers in tropical Africa was so few as to preclude serious administration. But even after the so-called second colonial occupation of the late 1940s and 50s, when administration was expanded to meet the new commitment to 'devel-opment and welfare', administrative services were very small, especially by comparison with what they were to become under independent governments (Kirk-Greene, 1980).

The colonial reordering of political space in South Asia was less drastic, partly because the indigenous traditions of territorial state for-mation were stronger. The British were more successful than any of their imperial predecessors in politically unifying the Indian sub-conti-nent, and in fixing northern frontiers where there had hitherto been conduits for invasions. But their territorial integration was incomplete: they placed an imperial resident in 550 or so princely states, covering about a third of the sub-continent, which acknowledged Britain as the paramount power but otherwise remained self-governing. The British also tolerated the vestiges of other European merchant empires, such as Portuguese Goa and French Pondichéry. Although Indian independ-ence is inescapably associated with the partition of the Punjab and Bengal, it was also a notable feat of state aggregation, which ratio-nalised and homogenised a political space more extensive than British India. The internal boundaries of the princely states disappeared when their rulers were cajoled or compelled into acceding to the Union in 1947–8; Pondichéry was rather grudgingly relinquished by the French in 1954; Goa was taken over by the Indian army in 1961.

But what of the longer-term political and economic processes within colonised societies? By the early twentieth century, Indian nationalist intellectuals had formulated the thesis of the 'development of underdevelopment' more commonly associated with the Latin American dependency school. In summary, they argued that the British Raj had drastically distorted economic processes for the benefit of British capitalists and consumers by incorporating the sub-continent into the international division of labour as an exporter of primary products and a captive market for Lancashire textiles and other British manufactures. The indigenous economy had, they argued, been 'de-industrialised' – or more aptly 'agrarianised' – by the widespread collapse of handicraft production, consequent on Britain's denial of export markets to Indian textiles. Once that had been accomplished, a political economy of free trade and laissez faire, secured in the last resort by military force, had hobbled industrial development by denying infant industries tariff protection and so perpetuated the agrarian 'bias'. The colonial relationship was a tributary one which 'drained' part of the economic surplus by the remittance of money capital to London; most of the rest had been appropriated by parasitic landlords – the collaborators of the Raj in the countryside – and money lenders, leading to a very low rate of investment. After 1947, this thesis supported two key planks of independent India's development strategy: an aversion to foreign trade and foreign inward investment and a leading role in economic management for the national state. The thesis remains a central orthodoxy of nationalist historiography. Bipan Chandra, the pre-eminent scholar of Indian economic nationalism, and his fellow authors write in their history of India since independence: 'A stagnating per capita income, abysmal standards of living, stunted industrial development and stagnating, low-productivity, semi-feudal agriculture marked the economic legacy of colonialism as it neared the end' (Chandra *et al.*, 2000, p. 16).

Nobody would challenge the accuracy of the descriptive terms, but whether stagnation and poverty can be ascribed *principally* to colonialism is very debatable. This is not a matter of resuscitating imperialist apologetics for the Raj but attending to the painfully obvious fact that ending colonialism was not a sufficient condition for eliminating poverty and raising abysmal living standards. Though Indian economic growth accelerated after 1950, under the stimulus of government intervention and public investment, the proportion of the population living below the poverty line did not decline. In 1973–4, it was 54.9 per cent, which was significantly higher than the 45.3 per cent in 1951–2 (Nayyar, 2006, p. 819). There was no clear trend in poverty reduction until the later 1970s. Indian legislators and governments had done less than their counterparts elsewhere in the 'developing world' to promote basic education and primary health care (which contribute significantly to poverty reduction) and were entirely responsible for their own failings (Drèze and Sen, 1995, pp. 38–40). But they were attempting to mobilise a huge agrarian economy – or more aptly a civilisation – where maintaining a low-level equilibrium around trusted routines smothered innovation and development. Like the British before them, they found their political power rested on an accommodation with agrarian social interests who were skilled in deflecting public interventions on behalf of the poor.

The dilemmas and shortcomings of the Congress Raj should help us place British colonialism in India in a relativist perspective. The British provided 'limited' government for a private enterprise economy in which most decisions about the allocation of resources were made by Indians. By all measurable criteria, the colonial state was small in relation to the wider society. In no decade between 1870 and 1947 did its annual share of gross national product average more than 10 per cent; usually it was less than that (Morris, 1983, p. 554). Except during the two world wars, the tax revenues amounted to a mere 5–7 per cent of the national income. British politicians and administrators, whose views on the proper business of government and on the prudent management of public finances were in any event conservative, understood the very definite limits to the extent to which an unrepresentative government could force increased taxation on to a poor country (Kumar, 1983, p. 905). Even the military costs of the British Raj were a relatively light burden for Indians: as a proportion of national income, peacetime spending on defence was less than Indian defence spending in the 1980s. (Military expenditure accounted for 2.4 per cent of national income in 1900–14, and for 3.87 per cent of GNP in 1988; see Dasgupta, 1993, p. 124.) Colonial India was far more sparsely policed than Britain; over large parts of the Indian countryside, there were no police at all. Civil order was enforced by local power holders operating outside the formal rule of law. Senior British police administrators admitted that extortion, fraud and perjury were commonplace amongst the police, while the legal process was commonly exploited by the powerful to ruin their opponents; villagers perforce relied on informal systems of policing and conflict resolution (Chandavarkar, 2007, pp. 450–2; Neale, 1962, pp. 193–202).

The nationalist paradigm, with its exclusive focus on colonialism as the driver of India's economic history, is no longer intellectually defensible. It overstated the tribute-taking characteristics of the post-1857 Raj and its capacity to impair economic production. But there has also been a great reaction, amongst economists and the Indian policy-making elite, against autarkic economic nationalism and a rehabilitation of the basic tenets of classical political economy, in which the British so firmly believed (up to 1920 at least).

It is now recognised that the economy would have grown more rapidly after 1950 had it been more open to world trade and had policy-makers been less hostile to market forces, both domestic and international (see, for example, Tendulkar and Sen, 2003). This reaction has prompted a redefinition of the link between economic history and modern India in which 'colonialism plays no essential role as a driver' (Roy, 2005, p. 178; Roy, 2002). To understand the snail's pace of economic modernisation we must grasp the constraints on Indian economic actors which arose from the sub-continent's resource endowments, the high cost of capital and the inherent uncertainties of monsoon agriculture on which the great majority depended for their livelihood. Beyond the major seaports, almost every aspect of trade was in the hands of Indian merchants operating on their own account or as agents. They, not foreigners, were best placed to take advantage of investment opportunities in modern industrial organisation and technology. Yet private investment was only 2–4 per cent of national income, and only 0.5 per cent was invested in machinery.

The crucial investment failure was in agriculture – by far the largest economic sector – which attracted less than a tenth of private investment in late colonial India (Roy, 2007, p. 244). This was a recipe for stagnant yields, low labour productivity and subsistence incomes. What discouraged Indians from investing more in the land, which provided the vast majority with a livelihood? The nationalist answer is 'colonial institutions': the land settlements imposed by the British to secure their revenue base either favoured a parasitic class of rent-seekers (the *zamindars*, who were awarded proprietary rights in exchange for tax-gathering responsibilities in parts of British India) or bore too heavily on peasant cultivators where they were directly taxed by colonial officials. It is true that the *zamindars* were never the improving landlords the British wished them to be, but the answer looks less persuasive given that the basic condition underlying agricultural stagnation, low and static yields per acre, was present for centuries before colonial institutions were imposed (*ibid.*, p. 240). Environmental conditions meant that subsistence could be won relatively easily, but it was much harder to intensify cultivation, raise yields and enlarge the agricultural surplus. The necessary investments were too costly for the tenant cultivator or proprietor to undertake without borrowing and the returns too low in relation to prevailing interest rates. The colonial state was not negligent with regard to agriculture, which attracted roughly one-third of public investment in the late nineteenth, early twentieth centuries, but this was mostly in canal irrigation, which extended the cultivated area but did not raise yields. A shift towards more intensive agriculture in South Asia came only when the state began to subsidise ground-water irrigation by tube wells and electric pumps, chemical fertilisers and the adoption of high-yielding varieties.

To explain the low rate of industrial investment nationalists pointed to the absence of tariff protection for 'infant' industries in colonial India, but again this can only be part of the answer. The Indian-owned Bombay cotton mills thrived during the period of greatest trade liberalisation, between 1882 and 1914. The growth rate of value added in factory manufacturing in 1900–13 was higher than in 1919–39, when industry enjoyed protection (Morris, 1983, pp. 553–8, p. 598; Lal, 1988, p. 192). More important in inhibiting investment was the low level of demand for industrial products in a poor society, where market signals were indistinct and profit-making opportunities rare. Much demand for manufactures was met by a vast handicraft sector, located in homes and small workshops, which drew upon abundant labour reserves. Moreover, Indian entrepreneurs operated in an imperfectly commercialised environment: well into the 1950s, about 40 per cent of total output was still being bartered in a large non-monetised sector. As economic policy-makers and planners discovered after 1947, the impression given by nationalist intellectuals of a domestic economy thoroughly penetrated by world market forces and capitalist imperialism was much exaggerated.

Scholarly assessments of the colonial impact on Africa diverge very markedly, partly because different disciplines impose different perspectives. While political scientists have usually regarded colonial rule as a great divide in African history, economic historians are more inclined to see the continuities between pre-colonial and post-colonial eras. In the early 1970s, Hopkins wrote in his classic *Economic History of West Africa*:

[T]here are sound reasons for thinking that colonial rule had a less dramatic and less pervasive economic impact than was once supposed. Little more than half a century elapsed between the end of the partition of West Africa and the beginning of independence. The first fifteen years of this period were devoted to pacifying recalcitrant peoples, the last fifteen years were spent trying to cope with African nationalism, and the intervening years provide plenty of evidence of the superficiality and impermanence of colonial rule, even though this was the time when the rulers themselves believed that their paternal control would remain unchallenged for several centuries. (Hopkins, 1973, p. 167)

The Nigerian historian, Jacob Ajayi, foreshadowed this judgement when he described European colonialism in Africa, as 'a transient phenomenon that did not significantly divert African societies from a trajectory of development underway before 1880' (Ade Ajayi, 1968, p. 194; see also Ade Ajayi, 1969).

Bruce Berman and John Lonsdale reached a diametrically opposed conclusion in their study of early twentieth-century Kenya: colonialism in Africa was 'one of the most consequential modern efforts to modify or create entire social structures, [which] continues to be of enduring importance for a large portion of humanity in defining their socio-economic and political circumstances' (Berman and Lonsdale, 1992, p. 144). In a similar vein, two American scholars, Mark Beissinger and Crawford Young, compared the impact of European colonialism on Africa with that of Soviet communism on Eurasia: both 'represented the high point of the tide of state power that swept the world in the early twentieth century, and both experiences involved attempts to impose a new social order through force'. In both geopolitical contexts, the state undertook 'extensive engineering of society for the dual purposes of modernization and control'. According to these authors, colonial legacies – or enduring intergenerational transfers from the past to the present – were 'glaringly visible in Africa' after forty years of independence (Beissinger and Young, 2002, p. 20).

However, Bayart, took a more qualified position in what is the single most influential monograph on post-colonial African politics: colonialism was no mere interlude, for by introducing money into every area of social life, instituting private property rights, and by making firearms a central and indispensable element of military technology, it radically transformed the resources, the modes and goals in all social struggles. Nevertheless, colonialism 'did not radically weaken the ability of African societies to pursue their own strategies to produce their own modernity'. Even after their military defeat, they were never the passive objects of a process of dependency: 'the colonial situation did not suspend the historicity of African societies' (Bayart, 1993, pp. 20–1). Pre-colonial modes of political action, domination and economic accumulation, which were deeply rooted in African material conditions, persisted through to the independent era.

Why do these characterisations of the colonial impact differ so markedly? One reason is that scholars tend to generalise from their specialist knowledge without sufficiently acknowledging that Africa was not all of a piece before the colonial occupation and that colonial rule varied considerably in its structures and impact. Pre-colonial West Africa (itself a huge, variegated region) had a well-developed market economy, a wide range of craft industries, substantial towns with sophisticated political institutions and civic associations, Muslim clerics literate in Arabic, and even extensive states (Asante, Dahomey, the Sokoto Caliphate). By contrast, East Africa was a region with very few centralised societies, and no substantial kingdoms or even permanent towns between the Islamised coastal fringe and the Great Lakes. State formation was inhibited by extremely low population densities and the precariousness of a shifting agriculture which involved the periodic movement of homesteads or villages. Economic and cultural links with the wider world came through long-distance trade, but this was often indistinguishable from predatory raiding in the later nineteenth century; young men were, typically, warriors on the defensive against intruders. In West Africa, the colonial experience gave an impetus to economic and social processes already under way; in East Africa, it switched the historical tracks.

The key variable in determining the divergent patterns of exploitation in colonial Africa was the presence or absence of European settlers, whose impact in British Africa was magnified by the practice of devolving self-government to colonists' representative institutions. It would be difficult to find more strongly contrasting agrarian societies than Southern Rhodesia, where self-governing whites were able to impose racial segregation on the land, and the Gold Coast, where customary land tenure became the central plank of government policy. Under Southern Rhodesia's Land Apportionment Act (1930) just over half the land was reserved for Europeans, about a fifth for tribal reservations where land was held under communal tenure, and less than a tenth designated as open to individual African purchasers. African squatters and sharecropping tenants were prohibited in the white areas. In the Gold Coast (and West Africa more generally) the colonial authorities had, by 1914, decided to forbid the alienation of land to Europeans, less out of humanitarian concern for African welfare than an appreciation of the limits on their power. They could muster the modest military resources needed to capture the political centre in states like Asante, but they lacked the intensive political power required to remould localised social institutions. The colonial administration was too 'thin' to function without the chiefs, whose authority would have been gravely impaired by the compulsory privatisation of communal land, and so could not impose the prerequisites of rural capitalism: a free market in land and a wage labour market. So long as Africans enjoyed customary rights of land use, they were reluctant to work for wages. The only politically viable basis on which to expand commercial agriculture was peasant production (Phillips, 1989). The political struggles to end colonialism reflected these different colonial situations. Because the Gold Coast's European population was small and transient, racial conflict was minimised and the transfer of power was evolutionary and orderly. Independence in 1957 was preceded by six years of close cooperation between Kwame Nkrumah and the colonial regime, when he took charge of internal self-government, the civil service was 'Africanised', and the expatriate companies operating in the Gold Coast adjusted their management policies to the inevitability of self-determination. In Rhodesia, the intransigence of the Rhodesian Front Party, and the unilateral declaration of independence in 1965, drove a divided nationalist movement into protracted armed struggle. Ndabanangi Sithole, the nominal leader of the more militant Zimbawe African National Union (ZANU), was imprisoned, and effective leadership passed to the exiled Robert Mugabe. Escalating guerrilla war and the white Rhodesian regime's growing isolation following the collapse of Portuguese power in neighbouring Mozambique eventually forced Ian Smith to negotiate with the nationalists.

Beneath the divergent patterns of exploitation, and the distinctive administrative practices in the different empires, lay certain family resemblances. All European rulers acquired their territories by conquest and imposed and extended their exiguous forces far more effectively than Africa's traditional rulers. In so doing, Europeans put a check on widespread social violence: great regions had been traumatised by escalating slave-raids in the mid- and later nineteenth century and fully merited Livingstone's description as 'the open sore of the world' (Iliffe, 1995, p. 182). The colonialists also instituted forms of legitimate violence that Africans had rarely experienced. Until the twentieth century most lived in communities with no concentrations of force to use against their citizens and where political space was pluralistic because the jurisdictions of the different authorities (over the land, over ancestral cults, over the rains) did not coincide (Lonsdale, 1986, p. 140). The colonialists unified social and political space by importing legal and administrative codes which authorised their officials to command labour and resources throughout a bounded territory. Where Roman

Law precepts were adopted (broadly, in French, Belgian and Portuguese Africa) colonial administrations could declare all waste land state domain; in British Africa, administrations were empowered to expropriate land without compensation for public purposes. The rulers' attitude towards their subjects was brusquely authoritarian: the *indigénat* (the native penal code in French Africa until 1945) prescribed summary punishment for any public act, statement, speech or chant disrespectful towards a European agent or representative of the state, or of a nature to undermine respect. In the Belgian Congo, both Africans and Europeans referred to the state as 'Bula Matari' ('smasher of rocks'). The term suggested the pulverising power of the European administration over native society. When Africans were evolving their own political culture in the late colonial period, their ideas of the aims and modalities of modern government inevitably refracted the colonial experience. In Tanganyika, for example, the African Association rarely met in the 1950s without demanding compulsion in some field (Iliffe, 1979, p. 443). The first generation of nationalist leaders found an authoritarian stance highly congenial: within a decade, nearly all made the 'emergency' powers of colonial governors (detention without trial, repression of political parties, trade unions and the free press) routine features of presidential, one-party rule. Their territorial officials aped the imperious style of the old district officers in their dealings with the peasantry.

However, authoritarianism at the apex of rule should not be confused with totalitarianism. Europeans were so few in number (even in settler territories) that they had no choice but to delegate local authority to African collaborators. As in colonial India, local policing was left largely to 'traditional' rulers and their agents who all too often abused colonial patronage to exploit 'their people' (Killingray, 1986). In the process, chieftaincies that had fallen into decay were revived and stateless peoples who had never acknowledged a central authority were compelled to do so. Indirect rule encouraged (or even required) the 'tribalisation' of African society. Missionaries, district officers and their creolised interpreters misperceived Africans' loose social affiliations as fixed and exclusive 'tribal' identities, and used them to facilitate religious conversion and administrative control (Amselle, 1998; Coquery-Vidrovitch, 1988b, p. 99). Africans subsequently created tribes – and invented histories and genealogies to give them legitimacy – in order to function within the 'tribalised' colonial framework. In Tanganyika, between the wars, men devoted as much energy to consolidating and advancing tribes as their children would later do to creating a nation

(Iliffe, 1979, p. 318). Under indirect rule, the customary restraints on chiefs decayed, with the result that the powers vested in them verged on the despotic in places. They levied taxes, coerced labour for public works and their private benefit, appointed policemen and were judges in the Native Courts. What Mahmood Mamdani has called the 'decentralised despotism' of indirect rule left an enduring institutional legacy in the form of a bifurcated legal order. In the towns, colonialism had introduced positive law and the germ of 'civil society', to which Africans could accede when the racial barriers to citizenship were removed at independence. But in the countryside, indirect rule had enhanced the executive and police powers of unelected chiefs, and recreated their legitimacy. Some radical nationalist regimes contemptuously demoted the chiefs, but elsewhere their powers were undiminished. In Uganda and Cameroon in the early 1980s, a poor peasant was ruled in the first instance by a chief who was simultaneously petty legislator, tax assessor, administrator, judge and policeman (Mamdani, 1996a, p. 54; Bayart, 1993, p. 60).

Post-colonialism

As a historical concept, post-colonialism is straightforward: its essential feature was the internalisation of sovereignty within colonised territories, usually by negotiating a conservative transfer of power to nationalists with an electoral mandate. Colonial boundaries were normally accepted as legitimate and conferred a national legitimacy on successor ruling elites. In Africa, this was not so much the transfer of state power as its inauguration. Colonial governments had monopolised collective violence within continuously bounded territories and were monolithic entities in their subjects' eyes, but they did not represent themselves in the international system and were not sovereign political units. One of their defining features had been political dependence on a metropolitan state, so that crucial functions of sovereignty were exercised outside the colony. From this it follows that the expression 'colonial state' is, strictly speaking, a misnomer, which can obscure the often surprising character of decolonisation. In the 1950s, many African territories were not expected to become states, even by their indigenous elites (Jackson and Rosberg, 1986, p. 9). The future of Francophone Africa appeared to lie in large federations within the French Union; the Portuguese were incorporating their African territories into Greater Portugal; the British bundled the colonies of Nyasaland and Northern

Rhodesia (now Malawi and Zambia) together with settler-dominated Southern Rhodesia into the Central African Federation, which was expected to move to independence as a dominion.

The doctrine of the modern state's untrammelled and indivisible sovereignty has been colonialism's most consequential ideological legacy, which nationalists wholeheartedly embraced (Young, 1994a). Sovereignty brought formal equality in the international society of states and the guarantee of inherited borders but it also empowered state elites against domestic rivals and regional autonomy movements. African leaders of sovereign states could claim an authority untainted by 'tribalism', superstition, or a reverence for ancestors. This gave them the confidence to deal more ruthlessly with the royal remnants of Africa's *ancien régime* than their colonial predecessors. For example, the uneasy compromise in Uganda between the populist nationalist, Milton Obote, and the Kabaka of Buganda broke down in 1966 when Obote ordered the storming of the Kabaka's palace. He later justified the destruction of the Bagandan kingdom as the triumph of the 'common man' over tribalism, feudalism and all that was divisive in the African past (Low, 1971). The price of the sovereign state's territorial stability in Africa has included international toleration of despotic regimes, xenophobia towards other African nationals and the collapse of pan-African dreams. Neighbouring states were well aware of the dreadful human rights abuses in Equatorial Guinea during the Nguema dictatorship (1968–79), but all adopted a scrupulous hands-off policy out of solidarity with their sister African micro-state (Decalo, 2000, p. 90).

Although the concept of post-colonialism is straightforward, the term is ambiguous. Prefixing any socio-historical expression with 'post' – whether it is 'feudalism', 'capitalism', 'communism' or 'colonialism' – opens up two meanings. The 'post' can signify either the definite closure of the phenomena (political, economic, ideological) to which the expression refers, so that they become of delimited historical interest, or it can signify that they continued to have a determining effect on human affairs long after they were formally terminated. In simpler language, 'post-colonialism' could mean either that colonialism was 'over and done with' after the transfer of power, or colonialism had so malformed Asian and African economies and societies that the new state actors were left no room for choice: a pattern of dependent development had been determined for them by the colonial experience and its institutional residue. This second sense of 'post' can be linked to the philosophical term 'sublation', which refers to the incorporation of a thesis in its dialectical antithesis, so that its effects are retained within a new synthesis despite its apparent negation. The sublation of colonialism within a world of independent sovereign states is more or less taken for granted within postcolonial cultural studies. While colonies are no longer with us, the consequences of colonialism purportedly remain so overwhelming that, according to Gayatri Spivak, the 'contemporary global condition' can be characterised as 'postcoloniality'. In this condition, even the urgent political claims of post-colonial nationhood, constitutionality, citizenship and democracy are 'recognised as coded with the legacy of imperialism' (Spivak, 1999, p. 172). For Robert Young, the term 'postcoloniality' 'puts the emphasis on the economic, material and cultural conditions that determine the global system in which the postcolonial nation is required to operate – one heavily weighted towards the interests of international capital and the G7 powers' (Young, 2001, p. 57).

Unarguably, we live in a world of extreme and morally reprehensible inequality: in 2005, all of Africa accounted for about 13.5 per cent of world population and 3.5 per cent of global GDP (taking account of purchasing power parity); India, Pakistan and Bangladesh together accounted for nearly 23 per cent of world population and 5.25 per cent of global GDP. Fifty-one per cent of the population of sub-Saharan Africa lived below a $1.25 a day poverty line; in South Asia the corresponding figure was 40.3 per cent (41.6 per cent in 'shining' India). More than seven out of ten of the world's poorest people lived in these two regions combined (World Bank, 2008a; Chen and Ravallion, 2008). But we should not assume from the persistence of mass poverty and economic 'backwardness' that post-colonial states were unable (or unwilling) to dictate the terms on which capitalist enterprises (whether foreign or domestic) operated within their national territories. Nor should we project the 'open' global economy of the late twentieth century back into earlier decades, when national governments controlled exchange rates and capital movements, and used tariffs and quantitative restrictions to limit imports. From the early 1950s, India's political elite set about vesting direct ownership and control of large-scale enterprise in the state, which owned more than three-fifths of industrial capital and nearly all the financial sector by the early 1970s. The active discouragement of foreign investment had reduced the share of multi-national corporations in the modern economy to very modest proportions (Bardhan, 1984). As a result of the inward-looking development policy, foreign trade (imports and exports combined) accounted for only 8 per cent of Indian GDP in 1970, as compared with 27 per cent in 2000. Although few African governments sought to achieve the same degree of autarky, they too exercised considerable economic discretion: there were more nationalisations and takeovers of foreign enterprises in Africa between 1960 and 1980 than in any other world region. The only states not to acquire at least one foreign enterprise were Côte d'Ivoire, Gabon and Liberia (Adedeji, 1981, p. 30). Some socialist and Marxist states sought to eliminate all private enterprise, whether African or foreign.

The blanket use of 'postcoloniality' not only obscures the autonomy of the post-colonial state in determining ownership of economic assets and external economic relations; it also deflects attention away from domestic policy failures which had important implications for development. It is surely astonishing that 40 years after independence over seven out of ten Indian women were illiterate (in Uttar Pradesh the figure was eight out of ten). This was in sharp contrast to the stated objectives and persistent rhetoric of Indian national planning documents and the achievements of other poor countries (including Sri Lanka, Vietnam, China and many African countries) in raising literacy rates (Sen, 1989, p. 377). Public expenditure is a fair reflection of the policy priorities of political elites. In India's case, it is evident that elites prioritised the strengthening of the state over citizens' education: in 1985, public expenditure on education accounted for 5.62 per cent of GDP, a proportion which *declined* to 3–4 per cent in the 1990s. In the later 1980s, military expenditure was over 8 per cent of GDP, and in 1990, 12.2 per cent (World Bank, *World Development Indicators*; Desai and Sreedhar, 1999, p. 113).

It is not a serious objection to the second (sublation) sense of 'post-colonialism' to say it is determinist: some version of determinism must be true for causal explanation to be possible. The objection is that it leads us into the elementary fallacy of asserting *post hoc ergo propter hoc*. Sequentiality is necessary, but not sufficient to demonstrate causality. Not everything that happened under colonial rule in South Asia and Africa happened because of colonial rule; nor should colonialism be elided with all the modernising forces purportedly emanating from the west in the later nineteenth, early twentieth centuries. The colonialists did not conjure up a market economy in South Asia or West Africa out of nothing and for much of the time did no more than provide political cover for the entrepreneurial initiative of indigenous economic actors. It is a commonplace observation, from the sheer variety of regime types in the independent Asian and African states and the disparities in their economic performance, that their political and economic elites have been neither prisoners of the colonial past, nor neo-colonial intermediaries between international capitalism and post-imperial dependencies. Some have skilfully managed their political arenas and the inherent conflicts of their plural, stratified societies; in so doing they created the political conditions for economic growth and rapid and pervasive improvements in material welfare. Others have disastrously mismanaged their economies, permitted the subversion of state institutions by private interests and failed to sustain such basic functions of governance as securing law and order and a sound medium of exchange.

Ghana and Malaysia – which both gained independence from Britain in 1957 – illustrate the spectrum of post-colonial trajectories. They are comparable, medium-size tropical economies: the Malay Peninsula has a somewhat larger population, more abundant land and a richer portfolio of natural resources than Ghana, and was decidedly more prosperous around 1960. But this only partly explains a far superior record of economic growth and development since then. Between 1960 and 1989, per capita GDP in Malaysia – measured in constant US$ and taking account of purchasing power parity – rose three-fold, while in Ghana it fell by a quarter (World Bank, *World Development Indicators*). Of course, estimates of per capita GDP tell us nothing about the social distribution of income, household consumption and the incidence of poverty. But, in this instance, they correlate with social indicators (infant mortality, expectation of life, access to safe water and health care) that point to increasingly divergent experiences in the everyday lives of Ghanaians and Malaysians. On a crude headcount index, poverty fell by half in Malaysia between 1970–5 and 1988–93, from 38 per cent to 16 per cent (World Bank, 1995, p. 212). It is difficult to put figures on the trend in Ghana, but knowledgeable observers report the remorseless impoverishment of broad social strata from the 1960s up to about 1983 (Rimmer, 1992, pp. 4–6). Even once-privileged public employees – such as senior civil servants and university professors – found their real incomes drastically reduced by the hyper-inflation of the late 1970s, early 80s.

In the late 1960s and early 70s, radical scholars regarded both Ghana and Malaysia as neo-colonies exhibiting a syndrome of underdevelopment supposedly characteristic of tropical economies which had been 'inserted' into the world market economy as primary producers (Kay, 1975; Amin and Caldwell, 1977). For those wedded to the concept of 'underdevelopment', it was an article of faith that primary production for world markets was an unequal trading relationship between the core and peripheral economies of the capitalist world system which resulted in the extraction of the surplus available for investment and the 'blocking' of capitalist development in the neo-colony. Given the intellectual currency of this concept, the least expected divergence in the post-colonial experience of these two states was the emergence of Malaysia as a substantial exporter of manufactures: in 1969, manufactures accounted for less than 7 per cent of total Malaysian exports by value, and 86 per cent of exports were classified as non-fuel primary products. By 1988, manufactures accounted for 45 per cent of Malaysian exports, while non-fuel primary products were slightly less than 40 per cent. The Ghanaian export sector remained structurally unchanged: non-fuel primary products were 96.5 per cent of exports in 1969 and 92.4 per cent in 1988. The relative weight of exports in the Malaysian economy had increased considerably in two decades: in 1969, the per capita value of Malaysian exports was about four and half times the per capita value of Ghanaian exports; in 1988, the per capita value of Malaysian exports was nearly 17 times greater (World Bank, *World Development Report*, 1995).

This is not to deny that post-colonial Malaysia has experienced acute ethnic tension and conflict, nor to overlook its authoritarian and frequently corrupt politics. At times, the Malaysian state has resembled the Ghanaian, but the likeness was superficial. Until the mid-1980s, the effect of state action in Ghana ensured that the great majority 'stayed poor': policy decisions taken soon after independence and fiscal irresponsibility in the 1970s were at the root of a general impoverishment which drove a fifth of the population (and probably a larger proportion of the workforce) into emigration (Rimmer, 1992, p. 213). For all its blemishes, the Malaysian state has provided the political conditions for a general improvement in material welfare. In alliance with the Malayan Chinese business community, it has repositioned the economy within the 'new international division of labour' that emerged with the de-regulation and internationalisation of financial markets around 1980, the accelerated growth of international trade in manufactures, and the relocation of production to low-wage economies. As has often been remarked, apart from Mauritius, no African economy has shown any sign of similar 'repositioning'; indeed, African economies are highly dependent on foreign trade yet marginalised within the international division of labour (Higgott, 1986; for a more recent analysis, see Collier, 2003).

The post-colonial phase in outline

Given the diversity of South Asia's and Africa's states and regions, can we sensibly generalise about the sub-continents' recent past? I think we can. A central contention of this study is that post-colonialism – in its literal sense – represented a reasonably discrete phase in South Asian and African history when sovereign state power was used to accelerate economic development and to nationalise or indigenise the commanding heights of the modern economy. Notwithstanding a ten- to 20-year gap between South Asian and African independence, the post-colonial phase was a temporal framework with real historical substance, and not a mere chronological stipulation (a point made by John Dunn, though I have generalised from it) (Dunn, 1978). The post-colonial political economy entailed a more or less explicit drive to correct the distortions – or perceived distortions – of colonial underdevelopment. Governments assumed responsibility for national economic planning, the mobilisation of capital investment in large-scale industry and infrastructure, and the transfer of savings from agriculture to industry, frequently by over-valuing their currencies at fixed exchange rates. Tariffs and import quotas were widely used to protect infant industries. By continuing and extending the colonial practice of making the purchase of agricultural produce a public monopoly, African governments imposed penal rates of hidden taxation on their farmers and manipulated the terms of trade between town and country. All post-colonial governments put their faith in state-led development and distrusted markets; African governments distrusted the immigrant entrepreneurs – Asians in East Africa, Lebanese in West Africa – who had cornered retail markets and service industries. South Asia, from the early 1950s, and Africa, from the later 1960s and 70s, experienced a 'golden age' of state capitalism, when public and parastatal enterprise was greatly expanded, and public sector and government employment grew much more rapidly than the economy as a whole. Since highly administered economies provide ample opportunities for the powerful to exploit public office for their own gain, it was also a 'golden age' of political rent-seeking.

To this broadly 'economic' generalisation I would add one that is broadly 'political'. Decolonisation changed the global order by greatly increasing the number of sovereign states but the appearance of fragmentation as the colonial empires broke up is deceptive: almost invariably acceding to sovereign statehood was a difficult and sometimes traumatic process of *political aggregation*. Witness the unstable union of

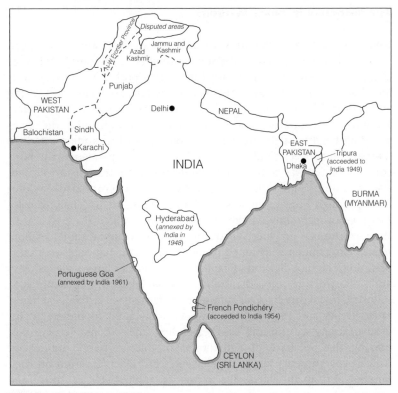

Map I.1 South Asia in 1948

Pakistan's two 'wings' and the ethno-regional strife in the Sudan, Nigeria, the Congo and other African states immediately after independence. Even India, where for historic reasons the sense of national integration had unusual depth, fits into a pattern of conflict-ridden state aggregation, and not just in Kashmir.

The most parsimonious explanation for these post-independence traumas lies in the transition from a 'mechanical' to an 'organic' relationship between rulers and subjects. As we have noted, modern colonial rule varied greatly in its forms and its impact on indigenous society and is difficult to characterise in general terms. In my view, it is best described as the cap-stone domination of plural and 'pillared' societies: it threw a canopy of European and 'native' law, police power and administration over different language groups, ethnicities, religious and cultural traditions which retained a high degree of autonomy.

Colonial administrations were small in relation to the population and cheap: they extracted little from the economy by comparison with contemporary national states (such as Japan) or successor states. Contrary to some accounts, they were often reluctant to unleash what were seen as destabilising and socially corrosive market forces, and sought to preserve indigenous traditions, not all of which were their own inventions. While the economic rationale of colonialism lay in extending and deepening the market economy, the moral justification of colonial rule lay in protecting the 'native' from the market. According to the East Africa Royal Commission, 'the dilemma confronting official policy lay in the fact that the desire to protect the African against the impact of modern influences conflicted with the desire to create the new income which alone could make possible a rise in his (*sic*) living standards'. 'Progress' required the introduction of foreign 'capital, organizing ability and technical skills', but safeguarding the African meant he had to be 'insulate[d] in the sphere of commerce and industry, from vigorous external competition' (East Africa Royal Commission, 1955, p. 391).

With the accession to national sovereignty – normally a protracted process – state administration invariably grew in size, social reach and modernising ambition. The fiscal 'take' from the economy rose to fund greatly increased public expenditure. Because the modern economic sector and civil society in the western sense were invariably small, public employment provided the main avenue of social advancement for the educated and ambitious. At independence, the successor regimes were expected to have an electoral mandate. India aside, democratic institutions proved fragile throughout the post-colonial world but, even when they were suppressed or suspended, national rulers were accountable to their publics in a way that their colonial predecessors had not been. These conditions enhanced the competition between poorly integrated sub-national communities for public office and public resources and raised the stakes in the internal struggle for political representation. Like all parsimonious explanations, this is liable to disappear into the mists of thick description when dealing with individual cases, but its heuristic core at a comparative level seems unassailable to me.

My third generalisation is surely uncontroversial: the post-colonial phase as I have defined it is now over. Since the 1980s, market liberalisation has effected a great retrenchment of state economic activity in both South Asia and Africa. In India, Rajiv Ghandi's premiership of 1984–9 initiated a break with the autarkic macroeconomic policies

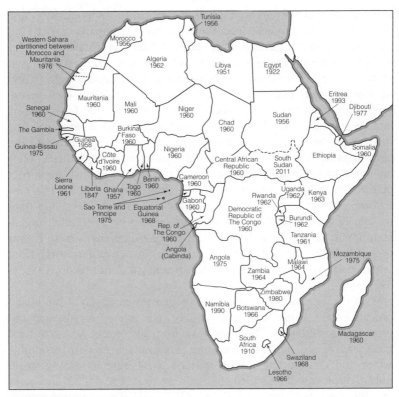

Map I.2 Africa, showing dates of independence

which had been pursued by Congress governments since around 1950. His government took the first, tentative steps to reduce the state's role in economic development and rely more on the market, with the declared aim of promoting efficiency, competitiveness and modernisation. The ulterior purpose was to curb the corruption and political rent-seeking which had become inextricable from the 'licence-permit-subsidy Raj' (Patel, 1987). The tectonic shift in the late 1980s from Congress dominance to an era of coalition politics opened the way for the more ambitious reform programme, introduced during of the premiership of P.V. Narasimha Rao (1991–6). This divested the government of economic functions it had been exercising for about 40 years. The economy, which had been protected by tariffs, import and exchange controls, and barriers to foreign investment, was opened up to world markets and global capitalism. The rupee was sharply devalued and made fully convertible on the current (though not the capital) account. Internal competition was encouraged by ending price controls and subsidies. The World Bank and International Monetary Fund had been urging reform on these lines for some time, and were given greater leverage over the Indian government by the depletion of its foreign exchange reserves, mounting international debts and a balance of payments crisis. But the initiative in going beyond what was needed to restore stability and alter fundamentally the relationship between the state and the economy was essentially Indian. Since the late 1970s, dissatisfaction with the meagre achievements of the inward-looking post-colonial political economy had accumulated amongst the policy-making elite. Before his assassination, Rajiv Gandhi had drafted a Congress election manifesto which anticipated the central points of the restructuring programme announced by the Finance Minister, Manmohan Singh. As he said, 'we are implementing our own agenda' (Nayar, 1998, p. 352).

Not so in Africa, where states were more indebted and the foreign trade sector was a proportionally larger part of most economies. The international financial institutions had relatively greater influence over Africa's exposed and weakened governments, which were reluctantly persuaded of the need for structural adjustment. This is discussed elsewhere (Chapter 4). Here, we must simply note that, while the economic role of African states has been much attenuated, their administrative capacity has been deeply eroded by the 'informalisation' of the economy, declining revenues and deteriorating infrastructure. In the 1990s, the most crisis-ridden states were unable to provide such essential public goods as law and security, enforceable contracts and a sound medium of exchange. About one African in five was living in a country disrupted by war or civil conflict (World Bank, 2000, p. 55).

Post-colonialism can now be viewed in a broad historical and comparative perspective to establish breaks and continuities with the colonial (and pre-colonial) past and the more recent transition from collectivist states aiming at societal transformation to the 'market opportunity' states of the present day. Whether they can still usefully be described as 'post-colonial' is a pertinent question. Crawford Young has argued that it is time to close the historical parentheses around the 'post-colonial' African state since little remains of the hegemonic state apparatus which African rulers inherited and initially sought to reinforce and expand as an instrument of rapid development (Young, 2004). With very different emphases, the argument also applies to South Asia. The state apparatus has certainly not shrivelled up in either

India or Pakistan; one malign symptom of its vitality is that they are nuclear states, with high levels of military expenditure in relation to GDP. In 1998, both courted international opprobrium by testing nuclear weapons and parading their capacity for mutual self-destruction. But government in India and Pakistan is no longer regarded as the orchestrator of economic development, as it was when Jawaharlal Nehru and Ayub Khan took personal charge of their countries' Planning Commissions and Indira Gandhi and Zulfikar Ali Bhutto launched their populist assaults on concentrations of economic power. The changes in the Indian political economy between 1980 and the early 2000s were so sweeping as to make it seem a different country to knowledgeable observers such as Francine Frankel (Frankel, 2005, p. xi). Pakistan in these years came to share some of the characteristics of the late twentieth-century African states: the state's authority ceased to run in extensive regions, not just in the tribal areas abutting Afghanistan but also in Karachi, where the proliferation of weaponry led to a 'Kalashnikov culture' and the violent criminalisation of politics. On the eve of the millennium, civilian officials could not undertake basic administrative tasks, such as taxing businesses, inspecting schools and compiling the census (or required the supervision of the army to so) (Talbot, 2000, p. 221). The military's continued dominance of political life is the outcome of a failure to institutionalise constitutional norms during the country's national history, which has obvious parallels with contemporary African states.

This book contributes to post-colonial history by trying to explain the distinctive patterns of change and persistence during the first generation of national independence. It combines political narrative with economic and social analysis in a reasonably accessible idiom. My method is to pose apposite questions and to try to answer them as far as the evidence allows. There are no satisfyingly succinct answers to the two overarching questions at the forefront of my mind when I embarked on this study because they involve huge counter-factual imponderables. (What would have happened to the Indian political economy had the British packed their bags in 1857? Would tropical Africa have developed differently had it remained under African rule after 1880?) The best we can do is to follow the 'play' of colonialism's institutional and economic legacies in the strategic choices of political actors in South Asia and Africa. They have not made their national histories under conditions of their own choosing, but they have made post-colonial history. Part I deals with South Asia up to the break-up of Pakistan in 1971 and the imposition of Mrs Gandhi's Emergency in

1975. With some temerity, I have included a chapter on caste in post-colonial India. It would be an exaggeration to say the institution was invented during the colonial era, but a Brahmin-dominated social order was, arguably, a legacy of colonialism. More to the point, caste in independent India has been functionally analogous to ethnicity in independent Africa. 'Casteism', used pejoratively by Indians to describe an unjust form of group solidarity which excludes other citizens, has the same kind of reference as 'tribalism' for Africans. The second part of the book, dealing with sub-Saharan Africa, was inevitably more difficult to focus. Chapter 4 offers a schematic chronology and thematic analysis of economics and politics in African states. There then follow three 'paired' case studies: Nigeria and Congo-Zaire; Rwanda and Burundi; and Angola and Mozambique (Chapters 5–8). It could well be argued that these case studies give a distorted impression of Africa's post-colonial experience by skewing the empirical material towards the calamities of civil war, military rule, ethnic violence and genocide, predatory rule, state failure and impoverishment. A different selection of case studies might well convey a more benign (and possibly more representative) impression of the post-colonial experience. In my defence, I would point out that the combined population of my chosen states is one-third of the African total, which is a substantial sample. Furthermore, they represent the variability of the colonial legacy in Africa and the variable degree to which its traditional institutions survived the colonial period (Burundi, for example, acceded to independence as a monarchy). They also exemplify broad themes in post-colonial history: the indigenisation of the economy, patrimonial rule, the attraction of Marxism to African radicals, the impact of Cold War rivalries and South African de-stabilisation, structural adjustment and market liberalisation. The final Summary and Conclusions try to take the measure of the growing divergence between South Asia and Africa, and offer a historical perspective on it.

1
Post-colonial Trajectories in South Asia

Introduction

India and Pakistan present a paradox for students of post-colonial history: they have a common colonial heritage but have followed different political trajectories since gaining independence on 15 August 1947. India was constituted as a secular state, Pakistan as a state for Muslims. In India, politics have observed democratic norms and power is transferred through competitive elections. The great exception was a period of emergency rule under Indira Gandhi in 1975–7, but even that was ended by her rash decision to call a general election. Pakistan, for most of its existence, has been governed by authoritarian regimes in which the military have played a dominant role; on four occasions army commanders have overthrown civilian governments. The Indian civil authorities have kept the military in strict subordination; senior military officers have never held ministerial office in New Delhi. India championed non-alignment in the Cold War; Pakistan allied with the USA. Of course, these are bald statements which require immediate qualification: Pakistan's founders were liberal secularists for whom Islam was a spiritual and moral framework, not a blueprint for modern jurisprudence. The Islamisation of the Penal Code, financial services and other civil society institutions was not attempted until the regime of General Zia ul-Haq (1977–88). Behind the contrasting constitutional façades, political life has exhibited disturbing similarities, including clientelism, pervasive corruption and criminalisation, and the alliance of religious militancy and xenophobic nationalism. Democratic and secular India has done only marginally better than authoritarian and Islamic Pakistan in preventing the recurrence of regional dissidence. In both countries, police abuse of the human rights of the poor goes unchecked. (See, inter alia, *Human Development in South Asia: The Crisis of Governance*, 1999.)

Nevertheless, the dissimilarities between Indian democracy and Pakistani authoritarianism are real and fundamental. If we applied the

42

principle that the same determinations cannot give rise to different outcomes, then it would be hard to see how 'the colonial heritage' could be the explanation for both. In fact, nobody would assert that colonialism alone determined the political characteristics of either state in the post-independence years. Colonial rule had overlain and entwined with indigenous traditions and institutions without obliterating them and had also provided a matrix for the evolution of representative politics and modern nationalism. The post-colonial political systems in South Asia resulted from a complex set of interacting determinations of which the institutional and cultural legacy of colonialism was only one. By the final years of their Raj, the British were not in control of events and were unable to impose their design for the post-imperial order on South Asia. There can be little argument that the structural conflicts within Indian society and politics led eventually to the creation of Pakistan (Bose and Jalal, 1998; Talbot, 1998). Partition represented a failure of British policy and the 'least bad' compromise between irreconcilable nationalist movements. The task of this chapter is to compare the different political trajectories of India and Pakistan from 1947 to 1971, when East Pakistan broke away to form the new state of Bangladesh, and to assess by way of an analytic narrative the factors determining the political development of each state.

The trauma of partition and the fragility of Pakistan

To explain the emergence of Pakistan is beyond the scope of this study. But to understand the brittleness of this two-winged state bifurcated by a thousand miles of Indian territory we need to grasp its improvised and even accidental character. Before the late 1930s, separatist nationalism did not seem a plausible political strategy to most Muslims. Though a recognised political category, with their own electorates, they did not cohere at the all-India level. Islam provided a spiritual canopy for the faithful, but its beliefs and rituals constituted only one component of social identity. Muslims were divided by region, language, sect, class and even caste. Many blended Islam with local traditions and symbols, not uncommonly of Hindu origin. Conservative theology was a barrier to modern political mobilisation because it preached the indivisibility of religious and secular rule and could not be reconciled with the nation-state.

The All-India Muslim League, which claimed to represent the Muslim 'nation', garnered only 4.4 per cent of the total Muslim vote in the

1936–7 elections and came close to extinction. Its core strength lay, not in the Muslim majority provinces of Punjab and Bengal, where Muslim politicians found their interests best served by regional parties and supra-communal alliances, but amongst the minority communities of the United Provinces, Bihar, Bombay, Gujarat and Madras. The League had no tradition of mass mobilisation and its leadership of urban professionals had deliberately eschewed civil disobedience. In September 1939, its leader, Muhammad Ali Jinnah, was still professing to be as much an Indian nationalist as Nehru; in January 1940 he could still write of India as the 'common motherland' for Muslims and Hindus (Moore, 1983, p. 537).

Three developments propelled Muslims towards an ambivalent separatism: the first was the formation, in 1937, of Congress Ministries in seven out of the 11 British Indian provinces and Muslim alienation by what was perceived as Hindu triumphalism. The second was the Raj's declaration of war in September 1939 without consulting Indian opinion, which it followed in October with a vague offer of post-war Dominion status. The League responded with its famous resolution of 23 March 1940, which demanded that the areas of Muslim majority in northwestern and eastern India be grouped together to constitute 'independent states', autonomous and sovereign. What exactly the League politicians envisaged is unclear, but it was certainly not the Pakistan of August 1947; most probably they anticipated the Muslim states federating with Hindu India. In August 1940, the government sought to allay Muslim anxieties by announcing that 'responsibilities' would not be transferred 'to any system of government whose authority [was] directly denied by large and powerful elements in India's national life' (quoted in Sarkar, 1989, p. 377). Of course, this was intended to divide further the League, which remained 'loyal', from Congress, which withdrew from the provincial ministries and forfeited its political leverage over the British. If the League could persuade the British that it was the 'sole spokesman' for Muslims, then it was tantamount to a League veto over the constitutional structure of the successor state (or states) when independence negotiations reopened on the outbreak of peace.

The third development was the League's explosive growth as a mass organisation following the crushing of the 'Quit India' movement in the autumn of 1942. The gaoling of the Congress leadership and arrest of about 90,000 militants created a void in which the League could operate; we might also speculate that the revolt itself persuaded Muslims that organising for independence was a matter of compelling urgency. For ordinary Muslims, 'Pakistan' came to represent freedom, equality and prosperity, and the League its champion. Exactly how *Islam* figured in the popular imagining of Pakistan is very difficult to say, but it is significant that the orthodox Islamic movement, Jama'at-i-Islami, was set up in 1941 to *oppose* the 'Pakistan idea' and counter the League's secular leadership (Talbot, 1998, p. 407). In Bengal, the League acquired a socially radical reputation by promising to abolish the rent-receiving rights of the *zamindars* (predominantly Hindu rentiers who performed no productive function in agriculture). Many Bengalis also flocked to the League because they expected the 'Pakistan idea' to be realised in two Muslim states. In Punjab, the League pledged an end to exploitation by Hindu *banias* and moneylenders. Small Muslim businessmen came to believe 'Pakistan' would protect them from the competition of established Hindu businesses. As Ian Talbot has remarked, by presenting 'Pakistan' as a universal panacea, the seeds were sown for the disenchantment so palpable in the post-colonial era (*ibid.*, p. 98). The 1946 election was, in effect, a plebiscite among Muslims on Pakistan and a mighty success for the League, which won 90 per cent of the Muslim seats. In Bengal, it polled so heavily that three-quarters of its opponents lost their deposits.

Jinnah entered the three-way negotiations hoping to use the demand for Pakistan to negotiate a new constitutional arrangement in which Muslims would have an equal share of power at a centre reconstituted on the basis of a partnership between two essentially sovereign states, Pakistan and Hindustan (Jalal, 1985). This strategy foundered on the insistence of Nehru and Sardar Patel on a strong unitary centre for independent India. They were all too aware of the sub-continent's potential for political fragmentation along its myriad fault lines of religious community, ethnicity and caste. They needed the Raj's powerful central apparatus to quell autonomy movements in the Hindu-majority provinces and incorporate recalcitrant princely states into the Indian Union (Jalal, 1995, pp. 15–16). The Gandhian ideas of non-party administration, decentralised power and authority, and village self-government had little appeal for the Congress high command. Their political 'vision' was resolutely statist; understandably so, given the ambition to establish India's sovereign independence, preserve its unity against secessionists and modernise its economy and social institutions. Nehru announced that Congress would not be 'fettered' by agreements with the British, which plainly indicated that Congress would use its majority in the newly created Constituent Assembly to write a constitution conforming to its ideas. What compelled the League and Congress to compromise was Britain's decision to bring

Independence Day forward to 15 August 1947 and escalating communal violence.

The circumstances in which Pakistan and India became independent states enormously influenced their subsequent political development. There is no calculus that would allow us to weigh these circumstances against the inheritance of mass poverty and illiteracy, a low level of economic development and a governing apparatus in which democratic nationalism vied with bureaucratic authoritarianism. I do not for a moment deny that the intended and unintended consequences of colonial policy and practice must have a central place in any causal analysis of South Asia's post-colonial history. But it would be perverse not to acknowledge the virtual autonomy of the nationalist elites by 1946, and their decisive roles in the sub-continent's partition, which resulted in India and Pakistan being constituted amid appalling communal strife and in mutual enmity. Killings were frequently accompanied by disfiguration, dismemberment and the rape of women from one community by the men of another (Khan, 2007, pp. 6–7). Estimates of the death toll vary from 250,000 to a million. Huge numbers were brutally shunted across the new international frontiers. During 1947–8, about 5.5 million Hindus and Sikhs crossed over from West Pakistan to India, while about 5.8 million Muslims travelled in the opposite direction. Every subsequent crisis in Indo-Pakistan relations prompted more to flee. By 1950, refugees or *muhajirs* constituted about 20 per cent of West Pakistan's population. The total number of migrations to and from East Pakistan can only be guessed at but probably exceeded a million. Some Bengali Hindu agricultural labourers fled *east* to Assam and the princely state of Tripura (which was not incorporated into the Indian Union until October 1949) where their presence added to the ethnic volatility of India's most restive region. The border between West Bengal and East Pakistan could be crossed without a passport or visa until October 1952 and many who fled their homes expected to return when communal peace broke out. In the west, the decision to migrate was irrevocable; in the east, it was more usually provisional. Permanent migrations tended to be a one-way traffic of Hindu landowners, civil servants and professionals who sensed their economic and career prospects in East Pakistan were dim: the bulk of the Hindu minority chose to stay put, and were about 22 per cent of the population in 1951. The 1971 civil war prompted a huge exodus, mainly to West Bengal and Bihar, though with significant numbers going to Assam.

The Kashmir conflict

The new governments wrangled over the division of the Raj's assets (particularly its military assets) and disputed control of the headwaters that irrigate some of West Punjab's best agricultural land. By late October, they were drawn into undeclared war in the state of Jammu and Kashmir where the Hindu prince ruled a Muslim majority and had hesitated to join either Pakistan or India. In late August, pro-Pakistan Muslims in western Jammu province staged an uprising; in response, Hindu communalists massacred an unknown number of Muslims in Jammu's eastern districts (where Hindus were in a majority), either at the maharaja's instigation or with his connivance. This prompted an invasion by *jihadists*, mostly Pathan tribesmen (armed and equipped by the Pakistani authorities) who matched religious zeal with an enthusiasm for pillage and indiscriminate rape (Guha, 2007, p. 67). When the *jihadists* and local insurgents threatened to overwhelm the maharaja's forces he called for Indian military assistance, which under law could not be provided unless he acceded to India. Muslims in Srinigar were so alarmed by the approach of their Muslim 'liberators' that they openly welcomed the Indian troops flown in to protect the capital. The *jihadists* were driven back and Indian ground forces moved westward to consolidate their control.

In a letter accepting Kashmir's accession, Mountbatten – the Governor General – wrote that 'as soon as law and order have been restored and Kashmir's soil cleared of the invader the question of the state's accession should be settled by reference to the people'. On 1 December, Nehru (who was of Kashmiri descent) reiterated this view in a private letter which envisaged either a plebiscite of the whole state, an agreed partition that reflected local sentiment or restoring an independent Kashmir (*ibid.*, pp. 71–2). Later in the month, he met with Liaquat Ali Khan, the Pakistani premier, in Lahore to negotiate a settlement, but the talks broke down over the question of the state administration in Kashmir: Delhi had installed an emergency regime under Sheikh Abdullah, leader of the National Conference, an intercommunal political movement in Kashmir, and a long-standing ally of Congress. Abdullah was a friend of Nehru, and both shared a secular vision of the modern nation-state; though not unambiguously in favour of accession to India, Abdullah was openly hostile to Pakistan. The Pakistanis argued that no plebiscite for which he had administrative responsibility would be free and fair, and insisted on his removal. Nehru confronted Liaquat with compelling evidence that the *jihadists* depended on Pakistani officials for arms and logistics, and that tens of thousands of armed tribesmen were under military instruction in West Punjab, preparing to engage Indian forces. When Liaquat denied any responsibility on the part of his government, Nehru's attitude hardened perceptibly. As soon as the talks broke down India warned that her forces would, if necessary, cross the frontier in pursuit of terrorists.

War between the two Dominions seemed imminent so Mountbatten, knowing Britain was unacceptable as a mediator, persuaded Nehru to refer the dispute to the United Nations Security Council. India's communication called for a plebiscite but also asked the Council to restrain Pakistan from assisting the invaders and from allowing its territory to be used for armed incursions against a neighbouring state. The internationalisation of the dispute made its peaceful resolution less likely because both sides used the UN as a forum for self-righteous inflexibility. India took her stand on the validity of the instrument of accession under international law and her sovereign prerogatives; her preconditions for holding the plebiscite became so strict as to arouse the suspicion they were intended to prevent it happening at all. Law and order had to be restored and parliamentary elections held in Kashmir *before* the plebiscite, which Indian and Kashmiri authorities would supervise and the UN merely observe. Until then, Abdullah's administration was to remain in place. These preconditions were totally unacceptable to Pakistan.

Open conflict between Pakistani and Indian troops broke out after the latter had moved against the Azad (Free) Government in western Kashmir, where Pakistani officers were organising local militias into a regular force. Pakistan's newly founded army went into action in May 1948 to ensure its borders and stabilise the situation. It drove the Indians out of western and northern Kashmir, but failed to over-run the central Kashmir valley. Hostilities continued until 1 January 1949, when a United Nations-sponsored ceasefire took effect, though with little prospect of a permanent settlement.

What, more than any other factor, prevented a peaceful settlement in 1947–8 was the intense mutual distrust of the Indian and Pakistani governments. Jinnah and his colleagues were convinced the Indians were bent on the piecemeal reversal of partition and the collapse of Pakistan: Kashmir was not the only instance where the sovereignty of a former princely State was in dispute, but failure to assert Muslims' right to self-determination there carried an existential threat to the state.

Pakistanis had heard harrowing accounts of the partition massacres from the refugees and public opinion gave the politicians no room for compromise. Nehru for his part looked on Kashmir's accession to India as the crucial test for the Union's secular character; the prospect of barbarous *jihadists* destroying the tolerant and urbane culture of the Kashmir valley horrified him. In acknowledgement of its Muslim majority and Kashmiri political aspirations, the State was granted a special status under the Constitution, which limited the Indian Parliament's legislative competence over Kashmir to defence, foreign affairs and communications. Kashmir retained its own flag and distinctive political titles, and Indian Kashmiri citizens had special rights. This status was from the outset repugnant to Hindu nationalists, who demanded unconditional loyalty to a state defined by its religious majority and opposed any constitutional rights or guarantees for minority communities.

The failure to achieve any of the options outlined in Nehru's letter of 1 December 1947 had baneful long-term consequences. The 'Kashmir dispute' proved to be one of the more rancorous and intractable in contemporary world politics: it has embittered relations between Muslims and Hindus, provoked communal violence and allowed bigots to manipulate religious solidarity. Pakistanis have never reconciled themselves to the inclusion in India of a principality with an overwhelmingly Muslim population on the say so of a Hindu maharaja. Indian-occupied Jammu and Kashmir could be retained in the Union only by military force and the occupying forces behaved with great brutality, especially after the emergence of the Jammu and Kashmir Liberation Front in the 1980s. India's political class connived in electoral fraud and the criminal violence of the security forces, with inestimable damage to the country's democratic and judicial processes (Guha, 2007, pp. 621–4).

We should note the sharp contrast between India's rationale for occupying Kashmir – to support the legitimate ruler – and its justification for the 'police action' taken in September 1948 against the principality of Hyderabad, where the Muslim Nizam ruled a predominantly Hindu population. Egged on by British Conservative politicians, the Nizam had asserted his treaty right to independence or even accession to Pakistan. His intransigence led to spiralling disorder and the flight of refugees to neighbouring states. The Indian army eventually invaded and overthrew his dynasty, an action legitimised by the will of Hyderabad's majority.

Constructing Pakistan's political economy of defence

Pakistan's geopolitical situation was inherently precarious: the east wing could not be defended in the event of Indian aggression and Afghanistan refused to accept the nineteenth-century treaties that demarcated the North West Frontier. The national elite were persuaded that the state's future could not be secured without huge military investment. In the initial year of independence, Pakistan spent more on defence than India (which had a far larger revenue base) and defence expenditure continued to impose a crushing burden on Pakistan's state budget throughout the first, vital decade of independence. Together with the cost of civil administration, defence accounted for more than three-quarters of the central government's budget – which left meagre public resources for development purposes. Barely 4 per cent of government expenditure was allocated annually to education, health and social services – a gross distortion of public spending justified by a climate of political paranoia. As a consequence, only a minority of children went to school and the adult literacy rate remained unchanged between independence and 1961 (when it was 16 per cent in West Pakistan and 21 per cent in East Pakistan).

Some time ago, the political theorist Hamza Alavi argued that postcolonial Pakistan inherited an 'over-developed' military-bureaucratic state apparatus designed by British rulers to subordinate the native social classes (Alavi, 1972). Though an enduringly influential notion, it is simply not true. At independence, the bureaucratic elite consisted of only 157 officers from the former Indian Civil Service and Indian Political Service; 50 were British nationals who remained behind on special contract. The officer corps was equally small and inexperienced: the infant state began life with ample soldiers at its disposal, but insufficient officers to command and organise them. Five hundred British officers were seconded to make up the shortfall and the first two commanders-in-chief were British. A Pakistani was not appointed commander-in-chief until General Ayub Khan assumed the post in 1951. The civilian elite of career politicians with experience of, or aspirations for, government office numbered a hundred or so men (Kochanek, 1983, pp. 46–7). Of course, the Pakistani state came into a legacy of institutionalised *practices* which were bureaucratic and authoritarian. Most senior officials had learnt their habits of rule in the service of the British Raj. But by any measurable criteria the state apparatus was 'under-developed' in relation to the national territory and wider society. It scarcely existed in Baluchistan, which the British had ruled indirectly through tribal leaders and institutions, and was rudimentary in the North West Frontier Province. The state had to be extemporised by an insecure central government that was desperately short of skilled personnel, which made extracting taxes from the provinces to fund escalating military expenditure even more difficult.

Constructing a political economy of defence led inexorably to the emergence of the army as a key governing institution. The army's sheer novelty was to its political advantage because it had no history as a pillar of the Raj, and so no anti-nationalist past to live down. It was seen as a body of Muslim patriots, who won plaudits for escorting refugees to the 'Homeland' during partition and acquitted themselves well in Kashmir. The undeclared 'state of emergency' during Pakistan's formative years proved highly consequential for its political evolution, since it enabled an unelected power elite to coalesce by cementing an alliance between the civil bureaucracy, the nascent officer corps and the judiciary. The balance of political forces was tilted towards the state's administrative arms and against its elected representatives. The latter lacked the collective confidence and even legitimacy to act as an effective check on the executive: both the constituent assemblies that sat during the parliamentary period from 1947 to 1958 were indirectly elected by the provincial assemblies and had 79 members at most, a tiny number in relation to a population of 75 million in 1951. Popular elections were held in the provinces but their results had no bearing on the composition of the first assembly, and little on the second. Although the failure of democracy was not pre-ordained, by 1950 there was already a tendency for the leading unelected officials to regard themselves as a 'shadow government', contemptuous of the venality and indiscipline of elected politicians.

The provisional character of the state's basic laws enhanced the inherited disposition to by-pass the political process and to govern by ordinance. By contrast with the speedy enactment of the Indian constitution, the ratification of Pakistan's was delayed until March 1956. Prior to that, the country was governed under the 1935 Government of India Act, as amended by the India Independence Act of 1947. This gave the Governor-General 'viceregal' powers over the provincial governments: before his death in September 1948, Jinnah had used them to deprive the provinces of their only elastic sources of revenue (the sales and income taxes and customs duties) and to dismiss two provincial chief ministers. Most damaging of all from the point of view of the country's precarious unity, he used his authority to impose Urdu, and Urdu alone, as the state language. In 1953–4, his successor, Ghulam Mohammed, exercised the same 'viceregal' powers to dismiss the Prime Minister and the first Constituent Assembly.

The economics of partition

The partition of the sub-continent was an economic, as well as a human disaster. In the short term, the violence and mass migrations disrupted food supplies and encouraged farmers to hoard their surpluses, while official price controls and rationing broke down amidst the administrative chaos. Consumer prices, which had already been driven up by inflationary financing in war-time, rose still further; by September 1948, they were about four times their 1939 level (Tomlinson, 1993, pp. 160–3). The longer-term consequences arose from the break-up of the sub-continent's common market and regional division of labour. What became Pakistan included some of South Asia's least economically and socially developed districts and for this reason physical and human capital was unevenly split between the two states. East Bengal, the world's largest producer of jute, was without a single jute mill; cut off from the industrial nucleus of Calcutta, it was what British officials called 'a rural slum' (Talbot, 1998, p. 98). West Punjab's cotton-growing areas were divorced from the mills of Bombay and Ahmedabad. Pakistan's sole economic advantage over India was greater food security: with 18 per cent of the population of undivided India it had supplied one-quarter of the food (Jha, 1980, p. 29). But it inherited only 10 per cent of the industrial base, much of which consisted of primitive agricultural processing plant, nearly all located in the west wing. Large-scale manufacturing accounted for only 1.5 per cent of total output in 1949–50 (the first year for which national accounts are available), while small-scale manufacturing accounted for 4.4 per cent (Bose, 1983, p. 997).

Before the great migrations, Hindus owned most indigenous industrial enterprises in the Muslim majority provinces and, along with Parsis and Europeans, dominated commerce and financial services. Their departure from Karachi and Lahore left an entrepreneurial vacuum, which was filled by *muhajirs* from the Muslim trading castes of western India. But the modern corporate economy and financial services had to be built from scratch: of the top 57 Indian companies on the eve of independence, just one was owned by a Muslim; the head offices of the major banks and commercial establishments were in

India. The prospects for Muslim capitalism were even dimmer in East Bengal than in the west, because very few Bengali Muslims had engaged in commerce or industry, which were largely controlled by Hindu Marwaris and Europeans (Kochanek, 1983, p. 21).

Monetary disunion and a trade war completed the commercial rift between Pakistan and India: in September 1949, following sterling's devaluation against the dollar, the Indian rupee was devalued while Pakistan kept to the old parity. Tariffs were introduced as part of a strategy of import-substituting industrialisation, which brought Indo-Pakistani trade almost to a standstill. Although a formal trade agreement was signed in April 1950, cross-border trade never regained its previous levels. Pakistan's leaders were determined to assert economic independence by excluding imports of Indian manufactures; exports to India of industrial raw materials (cotton, jute, leather) were substantially reduced.

By contrast with Nehru's India, the industrial strategy followed by Pakistan until the early 1970s put private enterprise at the forefront of development. The Industrial Policy Statement of April 1948 announced that state ownership would be confined to the munitions industry, hydro-electric power generation and the manufacture of railway cars and telecommunications equipment. All other industrial fields were to be left to private businessmen. The entrepreneurs who grasped this opportunity were, in the main, Gujarati-speaking *muhajirs* from endogamous communities (such as the Memons) noted for their frugality and industriousness. Wealthier members provided the capital and entrepreneurial skills needed for import substituting industrialisation. They were encouraged to shift from trade to industry by numerous state favours: an over-valued exchange rate, which effectively lowered the cost of imported machinery; tariffs for 'infant' industries, particularly those using local materials hitherto exported to India; tax exemptions on the profits of new enterprises. Where private capital could not be persuaded to take the initiative, the state-run Pakistan Industrial Development Corporation stepped in by raising capital for ventures that were sold to the private sector when fully operational.

Although the private sector was the vehicle for industrialisation, the government orchestrated the process through the bureaucratic allocation of foreign exchange. This gave it the power to determine every aspect of an industrial undertaking: its size, location, access to machinery and spare parts, and rate of expansion (Kochanek, 1983, pp. 76–7). Since domestic competition was weak, profitability was virtually guaranteed. In practice, the success of an enterprise depended more on its owner's ability to deal with bureaucrats than his managerial skills. Fortuitously, the Korean War stock-piling boom boosted the industrial strategy because revenues from raw jute and cotton exports soared and foreign exchange was relatively abundant. When the boom petered out, Pakistan faced a balance of payments deficit and sharply falling reserves, but chose not to devalue. Rather, the government introduced rigorous exchange controls and quantitative restrictions on imports, which further tightened its grip on the industrial boom.

From a very low base, large-scale manufacturing grew phenomenally between 1949 and 1955: cotton-spinning capacity rose nearly eight-fold and weaving capacity nearly four-fold. Production of jute goods rose from zero to over 54,000 tons. The converse of the industrial boom was agriculture's relative stagnation, due to lack of investment and artificially low prices for food and raw materials. Agricultural output rose by a meagre 1.4 per cent a year in West Pakistan between 1949 and 1958, much below the rate of population growth, and probably by the same in the East. Agriculture's share of total output was so large (53 per cent in 1950) that its stagnation depressed the economy as a whole. Despite the industrial boom of the early 1950s, the country's annual GDP growth rate throughout the decade was only 2.6 per cent. Internal terms of trade were deliberately turned against agriculture in order to transfer income to the industrial sector, and while agrarian living standards were depressed, those of the wealthier urban classes rose quite conspicuously (Noman, 1988, pp. 16–18). It was a striking example of the 'urban bias' so characteristic of post-colonial development, which bore particularly heavily on East Bengal. The transfer of its foreign exchange earnings to West Pakistan's industrialists became a symbol of regional exploitation. But even in the west wing, industrialisation was socially and ethnically divisive because it largely by-passed indigenous communities. Immigrant employers tended to favour immigrant workers: in 1959, nearly 70 per cent of Karachi's industrial workers were refugees, not local Sindhis; more than half industrial assets were owned by *muhajirs*.

Institutional continuities and discontinuities: India

Congress India inherited much from the British Raj: the central state institutions – the ministries, the Inland Revenue, Customs and Excise and various other economic services – were already in place; the administrative apparatus was taken over intact. The great majority of ordinary government officials had always been Indian, and the highest echelon of administration was substantially 'Indianised' before 1947. Unsurprisingly, therefore, the routines of *sarkar* (or government in general) were little affected by independence; clerks from the twice-born castes were as obnoxious as ever to illiterate and low-caste suppliants. Ministries were organised and functioned on British lines, with the politically neutral Indian Administrative Service acting as their 'steel frame'. Like its predecessor, the Indian Civil Service, this was an elitist bureaucracy, with a Gladstonian fiscal outlook and an ethic of public service. The banking system resembled Britain's (and not Germany's) in focusing on branch banking and having little involvement in industrial promotion (Joshi and Little, 1994, pp. 8–9).

The way the political system articulated with the state owed more to the 'Westminster' model of democracy than any other, largely because elements of it were already embedded in Indian political culture. The Constituent Assembly did consider alternatives: in his opening address, the Chairman anticipated greater attention being paid to the provisions of the American Constitution than to those of any other. In the event, the Assembly opted for cabinet, not presidential government, with the executive drawn from the party with a majority in the lower house (the Lok Sabha), which is elected on a first-past-the-post system. The decisive argument made against other forms of representative democracy was that India's 'constitutional traditions have become parliamentary' (cited in Morris-Jones, 1963, p. 298). And so they had: despite one-party dominance, the Union Parliament – and to a much lesser degree the state assemblies – proved an independent institution in the 1950s and early 60s, not an extension of government or party, in which opposition parties were surprisingly effective.

The 1950 Constitution was impressively innovative, while exhibiting strong elements of continuity with the 1935 Government of India Act (from which about 250 articles were incorporated virtually unchanged). Instituting universal suffrage in a vast society of illiterate smallholders was historically unprecedented. Roughly 13 per cent of the adult population had been enfranchised under the 1935 Act (though this included women who met a literacy or property qualification, so in this respect colonial India exhibited more gender equality than France or Italy). The constitution's statement of basic political principles marked a sharp break with the colonial past by eliminating separate electorates, listing the People's Fundamental Rights and drawing up the Directive Principles that the state should follow in making those rights effective (Brass, 1994, p. 2; the Constitution can be accessed on http://www.

india.gov.in). These principles included the distribution of the country's material resources in such a way as to promote the common good and avoid excessive concentration of wealth. 'Untouchability' and *begar* (the forced labour owed by tenants and others at the bottom of the rural hierarchy to their landlords and ritual superiors) were formally abolished, and the state was given an explicit obligation to ameliorate disadvantage amongst society's 'weaker sections ... in particular the Scheduled Castes and Scheduled Tribes'. Discrimination by the state on the grounds of religion, caste, sex and place of birth was prohibited under Article 15. After this had been cited in a legal challenge to Madras State legislation reserving a proportion of public jobs for the Scheduled Castes, the Constitution was amended in 1951 to permit *positive* discrimination on behalf of 'any socially and educationally backward classes of citizens'. Initially, this 1st Amendment was of little consequence but it eventually gave legal sanction to the 'rise of the backward castes', which so transformed Indian society in 1980s and 90s. (The Constitution's implications for caste are discussed in Chapter 3.)

The constitution reflected the secularism of the Congress high command by ignoring religious issues and precepts, with the significant exception of a reference to cow protection that was included against Nehru's wishes. The principle of free and compulsory education up to the age of 14 was endorsed and the states were directed to 'endeavour to provide' it within ten years (most failed lamentably to do so). With the subsequent passage of the Hindu Code acts (1955–6), a uniform civil code was established for all Hindus (and Sikhs), which represented a historic departure from religious and moral traditions (and was bitterly resisted by the religious right). It gave Hindu women the legal freedom to choose their marriage partners, to marry outside their caste and to divorce. Their entitlement to share in their husband's and father's property was substantially enhanced. Muslims retained their own system of Personal Law; to make them feel 'at home' in India, they were to be not only citizens with equal rights, but a religious community whose norms were recognised by the national state.

Running through the constitution is a contradiction between the citizens' rights it confers and the ample opportunity given to parliament to negate these rights during national emergencies, when the head of state can suspend the right to liberty and due process by introducing preventive detention (Brass, 1994, p. 3). Since the prime minister effectively determines what constitutes a national emergency, these provisions amount to a great concentration of coercive powers in the executive. They represented a striking element of continuity with the 'viceregalism' of the Raj, or the practice of the Centre ruling through administrative fiat. Moreover, the president can, in certain circumstances, suspend a state government and bring the state under Union control – so-called 'President's rule'. The family likeness to the Raj's coercive powers became even greater when, in the early 1960s, a Defence of India Act provided for the detention of anyone likely to prejudice the defence of India. In June 1975, when Mrs Gandhi suspended civil rights, ordered the preventive arrest of political opponents, imposed press censorship and outlawed 'extremist' organisations, she was acting *constitutionally*, just as she was when she dismissed non-Congress ministries in Tamil Nadu and Gujarat and imposed direct rule in January and March 1976.

Almost as consequential as the contradiction between freedom and coercion in the constitution has been the conflict between the socially egalitarian thrust in the Directive Principles and the inclusion of the freedom of property amongst the people's fundamental rights. Under Article 31, no property could be acquired for a public purpose unless the government paid compensation. Scholars have discerned a major pillar of state legitimacy in the protection given to private property: it helped insulate public institutions from revolutionary assault and ensured that politics has been dominated by legitimate political activity; peasant struggles have primarily had private property in view (Ludden, 1999, pp. 174–5). This thesis is persuasive in general terms, though the historical record is more complex than its proponents allow. Another and equally important pillar of the state's legitimacy has been promoting 'development', which has sanctioned the public appropriation of private and communal property. The 44th Amendment, passed during Mrs Gandhi's Emergency, actually removed the sub-heading 'The Right to Property' from the constitution, and greatly strengthened the government's powers of compulsory purchase. Her supporters argued this was necessary to give legislative teeth to the Directive Principles and redistribute land more fairly.

India was constituted as a federal Union in which the Centre and the States have recognised areas of competence. The Centre retained the more lucrative categories of taxation, but the States have responsibility for large areas of domestic government on which the national parliament cannot legislate. These include jurisdiction over public order, the administration of justice, education and communications. State governments are also responsible for agrarian governance, including such key subjects as land reform, agricultural credit, land revenue assessments and taxation of agricultural income. (Remarkably, the largest sector of the economy has been outside the independent state's fiscal reach: there has been no central taxation of land or agricultural income since 1950 and the States have taxed agriculture so lightly that it has made a negligible contribution to public revenues.) State assemblies passed the '*Zamindari* abolition' laws between 1950 and 1954, which ended the exploitative tax farming system in Northern India and represented the *only* serious measure of social reconstruction undertaken before the mid-1970s. (The process is examined in Chapter 2.) The Centre and the States share authority for subjects on the 'Concurrent List', which included social and economic planning. The federalism embedded in the constitution placed real restraints on the central government's social and agrarian policies and prevented a sweeping change of the social order by action from above. The strong powers vested in the Union government were more useful as a negative sanction in preventing open opposition by the States to basic principles of national policy than as a positive force for the effective implementation of central programmes (Frankel, 2005, p. 81). Federalism has been, in effect, socially conservative: it dovetailed with the legal and administrative framework inherited from the Raj in protecting the rights and privileges of diverse local elites.

The most pressing political problem confronting the Constituent Assembly was the integration of the 562 princely states into the Indian Union. Pakistan was a bitterly regretted aberration, which the legislators were determined not to see repeated. The Congress left wing despised the princes and aristocratic landlords as colonial collaborators and feudal relics, and favoured outright annexation. But Sardar Patel, the powerful head of the States Ministry, persuaded his colleagues to adopt a two-stage process by which the princes first acceded to the Union – that is, recognised its sovereignty in defence, external affairs and communications. Their territories were then integrated administratively, usually by posting in IAS and Police Service officials with extraordinary powers over local public representatives. As part of the concordat with the princes, the Constitution guaranteed them and their successors tax-free privy purses and the 'personal rights, privileges and dignities of the Ruler of an Indian State'. With the approval of the States Ministry, most Hindu princes continued to discharge the ceremonial and ritual duties they had performed as anointed kings. The concordat did little to placate their open hostility to the new regime. In Rajasthan, Madhya Pradesh and elsewhere, erstwhile rulers and their families exploited vertical ties of rank, caste and economic dependence to perpetuate an aura of political legitimacy. A significant number entered the electoral fray: 43 members of princely families contested parliamentary and state assembly seats during the period 1957–60, 51 during the period 1961–6 and 75 during the period 1967–70. Princely candidates enjoyed a success rate at the polls of almost 85 per cent. Such was their electability in the former British 'residencies' of central and western India, that all the major parties except the Communists sought their allegiance (Copland, 2007, p. 294). The shift to radical populism following Mrs Gandhi's smashing electoral victory of January 1971 put an end to the democratic state's concordat with the princes: the 26th Amendment (1971) abolished their privy purses and all their vestigial rights and privileges.

The end of princely India belies any simple thesis of continuity between the British and Congress Raj. Although the princely states had existed on British sufferance, their sham sovereignty and apparently voluntary obeisance to the King-Emperor rendered exemplary ideological service to the Indian Empire. The pompous rituals of allegiance allowed the Raj to project itself as the 'great arch' holding together India's diverse traditions and martial values, and the necessary source of order and authority amongst myriad principalities. These rituals underscored the idea that 'modern' national unity was a delusion. Princely India offended not just Congress's egalitarian ethos, but its centralising nationalism and desire for a state which could reach down into all regions and localities, rather than lord over them. This antithesis between imperial and national ideologies was so stark that we ought to pause over the assertion that bureaucratic authoritarianism was an enduring legacy of colonial rule (Jalal, 1995, p. 19). It is perfectly just in many respects, but misses the point that bureaucratic authority was what Congress wanted to exercise over large parts of India that had never experienced it.

Telangana: aborted agrarian revolution

We know the transfer of power took place without a national social revolution, or even widespread class conflict in the countryside, but we should not assume a fatalistic quiescence on the part of the socially oppressed. In specific political and social circumstances, the latent violence in the countryside could erupt into a sustained social struggle. By examining the most significant of these struggles, in the former princely state of Hyderabad, we can shed some light on why, at a national level, independence came without revolutionary upheaval.

As we have noted, Hyderabad was thrown into months of political turbulence by the Nizam's refusal to accede to the Union. At a local level, his regime was supported by a volunteer Muslim militia (known as *Razakars*) who, in alliance with the police, indiscriminately harassed the mainly Hindu villagers. Meanwhile, Congress and local communist militants intensified their political activity all over the state. While the former stepped up civil resistance (*satyagraha*), the latter resorted to terrorism, in which they were joined by a section of Congress and the socialists. Left-wing guerrillas took to arson, looting and murder, which drove rich landlords loyal to the Nizam into the towns for self-protection. Many village officials and well-to-do farmers migrated to neighbouring states, as much to escape the counter-terrorism of the Nizam's forces as the left-wing guerrillas.

When the Indian government finally took police action against Hyderabad on 17 September 1948, Communist parties throughout the world were under intense pressure from Stalin to break with 'bourgeois democracy' and the parliamentary road to socialism, and adopt a revolutionary strategy. Though more independent than many, the Indian Communist Party (CPI) was not immune to this pressure: in December 1947, it had decried independence as 'fake' and accused Congress of selling out to imperialism and feudalism. The party replaced its general secretary with a 'hard-liner', B.T. Ranadive, in February, and decided to continue the guerrilla war in the belief that the country was ripe for revolution. In May, the Nizam and urban party members struck an improbable tactical alliance against the common enemy, the 'bourgeois' Indian Union. The ban on the party in the state was lifted and gaoled communist militants were amnestied, on the understanding they would fight for Hyderabad's independence. After the police action, senior military, police and civil officials were drafted in by Delhi to lead an emergency administration, in a fashion highly reminiscent of their British predecessors. This almost certainly prolonged and widened the insurgency. Local circumstances dictated the tactics, but the enemy was now the national government. Landlords were either killed or driven out of the villages and their land redistributed among the tenants and poor, particularly in the Telugu-speaking districts, which gave their name the most extensive communist insurrection in the history of independent India. About 3000 villages spread over 16,000 square miles and with a population of 3 million were affected. For some years, large rural enclaves were controlled by a parapolitical regime of village 'soviets', which supervised the redistribution of about 1 million acres, prohibited forced labour and evictions for debt, and enforced a minimum wage for agricultural labourers. People were inoculated; public latrines were built; women's organisations were encouraged (Sundarayya, 1973). The guerrillas and government forces waged a savage little war until October 1951, when the communists were compelled by the real threat of political annihilation to reconsider their earlier assessment of the country's revolutionary potential. After consulting Moscow, Beijing and British comrades, the CPI changed its strategy to building a more effective legal organisation within the parliamentary system and forming united fronts with other leftist parties, though it did not rule out resort to violence in the future if the situation became favourable. For their part, the central and state governments appreciated that peasant grievances could not be allayed without radical change in the rural economic structure, and so introduced land reforms which struck at the power of the mainly Muslim magnates. Though the communists were branded as 'terrorists', the authorities had quietly learned lessons from their campaign of relief and uplift amongst the isolated villagers. Indian officials reached out to tribal groups whose previous experience of state administration was, at best, fleeting. The post-colonial state had set about crushing the Telangana revolution in the fashion of its predecessor, but was compelled to develop new strategies of pacification to bring it to an end (Sherman, 2007, p. 512).

Why did communist insurgency break out in a former princely state, and not in one of the erstwhile provinces of British India? Its initial impetus came from the nationalist movement but that does not explain its persistence over several years and in the face of drastic counter-insurgency measures. Much of the answer lies in the *jagirdari* system of land control that prevailed under the Nizam's feudal regime. *Jagirs* were originally land grants to Mughal officials that had evolved into hereditary holdings from which landlords could extract rent and state revenue without legal restraint. It was the extreme case of state support for landlords in pre-independence India, which gave tenants no legal protection, provided no institutions for conflict resolution or reform, and connived at the extortion of forced labour and payments in kind by Muslim and high-caste *deshmukhs* (revenue collectors turned landlords) from low-caste and tribal peasants and debt-slaves. The contrast with British India is instructive, for the colonial state had curbed the landlords' power and secured tenants' tenurial rights. Without much clear intention, British rule greatly expanded the social stratum with a legally recognised stake in the land, one that, though not an absolute property right, could be defended in the courts rather than by violence.

The electoral bases of the Congress Raj

The Indian National Congress is one of the world's oldest political parties, and was for many years one of the most successful. Its longevity as the party of national government in a functioning parliamentary democracy has been matched only by the Italian Christian Democrats and the Japanese Liberal Democrats. Congress was the outstanding example of a hegemonic political movement in an 'emergent nation', which provided both an umbrella organisation for diverse social groups and interests and offered them political and moral leadership. At its apogee under Nehru, Congress seemed like an entire party system in itself in which conflicting constituencies found expression, conciliation and compromise. It was the 'party of consensus' and the only political organisation from which a national government could realistically be formed; all other parties were 'parties of pressure' operating at the 'margins' of politics. Congress's synthesising nature undoubtedly contributed to the comparative stability of Indian politics in the first two decades of independence, and the successful working of elected parliamentary forms of government. 'One-party dominance' normally corrodes democratic institutions, but Congress was an exception: it gave legitimacy to the institutional framework of Indian democracy as a whole (Kothari, 1964).

Formally, Congress was a mass party with a dues-paying membership divided into primary and active members, and with an elaborate organisational hierarchy extending from the locality via the district and the State to the all-India level. It had prescribed mechanisms for allocating party nominations to candidates in Union and State elections, which functioned pretty effectively until the party split during Mrs Gandhi's first premiership. When Myron Weiner worked on his important study of Congress organisation in five scattered districts in the 1960s, he found that, though their organisational quality varied greatly, most district committees kept membership records in a functioning office and held periodic internal elections. The fundamental reason for the vitality of the party's local organisation was the expansion of governmental activities since 1947, coupled with the influence local parties could exert on their members' behalf over the local administration with respect to tax enforcement, issuing permits for the purchase of cement and fertilisers, and obtaining public employment. However, social altruism was still an aspect of party work: local Congressmen mediated disputes between landlords and tenants and many continued the Gandhian tradition of social work amongst the poor and 'untouchables'. We should also note the activism of the professional party workers in the state committees, who were constantly on tour, transmitting information and checking on the local parties (Weiner, 1967, pp. 461–5).

Under Nehru, economic development was the overriding concern of national policy and he projected an image of government by a dedicated but disinterested technocracy, serving citizens who would henceforth eschew the civil disobedience associated with the freedom struggle. As the 'natural' party of government Congress wished to be associated with modernity and civil discipline, but it could never be the political vehicle for a disinterested technocracy (as the Communist Party of the Soviet Union claimed to be) because its primary function was to mediate social cleavages and conflicting interests. The party was an arena for fierce political competition between ambitious individuals and their followings, and for this reason its formal organisation intermeshed at every level of political and governmental activity with an elaborate network of factions. Those hoping to secure the Congress ticket for State or Union elections had to forge links with the professional party managers on the one hand, and district Congressmen on the other. These 'faction chains' were often held together by kinship and caste and invariably lubricated by patronage. Congress chief ministers in the State legislatures were in grave danger of losing office if a rival faction took control of the party organisation: the Chief Minister of Uttar Pradesh was displaced in this way in 1961, much against Nehru's wishes (Kothari, 1964, p. 1164).

Congress owed its position as the 'natural' party of government partly to a 'first-past-the-post' electoral system giving an in-built advantage to the dominant party in multi-party contests. Under Nehru, Congress regularly secured 70 per cent of the seats in the Lok Sabha, and controlled the great majority of State governments, but with the active support of less than one-quarter of the electorate. Turn-out in the 1952 elections was 45.7 per cent and, in 1957, 47.8 per cent; on each occasion Congress received less than half the total vote. Women, particularly in the countryside, abstained more frequently than men; it would seem around one in three voted in the 1950s. Electoral support was mobilised 'vertically' within a deferential social hierarchy: Congress votes came from the land-controlling, twice-born castes at the top and from the Scheduled Castes, Muslims and disadvantaged minorities at the bottom. Doubtless, many illiterate villagers voted for Congress because it was 'the party of Gandhi', which was often the only political name recognised by rural Indians in the first decade of

Independence. But many others voted for Congress because they were instructed to by local patrons. Where the *jajmani* system survived, it facilitated 'vertical' political mobilisation by twice-born notables who manipulated client relations in the countryside to create veritable vote banks for Congress. This deferential form of electoral politics functioned all the more smoothly because Congress recruited very few active party members from amongst low-caste and disadvantaged groups, and the control of its local organisation usually lay with the traditional dominant castes. In the northern Hindi-speaking belt, they provided over half Congress members of the Lok Sabha until the early 1970s, though they were only a fifth of the population (Jaffrelot, 2000a, p. 86).

In terms of the percentage of popular vote garnered in national elections, the only party (apart from Congress) to scrape into double figures in the Nehru era were the Socialists, who were ideologically close to the Congress left. Opposition was, for all practical purposes, a regional phenomenon. In the Tamil-speaking south, the DMK (Dravida Munnetra Kazagham) emerged as the vehicle for ethno-regional (and anti-Brahmin) sentiment; Hindu communal parties had local bastions in the Hindi-speaking north. After the communists reverted to constitutional politics, they secured electoral bases in Kerala (where they established the world's first *elected* communist government in 1957) and in West Bengal (where they led a coalition after Congress's reversals in the state assembly elections of 1967). In the meantime, however, the party had split along its pro-Soviet, pro-Chinese fault line, which greatly impaired the communists' ability to challenge Congress at a national level.

The legitimacy of Congress under Nehru stemmed from having secured independence and from speedily introducing and then abiding by the Constitution. But its hegemony – meaning the process of maintaining the active consent of the 'political nation' – lay in its ability to operate simultaneously in two political cultures, each with its own idiom. The 'high' political culture – closely identified with Nehru in person – revolved around national integration, economic planning, secularism and non-alignment It was the political culture of an Anglophone intelligentsia that was both 'westernised' in its political values and 'anti-western' in its political ideology. Parallel to this was a 'low' political culture revolving around faction and caste, patronage and clientelism, nepotism and communalism. Modern political ideology was largely irrelevant to this 'low' culture and the grand issues of national development impinged on it only as opportunities to secure resources for one's locality and following. When operating in this 'low' culture, Congress accommodated itself with all kinds of social forces that were inimical in the 'high' culture. To take one example, between independence and 1956, Congress in the Gonda district of Uttar Pradesh was dominated by the ex-Raja of Mankapur, whose family owned one of the great talukdar estates in the region. The abolition of the old tax-farming system and the centre's theoretical commitment to land ceilings did little to diminish the ex-Raja's economic resources, his social power over tenants or his sheer pleasure in exercising power and authority in the grand manner (Brass, 1984, p. 95). There was nothing to distinguish him from the great landlords-cum-political patrons of West Pakistan.

The Congress 'system' under Mrs Gandhi

In late 1974, the political scientist Rajni Kothari published a reassessment of the Congress 'system' ten years after his original influential analysis appeared. Despite the political and social turbulence in the intervening decade he concluded that 'the system is still largely the same' (Kothari, 1974, p. 1039). Congress remained the single dominant party – no other organisation had the remotest chance of forming a national government – and it still assimilated heterogeneous social elements around an eclectic ideology. The party's staying power was remarkable because it had split in late 1969, following the rise to power of Indira Gandhi (1917–1984), Nehru's daughter. Mrs Gandhi had not been groomed for highest office: she owed her accession to the premiership after Lal Shastri died unexpectedly in January 1966 to the determination of the Congress Party president K. Kamaraj and his senior colleagues to exclude Morarji Desai, the able former finance minister who had been critical of Nehru's macroeconomic policies. Their expectation that Mrs Gandhi would be the pliant chair of a collective leadership was sorely disappointed. She effectively destroyed the clique of senior figures – the so-called Syndicate – who controlled the party's organisation and in the process transformed the Congress 'system'.

Mrs Gandhi's premiership began while the country was facing its gravest subsistence crisis since the Bengal famine of 1943 (discussed in greater detail in Chapter 2). Famine was avoided in the worst-affected State, Bihar, only by increased imports, mostly in the form of US food aid. Imports notwithstanding, food grain availability per head in

1966/7 was about a tenth below the 1960/1 level. When the country went to the polls in February 1967, food prices were rising at an unprecedented rate and acute distress was widespread; the electors' verdict on the government was understandably harsh. Congress's share of the popular vote in the Lok Sabha elections fell from 44.72 per cent in 1962 to 40.92 per cent (though the vagaries of a 'first-past-the-post' electoral system meant that its share of the seats fell from 73.07 per cent to 54.6 per cent). But in the State Assembly elections in Orissa, Bihar, Punjab and West Bengal Congress suffered much sharper reversals at the hands of anti-Congress 'fronts'. By the summer, coalition governments were installed in eight of the 17 states, which represented a watershed in the country's political evolution. Local results and surveys by the Institute of Public Opinion showed that Congress was losing support amongst the young, the uneducated and the poorest in the big cities, and amongst religious minorities. In urban India, the electorate was tending to polarise between the communist parties and the communal and conservative parties, with Congress occupying a contracting electoral space in the centre. It would, though, be wrong to impose too clear a pattern on the amorphous contours of the national political community: princes were voted into office in Madhya Pradesh, Rajasthan, Gujarat and Bihar, while revolutionary Marxists took the parliamentary road to power in Kerala and West Bengal. Hindu communalists roused enthusiastic support in the Hindi heartland, while militant anti-Hindi parties captured power in the south.

We can safely say that there was no disaffection with electoral politics as such: 61.3 per cent of the electorate voted in 1967 compared with 55.4 per cent in 1962. There was, though, a terrible degeneration of parliamentary politics at State level: the coalitions were usually unstable; individuals and factions were offered all kinds of inducements to 'cross the floor'; legislators sank into a morass of almost unlimited opportunism; the proceedings of local assemblies became more rancorous and sometimes violent and, when they were prorogued, conflicts within them spilt out into street confrontations between the supporters of rival factions and the police. The cost to the legitimacy of the democratic process – in growing public contempt for politicians, more frequent recourse by State governments to political arrests under preventive detention acts, police tear-gassings, lathi-charges and firings, and rule by executive ordinances as legislatures failed to function – was clearly very high (Frankel, 2005, p. 368).

This turning point in electoral and State politics took place against a backdrop of increasing social conflict and disorder. Political scientists have demonstrated that the ratio of riots to population – which had been relatively stable between 1954 and 1964 – rose slowly in the mid-1960s and dramatically from 1967 (Bayley, 1983; Rudolph and Rudolph, 1987, p. 238). Protests against food shortages, rising prices, hoarding and profiteering became much more frequent. The number of workdays lost to industrial strikes trebled between 1964 and 1970. Reported incidents of student 'indiscipline' rose ten-fold. More threatening to the political order and the landed hierarchy were the rural rebellions, usually involving tribal landless labourers, known as 'Naxalite' movements. They took their name from the bloody confrontation in the Naxalbari subdivision of Darjeeling, in March–July 1967, between landless cultivators, landlords they deemed to be in illegal possession of land and the police. The original movement was precipitated by local resentment at the failure to implement land reform and the installation of the first Communist-led government in West Bengal. Although soon repressed, it prompted similar Naxalite incidents, involving terrorist violence against large landholders, along the tribal belt running through West Bengal, Bihar, Andhra Pradesh and Kerala (Brass, 1994, p. 324; Guha, 2007, pp. 421–6). Though the Naxalite rebellions were crushed by force, more peaceful agrarian protests – usually involving the occupation of land that ought to have been relinquished under the land ceilings legislation – continued. A 1970 Home Ministry study stated that 'an explosive situation' existed as a result of the state governments' failure to implement land reforms, and warned that the patience of the cultivating classes was 'on the verge of boiling over' (quoted in Rudolph and Rudolph, 1987, p. 238).

In the wake of her party's electoral setback, Mrs Gandhi was obliged to accept Morarji Desai as her deputy prime minister and finance minister. His appointment exposed the widening ideological rift, within government and Congress, between the left – who were pressing for more state ownership, land reform, the revision of the Constitution and an anti-imperialist foreign policy – and the 'business-friendly' right, who were coming to see the public sector and bureaucratic regulation as dead-weights on enterprise and economic growth. Whether Mrs Gandhi aligned herself with the left out of intellectual commitment or (as her enemies alleged) to boost the cult of her own personality amongst the Congress youth wing, the radicalised intelligentsia and urban poor is difficult to judge. But her public advocacy of the left's programme, coupled with her polemical and divisive style of leadership, made a contest with the party bosses for control of Congress inevitable. Her opportunity came with the death of the President of the

Republic, Zakir Hussain, in May 1969. Presidents are elected by all members of parliament and State assemblies, who at that time were expected to vote on party lines for official party candidates. Mrs Gandhi defied convention and effectively called on her supporters to vote for an independent candidate (who was elected on the second ballot). In November, she was expelled from Congress for violating party discipline; in December, she and her supporters set up a break-away organisation, initially known as Congress (R). The 'old' party became known as Congress (O) – for 'organisation', the implication being that the Syndicate retained control of the party apparatus.

After the split, Mrs Gandhi put herself at the head of the radical left and, by her fierce denunciations of the old party bosses as the stooges of reaction and communalism, hastened the polarisation of politics. Her party routinely used the government-owned All-India Radio as a medium for Marxist polemics to discredit the opposition. The language of politics ceased to be conciliatory and consensual, and became stridently combative. The accommodative tone of the Nehru years was drowned out by the rhetoric of class confrontation, not least because communists and 'hard-line' socialists who had left the Congress in the 1930s and 40s re-entered the fold and took control of the Congress Forum for Socialist Action (CFSA). They became a key group of Mrs Gandhi's supporters, and the bête noire of her conservative opponents (Frankel, 2005, p. 433).

Three-quarters of Congress parliamentarians went over to Congress (R); some were attracted to Mrs Gandhi's political radicalism, but many calculated their chances of re-election were improved by identifying with the Prime Minister, who was making herself immensely popular with Congress's traditional electoral base and with illiterate women and men who had not hitherto voted. Mrs Gandhi lost her parliamentary majority but was sustained in office by the Communists. In late 1970, she called a Lok Sabha election 14 months ahead of schedule, thus for the first time uncoupling the election of a national government from state elections. The intention was to concentrate voters' minds on the Prime Minister's personality and the compelling political choice she offered the nation either to 'abolish poverty' (*garibi hatao!*) or conserve privilege. Congress (O) entered a discordant electoral pact with Swatranta (an anti-statist party that favoured economic liberalism), the socialists and Jana Sangh (the Hindu communalist party), so commentators expected less fragmented voting and a hung parliament, followed by an unstable coalition government. The results confounded these expectations: Congress (R) won 350 out of 518 seats; the opposing electoral alliance won 51 and the two communist parties 48. Once again, the first-past-the-post ballot 'amplified' the swing to the victorious party: Congress (R) secured 43.7 of the vote on a 55 per cent turn-out.

Following her victory, Mrs Gandhi consolidated her following on the left by moving the country diplomatically and commercially closer to the Soviet Union, which soon displaced the USA as India's main arms supplier and became an important source of development aid, as well as a major trading partner. A 20-year treaty of peace and friendship was concluded between the two countries in August 1971.

The Prime Minister's apotheosis came with the crushing military victory over Pakistan in late 1971 and the striking gains made by Congress (R) in the States elections of March 1972. In the preceding months she and her closest advisers had brought the party organisation at both national and State levels under their control, and they used the Congress 'ticket' to select candidates loyal to the Prime Minister and in sympathy with the radical policies she had pledged. The Congress Chief Ministers of Rajasthan, Andhra Pradesh, Madhya Pradesh and Assam were forced to resign in 1971–2 because of their 'rightist' leanings, though all commanded comfortable majorities. Mrs Gandhi's imperious determination to stamp her authority on the party lists was matched by the slavish desire of many candidates to win her approval: hundreds besieged the office of Central Election Committee in Delhi to press their claims. About 50 serving State ministers were denied the Congress ticket, while many last-minute defectors from other parties received it. Everywhere, the overriding criterion for selection was unquestioning loyalty to Mrs Gandhi (Palmer, 1972–3). The result was even greater electoral triumph than the national election: Congress (R) won over 70 per cent of the seats. Its proportion of the votes cast – 48.3 per cent – was higher than the undivided Congress had ever received. No opposition party had a national 'presence' and most had suffered reversals even in their local bastions. In the following months, Mrs Gandhi made further drastic changes in the party organisation and installed special committees in the States to supervise Congress chief ministers. This was an autocratic 'style' of one-party dominance that her father had never practised, or even desired. A diffuse and pluralistic structure of participation, which involved almost the entire political spectrum, gave way to a highly centralised apparatus of power in which the political parties (including Congress) and parliamentary bodies had much diminished roles. Political life at State and local levels lost its autonomy.

No other Indian prime minister has enjoyed quite the power and authority of Indira Gandhi in 1972–5, so it is rather paradoxical that she should have felt compelled to carry out what was effectively a coup d'état. More is said on the origins of the Emergency in the next chapter. Suffice to note here that the legitimacy of the political system was corroded from within by the corruption of some of Mrs Gandhi's closest associates (including her son, confidant and political heir apparent, Sanjay) and from without by extra-parliamentary agitations and social movements that reduced some States to near anarchy in 1973–4. Running parallel to this social crisis was a bitter contest over the Constitution, parliament's supremacy in the state and the independence of the judiciary. It arose from a Supreme Court ruling that a court could decide the question of 'adequate' compensation when an individual's property was compulsorily purchased. This opened a vista of staggering financial obligations should the state press ahead with a large-scale nationalisation programme (Rudolph and Rudolph, 1981). The Court based its ruling on the fundamental right to property written into the Constitution. The Congress left in the Lok Sabha argued that the urgent societal needs expressed in the Directive Principles could and should override individual property rights; in 1971, it pushed through the 25th constitutional amendment to that effect. The intention was to put laws implementing the Directive Principles outside the purview of the courts, in legal terms to make them no longer justiciable. In April 1973, the Supreme Court struck down this key provision of the 25th Amendment. The Prime Minister interpreted this as a direct challenge to her power and her supporters were convinced that any programme of radical social legislation faced legal jeopardy. They began to press for comprehensive constitutional change. Fortuitously, the chief justice was due to retire at the end of April, and Mrs Gandhi departed from established convention by ignoring judicial seniority and replacing him with a less experienced judge known to be sympathetic to the government's position. Her blatant intervention in the highest judicial appointment caused huge controversy. Opinion polarised between radicals urging authoritarian means to institute sweeping reforms, and an informal coalition of critics in civil society persuaded that constitutional freedoms were in danger.

To Mrs Gandhi's chagrin, India's anti-colonial tradition was the source of a 'counter-legitimacy' that came back to torment the duly elected national government. The Prime Minister's foremost extra-parliamentary opponent was 'J.P.' Narayan, a veteran of the freedom struggle and 'Mahatma' Gandhi's leading disciple. His political ideas for a 'partyless democracy' and 'Total Revolution' were very vague but his moral and political 'vision' was clear: peaceful agitation to overthrow corrupt government was an expression of the people's collective 'soul'. Against the unrepresentative outcome of formal democracy, 'J.P.' appealed to a higher good (Guha, 2007, pp. 479–83).

Pakistan: the failure to establish democracy

The first decade of parliamentary politics in Pakistan was marked by abject failure, due partly to the chaotic in-fighting and corruption of elected politicians, but more fundamentally to endemic conflicts between the central executive and the provinces and localities (Talbot, 1998, p. 126). Political processes were overwhelmingly provincial in character and in an ideal world the centre would have allowed resources to devolve to the provinces. But, given the state's strategic insecurity and financial exigencies, devolution was not something it could concede. Instead, the centre made revenue extraction its primary objective, and devoted most of its energies to administrative consolidation and expansion. The task of building a national party-based political system, capable of reflecting the country's linguistic and cultural diversities, was sorely neglected. It would, in any event, have been extraordinarily difficult because the Muslim League, the only party with a popular base in both wings, refused to transform itself into a party of government. In February 1948, the League's Council decided to debar government ministers from holding party office. Its organisation, which had little of Congress's strength in depth, began to atrophy. The country's first prime minister, Liaquat Ali Khan, was endeavouring to reactivate the League when he was assassinated in October 1951. His death hastened its decline as a nation-wide movement able to link the electorate with executive power, removed a politician of unusual probity and accelerated the drift to authoritarianism.

In the following months, a military-bureaucratic triumvirate grasped the reins of central state power: it consisted of the newly appointed Governor-General, Ghulam Mohammed, Ayub Khan, the Army's commander-in-chief, and Iskander Mirza, the Defence Secretary. All were 'non-party' men with little time for democratic politics. In April 1953, they removed the Prime Minister, Khwaja Nazimuddin, from office when he still commanded a majority in the legislature. Their impatience with Nazimuddin sprang from several causes: his constitutional proposals would have ensured a Bengali majority in the national legislative assembly, and also included provision for a board of *ulema* to advise the head of state whether or not any legislation was repugnant to Islam. This smacked of a religious veto over the legislative process, and was unacceptable to Ayub Khan and his colleagues, whose outlook was essentially secular. The Prime Minister could not unite a Cabinet increasingly factionalised between its Punjabi and Bengali elements and his government floundered in the face of social disorder resulting from food shortages, inflation and unemployment. It handled the Bengali language movement utterly ineptly. Additionally, the foreign policy orientation favoured by Nazimuddin diverged sharply from what the triumvirate considered to be in the state's best interests. They favoured Pakistan's entry into a Cold War-driven regional defence organisation sponsored by the United States; Nazimuddin would have preferred a pan-Islamic foreign policy. In his place, the triumvirate installed the ambassador to Washington, Mohammed Ali Bogra, a political nonentity from Bengal more concerned with promoting US interests than those of his own province.

Containing the Bengali autonomy movement: the dual crisis of 1954

The Constituent Assembly's refusal to recognise Bengali as a state language created an entirely avoidable problem. About 55 per cent of the population lived in East Bengal, where the overwhelming majority were Bengali speakers. Educated Bengali Muslims resented Urdu's status as the sole official language, not simply because of a justifiable pride in their own cultural and literary heritage, but because it effectively excluded them from the higher echelons of government service: candidates had to be able to speak and read Urdu. According to the 1961 census, only 1.3 per cent of the population of East Pakistan were Urdu speakers, compared with 14.6 per cent in West Pakistan, where Urdu functioned as the medium of literate communication. The privileging of Urdu perpetuated the historic disadvantages of Bengali Muslims. Under the British Raj, the Hindu *bhadralok* (or 'respectable people') had enjoyed a virtual monopoly on jobs in the administration of undivided Bengal: at partition, only *one* of the Muslim ICS officers opting for Pakistan was a Bengali Muslim. Bengali Muslims' resentment of their 'neo-colonial' situation was heightened by the posting of Punjabi officials to the east wing and the disdainful way the national elite dismissed their grievances as misguided provincialism – or evidence of an

Indian fifth column (Talbot, 1998, p. 134). To add insult to injury, the Constituent Assembly refused to hold sessions in Dhaka.

Agitation on the language issue began in 1948–9, when the government's inflexibility drove Bengalis who had long supported the Pakistan idea to quit the Muslim League and form the Awami (or People's) Muslim League. (To stress its secular character, 'Muslim' was later dropped from the title.) After a lull, the language agitation reached a crisis on 21 February 1952, when the police fired into a demonstration at Dhaka University protesting against the Urdu-only policy, killing three students and giving the Bengali cause its first martyrs. Thereafter, 21 February was commemorated as Martyrs Day, with ceremonies that invariably took on an anti-West Pakistan tone and marked a serious psychological rift between the two wings. Under constitutional proposals put forward in 1950 and 1952, they were to be allotted equal numbers of representatives in a bicameral legislature – a denial of the East's popular majority – without the substantial political autonomy that might have sweetened the pill of unfair representation. On both occasions, the opposition parties in the East organised province-wide protests against the proposals.

The electoral consequence of Bengali alienation was the overwhelming victory of the opposition United Front in the elections for the East Bengal Assembly in March 1954, and the Muslim League's near obliteration in the province. The Front was an alliance of convenience between the Awami League, the Krishak Sramik Party led by A.K. Fazlul Huq (the former premier of undivided Bengal), communists and a cluster of regional parties. It was riddled with ideological differences, though agreed on a 21-point programme demanding the adoption of Bengali as a national language, the recognition of East Pakistan as a sovereign and autonomous region, with the central government's authority restricted to defence, foreign affairs and the currency. In deference to the Front's left-wing components, the programme also called for the nationalisation of the jute industry, the uncompensated abolition of the *zamindars'* rental rights and the distribution of their holdings to landless peasants. Though the Front's motley leadership was generally conservative, it was buoyed up by radical populism, much of it directed against an arms agreement recently negotiated with the USA.

The United Front leaders interpreted their electoral mandate as a popular vote of no confidence in the Central Government and the Constituent Assembly, and called on both to resign. A new assembly would, they hoped, introduce a constitution that would respect

Bengalis' demographic preponderance. Not unexpectedly, the triumvirate and central premier rejected these demands. The political impasse
was broken by the Governor-General dismissing the United Front government, after it had served less than two months in office, and
imposing Governor's rule. Iskander Mirza was designated Governor of
the east wing and the Provincial Assembly was indefinitely suspended.
The pattern was set for subsequent coups: the deposed premier was
placed under house arrest and mass arrests followed. The Communist
Party was declared an unlawful organisation in both wings.
Censorship, including pre-censorship of the local press, was imposed.

The pretext for this coup de main was the allegation of treason – in
complicity with India – laid against the United Front's chief minister,
Fazlul Huq. He had, in fact, made no secret of a desire to heal partition
by reviving the old idea of 'India' as the common homeland of Hindus
and Muslims. Speaking at Sarat Bose Academy, in West Bengal, shortly
before his dismissal, Fazlul Huq proclaimed:

> We are fellow workers in a common cause. If we have a common
> cause in view, it is idle to pretend that I am a Bengali, someone is a
> Bihari, someone is a Pakistani and someone is something else ...
> India exists as a whole ... I shall dedicate myself to the cause of the
> Motherland and will work for those who will try to win for India –
> Hindustan and Pakistan – a place among the countries of the world.
> (Park and Wheeler, 1954, p. 31)

However baseless the treason accusation against Huq, there was a
certain rough justice in the dismissal of the United Front ministry, for
it had proved incapable of policing the industrial violence that swept
through the east wing during its tenure of office. In the worst incident,
some 400 people (including women and children) were killed during
riots at the notorious Adamjee jute mills. The violence had an ethnic
dimension because the appalling working conditions were conducive
to rivalry between Bengali and non-Bengali workers.

Shutting down Pakistan's democracy

Parliamentary government was effectively terminated in 24 October
1954, when Ghulam Mohammed dissolved the Constituent Assembly,
declared a state of emergency and formed a wholly unrepresentative
'cabinet of talents'. After the rout of the Muslim League in the east

wing, the state elite despaired of holding the country together by any form of party organisation, and looked to the army and bureaucracy to exercise power. The faction-ridden assembly was by this time utterly discredited in the eyes of the literate public. In a transparently self-serving manoeuvre, Bengali and Sindhi parliamentarians had secured the repeal of a law disqualifying corrupt politicians from office, while maintaining the existing ban on their political enemies. Ghulam was acclaimed a hero in the still comparatively free press and his promise of fresh elections accepted at face value. Educated patriots seem to have been wholly behind the coup, and not without reason: having been indirectly elected eight years previously, the Assembly was completely out of touch with the people; and five years of wrangling had demonstrated its inability to fulfil its responsibilities. The Supreme Court of Pakistan upheld the Governor-General's action, arguing that he was empowered to disband the Assembly and veto legislation it passed. Further support for the military-bureaucratic axis came from the Americans.

Temporarily, the coup defused the crisis in the east wing. United Front spokesmen were overjoyed by the dissolution of the assembly, which they took to be the prelude to the restoration of parliamentary provincial government. The new regime quickly sought to conciliate Bengali opinion by recognising it as a state language, while local languages in the west wing were recognised at the level of provincial government. But coupled to this conciliatory attitude was an unconcealed contempt for politicians, acquired during long years serving the British Raj. Iskander Mirza, who held the critical Interior Ministry, had spent 28 years in the pre-war Indian Political Service; in his view, Pakistan needed a 'controlled democracy', in which politics would keep out of administration and religion would keep out of politics. After the constitutional crisis was, apparently, resolved, a well-informed American political scientist described the new regime as 'an "official" Government, remarkably like that of pre-war British India, with the Governor General presiding over the Council, the Commander in Chief as Defence Minister, and no element of responsibility to a Legislature' (Wheeler, 1955, p. 5).

The immediate preoccupation of the triumvirate was amalgamating West Pakistan into a single administrative unit, with one assembly and one ministry for all the wing's provinces and states. The so-called one-unit scheme had been mooted since 1948 but the League's electoral humiliation in Bengal had made its implementation a matter of urgency. With a unitary West Pakistan, the Punjabi-dominated elites would be better positioned to pre-empt Bengali control of the centre and neutralise demands for greater provincial autonomy in the east wing. It would also be easier for civil and military bureaucrats to curb political provincialism in the west wing and militate against local forms of opposition. Politicians compelled to enter a larger arena would, it was hoped, adopt a broader national vision. Outside the Punjab, the scheme was bitterly opposed. The centre was able to force unification on West Pakistan in October 1955 only after it had flagrantly abused its political authority to convene a new, indirectly elected (and compliant) Constituent Assembly.

When the first constitution was eventually adopted, in March 1956, East and West Pakistan were accorded 'parity of representation' (i.e., 155 deputies each) in a unicameral legislature, which Bengalis grudgingly accepted under veiled duress. However, little was done immediately to reverse the cumulative effects of discrimination in appointments to senior civil service posts: in 1958, Bengalis held only 41 of these positions, as compared with the 690 held by West Pakistanis. For rather different reasons, Bengalis were even scarcer in the officer corps: in 1955, they numbered only 14 out of 894 officers in the Pakistani army, seven out of 593 in the navy and 60 out of 640 in the air force (Talbot, 1998, p. 162). The political import of this particular disparity became starkly evident after the 1958 coup, when the officer corps took direct control of the political arena.

Over time, the central state elite went far to meeting the aspirations of educated Bengali Muslims to a career in public service, but could not allay grievances which arose from increasing material disparities between the two wings. Nor could it contemplate Bengalis using a parliamentary majority in a democratic system to capture the central government. A democratic accommodation between the two wings was not attempted until 1970, when the first nation-wide general election was called. By then, the upsurge of Bangladeshi nationalism meant that the east wing could only be retained by military violence.

Democratic accommodation *within* the west wing was almost as elusive because West Pakistanis were a heterogeneous conglomerate of ethnicities and language communities whose primary political loyalties were clannish and provincial. Though the national language, Urdu, was widely understood amongst elite social groups, only about 7 per cent of the population spoke it as their mother tongue. Punjabis, with 48 per cent of the population, were the largest language-community. They were divided by class and region and we should not, therefore, exaggerate the homogeneity of Punjabi interests. Nevertheless, the British policy of favouring 'martial races' had nourished a distinctive Punjabi identity and resulted in Punjabis being disproportionately represented in the civil and military bureaucracies. Over time, their grip on the state's key echelons grew tighter. The landed elites of Sindh, Baluchistan and (to a lesser extent) the Frontier represented powerful centrifugal forces in opposition to the Punjabi-dominated central state apparatus.

After the constitution was promulgated, a general election could not be delayed indefinitely without resort to martial law. The governing clique maintained a parliamentary façade until 7 October 1958, when Iskander Mirza (by now President) dissolved the Legislative and Provincial assemblies, dismissed the central and provincial governments and imposed martial law (with Ayub Khan as its Chief Administrator). Political parties were outlawed and civil rights suspended. In justification, the junta cited the discreditable conduct of the parliamentary politicians, who were undoubtedly corrupt, mired in factional intrigue, and abused their power and privileges (Wilcox, 1965). In one shameful episode of parliamentary homicide, a fracas in the East Pakistan Assembly led to the death of the deputy speaker and the wounding of the speaker. The continuing regional and ethnic rivalry, and the tension between Islamists and secularists, gave the military additional reasons to intervene. But the demise of the parliamentary system was also rooted in an inherited ethos of administrative command and a compelling sense of the state's strategic vulnerability. Senior officers and bureaucrats anticipated both a major realignment of political forces after the general elections scheduled for 1959 and a drying up of the financial resources needed to maintain and expand the defence establishment. They acted to forestall both.

Mirza had informed the US ambassador, James Langley, in mid-May of the military high command's growing resolve to take over the state apparatus. The President's close relationship with the embassy over the coming months has, understandably, led scholars to conclude that the military's suppression of politics and political pluralism had at least the tacit approval of their international patrons (Jalal, 1990, p. 273). But the diplomatic correspondence between Washington and the Karachi embassy does not confirm this. The Secretary of State, John Foster Dulles, instructed Langley to inform Mirza that the US government neither endorsed nor disapproved of the proposed coup, for to do so would be an unwarranted intrusion in Pakistan's internal affairs. Nevertheless, Langley was to make clear that the United States considered democratic government to be in the long run superior, from the point of view of the people's welfare and development, to authoritarian government. Undeterred, Mirza confidentially advised Langley of preparations for the coup on several subsequent occasions. On 5 October, after being told by Mirza that it was imminent, Langley telegraphed the State Department: 'The Embassy has made no effort to influence Mirza's decision one way or another.' Dulles's deputy, Christian Herter, reiterated the instructions Langley had been given in May, adding: 'While in some instances democracies have had to depart temporarily from basic principles ... we do not have evidence to show this stage has been reached in Pakistan' (*Foreign Relations of the United States*, 1958–60, vol. xv, South and Southeast Asia, pp. 648, 665 and 667).

After a brief power struggle between the military and civilian elements within the junta, Mirza was sent into exile on 27 October and Ayub Khan assumed full power. The army was indisputably the dominant force in Pakistani politics.

Congress and the linguistic reorganisation of the Indian states

It would be misleading to compare too closely the authoritarian resolution of Pakistan's regional, linguistic and cultural conflicts with the democratic compromises reached in India. The discordant social forces were more intractable in Pakistan, and the inherited resources of skill, forbearance and mutual tolerance with which these forces could be coaxed into civil coexistence were more meagre. Nevertheless, there are comparable themes in the response of the Indian political class to the stresses of post-colonial political aggregation.

In a newly formed state with many languages, privileging one as the 'national' language is inevitably contentious. It confers an advantage on native speakers, but more importantly in a largely illiterate society it makes competence in writing the language a valuable symbolic skill. India has 15 major languages, most with scripts and literary traditions of their own. During the Constituent Assembly's heated debates on language, some urged adopting Hindustani, the lingua franca of northern India and commonly understood by Hindus and Muslims alike, as the national language. Its great merit was that it afforded a linguistic bridge between communities. But Hindi found greater favour: roughly one in three Indians spoke some variant of Hindi as their mother tongue. Perhaps more importantly, a standardised Hindi language written in Devanagari script had been integral to Hindu 'revivalism' under British rule and to the formation of a cultural identity that was self-consciously Indian as well as Hindu. Congressmen who resented the hegemony of English in administration and higher education urged that Hindi be designated the national language. Representatives of the regional languages resisted this, on the grounds that their languages were equally 'national' and non-Hindi speakers would be unfairly disadvantaged in competing for central government employment. They wanted to retain English for communicating with the central government, and expected to use their own languages in the provincial governments and legislatures. Anti-Hindi sentiment was particularly sharp in the Dravidian south. The Constituent Assembly compromised by granting Hindi the status of the official language, but postponing the final implementation of this decision for 15 years. In the interim, English was to be retained as a recognised language of administration.

Meanwhile, the central government was confronted by a more serious challenge to its authority on the part of language groups pressing for regional or state autonomy. Since 1917, the party had been committed to linguistic provinces in independent India; Nehru was temperamentally sympathetic to this proposal and Gandhi had urged the speedy reorganisation of the country into linguistic provinces shortly before his assassination. But the Partition crisis left the Congress leaders determined to preclude any further division of their political inheritance and suspicious of the particular claims of language communities. A committee of jurists and civil servants, under the direction of Sardar Patel, reasoned that linguistic provinces would impede the growth of nationalism and concluded they could not be supported (Guha, 2007, pp. 180–3). With many misgivings, the Constituent Assembly agreed to maintain the provincial boundaries of British India, which split some language groups among two or even three provinces, while incorporating others into large multi-lingual provinces such as Madras and Bombay.

The first major challenge to the status quo came from Telegu-speaking Andhras, who had long resented their subordination to better-educated Tamils in the multi-lingual Madras Presidency, and had demanded a state of their own even before Independence. Their claim to linguistic autonomy was impeccable: Telegu is the second most widely spoken language in the Indian Union, with a rich literature. In the early twentieth century, a common identity had been cultivated in Telugu speakers by cultural organisations. Nehru's initial reaction to the Andhra movement was to dig in his heels and insist on the immutability of the inherited boundaries. This stance cost Congress dear in the 1951 State Assembly elections when it won only 43 of the

145 seats in the Andhra region. Subsequently, the Andhra leader, Potti Sriramalu, orchestrated a campaign for statehood modelled on Gandhi's concept of *satyagraha*, or non-violent agitation inspired by the truth of one's cause. This moral force was difficult to resist. In October 1952, Potti Sriramalu began a fast to death. Three days after his demise in December, the government gave way and agreed to establish an Andhra state, though with great foreboding on Nehru's part. In a letter to the chief ministers, he warned that the 'fissiparous tendencies' of caste, community and language would tear India apart (Brown, 2003, p. 238).

Once the Andhras' claim was conceded, Nehru's government adopted a more conciliatory attitude towards linguistic and cultural pluralism, and appointed a States Reorganisation Commission to arbitrate on ethno-regional claims. In 1955, this recommended that the boundaries of the southern states be redrawn to conform more closely to linguistic regions. Its report brought into existence a comprehensively reorganised India, divided into 14 states on the basis of language. Kerala was established for Malayalam speakers; the old Mysore, now Karnataka, accommodated Kannada speakers; Madras, later renamed Tamil Nadu, was made a home for Tamil speakers. After bitter dispute between the main language communities, Bombay province was divided into the states of Gujarat and Maharashtra in 1960. For the first time in Indian history, sub-national political boundaries corresponded with linguistic-cum-cultural boundaries. The major regional languages, with standardised forms and literatures, became dominant in the government, courts, schools and the media of their respective states. Minority regional languages were frequently discriminated against by state governments, which clung to English when communicating with the centre and made little effort to institute Hindi as sole official language by the 1965 deadline. After much debate, English continued as 'an associate additional official language' and as an accepted medium of examination for the public services throughout the Union. In 1980, the English language press still accounted for a fifth of the newspaper circulation and remained the preferred language of elite communication.

One principle on which Nehru and his colleagues would not compromise was the secular character of the state; they refused to recognise autonomist claims on the part of religious communities. For this reason, they would not concede the demand made by the regional political party, Akali Dal, for a Punjabi-speakers' State in the north-western half of the Indian Punjab. It was, in effect, a claim for Sikh

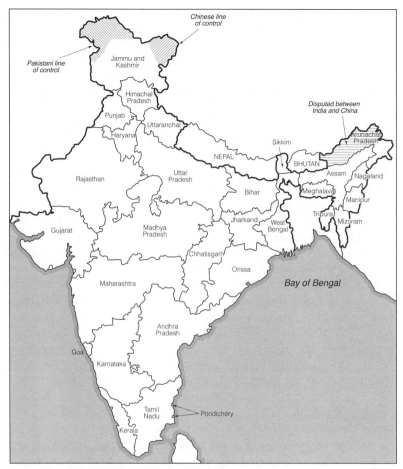

Map 1.1 India after states reorganisation (reproduced courtesy of Arun Ganesh)

autonomy: all Sikhs are Punjabi speakers (though not all Punjabi speakers are Sikhs). Punjabi written in the Gurmukhi script has a sacred character for Sikhs because it was the medium for their scriptures. Since Partition, and the mass migrations, Sikhs had been in a small majority in the northern Punjab which is both strategically and geo-physically sensitive (it borders Pakistan and agriculturally vital rivers run through it). Haryana to the south remained predominantly Hindu and Hindi-speaking.

Sikh aspirations for a recognised 'homeland' dated back to Akali Dal's formation in 1920. Historically, Sikhism had been a Hindu sect, rather than a distinct faith, and inter-marriage with Hindus had not been uncommon. Sikhism's divorce from the Hindu fold began around 1880, but proceedings were not finalised until the early twentieth century. Inter-communal relations were then embittered by the struggle to control what had been common spiritual property, the major Sikh shrines. Sikh identity became more militant and exclusive: autonomists sought to minimise the sectarian differences within Sikhism and reclaim for their community low-caste groups with no clear affiliation to either Sikhism or Hinduism. The holocaust suffered by Sikhs during Partition gave the 'homeland' aspiration a desperate urgency; henceforth, popular memory of that experience was embedded in the community's identity. The Akali Dal seized on the issue of language recognition to press for a Punjabi State (excluding Haryana) in secular terms. There were secularists within the party and we should not discount their sincerity. However, to Punjabi-speaking Hindus (who comprised about 40 per cent of the region's population) it was a thinly disguised claim for religious autonomy that would result in Sikh communal dominance. So they strongly opposed it. To the fury of the Akali Dal, many told the census officers that Hindi was their mother tongue. Though a few may have been confusing a regional variant of Punjabi with Hindi, for most language and religion had become congruent (Brass, 1974, p. 294). Naming one's mother tongue was a political choice. Punjabi – or more accurately, Sikh – demands were denied during the general reorganisation of states in the 1950s and early 60s. The central government relented only after Nehru's death, a change in the Akali Dal leadership and, perhaps crucially, the Indo-Pakistan War of 1965, when Sikh soldiers and the Sikh population played critical roles. As a reward for their national loyalty, Prime Minister Indira Gandhi agreed to the creation of a Punjabi Suba.

If we stop the historical record at this point, the comparison with Pakistan's failure to conciliate the East Bengali autonomy movement is rather flattering to India. By inflecting its centralising, statist nationalism with a large measure of linguistic federalism, Congress found a satisfactory means of maintaining national unity and the loyalty of most citizens. The nation's official rhetoric was modulated to reflect States reorganisation: cultural constructs of Indian identity in Republic Day pageants and school textbooks portrayed the nation as a kaleidoscope of regional sub-identities welded together by the state (Roy, 1999, p. 97). But in a wider and longer-term perspective, the record of Indian governments in dealing with regional, sub-national and religious dissidence is pretty dispiriting. The centre was so scarred by Partition that its only strategy when confronted by secessionist movements was to smash them with armed force. Between Independence and the late 1970s, the army was engaged in more-or-less continual warfare against separatist Nagas and Mizos in the tribal northeast. Moreover, Congress secularism served as a dogmatic rationale for rejecting out of hand autonomist demands based on religious differences. Tellingly, the word 'communalism' became the most vituperative in nationalist discourse; the fixation on extinguishing it wherever possible inevitably made the negotiation of communal differences more difficult.

The most harrowing confrontation between the central state and sub-national-cum-religious communalism was the 'not-so-small' war between Sikh secessionists and the security forces in Punjab in the 1980s and early 1990s, which is beyond the chronological limits of this chapter. Its origins lay in the internal dynamics of the Sikh autonomy movement, and the principal authors were Sikh fundamentalists who chose to assassinate the leader of a 'heretic' sect. The Janata government of 1977–80, and Mrs Gandhi after her return to power, dealt ineptly with Sikh autonomists, but the crisis was not of their making. However, Mrs Gandhi bears heavy responsibility for her disastrous decision to order the storming of the Golden Temple in Amritsar in June 1984, after it had been fortified by Sikh terrorists. About 3500 people died, mainly innocent pilgrims caught in the crossfire. After she was assassinated by her Sikh bodyguards on 31 October, Congress politicians in New Delhi – metropolitan councillors, members of Parliament, even Union ministers – led an anti-Sikh pogrom. They promised Hindu mobs willing to kill Sikhs money, liquor and loot (Guha, 2007, p. 571). In the ensuing years, the police and security forces crushed the Khalistan movement and quasi-insurrection with a staggering level of illegal violence, which the central government more or less openly condoned. It failed to pursue a political solution because of an obsession with national unity and territorial integrity rooted in a set of values associated with the idea of a strong centralised state. These values have justified the preservation of the Union by any and all means (Brass, 1999, p. 38).

The Ayub Khan regime: October 1958 to March 1969

The regime led by Ayub Khan between October 1958 and March 1969 was, in its day, warmly regarded by western political scientists as a model of benign authoritarianism in a developing country. It is still

hailed in some quarters as the most stable and least corrupt government in Pakistan's chequered history. According to this favourable estimation, it successfully combined rapid economic development with
social liberalisation, a degree of secularisation and a commitment to
curbing official venality. Some of this reputation is firmly grounded.
Ayub's religious outlook was progressive and pragmatic; he sought to
loosen the grip of Muslim traditionalism and improve the status of
married women; he permitted the public advocacy of birth control
(which deeply offended the *ulema*). He introduced a measure of land
reform and, as chairman of the newly created Planning Commission,
sponsored the Green Revolution, which brought impressive gains in
agricultural production.

Until 1962, Ayub governed under martial law, while combining the
roles of commander-in-chief, chief martial law administrator and president. The early years of his regime set something of a pattern for military interventions in post-colonial states. The legacy of coercive
instruments was deployed both to 'de-politicise' civil society and
restore a general sense of fairness: political parties were banned and
leading opponents temporarily detained without trial. At the same
time, the regime clamped down on hoarding, black marketing and
smuggling, and fixed the prices of milk, vegetables and ghee. Some 80
politicians suspected of graft escaped prison sentences in exchange for
voluntarily withdrawing from public life and automatic disqualifica-
tion from elective office until 1967. More constructively, Ayub instituted a system of 'basic democracies' to secure 'apolitical' grass-roots
support. This consisted of a multi-tiered hierarchy of legislative councils to represent all levels of society, from the village to the province. In
the countryside, villages were grouped into 'unions' of around 10,000
people, who directly elected the union councils, which constituted the
lowest but most important tier. (Though parallel union committees
were established for the cities, the system as a whole was designed to
marginalise the urban working classes and intelligentsia.) The union
councils then indirectly elected 'basic democrats'; each wing was
allowed 40,000 of them, later increased to 60,000. In January 1960,
they were asked to endorse Ayub Khan's presidency and to give him a
mandate to frame a new constitution.

When promulgated in 1962, the constitution ended martial law and
established a presidential form of government with a weak national
legislature. As president, Ayub exercised a wide range of executive, legislative and financial powers. He relied heavily on the country's civilian
bureaucrats, who formed the majority of his advisers and cabinet min-

isters, and his personal position was secure as long as he retained the confidence of the army. Senior military officers continued to enjoy various 'perks', and on retirement were often recruited to quasi-governmental bodies. Adult franchise was limited to the election of basic democrats, who constituted an electoral college for the president and for members of the national and provincial assemblies. A 'government party', the Pakistan Muslim League, was established to mobilise political support. Except for the communists, who remained proscribed, other political parties returned to legality, but those opposing the regime were under constant police surveillance and harassment. The press was muzzled.

Authoritarianism was combined with adroit political engineering, of which the union councils were the showpiece. They were made responsible for local government, including agricultural and community development, maintaining law and order through the rural police and trying minor cases in conciliation courts. They were supposed to cultivate a new rural constituency for the regime, which would endorse its political and economic agendas, but much evidence suggests that they fell under the sway of traditional local notables. When a British High Commission official was the guest of a local landowner in a village near Muzaffargarh in lower Punjab, his host, a patriarch of the powerful Qureshi family, told him that out of 57 union council chairmen in the area, 31 were now 'his men'. Most villagers lived in houses owned by the Qureshis, provided labour and services on a quasi-feudal basis, and voted for them and their nominees in local elections. Enrolment in the Pakistan Muslim League was a sham: membership forms were simply filled out by the chairmen of the union councils and the dues paid by the Qureshi patriarch.

Though authoritarian, the regime was by no means reactionary or socially conservative. The 1962 constitution created a more flexible framework for legislators than its predecessor by substituting a clause stipulating that no law should be enacted that was repugnant to the Koran and Sunnah with one stipulating that no law should be repugnant to Islam. To distance the state from religion, the title 'Islamic' was dropped from the country's name, though this did not withstand the vociferous objections of religious conservatives, who forced through a constitutional amendment restoring 'Islamic' in 1963. Despite the opposition of the Muslim clergy, the constitution restricted a husband's right to polygamous marriage and strengthened his wife's entitlement to judicial divorce if he married again without her consent. The ultra-orthodox Jama'at-i-Islami, and other elements of the religious right, were repelled

Table 1.1 Annual percentage growth of GDP in India and Pakistan, 1950–70

	1950–60	*1960–65*	*1965–70*
India	4.2	4.0	4.6
Pakistan (W)	–	7.1	6.9
Pakistan (E)	–	4.6	3.5

Source: World Bank, *World Tables*, 1976, Johns Hopkins University Press.

by the regime's secular liberalism. Relations became so bad that five prominent mullahs in West Pakistan were arrested in late January 1966 under the Defence of Pakistan Rules. Their offence had been to issue an edict instructing Muslims not to begin celebrating the religious festival of Eid on the day prescribed by an official committee. But more was in dispute than the timing of a moveable feast: behind the ostensible quarrel was a larger contest for authority between the state and religious establishment, which ended in stalemate. After a couple of months' imprisonment, during which press comment was repressed, the mullahs were released without any accommodation with the government.

Judged by the standard indicators, the economic progress made under Ayub's regime was impressive, though heavily concentrated in the west wing. In the 1960s, the GDP growth rate rose to 7 per cent in West Pakistan – which was higher than in India and above the norm for developing economies – and to 4 per cent in the East (see Table 1.1). Growth was checked by the repercussions of the 1965 war with India, but the decade as a whole remains the period of most sustained economic expansion in Pakistan's history (see Table 1.2). Manufacturing grew by 12.1 per cent a year in West Pakistan in the early 1960s, one of the highest rates of growth in the world at that time; though the pace slowed after the 1965 war, it was still respectable. The industrial workforce tripled in ten years. In East Pakistan, the manufacturing growth rate was 5.6 per cent in the early 1960s, followed by virtual stagnation. By 1970, domestic producers were supplying about 89 per cent of consumer goods sold in Pakistan, 85 per cent of intermediate goods and 38 per cent of investment or capital goods (Ahmad, 1972, p. 26). With the encouragement of the government, manufacturers of cotton and jute products also broke into export markets in the Middle East. To eliminate the disadvantages to exporters of an over-valued currency, they received import permits equivalent to 10–40 per cent of the goods they exported, which could then be sold on at a substantial premium. The

Table 1.2 Annual percentage growth in per capita GDP in Pakistan, 1960–73

	1960–5	*1965–70*	*1965–73*
E. Pakistan	1.9	0.6	–2.3
W. Pakistan	4.0	3.9	2.0

Source: World Bank, *World Tables*, 1976, Johns Hopkins University Press.

net effect was to boost exporters' earnings by 30–40 per cent. The share of manufactures in total merchandise exports rose from just under a quarter in 1960 to 57 per cent in 1970.

The better performance of Pakistan's agriculture was a basic reason for the acceleration in the GDP growth rate, as compared with the 1950s. As Table 1.3 demonstrates, agricultural output increased very rapidly during the 1960s in West Pakistan, while there was only modest improvement in the east wing. One reason for this discrepancy was that the technological package which combined high-yielding varieties with chemical fertilisers and ground-water irrigation only 'revolutionised' wheat culture, and scarcely any wheat is grown in East Bengal. But another was that West Pakistan had abundant 'waste' land or pasture it could convert to cereals. The area under wheat rose by about 1.34 million hectares between 1961 and 1971 or roughly 29 per cent; yields per hectare rose by about 32 per cent. Total output rose from 3.814 million tonnes in 1961 to around 7.3 million tonnes in the early 1970s. Additionally, West Pakistan increased its area under rice by about 20 per cent, and roughly doubled the rice harvest (which became an important export crop). In East Pakistan, the area under rice increased by about 17 per cent between 1961 and 1971 and yields fluctuated with the weather, without any clear trend (FAOSTAT). Other grains contributed only marginally to the total food supply. Consequently, the output of food grains per head of population declined by 0.8 per cent annually in East Pakistan during the 1960s, while it increased by 2.3 per cent annually in West Pakistan (Singh, 1990, p. 20).

It is often asserted that producers' gains from the Green Revolution were narrowly distributed and served largely to increase the power and affluence of West Pakistan's larger landlords (see, for example, Weinbaum, 1999, p. 91). But this gives a rather false impression. In West Punjab, substantial farmers with holdings of 25 to 50 acres – usually from the more prestigious cultivating castes – were to the fore in the Green Revolution. They represented 5.4 per cent of operational

Table 1.3 Annual percentage growth in agriculture and manufacturing in Pakistan, 1960–73

	1960–5	*1965–70*	*1965–73*
E. Pakistan – agriculture	3.2	2.8	0.8
W. Pakistan – agriculture	4.7	6.3	4.8
E. Pakistan – manufacturing	5.6	1.7	2.9
W. Pakistan –manufacturing	12.1	6.4	5.8

Source: World Bank, *World Tables*, 1976, Johns Hopkins University Press.

holdings in 1960 and 8.8 per cent in 1972, and owned roughly one-fifth of the farmed acreage (Singh, 1990, p. 70). They were an established entrepreneurial elite, not feudal magnates, and best placed to take advantage of the government's support for agricultural prices, its fertiliser subsidies and the cheap electric power which made investment in private tube-wells for irrigation so profitable (Noman, 1988, p. 42). Sustained agricultural expansion in the Punjab widened the circle of businessmen farmers who stood apart from the great landlords.

The regionalised pattern of economic growth led to great material disparities between West and East Pakistan, which did nothing to consolidate the national community. At Independence, the gap in per capita product between the wings had been a mere 4 per cent; by 1969–70, it had widened to 61 per cent (Bose, 1983, p. 1022). Some widening was to be expected because the west wing was more favoured by nature and geography, but there can be no question that the government's commercial policies and its allocation of investment greatly exacerbated inter-wing disparities. To industrialise, a poor agrarian country cannot rely on private savings: its government must either find a non-market mechanism for transferring resources from agriculture to industry or borrow from abroad. In practice, most developing countries have done both. Their favoured non-market mechanisms have been trade and exchange policies which discriminated against agriculture. Pre 1971 Pakistan was unique amongst developing countries in using these discriminatory mechanisms in a state structure that replicated the classic relationship between metropole and colony. East Pakistan ran a trade surplus with foreign countries by virtue of its agricultural exports, while West Pakistan had a substantial foreign trade deficit because of its imports of capital goods and industrial raw materials. However, it had a surplus in inter-wing trade because it supplied

East Pakistan with consumer manufactures. In this triangular pattern of trade, resources were transferred from east to west by exchange-rate manipulation and import controls.

The distribution of foreign aid (mostly loans at below market rates) and public investment also favoured West Pakistan. Ostensibly, private capital provided two-thirds of total investment during 1960s, but the state's role in capital formation was greater than that implies. Two public agencies, the Industrial Development Bank of Pakistan and the Industrial Credit and Investment Corporation, gave entrepreneurs access to cheap credit, and favoured them with tax holidays. Only 22 per cent of the Corporation's business loans went to the east wing between 1962 and 1967. Both agencies were conduits for World Bank loans that flowed predominantly to the west wing's private sector. In sum, the political economy combined a strong rhetorical commitment to private enterprise and free markets with a dynamic, authoritarian state that greatly influenced the fine detail of economic decision-making – and accentuated the regional imbalance. Foreign aid – which was proportionally bigger than India's – reproduced the same tension between free-market rhetoric and statist reality. The main bilateral donors were the USA, Japan and Federal Germany; with their aid came western academic advisers who saw Pakistan as a laboratory for liberal market capitalism in the 'Third World' and urged that social institutions be adapted accordingly (Talbot, 1998, p. 171). But the aid flowed to the government, which had its own priorities.

The private entrepreneurs who benefited from the regime's economic policies, and depended on officials for credits and licences, were a congeries of Urdu- and Gujarati-speaking immigrant families rather than a bourgeois class 'for itself'. They were too clannish to advance their common interests in effective business organisations. An industrial dynasty such as the Saigols, whose business empire centred on insecticide and fertiliser factories near Lahore, used their wealth to acquire political influence, and political influence to augment their wealth. They helped fund the Pakistan Muslim League and the family head, Rafique Saigol, was a PML member of the National Assembly for Lyallpur. Ayub Khan invited him to join the Cabinet in the autumn of 1966, but the family did not agree. They already had direct access to Ayub and no need for a man in the Cabinet. If the Saigols required foreign exchange for any project, Ayub would directly approve their request by telephone. They had no difficulty circumventing the law requiring the 'Pakistanisation' of their staff and employed about 100 French and German technicians in their chemical factories. The younger generation of Saigols were part of a plutocracy in the making: they were well educated, lived in great style and spent and entertained lavishly. They intermeshed socially with the landed hierarchy, the bureaucracy and the military elite through strategic marriages.

Even in West Pakistan, the economic achievements during the Ayub Khan years were far from unalloyed because a more uneven distribution of income and wealth was tolerated as the social price for rapid growth. By contrast with India's 'socialist pattern', the official development doctrine was one of 'functional inequality' that took a growing gap between rich and poor to be a positive virtue. Big landowners and industrial entrepreneurs enjoyed a remarkably benign fiscal environment and the measures taken to reduce landholdings had negligible effect. The land reform of February 1959 set a notably high ceiling of 500 irrigated acres or 1000 non-irrigated per person. Owners were compensated for land surrendered, but no serious attempt was made to break up large estates. Landlords used intra-family transfers to circumvent the regulations, and influenced local revenue administrations to deny tenants the right to buy. Slightly fewer than 1 million hectares of land were surrendered, of which a little more than 250,000 hectares were sold to about 50,000 tenants. Military and civil officials bought much of the resumed land cheaply by special arrangement; many resold it very profitably on the open market (Jalal, 1990, p. 305). Measures were introduced to give greater security of tenure and prevent distress sales of land by marginal farmers. The fragmentary evidence (reviewed in Singh, 1990) did not suggest any absolute impoverishment on the land, but there was certainly greater relative deprivation. Underemployed migrants were a burgeoning class in the cities. The government sought to head off urban unrest by the compulsory procurement of food grains at low prices.

After 1965, the regime was under mounting strain because migration and urbanisation created social forces that were increasingly difficult to manage and placate. Following the war with India, military expenditure increased by 17 per cent, imposing a crippling burden on an already slowing economy. The pace of industrial growth slackened, food shortages forced the government to import grain, foreign aid receipts declined and the price of basic commodities rose inexorably. The opposition deplored the concentration of wealth but the most devastating critique came from the chief economist of the Planning Commission, Mahbub ul Haq, in a widely reported speech on the economy in April 1968: 20 families – he claimed – controlled two-thirds of industrial assets and four-fifths of banking assets. The number was later revised to 22, and the accuracy of that figure was challenged (Kochanek, 1983, pp. 92–8). Nevertheless, '22 families' became a metaphor for intolerable private wealth amongst mounting penury. Nearly all opposition parties included the nationalisation of banking, insurance and certain key industries in their programmes when the country finally had a democratic election in 1970. The radical populism of the Bhutto government in Pakistan in the 1970s is traceable to the strong reaction against the former regime's 'functional inequality'.

The fall of the Ayub Khan regime

By 1966, the Ayub Khan regime was in trouble. The President's prestige and popularity fell sharply after the 17-day war with India in September 1965. Its origins lay in Indian-held Kashmir, where Pakistani guerrillas had sought to foment a rebellion that would either oust the Indians or at least force the dispute back onto the international agenda. Support among the Kashmiris was less than anticipated, but the fighting spread, and a process of escalation culminated in a full-scale Indian offensive towards Lahore on 6 September. The fierce engagements resulted in heavy losses of men and equipment for both sides until a UN-sponsored ceasefire took hold on 23 September. By tacit agreement, the east wing was excluded from the conflict, though the Bengalis' sense of their utter vulnerability vis-à-vis India added to their alienation from a Pakistan dominated by, and governed in the interests of the west wing.

Ayub's decision to accept a ceasefire outraged nationalist opinion and strained the allegiance of those army officers who felt the war had been aborted. When Ayub negotiated the Tashkent Declaration with the Indians in January 1966, he was roundly denounced by rioting students of Punjab University. The opposition parties condemned the regime for purchasing peace at the cost of national honour and betraying the 'just cause' of Kashmir. Within the army, the main pillar of his regime, Ayub's position was weakened by a division in the officer corps between those wanting to restore close relations with the USA and its pro-Chinese element. (The latter had been given a great boost by China's diplomatic support in the September war and its offer of military aid.) In the aftermath of the Tashkent Declaration, disgruntled officers of whatever persuasion were in no mood to pull Ayub's chestnuts out of the fire. By 1966, there was already talk of the commander-in-chief, General Yahya Khan, taking over.

Ayub's unpopularity deepened as his regime's reputation was increasingly tainted by corruption and nepotism. It was an open secret that the loyalty of serving and retired army officers was bought with offers of land and houses around Islamabad. Similarly, political friendships were cemented with licences to import foreign exchange and other perks. In an unfortunate demonstration of family loyalty, Ayub allowed his son to be released from the army to go into business where he quickly amassed a fortune. The corrupt enrichment of the few seemed all the more scandalous because living conditions for the majority were deteriorating, especially in the cities. Food prices rose sharply following a poor harvest in 1965 and the tapering off of American grain shipments. The need to divert foreign exchange to pay for food imports threatened to undermine the economic growth on which the regime had staked so much.

To the problems that were largely of the regime's own making were added endemic regional frictions. The most serious, and clearly the regime's most pressing internal difficulty, arose from the alienation of the east wing (discussed below). But Bengali dissidence was not the only threat to national unity. Local political leaders in the west wing were demanding its dissolution as a single unit and the restoration of the old provinces. The Sindh was a quagmire of regional discontents where the central state's representatives struggled to hold their own against local landowners and religious leaders – the Pirs, Makhdums and Syeds – who commanded absolute allegiance from their followers. The influx of refugees from Uttar Pradesh and Rajasthan, who competed with Sindhis for jobs, education and other resources, had destabilised Hyderabad and other cities. In the Sindh countryside, Punjabi magistrates, police superintendents and other state officials ruled, in the fashion of their British predecessors, as aliens in a foreign and turbulent land. In Baluchistan tribal life was disintegrating through the migration of young men to the cities and the decay of the traditional pastoral economy. The government was confronted by chronic unrest and spasmodic violence, which the police and the army brutally repressed. Camp-dwelling refugees from Indian-occupied Kashmir were another dissident minority: with some cause, they felt that the government was exploiting their plight for propaganda purposes while making little effort to rehabilitate and resettle them.

From the autumn of 1968, power and authority visibly drained away from the Ayub Khan regime in the face of industrial strikes, school and university closures, the defection of key allies and months of popular disturbances, focused mainly on deteriorating living standards, corruption and nepotism. The president finally resigned in late March 1969, after he lost the confidence of the army leadership. In a flagrant abrogation of the constitution, General Yahya Khan became chief martial law administrator and assumed the title of president. The national and provincial legislatures were dissolved, and political activities were temporarily banned, though it proved impossible to close the lid on political and social ferment. Yahya Khan's open admission that East Pakistan had received an inequitable share of public investment fuelled autonomist sentiment while his strictures on mounting economic inequality unintentionally encouraged greater labour militancy. At the end of November, he announced that democratic elections would be held in October 1970, that the national assembly would frame a new constitution, and that West Pakistan would be disaggregated into separate provinces. From January, all restrictions on political activity were to be lifted

Things fall apart: the break-away of Bangladesh

The Pakistani state founded in 1947 broke up in 1971 with the secession of the east wing (and the majority of its population) and the creation of the new sovereign entity of Bangladesh. We have become accustomed to the disintegration of multi-national entities, but before the 1990s secession from a modern state was an unusual occurrence. The East Bengalis succeeded where the Biafrans, Ceylonese Tamils and Turkey's Kurdish separatists failed. (In the early 2000s, we would have added the southern Sudanese to the list of failed secessionists.) What explains this? Pakistan's peculiar political geography decisively influenced the outcome of events in 1971 by putting formidable logistical difficulties in the way of retaining the east wing by force. Moreover, the exposed frontier enabled the Indians to intervene militarily on behalf of the Mukti Bahini separatists. But it was not simply geography that separated the two wings: there were irreconcilable differences in how educated East and West Pakistanis conceived the state to which they both belonged. Until quite late in the day, East Pakistanis could anticipate their democratic majority being mobilised to relocate the centre of political gravity in the east wing. West Pakistani elites never reconciled themselves to this eventuality. Their obstinacy was as much a cause of secession as Bangladeshi national sentiment. There had, too, been a marked divergence in the political socialisation of educated Pakistanis who came of age around 1970. In the east, their collective energies and ambition were channelled into a vociferous form of student-cum-street politics and animated by a strong sense of cultural identity; once mobilised, they were a difficult social force to contain. In the west, there were more diverse outlets for ambitious students and graduates: business, the law, public service, as well as politics. West Pakistani politicians gravely underestimated the strength of youthful radicalism in the east wing: Zulfikar Ali Bhutto, the former foreign minister, reportedly told Yahya Khan in the summer of 1970: 'East Pakistan is no problem. We will have to kill some 20,000 people there and all will be well' (quoted in Schendel, 2009, p. 124).

As economic conditions worsened after the 1965 war, the political temper of the autonomy movement rose. In May 1966, Sheikh Mujibur Rahman, the Awami League leader, launched a six-point programme for full provincial autonomy, with each wing having sovereign powers over taxation, currency issue and the operation of its own exchange account. The centre would have been left with responsibility only for defence and foreign affairs. Mujib justified these demands as consistent with the March 1940 resolution, and by reference to the widening economic disparities between the two wings and the under-representation of Bengalis in the state administration. The programme served to rally and unify his factionalised party and to canalise some of the seething discontent with the government's foreign policy. Anti-Americanism was especially vociferous amongst Bengali students and the political class, and outrage at the humiliating Tashkent accord with India was just as acute in the east wing as in the west. Paradoxically, the autonomy movement capitalised on a popular anger infused with radical, 'Third World' nationalism.

The national government interpreted the six-point programme as a demand for outright secession and attempted to restore its authority in East Pakistan by suppressing the Awami League's newspaper and arresting its leaders on charges of conspiring with India. Although Mujibur Rahman's contacts with Indian agents are now an established fact, the so-called Agartala conspiracy case backfired badly on the government. It was unable to gather sufficient evidence and withdrew the charges, but not until one of the alleged conspirators had died in custody and Bengali opinion had become further inflamed.

Whether, by early 1970, Bengali alienation was irreversible and a rupture of the state inevitable is hard to decide. There is much to suggest than an accommodation of the two wings was still possible and that events of that year created their own momentum, which carried the country towards civil war. The general elections promised by Yahya Khan had been scheduled for October, but severe monsoon flooding in Bengal followed by the terrible disaster of the November cyclone imposed a delay until December. The government was accused of inaction in the wake of this calamity, which racked up tension between the two wings, and allowed the Awami League to deepen its rural support. Its highly effective psychological propaganda portrayed the government as ineffective and uncaring. Yahya had anticipated that, with 25 parties contesting the elections, there would be no out-right winner and that his regime would continue to be the arbiter of Pakistani politics. He had announced his determination to be the judge of any future constitution by issuing a legal framework order empowering him to veto any document produced by the elected national assembly. Yahya Khan made it clear that the federating units could have all the autonomy they wanted provided this did not undermine the federal government's powers to discharge its legislative, administrative and financial responsibilities and to preserve the country's independence and integrity. It was an unsubtle ploy to corral the political process before it had started. The regime had no intention of transferring power to any political configuration that aimed at circumscribing the interests or reducing the dominance of the bureaucracy and the military, the main institutions of the state (Jalal, 1990, p. 309).

Yahya Khan's electoral forecast proved a massive miscalculation: the Awami League swept the board in East Pakistan and, because parliamentary representation now reflected the province's demographic preponderance, secured a majority of seats in the National Assembly (160 out of 300). The League's rhetoric had become more strident in the course of the campaign: the west wing was charged with monopolising foreign investment, dumping its manufactures on the east, and misusing the foreign exchange raised by jute exports. By polling day, the expectation that autonomy would be a panacea for all social ills was irrepressible. The Bengalis had responded to years of exclusion from the decision-making process by propelling to national power a party that stood diametrically opposed to the economic and political interests of the civil-military establishment. The election results in West Pakistan were almost as unexpected: Zulfikar Ali Bhutto's Pakistan People's Party (PPP), a left-wing populist movement launched as recently as 1967, gained 81 out of the 138 seats in the west wing. The Awami League had failed to win any seats in the west, and the PPP had contested none in the east, so the outcome of the election was the provincialisation of Pakistani politics.

Mutual suspicion, and the poor political intelligence given to Yahya Khan's government, created the conditions in which the country drifted into civil war. When Mujib refused to attend negotiations in West Pakistan in February 1971, this was interpreted as an intention to secede, although Mujib had yet to cross this Rubicon. On the 28th, he told the US Consul General in Dhaka that 'he did not want separation but rather a form of confederation in which the people of Bangladesh would get their just and rightful share of foreign aid' (*Foreign Relations of the United States*, 1969–76, vol. E-7, South Asia, 1969–72, doc. 121). The government seriously misjudged the intensity of popular support for the Awami League and its leader. Bhutto decided that the PPP would not participate in the National Assembly without a guaranteed share of ministerial power; increasingly, he appeared as the political ally of the military regime in its determination to resist the break-up of the country. In early March, the government, under pressure from Bhutto, decided to postpone the calling of the National Assembly and was shocked and angered when the Awami League established a parallel government in the east wing.

In response, a military crackdown was ordered on 25 March. The Punjabi and Pathan troops airlifted to the east wing acted with all the brutality of imperial masters chastising rebellious subjects. Hundreds of students were killed in an assault on Dhaka University's halls of residence; at least 250,000 Bengali women were raped by West Pakistani soldiers. The US Consul General in Dhaka reported to the Secretary of State on 28 March: 'We are mute and horrified witnesses to a reign of terror by the Pak military' (*ibid.*, doc. 125). His subsequent reports detailed the systematic elimination of the student leadership and the university faculty. Mujibur Rahman was captured, flown to the west and held on treason charges. By June, around 7 million Bengalis (many of them Hindus) had taken refuge across the Indian border; a further 3 million or so fled between June and December. The Indian army established camps in the border regions, where it trained and armed former servicemen, policemen and students who had been recruited to the Mukti Bahini.

Notwithstanding this paramilitary aid, the Indian attitude towards the insurrection was deeply ambivalent. Many refugees ended up in Bihar, where the Naxalites were conducting sporadic terrorism, and the Indian government feared that the refugee influx would further destabilise the state. During the summer and early autumn, the Indians sought to 'quarantine' and control the Bangladeshi freedom fighters, while aiding them in the separatist struggle. India's public position was that the crisis in Bangladesh could only be solved by negotiation between the Pakistan government and the imprisoned Mujibur Rahman. It insisted that its forces in the border region were there only for humanitarian purposes and (against all the evidence to the contrary) denied rendering military assistance to the Mukti Bahini.

Pakistan's military leaders were certain that India was waging an undeclared war in the east, as a prelude to annexing East Bengal. So they took a desperate gamble by opening hostilities with India in the *west*: Pakistani warplanes bombed Indian airfields along the western frontier on 3 December, while ground forces attacked Indian border towns, as well as invading Indian Kashmir. In justification, Yahya alleged the Indian army had launched a series of incursions into West Pakistan and Azad Kashmir. (The truth or otherwise of these allegations cannot be established, but American officials certainly believed them despite Mrs Gandhi's strenuous denial in a letter to President Nixon. In a telephone conversation with Nixon on 3 December, Kissinger, his National Security Advisor, said: 'It's more and more certain it's India attacking and not Pakistan.' Nixon concurred: 'Everyone' – he said – 'knows Pakistan not attacking India ... It's a tragedy the Indians are so treacherous.' Throughout the crisis, the United States regarded India as the aggressor; the Consul General in Dhaka, whose cables reported Pakistani atrocities, was withdrawn and demoted for insubordination (*Foreign Relations of the United States*, 1969–76, vol. XI, South Asia Crisis, 1971, doc. 221).)

India responded with bombing raids on Islamabad and the Karachi oil refineries and a military invasion of Bangladesh, which was formally recognised on 5 December. During the two-week war, Pakistan lost half its navy, a third of its army and a quarter of its air force. The Nixon administration suspended arms shipments and economic aid to India, but was unable to circumvent Congressional restrictions on supplying Pakistan, its nominal ally, with arms, aircraft and fuel. (A proposal that Iran should supply them and then be 'compensated' by the United States came to nothing.) The commander in Dhaka was compelled to surrender unconditionally on 16 December after Yahya agreed to the Indian ceasefire terms. This was after intense diplomatic pressure from the Americans, who feared the fragmentation of West Pakistan if the war was prolonged. The army's self-esteem was shattered and junior officers were openly hostile to the high command. Demoralisation was near universal, and many sensed a loss of national identity and purpose. There could be no question of another military man taking over the presidency of the truncated Pakistani state. Instead, Bhutto, at the high command's behest, assumed the post of president and chief martial law administrator.

Conclusions

The break-up of Pakistan is an appropriate point to pause in this narrative and draw out some conclusions. What factors propelled India and Pakistan on their distinctive political trajectories? The colonial legacy was clearly one of them; it could scarcely have been otherwise, given that British rule had left an array of 'anglicised' institutions (the bureaucracy, the judiciary, the army and police) which were incorporated into successor states. That legacy was also a matter of authoritarian habits of mind conditioned by the British style of rule. Bhutto's scathing denunciation of the elite echelon of the Civil Service of Pakistan as 'a class of Brahmins or mandarins unrivalled in its snobbery and arrogance, insulated from the life of the people and incapable of identifying with them' echoed the nationalists' animus against British officials during the independence struggle (quoted in Noman, 1988, p. 61). But the legacy had not just been a matter of 'hard' sovereign institutions and insufferable official hauteur. Open parliamentary-style elections had been part of the political life of British India since the early twentieth century. The idea that winning elections conferred legitimacy on rulers was imprinted on the nationalists' mental map, which goes far to explain the many continuities in the forms of Indian political life between the 1930s and the 50s. At independence, the nationalists inherited constitutional legislation their own elected representatives had done much to shape in the Round Table negotiations with the British.

The improvised nature of the Pakistani state, and the deep anxiety as to its viability, meant that 'hard' sovereign institutions were always likely to suppress electoral politics when unelected elites perceived the state to be in danger. Resort to martial law was not a destiny, but it was made more probable by the rapid decay of the Muslim League, the alienation of Bengalis from the West Pakistan establishment, and the formation of a military-bureaucratic nucleus at its core. The inherited authoritarianism of officials was complemented by that of the great landlords who expected unquestioning loyalty and obedience from their tenants. As Marxist theorists were wont to argue, class power and state power were 'configured' in West Pakistan. Gross errors of political judgement – such as the initial failure to recognise Bengali as an official language – exacerbated the structural faults in the bifurcated political formation.

We should also note how the political evolution of Pakistan and India was conditioned by their hostile coexistence in a sub-continent the British had unified as an empire. Their enmity grotesquely distorted government expenditure and endowed them with military apparatuses quite disproportionate to their security needs. Immediately after the 1971 war, India was allocating over a quarter of central government expenditure to defence and Pakistan nearly two-fifths (World Bank, *World Development Report*, 1990, Table 11). The Simla peace agreement of July 1972 did not result in a 'de-militarisation' of the sub-continent. Throughout the 1970s, the shrunken state of Pakistan had half a million men under arms, or roughly twice the number the British had required to dominate and to defend their entire Indian empire. India's defence forces numbered well over 1 million, while some 380,000 were enrolled in the paramilitary police forces. India tested its first nuclear device in 1974, claiming its purpose was entirely peaceful; by the 1990s, both states had diverted massive resources to develop nuclear armaments. The Kargil conflict of 1999, when the Indian army fought sizeable battles to repel Pakistani troops and Kashmiri guerrillas who had infiltrated the line of control, opened the terrifying prospect of a nuclear exchange in South Asia. The domestic outcome on the Pakistani side was another military coup, staged by the Chief of Staff, Pervez Musharraf, against the civilian government of Nawaz Sharif.

In a conspectus on post-colonial states, there was clearly nothing exceptional about Pakistan's political trajectory: Indonesia, Burma, Nigeria and many other African states went through a syndrome of democratic breakdown, ethno-regional conflict and political coup, followed by military or authoritarian rule. One explanation for this (to which I referred earlier) is that the colonial legacy left a state which was 'over-developed' – and over-bearing – in relation to the social forces of civil society. Here, I must register my dissent. As I argued in the introductory chapter, by all measurable criteria, the colonial state in South Asia was a 'capstone' edifice which left civil society largely to its own devices. Its fiscal 'take' was light by comparison with independent states such as Japan; the ratio of state officials and public servants to population was extraordinarily low; villages mostly policed themselves and settled disputes by informal tribunals. The nationalists came to power determined to institute an 'organic' state with the power and legitimacy to reach down and reorder society. In Pakistan, the initial impulse came from the imperatives of defence and national security, but under Ayub Khan planned industrialisation, agrarian modernisation and the experiment in 'guided democracy' gave further impetus to government intervention in the lives of the common people. Although post-war economic reconstruction was an immediate priority for India's new rulers, they planned in the name of 'development' far greater interference in society and customary social practices than the British had ever dared contemplate. In India's 'high' political culture, it was taken for granted that state would use its power to redistribute wealth, to reorganise resources and production, to develop industrial enterprises, to set ceilings on land ownership and to provide the sanction of force behind the legislative reform of 'untouchability' and social discrimination. India's 'low' political culture was immensely resourceful in frustrating and deflecting this programme, but it represented the great caesura between the colonial and post-colonial state. There was a step-jump in the scale and functions of government, which reached into social nooks and crannies never touched by the British. In Morris-Jones's beguiling metaphor: 'The little finger has become the whole hand. Government is everywhere and inescapable' (Morris-Jones, 1967, p. 16).

By the early 1970s, India's post-colonial state had at its command a formidable coercive apparatus and a diverse industrial base capable of producing high-technology goods (machine tools, automobiles, a nuclear 'device'). The proportion of the post-18 age group enrolled in tertiary education was about 9 per cent, which was very high for a developing country. Indian universities were training tens of thousands of engineers, scientists and economists to international standards. The senior civil servants who administered the 'organised economy' – effectively the public sector and industrial establishments employing more than ten workers – were highly competent and, with rare exceptions, incorruptible. Yet, for all its coercive and bureaucratic strength, the state was in crucial ways feeble and inept: it was unable to deliver universal basic education and health care or to ensure that children were adequately fed (national rates of stunting and wasting were amongst the highest in the world). Half or more of its citizens lived in extreme poverty. The economy remained overwhelmingly agrarian, and variations in the monsoon were the main cause of fluctuations in the growth rate. The notion of the post-colonial state's 'trajectory' has to accommodate this combination of coercive and bureaucratic power and relative socio-economic impotence. There is a temptation to think of the Constitution-makers plotting a set course which Indian democracy has followed reasonably faithfully but the historical process was more 'open-ended' and unpredictable than this scenario allows. No knowledgeable observer of India in 1976 regarded Mrs Gandhi's authoritarian regime as a temporary aberration since the Congress majority showed every intention of permanently altering the character of the state (see Chapter 2). When Zulfikar Ali Bhutto called a general election in January 1977 he boasted that Pakistan was giving a democratic lead to South Asia. (Bangladesh was under a military dictatorship at this time.)

Epilogue: the parallel elections of March 1977

Virtually simultaneous elections in neighbouring states, held in similar circumstances, provide ideal evidence for comparative political analysis. Pakistanis went to the polls on 7 March and Indians between the 16th and 20th. Since the introduction of Pakistan's 1973 Constitution, both had parliamentary systems with ceremonial heads of state. (Bhutto had exchanged the presidency for the premiership.) Both had been under emergency rule for some years. Observers initially expected routine plebiscites that would relegitimise authoritarian regimes and their strong, charismatic leaders. Instead, coalitions of heterogeneous parties were hastily assembled to offer voters an alternative national government, and campaigning was punctuated by 'waves' of anti-government protest. Mrs Gandhi and Bhutto stood on their records as radical social reformers and called on electors to choose between order and chaos; their opponents insisted the choice lay between democracy and prolonging dictatorship. At stake in both elections was not just the authority to form a government, but control of the state's institutional core. Mrs Gandhi had demanded personal loyalty from senior administrators; the PPP had colonised the bureaucracy and diverted huge sums from the public revenues to its coffers.

The big difference was that, whereas the Indian contest was wholly secular, both sides in Pakistan sought to mobilise religious sentiment. Three of the nine parties in the opposition Pakistan National Alliance (PNA) were of a strongly religious character and included the fundamentalist Jama'at-i-Islami. PNA spokesmen called for a legal code consistent with Sharia law, the outlawing of family planning and closer regulation of women in civic life. Not to be outflanked by the Islamist right, Bhutto dropped nearly all reference to 'Islamic Socialism' and asserted his nationalism and religious orthodoxy. Like the opposition, he called for Nizam-i-Mustafa (meaning 'Rule of the Prophet') which was the most potent slogan in political life. Bhutto also used the election to reconfigure his support base: many left-wing stalwarts were denied the PPP ticket in favour of so-called feudals from the traditional agrarian ruling class. (For valuable contemporary analyses see the contributions to the July 1977 number of *Asian Survey* by N.D. Palmer, Ziring, Weinbaum and Weiner.)

The results were a crushing electoral defeat for Mrs Gandhi, which led to the first non-Congress government since 1947 and a reinstitution of democracy, and a stupendous victory for Bhutto and the PPP, but of such obvious illegitimacy that the public outrage and political violence in the succeeding months induced another military intervention. 'First-past-the-post' exaggerated the Congress debacle; it won 34.5 per cent of the popular vote, as opposed to Janata's 43.17 per cent, and held its own in the South, where the social impact of the Emergency had been relatively light. But in Uttar Pradesh, Bihar, Delhi, Haryana and Punjab, Congress did not win a single seat. Mrs Gandhi and Sanjay both lost theirs. Huge numbers of Muslim, low-caste and 'untouchable' voters deserted Congress. Although there were some irregularities, the results were generally considered free and fair. The incoming Janata government chose to interpret the electoral verdict as a judgement on Congress state ministries, and dismissed nine of them in north and west India.

In Pakistan, protest at the fraud and intimidation which secured Bhutto's overwhelming majority escalated into a PNA-led mass movement demanding his resignation and fresh elections. The crisis appeared to have been resolved in mid-June when Bhutto agreed to elections in October, supervised by the army and judiciary, while the PNA agreed to his remaining in office. But Bhutto soon regretted his concessions and sought to revise the agreement in ways unacceptable to the PNA. On 5 July, Zia al-Huq, the chief of staff, broke the deadlock by declaring martial law, overthrowing the government and briefly detaining Bhutto, several ministers and the PNA leadership. The provincial governors were removed and all political activity temporarily banned. A four-man military council was formed to govern the country until the forthcoming elections.

Zia denied all personal political ambition but unintentionally set in train Bhutto's destruction (and his own 11-year rule) by lifting press restrictions. A muzzled and servile press had never pursued the many allegations that Bhutto had abused his power to intimidate and destroy opponents. Now it did so. On 3 September, he was charged with ordering the assassination of a political opponent in November 1974, though released on bail. Zia was shown documentary evidence incriminating Bhutto and, after much procrastination, decided that elections could not be held while the country's most prominent politician was charged with murder. Bhutto was rearrested on Zia's orders. He was determined to see Bhutto tried in a civil court, which would absolve the military of direct responsibility were he to be condemned to death. Hundreds of Bhutto's associates were arraigned for embezzlement, extortion and other crimes committed under, and to sustain, PPP rule. Zia announced that an election date would be decided only when Bhutto's trial was concluded, which put political life 'on hold' indefinitely. Bhutto was hanged on 4 April 1979. Martial law was not lifted until December 1985.

The parallel elections of 1977 were the most consequential ever held in South Asia. India's sixth general election repelled the most serious assault ever mounted on the democratic system and ensured the survival of its basic structure. Voting a Congress national government out of office temporarily ended the 'single-party' dominance of the historic nationalist movement. Pakistan's elections (which were the first held under a duly elected civilian government) demonstrated that political actors had not internalised legal norms and democratic conventions. Bhutto, his henchmen and rivals operated in a political culture that exalted the ruthless exercise of power and condoned extra-legal violence against those perceived as 'traitors' and 'enemies'. The army had been in disgrace since the humiliation of 1971 and its re-emergence as the ruling institution was a measure of the failings of civilian politics, as well as of its own autonomy and coherence. By respecting the independence of the judiciary, and not abrogating the constitution, Zia maintained a semblance of legal authority. He consolidated his power by pledging to institute an Islamic social order, which struck a consensual chord in an otherwise conflicted society. Koranic penalties were immediately decreed for various crimes while the Council of Islamic Ideology was reconstituted as an independent agency and charged with proposing Islamic social reforms. A formal programme of Islamisation was announced in February 1979. Although Jinnah's name was associated with this programme, it actually betrayed his explicit commitment to a state that would not concern itself with, nor discriminate between its citizens' religious beliefs and practices. For Jinnah, Islam was compatible with political and cultural pluralism, parliamentarianism and free expression – in other words, the balance between state and civil society represented by the 'republican' ideal. For Zia, that ideal represented a threat to Islam's integrity and authority (Ziring, 1984).

Islamisation accelerated the political, economic and cultural reorientation of Pakistan to the Middle East, which had begun with Bangladesh's secession. The direction it took after the pivotal crisis of 1977 could scarcely have been anticipated in the 1950s and 60s. All historical closures are, to a degree, arbitrary and we can point to several continuities between the Ayub Khan and Zia regimes, but there was also a real caesura, associated with the Soviet invasion of Afghanistan, the Iranian revolution and the effective reconstitution of Pakistan as an Islamic state.

2
Democracy, Economic Planning and Economic Stagnation in India: 1947–c. 1975

Introduction: economic planning and post-colonial consciousness

In the 1950s and 60s, Indian governments and their expert advisers attempted to implement a set of economic policies generally known as 'Nehruvian socialism' because of its close identification with the country's first prime minister. These policies were intended to end India's economic dependence and raise its abysmally low living standards by accelerating industrialisation; their chosen instrument was national economic planning. Planning would, it was hoped, create a self-reliant economy and assure national independence and security in world politics. The development strategy embodied in the second and third Five Year Plans (covering the years 1956–66) was overtaken by a double crisis of economic stagnation and political instability in the later 1960s. 'Nehruvian socialism' was not formally abandoned, and India remained one of the world's most highly regulated 'mixed' economies until the liberalisation of the 1990s. But there was a distinct watershed in 1966–70 that divided one political economy from another. The Nehru-era policies favouring cities, centralisation, bigness and capital-intensive industrialisation were modified by policies favouring agriculture, decentralisation and small producers. Here, I seek first to analyse a phase in India's history that was both 'post-colonial' and, in the working assumptions of the major political actors, self-consciously 'anti-colonial'; then to explain the transition to radical populism under Mrs Gandhi. The latter part of this chapter assesses the achievements and shortcomings of planned development.

Behind the Indian planning experience, in what we might term its ideological hinterland, was a reading – or misreading – of the economic record of the British Raj. Colonial rule had, it was believed, impeded industrial development by destroying native handicrafts and inserting India in the international division of labour as a primary producer. National wealth had been 'drained away' by unequal trade. When industrial enterprises were founded in the mid- and later nineteenth century, colonialism's dogmatic laissez faire had denied them the protection that most sovereign states accorded their infant industries. The Government of British India had failed to develop an industrial policy comparable to that followed in Meiji Japan. This reading of the colonial record overlooked the protectionist and dirigiste strands of economic policy in late Raj. In laying all India's woes at the door of colonial state, nationalists exaggerated its capacity to shape the subcontinent's domestic economy. Nevertheless, in reaction against what they took to be the 'open', laissez faire economy of colonialism, the nationalists constructed an autarkic political economy in which the central government and its bureaucracy became the dominant force in modern industry and finance, or broadly the 'organised economy'. India insulated herself from external economic forces by producing the consumer and capital goods she had once imported, by restricting foreign investment and by regulating external trade through exchange controls and import licensing. Until June 1966, the rupee's exchange rate was kept artificially high, which discriminated against exports. Largely as a result of these autarkic policies, India's share of world trade declined from 2 per cent in 1950 to 0.5 per cent in 1980. The policy recommendations of the 'structuralist' theorists of dependency were, unknowingly, being doggedly followed by Indian governments from the mid-1950s: the economy was 'de-coupled' from world capitalism. Obviously, this could not be a complete de-linkage. India had to import advanced industrial technology, modern weaponry and, in deficit years, food grains. Foreign aid accounted for a significant proportion of public investment in the 'organised economy'. Imports of American grains under the Public Law 480 programme, which authorised the sale of surplus crops for local currencies rather than dollars, were important in helping conserve foreign exchange reserves. During the near famines of 1966–7 in Bihar and Uttar Pradesh, many depended for their survival on food aid. But, within the limits of the possible, Indian governments pursued self-reliance, while eschewing totalitarian methods, and so provided a potent example for other 'emergent nations' in the 1960s. This makes the 'anti-colonial' phase of India's history as an independent state of particular interest for the broader themes of this study.

The origins and implementation of economic planning

The intellectual and ideological origins of planning lay in the 1930s when the 'modernising' left wing promoted the idea in Congress. That Nehru, who was then a Marxian socialist, should have been drawn to the concept of a planned economy was quite unsurprising. He wrote in his autobiography: 'In India, only a revolutionary plan could solve the two related questions of the land and industry as well as almost every other major problem before the country' (Nehru, 1936, p. 362). The Soviet Five Year Plans attracted worldwide interest and unstinting admiration on the left. Moreover, the global economic crisis and ensuing depression had created a progressive consensus in the liberal democracies in favour of the state regulating and intervening in the economy, which implied some measure of planning. Within Congress, Nehru and other proponents of socialist planning faced the scepticism both of businessmen wedded to laissez faire and Gandhians hostile to large-scale modern economic development. By early 1938, their objections were sufficiently allayed for Congress to resolve that the national state 'on the advice of a Planning Commission' would adopt 'a comprehensive scheme for gradually socialising our entire agricultural and industrial system in the sphere of both production and appropriation'. In October, the National Planning Committee was set up under Nehru's chairmanship. An impetus had been given to the planning movement when, with the formation of Congress state ministries in 1937, nationalists accepted responsibility for economic policy at the level of provincial government.

The National Planning Committee's work was cut short by the outbreak of war and Nehru's imprisonment, but the planning idea flourished in the 1940s. Its most unlikely proponents were the leading Indian businessmen who issued the 'Bombay Plan' in two parts, in January 1944 and January 1945. Their plan's chief objective was the doubling of per capita income in 15 years and its strategic focus was centrally directed investment in heavy industry, using deficit financing. Reducing dependence on foreign countries for capital goods was as important an aim as improving mass welfare. The first part of the Bombay Plan attracted great press attention and was immediately endorsed by the Federation of Indian Chambers of Commerce and Industry. The second part was frostily received by businessmen because it was remarkably forthright about the regulatory regime needed to ensure the inflationary consequences of deficit financing did not impose unequal burdens on different classes: 'Practically every aspect of economic life will have to be so rigorously controlled by government that individual liberty and freedom of enterprise will suffer a temporary eclipse' (quoted in Nayar, 1971, p. 855). It accepted that profits should be kept within limits and income inequality reduced through a steeply graduated income tax. In a remarkable passage, it anticipated most of economic controls for which the 'permit-licence-subsidy Raj' became notorious. Scholars have generally interpreted the Bombay Plan as signalling the 'national bourgeoisie's' willingness to subsume its class interests in the national interest. Vivek Chibber has convincingly shown that the plan's first part was conceived when businessmen feared social radicals would capture Congress; it was a defensive manoeuvre to forestall the socialisation of private enterprise by opening the way for *capitalist* planning. The hostile reception of the second part in business circles demonstrated a deep aversion to state ownership of industry and state direction of private enterprise (Chibber, 2003, pp. 94–105).

The Indian government had already begun piecemeal planning for post-war reconstruction, but was 'bumped' into a more comprehensive statement by the Bombay Plan. The *Second Report on Reconstruction Planning*, published by the Reconstruction Committee of the Council in April 1945, foreshadowed all the fundamental objectives and methods of the Five Year Plans of the 1950s. It both recognised the need for large-scale industry and envisaged state ownership of those 'new and necessary' enterprises 'for which private capital may not be forthcoming'. It gave priority to the development of power resources and 'of important capital goods industries'. The Industrial Policy Statement issued at the same time anticipated 20 major industries being brought under the control of the central government and the nationalisation of 'basic industries' if adequate private capital for their development was not forthcoming. There is little to distinguish this statement of intentions from the Industrial Policy Resolutions of 1948 and 1956 adopted by the government of independent India (Hanson, 1966, pp. 37, 40–5).

By independence, few amongst the educated and politically vocal dissented from the proposition that state economic planning was an essential component of national sovereignty. For its Indian proponents, it offered the means of marrying rapid industrialisation, which would free the country from dependence on foreign imports and the need for aid, with social justice and democracy. We should not exaggerate the level of public interest, in a predominantly illiterate country, in planning. During the first and second planning periods, the question of linguistic states generated far more popular excitement than did economic development (*ibid.*, p. 122). Nevertheless, planning became a key element of Congress hegemony. Its ideological role in India's domestic political economy was analogous to that of non-alignment in international politics. When defining the broad goals of political and economic development in November 1947, the All India Congress Committee stated that 'Our aim should be ... a social structure that can provide an alternative to the acquisitive economy of private capitalism and the regimentation of a totalitarian state.' Nehru later described India's approach to economic development as 'a third way which takes the best from all existing systems – the Russian, the American and others – and seeks to create something suited to one's own history and philosophy' (quoted in Frankel, 2005 pp. 18, 3). Planning promised fundamental changes in the economic and social structure of society and the removal of gross inequalities without the internal wars waged by communist regimes against landlords, kulaks and capitalists. It strengthened the state by underpinning a consensual, left-of-centre pattern of partisan politics that minimised the political salience of major social cleavages. Through planned development, Congress governments hoped to achieve a form of 'top-down' national integration that would accommodate India's myriad linguistic, religious and caste groupings.

Notwithstanding the influence of foreign models and thinking, the development strategy in the Nehru years was cast in a normative framework that was distinctive to the Indian nationalist movement because it fused Gandhian with Marxist ideals. Gandhi's disciples and the Marxist socialists in Congress shared certain basic assumptions about the immoral character of capitalist economic institutions. Both ascribed to the labour theory of value, not as a proposition of economic science, but as an ethical precept. Gandhians, like Marxists, equated private property in production with exploitation and profit-making with the 'theft' of labour value. There was, clearly, an intellectual chasm between Gandhi's abhorrence of modern industrial civilisation and the Marxists' belief that the expansion of the productive forces was the fundamental dynamic of social – and human – development. But in his later writings Gandhi had done something to bridge this chasm by acknowledging a place for modern industry in independent India, provided that it sub-served the villages and the village crafts. Here was a further point of compromise and fusion between the two social philosophies, for the socialists in Congress hoped to avoid the brutal blunders of Soviet modernisation by decentralising economic activity in so far as this was compatible with central planning. Like the Gandhians they sought to preserve – or revive – the village as the primary unit of social organisation in the belief that its communitarian values were indispensable to a humane social order.

Despite the passage of the Industrial Policy Resolution of April 1948, little was done to give economic planning immediate effect. The Resolution was a cautious document that envisaged a state monopoly of the defence industries, atomic energy and rail transport, and reserved new developments in a range of key industries (including minerals, metallurgy and heavy engineering) for the public sector. It listed 18 industries in which planning and regulation by the central government were necessary in the national interest. But the Resolution reassured private entrepreneurs in the key industries that their coopera- tion would be sought in executing a dynamic national policy. Their enterprises would be free to 'develop for a period of ten years', during which they would be 'allowed all facilities for efficient working and reasonable expansion'. If and when the state acquired industrial units, compensation would be 'awarded on a fair and equitable basis' (Hanson, 1966, pp. 448–9). These reassurances were essential in turbu- lent times when the new Indian government had reason to fear a flight of capital and the Cabinet was divided between a socialist left and a business-friendly right led by Sardar Patel. The Congress left wing inter- preted the Resolution as a kind of 'new economic policy' that accepted private enterprise as a temporary expedient and no more; to the right, it offered the entrepreneur and investor even more opportunities than they would be able to seize (*ibid.*, p. 451. 'New economic policy' was an allusion to the partial – and temporary – restoration of a market economy by Lenin and the Bolsheviks in 1921.) One reason for the hiatus in implementing economic planning was that Nehru did not achieve complete ascendancy over his cabinet colleagues until after Patel's death in December 1950. Only after his election as president of Congress in September 1951 was Nehru confirmed as ultimate arbiter of national policy.

The Planning Commission was eventually established in March 1950. Its basic terms of reference were derived from the constitution's egali- tarian and redistributive Directive Principles (see Chapter 1) and its primary duties were assessing the country's resources and formulating a plan for their most effective and balanced utilisation. This entailed deciding the overall level of savings and investment desired by govern- ment and the pattern of this investment. India did not have a 'command economy' and planning was essentially indicative, but the government had inherited from the Raj administrative controls over business, which it supplemented as its policies required. Critics of Indian planning, such as the development economist Deepak Lal, have portrayed it as the handiwork of a bureaucratic elite, imbued with the tradition of caste authoritarianism, which had stepped into British shoes (Lal, 1988, p. 222). This is to ignore the strain of Gandhian idealism in the planning ideology. In the Commission's view, planning had to articulate a popular consensus: a chapter in the Draft Plan entitled 'The Approach to Planning' emphasised the need for unanimity of purpose within the national community if resources were to be mobilised to the full extent. Planning had to be a democratic process, not just in the sense that the government would be responsible to the electorate, but in the active participation of the people in the formulation of the plans and their implementation. Local self-governing bodies, such as the village *panchayats*, were expected to play a vital part, and measures to promote their healthy growth were an integral part of planning (Frankel, 2005, p. 26).

Unlike the French Commissariat au Plan, the Commission was not a non-partisan body of technicians: it was chaired by Nehru until his death in 1964, and included a small number of powerful ministers throughout its years of greatest influence. Furthermore, it reported directly to the Cabinet, with which it shared its secretary. However, the Commission lacked executive power over the Finance and spending ministries and was unable to control the flow of information within central government and administration. Ministers and senior civil servants were reluctant to surrender their autonomy to the Commission, and for this reason it was a much less effective body than its counterpart in South Korea (Chibber, 2003, pp. 178–82). The First Plan began life as a six-year programme put before the Commonwealth Consultative Committee in September 1950 and was not finalised until December 1952. It was originally little more than a collection of projects, with some attempt to estimate future investment resources using a simple application of the Harrod–Domar growth model. Reasoning that the shortage of food and raw materials was the weakest point in the economy, the Draft Outline (issued for public discussion in July 1951) assigned highest priority to agriculture, rural development, irrigation and power: outlays under these heads accounted for 43 per cent of total expenditure. The planners ruled out the nationalisation of land for collective cultivation on the grounds of a 'tradition of free peasant ownership'. Less than 10 per cent of planned expenditure was allocated to industry and mining. The modest strategic aim was to raise the level of gross investment from 4 per cent of national income to 5.5–6 per cent over six years. On the basis of (as it transpired) unrealistic forecasts of population growth and capital–output ratios, the Commission estimated that per capita income could double by 1977 and consumption standards could rise by a little over 70 per cent of the 1950–1 level.

The inflationary climate ruled out any substantial reliance on deficit financing, so resources for development during the First Plan period (April 1951 to March 1956) were calculated on the basis of the normal expansion of government revenue, supplemented by running down the sterling balances and modest levels of foreign aid. Although India's total tax revenue was, as a proportion of national income, one of the lowest in the world, the Commission was reluctant to step up taxation since it did not wish to discourage saving and investment. This approach to fiscal policy precluded any large-scale programme for industrial development in the public sector. The Planning Commission looked mainly to the private sector to expand industrial production and, in the same spirit, gave a warm welcome to foreign capital. Unsurprisingly, the intellectual left was deeply critical of the plan's fiscal caution and political timidity.

In its final version, the First Plan prioritised the transformation of the institutional framework of agriculture to encourage greater productivity through the more efficient application of traditional labour-saving techniques. Yield levels had scarcely increased since the 1900s and the rate of increase in the output of food grains had lagged behind population growth in the subsequent half-century. Three-fifths of rural households either owned no land or had marginal holdings of one hectare or less; together they owned less than 8 per cent of the total area. The extreme parcellisation of holdings affected even large landowners who usually owned and operated (or leased out) a number of small plots rather than a single farm. To remedy this situation, the Plan proposed a significant redistribution of land (with a ceiling vaguely defined as three times the 'family holding') combined with the encouragement of cooperative societies. The ultimate goal was 'cooperative village management'.

Though the most limited of the Five Year Plans, the First was the most successful when judged by the criterion of meeting specified targets. Just how much this was due to the plan itself is difficult to assess. The economic improvement registered during the plan period (1951–6) cannot all be attributed to the plan, and much that was achieved laid the foundations for future advance and was not evident in statistics of production and income. The most spectacular success was in the production of food grains: output rose from 540,000 tons to 649,000 tons, which meant that the plan target was fulfilled by 143 per cent. However, the principal cause of increased food production was a succession of bumper harvests following favourable monsoons. Expenditure on irrigation actually fell short of the plan target by 29 per cent. There was also a serious shortfall in education: the percentage of schoolchildren in the age group six to 11 was up by 9.9 per cent at the end of the plan period, as against a targeted 18.8 per cent. Secondary education fell even shorter of target.

While the First Plan was being drawn up, the broad outlines of an indirect attack on the prerogatives and position of private enterprise emerged with the passage of the Industries (Development and Regulation) Act of 1951. This required all private industries to seek a licence from central government to set up a new unit or expand an existing unit substantially or change their product mix. The intention was to enforce a planned pattern of industrial investment, while fostering improvements, countering trends towards monopoly and protecting the interests of small-scale producers. It was a clear indication that the government proposed to increase its supervision and control of the private sector. In practice, licences were issued on a 'first come, first served' basis, and licensing simply resulted in delay, arbitrariness and corruption. Just applying for a licence involved a mountain of paperwork: each application had to be submitted in 15 copies, which the various departments and state governments took 400 days on average to process. The system had no discernible benefits in terms of accelerated development. When the industrial economy boomed during the Second and Third Plans, licensing had little effect on the pattern of investment, but after the recession of 1965–6 it created a formidable bias against large- and medium-scale investment, and in favour of small-scale investment (a point discussed further below).

Realising 'a socialistic picture of society'

During the latter half of the First Plan period, Nehru declared his intention to shift the balance of the mixed economy towards the public sector while accelerating the pace of heavy industrialisation. In November 1954, in a lengthy speech setting out his planning philosophy, he said: 'The picture I have in mind is definitely and absolutely a socialistic picture of society. I am not using the word in a dogmatic sense at all. I mean largely that the means of production should be socially owned and controlled for the benefit of society as a whole. There is plenty of room for private enterprise, providing the main aim is kept clear.' He added that poverty could not be eradicated by the gradual expansion of consumer goods industries based on imported machinery; an import substitution strategy had to include the basic industries and strengthen the domestic capacity for capital formation (quoted in Frankel, 2005, p. 117). About this time, he appointed as his economic adviser, the intellectually and politically congenial P.C. Mahalanobis, who was to be the principal architect of the Second and Third Plans. On December 1954, the Lok Sabha resolved that 'the objective of our economic policy should be a socialistic pattern of society' and that 'Towards this end the tempo of economic activity in general, and industrial activity in particular, should be stepped up to the maximum possible extent.' These pronouncements signalled the emergence of a distinctively Indian planning ideology. To arm itself for a big planning push, the government nationalised the Imperial Bank of India in 1955 (it was renamed the State Bank of India) and charged it with the task of expanding into rural areas. The following year the life insurance business was nationalised. A new Companies Act was drafted to give greater control over the private sector and create a more comfortable legal space for state-owned companies. Fiscal changes were prepared to increase the investment resources available to the public sector and restrict as far as possible consumption by all classes.

The basic strategic outline of Nehruvian socialism was spelt out in the Plan Frame that appeared on 17 March 1955. Heading the list of objectives was rapid, public sector-led, capital-intensive industrialisation 'to strengthen the foundations of economic independence'. The state or parastatal agencies would develop the key heavy industries, such as machine-building, and control the commanding heights of the economy. India had already achieved a high degree of import substitution in consumer goods; under the Second Plan, she would, it was envisaged, become

> independent, as quickly as possible, of foreign imports of producer goods so that the accumulation of capital would not be hampered by difficulties in securing their supply from other countries. The heavy industries must, therefore, be expanded with all possible speed. (Quoted in Gregory, 1961, p. 54).

The plan was framed while world market prices for India's primary products were in protracted decline and the planners assumed that traditional exports, such as tea, would stagnate for the immediate future. This reinforced their determination to achieve self-reliance, which they defined in practice as minimising foreign exchange requirements. A third of the planned investment allocations were earmarked for basic industries, as opposed to 18 per cent for consumer goods industries and 17 per cent for agriculture. Tariffs were tailored to underpin the development strategy: imported capital goods attracted the relatively low tariff of 27 per cent until 1973, while duties on intermediate goods ranged from 40 per cent to 100 per cent. Imports of consumer manufactures were banned. Though the goal was self-reliance, heavy dependency on external resources was unavoidable in the medium term, which made macroeconomic policy vulnerable to foreign exchange crises and the cessation of foreign aid (as occurred in 1965, when the United States suspended aid as a result of the Indo-Pakistan war). Furthermore, the strategy imposed a form of deferred gratification on the Indian people: public investment was concentrated in capital-intensive industries that offered only a distant prospect of the expansion of industrial employment or a more abundant supply of cheap consumer goods. Growing consumer demand was to be met mainly by developing cottage and village industries that would – it was hoped – diversify the rural economy and provide employment. Their products would be protected against competition from factory-made goods.

This strategic outline was given greater substance by the Industrial Policy Resolution of 1956, which demarcated three industrial categories, 'having regard to the part which the State would play in them'. The first comprised 17 'basic' industries whose future development would be the state's 'exclusive responsibility'. They included social utilities – irrigation, rail and air transport, and power – which were to be government monopolies, and producer goods industries, such as iron and steel and heavy electrical plant, in which all *new* units would be established by the state. This did not preclude the expansion of existing privately owned units or joint public–private enterprises in setting up new units. The second category scheduled 12 industries in which the state would 'increasingly establish new holdings', without denying private enterprise its opportunities. The industries included aluminium, ferro-alloys, bulk drugs and fertilisers. The third category embraced all remaining industries, which were to be open to both the state and the private sector.

Despite the emphasis given to the public sector, the Resolution was in some ways reassuring to private enterprise, which was guaranteed a secure place in the planned economy. The state's economic domain –

infrastructure and heavy industry – was not one private entrepreneurs generally wanted to enter. *Established* businessmen benefited handsomely from a highly protected domestic market to which entry was restricted by the licensing system, import restrictions and the control of capital issues. From under this bureaucratic blanket emerged a dependent form of private capitalism that relied on the patronage and protection of the state for its profits and security. The symbiosis between private capitalism and the state became still closer after the financial services were taken into public ownership in 1969–72 and private entrepreneurs relied on the lending policies and discretion of government-owned banks.

The Second Plan envisaged the sharp increase in the rate of investment that development economists were then specifying as a pre-requisite for 'take-off' into self-sustaining economic growth. Performance did not quite live up to that expectation. Measured against 1950, gross domestic investment (GDI) as a proportion of GDP at current prices roughly tripled over the decade (rising from 7.3 per cent to 17 per cent in 1960). But 1950 represented a nadir because foreign companies were then *dis*investing on a considerable scale, the calamitous after effects of Partition were still palpable, and Indian businesses faced an uncertain future. Most of the improvement in the GDI ratio occurred by 1955, when it was 14.1 per cent of GDP (World Bank, *World Tables*, 1976). Measured in constant prices, and using the now preferred concept of gross fixed capital formation, performance looks better: it was 11.2 per cent of GDP in 1954–5 and 17.5 per cent in 1965–6 (Bardhan, 1984, Table 10). But by East Asian standards, this was a *mediocre* effort: China was investing 23 per cent of its GDP in 1965 and South Korea 27 per cent in 1970.

The Indian public sector accounted for two-thirds of the increased investment. During the First Plan period, private investment in organised industries had been more than twice the amount of public-sector outlay. The Second Plan reversed this order of magnitude: public-sector investment in 1956–61 was about two and a half times the level of private-sector investment. Throughout the 1960s, the ratio of private to public-sector investment in the organised economy was approximately 40:60. Capital projects absorbed a greater share of the central government's expenditure than hitherto. Even before the Second Plan period had officially begun, outlay under this heading rose sharply; as a proportion of total government expenditure, it increased from 31.45 per cent in 1952–3 to 52.98 per cent in 1954–5. It then declined but rose again, and peaked at 54.64 per cent in 1958–9. Most capital expenditure was on heavy industry and agriculture was sorely neglected: the proportion of total outlay allocated to agriculture and irrigation fell from 34.6 per cent in the First Plan period to 17.5 per cent in the Second. This reflected the planners' misplaced confidence that the food problem had been solved after the bumper harvests of the early 1950s.

The financing of the Second Plan departed from the orthodox methods of the First both in projecting a greater measure of deficit financing and in the sheer vagueness of its budgetary calculations. One critic wrote that 'The alarming irresponsibility of the Second Five-Year Plan's chapter on "Finance and Foreign Exchange" represents the lowest point ever reached by Indian planning' (Hanson, 1966, p. 150). The plan's assumptions about the future price level and the financing of increased capital goods imports were patently unrealistic. This was not a matter of incompetence, but rather an effect of the political pressures on the planning process. The planners were more exposed to pressure groups demanding expenditure (but reluctant to pay for it) than they had been in the early 1950s, and were over-confident that the glaring gaps in the plan – as between agricultural investment and projected farm output, for example – could be filled by political will. In the event, deficit financing accounted for 20.4 per cent of plan outlays between 1956 and 1961, and external resources – or foreign aid – for 22.5 per cent. (If we include resources generated by the depletion of foreign exchange reserves, then they represented nearly 30 per cent of net investment.) Under the Third Plan (operative between 1961–6), external resources accounted for a still larger proportion of outlays (28.3 per cent). In the late 1960s, the contribution of external resources peaked at 35.9 per cent. But planning was principally financed by extending the tax base: the fiscal 'take' rose from around 6 per cent of national income in 1951 to 14.1 per cent in 1965–6.

While the Second Plan had been prepared in a mood of optimism, preparations for the Third in the later 1950s were overshadowed by a financial crisis, a foreign exchange crisis and a food crisis. By 1956, India had exhausted its sterling reserves and rising imports, especially of food, iron and steel and capital goods, combined with stagnating exports, led to a severe balance of payments of crisis in the winter of 1956–7. In January, stringent new controls had to be imposed to conserve exiguous foreign exchange reserves for the 'core' areas of steel, coal, transport and power. After two mediocre harvests, the monsoon failed in northern India in April 1957, leaving a badly damaged wheat crop and aggravating an already strained situation. Food grain production fell by almost 10 per cent between 1956–7 and 1957–8. The food minister admitted that 'we have passed through ... a year of scarcity the like of which did not occur in living memory' (Frankel, 2005, p. 143). Despite importing 4 million tons of food grains, the government could not make up the deficit and prices rose to unprecedented levels. In the Planning Commission's view, the planning strategy could be preserved only by price controls, and by the government procuring and rationing food grains. Since the speculative hoarding of grain was identified as an underlying cause of the food crisis, the Commission endorsed a proposal for the socialisation of the wholesale trade in food grains, but the government shrank from this radical step. Meanwhile, domestic inflationary pressures had pushed up the rupee costs of some industrial projects and compelled the planners to revise their financial calculations. Allocations to the social services, irrigation and power, and transport were cut to protect 'core' projects. Exacerbating the financial crisis was a growing discrepancy between the growth of central government revenue, drawn mainly from the urban middle classes, and the shortfall in the states' revenue, levied largely from agriculture. The states' assemblies had failed to meet their commitments to enhance the taxation of the countryside.

Underlying these inter-related crises was a population growth rate of over 2 per cent, which was twice the projected level. It meant that India approached the Third Plan period with a larger labour force than anticipated and a backlog of unemployment approaching 9 million. Despite the raft of problems confronting them, the planners clung to the 'heavy industrial' pattern of development in the belief that this was the quickest route to self-sustaining economic growth. Although the food crisis compelled that greater priority be given to agriculture and the production of fertilisers, the Third Plan was essentially a continuation and intensification of the Second. The public sector would, it was proposed, undertake 70 per cent of planned investment. Over half (52 per cent) of total investment was to be allocated to organised industry and minerals, power, and transport and communications. Machine-building was singled out for rapid development. Agriculture and community development would receive only 14 per cent of allocations. The Second Plan had had to be 'bailed out' by a consortium of foreign donors and creditors; in presenting the Third, the planners were quite frank that rapid economic development was more than ever dependent on external resources.

The planners had to specify the optimal balance in the allocation of resources between agriculture, industry and services, and between different industrial sectors. In retrospect, it is clear they failed to do this when formulating the Third Plan. By the mid-point in the plan period (late 1963), there were alarming bottlenecks in transport, inadequate increases in coal output and serious power shortages. It was evident that the plan's targets for agricultural output were unattainable: production had risen marginally in 1961–2, but fell back in 1962–3. Worse was to come: output recovered in 1964, but the 1965–6 harvest was a disaster. Food grain output fell by a fifth and total agricultural value added by 13.5 per cent. Grain output rose slightly in the following year, but agricultural value added actually fell again by about 2 per cent. Food constituted 22 per cent of imports in 1965. Real GDP in 1966–7 was 3 per cent lower than in 1964–5 (Joshi and Little, 1994, p. 73). Some of the shortcomings in industry might have been corrected in the second half of the plan period had the planners been dealing with wholly endogenous events and circumstances; unfortunately they were not. Two unanticipated wars forced a reallocation of public resources from development to defence. The first was the Chinese aggression on the North East Frontier in October–November 1962, when Indian forces were comprehensively defeated and the government was immediately compelled to double the defence budget. As a proportion of GDP, defence expenditures rose from 1.6 per cent in 1960–1 to 3.2 per cent in 1965–6 (*ibid.*, p. 48).

The crisis of 1965–6 and the planning hiatus

The second conflict was the Indo-Pakistan war of September 1965, which broke out while preparations for the Fourth Plan were under way. Its most unwelcome consequence was the United States' decision to suspend indefinitely all aid to both combatants. The Americans had, moreover, just refused to sign a fresh long-term agreement to provide India with food aid under PL 480. The Johnson administration, under pressure from Congressional opponents of concessional grain sales to India, adopted a 'short-leash' policy of doling out stocks sufficient only to meet a few months' requirements, and explicitly tied the continuation of food aid to India's adoption of policies aimed at increasing agricultural production and curbing population growth (Frankel, 2005, p. 286). India's recently appointed Food and Agriculture Minister, C. Subramaniam, needed no persuading that agriculture required a higher level of investment and willingly gave specific commitments to improve fertiliser use and allocate more foreign exchange to fertiliser imports. The suspension of American aid and the accompanying pressure on the balance of payments concatenated with the droughts of 1965 and 1966 to trigger a major crisis in the planning process that was eventually resolved by a demotion of the Planning Commission to the status of an advisory body and a partial retreat from the Nehruvian strategy.

The economic indicators show that the organised economy moved from rapid expansion to depression and prolonged stagnation. Industrial production, which had grown at about 9 per cent annually between 1959 and 1965, contracted in 1966 and in 1967. When growth revived it was much below the level of the early 60s. While the production of steel, cement and paper all went up by around 12 per cent a year between 1951 and 1965, it went up by a mere 1.4 per cent, 5 per cent and 4 per cent respectively in 1966–73 (Jha, 1980, p. 8). The increase in aggregate real investment dropped from an average of over 8 per cent annually between 1960 and 1966 to under 2 per cent per year between 1967 and 1972. Public-sector investment had been the fly-wheel of the industrial boom, so the deceleration in its rate of growth was particularly significant. Fixed capital formation in the public sector grew at an annual rate of 11.3 per cent between 1950–1 and 1965–6, but in the period 1966–7 to 1981–2 dropped to a rate that was less than half, 5.5 per cent (Bardhan, 1984, p. 24). Cutbacks in critical sectors such as railways and electricity were particularly severe.

When the scale of India's economic problems became evident, the governments of Lal Shastri (June 1964 to January 1966) and Indira Ghandi came under external pressure to effect 'structural adjustment'. Even before the subsistence crisis, the consortium of India's international donors had concluded that the country was at a development impasse. A World Bank mission had recommended devaluing the rupee, eliminating import controls and switching the emphasis in India's development strategy from heavy industry to agriculture. Mrs Gandhi reluctantly acquiesced in the 36.5 per cent devaluation in June 1966 (together with reductions in import duties and the liberalisation of foreign exchange controls) on the understanding that the donors would increase their project aid. When they reneged on this promise, she and her advisers felt the nation had been humiliated. The World Bank and the Johnson administration were reviled and Mrs Gandhi's hitherto cordial relations with the US President turned decidedly sour. The Indian government's lasting resentment palpably influenced economic management by strengthening the determination to rely as little as possible on aid and trade in future (Joshi and Little, 1994, p. 76).

In response to the multi-layered economic crisis and to donor pressure, the Indian government was forced to suspend the planning process, drastically reduce public spending on capital projects and relax some of the controls over the private sector. The next Five Year Plan went into hibernation and for three years (1966–9) the Planning Commission took a 'plan holiday', while it formulated annual plans. In real terms, planned investment was cut by 30 per cent during the 'holiday'. Not only was new capital investment out of the question, even the routine maintenance of industry was adversely affected by the government's inability to import sufficient machinery and spare parts. To stimulate private entrepreneurship, some of the controls under the 1951 Industries (Development and Regulation) Act were lifted, principally for agricultural equipment industries and light industries with a high export potential. Mrs Gandhi forsook her father's focus on public-sector industrial development, and set out to increase agricultural production by whatever means possible. The domestic imperatives to do so were compelling: during the seven years prior to the policy 'turn', the average annual increase in agricultural output was about half the rate of population growth, so there was constant upward pressure on food prices. As we noted in Chapter 2, there were large-scale food riots and rural insurgencies in eastern India.

After the electoral reversals of 1967, Congress lost control of eight states which led to more confusion and uncertainty in the political economy of planned development. Constitutionally, economic and social planning was on the 'Concurrent List' of functions over which the centre and states had joint authority. Raising revenue to finance the plans and implementing their proposals required a partnership between the central and state governments that deteriorated after 1967, chiefly because the coalitions in the states became embroiled in 'pork barrel' politics. Public resources were used to retain the loyalties of strategic voting blocs, whether by increasing the wages and allowances of public employees, or by bringing down food prices through government subsidies, or by providing scholarships for poor students. These relatively novel forms of clientelism drained the financial capacity of state governments to carry out development programmes. As substitutes for the rewards (and costs) of economic growth, they increasingly relied on providing symbolic satisfactions of collective regional grievances and aspirations.

From radical turn to social crisis: 1969–74

In retrospect, the liberalising interlude in macroeconomic policy in 1966–8 was a 'missed opportunity' to reduce the pervasive bureaucratic control of the organised sector, open industry to foreign competition, and move it on to the export-oriented path followed by South Korea and Taiwan in the 1970s and China in the 1980s (Kudaisya, 2002). The reason for this missed opportunity lay primarily in domestic politics: in her struggle with the 'Syndicate' for control of Congress, Mrs Gandhi adopted measures of public ownership and the closer regulation of private enterprise to consolidate her following on the left. As a prelude to this radical 'turn', she removed Morarji Desai, a fiscal conservative, from the Finance Ministry in July 1969. Following this, her allies in the Congress Forum for Socialist Action (CFSA) launched a strenuous attack on 'monopolistic capitalism' and urged extensive nationalisation to generate the investment funds needed for larger public-sector plans. To popular acclaim, the commercial banks were nationalised by presidential ordinance in July 1969 (the parliamentary instrument came later). The Monopolies and Restrictive Trade Practices Act of 1969 compelled firms with a certain level of capital assets and/or market share to seek official clearance before entering or expanding any line of production. This prevented industrial concentration, but by restricting the size of firms it prohibited economies of scale and reduced the amount spent on research and development. Applications took around two years to process, so the administrative costs to business and government were high. The managing agency system, which had been the key institution of western enterprise in Asia, was formally abolished in April 1970. Import controls became, once again, severely restrictive: all imports of intermediate and capital goods had to be used by the firm which imported them in its production process. The intention was to eliminate profiteering by intermediaries. Public agencies had a monopoly on imports of certain key inputs (including cereals, petroleum, fertilisers, and iron and steel).

Following Mrs Gandhi's electoral triumphs and the victory over Pakistan, she had almost imperial authority to pursue her assault on poverty, commercial monopolies and class privilege. The general insurance companies were nationalised in August 1972 and, by the following January, the entire coal-mining industry had been nationalised. The wholesale wheat trade was briefly, but disastrously nationalised in the spring of 1973. The Foreign Exchange Regulation Act of 1973 led to new restrictions on the investments that could be made by foreign firms and their subsidiaries. An array of regulatory measures was added to an already over-regulated economy, with the result that all basic management decisions in large-scale private industry were subject to government approval. A new industrial licensing policy entirely reversed the trend towards de-control started in the mid-1960s by with-drawing all previous exemptions from licensing requirements. The gov-ernment's entry into financial services enhanced its leverage over capital formation in the private sector. Very strict conditions were placed on business liquidation and the retrenchment of labour, so the public sector grew by taking 'sick' companies into public ownership.

In the foreign trade sector, the complex system of import allocations was matched by an equally complex system of export incentives. It operated by entitling the exporter to import licences that carried a premium, and so provided him (or her) with a subsidy. The system engendered 'rent-seeking' (that is, exploiting a political regulation of the market for private gain) and corruption. It also led to price distor-tions by subsidising exports made largely from imported materials, rather than those with a high domestic value added. In some instances, the foreign currency return from exports with a large import content were lower than the foreign currency cost of the imports embodied in them.

While the dirigisme of Nehruvian socialism was intensified under Mrs Gandhi, the strategic goal of inducing higher growth by concen-trating investment in heavy industry was sacrificed to the political pri-ority of raising mass consumption levels. When the Fourth Plan was being finalised in 1970, organised industry and mining represented only 15 per cent of GDP and the public and private sectors were together generating about 500,000 jobs per year, which was far fewer than the annual increment to the labour force. (The planners calcu-lated that an additional 65 million workers would enter the labour force by 1986.) Higher industrial investment could, at best, merely contain endemic rural underemployment; progress towards eliminating poverty could be made only by creating additional job opportunities within agriculture. On Mrs Gandhi's initiative, new programmes for rural development were hastily incorporated into the Fourth Plan, which inevitably siphoned off funds earmarked for industrial develop-ment. Alarmed by the jettisoning of their growth strategy, all members of the Planning Commission tendered their resignations following Mrs Gandhi's landslide election victory.

Despite the Prime Minister's immense personal power and prestige, her government's institutional and administrative capacity to imple-ment its social and economic policies was degrading for two reasons. First, at state level, there was neither the leadership nor organisation to implement the agrarian policy framework drawn up by the Planning Commission and approved by the centre. The split in Congress, and

Mrs Gandhi's autocratic style of political patronage, had destroyed the institutional network that mobilised support behind government policies in the Nehru era. Second, the quality of public administration was deteriorating because of Mrs Gandhi's insistence on a 'committed' civil service, loyal to her in person, and the efflorescence of political corruption, which seemed to constitute the 'milieu of the Indian polity' (Frankel, 2005 p. 475; Park, 1975). The main 'driver' of political corruption was the escalating costs of democratic election. Candidates' election expenses were limited by law, but not expenses incurred by third parties on their behalf. Faced with re-election, politicians looked to business for campaign contributions and political donations, while businessmen looked to politicians to help secure industrial licences, import quotas and public contracts. With the 'radical turn' in 1969, company contributions to political parties were banned, thus eliminating the legal financing of politics by business. As a result, 'number two' money accumulated by business tax evasion and black market operations became the principal source of political funding. Prices for licences or other permits were quoted in terms of the number of briefcases of cash required to obtain them. The Foreign Trade Minister, L.N. Mishra, who was Congress (R)'s chief fundraiser, became notorious for extorting 'donations' from uncooperative businesses by threatening them with raids from the Revenue Intelligence and Enforcement Directorate, which operated under the Cabinet Secretariat (Kochanek, 1987, pp. 1290–1). IAS officers unwilling to condone the corruption of their political bosses were demoted and moved to less sensitive posts. Mrs Gandhi was badly tainted by the award to her 22-year-old son Sanjay of the contract to build the Indian 'people's car', the Maruti, and the venture's subsequent collapse in a mire of financial malpractice. It was believed – and seems quite plausible – that the larger business houses bought off threats of nationalisation with illegal contributions to the Congress Party and to Mrs Gandhi herself. In an atmosphere of gathering demoralisation, the planning process became incoherent, politically manipulated and pulled apart by the conflicting demands for resources.

The tumultuous agitations which reduced some States to near anarchy in 1973–5 were projected on to a major economic and fiscal crisis. Its first, and most basic, cause was drought, which resulted in partial harvest failures in 1973 and 1975; net food grain availability declined by about 8 per cent between 1972 and 1973, and by about the same amount between 1974 and 1975. Inspired by the early results of the 'Green Revolution', the government had, in 1972, announced that the nation would henceforth be self-sufficient in food. Misled by its own rhetoric, and misinformed about the scale of the shortfall, it delayed importing grain until world prices had climbed to unprecedented levels. In an attempt to control prices and stamp out profiteering, private grain merchants were banned from the wholesale wheat trade which was taken under national control. The scheme was conceived by the Planning Minister, D.P. Dhar, a leading left radical, with the intention of giving the government a commanding position over the nation's food supply. It proved quite unworkable: wheat disappeared from the market in many regions and illegal trading took place on a vast scale. When confronted with the near universal resistance of the dealers, the government restored private trade. For consumers, the inevitable result of shortfalls in supply was food price inflation which hit the rural poor hardest: real agricultural wages declined by about a quarter between 1971–2 and 1974–5 (Joshi and Little, 1994, Table 5.8, p. 120).

The second, overlapping cause of the crisis was imported inflation due to the quadrupling of the international oil price in 1973. The cost of fuel, fertiliser and food imports rose steeply, putting a severe strain on both the balance of payments and public finances, which were already straitened by the burden of relieving the refugees from East Pakistan, escalating military expenditure and the virtual cessation of foreign aid. Between mid-1973 and September 1974, the annual rate of inflation was running at 33 per cent (*ibid.*, p. 105). The government adopted extremely tough fiscal and monetary policies: it cut public expenditure and froze wages and cost of living allowances in the organised sector (where it was the largest employer) while sharply increasing excise duties and rail fares. Real earnings in organised manufacturing fell by nearly 12 per cent in 1974–5, having already declined slightly in 1972–4. Companies' dividend distributions were restricted, the cost of borrowing rose and inflation eroded the real income from public bonds. To squeeze money out of the economy and drive down inflation, all income tax payers were required to deposit a proportion of their taxable incomes with the Reserve Bank. The government was determined to 'face down' labour militancy and uncompromisingly broke a three-week strike by over a million railway workers in June 1974. Its anti-inflationary stance hit secure urban workers, salaried employees and middle-class families who relied on dividends and government bonds for part of their income. The students who were the shock troops of the civil disobedience movements and anti-corruption agitations were, by and large, drawn from these relatively privileged social circles. Since students were predominantly from the 'forward' castes it would follow that most of the protesters were.

The Emergency of 1975

On all sides, there was growing impatience and despair with party politics. Despite massive Congress majorities at the Centre and in the States, Mrs Gandhi and her allies were increasingly paralysed by populist agitations to force the dissolution of factionalised and corrupt assemblies. In Gujarat, ten weeks of demonstrations – which led to 103 deaths and 8000 arrests – finally compelled Mrs Gandhi to dissolve the State Assembly in March 1974. A similar campaign, headed by the veteran Gandhian, 'J.P.' Narayan, was waged against the corrupt State ministry in Bihar: it brought administration to a halt between March and November 1974. The opposition in Bihar and elsewhere articulated both a moral distaste for the squalid 'wheeling and dealing' at State level, and conservative alarm at the radicalisation of the Congress Party's national politics and the electoral alliances it entered with the Communist Party of India in Uttar Pradesh and Orissa. The Prime Minister saw herself as an embattled left-winger assailed by bourgeois reactionaries in shady alliance with the foreign, 'imperialist' interests. She genuinely feared the sort of coup that had toppled President Allende of Chile (Frankel, 2005, p. 649). Order was restored in Bihar by imposing President's rule, despatching 40,000 troops to the state and sweeping arrests. In the following months, the Prime Minister and her coterie became persuaded that recourse to extraordinary powers at Union level was essential to cope with the growing incidence of extra-parliamentary agitations and political violence. What prompted the declaration of a State of Emergency was her conviction in the Allahabad Court in June 1975 on charges of corrupt electoral practices, and the ensuing national clamour for her resignation. On 25 June, the JP Movement called for a nation-wide campaign of mass disobedience, which would culminate in a *gherao* (peaceful blockade) of the Prime Minister's residence, thus forcing either her resignation or a massacre of demonstrators that would indelibly tarnish her reputation (Chandra *et al.*, 2000, p. 252).

With the imposition of emergency rule on 26 June, a government of independent India staged a coup against the political nation quite as draconian as the British crackdown on the 'Quit India' campaign of 1942. About 36,000 people were detained without trial at the beginning of the Emergency; according to one report, subsequent arrests brought the number behind bars to 80,000 (Guha, 2007, p. 505). All opposition leaders – and many Congress dissidents – were imprisoned; the fundamental rights guaranteed in the constitution were suspended, along with its federal provisions; the press was rigorously censored. What warranted this drastic repression, in Mrs Gandhi's eyes, was that she was both averting chaos and removing the obstacles to radical social reform. A 20-point economic programme, with the primary purpose of helping the rural poor, was announced. The highest priority was given to implementing land ceilings, aiding landless labourers, abolishing bonded labour and liquidating rural indebtedness. In urban India, the Emergency regime tried to instil a spirit of social discipline by enforcing punctuality at work, banning strikes and vigorously prosecuting smuggling and tax evasion.

From the present perspective, the Emergency was an aberration in India's post-1947 political history, but it gave every sign of being institutionalised in a durable authoritarian regime after an overwhelming parliamentary majority voted the 42nd Amendment Act in November 1976. This changed the state's official description to 'Sovereign Socialist Democratic Republic' and revised 59 clauses in the Constitution. Judicial review of any proposed constitutional amendment was ended; 'The People's Fundamental Rights' were made subordinate to an expanded set of 'Directive Principles of State Policy'; parliament was empowered to enact legislation banning 'anti-national' activities and associations, without giving any reason for so doing; the president could, at the prime minister's direction, further amend the Constitution by executive decree for a period of two years. The Supreme Court had already upheld the suspension of habeas corpus for the duration of the Emergency, which could be as long as the government wished under the amended Constitution, so for an indefinite future the judiciary could not determine the legality of someone's detention (Palmer, 1977a, pp. 166–9). The foundations of the political order established at Independence had been comprehensively undermined.

A US inter-agency intelligence memorandum judged Mrs Gandhi to be fully in control of political life and most Indians acquiescent in her rule. Were national elections to be called in 1977, Congress 'would almost certainly win overwhelmingly', because Mrs Gandhi's opponents were, if not in detention, 'isolated, weak and ineffective'. The government had ample internal security forces at its disposal and retained the loyalty of the military. The public applauded its energetic prosecution of corruption and economic crimes (hoarding, black marketing). Businessmen were pleased by the legal curbs on strikes, rural landlords by the high priority accorded to agriculture. Mrs Gandhi's domination of her Cabinet and Congress appeared unassailable: a recently appointed defence minister openly boasted that his loyalty was not to the office of prime minister but to Mrs Gandhi in person. She had indicated that censorship of the news media would continue indefinitely and had moved to ensure friendly coverage in large newspaper chains by exerting her influence over their editors. India's treaty partner, the Soviet Union, had openly endorsed the emergency and instructed the CPI to support Mrs Gandhi (*Foreign Relations of the United States*, 1969–76, vol. E-8, Documents on South Asia, 'India: Present Scene: Future Prospects', May 1976, doc. 229).

What stopped the institutionalisation of authoritarianism, it could be argued, was the alienation of Mrs Gandhi's strongest supporters amongst minorities, the Dalits (or 'untouchables') and 'Backward Classes' by a terrifying campaign of forced sterilisation, and her colossal misjudgement in calling national elections for March 1977.

The achievements and shortcomings of Nehruvian socialism

In what has been a political narrative of Indian development planning, its economic achievements and shortcomings have been neglected, and it is now time to assess them. The most signal achievement was the creation of an industrial base that, by the early 1970s, was remarkably diverse by Third World standards. While the established textile and agricultural processing industries expanded at a moderate pace in the 1950s and 60s, other lines of manufacture grew much faster. The expansion in the metallurgical, chemical and engineering industries was especially rapid. Many either did not exist in 1951 or were only rudimentary. Taking 1950–1 as the base year, the general index of industrial production rose to 137 in 1955–6 and 194 in 1960–1, while that of machine production had soared to 503. Throughout the first two plans, industrial production grew at an average rate of 7 per cent annually. It must, though, be emphasised that India remained a vast, overwhelmingly agrarian economy in which manufacturing's share of net domestic product rose quite slowly: in 1950–1, it was 10 per cent, by 1965–6, 14.7 per cent, and in 1970–1, had receded slightly to 13.4 per cent (Bardhan, 1984, Table 5). Furthermore, around 1980, more than a third of manufacturing output still came from unregistered workshops – that is, establishments employing fewer than 25 workers and not using power or establishments employing fewer than ten workers but using power. Trade, hotels and restaurants contributed more to the national product than the registered manufacturing enterprises right up to the mid-1980s.

As a result of import substitution and industrial diversification, India ceased to rely on finished industrial imports; she was thereby freed from the dependence on particular trading partners that characterised her colonial trade. Furthermore, despite substantial absolute external borrowings, India avoided the levels of indebtedness to foreign creditors found in other large developing economies. Debt service payments as a ratio of exports were much lower than in Mexico and Brazil, for example. Investment dependency was minimised by limiting the proportion of equity that foreign capital could hold in Indian firms, and by steering the acquisitions of foreign technologies in the direction of agreements allowing co-production.

Nehruvian socialism met one of its crucial political objectives by enabling the state to create and occupy the commanding heights of the organised economy. In 1951, there were fewer than ten firms in the public sector; by 1978, their number had grown to 745, and by 1982 to 894 (Lal, 1988, p. 257; Rudolph and Rudolph, 1987, Table 5, p. 29). The central government undertook giant projects – such as the Bhakra-Nangal irrigation and power complex – but state or local governments owned rather more than half of productive capital in the public sector. During the first three plans, public-sector growth was predominantly a matter of creating new enterprises but, in the 1970s, the sector was also extended through the nationalisation of declining or sick industries and the creation of joint public–private enterprises. Of the top 12 industrial firms, in terms of their sales, around 1982, ten were government owned; their net sales were about six times greater than those of the ten largest private-sector firms. The larger the firm, in terms of capital employed, the more likely it was to be publicly owned: public-sector enterprises accounted for 62 per cent of all productive industrial capital, and 58 per cent of gross fixed assets in 1978–9, though only 26.7 per cent of registered industrial employment (Bardhan, 1984, Tables 13 and 14). The state had total monopolies of power generation, rail and air transport, life and general insurance, and a near monopoly of banking. The leading firms in iron and steel, oil, natural gas and the heavy electrical industry were all in the public sector.

Behind this impressive edifice of public-owned enterprise lay several structural weaknesses that were increasingly evident during the 1970s as the public economy became an elaborate network of patronage and subsidies. Budget management on public-sector projects was poor: most cost up to 40 per cent more and took two years longer to complete than was anticipated, and they were frequently subject to mid-stream changes (Jha, 1980, p. 73). In following their penchant for capital-intensive investment, the planners were insensitive to the social opportunity cost of capital. While the first generation of projects were evaluated according to rational economic criteria, there was a conspicuous lack of realism on the part of central and State governments as to the costs and benefits of second- and third-generation projects. The location of industrial plants was often determined by political rather than economic considerations, and they usually operated less efficiently than their private-sector counterparts. From the late 1960s, the public-sector industries were plagued by problems of overcapacity, underproduction, inefficient management, poor labour relations and supply shortages. Unsurprisingly, the rate of return on public investment declined.

To which we must add that public-sector employees became a large, powerful and relatively well remunerated vested-interest group. In 1980–1, they accounted for 6.8 per cent of the labour force and earned very nearly 40 per cent of the wages and salaries in the entire economy (Kelgama and Parikh, 2003, p. 106). Public-sector pay was not systematically related to either productivity or profitability. Since more than seven out of ten workers in the organised sector were in public employment, its wage rates had a 'knock-on' effect on private industry. This reinforced the tendency for employers and managers to opt for capital-intensive labour-saving techniques, a choice completely at odds with the abundance of labour and relatively high cost of capital. Most of the country's modern economic infrastructure was controlled by highly organised public workers, who had exceptional job security. Under the 1947 Industrial Dispute Act, any firm (public or private) with more than 100 employees required the permission of the relevant State government to make workers redundant, permission which was rarely given. Unsurprisingly, when the Narasimha Rao government embarked on its economic reform programme in the early 1990s, public-sector workers were formidable opponents of privatisation.

Development economists have drawn attention to the rising capital-incremental output ratio in the Indian economy and most have seen it as a symptom of serious economic malaise. (The ratio relates increases in output to the investment required to achieve that output, and is a measure of the productivity of investment.) Rising capital-output ratios were, to be sure, a global phenomenon in the early 1970s, especially after the quadrupling of fuel prices, and are an inevitable consequence of investment in more complex and expensive technologies. But India's problem was *sui generis*: she had one the highest capital-incremental output ratios amongst developing countries, and there is no doubt that a major factor in this trend was the inefficiency with which capital was utilised and managed (Bardhan, 1984, p. 27). International comparisons in these matters are hazardous, but can be used to underline the lamentable performance of Indian industries: while total factor productivity growth in South Korean manufacturing averaged 5.7 per cent a year between 1959 and 1979, in India productivity growth was *negative*, and ranged from –0.2 per cent a year to –1. 3 per cent (Lal, 1988, p. 263). Nearly all industries, whether publicly or privately owned, were cocooned either by tariffs or quantitative restrictions, which contributed to their inefficiency and high capital–output ratios. Nevertheless, the declining productivity of investment was particularly evident in public-sector enterprises: where they coexisted with private companies, they utilised their capacity 15–20 per cent less efficiently, and generally failed to generate a surplus for reinvestment. Some public-sector units owned by the central government were staggeringly inefficient: throughout the 1970s, at least 30 recorded losses every year. As many as 33 units accumulated losses that more than wiped out their entire share capital base (Bardhan, 1984, p. 63). The political and administrative mismanagement behind this dismal record was even worse in enterprises run by the states. Any historical assessment of the public sector and import substitution in India's economic development should recognise their dynamic roles in fostering skill-formation and learning-by-doing in a range of sophisticated industries, but these positive effects were remorselessly attenuated after about 1970.

From the point of view of the social welfare of the Indian people, the major drawback of the capital-intensive, heavy industry strategy was that it created little new employment and so failed to soak up the surplus labour coming onto the market. Simply to prevent unemployment from increasing, at least 2.5 million jobs were needed each year, a number far greater than the annual increments to the industrial workforce. Between 1951 and 1971, nearly three-quarters of the increase in the labour force was absorbed by agriculture, and the structure of output and employment did not change markedly. As its critics have argued, the heavy industry strategy was implicated in the painfully slow decline of poverty, which was mainly attributable to the failure to increase substantially the demand for non-agricultural labour.

Paradoxically, the strategy had the further, unintended consequence of accelerating the growth of employment in the public services in a politically driven effort to absorb surplus labour. More and more 'white collar' posts were created, irrespective of the real need for them, by all levels of government. While national income grew by around 42 per cent between 1960–1 and 1972–3, employment in the government sector grew by 69 per cent. Because wages in this sector were protected against inflation by 'dearness allowances', the salary bill of the central and state governments rose by 15–18 per cent a year throughout the 1960s and by even more in the 70s (Jha, 1980, p. 66). The GDP (at 1971 prices) for public administration and defence multiplied nearly seven times between 1950–1 and 1980–1, while the total GDP at factor cost multiplied less than three times in that period. By 1980, two-thirds of workers in the organised economy were employed either in government services or public-sector enterprises. Although a bloated public workforce had obvious welfare benefits, they came with a huge 'opportunity cost' in terms of forgone investment in productive industry. The average pay of a central government employee was around 5000 rupees a year, about a third of the investment required to create a 'real' job in industry. According to one calculation, had it not been for the reckless creation of bureaucratic sinecures, an additional 15 million productive jobs could have been created, mostly in the organised sector (Jha, 1980).

During the most dynamic decade of Nehruvian socialism (1955–65), private enterprise flourished below the commanding heights of the organised economy, chiefly because public-sector demand stimulated private-sector investment and output. In response to the state's industrial strategy, entrepreneurs invested heavily in the cement, chemicals, aluminium, copper and engineering industries; by the early 1960s, about half their output was being purchased by the government. Businessmen were guaranteed sales in a highly protected market so they had a powerful incentive to jump over the bureaucratic hurdles in the way of private investment, which outpaced all the official forecasts. (The fact that businesses grew chiefly through reinvesting profits also tended to nullify the licensing system.) Private firms were dealt a severe blow by the cut-back in public investment in 1966, and the announcement of a plan holiday triggered a wave of bankruptcies. For years, private industry was plagued by excess capacity.

The private sector's recovery was retarded by the overt hostility of Mrs Gandhi's government to big or 'monopolistic' business after 1969 and the increasing bias in industrial policy against large-scale private

Table 2.1 Value added in manufacturing as a percentage of GDP in selected Asian states

	1970	1975	1980	1985
India	14.16	15.75	16.72	16.51
Malaysia	12.44	17.60	21.55	19.32
S. Korea	17.79	21.65	24.45	27.31
Indonesia	10.29	9.80	12.99	15.98
Pakistan	16.06	16.70	15.93	15.90

Source: World Bank, *World Development Indicators*.

investment and capital conglomeration. The dirigisme of Nehruvian socialism now started to exert a major influence on the structure of private enterprise and the pattern of investment. As we have noted, the Monopolies and Restrictive Trade Practices Act of 1970 prohibited the larger companies from expanding their existing lines of production without special licence; to grow, they had to enter new industries. Meanwhile, it became progressively easier to create small and medium-sized enterprises. The capital threshold below which a business was exempt from licensing was raised and the field of enterprise reserved for small businesses greatly extended. By the 1980s, 830 items (ranging from garments for export to lamps and the simpler agricultural implements) could be legally produced only by small-scale businesses, which were given preferential access to low-interest credit and priority in the allocation of scarce raw materials. There were fraudulent ways around product reservation, but it actively encouraged the 'involution' of industry and commerce through the proliferation of small and medium-size enterprises. There were 47,210 registered private-sector firms in 1978, a number that ballooned to 70,795 by 1982. The web of controls undoubtedly contributed to the *comparatively* slow growth of manufacturing in India in the 1970s and early 80s (see Table 2.1). An industrial firm wishing to develop new product lines with imported machinery required a licence from the Ministry of Industry allowing new investment to take place, a licence from the Ministry of Commerce to import capital goods and authorisation from the Reserve Bank of India to buy the necessary foreign currency. If the firm wanted to raise more capital from its shareholders, it required the permission of the Comptroller of Capital Issues. All the instruments of industrial policy tended to reinforce each other in diverting private investment, first, from basic towards consumer industries (often producing luxuries), from large-scale to small-scale enterprise and from industry to trade (Jha, 1980, p. 90).

Poverty and the land

The most damning indictment of 'Nehruvian socialism' was that it failed in its central objective of alleviating mass poverty. This was partly a matter of the low rate of growth in per capita GDP, which, during the heyday of national planning, was below that in Pakistan and below the average for developing countries as a whole. More specifically, it was due to the glacial pace of structural change in the labour force, which condemned huge numbers to a life sentence in low-yielding, smallholder agriculture. Just over three-quarters of the labour force was employed in the primary sector in 1961, a proportion that fell to about 65 per cent in the early 1990s. The decline was steeper for male workers than female, but the large majority (58.3 per cent) of males were still employed in the primary sector at the latter date. In the countryside, regular employment of any kind was very exceptional: the overwhelming majority of workers (both male and female) were classified as either 'self-employed' or 'casually employed'. In the towns, just over half (50.7 per cent) of male workers were classified as 'regularly' employed in 1972, but the proportion declined to 42 per cent by the early 1990s (Dev, 1997, Table 2). In both urban and rural India, the fastest-growing sector was, not industry, but services, where the great majority eked out a hand-to-mouth existence in the 'unorganised sector'.

India is the only developing country for which we have national household sample surveys running from the early 1950s to the present, and the data on consumption expenditure have been used to deduce the incidence of poverty over time. Interpreting the numbers and specifying a poverty line has generated a large and contentious literature, but there is general agreement that there was no significant trend in the incidence of poverty between 1951 and the early 1970s. At any one time, about half the rural and two-fifths of the urban population were too poor to secure a nutritionally adequate diet. The considerable variations about these averages were due entirely to the weather: good monsoons led to bumper harvests and lower food prices, which lifted many above the poverty line for a while; drought, crop failures and high prices drove them below it (Dev, 1997, and Nayyar, 2006, are useful overviews). The landmark study by V.M. Dandekar and N. Rath differed from other investigations in concluding that the higher cost of urban living meant the incidence of poverty was greater in the towns than in the countryside: they estimated that, in 1960–1, 38 per cent of the rural population and about 50 per cent of the urban population lived below an income level of 50 paise per day – that is to say in destitution (Dandekar and Rath, 1971).

There are indications that, with falling real wages in agriculture, the living standards of the poorest 40 per cent actually worsened during 1960s and that the proportion of the population below the poverty line rose substantially (Nayyar, 1998). Rural poverty probably peaked around 1966–8 when, according to one respected estimate, 56.5 per cent of the population in the countryside could not meet their minimum calorie needs. This 'peaking' is what we would expect given the crop failures in 1965–6 and the ensuing near famine conditions in many areas, though it is not confirmed by other estimates (see Bhalla and Vashistha, 1988). Whatever the lived experience behind the figures, when Mrs Gandhi pledged to 'abolish poverty' she was implicitly condemning the cardinal failure of her father's development strategy. In 1972, the Planning Commission reckoned that absolute poverty (defined in terms of per capita consumption of less than 40 rupees per month at current prices) afflicted at least two-fifths of the population, a minimum of 220 million people (Frankel, 2005, p. 493).

We know that a substantial and apparently permanent reduction in poverty was achieved in India by the end of the century, but specifying when this 'structural' amelioration began is not easy (see Table 2.2). The turning point was probably the mid-1970s and the principal cause the falling real price of food because of impressive increases in output during the Green Revolution, though the anti-poverty programmes initiated by Mrs Gandhi's government may have been a contributory factor. The Green Revolution was at first confined to Punjab and Haryana and accentuated long-standing regional variations in poverty. In the early 1970s, the 'headcount' incidence of poverty in rural Punjab was about half the national rural average; by the late 1980s, it had fallen to below one-third. In rural Haryana, the corresponding fall was from roughly three-fifths to two-fifths of the national average (Dev, 1997, Table 11). In rural Bihar, by contrast, the gap between the state's incidence of poverty and the national average grew wider; an already poor region became *relatively* poorer. Between 1973 and 1993, poverty

Table 2.2 Incidence of poverty in India: 1973–2000, percentage below the poverty line

	1973–4	*1977–8*	*1983–4*	*1987–8*	*1993–4*	*1999–2000*
Rural	56.4	53.1	45.7	39.1	37.3	27.1 [30.0]
Urban	49.0	45.2	40.8	38.2	32.4	23.6 [24.7]
Total	54.9	51.3	44.5	38.9	36.0	26.1
Total number below poverty line (million)	321.3	329.0	323.0	307.0	320.4	260.2

Source: National Sample Survey and Planning Commission, given in Nayyar, 2006. The bracketed figures in the last column are adjustments made by Angus Deaton and Jean Drèze to reflect changes in NSS sampling methodology.

in rural Bihar fell by about 5 per cent, across rural India as a whole by about 19 per cent. These divergent experiences added to the 'Green Revolution pessimism' of many commentators, who warned that landless labourers would be rendered destitute by the curtailing employment opportunities. These fears proved groundless: the demand for labour in Punjab and Haryana was such as to attract heavy inward migration from Bihar and eastern Uttar Pradesh. Over time the evidence became clear that the expansion of agricultural output reduced rural poverty; it was a rare example of 'trickle-down' development actually trickling down (Singh, 1990, pp. 26–7).

Widespread absolute poverty coexisted with comparative equality, for the Indian distribution of income was among the more nearly equal by international standards. The share of national income going to the poorest 40 per cent of the population was about 18 per cent, whereas in richer countries, such as Brazil and Mexico, it was in the range of 8–10 per cent. Again by stark contrast with these societies, the wealthy in India were becoming comparatively less well off. According to Lal, income inequality decreased between the 1950s and 1980, not because of any transfer of consumption from rich to poor, but because of an absolute fall in the living standards of the top 15 per cent of the rural and urban population (Lal, 1988, p. 272). One important implication of India's relatively egalitarian income structure was the limited possibilities for redistributive policies: only about a tenth of the population had sufficient surplus income to be able to forgo it without serious impoverishment. Another implication, one might suggest, was that political ideologies foregrounding class conflict would have limited appeal to the Indian electorate. Not only was income relatively evenly distributed, about two-thirds of the poor had a stake in the private property system in the form of a tiny plot of land. The distance, in purely economic terms, between them and the not so poor was too narrow to mobilise great masses around a political assault on property and wealth. Except in specific localities, poor peasants and agricultural wage labourers did not organise themselves, but remained locked into clientelistic relationships with the more prosperous farmers who were their seasonal employers and, usually, creditors. More often than not, the poor in the countryside were mobilised by farmers' movements in agitations for lower taxes, higher prices and better subsidies – demands that primarily represented the interests of the larger, more prosperous landowners. Even the left-wing parties usually followed an electoral strategy of appealing to an agrarian community of richer farmers, marginal peasants and wage labourers, and blurring the real conflicts of interest between them. The rhetorical fire of the left was directed at a phantom feudal class.

In terms of raising the welfare of the great majority, the favoured international comparison by which to judge the achievements of 'Nehruvian socialism' is with Communist China. Nehru and his colleagues on the Planning Commission would have been the first to acknowledge the legitimacy of that comparison. They considered that the historical experiences and current problems of the two nations were highly similar and were keenly interested in Chinese economic policies and progress. Mahalanobis came away from a visit to China in the mid-1950s convinced that it 'provided a better model of development for India than the advanced western countries' (Frankel, 2005, p. 125). On most social indicators, the comparison highlights the shortcomings of 'Nehruvian socialism', which served the Indian people less well than Maoist communism did the Chinese. Indians were spared such catastrophes as the 'Great Leap Forward' and the 'Cultural Revolution', but denied the impressive advances made in health care and nutritional status in China. Around 1950, average life expectancy in both countries was about 40 years. In 1970, the expectation of life in India was still only 48 years and the infant mortality rate per 1000 live births was 139. The corresponding figures for China were 59 years and 69 infant deaths per 1000 live births. Between 1960 and 1980, the proportion of Chinese adults who were literate rose from 43 per cent to 69 per cent; in India, it rose from 28 per cent to 36 per cent (Dasgupta, 1993, Table 5.4, p. 118; Drèze and Sen, 1995, ch. 4).

A further contrast with China is worth dwelling on. Communist China's land reform was the greatest act of expropriation in human history: at least 200 million acres were distributed to about 75 million families (Gray, 1990, pp. 291–2). Hundreds of thousands of landlords were denounced as counter-revolutionaries and suffered the severities of proletarian justice. In India, Congress-controlled federal and state governments were loath to promote class conflict on the land and generally respected agrarian property rights. The redistribution of land, which the Planning Commission regarded as necessary to eliminate endemic poverty, was approached very gingerly. In 1953, the Commission advocated a ceiling on holdings of three times the average family farm, while recommending that small and medium-sized farmers be assisted to group themselves voluntarily into agricultural cooperatives. Detailed recommendations for legislation were not made until 1956; and most states did not pass enabling legislation until 1960 or 1961. Except for moderately successful measures in West Bengal and communist-controlled Kerala, this 'ceilings' legislation was ineffective. The long delay between proposing and passing the new laws gave landlords ample time to arrange the partition of family holdings between individuals, and so to circumvent the ceilings. Up to 1972, a total of only 2.3 million acres of surplus land had been formally transferred from private landowners to government for redistribution to the landless.

Before the 1970s, the only significant transfers of land ownership in independent India resulted from the *zamindari* abolition legislation of 1950–4. Where the *zamindari* system had existed on a large scale, this did accomplish major changes in the pattern of landownership, though it fell far short of an agrarian transformation (Frankel, 2005, pp. 190–4). The legislative provisions did not allow for the outright expropriation of the *zamindars*, who were generously compensated for their lost revenue rights and permitted to keep land they personally cultivated (the 'home farm'), usually without any ceiling. Where *zamindars* were absentee rentiers without a 'home farm', State governments allowed them land for personal cultivation subject to a ceiling. The former *zamindars* gained full ownership rights of this land, but their tenants were confirmed only in the legal rights they enjoyed on the date immediately preceding vesting. The main beneficiaries of the reform process were the more substantial occupancy tenants from the Sudra castes. They were elevated in economic standing relative to the resident upper-caste ex-*zamindars* who were left with reduced estates. For tenants-at-will, who were amongst the most vulnerable of the rural poor, *zamindari* reform often brought greater insecurity into already insecure lives, since evictions to exaggerate the proportion of 'home farm' under personal cultivation were common. Francine Frankel, a close observer of Indian development planning, wrote: 'It is a sound assumption that the relatively small number of tenants who acquired superior occupancy or ownership rights under the legislation were outnumbered by those who lost their holdings to landlords under provisions permitting resumption for personal cultivation' (Frankel, 2005, p. 194). That is the only logical explanation for the sharp decline in the number of recorded tenancies between 1954 and early 1960s. There is little reason to believe that the incidence of unrecorded tenancies actually decreased; rather, registered leases were converted into oral, informal agreements that effectively deprived the cultivator of any protection under State tenancy acts.

Where we can follow the process of *zamindari* abolition at the village level, and assess its consequences over several decades, we find strong continuity in the distribution of land (and power) between the British Raj and the Congress Raj. In Palanpur, in Uttar Pradesh, those who gained most were substantial leaseholders whose families had secured hereditary tenure by virtue of inter-war legislation. Households belonging to service castes and agricultural labourers gained nothing. *Zamindars* had been compensated for the loss of their proprietary rights with the payment of a sum equal to eight times the annual rental, plus a rehabilitation grant. In the 1970s, Palanpur's erstwhile *zamindars* remained large and prosperous farmers dwelling in neighbouring villages. Palanpur had not been 'timeless' and static: it had seen many changes in its agriculture and land ownership since Independence, but within a pattern an ICS district officer would have recognised. Material goods that embodied both prestige and utility became more widely distributed: in 1974–5, there were 74 watches and 38 bicycles in the village compared with only one watch and not a single bicycle in 1957–8 (Bliss and Stern, 1982).

For the Congress left, an unwanted consequence of *zamindari* abolition was to set up a formidable social barrier to further social reorganisation on the land. The peasant elite from the superior cultivating castes, who gained most from abolition, became the conservative pillar of the new rural order, and its representatives were increasingly influential in the State legislatures. Though smallholders by western standards (usually with holdings of between 5 and 25 acres), they were less than a fifth of the rural population and normally controlled half or more of the cultivated area. Labourers and marginal cultivators proved unable to mobilise themselves politically and allowed the rural elite to manipulate the diffuse loyalties of kinship, caste and faction to maintain personal retinues. By this means, elite farmers dominated the village cooperative and *panchayat* bodies and were usually able to deliver the vote at State and national elections. The defeat of Congress in almost every north Indian state in the 1967 elections was widely attributed to their deserting the party. It was another incentive for Mrs Ghandi to provide public support to the better-endowed farmers and regions by way of subsidised inputs (fertilisers, seeds, water and electric power), cheap credit and procurement prices that ensured high returns for producers. These were, in a sense, political tribute to the electoral power of the country's commercial farmers.

Just as it was wrongly believed that the Green Revolution entailed deepening pauperisation, so it was feared that the accelerating commercialisation of agriculture spelt greater inequality in land holdings and a rising proportion of the rural population who were landless. Frankel, who used the evidence of the National Sample Survey, affirmed that land was becoming more unequally distributed. Between 1961–2 and 1970–1, the proportion of holdings which were less than 2.5 acres rose while the proportion of holdings over 25 acres declined, but occupied a larger fraction of the cultivated area (Frankel, 2005, p. 493). In a longer-term perspective, it is evident that these conclusions were premature; the short-term fluctuations masked the secular trend in independent India towards the *more equal* (or less concentrated) distribution of land, brought about principally by population growth and the equal division of holdings amongst heirs. Landlessness has actually diminished. Let me reiterate that the country inherited a very unequal structure of landholding, though one in which landowning and landless households quite frequently changed their status over one or two generations. According to the first extensive survey on land ownership undertaken in 1954–5, 22 per cent of rural households owned no land at all; another 25 per cent owned fragments of less than 1 acre; an additional 14 per cent owned uneconomic or marginal holdings of 1 acre to 2.5 acres. The upper 13 per cent who had more than 10 acres owned 64 per cent of the entire area (Frankel, 2005, p. 97). Twenty years later, an estimated 12.3 per cent of rural households were landless while a further 34 per cent occupied marginal and sub-marginal holdings. The top 18.6 per cent owned 60.4 per cent of the cultivated area (Bardhan, 1984, Table 17, p. 107). The two sets of data are not entirely consistent and may exaggerate the decline of landlessness, but there is no doubt that the proportion of the rural population not owning any land fell significantly (Vaidyanathan, 1983, p. 978). Landless house-holds acquired land more frequently than small households lost their land. Deepak Lal cites studies undertaken in five states which showed land ownership becoming more dispersed both through a decline in the numbers and average size of the largest-sized holdings and an increase in both average size as well as in the number of small-sized holdings (Lal, 1988, p. 277). Land markets worked in favour of small and marginal farmers, rather than against them; public intervention tended to work against concentrated ownership. According to Inderjit Singh: 'Fear of the imposition of ceilings on landholdings, opportuni-ties for profitable intensification of land use, and tenancy legislation that made it easier for tenants to acquire land in a number of states all made it less desirable and more difficult for larger owners to enlarge their holdings' (Singh, 1990, p. 50). Between 1960 and 1990, state poli-cies and land competition shrank the proportion of cultivated land in operational holdings over 25 acres from 31 per cent to 17 per cent, while holdings of less than 2.5 acres increased by roughly the same proportion, from 19 per cent to 32 per cent.

Many holdings were too small to support a family without recourse to wage labour, so the proportion of rural households depending pri-marily on wage employment inevitably increased. By 1985, more than two-fifths of the working population in the countryside were classified as 'rural labourers', compared with about 30 per cent in 1951, though about one in four were also operating land as farmers or tenants. About 13 per cent of 'rural labourers' worked in non-agricultural occupations (Singh, 1990, p. 77). While there was certainly a trend towards the 'proletarianisation' of the agricultural workforce, it was inter-woven with the increasing interdependence of the wage labour market with the market for leasing land in and out. In most regions, it would have been difficult to draw an objective, economic class boundary between those who hired and those who did not hire labour. Many hired out their labour at certain times of the year, but hired labour in when it was needed. Ritual prohibitions against manual labour meant that even very small and impoverished landowners belonging to the upper castes did not usually cultivate but depended on tenants and labourers. (In West Bengal, nearly a quarter of farmers hiring labour had holdings not exceeding 2.5 acres.) Even amongst the lower castes, families some-times refrained from work considered polluting or injurious to femi-nine virtue, and hired labourers from still lower social categories to do it. Buying and selling wage labour was often not a pure cash nexus but had an element of 'ritual' transfer. An agricultural employer would sometimes limit recruitment to the immediate neighbourhood, even when wages were lower outside, and by providing local workers with credit and emergency help, nurture their loyalty and consolidate his social control.

Over and above these cultural constraints on hiring labour, we must note that the persistence of the small farmer, owning his land, with modest capital and relying largely on family labour is one of the most salient features of contemporary Indian society. It has reflected and reinforced an ideological consensus idealising the village community in which families privately own and farm their land under the protection of the state. This social model has been a template for land reform, guided the implementation of the Green Revolution and served as a prophylactic against social revolution. The architect of *zamindari* abolition in Uttar Pradesh claimed that:

> by strengthening the principle of private property where it was weakest, i.e. at the base of the social pyramid, the reformers have created a huge class of strong opponents of the class war ideology. By multiplying the number of independent landowning peasants there came into being a middle of the road stable rural society and a barrier against political extremism. (Quoted in Ludden, 1999, p. 176)

Conclusions

During the first generation of Indian independence, the nationalist elite constructed a political economy they regarded as antithetical to colonialism. Their chosen instruments of national self-assertion were state economic planning, public-sector led heavy industrialisation and non-alignment in international politics. They intervened on behalf of the poor more vigorously than the colonial state had ever done, especially when the shortcomings of the heavy-industry strategy became evident. To finance this effort, Indians had to be more highly taxed, with the result that the state's 'fiscal take' increased much more rapidly than the growth in national product in the 1960s and 70s. But the nationalist elite did not begin state-building *de novo* in August 1947. It had inherited governing institutions and practices from the Colonial Raj and needed to accommodate the regional, linguistic and cultural diversity of India's many societies. Inevitably, the policies and practices of nationalist government exhibited several continuities with its predecessor; it could scarcely have been otherwise. Import substituting industrialisation behind tariff barriers began, not in the 1950s, but in the inter-war years. On the land, the agricultural modernisation which got off to a limping start around 1960 conserved basic elements of the property 'settlement' that had evolved under British rule. The Nehruvian state was, therefore, 'post-colonial' in a dual sense: it consciously repudiated the political economy of colonialism while adopting many of its precepts and practices. The great discontinuity was a matter of *size*: the colonial state had been too under-resourced to manage economic development on a sub-continental scale; the functions, powers and personnel of the Nehruvian state grew exponentially to meet that task. The bureaucrats who administered the 'permit-licence raj' were far more powerful than the business owners and managers in the private sector.

The historical phase we have considered did not have an end as clear-cut and determinate as, for example, the break-up of Pakistan. Nevertheless, there can be no doubt that Indian politics and the political economy were radically transformed after 1966 and still more decisively after the victory over Pakistan in 1971. By her assault on so many of her father's old allies and the democratic institutions created in 1947, Mrs Gandhi redrew the ideological map. Under 'J.P.' Narayan's leadership, the moral force of the nationalist movement, and its agitational tactics, were brought to bear on a national, democratically elected government, and democratically elected governments in the states. New fault lines were opened within the Indian body politic: between corruption and anti-corruption, radical populism and the clientelism of party bosses. While there was little evidence of either a general class polarisation or an impending class war in the countryside, the resentment of landless labourers and marginal peasants led to a rash of agrarian disturbances, particularly in the 'tribal' regions.

The post-colonial political economy began with the imposition of 'democracy from above' on a largely passive electorate by an enlightened elite drawn to state socialism and modern industrialism, but repelled by the inequalities of market capitalism. The post-colonial political economy ended with democracy 'welling up from below' because the promised development did not materialise: vast numbers socially excluded by their poverty, illiteracy and inferior caste status began to use their electoral strength to make demands on the political system. Under Nehru, the central state elite could adopt a stance towards the nation reminiscent of Platonic guardians; under his daughter the centre had to be more responsive to the increasingly clamorous electorate. It also had to be better prepared to respond to rural violence and disorderly politics with coercion. One of the great paradoxes of post-colonialism is that independent, democratic India became a more intensely policed political community than it had ever been under the British. The cost of the rapidly expanding police and paramilitary forces rocketed in the 1960s and 70s: per head of population, total expenditure on policing rose by 70 per cent in constant prices between 1960–1 and 1981–2. By then the civil police forces, which are officered by the elite Indian Police Service under the Centre's control, numbered about 750,000; the paramilitary units under the control of central government ministries made up another 350,000–600,000; and the armed constabularies in the states accounted for about 400,000 (Frankel, 1989b, p. 499). This surge in policing was directly related to what we might call 'the street-cum-village politics of scarcity': in an environment of chronic want, where the market failed to secure the basic nutritional needs of so many, government was the focus of both hope and anger. It represented the possibility of social amelioration, but its very salience in the economy and society made it the obvious target for popular grievance. There was a continuum between the democratic mobilisation which made the subaltern castes an electoral force to be reckoned with, and the riotous disorder which came to characterise Indian politics in the 1970s.

3

Caste in Post-colonial India

Introduction: constitutional secularism and the ritual hierarchy

In 1947, India's new leaders sought to institute secular, democratic government in history's most durable social and religious hierarchy. They were egalitarians devising the basic political arrangements for a civilisation permeated by inequality in every sphere and in which the marks of inequality were visible in every form of collective life. To a degree unparalleled elsewhere, the inequality of what the Constitution called the 'socially and educationally backward classes of citizens' was an attribute not of individuals but of self-perpetuating communities that we call 'castes'. This chapter explores the complex *history* of caste in post-colonial India. I emphasise 'history' because there is an understandable presumption that caste is a primordial Hindu institution that has maintained its essential characteristics while all around has changed. This presumption must be discarded at the outset. In the post-Independence generation, caste practices and ideologies were subject to intense selective pressures: agrarian development and reforms weakened the material position of upper-caste landowners in the rural hierarchy; the middling castes of 'bullock capitalist' used their numerical strength in a democratic electoral system to seize control of village and rural institutions; positive discrimination by the federal and State governments undermined the ascribed status of the traditional 'writing' castes as India's 'natural' bureaucrats. The religious aura and legitimacy of caste was challenged by secular nationalism, 'up-lift' movements of the outcaste and, from the late 1970s, militant Hindu nationalism. Caste remained central to the patterning of everyday life, and its political salience was scarcely diminished, but the institution was fundamentally transformed by a process of competitive selection. This chapter will try to capture that transformation and place it within the dual perspective of India's colonial past and post-colonial history.

Whether modern colonialism constructed *the* Brahmin-dominated caste system is a matter of debate. Susan Bayly argues that caste as an ideology legitimising hierarchic rule was a real and active part of political life in the Indian kingdoms in the century or so before the British began extending their territorial power. From about 1650, the caste values associated with the Kshatriya or warrior archetype were synthesised with Brahminical ideals in the royal courts and became more widely diffused amongst military power holders at large. 'Brahminism' was 'far from being an invention of the Brahman-fearing colonial imagination'. She does, however, consider that 'untouchables' emerged as a social category in the nineteenth century with the hardening of the pollution barrier; 'untouchability' as we understand it was 'very largely a product of colonial modernity' (Bayly, 1999, p. 34, p. 371, p. 226). Nicholas Dirks credits the 'colonial imagination' with much greater potency. In a trenchantly postcolonial analysis, he maintains that 'it was under the British that "caste" became a single term capable of expressing, organizing, and above all "systematizing" India's diverse forms of social identity, community and organisation'. The most influential colonial accounts of caste asserted that its centrality in Indian social life precluded the liberal individualism that was the basis for a self-governing civil society and thus constituted a barrier to national development. Hindus, accordingly, 'required' an imperial power above the caste system, which was 'a specifically colonial substitute for civil society that maintained a vision of India in which religion transcended politics, society resisted change, and the state awaited its virgin birth in the late colonial era' (Dirks, 2001, p. 5, p. 60).

I am not able to say whether Dirks has interpreted the colonial archive judiciously, but I would suggest that secular nationalists had a political aversion to caste that was homologous with the account of the institution just cited. Nehru declared in 1955: 'so long as the caste system continues to exist... democracy and people's rule have absolutely no meaning... How can the concept of equality and of equal opportunities for all exist side by side with the caste system?' (quoted in Brown, 2003, p. 230). In the secular, nationalist vision of India, the strong, liberal state would stand above the caste system and, by combining universal rights with positive discrimination, end inherited inequality and injustice. The great paradox of post-colonial history is that caste mobilisation has actually democratised India's political culture by enabling under-privileged groups to aggregate and articulate their collective interests. In the early 1950s, there was a two-fold democratic deficit in Indian politics: roughly half adults did not vote in national and State elections; and the great agrarian mass was sorely under-represented in the elected elite. The politicisation of caste has gone far to wiping out this deficit.

The Constitution combined the ideal of equal citizenship with the realistic appreciation that society's most oppressed members could fully participate in the new political order only if they were accorded special group privileges. Hence, while all citizens were to vote on the same electoral rolls whatever their religion or caste, seats in the federal and State assemblies were reserved for the Scheduled Castes and the Scheduled Tribes in proportion to their total population within a State. (Seventy-two seats out 495 in the Lok Sabha were reserved and 477 out of 3283 seats in the State Legislative Assemblies.) In a reserved constituency, only persons from designated outcaste or tribal groups could stand for election, though all adults were eligible to vote. The enforcement of any disability arising out of 'untouchability' was declared illegal, as was caste discrimination in access to shops, restaurants, hotels and places of public entertainment, and in the use of public facilities such as wells, bathing ghats and roads. Hindu religious institutions of a public character were thrown open to all classes and sections of Hindus. The occupational exclusivity enforced by many castes was proscribed, and all citizens given the right to practise any profession or carry on any occupation, trade or business. The much-debated Article 46 pledged the state to promote with special care the educational and economic interests of 'the weaker sections of the people and, in particular, of the Scheduled Castes and Tribes'. It thereby laid the basis for the transfer of privilege from caste Hindus to 'untouchables' and the backward castes through positive discrimination in recruiting to educational institutions and government employment. Twelve and a half per cent of the vacancies filled by open competitive examinations in the Central and All-India Services were reserved for members of the Scheduled Castes (Srinivas, 1957, p. 547).

But though the Indian state pioneered 'positive discrimination' in recruiting its personnel, we must recognise that 'the more things changed, the more they stayed the same'. Given the stringent educational qualifications required for senior posts in state service, those at the higher administrative levels were drawn predominantly from the 'twice-born', scribal castes just as they had been under British rule (Bayly, 1999, p. 321). Indeed, the bureaucratic expansion of the 'licence-permit-quota raj' made the first four decades of independence a 'golden age' for the academically well-qualified children of the upper castes. Their hysterical reaction to the caste reservations proposed by the Mandal Commission (see below) is fully comprehensible only if we bear that in mind.

The 'anti-caste' provisions in the 1950 constitution followed colonial precedents and were the outcome of a long struggle within the all-India political community for civil rights for the low caste and out-caste. When they devolved power to representative institutions, the British ensured that constitutional legislation protected the interests of the oppressed and so created the conditions in which castes and communities assumed political identities. Seats were reserved for representatives of the 'Depressed Classes' in provincial legislatures set up in the early 1920s, while several provincial governments began reserving a certain percentage of official posts for the non-Brahmin castes (Srinivas, 1962, p. 21). Most consequentially, special representation was accorded the Scheduled Castes and Backward Tribes by the 1935 Government of India Act. This was in response to the agitation, led by B.R. Ambedkar, on behalf of the 'untouchables', those diverse groups, considered congenitally unclean by caste Hindus, who stood outside but were defined by the ritual hierarchy. 'Untouchables' were usually denied entry into temples and endured lives of multiple deprivation and humiliation. In the south, they had in recent memory been prevented from living in brick and tile houses, and from clothing their upper body and wearing silk garments. 'Untouchable' women were, in places, expected to wear stone beads as a sign of their degradation. Ambedkar came from the rural Mahars and was the first Indian from an 'unclean' caste to be professionally educated. In the later 1920s, he launched increasingly bitter attacks both on 'caste oppression' and on Congress, whose leadership he thought pusillanimous in its unwillingness to condemn caste unreservedly. In 1927, he caused a sensation by publicly burning the *Laws of Manu*, which are revered in the Hindu tradition as a guide to moral conduct but are also the principal scriptural source of theological justifications for caste and the pollution barrier.

The formation of the Depressed Classes Federation in 1930 to militate for 'untouchable' political rights and civil equality exposed some of the communal fractures within the nationalist movement and the inability of Congress to speak for all Hindus. In the constitutional negotiations of 1931–2, Ambedkar had originally claimed separate electorates for 'untouchables', which Gandhi opposed so adamantly he was prepared to fast to death over the issue. The compromise – known as the Poona Pact – struck between Ambedkar and Gandhi was the reservation of 148 seats in the provincial legislatures for the Depressed Classes, a guarantee concerning their representation in any federal assembly and the promise that monies would be earmarked in every provincial budget for their education. Ambedkar was compelled to yield on the issue of separate electorates, which blocked any attempts by the 'untouchables' to act as a distinct community *outside* Hinduism. Gandhi subsequently underlined the passivity of the oppressed by making the campaign against 'untouchability' a moral duty of penitent caste Hindus, who were supposed to bestow social equality on their religious inferiors as a gift, rather than a right (Frankel, 1989b, p. 491). With unintended condescension he dubbed the 'untouchables' Harijans or 'children of God'; the term 'Dalits', meaning 'the oppressed', is now much preferred. The Poona Pact was substantially embodied in the 1935 Act. In the following year, the authorities undertook the mammoth exercise of listing or 'Scheduling' for the new caste-based constituencies, with the aim of identifying every depressed community so as to calculate how many seats to reserve in the provincial legislatures (Bayly, 1999, pp. 262–3).

Despite his sharp, even rancorous differences with Congress, Ambedkar was given a key role in devising the 1950 Constitution and was responsible for its 'untouchability' provisions. These heralded an attempt to engineer a more just social order and were a public formulation of the goal of a 'casteless society'. In this latter respect, they were massively discordant with the realities of Indian associational life. For the overwhelming majority of Hindus, and for most Muslims, Christians, Sikhs and Jains, caste – or more accurately one's *jati* – was what constituted the effective arena of social life and gave it cohesiveness over time. It is no exaggeration to say that a social system without *jatis* was unimaginable. A villager's relations with other human beings were mediated through their *jati*, just as their relation with the external environment was mediated through agriculture (Srinivas, 1976, p. 165). A *jati* was (and frequently still is) an endogamous, hereditary and usually localised birth group, having a traditional association with an occupation, and a particular position in the local hierarchy of *jatis*. Members of a *jati* had a common dietary code and rules prescribing with whom one could dine and from whom one could accept drinking water. What made these rules so compelling was fear of polluting one's spiritual being by contact with somebody considered unclean by virtue of their birth and occupation.

There were about 3000 *jatis* in the 1950s (Srinivas, 1962, p. 65). Some, though by no means all, had a ritual status that could be mapped onto the *varna* conception of the social order found in the Vedic scriptures and the *Laws of Manu*. (*Varna* means colour; whether the term derived from the colour consciousness of fairer skinned Aryan invaders or had a purely symbolic reference is a matter of debate.) According to this conception, the social and ritual hierarchy consisted of four hereditary orders, each with a distinct moral quality and calling: the Brahmin or priestly order; the Kshatriya order of rulers or warriors; the Vaishya mercantile order; and the labouring order of Sudra. The first three are considered 'twice-born' and entitled to wear the sacred thread at the Vedic rite of *upanayana*; Sudras are not. Gandhi – we should note – could not envisage Hinduism without the *varna* order, which he considered 'fundamental, natural and essential' (quoted in Jaffrelot, 2003, pp. 17–18). This schema is what many in the west understand by the caste system, but it can be deeply misleading as to caste's historical origins and present-day realities. Invoking the Vedic scriptures suggests an ancient hierarchical form persisting through millennia, whereas historians now insist that ideologies of caste, which legitimised elaborately ritualised schemes of social stratification, only gelled in recent centuries. In the villages where the great majority lived, religious traditions have been oral, localised and often inflected by non-Hindu beliefs and practices. These 'little' traditions have frequently borne only a tenuous relationship with the 'great' tradition derived from the Vedas. The *jati* system encountered at a parochial level exhibited little of the fixity of the *varna* categories: the blanket term Sudra covered a range of disparate *jatis* from prestigious, landowning peasants (who in places passed themselves off as Kshatriyas) to artisan or service *jatis* just above the untouchability line. In the local hierarchy of a dozen or more *jatis*, only the extremes were fixed with any degree of firmness and the position of all others was ambiguous. Because of uncertainty as to mutual rank, and competition for prestige and social power between *jatis*, socio-cultural stratification had a dynamic quality missing from the *varna* scheme. By adopting vegetarianism and teetotalism, and by 'Sanskritising' its ritual and pantheon, a low caste could rise in the hierarchy over a generation or two (Srinivas, 1956). Even the distinction between the 'clean' and 'unclean' castes was not as definitive as is often assumed: by taking up different occupations and changing their style of life to conform with Vedic norms, castes such as the Iravas of Kerala and the Nadars of Madras upgraded their ritual status from 'unclean' to 'clean' over two to three generations (Rudolph and Rudolph, 1967, p. 132).

Only western-educated secularists had a principled objection to caste and even their attitudes tended to be ambivalent. As a system of ascribed status and hierarchical ranking, it offended their egalitarian and democratic principles. Moreover, Congress shunned all forms of communalism, and for this reason its 1955 national conference resolved that no active member could simultaneously be a member of a caste organisation. Nevertheless, caste was an indigenous institution, rooted in an ancient but still vibrant Hindu civilisation of which educated Indians were intensely proud, that had enabled them to deflect the imperious 'westernisation' and rampant individualism of their European conquerors. Caste allowed Indians to preserve a corporate identity while fully participating in bureaucratic institutions and the liberal and scientific professions. Through the caste associations that proliferated in the later colonial period, many men from the urban middle classes had furthered their education, acquired marriage partners and advanced professionally. The revolution in physical and symbolic communication under the British had promoted the horizontal solidarities of the literate castes: educated leaders had started caste journals and organised caste conferences. Caste hostels, hospitals, cooperative societies became common features of urban life. By the inter-war period, a fairly small Brahmin *jati* known as the Saraswats, many of whom had migrated to Bombay to take up government employment, had launched India's first cooperative housing society, and established a cooperative bank, a social club, schools and scholarship funds – all predicated on caste membership (Conlon, 1977, pp. 184–94).

The framers of the constitution assumed that caste referred, not to a group bound by social ties, but to the occupants of a place in the Hindu ritual order or to Hindus ritualistically excluded by the pollution barrier. Until 1964, when the law was amended, converts to other religions were deemed to have 'lost' caste and, in the eyes of the courts, non-Hindus were ineligible for the 'privileges of backwardness'. This religious conception of caste was seriously discordant with social realities: in many regions, Muslims were a recognised *jati* within the village hierarchy, and where they formed concentrated communities Muslims were usually divided into several *jatis*, ranked according to descent, traditional occupation, education, wealth and observance of purdah. Moreover, the untouchables embraced two fairly distinct categories of disadvantaged people: one comprised those hereditary groups following 'unclean' trades (such as leather working) or providing services regarded as polluting by nearly all Hindus. Where the *jajmani* system of patron–client relations still functioned, many performed menial tasks – such as ordure collection, removing carrion and barbering and tonsuring – for caste Hindus in return for annual payments of grain. A broader category within the Scheduled Castes, however, consisted of landless labourers or sharecroppers who were the descendants of former serfs or slaves (such as the *paraiyans* of south India). At Independence, many remained bonded labourers in fact if not in law and were mostly found in regions where tilling the soil was itself considered defiling. Together, these two categories constituted about 14 per cent of the total population in 1951, though the proportion varied considerably between states. Scheduled Castes accounted for about 6 per cent of the population in Maharashtra, but 21 per cent in Uttar Pradesh.

The Scheduled Tribes (or Adivasis) were a smaller minority (6 per cent of the population) of descendants of the sub-continent's aboriginal people who lived on the margins of Hindu society, usually in isolated ecological niches. At Independence, and for some decades thereafter, each tribal community retained its own social organisation, its own customs, its own religion and, above all, its own language (Béteille, 1983, p. 113). Because they were more concentrated than the Scheduled Castes, tribal people interacted differently with the system of political representation. Prior to 1962, reserved seats were in double-member – and therefore larger than normal – constituencies, with one seat treated as open and the other as reserved. Thereafter, reserved seats were in single-member constituencies of normal size. In tribal areas, electorates were more homogeneous, and in some instances tribal peoples were sufficiently concentrated to constitute a majority. The Scheduled Castes were much more dispersed and nowhere formed a majority.

While the Scheduled Castes and Tribes were well-defined categories, what the Constitution called the 'other backward classes' were not. They were a large and residual category of poor people with unclear and elastic boundaries. In 1953, the Union government set up the first Commission to recommend ways of improving the economic and social status of the Backward Classes (a second was created in 1978). When it reported in 1955, the Commission expressed doubts about adopting 'caste as the basis for identifying backward classes', but nevertheless 'identified 2,399 castes as socially and educationally backward', and proposed reserving between 25 per cent and 40 per cent of posts in government services for these deprived groups. The government rejected this recommendation, on the grounds, first, that with the achievement of a socialist pattern of society social distinctions would disappear and, second, that the commission had not provided any objective test for identifying the Backward Classes. The report was not discussed in Parliament until 1965, when the Congress government failed to support its recommendations. Nevertheless, the advocacy of preferential treatment for the 'backward' gave a sharp stimulus to the political mobilisation of the low castes by the Samyukta Socialist Party in Uttar Pradesh and Bihar.

At Independence, only a sixth of the population lived in towns so the ambit of caste for the great majority was the village and neighbouring villages, where the ritual hierarchy was *perceived* as immemorial or at least stable over many generations. How accurately this perception accorded with historical realities is difficult to determine. Large-scale migrations – sometimes prompted by famine – had frequently made local caste structures quite fluid across the generations. The enlistment of over 2 million men in the Second World War and the massive population movements at Partition had brought an exceptional degree of geographical mobility in northern India. Nevertheless, probably nine out of ten adults were living in the district of their birth around 1950. For them, the physical limits of everyday experience were set by proximity to metalled roads and bus routes. Even in North Kerala, where villages were dispersed settlements and so less self-contained than their counterparts elsewhere, 'every village retained a nucleus of families from all castes who have lived there from time immemorial. Immigrant families were remembered as 'foreigners' even down to the fifth generation though they may have intermarried extensively with native families of their own sub-caste' (Miller, 1960, p. 53).

How the ritual hierarchy was constituted – or what has been called the caste profile – varied considerably between different regions, and these variations greatly influenced political divisions and mobilisation in the States. In the Hindi-speaking Indo-Gangetic heartland, Brahmins and other twice-born castes formed a substantial minority in a hierarchy that was more or less continuously graded. In the Tamil-speaking, Dravidian south, the hierarchy was discontinuous: Brahmins were both a smaller fraction of the population and often the only representatives of the twice-born. With their fairer skin, sharper features, distinctive patterns of speech and particular style of dress, Brahmins in the south were physically and socially distinct from non-Brahmins, which was reflected in the adage 'Dark Brahmins and light Paraiyans are not proper' (Béteille, 1965, p. 48). The fact that in the north castes tended to spread across state boundaries, whereas in the south castes were usually bounded by them, also affected political mobilisation. In the mid-1960s, the American scholars, Susanne and Lloyd Rudolph, observed that anti-Brahminism had flourished in regions characterised by steep and discontinuous social hierarchies – such as Madras and

Maharastra – and this in turn had fostered the political mobilisation of castes lower in the ritual hierarchy. By contrast, they suggested, regions with relatively higher proportions of twice-born castes and more gradual and continuous social landscapes were less susceptible to horizontal mobilisations from below of ritually deprived castes seeking opportunities, status and political power (Rudolph and Rudolph, 1967, pp. 78–9). For reasons I discuss below, this rough correlation to which the Rudolphs drew attention was less evident after the Congress split in the late 1960s. This analysis will consider the two decades or so after 1947, when the political alignments of caste dovetailed with the 'Congress system', and then turn to the factors that led to the disintegration of the system.

The *jatis* in Indian villages

We must first observe, however, that at a village level the gross differences in caste profile between the Hindi north and Dravidian south gave way to much more complex variations determined by many factors, including geographic isolation and natural ecology, proximity to towns and modern means of transport, the ethnic and linguistic 'mix' within the village. Significantly, though, the recent historical experience of being part of the British Indian Empire was not amongst these factors. The ethnographic case studies in *India's Villages* (1960), a collection edited by M.N. Srinivas, were drawn both from the erstwhile provinces of British India and from the princely states, but the reader would be hard pressed to discern any difference in the caste hierarchy on these grounds. Whatever the external political regime had been, villages had exercised a large measure of self-government: they normally depended on village and caste councils, and hereditary officials and priests, for law, order, social and religious leadership, and basic administration.

An Indian village was usually a vertical unity of many, interdependent *jatis*, each one of which was a horizontal unity, with its alliances going beyond the village. The settlement pattern normally reflected the basic cleavage between the 'clean' and 'unclean' castes. In Rampura, in Mysore, where Srinivas spent a year in 1948, there were 17 *jatis*, all with distinctive traditions and strong ties with the same *jati* in nearby villages (Srinivas, 1960, 1976). 'Untouchables' lived apart in one compact area. Ritual codes were enforced by *jati* courts, which normally worked closely with the village authorities, and had the power to excommunicate the most blatant offenders. The *jati* hierarchy over-lapped, albeit imperfectly, with the marked inequalities in land owner-ship, since the richer landowners were generally of Brahmin, Peasant or Lingayat status, while landless labourers were frequently untouchables. But a few members of the lower rungs of the ritual hierarchy owned reasonable amounts of land and several peasant and shepherd families on the middle rungs were landless. The interdependence of the *jatis* was partly a matter of occupational specialisation in a local economy where money had only a limited role and many services were still bartered. The carpenter, washerman, potter and barber (who each belonged to separate *jatis*) were all paid annually in paddy and straw by the families they served. The Brahmin and Lingayat priests of three important temples in the village were also paid a small quantity of paddy and straw annually, but enjoyed the benefit of land that had been endowed to the temples. Parallel to this occupational interde-pendence were the vestiges of a hereditary servitude that had formerly linked 'untouchable' and upper-caste families in a master–servant rela-tionship. The servant – called the *halemaga* (old son) of the master – had certain duties on ritual and social occasions, for which he was paid a quantity of paddy and straw at the harvest, and was also entitled to the carcass of any cow or bullock that died on the master's property. When Srinivas stayed in Rampura in 1948, the *halemaga* system was in advanced decay because 'untouchables' were refusing to perform tasks they considered degrading, though we should note that this was one of many sources of friction in the *jati* hierarchy since their erstwhile masters wanted to maintain the servile relationship. Most despised of all *jatis* were the smiths: they could not perform their weddings in the village, and were excluded from village assemblies, prayer parties and marriage houses. Any attempt by the smiths to assert their equality usually led to a fight.

Amongst the regions and localities discussed in *India's Villages*, North Kerala stood out because as many as two-thirds of the population belonged to the 'polluting castes', which fell into two broad groups: a superior group that included *jatis* of small tenants, carpenters and smiths; and an inferior group, of which the most numerous compo-nent were 'untouchable' landless labourers whose recent forebears had been agrestic serfs, tied to particular blocks of land and automatically transferred to the new owner if the land was sold (Miller, 1960, pp. 44–5). The village usually contained a cross-section of 15–25 interde-pendent *jatis*, each with a caste rank closely associated with land ownership, especially paddy land. Around 1950, the hereditary head of the village was almost invariably the chief landowner, the bulk of whose land was parcelled out among tenants, who either cultivated it themselves or sub-leased it. Village-headships were monopolised by the Nayars, who combined political authority with economic control and an extraordinary ritual aura. For someone from the lower castes to approach a Nayar closer than 64 feet was considered polluting. The Nayars' power was buttressed ritually by their trusteeship of the chief temples. Inter-*jati* relations were complementary, involving tradition-ally ordained and clear-cut rights and obligations, authority and subor-dination. Unsettled disputes inside a low-caste *jati* tended to be referred upwards to a higher-caste *jati*. The caste system did not engender any sense of injustice (or, at least, the anthropologist who left this account did not detect any). Resentment was felt only towards the individual who had exceeded his rights and did not extend to a cleavage between *jatis* or between ruler and subject. The society was united by the common philosophy of *dharma*, which held that the greatest good is to behave according to one's station in life (*ibid.*, p. 47). Whether this assessment would have been made a few years later is rather doubtful: from our perspective, it is surely unsurprising that the communist parties found natural constituencies amongst Kerala's large, impover-ished rural proletariat (Brass, 1994, p. 79).

Caste and political mobilisation in the Congress system

Until the Indian Union was constituted, the great majority of villagers had experienced the state – whether they lived in a native principality or a British-governed province – as a remote monolith that impinged on their lives only to demand taxes and settle those rare disputes that could not be arbitrated by village institutions. Under this 'capstone' form of state, caste relations and institutions mutated in an 'unguided' fashion, through interaction with the market, group migration and the 'Sanskritisation' of upwardly mobile castes. One should add that, because of the restricted franchise, electoral competition in British India appears to have had little impact on caste relations at the village level. Independence brought, not immediately but by the early 1950s, a new kind of state to the countryside, one that had an organic relation-ship with India's multifarious societies through its electoral mandate and its commitment to economic development and social equality. The national Congress leaders had the collective ambition to reach down and remould social relations and institutions at the village level.

Because independence brought universal suffrage, more intense electoral competition and the cultivation of constituencies, the state's elected representatives became a palpable presence in village life. To give one example: before 1948, the highest official ever to have visited Rampura was the (unelected) deputy commissioner; by 1952, villagers had become so used to visits by state ministers that they affected indifference (Srinivas, 1976, p. 242). Rampura was on a bus route and about 30 miles from Mysore city; more isolated villages were insulated from the full impact of democratic politics for much longer. But nowhere in the Indian Union could remain fully immune.

The Congress's ideological commitment to a casteless and classless national community was virtually irrelevant to the lower tiers of a federal political system where caste-aligned factions ruthlessly competed for public office. Though local factions could not dispense with the party's imprimatur, its organisation and activities were often controlled by people with no clear ideas about the principles their leaders propounded at the all-India level. As Béteille noted, the Congress had such a vast tradition and organisation, and had been associated with so many shades of ideology, that very few villagers found any difficulty in identifying themselves with it (Béteille, 1965, p. 177). Caste was so 'naturalised' in social life that it intersected with every strand of the political process and was 'everywhere the unit of social action' (Srinivas, 1957, p. 548). In selecting candidates for State assemblies, rival political parties (including the communists) tried to match caste with caste as a part of their electoral strategy. When canvassing, candidates and their supporters appealed to caste loyalties and exhorted electors to vote for caste fellows. When constructing provincial cabinets, party leaders tacitly accepted the principle that each major caste in the State should have a minister. The distribution of public resources by elected officials was affected by caste-based clientelism: Srinivas was informed that electors in Mysore who voted on a caste basis expected an elected minister to help his caste-fellows (Srinivas, 1976, p. 72). Like ward bosses elsewhere, leaders of the dominant castes in rural areas could deliver the vote for politicians, and expected favours in return: whether it was licences for buses and rice mills or places in medical and technical colleges for their kinsfolk. In the intersection of caste and State politics, the traditional authority and functions of the *jati* declined, but those of the caste associations grew by combining the roles of voluntary organisation and secular pressure group. They had offices, membership lists, publications, and aggregated and expressed caste interests through conferences, delegates and resolutions. They attempted to have their members nominated for elective office, either by working through existing parties or forming their own, and sought to maximise caste representation and influence in State cabinets and lesser governing bodies. Most significantly, they helped extend the principle of organised representation into a largely illiterate mass electorate (Rudolph and Rudolph, 1967, pp. 32–6).

To put things in simplified terms, caste in post-colonial India was politicised and transformed in response to 'top-down' initiatives emanating from the state and 'bottom-up' pressures emanating from party and electoral politics. As has been noted, state commitments were embedded in the articles of the constitution outlawing 'untouchability' and caste discrimination, but these had negligible immediate effect. As Béteille admitted when giving the Ambedkar Memorial Lectures in 1980: 'The stigma of pollution, the segregation of the Untouchables and the isolation of Tribals persist in practice, no matter what the law lays down' (Béteille, 1983, p. 117). It was otherwise with *zamindari* abolition, which struck hard at the prestige and economic position of petty *zamindars* and tenure holders from the upper castes who lost the right to collect rent from lower-caste tenant-cultivators. Brahmins in Bihar, for example, attributed the decline of their previously unquestioned authority to *zamindari* abolition. The twice-born castes in the state found it impossible to assert the subordination of economic standing to ritual status and could no longer subject low-caste landowners to social abuse (Frankel, 1989b, p. 95). We must add, however, that other social relations in the state were virtually unchanged: through borrowing money at usurious interest rates, Scheduled Caste labourers were kept in 'informal bondage' and compelled to provide free labour to twice-born landlords.

At an all-India level, the most consequential of the 'top-down' state initiatives was the institution of a system of democratic local government known as the *Panchayati raj*. The village *panchayat* (roughly council or corporation) was an ancient institution through which the traditional dominant castes (usually Brahmin or Kshatriya landowners) had manipulated the ritual hierarchy, and the ties of kin and economic dependence with which it overlapped, to mobilise the village and district into 'vertical' personal followings. What gave a considerable impetus to a process of caste succession at village level was the proposal, put forward in the First Five Year Plan, to give the village *panchayat* a central role in planning and implementing rural development, as part of a wider policy of reviving community values and restoring the corporate character of village life. *Panchayats* were to be reconstituted on the principles of universal membership and adult suffrage and, together with the agricultural cooperatives proposed at the same time, were to form the basic political units of a 'Gandhian' national community in which all would participate regardless of caste. Individual village *panchayats* were to be linked to administrative divisions known as Blocks, and the latter to Development Districts. It was envisaged that, in a period of rapidly expanding education, democratically elected *panchayats* would encourage the 'horizontal' mobilisation of the agrarian lower classes, which would bring their power of numbers to bear in a non-violent way behind the Congress government's reform programme (Frankel, 2005, pp. 104–5). The implementation of the new local government regime in the later 1950s was quite protracted, since it depended on State legislation, and in places it did not start functioning until 1960.

In the event, widening participation in electoral politics and instituting *Panchayat raj* did effect a shift in the locus of power and influence from the castes at the top of the ritual hierarchy to the numerically stronger castes in its middle and lower echelons (Bhatt, 1977, p. 303). Village studies carried out in the late 1940s and early 50s showed that the traditionally high castes remained, in the majority of cases, dominant. By the mid-1960s, most commentators were agreed that a process of caste succession had either occurred or was in train. When it became evident that the new institutions dispensed valued resources, *jatis* in the villages used the ballot box to secure their share. Since representation was by ward, settlement patterns usually ensured that each *jati* – including the Dalits – could normally secure at least one seat, though it seems to have been commonplace for 'untouchable' councillors to sit apart (Béteille, 1965, p. 153). The principle of representing all castes in government travelled back from the provincial capitals to the *panchayats* and to the higher level representative bodies (known as Union Councils) instituted at the same time. (Normally, some 40 or so village *panchayats* were represented in the Union Councils, which were empowered to co-opt untouchable and female members.)

Caste profiles were caught and compressed between the pressures of the interventionist state emanating from 'above' and those of democratic politics welling up from 'below'. Men who derived their power from the support of numerically stronger groups, and their connections with a political party and government officials, successfully challenged those whose power stemmed from ritual status and land ownership (or a combination of the two). While a large-scale survey of four states

(Andhra Pradesh, Gujarat, Uttar Pradesh and West Bengal) in the early 1970s showed non-agricultural high-caste groups were more advanced in terms of education, occupation, income and urbanisation, they had tended to withdraw from involvement in politics and public affairs. They had been deprived of their customary bases of influence – in that high ritual status ceased to command automatic respect and twice-born families had lost land – and rarely mustered the numbers to control village *panchayats*, cooperative societies or other elected institutions. Where a high-caste group still exercised dominance, it did so because of its pivotal place in a local coalition rather than its ritual status. Two-thirds of respondents to this survey considered the chairman of the village *panchayat* to be the most powerful person in the village, as against 14 per cent who nominated the leader of the traditional dominant caste. The political sociologist who reported these results affirmed: 'The middle, lower middle and the low caste groups are the dominant caste groups in India today' (Bhatt, 1977, p. 303).

Since it was most unusual for any middle-ranking *jati* to command an absolute majority in a locality, those seeking to challenge the hereditary privileges of the twice-born had to enter electoral alliances, which encouraged the informal coalescence of adjacent segments within the caste system. New, broader caste categories emerged that expressed the common material interests of, by and large, India's bullock capitalists (Jaffrelot, 2000b). One such category was the *Yadavs*, a Sudra caste of north India who acquired a new, shared identity that crossed regional, sect and sub-caste lines. Observers of the phenomenon of 'caste compression' considered that it was in the long run likely to affect other aspects of inter-caste relations such as commensality and inter-marriage. There are documented instances of caste alliances consciously breaking down pollution barriers: the Kshatriya Sabha in Gujarat, for example, which sought to federate the state's 'high' and 'low' cultivating castes under the Kshatriya label, insisted that aristocratic Rajputs and semi-tribal Bhils sit together at common festivals (Kothari and Maru, 1965). Generally, the political coalescence of cultivating *jatis* encouraged their militants to identify themselves with what the Constitution called the 'other backward classes', and to demand the privileges of backwardness in terms of positive discrimination in access to public employment and educational institutions. Rather amusingly, the Gujarat Kshatriya Sabha used the 'warrior' archetype to raise the social consciousness of economically depressed cultivators while demanding the state government reclassify the Kshatriyas as 'Backward Classes'.

When Béteille stayed in Sripuram, in the Tanjore district of Madras, in the early 1960s, he observed the process of caste succession at close quarters. Until Independence and beyond, resident Brahmins were the village political elite, thanks to their ownership of land, ritual status and superior education, but with the coming of local democracy they had been displaced by the middling castes of Kallas and Vellalas. The *panchayat* president was a Kalla 'tough' who won his political laurels – and kudos with local Congress leaders – during the 'Quit India' movement of August 1942 (when he was briefly gaoled). His authority in the village depended partly on the strength of these external political ties but, conversely, his command of a fairly large block of votes put him in good standing with candidates for the state assembly and local party bosses (Béteille, 1965, pp. 152–7). As the power and prestige of the Kallas rose throughout the district, the Brahmins increasingly withdrew from *panchayat* affairs, and many moved permanently to the towns. With myriad regional variations, basically the same change was occurring throughout the Indian States: the more substantial peasant proprietors from the Sudra castes, who relied mainly on family labour, were becoming the new dominant castes in the countryside. In Uttar Pradesh, the most populous state, the once powerful landlord castes of Kshatriyas, Bhumihars and Brahmins were superseded, in terms of political weight, by their erstwhile tenants from the middling castes of Ahirs, Jats, Kurmis and Koris. The Jats, Marathas and Patidars similarly replaced the Kshatriyas and Brahmins as dominant castes in the states of Rajasthan, Maharashtra and Gujarat, respectively (Singh, 1977, p. 142).

Most accounts indicate that this shift in village power structures did little or nothing to improve the standing of Scheduled Caste landless labourers and sharecroppers. Legislation to protect sharecroppers was openly flouted in Bihar, where revenue officials were in the pocket of the landlords. Sharecropping tenants were shifted from plot to plot to prevent them claiming occupancy rights and compelled to divide the crop on the landlord's premises. Illegal exactions often left the sharecropper with a nominal amount of grain, and an obligation to render unpaid labour to the landlord. Landless labourers were treated even more callously. They suffered as much social and physical abuse from the rising Sudras as from the twice-born; the State became notorious for the sexual exploitation and abuse of Scheduled Caste women (Frankel, 1989a, pp. 96–7, 99). I will revert to the origins of Bihar's 'caste wars' in the penultimate section of this chapter, but before that we should consider the peculiar configuration of caste and politics in Tamil Nadu.

'Non-Brahminism', Dravidian ideology and Dalit assertiveness in Tamil Nadu

'Non- (or anti-)Brahminism' has a long history in the south Indian State of Tamil Nadu (known until 1968 as Madras State), where it has been inter-woven with the Dravidian autonomy movement, opposition to the designation of Hindi as the national language and a general sense of southern 'separateness' from the 'Brahmin-dominated' north. As has been mentioned, the ritual hierarchy of the Dravidian south was distinctive in presenting a sharp discontinuity between the tiny Brahmin elite and other castes, while 'untouchables' were 18 per cent of the population (compared with an all-India average of 14 per cent). About three out of five 'untouchables' were *paraiyans*. In the popular imagination, the Brahmins represented 'Aryan' conquerors who for too long held the indigenous Dravidians in thrall; however mythical its basis, this belief has had tangible consequences for political attitudes. Ideologically, it helped 'make sense' of the Brahmins' status in the mature colonial society of the Madras Presidency: Brahmin landowners rigidly observed the prohibition on working the land and were frequently absentee landlords, dwelling in the cities. When recruitment of Indians to government service and the liberal professions took off, Brahmins used their early mastery of western education to establish a presence in administrative and professional life quite disproportionate to their numbers in the wider society, one which they consolidated by recruiting their own kind. In 1914, 70 per cent of both district public officials and the registered graduates of Madras University were Brahmins, though they were only about 3 per cent of the total population (Béteille, 1991, pp. 92–3).

In 1916, the Non-Brahmin Movement was formally launched in Madras with the issue of a manifesto denouncing the concentration of Brahmins in the public services; the following year, the Movement assumed political form with the formation of the Justice Party to challenge the Brahmins' pre-eminence in 'modern' civil society and the bureaucracy. The party was most definitely not the vehicle of the socially down-trodden: its founders came from castes that by education, income and political sophistication felt themselves equal to the Brahmins but were excluded from leading positions in modern life. It was an elite grouping dominated by urban, western-educated, landowning and professional people, which included Christians and Muslims as well as 'non-Brahmin' Hindus. In the 1920 elections, the party won control of the Madras Presidency and sought to improve the position of non-Brahmins by legislation and executive action. A 'reservations policy' secured a proportion of jobs in the public services and local bodies for non-Brahmins, and places for them in educational institutions. Its impact was wholly confined to the principal towns; the Brahmins continued to dominate the village hierarchies by virtue of their ritual status and (in some districts) their ownership of land until independence and the institution of democratic suffrage. Before then, organised politics was the prerogative of the western-educated urban elites.

Principally because Congress was dominated by caste Hindus, the Justice Party was anti-nationalist and favoured by the British; indeed, all its leading figures came from families that had served the British for generations. The party was overwhelmed by the Congress-led nationalist upsurge of 1936 and apparently confined to oblivion after Brahmin Congressmen took the leading posts in the provincial government formed in 1937. But the 'communal' or caste idiom which the Justice Party introduced into south Indian politics did not go away. In the Tamil-speaking region, political rhetoric remained premised on a three-fold division of society into Brahmins, non-Brahmins and Dalits. The non-Brahmin movement encouraged the defensive coalescence of the Brahmins and created a lasting impression that in virtually every political context it was important whether a person was a Brahmin or a non-Brahmin. This gave south Indian politics after independence its distinctive character. The reservations policy initiated by the Justice Party was broadened by the Congress-led Madras government in 1947 when it introduced separate reservations for what were called 'Backward Hindus' (who were not to be confused with educated 'non-Brahmins'). This was the first recognition by one of the Indian States of the emergent social grouping of lowly Sudra castes that had no counterpart in the *varna* order. Two Brahmins challenged the reservation order in the courts on the grounds that it discriminated against certain classes of citizens. In 1950, the Supreme Court upheld their petition and quashed the order. This soon led to the new constitution being amended so that it could not inhibit the state positively discriminating on behalf of 'any ... backward classes'. In 1951, the Madras government was able to make an order reserving 25 per cent of State government posts for the backward castes and 16 per cent for the Scheduled Castes without being challenged in the courts (Brennan *et al.*, 2006, p. 134). In terms of reserving public jobs for the 'Other Backward Classes' (or 'OBCs'), Madras was decades ahead of the States in the Hindi belt.

Congress in Madras was spurred into an energetic reservations policy by the emergence in the 1940s of the militant secessionist movement, Dravida Kazagham, which was ideologically committed to the destruction of the caste system. The DK had originated in the Self-Respect Movement founded by E.V. Ramaswami Naicker (known as EVR) in 1926, which strove to liberate the Dravidian depressed castes psychologically from their habitual servility in the face of ritual oppression (though EVR was himself from the Nayak warrior caste). He renamed 'untouchables' Adi-Dravidas (the first Dravidians) and, with great public fanfare, performed marriages between them and caste Hindus. EVR had been Congress President in Madras, but quit the party because of Gandhi's equivocal attitude to the separate dining of Brahmin and non-Brahmin pupils in Congress-sponsored schools. Henceforth, EVR's detestation of caste was charged with strident atheism, utopian social radicalism and venomous denunciations of 'Brahminism'. In 1937, he repudiated Indian nationalism entirely after the Congress government of the Madras Presidency made Hindi compulsory in schools. EVR and about 1000 supporters were briefly imprisoned for organising protests against the language policy. The episode made him still more resolved to oppose northern domination of Indian politics, culture and religion.

When launched in 1944, the DK stood for a Dravidian nation-state but it was conceived as a 'consciousness-raising' movement above the electoral fray. In 1949, those followers of EVR bent on contesting Congress's electoral dominance parted company to form the Dravida Munnetra Kazagham (or Progressive Dravidian Federation). Until 1962, the DMK was a marginal force in southern politics and from the centre must have looked like the lunatic fringe. But in the general elections of that year the DMK won seven Lok Sabha seats and 50 in the Madras Legislative Assembly. Furthermore, secessionism became a hopeless cause in the national hysteria following the calamitous war with China in October, so the DMK abandoned its demand for independence in favour of greater state autonomy. The party espoused a nebulous socialism laced with anti-Brahmin rhetoric that had racist undertones. Tamil Brahmins occasionally described themselves as the Jews of south India and one might suggest that anti-Brahminism was functionally analogous to anti-Semitism in central Europe in that it enabled the heterogeneous followers of Dravidian ethnic nationalism to cohere in the face of a stereotypical 'hate figure'. Like the DM before it, the DMK preached and occasionally practised violence against Brahmins, who had to be escorted to the polling booths in parts of Tamil Nadu during the 1962 elections (Béteille, 1991, p. 94). Behind the DMK's electoral surge lay patient organisational work at local level and close links with the hugely popular Tamil-language film industry. The fan clubs of the adored M.G. Ramachandran (MGR), who had risen to stardom by portraying the saviour of the poor, often doubled as local party branches. The DMK was given a great fillip by leading the state-wide agitation in 1965 against the proposal to formalise the status of Hindi as the sole official language of the Union. In 1967, it swept to power in the Tamil Nadu State Assembly, capturing 138 out of the 234 seats in alliance with Swatranta, the CPM and some smaller parties, while reducing Congress to 49 seats. Before taking office, it had toned down its anti-Brahmin rhetoric, while self-interest had moved some Brahmins towards cautious support for the party.

In electoral terms, the party's ascendancy was typical of the process of 'caste succession' occurring across rural India: it relied principally on the support of the intermediate *jatis*, such as the Vanniyars and Nadars, who were being lumped together as the OBCs. What set the DMK apart was the Dravidian ethnic label which, since 1967, has been essential for any party hoping to command a majority in the State Assembly. The ambiguity of the OBC acronym – which can mean either 'Other Backward Classes' or 'Other Backward Castes' – indicates the ambiguous relationship between the party and its main constituency. To a degree, it represented the common economic interests of the peasant castes who were prospering from the Green Revolution, but it also articulated more diffuse status aspirations and anxieties that went with 'Dravidian' ethnic consciousness. As petty landlords and employers, the superior Sudra castes had a common interest in resisting their landless labourers' demands for better wages and access to land, but they also had their own social dignity to affirm against the 'Forward' 'twice-born' castes on the one hand and assertive *paraiyans* on the other.

With its anti-caste rhetoric, the Dravidian national movement had encouraged the emergence of Tamil Nadu's 'untouchables' as social and political actors in their own right, though we should not assume a strong community of class interest. Members of the Scheduled Castes were statistically more likely to be landless labourers than the 'clean' castes, but landlessness and untouchability were not coterminous: in 1961, only 47 per cent of landless labourers were 'untouchables', while the majority of untouchables were marginal landowners. The Thanjavur district was exceptional in having a close correlation between landlessness and 'untouchability', and there communist militants succeeded in mobilising the 'unclean' rural proletariat behind demands for better wages, access to land and the end to caste discrimination. Violent class confrontations occurred between labourers and thugs in the pay of clean-caste landowners. The worst outrage happened during a communist-led strike in Kilvenmani, in Eastern Thanjavur, in January 1969, when 42 Dalits – men, women and children – were herded into a hut and burnt to death. Twenty-three local landlords were accused of the atrocity and all were eventually acquitted in Madras High Court, a verdict which evoked little consternation in the State. Elsewhere, however, Dalit assertiveness was shaped by and contained within the Dravidian movement. 'Untouchables' were enthralled by the fantasy world of the Tamil-speaking cinema: they ran their own MGR fan clubs and often rode on bicycles to see the movies in bamboo-thatched cinemas. An American anthropologist was informed that, as a consequence of broadening social horizons, they 'do not show any meek worship to the caste Hindus'. One informant, a prosperous landowner, told her:

> Times have changed. The poor do not show any respect to the rich. I cannot dismiss my *padiyal* [day labourer] without any reason. If I do so, he would abuse me in filthy language face to face ... The poor are not as ignorant as they once were. The political parties have taught them they are equal to the rich in society. So they have started developing a contempt for us. (Mencher, 1974, p. 475)

Whether Dravidian governments brought 'untouchables' anything more than symbolic advantages is debatable. After 1970, no DMK or ADMK government was formed without at least two ministers from the Scheduled Castes, and other public offices were distributed to ensure their communal representation. For example, the Madras Municipal Corporation adopted the convention of rotating the mayoralty between one Brahmin, two non-Brahmins, one Dalit and one Muslim. Writing in the later 1980s, David Washbrook argued that such token political gestures were a substitute for serious public intervention to improve the material position and overcome the social exclusion of 'untouchables', which had tended to worsen under Dravidian government rule. 'Untouchability' had ceased to be a central political issue, and its continuing social evils were rarely denounced in public (Washbrook, 1989, p. 207). However, by the late 1990s, it was evident that Tamil Nadu's 'untouchables' were sharing in the state's generalised prosperity. Material deprivation was still heavily concentrated amongst *paraiyans*, nearly two-thirds of whom had a 'low' standard of living, but a third had a 'medium' standard. The other Scheduled Castes had fared rather better. Although the correlation between socio-religious status and economic prosperity remained strong, it was far from absolute (Brennan *et al.*, 2006, p. 140).

The OBCs' most eye-catching 'reward' for their electoral support for the Dravidian parties was an exceptionally vigorous policy of 'reserving' public-sector jobs and educational places for the 'backward' classes or castes. By 1980 over 70 per cent of appointments in the state bureaucracy were being made on the basis of community quotas for the Backward Classes and Scheduled Castes and Tribes rather than competitive merit. The same was true of the distribution of scholarships for education and university and college places. Far from destroying the caste system, the reservations policy enhanced the importance of caste. It led to an extraordinary inflation of the number of castes categorised as 'backward' and the introduction of ever finer distinctions to accommodate their conflicting claims. In 1883, when the Madras Presidency government first drew up a list of the 'backward classes', 11 castes were so classified (including what were later designated the Scheduled Castes and Tribes). By 1988, the list of 'Other Backward Castes' drawn up by the Tamil Nadu government had expanded to 323 castes (Kumar, 1992, p. 295). A more or less permanent line of conflict between 'Backward' and 'Forward' castes had been built into the State's political system. Well-informed observers considered the reservations policy led to 'painfully low' academic standards in most south Indian universities and promotion, not on merit, but according to caste quotas. Dharma Kumar, the doyenne of India's economic historians and a formidable critic of reservations, was told of one instance in Madras where an excellent OBC candidate could not get the university post he deserved because it was reserved for a candidate from a Most Backward Caste (*ibid.*, p. 296). Tamil Brahmins more or less withdrew from public-sector employment and State politics, although their high educational qualifications meant they were still well represented in the professions. Many Brahmins migrated to other parts of India and abroad, to the detriment of Tamil Nadu's intellectual and academic life, and its pool of scientific and technological expertise (Chandra *et al.*, 2000, p. 302).

Bihar: the origins of the 'caste wars'

In recent decades, Bihar has become notorious for the proliferation of private caste armies and so-called caste wars involving the state's

Forward and Backward castes (or classes) and its Scheduled Castes and Tribes. To call the endemic conflict in Bihar 'war' is no hyperbole: between 1989 and January 1995, more people were reported killed in the state's inter-communal violence than in six years of conflict between Muslim separatists and the Indian security forces in Kashmir (Bayly, 1999, p. 345). But the social violence in Bihar's countryside is diffuse, many-sided and multi-causal: it shades into ruthless electoral competition, the criminalisation of politics, police terrorism and pure dacoitry. To explain its origins simply in terms of caste would be a crude simplification; the preconditions for the breakdown of social order included economic backwardness, explosive population growth, deepening immiseration, and linguistic and ethnic divisions. Much of the violence had its source in class conflict: landlords attempted to reassert their coercive power over marginal tenants; Scheduled Caste labourers banded together to resist the humiliations heaped on them by the 'clean' castes of all descriptions. Nevertheless, caste interests and identities are an essential element in any explanation, and it is appropriate that they are considered here.

Until the later 1960s, political and economic power was conjoined with ritual status in Bihar. Although the economic standing of the twice-born castes varied greatly, the biggest landowners were, in the great majority, from the Brahmin, Rajput and Bhumihar castes. Exceptionally amongst the twice-born, Kayasthas were rarely landowners but a scribal caste, from which was drawn the professional and bureaucratic elite and Bihar's first generation of nationalist leaders. These four castes constituted about 15 per cent of the population, but were culturally and economically heterogeneous. Brahmins were divided by language and sectarian tradition north and south of the Ganges, and rarely married across this divide, let alone into other castes. Rajputs were traditionally a warrior caste, whose culture exalted masculine prowess and the seigniorial leadership of their tenants. Most twice-born landowners had medium-size holdings of 2.5 to 10 acres, and a substantial minority had holdings of 2.5 acres or less. In economic terms, there was nothing to distinguish the latter from Sudra smallholders.

The Sudra or 'Backward' castes made up about 48 per cent of the population, and were fragmented into numerous *jatis*, the largest being the Yadavs and the Koris. The great majority were either landless or marginal smallholders, but about 10 per cent owned medium plots, and a few 10 acres or more, which made them large landowners by Bihar's standards. They were an elite of skilled and enterprising agriculturists, formed by the exodus of Muslim landlords during partition and the transfer of *zamindari* land from the twice-born (Kohli, 1990, pp. 218–20).

The Scheduled Castes were 14 per cent of the population and the Scheduled Tribes a further 8 per cent. Both were wretchedly exploited but in rather different ways: 'untouchables' were scattered in hamlets throughout the state, and vulnerable to the usurious landlords, thugs and sexual predators amongst the 'twice-born' and Backward classes. Tribal settlements were more compact, less exposed to personal indignities and better able to assert themselves as communities. Impoverished Muslim villagers, who made up a further 15 per cent of the population, were ascribed a demeaning status comparable to the Scheduled Castes'. Landlessness, and its accompanying impoverishment, cut across the status divide between the 'untouchables' and the 'backward': whereas some 70 per cent of the Scheduled Castes were landless, roughly 40 per cent of landless labourers were from the Backward but 'clean' castes.

Until the 1967 elections, Congress enjoyed unchallenged supremacy in the Bihar Legislative Assembly, thanks in no small measure to its virtual monopoly over two 'vote banks': the Scheduled Castes and the Muslims. Both voting blocs deferred to their communal leaders, who remained loyal to the party of Gandhi. Furthermore, the system of reserved seats worked in ways that subordinated Scheduled Caste Assembly Members to Congress's twice-born leaders. Because 'untouchables' were scattered throughout the state, reserved constituencies were actually dominated by 'clean' caste electors. In allocating the party ticket, Congress leaders sought candidates who could appeal to voters across caste lines. They were generally found amongst the tiny number of educated and prosperous 'untouchables' who were cautious about advancing their communities' sectional interests. ('Uncle Toms' would be a not unfair analogy.) As the party of government, Congress was able to deflect any challenge from the Backward Sudra castes by offering their leaders contracts, business licences and, most alluring of all, Congress tickets. This situation ensured the preponderance of the traditional elites: more than two out of five Congress MLAs were from the twice-born castes. Factions from these castes struggled amongst themselves for control of the State's Congress organisation. Caste-based coalitions dominated by the Bhumihars, on the one hand, and the Rajputs, on the other, contested the party leadership and ministerial control in the State Assembly.

The 1967 elections were a major reverse for Congress in Bihar, where the State government had attracted huge unpopularity through its failure to manage the 1965–6 famine: Congress's share of the vote fell from 41.4 per cent to 33.1 per cent, and its share of seats from 58 per cent to 40 per cent. The Yadavs and other low castes increased their representation and helped form a coalition of socialists, communists and the Jana Sangh. It was highly unstable because Backward caste affinities were stronger than party discipline: B.P. Mandal, a Yadav (who later chaired the second Backward Classes Commission), almost immediately defected from the socialists to form a party of Backward dissidents. This set a precedent for literally hundreds of defections and counter-defections that reduced assembly proceedings to chaos and made effective government impossible. Over the next four years, nine coalition ministries were formed and President's rule was imposed for three periods. One discernible constant in the confusion was the determination of Backward caste leaders to increase their representation in the various State ministries. Since the publication of the Backward Classes Commission's report in 1955, the younger generation had lost interest in improving their status by Sanskritisation and turned instead to secular goals, particularly reservations in professional and technical institutions and government employment. Very quickly, they shifted their reference group from the upper castes to that of the 'Backward Classes'. This attitudinal shift proved divisive rather than solidaristic: affirmative action promised educational privileges and secure employment for a tiny minority but was no basis for collective action by the Backward Classes as a whole. The Sudras were divided amongst themselves and failed to coalesce with the Scheduled Castes and Tribes and Muslims. Rather than concerting the interests and political unity of the poorer classes, the growing preoccupation with reservations policy accentuated their political fragmentation (Frankel, 1989a, pp. 95–6).

Mandal's appointment as Chief Minister in February 1968 was a sign of the changing balance of socio-political power. He was the first person from the Backward Classes to hold this position and, though short-lived, his government represented a watershed in the state's factional politics. In the following years, the great majority of chief ministers were not from the twice-born castes. After Mandal's defeat on a 'no confidence' motion, he was succeeded by a Dalit, a protégé of twice-born Congressmen who aligned themselves with Scheduled Caste leaders to resist Backward assertiveness. In political rhetoric, 'Forward' and 'Backward' became polar terms, implying a mutual repulsion that overrode any common interest, whether of class or ideology. The rhetoric was grossly simplifying – because coalition-building required constant horse-trading between Forward and Backward factions – but had the quality of self-fulfilling prophecy. According to one political scientist, the rhetoric of Forward v. Backward conflict actually aimed at *creating* caste-based political blocs out of a heterogeneous social base (Kohli, 1990, p. 222). Following the national split Congress in November 1969, supporters of Mrs Gandhi's Congress (R) in the Bihar State Assembly had to court the representatives of both the Backward Classes and Scheduled Castes to form a viable ministry. The political 'price' of their support was the appointment of a Backward Classes Commission to make recommendations for reservations in educational institutions and State government services. It was insufficient to satisfy competing factional claims for office and the ministry collapsed within ten months, but the commission represented a tangible focus for Backward aspirations.

The radicalisation of national politics after Mrs Gandhi's smashing electoral victory of March 1971 overlay the factional turbulence in Bihar's political arena, and gave it a certain 'shape' and direction. She had succeeded in identifying herself with the compelling slogan 'Abolish poverty!' and the main national opposition parties with vested interests. Scores of deputies in the Bihar assembly were prompted to desert the Congress (O) fold and align themselves with the triumphant Prime Minister. If they anticipated the lustre of her name would guarantee sweeping success in the state 1972 elections, they were disappointed. The popular vote for Congress (R) in Bihar was only 32 per cent, though it sufficed to secure a small majority in the State Assembly. Once restored to ministerial power, however, the Congress leaders overlooked their relatively narrow electoral support to revive the old coalition of Brahmins, Scheduled Castes and Tribes, and Muslims around a socially radical programme. This did nothing to raise the 'tone' of state politics. The unseemly spectacle of carving up ministerial appointments was characterised by the *Times of India*, in September 1973, as a 'no holds barred struggle between rival factions to capture office with the object of making money, enjoying official privileges and distributing jobs and patronage among relations, friends and hangers on' (quoted in Frankel, 1989a, p. 102).

The factional struggle in the assembly redounded on society when Bihar's students – drawn overwhelmingly from the urban middle classes – called upon 'J.P.' Narayan, the Mahatma's veteran disciple, to lead the protest movement demanding the state government's resignation. Bihar soon became the epicentre of the 'J.P.' movement: the massive demonstrations against the state ministry between March and November 1974 eventually provoked the central government into drastic repression and the declaration of a national emergency. How we interpret the 'J.P.' movement is controversial: Narayan had unquestionable moral authority yet, according to Francine Frankel, within Bihar, '[the movement] amounted to little more than another manifestation of caste group rivalry, involving a temporary alliance between leading politicians of the Backward Classes and their rivals among Bhumihar, Rajput and Kayastha groups, all of whom had been excluded from power by Mrs Gandhi's Brahman-led coalition' (*ibid.*, p. 103). Activists and those who remained aloof were, Frankel asserts, distinguishable along caste and class lines: student demonstrators were predominantly upper caste (though not Brahmin) or from the newly prosperous ranks of the Backward Classes. Those indifferent to the movement were, by and large, from Mrs Gandhi's bedrock of popular support amongst the Scheduled Castes and Tribes, Muslims and the poorest peasants, landless and casual labourers, and industrial workers.

During the nineteen-month Emergency, caste resentments were exacerbated by the decision of the Brahmin-led state government to ignore the Backward Classes Commission's recommendation that 26 per cent of government posts be reserved for the Backward Classes. At the same time, the aggressive implementation of Mrs Gandhi's 20-point programme for reducing rural poverty alarmed the more substantial landowners amongst the Forward *and* Sudra castes, who both objected to the redistribution of land to 'untouchables', the cancellation of their debts and the energetic enforcement of minimum wage legislation. The central government's social radicalism, rather than its high-handed authoritarianism, may have been why, in the unexpected elections of March 1977, the landowning Forward and Backward castes suspended their differences and joined in the tidal wave that swept Mrs Gandhi from power. Only the bulk of the Dalits remained loyal to her.

The 1977 elections have acquired a historical aura as the moment when the democratic spirit of the national community reasserted itself; events at the polling booths were actually less edifying. Fraudulent practices and 'booth capturing' by criminals, some of whom stood as candidates, were widespread. Mrs Gandhi's supporters were often physically prevented from casting their votes by Bhumihar, Rajput and Yadav thugs, who were determined to put 'unclean' upstarts in their place. The fissiparous coalition that won a two-thirds majority in the Bihar state elections of June was almost immediately beset by renewed conflict between the Backward Classes and Forward Castes. Resentment stemmed partly from the fact that a Brahmin, Morarji Desai, was chosen to head the central Janata government over Charan Singh, a

Backward Class jat with, as he saw it, a better claim on the premiership. In the subsequent horse-trading, Janata's national leadership imposed a Backward Classes politician on the governing coalition in Bihar, who drastically reduced Forward representation when forming his cabinet. Janata's national election manifesto had included a pledge to implement the recommendations of the (national) 1955 Backward Classes Commission Report. After prolonged indecision, the Bihar State government announced a reservation policy of 25 per cent of government posts and places at government colleges for the Other Backward Classes, which immediately provoked large-scale rioting by Forward Caste youths. Reservations actually affected a few thousand people in a state with a population of 80 million, but perceptions were shaped by the policy's symbolism rather than its content. At stake was, apparently, the class status (and material advantages) that came from investment in human capital. Many rioters were from Kayastha families with long traditions of educating sons for public service and the liberal professions. Senior Janata figures refused to accept the reservations policy and tacitly encouraged the rioters, which helped polarise relations between Forwards and Backwards throughout the state. More than 100 people died during bloody clashes that accompanied the elections to *panchayat* Block councils in late 1978. After this point, according to Frankel, neither side saw the conflict as amenable to compromise:

> The Forwards had already experienced an erosion of social prestige, economic affluence, and political power in the villages. Against this perspective, they viewed the demand for reservations by the Backward Classes as an assault on their overall primacy, which would end, after some 20 to 30 years, in the destruction of upper caste dominance in society and power in the state ... The leaders of the Backward Classes ... became convinced that only the displacement of the Forward Castes from positions of power could open up opportunities for social mobility. (Frankel, 1989a, p. 110)

Running parallel to this urban conflict over reservations was an escalating Naxalite rebellion which set politicised 'untouchable' labourers against landowners from both the Forward and Backward castes. Maoist militants organised the Dalits into agricultural labour fronts which demanded higher wages, shorter hours, access to common land and an end to the sexual molestation of 'untouchable' women by Bhumihar and Rajput landlords. The conflict inevitably extended to Yadav and Kurmi farmers, who were no less abusive of the Dalits than the Forwards. Out of the spiralling violence came five or so private armies, known as *senas*, with strong caste identities: the Lorik Sena was identified with Yadavs; the much-feared Bhoomi Sena with Kurmis; the Brahmarishi Sena with Bhumihars; the Kunwar Sena with Rajputs; the Lal Sena, with landless labourers. Only the Brahmins did not have a private army. The term *sena* has strong devotional connotations, evoking the ideal of the Hindu warrior who fights for his lord in a spirit of selfless piety. Though their main function was to terrorise Dalit set-tlements with the open complicity of the police, these self-professed armies of the righteous represented themselves as defenders of caste-defined 'community' interests against the depredations of an unclean, Naxalite enemy (Bayly, 1999, pp. 346–7). They reflected and reinforced what has been termed the 'substantialisation' of caste.

The dissolution of Bihar's 'Brahminical social order' left a socio-moral vacuum. Bribery became the only means of moving the administrative machinery in all public institutions. Elected officials patronised crimi-nals who were essential to their prospects at election time. Ministers abused their power to favour family members and siphon off public funds, and clung to office by corruption and coercion. Strength in numbers brought the Yadavs political leverage, but their pretensions to Kshatriya status went unrecognised and they could not impose their authority in the fashion of the 'traditional' dominant castes. The moral cement which had held the old hierarchy in place crumbled away and politics degenerated into a brutal contest between hired thugs. With the decay of Congress, there was no overarching organisation able to incor-porate disparate caste, class, ethnic and religious groups into a single movement. Bihari society was immobilised by growing, if localised vio-lence, and trapped in a political cycle of rebellion and repression. Its history since 1980 is peppered with gruesome massacres perpetuated by one caste-cum-class group upon another; in 1996 and 1997, more than 150 were killed in these outrages (Guha, 2007, p. 619).

'Mandalisation' and after

The expectation that a casteless nation could be 'constituted' in inde-pendent India has been belied by events. Although caste has been transformed – and in many ways 'modernised' – it still shapes social relations, influences who marries whom, who gets educated to what level and who gets what job. Some people are still deemed inherently polluting: to cite one vignette among many, a nurse practitioner employed in the 1990s on a public pre-natal care programme refused to enter the homes of Scheduled Caste patients because she would have to bathe afterwards (Desai and Sreedhar, 1999, p. 112). Two scholars called the first chapter of their history of India since 1989 'The Recalcitrance of Caste' – which admirably captures the institution's truculent refusal to spare modern, highly educated Indians further national embarrassment and simply go away (Menon and Nigam, 2007). What, more than anything, accounted for the discomforting centrality of caste to public argument (especially argument conducted in the English-language press) in the 1990s was the huge controversy surrounding the implementation of the Mandal Commission's recommendations. B.P. Mandal (the former chief minister of Bihar) had been asked by Morarji Desai to chair the second Backwards Classes Commission in 1979. His brief was to 'determine the criteria for defining the socially and educationally backward classes' and 'to examine the desirability or otherwise of making provisions for the reservations of appointments or posts in favour of such backward classes of citizens which are not adequately represented in the public services'. The appointment of the commission was a tribute to the rise of the OBCs as an electoral force to be reckoned with in northern India. Owner-cultivators from the Sudra castes were by then well represented in State legislative assemblies and the Janata coalition. Their champion in government was Charan Singh, the Finance Minister, who had long experience with organising farmers' interests groups (known as *kisan* unions). Mandal concluded, on very questionable grounds, that the 'Backward Classes' were coterminous with the low (but not Scheduled) castes, representing 52 per cent of the population. He recommended that 27 per cent of the posts in the civil service, the public sector, universities, colleges and in private-sector undertakings which had received public financial assistance be reserved for them. (The Supreme Court had earlier ruled that reservation quotas could not exceed 50 per cent of jobs.) The Janata government fell before it could act on the report and the Congress governments of Indira and Rajiv Gandhi refused to publish it, probably because they feared alienating their Forward caste supporters.

The report was published by the National Front coalition government (led by V.P. Singh), which came to power in 1989. Janata Dal, the Prime Minister's party, had already committed itself to implementing Mandal's recommendations and had set an example by allotting 60 per cent of party tickets in the general election to 'the weaker sections of society'. Singh formally announced a reservation policy (which excluded the private sector) in his Independence Day Address on 15 August 1990. He acknowledged its social impact would be limited, since 'Government jobs account for only one per cent [of the total] ... But our outlook is clear ... We want to give an effective share in the power structure and the running of the country to the depressed, down-trodden and backward people' (quoted in Jaffrelot, 2000b, p. 95). The announcement provoked an extraordinary wave of protest across the Hindi belt (with over 100 suicides on the part of upper-caste students), an acrimonious debate in the press and caste polarisation when the OBCs mobilised in favour of Mandal's recommendations.

A striking feature of the furore was a reversal of customary roles: in the past, the Brahmin and other 'twice-born' castes justified their exalted social position in terms of their innate purity; now, they defended their near monopoly of elite administrative posts in terms of merit and efficiency. They vehemently denied any link between the ascribed hierarchy of caste and the bureaucratic hierarchy, despite the fact that candidates from the upper castes (who accounted for about one-fifth of the population) secured 95 per cent of elite administrative jobs. It was now the OBCs calling for reservations who were accused of flaunting the banner of caste and seeking privileged treatment. The upper castes identified themselves with modern, meritocratic secularism; caste reservations were deplored as 'atavism' (Menon and Nigam, 2007, pp. 17–18). It was a glaring example of cognitive dissonance: the OBCs represented nearly three-fifths of the population, yet fewer than one in 20 government posts were filled by people of OBC origin.

The Mandal quotas began to be implemented after the Supreme Court upheld the principle of affirmative action in 1992, though protest was now more muted. This was partly because, with the liberalisation of the economy, careers in the private sector (where quotas do not apply) became more attractive to upper-caste graduates. In relation to the total labour force, of which only a tiny fraction is educationally qualified for government service, reservations are a symbolic issue. They have made a difference *within* the bureaucracy and education, but are practically irrelevant to the employment chances of the great mass of the disadvantaged. Thus, by the 1990s, over 13 per cent of grade A posts in the Indian government's administration were occupied by people from the Scheduled Castes whose forebears were considered 'untouchable'. But only about 0.3 per cent of the Scheduled Castes had gained a BA or BSc, which was the minimum educational requirement for these posts. The link between caste and literacy has proved very durable: by the early 1990s, some privileged castes in Uttar Pradesh and

West Bengal had enjoyed near-universal adult literacy for several decades, while literacy rates were still close to zero amongst disadvantaged castes, especially their womenfolk (Drèze and Sen, 1995, p. 97). Across the nation, the literacy rate for rural Scheduled Caste women was only 19 per cent in 1991.

For those at the bottom of the ritual hierarchy, caste still sanctions daily oppression in the countryside where men claiming warrior descent treat their field labourers as personal retainers, demand sexual access to their women and use force to exact *begar*-like services. The legal and constitutional proscription of 'untouchability' has not weakened the internalisation of its norms: researchers have shown that high or 'clean' caste people consistently regard all whom they know to be of Dalit origin as permanently polluted and ritually unclean, without any further differentiation between them. Furthermore, those belonging to Scheduled Caste groups reportedly do not question or reject the concept of ritual pollution itself, though they differentiate between the quality of their own and other people's untouchability. Typically, they regard other Dalit groups as inherently and irredeemably polluted, while considering their uncleanliness as contingent on having accidentally violated a norm of dharmic conduct, and therefore reversible. Perhaps for this reason, there is little evidence of a sense of common identity uniting those who belong to different 'unclean' groups (Gupta, 2000, pp. 1–6).

The *jati* hierarchy with its Brahmin apex no longer dominates parochial life, but caste has become if anything more prominent in the larger milieus of the state and region. It has proved an effective tool and resource for the creation of common interests across the boundaries of region, language, faith and economic status (Brass, 1994, p. 4). The social relationships of caste have adapted to democratisation and electoral politics and, ironically, contributed to the success of Indian democracy by helping the mass electorate to participate meaningfully and fully. The OBCs in the Hindi belt *were* grossly under-represented in the Congress system at its apogee, while the twice-born castes were over-represented; only by mobilising electorally in caste coalitions did they change this state of affairs (Jaffrelot, 2003). Caste relationships have also intermeshed with the political clientelism endemic in a state-administered economy undergoing modernisation from above. The state's efforts to bring about land reform have generated what can be loosely termed 'caste conflict' in the countryside, principally because 'clean' caste groups have coalesced and mobilised to resist the redistribution of land to the lower castes and 'untouchables'. It is no exaggeration to say that many of India's most socially vulnerable rural citizens have been terrorised by their neighbours. Moreover, affirmative action policies have provoked a vociferous backlash on the part of urban families from the scribal castes with traditions of professional training and white-collar employment. To their dismay, they have seen the white-collar middle classes grow and diversify by recruiting from the children of the old rural elites, from the OBCs and Scheduled Castes. The prospects of material advancement through job reservation have led to a kind of competition for backwardness among castes at the middle level of the hierarchy. Universities, medical schools and other state educational institutions have internalised the caste tensions in the wider society. In principle, educated liberal Indians deplore 'caste' as sincerely as western liberals deplore racism: the English expressions, 'casteism' and 'casteist', are always used pejoratively in public discourse. (Their connotations are analogous to 'tribalism' and 'tribalist' in contemporary Africa.) Yet, informed observers are in little doubt that for many Indians the idea of pride in caste as an expression of selfless virtue has undergone a real revival. Many have come to see their caste identities as fixed, inherent and immutable. Like the Hindu nation, caste has come to operate as an imagined community, a bond of idealised allegiance.

4
Politics and Economics in Independent African States

Introduction

Are Africa's states still 'post-colonial'? In certain obvious ways 'yes': as territorial entities, all but a few were created by European colonial powers and are inconceivable without their prior existence as colonies. In 1963–4, the Organisation of African Unity (OAU) reached a consensus on the immutability of their boundaries, which preserved the continent's political geography in colonial aspic. Nearly every state inherited an organisational core from the colonialists and a European language for public administration, together with an ideology of sovereignty alien to indigenous political traditions. National identity was nowhere the organic outgrowth of a common language and culture, but a reflection of the identity of the colony in the minds of an educated elite. Independence by-passed Africa's historic political nations, such as the Asante, the Baganda and the Bakongo, which underscored the foreign and derivative character of the post-colonial state. In electoral terms, most successor regimes represented minorities: a telling example is Kwame Nkrumah's Convention People's Party – one of the more broadly based nationalist parties – which before 1957 won the support of no more than 35 per cent of the Gold Coast's enfranchised electorate (Rathbone,1978, p. 22). Modern nationalism's political base was, typically, an even narrower urban stratum because (Lusophone Africa and Zimbabwe apart) independence movements were not tested by protracted military struggle and had rarely extended their support into the rural hinterlands.

Yet, in equally obvious ways, the Africanisation of the state has severed its ties with the colonial past, and the 'post' in 'post-colonial' means 'over and done with'. Veterans of the independence struggles have all but disappeared from the political scene in the 28 states created between 1957 and 1965. With the exception of Zimbabwe, anti-colonialism is no longer foregrounded in political ideology and – as far as we can tell – is a marginal theme in popular opinion (see Introduction, this volume). 'Neo-colonialism' has virtually dropped out of the radical lexicon, which seems a tacit admission that it no longer represents a threat to African sovereignty. Although African states have been weak, fissiparous and unable to direct structural economic trans-formation, they are effective instruments for ensuring that local elites profit from commerce and production and political rents accrue to powerful Africans. Despite the continuing presence of foreign business, the significant levers over the economy have long been in African hands (see, inter alia, Rimmer, 1984, p. 253).

The argument that Africa's contemporary linkages with the world economy perpetuate the external economic relations of colonialism is superficially plausible, but will not withstand close analysis. What Bayart has called the 'strategies of extraversion', followed by the domi-nant coalitions of politicians, bureaucrats, traders and military men, are neither externally imposed nor determined by inexorable historical forces. The sub-continent's many-sided dependence on the wider world for imports of food, consumer goods, technology and development capital is constructed and maintained as much by Africans as by the foreign actors who profit from external economic relationships. Africa's traditional rulers struggled to squeeze a surplus out of shifting, subsis-tence agriculture and internal trade; they drew their revenues from taxing international trade and, not infrequently, exporting surplus people. Their post-colonial successors similarly seek to compensate for the inadequacies of their domestic economies by mobilising resources derived from their relationship with the outside world (Bayart, 1993, p. 26; Bayart, 2000, pp. 217–67).

In this chapter, I will argue that the present political situation of the African countries cannot be considered the continuation of an unbroken 'post-colonial *period*'. History has gone on all the time in Africa, and to continue characterising the recent past simply as poste-rior to the European occupation is misleading and intellectually lazy. Not to recognise the major discontinuities in the last four decades would be rather like ignoring the ending of the 'post-war period' in Europe. Unquestionably, 'post-colonialism' in the 1960s and 70s was a time when history in Africa appeared to have real coherence and 'direc-tion' (Dunn, 1978, pp. 1–21). Political self-determination and eco-nomic growth seemed to proceed hand-in-hand in 1960–73. In the eight years prior to the great oil shock, real per capita GDP in Africa grew at two and half times the rate in South Asia (World Bank, *World Development Report*, 1990, p. 11). By most basic measures of human welfare – life expectancy, literacy rates, access to medical care – Africa's independent rulers presided over considerable social progress. In 1960 tropical Africa had one qualified doctor for every 50,000 people; in 1980 one for every 20,000. Child death rates fell from 38 per thousand in 1960 to 25 per thousand in 1980, and life expectancy rose from 39 to 47 years (World Bank, 1981, p. 14). But the great success story of independence was education: between 1960 and 1983 primary school enrolment in sub-Saharan Africa roughly quadrupled, secondary school places multiplied six-fold and the number of university students increased twenty-fold (Iliffe, 1995, p. 263).

However, the African states' common history has been punctuated by political radicalisation, internal crises and external shocks whose cumulative effect has been to 'suspend' or even reverse their economic and social development. The macroeconomic data demonstrate an abrupt change in material life at the end of the 1970s, when demographic expansion began to outstrip the export-led growth inherited from colonialism. For reasons I will examine in greater detail, agriculture was insufficiently responsive to population increase and per capita output of food and cash crops declined. This was a major factor – though by no means the entire cause – behind the sharp fall in living standards for the great majority in the 1980s and early 90s. Primary school enrolment rates began to fall from the early 1980s because impoverished parents could no longer afford school fees or forgo their children's earnings. By 1989, 13 countries with a combined population of a third of the sub-continent had an income per head lower than at independence (World Bank, 1989, p. 18).

To which we must add that across a swathe of central and southern Africa, the HIV/AIDS epidemic has virtually annulled the public health gains of the mid- and later twentieth century. By 2000, two countries (Botswana and Zimbabwe) had HIV infection rates in excess of one-quarter of the adult population. Average life expectancy, which rose continuously in Africa from the 1940s until the late 80s, has declined in the last 25 years. The biggest reversal has been in Botswana, where life expectancy reached 64 years in 1985 but had fallen back to 36 years by 2005. In Zimbabwe, life expectancy fell from 61 years to 37 years in the same period. In Kenya and Côte d'Ivoire life expectancy fell by 11 and eight years respectively. Aids orphans made up 11 per cent of the population in the most afficted countries (World Bank, 2008b, Table 2.2). The epidemic's full impact on economic production has yet to be felt: unless treatment expands substantially, 19 countries will lose 10 per cent of the workforce by 2015 (Commission for Africa, 2005, p. 204).

There is no easy way to sum up the change in historical 'direction' taken by African countries since the late 1970s, but it is legitimate to ask what the first generation of independent leaders intended for the societies in their political charge, and how and why their intentions were thwarted. The crucial lesson they had learnt from the humiliation of colonisation was the need to overcome economic and technological, as well as political and military weakness. All – as far as I know – wanted to accelerate modern development by import-substituting industrialisation; this common ambition overrode their often sharp ideological differences in the 1960s (Young, 1982a; Ake, 1996). Nkrumah set himself a domestic programme of state-led industrialisation, believing – in his biographer's words – 'that Ghanaians would never be happy until industrial smoke and grime made it impossible to see from one side of the Volta river to the other' (Birmingham, 1990, p. 64). Félix Houphouët Boigny did not envisage a radically different future for neighbouring Côte d'Ivoire; what was at stake in his celebrated wager with Nkrumah was the advantage (or otherwise) of remaining closely tied to the former colonial power, not the desirability of industrial growth (Woronoff, 1972). No African nationalist of any political consequence has followed Gandhi in idealising peasant simplicity and in seeing the real enemy, not as imperial domination, but as modern industrial civilisation in its entirety. Modernisation was the intention, and served to justify 'squeezing' the peasantry in order to transfer resources to industrialising sectors (Bates, 1983, pp. 118–19).

As an abstract concept, 'modernisation' is vacuously tautological, but in a situation where governing elites are acutely aware of their country's comparative economic backwardness, it is an apt enough term for their endeavours to 'catch up' with the industrialised countries. By common consent, these endeavours have run into the sand. Structural transformation or the shift of labour from agriculture to industry stalled in the late 1970s and – except for Mauritius – no African country was able to enter the new international division of labour as a low-cost producer of manufactured exports. Indeed, the most crisis-ridden (Angola, Somalia, Sierra Leone, Liberia, the Democratic Republic of the Congo, Chad, Zimbabwe) were locked into a process of 'de-modernisation' in the 1990s. Its symptoms included the decay of the monetised market economy imposed by the colonialists, a deteriorating infrastructure and the state's inability to provide such essential public goods as law and security, enforceable contracts and a sound medium of exchange. Political mafias had 'hollowed out' weak states from within: they could not maintain their monopoly of legitimate volence, and patently criminal practices had become routinised at the heart of political and governing institutions (Bayart *et al.*, 1999; Mbembe, 2001, pp. 67, 73–7, 85).

What follows is, first, a chronological framework for analysing the political economy of post-colonial Africa, second, a thematic discussion of key issues. The chronology is unavoidably schematic: Africa is the world's most politically segmented region, and there are limits to what can be usefully said about its 48 states as a whole. They vary greatly in their populations, resource endowments and economic opportunities. Land-locked, resource-scarce states (Malawi, Burkina Faso, the Central African Republic) defy economic logic; elsewhere in the world they would be 'backward' hinterlands of more viable national economies. Furthermore, the chronology oscillates between the 'economic' and the 'political' without giving primacy to either because it is open to question whether an 'economy' as an autonomous sphere of productive activity (over and above subsistence and local trade) has actually existed in post-colonial Africa. As has often been remarked, political power gives rise to economic power, rather than the reverse (Bayart, 1993, p. 70). The use of official positions within the post-colonial state to advance business interests has been more or less the norm. Class relations were, in the final analysis, determined by relations of political power, not production (Sklar, 1979, p. 537). Conversely, of the many constraints inhibiting indigenous African capitalism, by far the most important was the ineffective yet frequently obstructive nature of state power, wielded by often corrupt political leaders suspicious of market institutions. Until the mid-1980s, many were wary of the emergence of an autonomous class of African entrepreneurs, those influenced by radical socialism and Marxism were openly hostile (Kennedy, 1994).

We are now in a better position to gauge the econometrics of poor governance thanks to the multi-authored study undertaken by the African Economic Research Consortium (AERC). The 'big question' the authors address is why Africa's economy scarcely grew between 1960 and 2000, by the standard measure of real per capita GDP at international purchasing power parity. As they stress, stagnation was *not* the norm; the average conceals emormous variation between countries and over time. More than a quarter of African countries experienced at least one extended episode of extremely rapid growth after 1960 (Ndulu *et al.*, 2008, p. 8). Côte d'Ivoire went full circle from 'economic miracle' in

1960–79 to prolonged decline in 1980–2003: according to one estimate, real per capita GDP in 2002 was lower than in 1964 (Bogetic *et
al.*, 2007, p. 2). At a continental level, geography, climate, disease and
demography explain a great deal. Around three in ten Africans live in
land-locked, poorly endowed economies at a considerable distance
from navigable waterways or the sea. Inland transport costs are
inevitably high, which has frustrated the extension of the market and
the regional division of labour. Africa's farmers have to cope with
leached and fragile tropical soils, so they use land comparatively
unproductively, and are often debilitated by parasitic infestation and
chronic disease (Sachs and Warner, 1997). Africa is only just entering
the demographic transition from high fertility and mortality to low
birth and death rates and has the world's highest youth-dependency
ratios. But when Africa's economies are categorised as 'coastal', 'land-
locked' and 'resource-rich' and compared with similarly categorised
developing economies elsewhere, then it is clear much remains unex-
plained. The contrast between the economic upsurge in the developing
world's coastal economies after 1980 and regression in coastal Africa is
particularly striking.

According to the AERC authors, economic growth was stymied by
'dysfunctional political-economy configurations' which they term 'syndromes'. These were 'salient episodes of purposive failure attributable
to human agency within the society – whether by leaders, governments, or groups outside government such as rebel movements'
(Collier and O'Connell, 2008, p. 89). One syndrome involved the
repressive regulation of economic activity. Unsurprisingly, this was
especially evident under socialist or Marxist regimes which instituted
'hard controls' by nationalising the banks and other 'commanding
heights' of the economy, but even regimes with large private sectors
often instituted 'soft controls', such as administered prices. A second
type of syndrome they identify with the redistribution of income
between ethno-regional groups, which was particularly deleterious
where the economic returns to political power were so inflated that
substantial resources were devoted to 'rent-seeking'. In its extreme
form, the redistributive syndrome resulted in the 'looting' of public
resources, which we intuitively associate with predatory autocrats,
although the authors consider the most serious single episode of
looting occurred during Nigeria's second, democratic republic of 1979–
83 (*ibid.*, p. 93) (see Chapter 6 of this volume). The third type of syndrome was 'intertemporal' or what we could call mortgaging the future.
It usually took the form of governments misconstruing temporary

increases in national income as permanent and undertaking massive public expenditure on the basis of foreign loans. Two examples are the public spending sprees in Nigeria during the first oil cycle (1973–6) and in Côte d'Ivoire during the cocoa and coffee boom (1975–7). The fourth type of syndrome was state breakdown, ranging from an inability to control crime to civil war. Over the decades 1960–2000, about three-quarters of Africa's population were living in a country affected by one or more of these syndromes; during the 1970s and 80s, about nine-tenths were. Though being syndrome-free did not guarantee growth, it was a necessary condition for it.

Africa's five-phased trajectory since 1960

There is no such entity as the typical African state, but African states have, to a greater or lesser degree, been affected by common economic and political trends. These can be analysed in terms of five phases, which should be seen as overlapping and intertwined processes, rather than rigidly sequential stages.

Phase I: c. 1960–c. 1968

In this phase the constitutional settlements agreed at independence almost universally broke down. They turned out to be transitional arrangements between one form of authoritarianism and another. By 1970, Africa's independent states were, with few exceptions, under one-party government or military rule. The near total failure of multi-party democracy must be seen in the light of the immense challenges confronting African leaders and their insecurity, given their narrow electoral bases in ethnically divided societies where the sense of nationhood was shallow. Independence was everywhere a revolution of rising material expectations, which the nationalist movements greatly encouraged but were ill-equipped to satisfy. Their own cohesion – and that of the political class more generally – was sundered by intense competition for public office and resources. Factionalism induced chronic insecurity and made authoritarian solutions to the problem of maintaining political order all the more attractive. Nkrumah believed a monolithic CPP was necessary to prevent the young ex-colonial state 'dissipat[ing] its national energies in senseless wranglings' (quoted in Zolberg, 1966, p. 58). He instituted a de facto one-party state in 1961 as part of the regime's 'big push' for state-led industrialisation. The territorial administration had already been politicised – and the government's grip on the localities tightened – by ensuring district officers and administrators were CPP appointees. The TUC and the Farmers' Council were incorporated into the party. In a move that was paralleled throughout Africa at this time, the country was formally proclaimed a one-party state in 1964.

Political pluralism – in the shape of a multi-party system – was often proscribed for honourable reasons: competitive, partisan politics were an imported luxury that would mirror and politicise ethnic, regional and religious cleavages, and divert the new nations' political energies from the tasks of development. Monopoly parties – it was claimed – 'internalised' democracy in a way that accorded with an African tradition of consensus. Tanzania's Julius Nyerere – one of Africa's most respected leaders – argued that 'where there is one party, and that party is identified with the nation as a whole, the foundations of democracy are firmer than they can ever be where you have two or more parties, each representing only one section of the community' (quoted in Decalo, 1992, p. 10). In practice, the monopoly party tended to be a network through which the ambitious sought to maximise their access to state resources. Its exclusive position in the state rendered legal transfers of governing authority virtually impossible. The normal method of changing regimes became the military coup d'état: there were eight in 1966 alone. Coups or attempted coups were as frequent in Anglophone as Francophone states, which indicates that their background causes lay less in specific features of the colonial legacy and more in the general fragility and uncertain legitimacy of the new states. The Ghanaian army removed Nkrumah in late February, two days after Milton Obote's coup against the Kabaka of Buganda and six weeks after the Nigerian majors had murdered the Federal Prime Minister and other leading officials. Around this time, successful coups occurred in the Democratic Republic of the Congo, Benin, the Central African Republic and Burkina Faso. (For a comprehensive listing of African coups, see McGowan, 2003.)

While political trajectories in the former French and British colonies were very similar, they followed different paths to economic decolonisation. Francophone political elites had closer ties with the metropole and took charge of less-developed economies, with more exiguous resources of trained manpower than in Anglophone Africa. (In 1960, fewer than 10 per cent of adult Ivorians were literate, as compared with 27 per cent of adult Ghanaians.) With the exception of Sekou Touré in Guinea, they saw considerable advantage in maintaining monetary, commercial and financial links with France and providing a hospitable environment for French businesses. French experts drew up their development plans, while cooperation agreements ensured a high level of French aid, mostly in the form of grants, as well as a remarkable degree of institutional, administrative and socio-cultural continuity. (Until the early 1980s, four out of five secondary school teachers in Côte d'Ivoire were French expatriates.) Exports from the African franc zone to France – and the EEC – were given price and quota preferences (Coquery-Vidrovitch, 1988a; Basso, 1992). The value of the CFA (Communauté financière africaine) franc remained pegged to the metropolitan, and France guaranteed its unrestricted convertibility, circulation and transfer, while subsidising the state budgets of the poorest ex-colonies to ensure monetary stability. But in return France insisted on the free transfer of profits and capital within the franc zone and the maintenance of strict control over the new states' financial reserves, which were deposited in French francs on account with the French Treasury. The two issuing banks of the former French African Federations were, in practice, branches of the Bank of France.

The monetary and commercial ties between Britain and its former colonies were much looser. They had agreed, as part of the decolonisation 'pact', to place their reserves in London and peg their currencies to sterling, but the pound's forced devaluation in November 1967 ended its role as a reserve currency. The ex-colonies revalued their currencies to maintain the existing dollar exchange rate and moved their reserves from London. The Imperial Preference System had been dismantled under the General Agreements on Tariffs and Trade (GATT) before decolonisation, so imports from the ex-colonies did not enter Britain on preferential terms (Fieldhouse, 1986, pp. 58–9). As a trading partner, Britain was much less important to them than France was to the Francophone countries. The former British colonies also diversified their sources of foreign aid more rapidly.

The move to single-party states did not dim the bright economic prospects during this phase. Independence came during the long boom in the world economy when demand for African commodity exports, which typically accounted for 20–5 per cent of total output, was buoyant. Export volumes grew at 5.3 per cent a year during the 1960s, while their purchasing power increased by 7.6 per cent annually because import prices rose more slowly than export prices. The net barter terms of trade improved by 2.9 per cent a year. Mineral-exporting countries, such Zambia, did exceptionally well: the purchasing power of their exports rose by 11.1 per cent a year and their net barter terms of trade improved by 6.5 per cent annually (World

Bank, 1981, Table 3.2, p. 18). In the first fiscal year of independence (1964–5), Zambia's revenues were about three times greater than in the last fiscal year prior to independence: it received taxes that previously went to the federal government, renegotiated to its benefit the royalties agreement with the British South Africa Company and was the beneficiary of soaring copper prices. Its capital funds increased dramatically (Bates,1974, p. 20). Under the spur of rising prices, mining everywhere attracted new investment, often in the form of joint ventures between African governments and foreign consortia, and the industry diversified into new fields (such as bauxite in Guinea, copper and nickel in Botswana). The net barter terms of trade for agricultural exporters improved by 1 per cent annually during the 1960s, but because export volumes rose by 4.7 per cent a year their income terms of trade improved substantially. Between 1960 and 1970–2, African producers increased their share of world trade in coffee, cocoa, tea and cotton. However, their share in palm oil trade plummeted from 63.2 per cent to 20.8 per cent, due to the collapse of the commercial agriculture in Congo-Zaire and increased domestic consumption in West Africa, while their share in groundnuts trade also fell.

The favourable international economic environment boosted the optimism of African political leaders and their western advisers that development could be accelerated by strategic government intervention. There was an affinity between the leaders' 'vision' of economic modernisation and the model held by many economists which construed development as a discontinuous process of structural transformation (Killick, 1978). To break out of the low-level equilibrium in which poor countries were trapped required a 'big push' or 'critical minimum effort', the principal ingredient of which was a massive increase in the ratio of investment to national income, which only governments could engineer. Once a certain level of per capita income was reached, growth would be self-sustaining. A professional consensus in favour of planning and state interventionism brought mainstream development economics and African economic nationalism still closer. Market mechanisms in advanced societies were deemed imperfect; in subsistence-oriented agrarian societies, they were considered hopelessly inadequate as a means of initiating rapid growth. Central planning, which had swiftly transformed the Soviet-bloc countries from agrarian to industrial economies, was in vogue. The African press and political leaders in their speeches harked constantly on the need for planning, which was usually opposed to the selfishness of the profit motive (Hunter, 1962, p. 289). African governments, generally with full donor support, drew up comprehensive five-year plans, increased their spending on infrastructure and administration and invested in large, state-run core industries. They viewed agriculture as a backward sector that would provide surpluses – in the form of taxes and labour – to finance industrialisation.

Manufacturing value added grew on average by 8 per cent annually in the 1960s, which was nearly double the rate of GDP growth. By 1965 manufacturing accounted for more than 15 per cent of GDP in 12 countries (including Côte d'Ivoire, Ghana, Kenya, Senegal, Togo and Congo-Zaire) and by 1973 in six more (World Bank, 1989, p. 110; Hawkins, 1991). African governments offered foreign companies generous incentives to invest in manufacturing (tax credits, accelerated depreciation allowances, subsidised interest rates, preferential duties on capital equipment), though the major inducement was prohibitive tariffs on finished goods. Textiles, bicycles, processed foods and beverages, footware and clothing were particularly favoured: the protection accorded them frequently exceeded the value added in processing and manufacturing. Because development programmes generated sharp increases in demand for imports, governments sought to control import spending by extending controls over foreign trade and payments, measures that were to continue in one form or another until the 1980s.

Phase II: c. 1968–c. 1978

In the second phase, African governments sought to bring the economy's commanding heights under their control. Politics veered sharply to the left with the 'second decolonisation' of the late 1960s, early 70s, when the neo-colonial arrangements made to defend French, British and Belgian interests in Africa came under fire and were partly dismantled. In response to African complaints that the rules of the franc zone put a financial straitjacket on development, they were liberalised in 1972–3 to give member governments greater control over credit policy, while Africans replaced Frenchmen on the boards of the two issuing banks (Walle, 1991, p. 390). The development plans adopted in this second phase reflected the ambitious goals of self-reliance and socialisation (Ake, 1996, p. 19). Tanzania's Arusha Declaration of 1967 and Zambia's Mulungushi Declaration of 1968 were early manifestos of this left-wing economic nationalism, prompted partly by the western powers' tepid support for previous development plans. By the mid-1970s, 80 per cent of medium- and large-scale economic activity in socialist Tanzania lay in the public sector, which accounted for 80 per cent of total investment. Coupled with this was a 'hard' control regime which included the collectivisation of agriculture, the nationalisation of all large rented buildings, the nationalisation of the press and what one expatriate academic admiringly called 'a sustained effort ... to nip in the bud the emergence of *any* African entreupreneurial group whatsoever' (Saul, 1973, p. 244, his emphasis). Except for the CFA countries, states dispensed with externally imposed 'agencies of economic constraint', such as independent currency boards, and brought their central banks under local political control. There ceased to be autonomous agencies empowered to protect public assets from depletion, prevent the inflationary printing of money, control corruption and shelter socially productive groups from exploitation (Collier, 1991). Political radicalisation accelerated when military coups installed regimes that were officially Marxist-Leninist in Congo-Brazzaville (1969), Somalia (1970), Benin (1974), Madagascar (1975) and Ethiopia (1974–6), while revolutionary movements swept to power with the ending of the wars of liberation in Lusophone Africa (1974–5). Most states that had not already done so sought to 'indigenise' their economies, either through outright nationalisation or by the exclusion of foreigners from participation in scheduled industries. Zambia had led the way with the nationalisation of its mining companies, though at the expense of incurring a huge debt in compensation payments to foreign shareholders and the hostility of expatriate managers. Immigrant entrepreneurs were squeezed out of commerce and light-industrial sectors. In Uganda, the despot Idi Amin simply confiscated Asian assets and then handed them out in an informal fashion as state patronage. In Kenya, the Africanisation of distribution was effected by a Trade Licensing Act which excluded non-citizen Asians from domestic commerce.

Outwardly, states became 'Leviathans': as a proportion of GDP, state expenditure rose inexorably in the 20 years after independence. During the 1970s, spending on public administration and defence, which with education were the largest components of the government sector, grew on average at 9.9 per cent annually, and in some of the poorest countries at a substantially higher rate. By the end of the decade, the total resources marshalled by governments typically exceeded a quarter of GDP, and in many cases two-fifths (World Bank, 1981, p. 41; Collier and Gunning, 1999b, Table 4, p. 70). Government consumption and spending was proportionally higher than elsewhere in the developing world, and several times greater than during late colonialism. The public sector grew through bureaucratic expansion, the widening of public services (such as education and health care) and the extension of the state into manufacturing, mining, transport and marketing. Even in countries committed to private enterprise the public sector dominated the modern economy and state agencies closely regulated export agriculture. Côte d'Ivoire's 'economic miracle' (1960–79) is often ascribed to 'farmer- and market-friendly' policies which reflected the social interests of the indigenous 'planter' class (Bates, 1981, p. 95). In fact, the practical similarities between the Ivorian and other African states were more striking than the differences. It pursued a highly dirigiste, planned growth strategy, in which a parastatal agency, the Caisse de Stabilisation, imposed farm-gate prices on cocoa and coffee farmers and appropriated the difference between world prices (which was 50 per cent or more). Much of this surplus was invested in state-owned enterprises (Crook, 1989, pp. 208–20). Ghana's socialist growth strategy under Nkrumah depended on the same mechanism to accumulate capital. The Ivorian 'miracle' is attributable not to a distinctive macroeconomic policy, but to 'open-door' immigration which ensured abundant labour from the Sahel, the monetary and financial stability which came from franc zone membership and the greater political and administrative capacity of the state elite. Whatever their ideological complexion, governments generally preferred bureaucratic regulation to market liberalisation. Those committed to supporting the indigenous private sector assumed that it should be manipulated from above and develop alongside an expanding public sector (Kennedy, 1988, p. 78). Measures to assist local business were either soon abandoned or implemented so as to favour political 'insiders' and government officials, or the latter's own supporters and clients. Underpinning the 'anti-business' stance was fear and suspicion of potential rivals and a belief that, since African economies were poor and undeveloped, individuals and groups could gain only at the expense of others.

Public employment was the main source of job opportunities for graduates and secondary school leavers. Central government salaries were high in relation to average incomes (the usual ratio was about 6:1 in 1980, compared with 2.5:1 in South Asia) but public office was prized no less for its perks: cars, housing, bursaries for children, health care and overseas travel. The state became the major avenue of upward mobility to wealth and status; it soaked up administrative capacity, which was the scarcest resource in many African economies, and deployed it inefficiently and expensively. As public administration expanded, and its functions proliferated, so its efficiency and probity declined. Inexperienced staff were promoted too rapidly and, not infrequently, as a result of ethnic favouritism, political patronage and nepotism. Governments took control of the communications media, intervened in religious and cultural life, in some cases ordered considerable rural populations to relocate, and in others expelled immigrant communities. Dysfunctional 'regulatory syndromes' and autocratic leadership went hand in hand.

This phase of radical 'Africanisation' and social revolution effectively ended the old colonial dependency: where financial, monetary and military ties with the former imperial power remained close – as they did in the franc zone – this was a matter of elite self-interest on the African side. Furthermore, during this second phase, politics became systematically patrimonial: 'big men' in positions of power exploited public resources as if they were private assets, lining their own and kinsmen's pockets while redistributing social goods to favoured clients. Presidential regimes were instituted in which the head of state personally disposed of substantial revenues and decided foreign exchange allocations. The monopoly political party not infrequently became a tattered 'front' for an autocrat's personal rule, legitimated by an eclectic appeal to a purportedly traditional notion of the wise leader and a modern claim to be the presiding genius of national development. But politics was usually oligarchic, not dictatorial. The president was one amongst 'cronies' – politicians, businessmen, military officers and bureaucrats – who used clientelistic networks to build mutual support. 'Crony statism', as it has been called, ensured a fluid, two-way exchange of political power and wealth between elites, without wholly forfeiting popular acquiescence (Callaghy and Ravenhill, 1993).

After the first oil 'shock' of 1973–4, and well before the disasters of the 1980s, it was evident that economic prospects in many African states were dimming. Per capita GDP growth in the sub-continent as a whole just about kept pace with population growth for the rest of the decade, but a few states boomed while most stagnated. Nearly all the GDP growth can be accounted for by the huge increase in the value of oil exports, principally from Nigeria. Fifteen countries recorded negative rates of growth between 1973 and 1979. In the poorest countries per capita GDP declined by –0.3 per cent a year, and in the 'middle-income' countries not blessed with oil wealth by –0.5 per cent a year (World Bank, 1981, pp. 8–9). The drastic fall in the copper price in 1975 impacted severely on Zambia, which depended on copper for 90 per cent of its export earnings, and on Zaire. Ghana plunged into the abyss of national poverty in the 1970s when run-away inflation and government corruption assumed enormous, socially destructive proportions (Rimmer, 1992, ch. 7). By the turn of the decade, economic malaise was affecting hitherto 'success stories', such as Kenya, Malawi and Côte d'Ivoire: they faced mounting balance of payments deficits and indebtedness, and were compelled to design programmes to restructure their economies.

At this point, I must mention – almost in parenthesis – two powerful 'external' agencies with their own temporal rhythms which 'bridged' the second and third phases. The Cold War intruded more sharply into African politics from 1975, when the Soviet Union and Cuba supported states of 'socialist orientation' and the west favoured regimes and rebel movements willing to stand against Soviet influence. At the same time, South Africa opted to defend the white laager by the aggressive desta-bilisation of neighbouring states. Both intensified the continent's mili-tarisation and led, inevitably, to a 'step-jump' in the scale of organised violence. From the 1970s, expenditure on conventional arms rose faster in Africa than in any other region largely because of the military aid furnished by the superpowers. During the 'Second Cold War' of the Reagan–Brezhnev–Andropov years, 'security assistance' – a euphemism for arms supply – accounted for between one-half and two-thirds of the US aid budget. The Soviet Union provided nearly $2.1 billion in eco-nomic assistance to sub-Saharan Africa between 1980 and 1984, while its arms deliveries were worth more than $5.9 billion (Furedi, 1988, p. 127; Clapham, 1996, ch. 6). At the height of the wars in Angola, Ethiopia and Mozambique, military spending absorbed half or more of these countries' national budgets and anything from 12 to 28 per cent (in Angola) of GNP. The foreign exchange costs, both directly in arms purchases and in more indirect terms, were enormous; they competed with development needs and led to large military debt burdens (Luckham, 1994, p. 52). In 1989, about one-fifth of Africa's external debt of $230 billion had been incurred for arms procurements. Though Africa's arms race generated few state-on-state wars, protracted conflict within states displaced vast numbers and drove many over interna-tional borders. In the late 1980s, there were some 4 million refugees and a further 12 million displaced persons in Africa (World Bank, 1989, p. 22).

Phase III: c. 1979–c. 1989

What 'Africanisation' did not do was lessen the sub-continent's vulner-ability to external economic shocks or create the domestic conditions for industrial 'take-off', such as occurred in South East Asia in the 1970s and 80s. On the contrary, while many of the world's poorest countries enjoyed sustained economic growth, sub-Saharan Africa endured a decade or more of 'lost development'. It was the only developing region to experience such prolonged economic decline and social immiseration. The proportion of Africa's population living on less than $1 a day rose from 42.6 per cent in 1981 to 47.5 per cent in 1990; the number from 169.4 million to 245.2 million. In South Asia, the proportion of the population living below this international poverty line fell from 41.9 per cent to 34 per cent in the 1980s (Chen and Ravallion, 2008, Tables 7, 8). Patrimonial states were gravely weakened by this protracted economic crisis which deprived them of export revenues, the political rents needed to sustain clientelistic networks and the capacity to maintain the material infrastructure. The vulnerability of import-substituting industrialisation to foreign exchange shortages had already been exposed in oil-importing countries after 1974; ten of them were 'de-industrialising' in the later 1970s, when their manufacturing output declined. A further 11 countries 'de-industrialised' in the early 1980s, including Nigeria where manufacturing was crippled by the dearth of foreign exchange after the value of oil exports fell by three-fifths between 1980 and 1983 (World Bank, 1989, p. 110).

Investment ratios declined across the continent: in Côte d'Ivoire, combined public and private investment had peaked at 33 per cent of GDP in 1978; it fell to a nadir of about 7 per cent in 1991. In real terms, the value of the physical capital stock per Ivorian worker dropped by about two-thirds between 1979 and 1999, output per worker by about a third (Bogetic *et al.*, 2007, p. 13). In Zambia, gross domestic investment had averaged 25 per cent of GNP between 1965 and 1980, but was only 11 per cent by 1987. With insufficient foreign exchange to import spare parts, fixed capital deteriorated: Zambia's copper mines were so run-down that when the copper price rebounded to a near record high at the end of 1980s, they could not raise output: Zambia produced only 400,000 tonnes of copper in 1989, as compared with 720,000 tonnes in 1969. The rural infrastructure was just as neglected (Martin, 1993). With short-term fluctuations, real per capita GDP in Zambia declined up to the end of the century, when it was it about 40 per cent below the 1970 level (World Bank, *World Development Indicators*, 2008).

Mounting public indebtedness compelled governments to enter deeply unpopular 'restructuring' agreements – more honoured in the breach than the observance – with the international financial institutions (IFFs). These undermined their legitimacy and their ability to purchase popular support through food subsidies and educational and welfare services. The struggle between 'big men' to appropriate public resources and redistribute them amongst their clients became more intense. As institutional clusters, states lost much of their coherence, capacity and authority, and corruption became one of their defining features. Presidential governments decayed into highly personal, ramshackle affairs, unable to transform allocated public resources into intended policy aims. The writ of government often no longer extended to all parts of the country, and where it did was irregularly observed (Jackson and Rosberg, 1986). As the World Bank noted, in many countries the administrations, judiciaries and educational institutions were mere shadows of their former selves by the late 1980s (World Bank, 1989, p. 22). Academic visitors were struck by the dilapidation of universities which had once epitomised African modernity and the impoverishment of African colleagues. Like other public-sector employees, they experienced the savage adjustment of the state's salary bill to its diminishing revenues in the 1980s. By the end of the decade, public-sector wages were barely enough for subsistence in several countries (*ibid.*, p. 29). The educated unemployed became a highly visible presence in African societies as the growth of the clerical labour force outstripped job creation. Public institutions which could not employ graduates and secondary school leavers were drained of their remaining legitimacy and credibility.

At the close of this phase, Africa was simultaneously a marginal participant in the global economy and acutely vulnerable to global economic fluctuations. Its share of world trade had fallen from 3 per cent in 1960 to less than 1.5 per cent and the sub-continent attracted around 0.3 per cent of the world's foreign direct investment (*ibid.*, p. 37). Yet, it was even more dependent on a narrow range of commodity exports than in the 1960s. World prices for the tropical staples (cotton, coffee, cocoa and sugar) went into long-term decline around 1978/80: over the next two decades they fell by between one-half and three-quarters in real terms. Even more damaging than the secular trend were the violent fluctuations in commodity prices: between 1986 and 1989, Africa lost the equivalent of 15–16 per cent of its GDP because of price falls for its exports (Commission for Africa, 2005, p. 109). African economies were poorly equipped to absorb an external shock of this magnitude: on average, the physical capital stock per worker in 1990 was less than half the level in South Asia (which was itself far below the East Asian level). The poor rates of return on private investment had been an incentive for wealthy Africans to move their capital abroad: by 1990, 39 per cent of private wealth had been relocated outside Africa, an astonishing level of capital flight matched only by the Middle East (Collier and Gunning, 1999b, Table 8, p. 93).

The franc zone countries, which had appeared better able to weather the storm at the beginning of the decade, were in as dire straits as the rest of Africa after 1986, because the metropolitan franc began to appreciate against the dollar, dragging the CFA franc with it. The Francophone political elites had learnt to evade the fiscal and monetary discipline once entailed by franc zone membership and virtually bankrupted their domestic lending banks by compelling them to extend credit to unprofitable public enterprises; only susbidies from the French treasury stopped the banks foundering in a morass of 'non-performing' loans. French private investors began repatriating their capital from 1985 onwards; by 1988, three-quarters of them wanted to pull out of Africa altogether. The World Bank urged devaluation of the CFA franc to make exports competitive (and halt large-scale smuggling into neighbouring countries that had devalued). This the political elites refused to contemplate: an over-valued currency suited the interests of the urban middle classes (not infrequently state or public-sector employees) who were the regimes' core supporters. The French treasury was spending about $1 billion a year to maintain the value of the CFA franc by the late 1980s, a price President Mitterand and his advisers deemed worth paying to sustain metropolitan influence over the former colonies (Walle, 1991). Devaluation was – foolishly – delayed until 1994.

Africa's geo-strategic significance had also greatly diminished with the superpower détente and Gorbachev's decision to terminate Soviet involvement in Africa. African autocrats, such as Mobutu in Zaire and Mengistu Haile Mariam in Ethiopia, had skilfully exploited Cold War rivalries to secure financial, diplomatic and military aid; after 1989, it was no longer possible for ruling elites to resist internal pressure for change by manipulating external patronage.

Phase IV: c. 1988–c. 1994

In the fourth phase, Africa's authoritarian, unaccountable states were confronted by popular political movements of a type not seen since the mass nationalism of the late 1950s and early 60s. The demand for 're-democratisation' and political accountability originated in Africa but quickly partook of the global challenge to authoritarianism, the so-called third wave of transitions to democracy. When the Berlin Wall fell, 38 sub-Saharan states were under one-party rule and, to a greater or lesser degree, authoritarian. Military coups were then the main mechanism for the circulation of elites (Decalo, 1992, p. 9; Luckham, 1994, p. 26). Eighteen months later, over half these states had committed themselves to competitive multi-party elections and major limitations on executive powers. Benin set an example for the Francophone states when President Kérékou, head of a nominally Marxist-Leninist regime since 1974, was compelled by state bankruptcy and months of student demonstrations to convene a National Conference in February 1990 and end the monopoly of the Parti Révolutionnaire du Peuple du Benin. The Conference declared itself sovereign and drew up a new constitution. President Mitterand's announcement at the Franco-African Conference in June 1990 that henceforth French economic aid would be linked to democratisation gave the reform process an additional impetus. Although democracy was fully restored in only a handful of states, the political atmosphere was suffused with great ferment, expectation and even optimism. South Africa's peaceful transformation to multi-racial democracy was inspirational. All the People's Republics followed Benin's example by renouncing Marxism and the vanguard role of the single Marxist-Leninist party, and moving to restore a market economy. Across sub-Saharan Africa, governments set about privatising the public sector.

Neither the democracy 'wave' nor economic liberalisation fulfilled all the hopes vested in them (Young, 1999). Multi-party elections were often grudgingly instituted at the behest of international donors, who insisted that further aid would be made conditional on popular accountability, and became instruments of factional mobilisation. Military coups were as frequent as ever, since weakly institutionalised democratic governments were just as likely to experience them as their autocratic predecessors: between 1990 and 2001, there were 50 attempted coups in sub-Saharan Africa of which 13 were successful (McGowan, 2003, p. 349). Côte d'Ivoire, a land of fabled political stability under the 'benign' autocrat Houphouët-Boigny (d. 1993), experienced its first military coup in December 1999, after a seemingly orderly transition to multi-party democracy. This was followed by a second coup in September 2002 and full-scale civil war. Autocrats and military power-brokers proved quite adept at deflecting democratisation; plebiscitary presidentialism was a common trend in African countries in the 1990s. The widely predicted explosion in political participation did not occur, and decision-making in the new democracies strongly resembled the patrimonialism of the old one-party states. The privatisation programmes provided opportunities for the politically powerful, military and civilian bureaucrats, and well-connected businessmen to appropriate public assets at bargain prices. Macroeconomic reforms led to lower tariffs, greater trade openness, more competitive exchange rates and reduced fiscal deficits, but they did not reverse the deterioriation in the quality of public institutions. Civil service morale and service delivery remained very poor (World Bank, 2000, p. 37). Moreover, the mobilisation of popular discontent, coupled with the decay of the military and police establishments, had profoundly negative, as well as positive consequences. With the erosion of the state's coercive capacity, organised violence was 'privatised' and generalised. Regimes were confronted by jacqueries, warlords and more or less criminal armed rebellions on an unprecedented scale.

The early 1990s were a time when African states were both experiencing a revival of popular democracy *and* entering a terminal crisis of 'de-modernisation'. Congo-Zaire is an extreme, but not unrepresentative instance, which is discussed in detail elsewhere. It was one of 20 African countries where the local currency was effectively worthless by the early 1990s and where the elite used the dollar for formal transactions while ordinary consumers resorted to barter. Few of Africa's long-serving autocrats were quite so adept as President Mobutu at remaining in office while their countries slid into ruin, but political recidivism was painfully evident thoughout the decade. Long-serving autocrats such as Omar Bongo in Gabon and Paul Biya in Cameroon 'rode out' the democratic ferment and the formal installation of multi-party systems by an adroit mix of electoral fraud, intimidation, ethnic favouritism and repression (and in Bongo's case by calling on French troops to restore order: he died in office in 2009, after 42 years in power, and was succeeded by his son). Daniel arap Moi, Kenya's president since 1978, conceded multi-party elections in late 1991 after western donors withdrew all financial support following high-profile political assassinations and a mounting crisis of legitimacy. (Two of Moi's closest associates were charged with the murder of the Foreign Minister, Robert Ouku, in February 1990, after he had compiled a dossier on high-level corruption. They were released 'for lack of evidence' and Moi abruptly dissolved the commission of enquiry into the crime.) But the opposition was hopelessly divided on ethnic and personal lines, and could not agree on a single candidate for the presidential election of December 1992, which Moi won on 37 per cent of the vote. He remained at the head of a quasi-democratic kleptocracy until 2002, thanks to the manipulation of the ethnic patchwork and the control of government resources, the state-owned media, the police and the electoral machinery (Meredith, 2005, pp. 398–404; Nugent,

2004, pp. 409–11). Where they were instituted, multi-party elections did little to restrain the corrupt exploitation of political office: Moi colluded in the notorious 'Goldenberg' scheme to defraud the public treasury of $600 million by paying government subsidies for exporting gold that had been smuggled in from Congo-Zaire. The governor of the central bank, head of the treasury, and many senior officials and politicians were implicated (Ellis, 2006, p. 204; see also the Wikipedia entry on 'The Goldenberg scandal'). After Moi left office in 2002, his successor, Mwai Kibaki, commissioned Kroll Associates UK to investigate the wealth of the Moi family: their report was not formally published but 'leaked' by Wikileaks in August 2007. It indicated that the ex-president's relatives and associates had siphoned off more than £1 billion of public money. (See 'The Looting of Kenya', *The Guardian*, 31 August 2007.) Elsewhere, heads of state became involved in smuggling drugs, guns and other illicit goods, exploiting all the advantages of state sovereignty: diplomatic passports and bags, immunity from prosecution, access to central banks to launder money (Bayart *et al.*, 1999).

Phase V: c. 1992–c. 2002

The fifth phase was marked by both the unprecedented regionalisation of civil wars and ethnic conflicts *but also* by resurgent economic growth after 1995 in states that avoided civil strife. Seventeen wars were fought in Africa in 1990–8: three were inter-state (Chad and Libya, Rwanda and Uganda, Ethiopia and Eritrea) the rest were intrastate, but frequently spilt over international frontiers. On the eve of the millennium, 11 African countries were experiencing prolonged political crises and turbulence and a further 18 were engaged in armed conflict or civil strife. Sixteen million people had been displaced by fear of violence and 3 million were refugees. An estimated 20 million landmines had been laid, including 9 million in Angola alone (World Bank, 2000, p. 55; Newbury, 2002, p. 5).

The worst of the regional conflicts was in the eastern provinces of the DRC where, between 1998 and 2002, 11 countries were involved in Africa's so-called 'First World War' (Prunier, 2009). It originated in the huge social crisis in the Great Lakes region following the Rwandan genocide and the flight of Hutu refugees, under the diktat of genocidal militias, into the eastern Congo after the Rwandan Patriotic Front's (RPF's) victory in the civil war. But a further precondition was the total decay of the Mobutist state, which neither policed its national territory nor protected the population. It could not contain the refugee influx, nor disarm the *génocidaires* amongst them, nor stop RPF forces from crossing the border. After Laurent Kabila fell out with his erstwhile backers in Kigali, a large swathe of eastern Congo was occupied by armed forces from Rwanda, Uganda and Burundi, assisted by a Congolese rebel group (the Congolese Rally for Democracy), while the Kinshasa government was supported at various times by Angola, Zimbabwe, Namibia, the Central African Republic and Chad. Military commanders on both sides looted Congolese mineral resources, with the connivance of their own governments; their troops stole and raped with impunity. The depredations of 'freelance' militias created vicious circles of barbarism: they terrorised adolescents into their ranks by forcing them to commit heinous crimes (such as killing parents or relatives) and unleashed horrific sexual violence against women and girls. They were raped, mutilated and forced into 'domestic' servitude to control their communities through humiliation, fear and despair (Human Rights Watch, 2002). West Africa's regional conflict of the 1990s was characterised by the same barabarism, destabilisation of neighbouring states and plundering of mineral resources.

The mortality attributable to the sprawling conflict in Central Africa is a matter of considerable controversy amongst demographers. The International Rescue Committee (IRC), a highly respected NGO, undertook a series of sample population surveys from which it concluded there were 5.4 million excess deaths in the DRC between August 1998 and April 2007, with an estimated 2.1 million occurring after the formal end of the war in 2002. It reckoned that, up to mid-2001, about 10 per cent of deaths in the east were directly attributable to violence; this implies the shockingly high figure of c. 350,000, but most deaths were due to the greater incidence of preventable and curable disease, especially amongst infants and children. According to the IRC analysis, the war killed, in the main, by displacing populations, degrading infrastructure and denying access to health services (International Rescue Committee, 2008). The headline total – 5 million excess deaths – is frequently cited in the press and other media without any awareness of its dubious methodological basis. For it is arrived at by assuming that, without the war, the crude death rate in the DRC would have been the average for sub-Saharan Africa. Two Belgian demographers have demonstrated that the headline total is impossibly high by comparing the registration of electors in 2005–6 with the last population census in the DRC in 1984. Electoral registration was compulsory for everyone over the age of 18 and the elector's card is a sought-after means of identification, so very probably 95 per cent of the adult population was registered. By projecting forward age and gender-specific mortality rates from the 1984 census they cautiously estimate that the demographic deficit attributable to the war was around 300,000 (Lambert and Lohlé-Tart, 2009). They do *not* question the accuracy of the mortality data in the IRC surveys; it is the counter-factual deduction that the population would have been 5 million greater without the war which they deny. They argue that expectation of life in Congo-Zaire peaked around 1979, and then declined with general impoverishment, the collapse of health care and social services, and the onset of the HIV/Aids epidemic. This demographic regression long preceded the outbreak of the conflict and its basic cause was the decay of the Mobutu regime. The one cheering finding in this as yet unsettled controversy is that by 2008 violent death was quite *rare* in the DRC: of the 2898 deaths tablulated in the most recent IRC survey only 14 (0.4 per cent) were due to violence.

An exclusive focus on war and regression in millennial Africa would be very misleading. Until 2008, Africa was experiencing the longest episode of strong economic growth since the 1960s and there was cautious talk of the sub-continent having reached 'a turning point' (Arbache *et al.*, 2008). Per capita income grew on average by 1.6 per cent a year in the late 1990s and by 2–3 per cent a year in the early 2000s. During 2000–6, about 26 countries, accounting for about 70 per cent of the region's population, had GDP growth rates exceeding 4 per cent a year, while as many as 14 exceeded 5.5 per cent. The underlying cause was improving prices for Africa's commodity exports, which more than cancelled out the impact of rising oil prices on oil importers, coupled with a below double-digit rate of inflation. A novel factor spurring on the commodity boom was Chinese demand for minerals and other resources, and Chinese investment in mining and infrastructure. Chinese–African trade grew five-fold between 1997 and 2006, by when China had replaced Britain as Africa's third most important trading partner (after the USA and France). In the first ten months of 2005, Chinese–African trade grew by a staggering 39 per cent. We should note, though, that at this date Chinese–African trade represented only two-fifths of the US–African trade volume. Over a quarter of Chinese trade was with Angola, which supplied about 13 per cent of China's oil imports in 2004. Chinese companies have been less averse than their western counterparts to investing in 'risky', war-torn and unstable countries (such as the DRC) and have undertaken infrastructural projects that are not strictly commercial, but financed through 'tied' Chinese aid. African governments regard China as a more congenial trading partner and donor than the West because Chinese officials are punctilious about respecting national sovereignty, do not attach political conditionalities to aid, and do not criticise African corruption in public (Tull, 2006).

Whether economic growth stemmed the rising tide of impoverishment is debatable. The Commission for Africa noted in 2005: 'Poverty and hunger are deepening in sub-Saharan Africa. The number of poor people is expected to rise from 315 million in 1999 to 404 million people by 2015' (Commission for Africa, 2005, p. 102). However, World Bank economists more recently estimated that the proportion of Africa's population living below $1.25 a day *fell* from 58.7 per cent in 1996 to 51.2 per cent in 2005 (Chen and Ravallion, 2008, Table 7). In South Asia, the corresponding fall was from 47.1 per cent to 40.3 per cent. It is worth noting that the proportion living below $2 a day was virtually identical in both regions (73 per cent in Africa, 73.9 per cent in South Asia), from which we can deduce that Africa's poverty is 'deeper'. But on this evidence, the trend was positive; whether it will continue, given the contraction in world demand, is another matter.

Having sketched out a chronological framework, I will now look more closely at three key issues.

Stagnant agriculture and the climacteric of the later 1970s

The general crisis that overtook Africa from 1979 was first and foremost an agricultural crisis. The great majority of Africans earned their livelihood from agriculture and subsistence-oriented production still accounted for more than half of farm output. National accounts invariably underestimated agriculture's share of GDP because agricultural output was valued at the prices governments paid to producers, which were below export or import prices, while the value of production in industry and services was inflated by subsidies and protection. The World Bank's report on *Accelerated Development in Sub-Saharan Africa* was surely right to assert: 'Agricultural output is the single most important determinant of overall economic growth and its sluggish record of recent years is the principal factor underlying the poor economic performance of the countries of this region' (World Bank, 1981, p. 45). From 1970 to 1985, the expansion of agricultural output averaged only 1.4 per cent a year, while population growth accelerated to 3.2 per cent annually.

The most visible symptom of stagnant agriculture was mounting food deficits: 23 African countries faced serious or even dire food emergencies in 1983, when cereal production was its lowest since 1973.

Mass famine mortality returned to the sub-continent after nearly half a century without widespread famines. By the late 1980s, about one in four Africans (over 100 million people) faced chronic food insecurity (Iliffe, 1987, p. 230; World Bank, 1989, pp. 10, 89). It was, to be sure, a natural disaster: the southern African drought of 1983 was the worst in recorded history. But it was also the result of a decline in per capita food output with social causes. In about two-thirds of African countries, food output and availability per head fell during the 1970s, in the worst affected by as much as 30 per cent or more. Nearly half faced serious shortages by 1980 – *before* the great drought – when grain production per capita in the 24 most seriously afflicted countries averaged about one-fifth less than in 1970 (Eicher, 1986; Lofchie, 1987; Commins *et al.*, 1986). Africa was the only major world region to experience such a reversal in food production and availability: the increase in basic cereal productivity in Africa in the decade 1973–82 was less than one-third of that achieved in Asia. In 1973, Africa – with 9.4 per cent of the world's population – produced 4 per cent of the world's cereals; in 1983, it produced 3.9 per cent with 11 per cent of the world's population (Christensen and Witucki, 1986). To meet the food deficit, cereal imports rose from 1.2 million tons a year in 1961–3 to 4.1 million in 1974 and to 8.1 million in 1986, when 3.1 million tons were provided as food aid. Commercial imports of food grain grew more than three times as fast as population in the 1970s.

For food production to have kept pace with population increase would have been a real achievement, given that there so many more dependents to feed. But for it to lag far behind, while South Asia was achieving self-sufficiency in food grains, stands in need of explanation. The environmental checks – the encroachment of deserts, the deterioration of fragile soils – were severe, but more fundamental was the dysfunctional 'regulatory syndrome' which inhibited agricultural development. State intervention in produce markets and over-valued exchange rates created disincentives for farmers to increase production. The monopoly marketing agencies for staple food crops, which most countries instituted, did not in themselves seriously distort markets: their operations were easily evaded because food is grown virtually everywhere and has many outlets. Probably no more than 10–30 per cent of the food crops designated for government control passed through official channels, though by imposing official, *country-wide* prices they compelled food producers living near towns to absorb the transport costs of more remotely located farmers. Tanzania, for example, paid farmers everywhere a uniform price for maize, which discouraged regional specialisation, increased transportation costs and encouraged smuggling across borders.

However, the basic cause of sluggish output lay in the internal terms of trade between agriculture and industry. The prices food producers received deteriorated relative to the prices they paid for basic consumer goods, agricultural implements and other farm inputs. Import-substituting industrialisation created highly protected domestic markets for local manufacturers, who were under no compulsion to improve efficiency and lower costs or even fully satisfy rural demand. Price controls on foodstuffs in urban markets inhibited the tendency for prices to equilibrate. Over-valued exchange rates gave food importers a market advantage over domestic producers. In short, the terms of trade were systematically biased against rural producers and in favour of urban consumers, who benefited from food subsidies and minimum wage legislation. In some countries, the basis of reciprocal trade between town and country had eroded away by the early 1980s with the disappearance from the countryside of such consumer items as soap, cloth, sugar, radio batteries, bicycle tyres and cooking oil. Once instituted, the anti-agricultural bias in import-substituting industrialisation was self-reinforcing: the ongoing capital requirements of infant industries (which never grew up) starved the agrarian economy of investment, while the poor returns of farming deepened rural poverty and hastened the drift to the towns.

Less visible than food shortages, but equally symptomatic of stagnant agriculture, was the falling quantity of agricultural exports. During the 1960s, exports volumes grew at nearly 2 per cent a year. They declined by 3 per cent a year between 1973 and 1980, and for the rest of the decade they were between one-quarter and a fifth below the quantities exported in the later 1960s. Africa's share of non-fuel exports from developing countries was halved between 1970 and 1978 (falling from 18.6 per cent to 9.2 per cent) because competitors in South East Asia and Latin America proved more adaptable to changing market conditions. Between 1970 and 1984, Africa's share of world markets for coffee, cocoa and cotton shrank by 13 per cent, 33 per cent and 29 per cent respectively. The only commodity in which it increased market share was tea (World Bank, 1989, pp. 19–21). The export volumes of the staple tree crops of former British West Africa fell precipitously: cocoa exports from Ghana and Nigeria were halved between 1965 and 1980; Nigeria's palm kernel exports shrank by over three-quarters. The staple exports of Senegal (groundnuts and groundnut oil), of Uganda (coffee and cotton) and of Angola (coffee) also fell sharply. The agricultural trade of some countries boomed: Kenya's coffee exports doubled in volume between 1965 and 1980 and cocoa exports from Côte d'Ivoire rose two and half times. But, for sub-Saharan Africa as a whole, the marketed volumes of the major agricultural exports were no higher at the end of the 1970s than in late 1950s. Increasing domestic consumption and processing accounted for a small fraction of falling export volumes, which were essentially a matter of stagnant production.

Why did production stagnate? One answer might be that international demand flattened off, which was reflected in deteriorating terms of trade for primary producers. During the early 1980s world market prices for many agricultural commodities fell to their lowest level since the Second World War: though they recovered somewhat by the end of the decade, average prices were still 33 per cent lower in 1989 than in 1980. The decline in the terms of trade was most pronounced in sub-Saharan Africa and Latin America, regions which had been relatively favoured in world markets in the 1970s. But the deteriorating terms of trade do not fit the chronology of Africa's agricultural decline: exports volumes began to fall in 1973, when – as we have seen – world market prices for many primary commodities were rising. Between 1974 and 1977, many African countries were cushioned from escalating energy costs by large price rises for such commodities as coffee and cocoa. Because of the cocoa boom, Ghana's commodity terms of trade improved by 5.5 per cent a year between 1969–71 and 1977–9, though this commercial opportunity was squandered by the precipitous decline in the volume of cocoa exports. Côte d'Ivoire's commodity terms of trade improved by 2.9 per cent a year in the same period; with increasing exports volumes, Ivorian income terms of trade rose by 8.3 per cent annually. For a brief period, OPEC's example and the commodity boom created an illusion of economic power shifting to 'Third World' primary producers. It gave African leaders the confidence to accelerate their indigenisation programmes, nationalise key industries and borrow heavily from abroad to finance development in the expectation that buoyant public revenues would cover interest charges. The adverse terms of trade in the 1980s exacerbated and prolonged Africa's agricultural crisis, but it originated endogenously, in the farm-gate prices producers received and the public-marketing agencies to which they were obliged to sell.

Most states inherited or created public monopsonies for their export crops, with the result that parastatal agencies handled about 90 per cent of palm oil exports, 80 per cent of coffee exports, 70 per cent of cocoa exports, 65 per cent of tea exports and 60 per cent of raw cotton exports (Bates, 1981, p. 12). Distrust of commercial markets was so pervasive that it was not uncommon for a dozen public-marketing agencies to be operating in a country's rural sector, many with such additional responsibilities as providing credit to farmers, distributing inputs and conducting agricultural research. The price paid to the producer was usually between one-third and two-thirds of the international 'free on board' (FOB) price – a differential that frequently widened in the 1960s and 70s and became a powerful incentive for smuggling, though the parastatals' operations were difficult to evade because export crops were grown in particular regions and had few marketing outlets.

Marketing surpluses were rarely used to compensate farmers for downward fluctuations in world prices. After legal restrictions on the use of accumulated funds were relaxed in the 1960s, most surpluses were transferred to governments and became a source of investment for import-substituting industrialisation. Export agriculture accounted for about half of the growth of real output between the mid-1950s and late 1970s, and generated between 20 per cent and 40 per cent of state revenue, but received a disproportionately small share of public investment. Development expenditures were invariably concentrated in urban areas, the most extreme instance of this bias being in Ghana, where less than 5 per cent of capital spending was in the rural sector (*ibid.*, p. 18). To promote local processing industries, monopoly marketing boards were commonly required to supply favoured public enterprises with copra, coffee, sisal and other commodities at artificially depressed prices in order to lower their costs (*ibid.*, p. 25).

To Robert Bates, the most influential academic critic of the state monopsonies, they appeared inefficient, over-staffed and often riddled with malfeasance. Their failings included long delays in payments to farmers or payments in worthless scrip, ruinously high operating margins, extortion from their clients and woeful standards of accountability (Bates, 1983; Lofchie, 1986). Monopoly marketing was the principal factor in the continuous decline of producer prices as a proportion of export prices. Cocoa and coffee producers received on average from 60–5 per cent of the export price in 1960, but around 40 per cent in 1980. The trend varied from country to country, but even in 'farmer-friendly' countries such as Côte d'Ivoire, Cameroon and Togo it was downwards. Only cotton escaped the trend, but largely because the farmer's return was miserably low in the first instance: as a proportion of cotton export prices, producer prices rose from 22 per cent to 26 per cent between 1960 and 1980.

What needs emphasising is that states' 'take' from export agriculture grew during the 1970s largely from the marketing agencies' failure to pass on the considerable increases in international commodity prices to farmers. Economic 'exploitation' – in the sense of denying farmers part of the return they ought to have gained from world markets – came from the state controlling the 'gate' to these markets. In Francophone Africa, the scale of the levies enabled the price 'stabilisation funds' to increase their role in the economy. From being straightforward agencies for market regulation they became institutional investors. Objectively speaking, inter-sectoral transfers were not irrational, but expenditure tended to rise to whatever level was consonant with total revenue, and the volatility of such sources of finance was a major reason for deteriorating financial balances during the later 1970s (Contamin and Fauré, 1995, pp. 150–1).

The progressive over-valuation of currencies imposed a further, hidden tax on export producers. At independence, exchange rates had fairly reflected the buoyant demand for African countries' exports and their adequate reserves of foreign exchange. However, in the 1960s and 1970s, domestic inflation, generated by budget deficits, oustripped foreign inflation: the purchasing power of African currencies abroad (converted at the official exchange rate) became greater than at home. In Ghana, Uganda and Zaire, for example, the exchange rate appreciated by over 100 per cent between 1963 and 1978 (World Bank, 1981, p. 25). Official exchange rates could only be maintained by controls, and the black-market premiums on hard foreign currency averaged about 300 per cent in the early 1980s (the highest premiums in the developing world). Parities were much less distorted in the CFA countries, where domestic inflation was held in check. As the domestic purchasing power of money fell, farmers exchanged their crops for a diminishing bundle of goods. Faced with poor, and increasingly uncertain returns, they either diversified into petty trade or joined the drift to the cities. If they stayed on the land, their own food security depended increasingly on non-farm activities. They were reluctant to invest labour and capital in long-term projects, such as soil conservation, water-control or better grain silos (Berry, 1993b). Urban bias produced a disgruntled peasantry, too poor to raise farm productivity or create an expanding domestic market for urban products.

What must strike any historian of post-colonial Africa is the stubborn persistence, in predominantly rural societies, of policies patently biased against rural interests. In 1989, World Bank economists ruefully noted that 'the unsuccessful agricultural policies of the 1960s and 1970s [which depend excessively on public administrations unequal to the task] are still common today' (World Bank, 1989, p. 90). Administered prices, parastatal export marketing and price-distorting subsidies were singled out for criticism – much as they had been at the beginning of the decade. Why did African rulers countenance such counter-productive policies for so long? They were under no pressure to relinquish them because illiberal political systems stifled dissent, but they were also wary of the mass volatility of urban consumers. Between 1960 and 1980, the total urban population grew by about 6 per cent annually, while the population of capital cities mushroomed by 8.5 per cent a year. Migrants were attracted to cities by the great disparity between rural and urban life chances: urban wages were substantially higher than smallholders' incomes (until structural adjustment induced a near-universal collapse of real wages in the 1980s) and infant and early-child mortality were lower in the cities. To a privileged minority of employees in the formal sector, the cities offered state-enforced minimum wages and heavily subsidised amenities such as public housing, piped water, electricity and medical care. These social goods were mostly unavailable to the under-employed majority eking out a living in the informal sector and, because inequalities were so transparent in the cities, their sense of relative deprivation was acute. Amongst an already discontented population, rising food prices frequently triggered unrest and riot. The spectre and reality of popular anger induced a siege mentality amongst politicians, soldiers and bureaucrats. Their own political survival depended on short-term palliatives for urban discontent (such as food subsidies) and few governments contemplated serious reform of their agricultural pricing systems. Even famine conditions in the countryside did not deflect them from the policies that were the principal cause of the agricultural crisis; mass distress was used as a source of leverage on donor agencies rather than a signal for reform. The urban coalition with an interest in cheap food carried greater political clout than the isolated rural majority. Moreover, anti-rural policies were inextricable from 'crony statism': the parastatal marketing agencies contributed significantly to government budgets and provided highly paid employment to political cronies who diverted public funds to clientelistic networks.

De-regulating agriculture: winners and losers in the 1990s

The proportion of Africa's population affected by the 'regulatory syndrome' fell steeply in the 1990s: in the coastal countries from 72 per cent to 19 per cent and in the landlocked countries from 57 per cent to 13 per cent (Collier and O'Connell, 2008, Table 2.10, p. 99). Parastatal marketing agencies were dismantled and farm-gate prices for agricultural exports moved closer to world prices, which were themselves rising. This was not just a consequence of indebted African governments doing the bidding of the international financial institutions (IFFs): so-called external conditionality was only effective in bringing about market reform where there was a strong domestic movement for change. Farmers' prices improved dramatically in Ghana after Jerry Rawlings's government performed a volte face in 1983 and embarked on economic reforms; similarly, Nigerian farmers' prices improved when General Babangida launched a structural adjustment programme in 1986 (see Chapter 6, this volume). A more general improvement in real producer prices for exports followed the democracry wave of 1989–92. When it tabulated price movements in 19 countries up to 1995–7, the World Bank found that farmers' real prices for their export crops had risen in 15 (in Uganda, Tanzania, Mozambique and Nigeria by 50 per cent or more) (World Bank, 2000, Fig. 6.3, p. 183).

Kenya was a notable exception: the introduction of competitive politics in the early 1990s appears to have worked against 'farmer-friendly' reforms by provoking ethnic tensions revolving around land ownership and the control of the state. The regime of Daniel arap Moi sought to redistribute income and wealth away for the Kikuyu, who had been the main beneficiaries of economic growth in the 1960s and 70s, and towards his Kalenjin-led ethnic coalition. This 'regime shift towards redistribution for political expediency destroy[ed] the policy environment and the incentive structure for economic agents' (Mwega and Ndung'u, 2008, p. 326).

In Côte d'Ivoire modestly improving prices for export producers in the 1990s did not wholly compensate for the price falls in the 1980s. The country's failure to recover economically in the later 1990s is especially poignant, given its impressive record as an agricultural exporter in 1960–79 and as the industrial hub of Francophone West Africa. The economy received a short-term boost from the 50 per cent devaluation of the CFA franc in 1994 but GDP per person employed declined every year from 1999 to 2006; the cumulative fall was about 20 per cent. The proximate cause was acute political and ethno-regional conflict from 1999, which culminated in the civil war of 2002–3 and de facto partition between the insurgent-controlled north and government-controlled south. But behind the anti-immigrant feeling and virulent sense of indigenous identity (*l'Ivoirité*), which political leaders unscrupulously manipulated, was an economy in thrall to the world price of cocoa and a social fabric perilously frayed by the 'open' immigration needed to cultivate the crop. Between 1960 and 2000, Côte d'Ivoire's share of the world cocoa market rose from about 7 per cent to 40 per cent. Cocoa occupied over half the permanent crop land by the late 1990s, and accounted for over 50 per cent of exports and 21 per cent of GDP. By normal commercial criteria, over-specialisation in cocoa made little sense, because from 1985 onwards its real international price was consistently below the price level in the 1960s. However, to the Burkinabé and other Sahelian immigrants into the forest belt, cocoa represented the opportunity for greatly improved living standards. Using a customary contract, they had obtained use rights to communally owned land, which Houphouët-Boigny openly encouraged them to regard as their 'own'. Immigrant land ownership became a socio-political time-bomb. In 1998, a law was passed stipulating that only Ivorians could own land. Immigrants could retain lifetime usage rights, but their land would revert to the state after their deaths, without compensation to their heirs. By this date, immigrants – so-called – were 26 per cent of the population, though nearly half the Burkinabé and Malians were Ivorian-born and many Ivorians were of mixed immigrant-indigenous parentage. At stake in the unresolved conflict is the redefinition of Ivorian citizenship and sovereignty.

The business of politics and the patrimonial state

Whether African states were ruled by civilian presidents or military men, their political life exhibited a strong family resemblance. Political ideology was rarely a powerful integrative force either within the political class or between political leaders and led. Mozambique and Angola, after FRELIMO and the MPLA declared themselves Marxist-Leninist vanguard parties, were ideological states in that sense, but they were exceptional. Elsewhere, ideology was superficially smeared over a body politic held together by patron–client networks and animated by political rent-seeking. Once the grand objective of independence had been achieved, what motivated African politics – not entirely but to a pervasive degree – was the pursuit of public office for private gain, both for oneself and one's kin and for a wider network of clients. Politics was personalistic, materialistic and opportunistic. Political life revolved around chains of connection between those in positions of power within the state apparatus and those seeking to use their connections to enhance economic and social power outside. The arena of politics was much wider than the sphere of formal political activity because the state – in Bayart's analogy – grew like a 'rhizome' beneath the surface of society (Bayart, 1993, pp. 218–19). Douglas Rimmer's comments on West African states apply to Africa more generally: 'Whatever the matter at stake – an industrial licence or a school building, an irrigation project or a clinic – what counted was having one's own man in a position of authority, whether in political office, the party, the public service or a parastatal body. The dominant purpose of electoral activity was the control of such preferment' (Rimmer, 1984, p. 215). The disappearance of party politics made little if any difference. One-party states resulted not only from the intolerance of governments for opposition, but also from the disinclination of the oppositions to be automatically excluded from government patronage. We should not overlook the redistributive function of this form of political life and its capacity to attenuate social contrasts that would otherwise have seemed unbearable. As was drily remarked of Côte d'Ivoire: 'A number of the high functionaries of the regime and a great body of petty officials are ... paid for doing nothing. The better-positioned among them ... accumulate relatively vast fortunes but, at the same time, the system ensures a significant redistribution of wealth' (Coquery-Vidrovitch, 1988b, p. 105).

What accounts for this state of affairs? One way of approaching the answer is to insist that politics was not so different elsewhere. To cite a contemporary parallel in the heartland of post-war Europe, the hegemony of Christian Democracy in the first Italian Republic was marked by intense factionalism within the dominant party, clientelism and systemic corruption. Italy's public and parastatal sector was invaded by clientelistic networks; regional party bosses distributed public employment and other 'goods' to their followings. Given these underlying similarities, African politics needs to be 'banalised', its political actors seen as ordinary men with ordinary motives for what they do (Bayart, 1993, p. 268). This is a salutary corrective to accounts which treat African politicians as an exotic species: they are not innately more grasping than politicians elsewhere and their notorious corruptibility does not arise from inherent moral flaws. Many African social organisations are run with exemplary probity by their officials, who are routinely entrusted with large sums of money. But we also need to recognise that Africans act politically within culturally transmitted mentalities and structures which are distinctive to the sub-continent's history. Its abundant land and small populations have determined that wealth and power were accumulated through the control of people. What set the 'big man' apart in Africa's political communities were the number of his (usually conscripted) dependents: wives, children, pawns, slaves, kin and non-kin. 'Big men' presided over intricate networks of clientage involving reciprocal but unequal relations with 'small boys'. When the Europeans imposed their wafer-thin administrations on African societies, 'big men' were indispensable collaborators. They became clients of their European patrons in the territorial administration and were rewarded with salaries, titles and legitimacy, but also with the despotic power to command African labour and deny access to land. This dimension of colonial rule proved a crucial precondition for post-colonial politics because it made authoritarian patron–client relations the basic mode of access to the state and its resources (Berman, 1998).

Interlaced with the 'big man' syndrome was the construction of ethnicity in the colonial period, when Africans took on social and political identities with a broader, more inclusive frame of reference but which also delineated them more clearly from other groups. Many of the processes which ostensibly should have blurred the sense of ethnic identity in colonial Africa accentuated it: labour migration, mission schooling, the coming of literacy and the standardisation of vernaculars, the competition for jobs in the lower echelons of the bureaucracy – these all drew co-ethnics together, and tended to set them apart from people of different speech, customs and myths of origin. An exemplary account of 'ethnogenesis' is J.D.Y. Peel's study of the Yoruba-speaking area of Western Nigeria. He found that the vast bulk of people who now know themselves as Yoruba did not do so in 1900. Originally the word referred to only one Yoruba grouping, the Oyo. Other Yoruba-speaking groups (such as the Ijeshas) began to adopt this ethnic identity from the 1920s, as migration, cash cropping, education and conversion to the world religions drew more people into a Nigeria-wide sphere of social relations. From the late 1930s, when nationalism really began to get under way, the Yoruba began to shape themselves politically against other ethnicities, especially the Igbo in the political crucible of Lagos (Peel, 1983, 1989). Paradoxically, consciousness of being Nigerian came (usually through migration) with an *increased* rather than a diminished ethnic consciousness as Yoruba. In Peel's account, colonialism, by extending the ambit of social interaction and by linking communal leadership to western education, provided a necessary context for the construction of modern ethnic identities, but the Ijeshas were the main actors in their own drama.

The national movements believed (or, at least, said) that 'For the sake of the nation, the tribe would die', but the advent of independent states did not dissolve patron–client ties, nor loosen their articulation around notions of ethnic solidarity and intra-ethnic competition. As a moral community, one's ethnic group was more deeply felt than the nation: it was a source of honour and respect to which a migrant could look for support and to which he owed obligations. It guaranteed him access to land on his return to his natal village and provided him with a bride. The converse of 'moral' ethnicity was political 'tribalism': the stereotyping and distrust of people of other ethnicities with whom one increasingly competed for jobs, scholarships and commercial opportunities. Unsurprisingly, the crucible of 'moral' ethnicity and political 'tribalism' was the modern commercial and administrative city, where immigrants acquired an acute sense of their own and others' social identities. Modern institutions, such as universities, which ought to have been oases of supra-ethnic sentiment, were important sites for the articulation of political 'tribalism'. Kenneth Dike, the first black African to gain a PhD in History and a founding professor of African history at Ibadan University, bitterly complained: 'It must be said to our shame that the Nigerian intellectual, far from being an influence for national integration, is the greatest exploiter of parochial and clannish sentiment' (quoted in Joseph, 1987, p. 52).

Some 30 years ago, the Nigerian political scientist, Peter Ekeh, argued that a structural legacy of colonialism for African politics was the existence of two 'publics'. One was the 'primordial' public of one's ethnic community in which the same moral imperatives operated as in the private realm of family and kin. Under colonialism, it was legally defined by 'native' or 'customary' law. The other was the 'civic' public historically associated with the colonial administration, and in post-colonial societies with the national state, which was legally defined by western, positive law. This 'civic' public – Ekeh argued – had no moral linkages to the private realm and lacked generalised moral imperatives. 'Natives' had been excluded from the colonial 'civic' public; when admitted to it as nominal citizens of the new national states, they conceived the 'civic' public more as a Hobbesian arena of struggle than a community of rights and obligations. Political actors straddled these two 'publics': in competitive elections, their bases of support were found in 'primordial' publics to whom they had moral obligations, but the material rewards of political action were to be found in the Hobbesian arena. It was not that there were no moral sanctions within the 'civic' public on corruption and malfeasance; rather, moral repugnance was always inflected by loyalty to one's 'primordial' public. Behaviour which to others appeared grossly self-serving could, from the perspective of one's clients in the 'primordial' public, seem quite laudable if it sustained the reciprocal obligations of patronage (Ekeh, 1975).

Even before independence, moral ethnicity and political tribalism were undermining the solidarity of the nationalist coalition. The ethic and language of nationalism had been socially radical; its values were redistributive, egalitarian and democratic. In practice, while agitating to overthrow the colonial regime, the disparate elements in the nationalist coalition – which were usually ethnically or communally defined – were trying to block one another from appropriating the colonial legacy. Competitive elections and the Africanisation of the bureaucracy began to make ethnicity increasingly important as a basis of political support and access to the higher levels of the state. In West Africa – the most politically advanced region – competition amongst the nationalist groups dominated political life after self-government was introduced in the 1950s; the colonial power became a referee rather than the opponent. Independence enhanced the centrifugal tensions because the material rewards of political control of the sovereign state in highly administered economies were so great, and the disadvantages of being excluded from political control over the economy were so palpable. In the words of Claude Ake, the Nigerian political scientist: 'The struggle for power [within the political class] was so absorbing that everything else, including development, was marginalized' (Ake, 1996, p. 7). The electoral struggle in the Hobbesian terrain of the 'civic' public was marred by violence, vote rigging, the intimidation of opponents' supporters and other abuses; unsurprisingly, the victors lacked legitimacy in the eyes of their opponents. The elites who won the struggle for public office had power, but not authority. They found themselves increasingly isolated, and ever more reliant on 'extra-legal' and executive measures to suppress opposition: preventive detention, detention without trial, the declaration of states of emergency which permitted censoring or closing the free press. The degeneration of political competition into internecine war paved the way for military coups, which essentially formalised a reality that was already firmly established. 'It was not the military that caused military rule by intervening in politics; rather, it was the character of politics that engendered military rule by degenerating into warfare, inevitably propelling the specialists of warfare into the lead role' (*ibid.*, p. 6).

The terms 'the politics of the belly' and 'crony statism' have been widely used to describe the form of political life I have described. They carry rather different connotations; the former conveys the gluttonous striving after 'a slice of the national cake' – to use the popular Nigerian expression – and gets us deeper into the everyday lived culture of politics; the latter refers to the use of clientelistic networks of politicians, businessmen and bureaucrats to build mutual support through the extraction and distribution of political rents. Interrelated characteristics of 'crony statism' were the expansion of the size of the state, including the creation of an extensive parastatal sector; and the purchase of primarily urban popular support through state welfare services and food subsidies. There were clearly intimate connections between the two: the 'politics of the belly' ensured popular acquiescence in the exchange of political power and wealth between elites under 'crony statism'. Of course, the great unintended consequence of 'crony statism' was the debilitation of African states: most were transformed in a way that made them 'over-mighty' yet administratively weak. They became highly personalistic and authoritarian, but ineffective instruments of positive government – what Thomas Callaghy dubbed 'lame Leviathans' (Callaghy, 1989). The authoritarian forms of rule which prevailed in them resulted not from high levels of power and legitimacy, but from the tenuousness of public authority. Typically, dominant elites 'recreated' centralising administrative states – closely resembling their colonial predecessors – and patrimonialised them. In the process, autonomous political movements, normally based in the towns, which expressed emerging class interests and divisions, had either been dissolved or incorporated into the single, ruling party. In their turn, ruling parties had increasingly become the hollowed-out instruments of the country's president and his ruling clique, and central executive authority was personalised around a presidential ruler.

Academics vigorously debated how best to characterise the state and the ruling class without reaching any consensus. Marxists usually conceived of the state in functionalist terms as 'the institutional ensemble ensuring the reproduction of the social relations of production' and their favoured formulae for the ruling class were the 'national', 'bureaucratic' or 'comprador' bourgeoisie. It was recognised that African rulers exercised 'relative autonomy' vis à vis their own societies and the international economic system, but in the final analysis they were agents or proxies of metropolitan capitalist interests and the multi-national corporations. Richard Sklar challenged the fundamental Marxist premise that the social relations of production determined class formation: political and military power were independent determinants of class relations and irreducible to economic structures. By seizing control of the state, he argued, African rulers consolidated a dominant class which engaged with foreign capitalists out of self-interest, not subservience (Sklar, 1979; see also Young, 1982b). The notion of the state serving some 'functional' purpose on behalf of the capitalist mode of production was utterly ridiculous with respect to 'failing' states, like Uganda under Idi Amin (1971–9) or Ghana under Colonel Acheampong (1972–8); in both, misgovernance led to a regression from commodity to subsistence production, rampant hoarding and a massive exodus of skilled and professional workers (Jefferies, 1989). Even in better-governed states, ruling regimes were patently not instruments either of the 'national' or the 'international bourgeoisie'; foreign entrepreneurs and multi-national corporations often found them unreliable and difficult partners. In an effort to make political theory more congruent with African realities, Callaghy and others argued that the ruling class in most states was 'a political aristocracy': its basic values, its power and its economic base resulted from its relationship with the state, which was the major avenue of upward mobility, status, power and wealth (Callaghy, 1989, p. 92).

In a stimulating paper, Bruce Berman argued for a persistence in the post-colonial states of the unique linkage forged under colonialism between bureaucratic authoritarianism, patronage and clientelism, and ethnic fragmentation and competition. The continuity of institutions, identities and power relations proved more consequential – he argued – than the disruption of independence. Writing in the late 1990s, he forecast that without a trans-ethnic public arena grounded in universalistic norms, African politics would continue to be plagued by 'uncivil nationalism' in which the desire for communal identity and social responsibility would conflict with the tribal competition for the levers of state patronage (Berman, 1998, pp. 309, 334–8).

Structural adjustment and after

Africa's total external debt increased from $6 billion in 1970 to $134 billion in 1988, which was roughly equivalent to its GDP and three and a half times export earnings. Though the absolute level of debt was higher in Latin America, in relative terms Africa was the world's most indebted region (World Bank, 1989, p. 20). Until late 1982, the economically stronger states could borrow commercially to cover what they hoped were temporary shortfalls in their balance of payments (nearly half the commercial debt was incurred by Nigeria). But this source of funding dried up when the adverse movement in Africa's terms of trade made commercial lending too risky.

This level of debt had not been incurred because African governments were invarariably incorrigible spendthrifts; many had been encouraged by the IFIs to borrow abroad to finance development at a time when real world interest rates were negative. It was their inability to service their debts in the world recession of the early 1980s, when real interest rates turned positive and credit conditions became harsher, which made the debt problem so critical. Public expenditure could not be maintained at existing levels without borrowing and budget deficits in excess of 7 per cent of GDP soon became the norm. Between 1980 and the early 1990s, indebtedness compelled over 40 African countries to apply to the IMF and/or the World Bank for loans to support their balance of payments and cover their deficits. (The first to do so was Senegal.) These loans were made conditional on changes in economic policy and practice, which were intended, in the first instance, to correct external imbalances (that is, bring exports and imports into line) and reduce budget deficits and, in the longer term, to restructure economies to give greater weight to private economic actors and market forces. Governments pledged – *inter alia* – to devalue and float their currencies, curb public expenditure, dismantle monopoly marketing organisations, cut food subsidies to urban households and fertiliser subsidies to farmers, and charge their citizens for welfare services. The privatisation of state-owned enterprises was also a common condition for further lending, although rather few were sold off before the mid-1990s because indigenous buyers with sufficient capital were hard to find.

Western governments, which in the final analysis underwrote lending to Africa, were generally happy for the World Bank to take the lead role in pressing for reform. (The exception was France, and the chief cause of friction was the CFA franc.) Structural adjustment had many losers – particularly amongst urban elites deprived of cheap imports, subsidies, political patronage and even secure employment – and the Bank acted as a 'lightning rod' for their anger and resentment. Moreover, it could plausibly claim to be an apolitical institution, making recommendations on technical grounds. The Bank's articles of agreement prohibit interference in the political affairs of any member state by its officials who should not be influenced by a state's political character in reaching their decisions. 'Only economic considerations shall be relevant' (given in Lancaster, 1997, p. 187). Its landmark report, *Accelerated Development in Sub-Saharan Africa* (World Bank, 1981, also known as the Berg Report after its principal author, Elliot Berg) was an *implicit* condemnation of state-led development, and a rationale for structural adjustment lending. But the Bank did not condemn single-party authoritarianism, nor state ownership of the economy as such. When, around 1990, it began pressing for 'good governance' as a pre-requisite for sustained growth, the issue was not raised with respect to individual states or governments, and the critique of 'poor governance' was restricted to the civil service, public administration and the legal system. Political reform was not the Bank's concern.

Fifteen years or so ago no issue stirred more controversy in African studies than structural adjustment. Africans bitterly (and understandably) resented the usurpation of national sovereignty by the Bank, whose staff effectively designed the reform programmes, and their continent's informal recolonisation by an army of expatriate 'experts' lacking any democratic accountability. Sympathetic western academics were appalled by the amoral economism of the Bank's prescriptions, which appeared to be sacrificing social welfare on the altar of market efficiency (Ferguson, 2006, ch. 3). When published in 1994, the Bank's account of *Adjustment in Africa: Reforms, Results and the Road Ahead* (World Bank, 1994) was received with anger and derision on the left. The editors of the *Review of African Political Economy* insisted that Africa's problems were predominantly 'external' in origin and deplored the Bank's crude application of a standard package of measures to a general set of putative internal 'deficiencies', when specific measures tailored to particular circumstances were needed. They accused the Bank of 'attempting to force its ideological hegemony on development history, theory and policy'; constructing 'the statistics and evidence to bolster its own version of reality'; and '[refusing] to allow the facts to interfere with its view of the world' (Loxley and Seddon, 1994).

Today, it seems as if the parties to this controversy were shouting past, rather than at each other. Rereading some of the contributions, we would be forgiven for thinking that Africa had been malovently singled out for structural adjustment. In point of fact, many Asian developing economies (Indonesia, South Korea, India) were constrained by similar circumstances (indebtedness, trade imbalances, fiscal deficits) to adopt more or less the same neo-liberal package. Indeed, structural adjustment usually cut deeper into the statist political economies of developing Asia, and effected a more thoroughgoing economic transformation. A key difference, however, was that there were domestic constituencies for 'market-friendly' reforms within Asia, and they were not simply imposed from without. To cite one example, while the Indonesian intelligentsia was promoting the policies needed for international competitiveness, the Nigerian intelligentsia was deriding them. Partly for this reason, Indonesia's relations with the IMF and World Bank were radically better than Nigeria's (Bevan *et al.*, 1999, p. 278).

For African governments, it was politically expedient to claim they were powerless in the face of 'Washington consensus' and to attribute dilapidated public services and plunging civil service salaries solely to structural adjustment; popular discontent was thereby deflected away from their own incompetence and unaccountability. In fact, they retained greater autonomy than the people were given to believe, for the World Bank was reluctant to terminate adjustment lending or cancel adjustment programmes even when borrowing governments failed to comply with loan conditions. Often the threat of urban unrest if austerity bit too deep was more potent than the penalties the IFIs could bring to bear. Zambia is an instructive example: the Kaunda regime became a by-word in the IFIs for incorrigible back-sliding and lacking the political will to adjust demonstrated by Rawlings in Ghana. This simplistic judgement overlooked the different societal constraints on the Zambian government and the intractability of its economic problems. Though Zambia had borrowed from the IMF in the 1970s and early 80s, it resisted pressure to 'adjust' until 1985, when the standard 'reform' package was reluctantly adopted. The kwacha was devalued to reduce imports and increase export earnings, and the government promised to remove price controls and subsidies, freeze the wages of civil servants and raise interest rates to give a positive return to capital. These promises could not be kept in the face of popular discontent. When, in December 1986, the government announced it would stop subsidising 'breakfast meal', a staple of the local diet, 15 people died in the ensuing riots. The subsidy remained. The kwacha's precipitous devaluation impacted so severely on the urban poor that the government severed relations with the IMF and reversed its monetary and financial policies: the kwacha was revalued in May 1987, controls on prices and interest rates were reimposed and a ceiling of 10 per cent of exports set on debt-service payments. The results of this policy reversal were disastrous: the vicious circle of inflation, budget deficit, scarcity of essential commodities and unemployment was exacerbated. At the end of the 1980s Zambia was ineligible to borrow from the World Bank or the IMF, and most of the big donors refused to help until Zambia had regained IMF approval. Meanwhile, relentless impoverishment continued: in 1993, 84.6 per cent of Zambians were living on less than a dollar a day (a proportion exceeded only in Guinea-Bissau) and the poverty 'gap' – or the mean shortfall below the poverty line expressed as a percentage of the poverty line – was the widest in Africa.

Where the World Bank's critics saw a neo-liberal juggernaut, its economists harked on the incompleteness of the reform process: in their view, no African country had achieved a good macroeconomic stance by the early 1990s, though there had been improvements. Fiscal balances were still fragile, inflation was above international levels, and the parallel market premium for foreign exchange remained in most countries (World Bank, 1994, pp. 44, 58, 184). The 'striking finding' of seven country case studies of adjustment was that 'the global wind of change that is redefining the role of the state has not yet swept these countries, at least by contemporary standards' (Husain and Faruqee, 1994, p. 427). Their basic dilemma was that they needed a smaller state, but one which deployed scarce technical and administrative skills more effectively. These desiderata tended to conflict because reducing the public pay roll, and dispensing with public servants' fringe benefits, lowered civil service morale. Across Africa, vast cadres of de-motivated civil servants were either unable or unwilling to implement reforms.

Even Ghana, the 'best performer', received a lukewarm endorsement. From 1983, President Jerry Rawlings had driven through a series of austerity-plus-liberalisation packages with the zeal of the convert. Their benefits were 'large, visible and widely shared' (Leechor, 1994, p. 153). The cedi underwent several drastic devaluations and the parallel market in foreign exchange was eventually eliminated. The prices farmers received for their cocoa had quadrupled in real terms by 1988. Real per capita GDP rose from 1984, inflation was sharply reduced (from 122 per cent in 1983 to 21 per cent in 1990) and investment picked up (from 3.7 per cent to 14.5 per cent in the same period). But Ghana's external debts more than doubled during the 1980s through rescheduling and the ratio of debt service to exports was 48.5 per cent at the end of the decade (Martin, 1993). Moreover, ten years into the reform programme, more than 300 public enterprises were still being subsidised, the civil service was over-staffed, investor confidence was generally low and conditions for attaining growth without foreign aid were unpropitious. Nearly two-thirds of employees in the organised modern sector still worked for the government and public enterprises. The latters' tax privileges and quasi-monopoly status crowded out private investment, which was less than 8 per cent of GDP in 1992 – way below the norm in low-income developing countries. Far from 'reining in' or 'curtailing' the state, structural adjustment had rescued it from ruin: in 1982, at Ghana's economic nadir, government revenue was less than 5 per cent of GDP because the over-taxation of cocoa had eroded away the fiscal base; by the later 1980s, revenue was about 13 per cent of GDP. Government spending expanded continuously during the first four years of reform; social expenditures rose in real terms and as a per centage of GDP. The main social indicators (child mortality, expectation of life) improved, as did the primary school enrolment rate (Leechor, 1994, pp. 153–92).

Whether that was despite, not because of structural adjustment is a moot point, since in most African countries the primary enrolment rate was lower in 1995 than in 1980; it was the only region to experience such a widespread reversal. The educational opportunities of poor children were disproportionately narrowed; enrolment in secondary and tertiary education, which mainly benefited the better off, improved slightly in this period (World Bank, 2000, pp. 105–6). This was grist to the mill of those who maintained that state welfare services atrophied under structural adjustment, and virtually disappeared from the countryside. The objective reality of decrepit schools without textbooks and clinics devoid of medicine is indisputable. Nevertheless, comparative data suggest that we need a more nuanced account of social welfare services in the 1990s than blanket pessimism. *Total* health spending in Africa was 5.6 per cent of GDP, the average for all low- to middle-income countries and distinctly higher than the 4.1 per cent of GDP spent on health in South Asia (World Bank, 2000, Table 4.3, p. 114). Nearly all capital investments in health in the African public sector were financed by donors and NGOs, but even public spending on health was, on average, proportionally higher in Africa than in South Asia. In India and Pakistan, it was less than 1 per cent of GDP; in Zambia 2.3 per cent, Zimbabwe 3.1 per cent, Côte d'Ivoire 1.4 per cent, Ghana 1.8 per cent. Nigeria, at 0.2 per cent, was a large and puzzling exception (World Bank, *World Development Report*, 2000, Table 7, p. 286).

Falling school rolls notwithstanding, public expenditure on education in Africa in 1997 was proportionally higher than in South Asia (4.1 per cent as opposed to 3.1 per cent). There was great variation around the average and educational spending had fallen since 1980 in several African countries: in Côte d'Ivoire, from 7.2 per cent to 5 per cent of GDP, in Zambia from 4.5 per cent to 2.2 per cent, in Nigeria from 6.4 per cent to 0.7 per cent (a fall so staggering that it cries out for further investigation). In Kenya, it had fallen from 6.8 per cent to 6.5

per cent, but this was still proportionally twice as large as public educational expenditure in India (World Bank, *World Development Report*, 2000, Table 6, p. 284). Of course, the raw data tell us nothing about the efficacy with which public funds were allocated, nor their relationship with objective need. African dependency and sickness ratios were higher, so more needed to be spent on education and health. And, clearly, the South Asian states' record in promoting citizens' welfare was not something to be emulated.

In a longer-term perspective, it is evident that African governments found ways of responding to imposed adjustment policies which allowed them to gain political advantage from the process. Half-hearted reform, or even outright non-implementation, carried few penalties because the conditionality attached to restructuring loans proved toothless: aid continued to flow and debts to be rescheduled, however poor a government's record. The language and targets of privatisation programmes were skilfully manipulated in order to perpetuate patronage systems. As intended, structural adjustment restrained the economic activity of governments, which spent less on infrastructure and public works and allowed many developmental functions to devolve to donors and NGOs. Public investment in the 1990s was less than half what it had been in the 1970s. Yet the goal of 'rolling back the state' was only partly achieved and overall government consumption and development expenditures did not decline. This was chiefly because of the influx of foreign aid, which grew by over 5 per cent annually in real terms between 1970 and 1995. Africa received 24 per cent of total Overseas Development Assistance in 1980 and 37 per cent in 1993. Excluding Nigeria and South Africa, the average African country received the equivalent of 12.3 per cent of its GDP in ODA in 1996 (Walle, 2001, p. 7). Aid came mainly as goods and services to governments and, if these are included, the overall resources controlled by governments probably rose by several percentage points of GDP in the 1980s and 90s. Aid enabled governments to 'look after their own' by concentrating their increasingly limited revenues on so-called sovereignty expenditures – central administration, policing and defence – which helped maintain the unity of the political elite. Nicholas van de Walle concluded in 2001 that 'Thanks in part to substantial donor support to state structures, twenty years of crisis have resulted in a bigger state that does less for its citizens, particularly its poor and rural ones' (*ibid.*, p. 65). The flow of aid to African NGOs likewise had the unintended consequence of sustaining elite cohesion because in many countries supposedly private organisations are offshoots of the 'rhizome state', staffed by the clients and kinsmen of the 'big men' in government offices.

Conclusions: the end of post-colonialism in Africa

In 2002, when introducing an essay collection comparing post-independence Africa with post-Soviet Central Asia, Crawford Young remarked that 'Colonial legacies' – which he took to be enduring inter-generational transfers from the past to the present – 'are glaringly visible in Africa after forty years' (Beissinger and Young, 2002, p. 21). Yet, a mere two years later in an article in *African Affairs*, Young asked whether 'post-colonial' was still a serviceable designation for the African state, which had become a far less dominating, agenda-setting actor. In view of the dramatic deterioration in its legitimacy and functional capacity since about 1990, we need – he argued – to recognise the historical closure of the African 'post-colonial state' (Young, 2004).

The contradiction between these statements is, I think, more apparent than real. The colonial legacies – embodied mainly in the sovereign territorial state – persist but the historical *situation* of 'post-colonialism', with its distinctive political economy, is irrecoverable. Whatever their current travails, Africa's states, with their inherited boundaries, European administrative languages and bureaucratic trappings, look like lasting into the foreseeable future. Guinea-Bissau aside, it seems unlikely that any state will follow Somalia by imploding into functional anarchy. Chad has long threatened to fragment into ethno-regional units, but has somehow held together. Mozambique and Uganda in the 1990s, Sierra Leone and Liberia in the 2000s have shown that, even at its most dire, state 'failure' is not irreversible. Eritrea was the only African state established by a war of secession until July 2011, when it was joined by South Sudan. The Sudanese peace agreement of March 2005, which ended over two decades of civil war, had provided for the referendum held in January: the result was an overwhelming mandate for southern independence which the Khartoum government respected. Though we cannot be certain, it seems unlikely that there will be further revisions to the political map of Africa. On the other hand, the prospects for regional integration through pooling sovereignty in inter-state institutions are poor. The level of international trade within Africa is below its potential, and seems likely to remain so. Africans, it would appear, are stuck with states they can neither do without, nor supersede. They remain institutional clusters to be captured and manipulated for individual and communal benefit, but inspire little trust and scarcely any confidence they will promote development. According to Mbembe, 'the state no longer has credit with the public'. Its legitimacy has been eroded by the contraction of the public sector and the privatisation of what used to be public services: governing elites have far fewer 'goods' and amenities to redistribute amongst the population. 'All that is left [to them] is control of the forces of coercion, in a context marked by material devastation, disorganisation of credit and production circuits, and an abrupt collapse of notions of public good, general utility, and law and order' (Mbembe, 2001, p. 76).

But it would be wrong to conclude on this deeply pessimistic note. Not only are there heartening 'chronic' exceptions, most obviously Botswana, but governance in some African states is *dramatically* better than in the not-so-distant past. Uganda is a good example which, though it certainly raises troubling reservations, warrants a more optimistic conclusion. Under Idi Amin (1971–9) and Milton Obote (1980–5), Ugandans were not so much badly governed as arbitrarily terrorised by men in uniform, who could kill ethnic and political 'enemies' without restraint but could not impose a semblance of civil order (for banditry flourished amidst economic devastation). Yoweri Museveni, who came to power at the head of armed insurgency, was able to break the vicious circle for two reasons: first, discipline in his National Resistance Army had been strict, with harsh punishments for brutalising civilians, so his moral stock was quite high. Second, he constructed a very broad-based government, built on an alliance of Bantu southerners, but with the Baganda and all former political parties represented – though he soon made clear his preference for 'no party' government (Low, 1991a, pp. 324–5). By the late 1990s, he was recognised as one of a cluster of 'new' political leaders who had pragmatically discarded failed development models (Museveni was once a Marxist) in favour of piecemeal reconstruction (Ottoway, 1999). Museveni went far to restoring the popular legitimacy of government after being elected president in 1996 on a platform of basic education for all and delivering on his promise. Every household became entitled to free schooling for up to four children. Market liberalisation made cash-cropping profitable once again: with the abolition of the state monopoly marketing agency, the share of the export price going to coffee producers increased from 15 per cent to 75 per cent. Asian businessmen were persuaded to reinvest in the country. In a remarkable example of 'slimming down' the overgrown state, the government shed over a third of its payroll in 1994–5 without serious political or poverty consequences and demobilised a substantial proportion of its army without any increase in crime or violence. Museveni's government tackled the Aids pandemic with a clarity and vigour that put the evasive and irresponsible pronouncements of South Africa's Thabo Mbeki to shame. The deeply disquieting aspects of an otherwise impressive record were Ugandan participation in the war in the eastern Congo and the regime's drift to presidential authoritarianism. In 2005, Museveni reneged on a promise not to seek a third term as president and amended the constitution to enable him to do so. The ensuing election was marred by apparently trumped-up charges of treason and rape against his main opponent. Museveni was re-elected with 59 per cent of the popular vote, which almost certainly reflects the support he continues to enjoy, but even sympathetic observers fear he is succumbing to the 'big man' syndrome.

5
Nigeria and Congo-Zaire, 1960–c. 1975: Decolonisation, Civil War and State Recovery

Introduction

Why compare Nigeria and Congo-Zaire?[1] Their sheer demographic weight is one reason: in 1960, their combined population was 26 per cent of the total population of sub-Saharan Africa. Nigerians numbered about 42.4 million, the Congolese 15.5 million. By 2005, their numbers had grown to 141.4 million and 58.7 million; together they were 27 per cent of the African total. So, these states encompass a large part of Africa's human experience. Then, there is their quintessentially post-colonial character: neither could conceivably have evolved out of the indigenous polities or empire-building traditions that once flourished within their present territories; their 'internal nations' had different legends of origin, histories and institutions. As political formations, they are the handiwork of European colonialists, who set their boundaries and endowed them with administrative languages and apparatuses. Each has a small number of major indigenous languages and hundreds of minor ones; in both, assimilating primordial cultural identities with the national state has been a conflicted process. Finally, there are parallel events which repay comparative analysis. Both came close to disintegration after independence, in Congo-Zaire's case within weeks of the transfer of power, in Nigeria's after several years of deepening regional and ethnic tension. In each country, a major territorial region attempted to secede and horrendous civil wars were fought to maintain the state's integrity.

These post-colonial crises were alike in expressing the contradictions between cultural pluralism and the neo-national state, in contexts where

---

1. President Mobutu changed the cournty's name to 'Zaire' in Otober 1971 in the mistaken belief that it was more 'authentic' than 'Congo'. Laurent Kabila reverted to the original name after he overthrew Mobutu in May 1997. Most place names were permanently changed during the early 1970s.

the sense of nationhood was shallow, but also very different. The Congo crisis was immediately internationalised, and enveloped in the Cold War; the Nigerian civil war was a wholly domestic affair. Neo-colonial interests sustained Katanga's secession, but not Biafra's. Furthermore, the regimes which emerged triumphant from the crises were very dissimilar at their apex. After seizing power in November 1965, Colonel Mobutu Sese Seko imposed a personal dictatorship that lasted for three decades. For much of this time, he ruled as an uncrowned absolutist monarch through a political aristocracy who depended on state favours for their wealth. His army background notwithstanding, the military was only one (rather rickety) element in a patrimonial regime.

The Nigerian military, by contrast, were the arbiters of Nigerian politics between the coups of 1966 that liquidated the First Republic and the election of a civilian president in 1999. Federal military governments ruled for 28 of the intervening 33 years. Although power and responsibility were delegated to senior civil servants and co-opted politicians, the military did not relinquish their self-appointed duty to cleanse the political stables when they became too squalid. In 1979, they permitted a return to civilian rule but the Second Republic was in its turn dissolved by a military coup in December 1983. When General Ibrahim Babangida took over the leadership of the military junta in August 1985, he instituted a protracted transition to democracy that culminated in the presidential election of June 1993. The democratic interlude was still-born: in November, General Sani Abacha seized power.

Understanding Nigerian and Zairian politics is a difficult enough task when each is studied in isolation; comparison complicates matters for the reader. The point of the exercise stems from this central paradox: the two states emerged from very dissimilar colonial backgrounds with dissimilar political and economic legacies, yet their historical trajectories were remarkably similar over the longer term. This convergence is all the more striking because decolonisation followed different patterns. Nigerians acceded to independence with nearly a decade's experience of competitive party politics and democratic elections; their political leaders were well versed in the exercise of executive power, thanks to the incremental devolution of self-government from the late 1940s. By the mid-50s, political conflict between regionally and ethnically based parties had virtually eclipsed the nationalist struggle. Economic life became politicised with the expansion of the public sector, the government's increasing role in promoting development and, crucially, the assumption by Nigerian politicians of control of the produce marketing boards (Rimmer, 1978). The Nigerianisation of the civil service was well advanced by independence.

By contrast, the transformation of the Belgian Congo from tropical Africa's most European-dominated (and seemingly docile) colony to an independent and highly Africanised state was unanticipated as late as 1956. The Belgians remained calmly confident that, in the midst of upheaval elsewhere, their formula for colonial stability still worked. It consisted of so improving the material well-being of the Congolese that they would not aspire to democratic and national rights, though they were not, in theory, to be denied them in perpetuity. The évolués – French-speaking Congolese with secondary education, often employed as clerks in the public administration – had so internalised the colonialists' values that they envisaged the political future in Belgian terms. In February 1956, Patrice Lumumba, then Président de l'Association des évolués, circulated a pamphlet urging that:

> All the representatives of Authority ... have a right to our acknowledgement, to our esteem and to our sympathy. We must remain closely attached to them, in order to construct in a spirit of perfect loyalism, a veritable overseas Belgium. We do not have the right to undermine ... the labour of those who are continuing the benevolent work of Leopold II, the work of uplifting, enfranchising and liberating the native population. (Quoted in Stengers, 1989, p. 279)

Some four years later, Lumumba was installed as the Congo's first prime minister and the formalities of the Independence Day ceremonies were shattered by his bitter denunciation of Belgian colonialism.

Contrasting colonial legacies

As a single entity, the Congo dates from the 1880s; Nigeria was a more recent fabrication. The Northern and Southern Protectorates were not amalgamated until 1914, as the men who led the country to independence well remembered, and were separately administered until the late 1940s. The novelty of this colonial formation partly explains its friability. The Hausa-Fulani north had been oriented culturally to the Muslim world and commercially to the trans-Saharan trade routes; the Delta states and the coastal hinterland had been exposed to the Atlantic slave trade and more open to Christianity and 'legitimate' commerce. Except in Lagos (a Crown Colony) the British ruled by placing an imperial arch of western legal norms and military power over native authority structures and customary law. In the emirate North, their suzerainty was imposed on 'one of the most effectively organized systems of indigenous rule south of the Sahara', where a trained judiciary administered the Maliki school of Muslim law (Hailey, 1957, p. 453). After the emirs had agreed to suppress slave-raiding and trading, their fiscal, judicial and administrative powers were confirmed by the Native Authority system, which largely insulated the North from Christian missions and western education, and allowed the Hausa-Fulani aristocracy to retain the leadership of a deferential social order. According to Ahmadu Bello, the North's leading politician in the 1950s: '[The British] made no drastic changes, and what was done came into effect only after consultation. Everything went on more or less as it had done before, for what could one Resident, an assistant and a few soldiers in Sokoto do to change so vast an area as the Sokoto Empire' (Bello, 1962, p. 19).

Indirect rule through Native Authorities worked less smoothly in the Yoruba-dominated southwest, and not at all in Ibo-dominated southeast, but even in these territories the colonial regime held diverse communities on a loose rein without greatly affecting their institutions or ways of living. The thinly staffed bureaucracy made little attempt to regulate native agriculture. Less than 1 per cent of the territory was alienated to Europeans, who were refused permission to establish plantations. After 1947, expatriate employees were admitted on a strict quota basis and only when the immigration authorities were satisfied the vacancies could not be filled by Africans. In the Western Region, recruitment of expatriate colonial administrators ceased in 1953; by 1960, all but one administrative post had been Nigerianised. The number of secondary grammar schools in the Region trebled between 1954 and 61 to meet the demand for an education that qualified the young for government service (Lloyd, 1975, p. 556).

The 'open' colonial economy was based on peasant production, the main driver of economic growth up to independence. Cocoa, groundnut produce and palm produce constituted three-fifths of exports in 1960, followed by tin and rubber. Under the stimulus of improving terms of trade, export values in current prices rose twelve-fold between 1946 and 1966, which brought modest but widely diffused prosperity, despite heavy taxation by the Marketing Boards. Per capita income rose by about 2 per cent annually in the 1950s and early 60s. The social distribution of income was relatively even, but geographically skewed in favour of the cocoa-producing Western Region, where income per head was about twice as high as in the North. At independence, oil exports from the Niger delta were inconsequential, but accounted for a third of exports by value by 1966. They were expected to secure abundant foreign exchange and so unshackle the economy from the restraints of capital dearth. By virtue of its large population and well-developed transport system, Nigeria was Africa's second largest market.

Manufacturing was the fastest-growing sector of the late colonial economy, though from a base so low that it accounted for less than 5 per cent of total output in 1964 (see Table 5.1). Industrial investment by the giant trading companies had been induced mainly by tariff protection and the greatly enhanced role of government in economic management. Setting up the Federation in 1954 fundamentally altered the political environment in which foreign enterprises operated by devolving key controls over business to Nigerian politicians, who energetically pursued industrialisation and public investment in infrastructure. They aimed to indigenise the economy by public ownership of its 'commanding heights' but the public corporations established in the mid-1950s to undertake production performed poorly. The politicians were reluctantly persuaded that developing the modern sector would depend on foreign-owned companies for the time being, though these were constrained to Nigerianise their staff and sell minority shareholdings to government (Schatz, 1977, pp. 5–7). The establishment of new retail enterprises was effectively barred to non-Africans, although it was to be some time before Nigerians were able to compete with the Lebanese and Asian businessmen who were the main intermediaries between the large expatriate companies and African consumers.

Table 5.1 Sectoral output as a share of Nigerian GDP, 1950–77

	1950	*1964*	*1971*	*1977*
Agriculture, livestock, fishing, forestry	67.5	61.9	48.8	27.3
Mining and oil	1.1	2.8	10.2	29.3
Manufacturing and utilities	0.6	4.7	7.9	12.2
Transport and communications	4.5	4.7	2.8	3.3
Building and civil engineering	3.0	3.2	5.8	6.4
Government	2.2	3.5	6.2	7.0
Other services	18.8	16.8	5.6	5.4
	100	100	100	100

Sources: Kilby, 1969, p. 11; Kirk-Greene (with D. Rimmer), 1981, p. 64.

Nigeria's crucial constitutional legacy from the late colonial period was its federation into three virtually autonomous regions, with separate governments, legislatures, judiciaries, civil services, produce marketing boards and development plans. Apart from the Federal Civil Service and Foreign Service, only the army appeared to be a genuinely national institution. The Eastern and Northern Regions were effectively single-party states: the former was dominated by the National Council of Nigeria and the Cameroons (NCNC – renamed the National Council of Nigerian Citizens in 1962), the latter by the Northern People's Congress (NPC). The NCNC had been established by an Ibo, Dr Nnamdi Azikiwe, in 1944, on a platform of left-wing, unitary nationalism, but was too closely identified with Ibo ethnicity and culture to function as a pan-Nigerian 'umbrella organisation'. The NPC had been organized in 1951 by a small group of western-educated Muslims, but at the behest of the emirs and primarily to protect the interests of the Hausa-Fulani elite and its conception of the northern 'way of life'. The party's structure dovetailed with traditional networks of aristocratic patrons and commoner clients, and became *the* conduit of public patronage for those seeking office, loans, scholarships or contracts. The situation in the Western Region was more complex: the main vehicle for Yoruba political activism was the Action Group (AG), set up by Chief Obafemi Awolowo, which had a solid majority in the Regional Assembly. But Awolowo did not wish the AG to be stigmatised as 'tribal' and had some success in recruiting across ethnic lines. Conversely, the NCNC campaigned strongly in the west, and narrowly won the federal election there in 1954.

The regionalisation and democratisation of government took place against a backdrop of solidifying ethnic consciousness and mounting ethnic suspicion that easily spilt over into attacks on 'strangers'. Ibo migrants in the North, where they were well established in the modern economy as traders, motor mechanics, clerks and the like, were particularly exposed to mob violence, for they lived apart in 'stranger communities' and tended to be physically distinct from the local Hausa. Within each region, ethnic minorities clamoured for states they could call their own, sometimes enlisting the support of a dominant party from another region. At the federal centre, the NPC was the major partner in coalition governments; the first, formed in 1957, embraced the three major parties, the second was put together after the 1959 elections with the NCNC alone. Acceding to independence was merely an interlude in a political drama that began in the early 1950s and came to a dénouement in 1966–7.

There was a further continuity in what we might call the 'texture' of politics. By the later 1950s, the elected politicians' venal abuse of public office was well documented. Official enquiries into the running of the town councils of Lagos, Port Harcourt and Onitsha (which were democratically elected from 1950) found considerable evidence of bribery in allocating public contracts and other malfeasance. The British became obsessed with the politicians' 'mania for self-enrichment' but were increasingly reluctant to intervene in Nigerian politics to curb corruption (Tignor, 1993). In fact, the graft associated with development policies at every level was for the most part 'solidaristic': either directly or through the medium of the parties, men in authority benefited their home communities by providing amenities, misappropriating funds and local favouritism in appointments. 'They received fealty and delivered largesse' (Douglas Rimmer, cited in Joseph, 1983, p. 31). Once national independence was beyond doubt, what animated politics was the competition between rival patrons, and their clients and associates, for the control of public resources and political rents. The leading protagonists straddled the 'civic' and 'primordial' publics (Ekeh, 1975). Prior to independence, serious corruption allegations were levelled against Azikiwe and Awolowo, which would have terminated their careers had the 'civic' public been the source of the ethical standards by which politicians were judged and found wanting. Both diverted public money for party political purposes while they were regional premiers. The Awolowo case was straightforward: overwhelming evidence was presented to a commission of enquiry in 1962 that he had appropriated vast sums from the Western Region statutory corporations to fund the Action Group. His supporters were neither greatly surprised, nor shocked. Not without reason, they regarded the commission as partisan and its judgement as a politically motivated attempt to destroy Awolowo and the Action Group; I revert to this below (Diamond, 1988a, p. 104).

Azikiwe's case was more 'borderline': he was accused (by the chief whip in his own government) of investing £2 million of public money while premier of the Eastern Region in a loss-making bank he directed and partly owned. The bank was financing the Zik Group of Companies which owned the newspapers controlled by Azikiwe. An official enquiry accepted that his primary motive was to support an indigenous bank that would liberalise credit for Nigerians, but judged Azikiwe 'guilty of misconduct as a Minister' in not relinquishing his financial interest in the bank when the proposal to inject public money was first mooted (Willink Report, 1957–8, Cmnd 51, paras 194–7). This

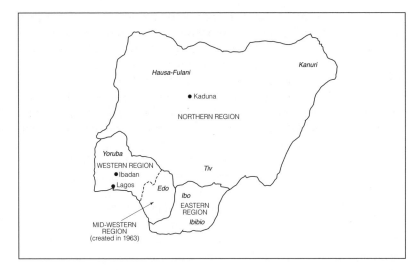

Map 5.1 Nigeria at independence

admonition did not affect Azikiwe's career in the slightest; the NCNC shortly won a substantial majority in the Eastern Region elections and his internal party enemies were routed. Azikiwe and (in the longer term) Awolowo survived these scandals because, in the judgement of their ethnic constituencies, they remained trusted men of honour. It was not, I must add, that Nigerians were cynically indifferent to venality in public life; but the political culture was so fiercely antagonistic, and so ethnically charged, that accusations of corruption were normally a tactic in partisan warfare, rather than the expression of a gross affront to common public standards. Just about every area of public life was politically contested.

In turning to the Belgian Congo we must first dispose of the common misconception that 'of all African colonies [it was] the least developed' (Westad, 2007, p. 137). In fact, by the normal criteria of capitalist development, its economy was more 'advanced' than Nigeria's. The Belgians invested more on a per capita basis in their African subjects than any other colonial power, and so created the largest industrial sector outside South Africa and the settler colonies. While public investment was principally in transport, communications and public utilities during the 1950s, private investment spread beyond commercial agriculture and mining into supplementary industries (chemicals, metals, electricity, coal and cement) and consumer goods manufacture (textiles, beer, tobacco, food and cheap furniture). Industry, including agricultural processing, accounted for over 10 per cent of GNP by 1959 – a far bigger proportion than in Nigeria – and satisfied more than two-fifths of consumer goods demand (Peemans, 1975, p. 186). At that date, the value of Congolese exports exceeded the value of Nigerian exports and represented 39 per cent of GDP (as opposed to 19 per cent in Nigeria). The ratio of mineral to agricultural exports was roughly 3:2. Mining, metallurgy and commercial agriculture were dominated by concessionary companies, and corporate capital was exceptionally concentrated; between the early 1930s and independence, four financial groups controlled, in association with the state, 75 per cent of the capital in the colony (Anstey, 1966, p. 113). Many of the companies were inter-connected via Belgium's premier capitalist institution, the giant holding company, Société Générale.

The colonial administration was a major shareholder in the corporate economy, having inherited the Leopoldian regime's portfolio, along with its mineral rights and a huge public domain. This did not make for a 'mixed economy' in the usual sense because the administration was a passive investor, and left business decisions to company managers. However, what survived from the Leopoldian era in mineral-rich Katanga was 'mixed' public and private government. The Katanga Company, the largest of the concessionary companies, had been granted freehold rights over a third of its territory, assigned one-third of the revenues and entrusted with administrative functions. In an arrangement which lasted up to independence, the province was administered by a joint body, the Comité special du Katanga (CSK), on which the Company had one-third of the representation (and the colonial government two-thirds). The CSK set up, and became the major shareholder in the mining company, Union Minière du Haut Katanga (UMHK), the single most important business enterprise in the Congo. This complex meshing of concessionary and industrial companies and the colonial state was the source of Katanga's distinct identity, and a historical precondition for the neo-colonialist bid for secession in 1960.

African wage-earners numbered about 961,000 in 1959, roughly twice the number in Nigeria for population just over one-third its size (Hunter, 1962, Table IV). More than one in three adult males lived in urban areas in 'extra-customary centres' (meaning they were not under the authority of a chief); with family dependants, they constituted one of the largest and most stable working classes in Africa. The living standards of regular employees in mining and industry compared favourably with those of wage-earners anywhere in the developing world (Young, 1965, pp. 211–12). They were not confined to unskilled labour; Congolese tradesmen and technicians held the sort of jobs reserved for Europeans in neighbouring colonies. Nearly 20,000 adolescents were enrolled full time in trade and technical schools in 1959–60. The social infrastructure of elementary schools, clinics and dispensaries was amongst the best in tropical Africa (*ibid.*, pp. 50–5). Thanks to the Catholic teaching orders, which were subsidised for their educational work by the colonial administration, the proportion of Congolese children attending primary school by 1960 was around 70 per cent (Hunter, 1962, p. 244). This was lower than in Nigeria's southern regions, which had introduced free, universal and, in the case of the Western Region, compulsory primary education on attaining full self-government in 1957, but still high for colonial Africa. In the early 1950s, the Congolese school enrolment rate had been second to none; such was its cumulative effect that 49 per cent of Congolese adult males were literate in 1960 as compared with a quarter of Nigerian men (Cooper, 2002, Table 2, p. 114).

Unlike the West African states, where the modernising elite included university-trained professionals, the Congo became independent when its first universities had produced only 16 (very recent) African graduates and were educating about 450 African students (Stengers, 1989, p. 188; Anstey, 1966, p. 207). Before then, the Catholic seminaries represented the only opportunity for Africans to acquire a higher education, so the colonial legacy included a substantial African clergy.

Since 1918, Belgian colonial rule had officially been 'indirect'. The basic administrative unit of 'customary society' was the chieftainship, which was responsible for summary justice, census-taking and taxation, and had a treasury and police force. But this administrative network had been imposed on communities depleted and demoralised by epidemics and forced deliveries; rather than local autonomy, it secured control 'from above'. To extract labour from a sparse population, and in the belief that native indolence could only be remedied by 'cultures éducatives', the regime had instituted strict agricultural regulations and harsh punishments for violating them. Beating supposedly recalcitrant Africans was commonplace. Far from relaxing, the bureaucratic control of native agriculture became even closer in the 1950s, with a system of land apportionment to peasant families who were required to follow a pre-established crop rotation. Compulsory cotton cropping was still enforced in 1959. Congolese farmers were both dragooned into the market economy and denied an active role: they were excluded from credit, from private ownership of urban land and from the right to hire employees.

Europeans were a substantial presence with an ostentatiously comfortable lifestyle: their numbers peaked at 114,341 in 1959 (having risen from 35,000 in 1945). The average European salary was about 44 times the average African salary (Stengers, 1989, p. 189). Nine per cent of the colony's territory had been alienated or reserved for European occupation (Hailey, 1957, p. 687). Yet Europeans had no formal political rights and little political influence in a system of colonial government highly centralised in Brussels. Settlers questioned by the Belgian Institute of Political Science on the eve of independence bitterly resented the indifference with which their opinions were treated (Hunter, 1962, p. 281).

It is customary, but incorrect, to date the decolonisation process to the Léopoldville (now Kinshasa) riots of 4 to 10 January 1959. In fact, Belgian policy-makers were already committed to an accommodation with Congolese nationalism. In October 1958, Lumumba and other évolués set up the Mouvement National Congolais (MNC) which sought independence within a reasonable timescale and through peaceful negotiations. The Belgians responded promptly and positively, despite the movement's still limited social base. A fact-finding mission on behalf of the Minister of the Colonies concluded in late December that the demand for independence was irresistible; it proposed offering the Congolese the choice between complete independence and continued association with Belgium. When this choice would be made it did not say, but having observed the Dutch and French vainly struggle to suppress nationalist movements in South East Asia and North Africa, the Belgians were determined to avoid similar errors. They would move their colony to independence in amity, while extending a fraternal hand to their erstwhile charges.

The explosion of popular fury in Léopoldville transformed an evolutionary situation into a revolutionary one. Europeans were shocked to find themselves objects of African hatred and astonished by what one witness called 'an incredible acceleration in the growth of the political consciousness of the masses' (Stengers, 1989, p. 248). Within a week, the government announced its intention of 'organising a democracy in the Congo, able to exercise the prerogatives of sovereignty and decide on its independence'. It was generally assumed that the transfer of power was several years away, but decolonisation acquired such a hectic momentum in the ensuing months the timetable was drastically curtailed: in December 1959, the government scheduled a Belgian-Congolese Round Table Conference for January–February 1960, with independence fixed for 30 June.

The pace of change was accelerated by the frenetic politicisation of the Congolese masses in 1959, the breakdown of colonial discipline and the increasingly insistent demands of the emerging political class. The prospect of independence released an extraordinary political energy: dozens of parties were formed, manifestos drawn up and congresses organised. The accusation later levelled against the Belgians of 'scuttling' overlooks the fact that Congolese party leaders made the speedy transfer of power a condition for continued collaboration with them. They were under intense pressure from the people's soaring aspirations, and sought to outbid each other in the radicalism of their demands. For the peasants and rural workers, independence became inextricable from an inchoate revolt against the oppressive, omnipresent colonial system: they sought an end to being coerced into a modern market society. Rural folk were gripped by a utopian expectation of a new order: within a few months the Kuba people administered the poison ordeal to 500 suspected witches, in the hope of cleansing the social system of its colonial past and entering a happy millennium (Vansina, 1990, p. 248).

The political torrent sweeping away Belgian colonialism had several cross-currents. Pulling against the territorial nationalism of the MNC, which aimed to take over the unitary state, were ethno-regional parties militating for a federalist post-colonial order. The dominant party in Lower Congo was Abako (an abbreviation of Alliance des Bakongo) led by Joseph Kasavubu. It had originated in a cultural organisation of Kikongo speakers which transformed itself into a political party in 1956, and was the first to demand immediate independence. During 1959, Abako was often the Belgians' most intransigent opponent, but its federalism was sometimes barely distinguishable from separatism (Anstey, 1966, p. 232). Federalist claims were asserted in Katanga by the Confédération des Associations Tribales de Katanga (abbreviated as Conakat), set up to represent 'native' ethnic groups resentful of the immigrant 'strangers', especially from Kasai, who had been recruited by Union Minière. In July, the Union Katangaise, an organisation which represented the 3000 or so European settlers, was officially admitted to Conakat. In December, Moise Tshombe, the son of a wealthy Lunda businessman, was elected party president. Conakat was not yet a separatist movement: Tshombe publicly accepted 'the idea of federal unity', provided the traditional chiefs continued to play a fundamental role in post-colonial Katanga, which would in any event 'seek a community with Belgium' (Gérard-Libois, 1966, p. 33). Meanwhile, an ideological division had opened in the MNC between Lumumba's 'radicals' and the 'moderates', led by Cyrille Adoula and Joseph Ileo, who accused him of communist sympathies and dictatorial tendencies. In October, the moderates asked Albert Kalonji, the Baluba leader in South Kasai, to head a new MNC 'wing', known as the MNC (K), which rapidly became a vehicle for Baluba interests.

The pillars of the colonial state – the administration, the Church and the colonial business corporations – were resigned to their diminishing influence with the Belgian government and parliament and their evaporating authority over the Congolese masses. The companies' passivity is especially noteworthy. It can partly be explained by confidence in their own indispensability: so crucial was their role in mining, transport and manufacturing that they felt certain of remaining in place whatever the political outcome. To ingratiate themselves with the Congo's future political masters, the companies began indiscriminately subsidising all political parties. Before the secession of Katanga in the summer of 1960, Belgian industrialists were financing both Tshombe's Conakat and its rivals (Stengers, 1989, p. 256).

The Round Table Conference held in Brussels in early 1960 was a confrontation between Congolese party leaders bent on wresting immediate independence and Belgian ministers and parliamentarians seeking an amicable transfer of power. The constitution, drawn up by a special commission, replicated Belgium's in having a three-fold division of powers: between the central government and the six provinces, between the Senate and the Chamber of Representatives, and between the prime minister and president. In theory, executive power was vested in the prime minister and the president was a largely ceremonial head of state; in practice, this arrangement led to a major conflict of jurisdiction. National and provincial elections were scheduled for May, on the basis of universal suffrage. Congolese sovereignty was to be untrammelled by any remaining Belgian competencies for defence, diplomatic representation or finance after 30 June. The final settlement was remarkably generous on Belgium's side (Young, 1965, p. 182). It assumed heavy financial obligations to the independent state, which expected to retain its European bureaucrats until educated Africans could replace them. Recruitment to the senior administration was to remain graduate-only, so its Africanisation would be painfully slow, given the tiny numbers graduating from Congolese universities.

The election results confirmed the nationalists' disastrous fragmentation, principally on ethnic lines but cross-hatched by the political rift between radical unitary nationalists and conservative federalists. Kasai was divided between deputies representing the Lulua and Baluba;

CENTRAL AFRICAN REPUBLIC

Orientale

Équateur

● Stanleyville

REPUBLIC
OF THE
CONGO

RWANDA

Kivu

BURUNDI

Léopoldville

Kasaï

★ Léopoldville

Katanga

ANGOLA

Elizabethville
●

NORTHERN RHODESIA (ZAMBIA)

Map 5.2 The Democratic Republic of the Congo at independence

Léopoldville province between its Bakongo and Bangala deputies; and Katanga was split between separatists and unitarists. The results gave nine parties seven or more seats in the 137 seat Chamber. The Belgian official in charge of the transition wanted Kasavubu to be prime minister, but the post went to Lumumba who controlled a slim parliamentary majority, thanks to the alliance of the MNC (L) with smaller parties. Kasavubu got the presidency. The two men represented discordant and geographically distinct constituencies: Lumumba's ethnic group, the Batetela, was too small to serve as a political base. Once the advocate of collaboration with the colonialists, he had been converted to supra-ethnic nationalism and radical populism by Nkrumah's inspirational example. His party's electoral bastion was Orientale province, the only one where it won a solid majority in the provincial elections, and his most committed followers were the industrial workers of Stanleyville (now Kisangani). The MNC (L) attracted little support in Léopoldville, which had a crucial bearing on later developments. Kasavubu's ethnic base was the Bakongo, one of Central Africa's largest historic nations, which had renewed its cultural cohesion in the colonial period, so he had an ingrained sympathy for federalism. His record of anti-colonial militancy was impeccable, but he tended to align with the 'moderates' in intra-Congolese disputes.

The crisis of the first Congolese Republic

The independence settlement lasted less than a week, for, on 5 July, the Force Publique, which should have guaranteed the expatriate community's physical safety, mutinied against its European officers. The Force's Commander provoked the mutiny by striding into a room in which about 200 Congolese NCOs were assembled and writing on a blackboard 'After independence = Before independence'. His astonishing arrogance insulted the class of men on whose goodwill the independence 'compact' rested. A political superstructure of African ministers and legislators had been placed on top of the colonial apparatus, whose leading cadres would remain European for some time. At independence, there was not a single Congolese officer in the Force Publique and the highest category of the bureaucracy remained entirely European. (By contrast, Nigerians held about 2600 senior civil service posts.) The ambitious, literate and recently politicised men serving on low pay as NCOs or petty functionaries could expect neither promotion, nor the glittering prizes which independence brought the elected politicians. (The first legislative act of the Congolese parliament, we might note, was to triple its own salary over the amount specified in the provisional constitution.) The NCOs' collective resentment made it impossible to isolate the indiscipline or prevent it being directed against the conspicuous manifestations of European power and privilege.

Lumumba took drastic steps to retain the army's loyalty: the officer corps was Africanised and all enlisted men were promoted to the next higher rank. On 9 July he appointed his protégé, Joseph-Désiré Mobutu, chief of staff of the renamed Armée nationale congolaise. These measures did not stop the mutiny spreading throughout the provinces, nor the intimidation of Europeans. Ostensibly to protect their lives, Belgium despatched two companies of paratroopers to

Léopoldville, an intervention which Lumumba denounced as unwarranted aggression and a breach of the Treaty of Friendship and Cooperation. On 11 July, Belgian ships bombarded the port of Matadi, which had been evacuated by Europeans, in a ham-fisted attempt to overawe the mutineers. Lumumba's government was persuaded that Belgium was attempting to reoccupy the country. Greatly exaggerated accounts of the fatalities at Matadi spread with extraordinary speed, and exposed Europeans to a worsening cycle of abuse and humiliation. In less than a month, about 60,000 fled the country. They included most magistrates and civil servants, who were prompted to leave after the Belgian ambassador promised their integration into the metropolitan civil service in a radio broadcast on 12 July. The European population fell to 20,000 by August, and was heavily concentrated in Katanga, which had declared its independence. (Significantly, the promise of integration did not apply to Belgian civil servants in Katanga.) The flight of the European administrators brought sudden, unanticipated promotion for thousands of Congolese civil servants.

The mutiny was Tshombe's pretext for proclaiming Katanga's independence on 11 July, which he coupled with a request for Belgian aid. Secession had been bruited for weeks and made more likely by the election results and the meagre allocation of portfolios to Conakat in Lumumba's governing coalition. European 'ultras', who had some influence with Tshombe, had long advocated secession, but he and several provincial ministers took the decision. Without their agency, secession would not have been possible. A powerful motive was retaining local control of Katanga's mineral royalties: they had figured large in Conakat's election campaign, which blatantly appealed to provincial self-interest. The Belgian Foreign Minister publicly opposed secession, because it imperilled Europeans in other provinces and rendered the Congo economically unviable (Gérard-Libois, 1966, pp. 97–8). Once it was a fait accompli, however, the Belgian government was committed to Katangan independence: it withheld formal recognition but, through the legal fiction that any province could receive Belgian technical assistance if it so desired, provided crucial military and administrative support. Under Belgian supervision, immediate steps were taken to convert the Katangan Gendarmerie into an effective force, with a cadre of mercenary officers recruited in Brussels. Belgian civil servants administered what was effectively a client state. Essential financial support came from Union Minière which immediately advanced Tshombe's government 1.25 million Belgian francs and began paying its taxes directly to Elisabethville (now Lubumbashi). The company could not operate without the political security enforced by the Conakat regime, and Katanga was not viable without Union Minière. Their symbiosis and convergence of interests created an image of Katanga 'as a mere creature of Union Minière and sacred ground for neocolonialism' (*ibid.*, p. 283).

Katanga was not the only dissident region: a further blow to the Congo's territorial integrity came when the Baluba zones of South Kasai seceded on 9 August (Nzongola-Ntalaja, 2002, pp. 101–6). The Baluba bear comparison with the Ibos of Nigeria in that they had taken with zest to the modern economy and migrated to the larger towns, where they worked as traders, clerks and technicians. Their relative material success and ethnic solidarity had made the Baluba many enemies. Even before independence, they were returning to the security of their homeland. Ironically, their bitterest rivals in South Kasai were the Lulua – a group with whom they shared a language, culture and myths of origins. The two had only invented separate identities in the colonial period. The Baluba's political loyalties depended largely on the local ethnic context in which they found themselves. In their South Kasai homeland, they were mobilised around Kalonji's dissident wing of the MNC, which militated for a separate 'Baluba' province after it failed to secure a majority in the Kasai provincial assembly in the May elections. The break-down of central government authority and Katanga's secession encouraged Kalonji to raise his sights from leading an autonomous province to presiding over an independent state, with his legitimacy confirmed by the Baluba chiefs in a 'reinvented tradition'. Baluba separatism only made political sense, however, where they were a majority. In neighbouring Katanga, Baluba migrants were organised by Balubakat, a staunchly unitarist and radical nationalist party opposed to Tshombe's Belgian-backed secession.

South Kasai included the most important diamond-producing area; the copper belt lay in Katanga. When they broke away, the economic and fiscal viability of the Congo became highly questionable, since these regions accounted for about 40 per cent of central government revenues and over half export earnings.

With the national army in disarray, Lumumba was powerless to end the Katangan secession or resist the Belgian take-over of the capital's airport and European quarter. At the suggestion of the US Ambassador, he and Kasavubu telegraphed the UN Secretary General, Dag Hammarskjöld, on 12 July, requesting assistance to restore order and resist Belgian aggression. The first UN troops landed in Léopoldville on 15 July, with a mandate to aid the civil authorities but not, at this stage, to terminate the secession. Meanwhile, Kasavubu and Lumumba had severed diplomatic relations with Belgium and telegraphed the Soviet leader Nikita Khrushchev, intimating they would request Soviet help if Belgian aggression did not cease. Subsequently, they handed UN officials an ultimatum threatening Soviet intervention if all Belgian troops were not removed from the Congo by midnight on 19 July.

The telegram and the ultimatum aroused American anxiety that Lumumba – and much of Central Africa – was about to 'go communist' and were a momentous step towards embroiling the crisis in the Cold War. The Eisenhower administration had hitherto ignored tropical Africa, where the United States had no strategic and few economic interests, and where it never contemplated deploying US troops. Its political sympathies lay with moderate African nationalism against European neo-colonialism. The UN mission internationalised the crisis in a way the administration could warmly endorse: it promised to curb Soviet expansionism without implicating the United States in Belgium's disreputable venture in Katanga. The US government provided substantial logistical support for the mission and underwrote much of its cost. Some critics allege that the General Secretariat under Hammarskjöld was little more than a 'front' for American interests and charge the UN mission with complicity both in undermining Lumumba's government and his subsequent assassination – charges which the former UN official, Brian Urquhart, has vehemently contested (Urquhart, 2001).

On 22 July, Lumumba impulsively travelled to New York, where he conferred with Hammarskjöld, and then went on to Washington where he met the US Secretary of State, Christian Herter. The Americans tried to persuade him that all military aid to the Congo should be channelled through the UN. Though Lumumba's public reception was cordial, the private assessment of him by American officials was damning. In a secret telegram to the US Embassy in Brussels, Herter made clear that Lumumba was considered too unreliable to be a satisfactory partner for the West and that the search for a more trustworthy alternative was on. Soon after Lumumba's return from the United States, his quarrel with Hammarskjöld became an irreconcilable breach after the Secretary General persuaded the Katangan authorities to admit UN troops, who took control of Elisabethville airport from the Belgians. Lumumba was infuriated: Hammarskjöld had negotiated with Tshombe without his government's knowledge and the Secretary General's reception in Katanga appeared to confer legitimacy on the break-away regime. Far from ending the secession, UN troops would, so it seemed to Lumumba, provide security against any attempt by the central government to seize the airport.

On 15 August, having publicly announced his government's loss of all confidence in the UN, Lumumba secretly requested Soviet military aid to restore control over the secessionist provinces. Soviet aircraft, personnel and weapons began arriving in Stanleyville on the 23rd, in sufficient quantities for Lumumba to order an assault on South Kasai (which was en route to Katanga). Meanwhile, at a meeting on 18 August, Eisenhower had ordered the CIA to eliminate him. Although American agents were not, in fact, implicated in his assassination, several CIA plots to murder him have been exhaustively documented. Substantial resources were channelled to the US Embassy in Léopoldville to subsidise pro-western politicians and political groups. On 26 August, the head of the CIA instructed his station chief there: '[Lumumba's] removal must be an urgent and prime objective and ... under existing conditions this should be a high priority of our covert action' (Kalb, 1982, p. 65).

Whether Kasavubu was responding to American prompting when he dismissed Lumumba, along with the vice-premier Antoine Gizenga and several key ministerial allies, on 5 September is debatable. Kasavubu was not an American client and had waited until opposition to Lumumba's policies, within and without the governing coalition, had mounted to a crescendo (*ibid.*, p. 72). In the radio broadcast announcing Lumumba's dismissal, Kasavubu accused him of 'governing arbitrarily and plunging the country into civil war'. These were not idle charges: Lumumba had used emergency powers to arrest political opponents, and national army units reoccupying South Kasai had massacred Baluba civilians. While he could not be blamed for their murderous indiscipline, he was responsible for their being there. The leading UN officials were forewarned of, and acquiesced in Lumumba's removal, despite its dubious legality.

Kasavubu nominated a leading moderate, Joseph Ileo, as the new prime minister, though he had no real chance of securing a parliamentary majority, while appointing Mobutu head of the army. Lumumba's cabinet responded to Kasavubu's coup by accusing him of high treason and voting to dismiss him. Parliament refused to confirm the dismissal of either Lumumba or Kasavubu and sought to reconcile them. After a week's deadlock, Mobutu announced on 14 September that he was assuming power until the end of the year in order to 'neutralise' both Kasavubu and Lumumba. He denied staging an army coup and insisted his was a 'peaceful revolution' during which the country would be run by a group of technicians. Although a protégé of Lumumba, Mobutu had aligned himself with the moderate, pro-western unitarists and enjoyed the support of the Americans, who had been grooming him for weeks. He immediately ordered the departure of Soviet-bloc diplomatic personnel and the release of political prisoners arrested by Lumumba. Parliament was suspended and Lumumba detained in his official residence behind a protective cordon of Ghanaian UN troops. Hammarskjöld refused to recognise Mobutu's coup or permit Lumumba's arrest by ANC soldiers who formed a second cordon around the Ghanaians. With Kasavubu's tacit approval, Mobutu installed the so-called College of Commissioners on 29 September, which was a government composed largely of students and recent graduates. Unsurprisingly, its legitimacy was denied by Lumumba's supporters, particularly in the MNC bastion in Stanleyville, and by the more radical African states and communist countries.

By November, the Congo had broken into four entities: South Kasai and Katanga were in the hands of ethno-regional separatists, while Léopoldville and Stanleyville had become rival power centres for those wanting a unitary state. The moderates had rallied to the Mobutu government in the capital; Stanleyville was in the hands of Lumumba's radical followers. A separate government was formed in the East after the UN General Assembly ratified (under strong American pressure) the accreditation of the UN delegation appointed by Mobutu. In effect, the international community was endorsing Kasavubu's coup against Lumumba, and blocking his peaceful return to office. On 27 November, Lumumba escaped house arrest and set out by car for Stanleyville, where Antoine Gizenga had formed a rival administration. He was apprehended by troops loyal to Léopoldville when he was about to cross the Sankuru River. UN peacekeepers, who witnessed the incident, refused his appeal for protection. Lumumba was then imprisoned as a common criminal, while his domestic and foreign enemies pondered how best to dispose of him. Responsibility for transferring Lumumba to Elisabethville, where he and two associates were murdered on 17 January 1961, lay with Harold d'Aspremont Lynden, Belgium's African Affairs Minister and the head of the 'technical mission' to Katanga. Contrary to what was claimed at the time, this was not an 'all African' affair: Tshombe agreed to admit Lumumba only under intense Belgian pressure; Belgian police officers oversaw the killings and the disposal of the bodies. D'Aspremont Lynden had called for Lumumba's 'definitive elimination' in a memorandum which was widely circulated in the Belgian government; its complicity has been acknowledged by a Belgian parliamentary committee of enquiry. The Belgians acted entirely independently of American agencies (Witte, 2001, p. 78).

The announcement of Lumumba's death on 13 February prompted anarchy in many areas, but helped Gizenga consolidate his regime, which was officially recognised by the Soviet bloc, China and a number of African countries. The Tshombe government, on the other hand, remained diplomatically isolated. The fragmentation of the country was accompanied by escalating political violence and summary executions. In the north of Katanga, Baluba dissidents attempted to 'break away' from the informal Belgian protectorate; when the Belgian-led Gendarmerie repressed the uprising, it devastated the region.

The reunification of the Congo in the following two years was a tangled process which I can only outline here. Fear of the country's permanent disintegration led to an uneasy rapprochement between Kasavubu and the Lumumbists in Stanleyville, the reconvening of Parliament and its unanimous vote for Cyrille Adoula as Prime Minister on 2 August 1961. This resolved the constitutional crisis triggered by Lumumba's dismissal. Adoula represented the moderate, pro-western unitarists and, to secure his election, the Americans spent considerable sums bribing parliamentary delegates (Kalb, 1982). South Kasai's secession was ended by a military revolt in Kalonji's army in September 1962, with the backing of the Léopoldville government. The Katangan secession was ended by UN forces in early 1963. The international revulsion at Lumumba's murder had goaded the Security Council into resolving to use 'force' if necessary 'to prevent the occurrence of civil war in the Congo'. Additionally, it recognised the 'imperative necessity' of restoring parliamentary institutions in accordance with the constitution and called for the removal of foreign advisers and mercenaries. Since both the United States and the Soviet Union supported the Congo's reintegration, the international pressure behind reunification appeared irresistible to Tshombe's Belgian backers, who urged him to make an accommodation with Léopoldville. Eleven months elapsed before he capitulated, but on favourable terms, since he and the national and provincial deputies who supported him retained their parliamentary mandates. Tshombe retired to Europe without any judicial charges being brought against him. Nearly all the gendarmes went into exile in Angola, presumably because they feared popular vengeance: as the military arm of an all too evidently neo-colonial regime, they had brutally repressed dissent amongst the mining and industrial workforce.

The demand for a 'second independence'

In early 1964, huge regions were engulfed by rural rebellion, in what was a rare instance of abortive social revolution welling up 'from below' in sub-Saharan Africa. The political and socio-economic conditions for revolt lay in the near-universal disappointment with the results of independence and popular contempt for the new political and bureaucratic masters. While the political parties fragmented and lost all touch with their nominal constituencies, party politicians created and occupied an inordinate number of well-paid political offices. In an attempt to defuse ethnic animosity, the six old provinces inherited from the Belgians were split into 21 new ones in 1962, on the basis of a modified system of ethnic self-determination, each with its ministry, military force and bureaucracy. The centralised system of government and public financing was abandoned, and the *'provincettes'* became little political worlds, where the former évolués appointed themselves to plum public positions on European salary scales. A class divide opened up between those in white-collar public employment, who could protect themselves against inflation, and workers and peasants hit by widespread unemployment, the disruption of rural trade networks and inexorably rising prices due to falling production and an expanding money supply. This class divide was often perceived in ethnic terms and the sense of injustice it engendered was frequently framed within a millenarian religious consciousness.

The first uprising broke out in Kwilu province in January under the charismatic leadership of Pierre Mulele, Lumumba's erstwhile Minister for Education and Africa's first prominent Maoist. The biographical details are hazy, but we know he travelled to China in 1962 for instruction in revolutionary guerrilla warfare (Fox *et al.*, 1965; Nzongola-Ntalaja, 2002, pp. 128–30). Following the reconciliation of the Léopoldville and Stanleyville governments, Mulele was appointed to the Kwilu provincial government in the summer of 1963, but disappeared into the bush where he organised camps for training and indoctrinating partisans. His followers imbibed a simplified Marxist-Leninism and Maoist revolutionary doctrine, but the rebellion's aims, ethos and tactics were authentically Congolese. The rebels demanded the 'Second Independence', which would realise the aspirations of 1959–60; their prime targets were those Congolese who had stepped into the colonialists' shoes. The movement embraced most of the socially dispossessed in Kwilu province, but was largely confined to the Bapende, Mulele's ethnic group, and the Bambundu, who had supported Gizenga's Parti solidaire africain. Recruits were baptised with 'Mulele' or 'Lumumba' water, which was supposed to confer invulnerability to bullets, and Mulele was credited with magical powers. The insurgents quickly eliminated all governmental authority over a large area of south Kwilu, but their ethnic solidarity meant the uprising became self-containing: as the Bapende and Bambundu bands moved out of their home areas, local people saw the revolt as directed not against the Léopoldville government, but against themselves. The ANC was able to push the rebels back to south Kwilu, where a Mulelist *maquis* continued to operate until 1967.

The rebellion in eastern Congo that broke out in May was a greater threat to the central government and more like a conventional civil war, with a regular insurgent army, a rebel strategy of seizing key towns and the formation of a revolutionary government in Stanleyville. The military uprising was organised by Nicolas Olenga, hitherto an unknown, but its political direction fell to Gaston Soumialot, one of Lumumba's lieutenants and the principal organiser of the MNC (L) in Kivu province. The insurgency was plotted outside the country, initially by radicals who formed the National Liberation Council in Brazzaville, later by Lumumbist and PSA dissidents who took refuge in Burundi. Olenga's 'simbas', like Mulele's fighters, enjoyed magical immunity to bullets, and had astonishing initial successes: by September, they controlled nearly half the Congo's territory and seven out of the 21 local capitals. The rebellion was once seen by the western left as a struggle to realise the socially egalitarian goals of radical nationalism in Central Africa, which was brutally extinguished by a neo-colonial reconquest. However, this seems naively utopian given the evidence that the revolutionary regime undermined its popular foundations by wanton violence, ethnic favouritism and its lack of any coherent social policy. The insurgents were led locally by violent young men, wreaking furious vengeance on the so-called intellectuals who dominated a post-colonial order that excluded the illiterate or poorly educated. ('Intellectual' had displaced the colonial term évolué and meant, in practice, anyone deemed to have been westernised.) In Stanleyville, the regime authorised or condoned numerous executions on the basis of the victims' class identity. Crawford Young, who visited the city soon after the regime was recaptured by the ANC, estimated that roughly 20,000 were killed, often with grotesque cruelty. 'The intellectuals were the primary targets – provincial politicians, civil servants, or indeed anyone wearing a white shirt and necktie at the wrong moment' (Young, 1966, p. 40).

The rebellion had the unforeseen consequence of reversing Tshombe's political fortunes. Kasavubu and Mobutu summoned him from exile to replace Adoula as prime minister in July 1964 because, they calculated, he could call on Belgian military and technical advisers and had unrivalled contacts with European and South African mercenaries. He also commanded the loyalty of the Katangan gendarmes, who were recalled from Angola and integrated into the ANC, alongside about 500 white mercenaries. Belgian military and civilian officials who had guided the secessionist government returned to serve Tshombe as central prime minister. The USA supported the ANC offensive with transport aircraft, and supplied the Léopoldville government with fighter-bombers and helicopters flown by Cuban exiles. With its superior military assets, the ANC began to recapture rebel strongholds, but as it did so the fighting became more indiscriminate and civilians were atrociously brutalised by all armed forces. The offensive culminated on 24 November in the most internationally controversial episode during the Congo's internal wars: the dropping, from US planes, of a Belgian parachute force on Stanleyville, to rescue 1600 European hostages, an operation timed to coincide with the arrival of ANC and mercenary units. With the capture of Stanleyville, Soumialot fled to Cairo and the eastern rebellion was reduced to isolated pockets of resistance. The operation represented a watershed in US–Congolese bilateral relations: henceforth, whenever European military intervention became necessary, the United States stood ready to offer political support for the central government as well as logistical and military assistance – but no American troops (Schatzberg, 1991, p. 29).

Western military intervention had considerable repercussions within Africa's emerging international system which the newly independent states were trying to regularise through the OAU. African foreign ministers who had been seeking the hostages' release by peaceful means were outraged by what they saw as the racially selective nature of the West's humanitarianism. The episode also touched on a deep political sensitivity by exposing the brittleness of Congolese sovereignty: the state could not enforce a monopoly of legitimate violence in its territory, nor make its borders an effective barrier against subversion from without; it was a state in international law rather than empirical fact. All African leaders could recognise this dilemma, and collectively insisted on non-interference in other states as a cardinal principle of their international system. In practice, they were split between pro-western states that acquiesced in a legitimate head of government soliciting external assistance and the more radical states that opposed all neo-colonialist intervention.

Mobutu's second coming

Tshombe intended to consolidate his position in Congolese politics by challenging Kasavubu for the presidency, after his national popularity had been demonstrated in the free and fair legislative elections held in May 1965. Tshombe had put together a loose alliance of 49 parties from among the 223 that mushroomed into existence to contest the elections, and secured a parliamentary majority. Following months of friction, not least over the continued presence of white mercenaries in the army, Kasavubu dismissed Tshombe in October and nominated one of his leading opponents as prime minister-designate. A constitutional deadlock, virtually identical to that of September 1960, ensued: Tshombe still commanded a parliamentary majority, which refused to endorse Kasavubu's nominee, while the president refused to give way. Mobutu broke the impasse by seizing power for the second time on 25 November. He declared himself president for five years under a state of emergency and appointed a new 'government of national union'. The coup had been prepared in the army high command, and there was little to distinguish it from the rash of military interventions elsewhere in Africa at this time. Tshombe, Mobutu's most dangerous rival, went into exile for a second time. Party political activity was suspended, although the parties were not yet dissolved. Parliament gave the new government overwhelming approval.

Why was Mobutu able to consolidate his 1965 coup, and create one of Africa's most durable post-colonial states, when in 1960 he had allowed the party politicians to retake control of the central government? Part of the answer lies in his youth and inexperience in October 1960 – when he had just turned 30 – and the fact that the ANC was then a mutinous rabble. In the subsequent years, the army and the security police became more efficient coercive instruments, which enhanced their political role and strengthened Mobutu's institutional base. Moreover, between 1961 and 1964, he and senior officials from the Interior Ministry, the police and the National Bank formed a political clique – known as the Binza group from the Léopoldville suburb where they lived – which covertly exercised considerable power through the control of the central bureaucracy, rather than through party political organisation. The Americans enthusiastically supported him in 1965 (as they had five years earlier) but with the perhaps crucial difference that his ascendancy appeared altogether more conducive to broad western interests than Tshombe's.

There is, however, a further, banal reason for the consolidation of Mobutu's power after the 1965 coup: the sheer relief with which the great majority of Congolese greeted the demise of a polity that had served them so badly. 'Politicians' became a term of abuse during the first republic: they had presided over general impoverishment and mounting social inequality, while exposing the state to sundry external machinations and debasing its institutions with their opportunism and venality (Young and Turner, 1985, p. 52).

The endemic disorder had inevitable structural consequences for the economy, the most serious being the breakdown of the division of labour between town and country. Peasants in the more remote areas ceased producing for the market when their inter-sectoral terms of trade deteriorated. Marketed agricultural output fell by a third between 1959 and 1965; the resulting food scarcities drove up urban prices and added a further twist to spiralling inflation. Prices climbed nearly five-fold on Léopoldville's markets between June 1960 and December 1965, while workers' nominal wages rose only three-fold; in real terms, their incomes declined by about a third. Underlying the price inflation was a three and a half-fold increase in the money supply combined with falling output. State officials were unable to relieve the inflationary pressure through higher taxation, and worsened matters by reducing public investment and increasing unproductive expenditure, mostly on public service salaries. Declining exports led to a deteriorating trade balance, the introduction of exchange controls and import licensing, and two currency devaluations. The wages of civil servants and military personnel were protected against inflation, while many clerks and NCOs benefited from the wholesale promotions from the lower to the upper ranks. Merchants who acted as privileged middle-men between state officials and the expatriate companies were the only other group to prosper amidst the general economic decline. Thus, the new political class adroitly shifted the burden of economic regression on to the most vulnerable social groups: unorganised rural and urban workers and the peasantry.

Mining and its ancillary industries were less affected than commercial agriculture by the prevailing disorder: mineral exports declined by only 17 per cent between 1958 and 1966, although mining employment fell by two-fifths. The expatriate companies were relatively immune from the political and social turbulence of the First Republic because the Congolese elite recognised it lacked the technical competence to operate the mining and industrial complex without them. Though national leaders pledged themselves to a socialist future, they stopped well short of any immediate threat to the corporate sector: the engine of modernity had to be kept running (Young, 1965, p. 203).

Mobutu's central achievements after 1965 were reversing economic decline and stabilising the financial situation, and reconstructing the power of the central state, which provided a spring-board for the robust assertion of economic nationalism. Fortuitously, the onset of his regime coincided with an exceptional improvement in the terms of trade for Congolese mineral exports: the index climbed from 105 in 1964 to 204 in 1970 (1953 = 100) (Peemans, 1975, Table 5, p. 175). Export levies were the central government's principal source of revenue, so public finances automatically improved, but the regime also increased the rate of export duty, thus enabling it both to balance the budget and finance a surge of capital investment. The economic turning point for Mobutu's government was the monetary reform of June 1967, when a new currency was introduced, along with a swingeing devaluation in relation to the US$. The intention was to bridge the gap between the official and black-market rates of exchange, to restore the profitability of export enterprises and to control inflation. Devaluation was coupled with the ending of the import licensing that had been introduced by the First Republic, the easing of restrictions on the remittance of profits abroad and the promise of 40 per cent increase in the legal minimum wage. The stabilisation package was put together with the advice of the IMF and its adoption strongly urged by western embassies. The operation's success contributed decisively to the regime's credibility by effecting a revival of production and employment (Young and Turner, 1985, p. 280).

While being advised by the IMF on financial stabilisation, the Mobutu regime was reasserting the state's role in the economy and extending its sovereignty over the expatriate companies. During the Round Table Conference, there had been no agreement on the transfer of the colonial administration's share portfolio to the Congolese state, or on its taking over the public debt, or on the status of the colonial charter companies. These contentious issues had all been left to inter-governmental negotiations. Tshombe had eventually resolved them, but at a price Congolese nationalists deemed outrageous, for it included compensating the owners of the charter companies for their formal dissolution, though these discredited relics had repaid Belgian bondholders many times over. Mobutu immediately adopted a more aggressive stance towards the economic remnants of colonialism. In 1966, legislation was passed making all public land a domain of the Congolese nation-state and formally extinguishing all land grants and concessionary powers delegated by the colonial state. Companies were given a month to file claims for confirmation of rights to lands actually developed, which was usually granted, but lost all land and mineral rights held 'in reserve'.

This was followed by taking into public ownership Union Minière, which provided 50 per cent of state revenues in 1965 and 70 per cent of the country's foreign exchange (Young and Turner, 1985, p. 289; Rood, 1976, p. 432). It had been the fiscal prop of secessionist Katanga, and an important political motive for nationalising UMHK was to prevent Tshombe using the company's resources to return to power. Title passed to a new public corporation – the Générale Congolaise des Minérais (later known as Gécamines) – in which a 40 per cent share was held open for foreign partners, though as none were forthcoming it became completely state-owned. State appropriation was a popular move which cemented the nationalist consensus amongst the regime's elite and confirmed its radical credentials with students and 'intellectuals'. Negotiations began over the division of UMHK into its Belgian and Congolese components, but foundered on the ownership of a very large quantity of copper already exported but not yet marketed. When UMHK appeared obdurate, Mobutu seized its bank accounts and installed a management board to run the mines. Six weeks of economic warfare ensued, during which UMHK enlisted the support of the Belgian government in imposing a Common Market embargo on Congolese copper imports, while the Mobutu government sought a minority foreign partner to help run the enterprise. The United States offered its good offices in the dispute. Its resolution was apparently a victory for economic nationalism since UMHK accepted that Gécamines would have a monopoly on mining in Katanga and agreed that it would have no part in managing the state corporation. There was, however, a proviso which made this something of a pyrrhic victory: the management service contract went to an affiliate of the Société Générale group that was, in effect, a sister enterprise of UMHK. It was paid a percentage of the sales revenue of Gécamines far in excess of its costs, and the surplus was used to compensate UMHK – handsomely, as it transpired. The company's annual reports apparently show that its profits from the Congo were not affected by the nationalisation (Young and Turner, 1985, p. 293). Nevertheless, the Mobutu regime had put itself in the vanguard of 'Third World' states demanding public ownership of their natural resources.

Nationalising UMHK was part of a systematic policy of state participation in the economy: by 1970, the state owned nearly nine-tenths of the capital in mining, an even larger share in the metallurgy and electricity industries, and about four-fifths in transport and communications. State participation had also advanced in banking, insurance and commercial importing. The regime's goal was not to exclude foreign private enterprise, but to reinforce its bargaining power vis à vis the multi-national corporations, whose investment it was energetically soliciting. A relatively generous investment code was promulgated in 1969 which offered exemption from import duties on capital equipment, as well as the waiving for five years of corporate taxes and income taxes on expatriate salaries. This was a powerful inducement for multi-national corporations to invest in import-substitution manufacturing: General Motors, Leyland and Renault established vehicle assembly plants, Goodyear set up a tyre factory, Krupp invested in a palm oil and soap enterprise. New Japanese and American investors were found to develop hitherto unexploited copper reserves, using the time-honoured device of the concessionary company, with the state taking a minority share. Much the larger share of capital investment, however, was on public account, with foreign contractors bidding for 'turnkey' projects.

Agriculture, both commercial and peasant, atrophied during the investment boom, when the rural infrastructure was allowed to deteriorate. The share of agriculture in monetised GNP fell from 40 per cent in 1958 to 22 per cent by 1972, though it is scarcely credible that total agricultural production declined quite so precipitously. Peasants were offered such poor official prices that some reverted to subsistence, while others smuggled their crops over borders and traded them illicitly. However, there can be no doubting the steep fall in agricultural exports, such as palm products, and the massive contraction of employment: agricultural wage-earners were 55 per cent of all employees in 1959 and only 30 per cent in 1968 (Peemans, 1975, Table 13, p. 178). The Congo, which had exported a small food surplus before 1960, ceased to be self-sufficient in food; by 1977, food imports cost about $300 million. State distortion of produce markets was an underlying cause of agricultural malaise. To control inflation and placate urban consumers, administered prices and monopoly purchasing were imposed on food producers, though the principal beneficiaries were traders able to buy from peasants at fixed prices while evading price controls in urban markets. To add to peasant resentment, compulsory unpaid labour on 'development' projects for one afternoon a week was instituted in 1973. According to official rhetoric, 'authentic' communal values and solidarity were being restored; in practice, it was an opportunity for chiefs and local bureaucrats to extort a labour tribute for private purposes. The resemblance to the Belgian regime was all the greater because rural administrators aped the ways of their colonial predecessors. In a speech of rare candour, delivered in September 1974, the Commissioner of Political Affairs admitted his territorial agents acted 'in their jurisdictions as if they were in a conquered land [and] treat[ed] the population with arrogance and condescension' (quoted in Callaghy, 1984, p. 169).

Nigeria 1960–6: the crises of the First Republic and the road to civil war

The Congo's disintegration was a stark warning to other African leaders of what could befall their own countries. On dissolving the Nigerian parliament in December 1964, President Azikiwe denounced the corruption and intimidation which had marred every Nigerian election since 1954 and 'venture[d] the prediction that the experience of the Democratic Republic of the Congo will be child's play if it ever comes to our turn to play such a tragic role' (quoted in Kirk-Greene, 1971, vol. 1, p. 21). What Azikiwe could not have predicted was that his own Eastern Region would secede in late May 1967, with the overwhelming support of fellow Ibos. Hitherto, they had been in the vanguard Nigerian nationalism: they were the first to embrace the idea of a unified Nigeria wholeheartedly and to identify with its survival and progress as a political entity (*ibid.*, p. 4). Ibos were disproportionately present in the army officer corps, the federal bureaucracy, the universities, and had migrated throughout Nigeria in search of economic opportunities. Biafran nationalism was the overnight invention of Ibo lecturers at Ibadan University who began meeting in April 1966 to elaborate the rationale for secession; it had no historic roots because the Ibos were a 'de-centralised' people with no tradition of state formation. In short, Biafra's secession had no long-term, structural causes; it was contingent on events following the coup attempted by a group of young army officers on 15 January 1966, when the Federal Prime Minister, the Northern and Western regional prime ministers and seven senior army officers were assassinated.

The political crisis which the young officers sought to resolve, and bloodily exacerbated, did have long-term causes. In explicating them it is difficult to disentangle the objective conditions which made Nigerian unity so precarious from the subjective prejudices and animosities of the political actors struggling to dominate the federal and regional arenas. As Anthony Kirk-Greene explains:

> The Nigerian tragedy has been bedevilled by a set of oppositions – generalised, stereotyped, not necessarily of the same order and maybe imaginary, yet each widening the wound and reducing the hope of healing it: North v. South, Islam v. Christianity, alleged feudalism v. assumed socialism, federal v. unitary preferences, traditional authority v. achieved elitism, haves v. haves not, each with sinister undertones of tension, irreconcilability and threatened withdrawal. None was entirely accurate. Nevertheless each opposing set had sufficient seed of truth within it to permit, and even fertilise, the growth of feared fact from the semi-fiction of its existence. (*Ibid.*, pp. 5–6)

The most fundamental of Nigeria's political problems was that it acceded to independence with a constitutional structure that encouraged the country's many socio-cultural conflicts to crystallise around the North–South divide. This same structure enhanced the power of the ethnic majority in each of three regions, and led to inherently unstable coalitions at the federal centre. In retrospect, it is evident that, had the nationalists agreed to split the regions into smaller states, then a more flexible structure, one more responsive both to the ethnic pluralism within the regions and Nigerians' common interest in maintaining national unity, would have resulted. Unfortunately, the Willink Commission of 1958, set up to consider the fears of minorities in the regions, refused to recommend the creation of new states on the grounds that they would perpetuate separatism and tribalism, which 'might otherwise disappear' (Willink Report, 1957–8, p. 87). In the early 1960s, the three regions had many of the appurtenances of sovereign states within a mini diplomatic system; in terms of their populations and resources, they were as independently viable as the constituent parts of the French West African Federation that broke into national states.

The constitutional structure was made particularly unwieldy by the Northern Region's preponderance: it accounted for three-quarters of Nigeria's territory and about half its population, which inevitably gave its dominant party a plurality of seats in the federal legislature. Northern leaders took federal office primarily to defend the North's 'unity' and 'traditions'; revealingly, the most powerful, Ahmadu Bello, who held the honorific title of *Sardauna* or war leader of Sokoto, chose to remain the Regional Prime Minister, rather than become federal premier. In the ideological cartography of Nigerian politics, the North appeared a monolith looming over the Federation; to its detractors, bigoted and backward, to its admirers, morally and socially cohesive and at peace with its religious tradition. Behind the monolithic appearance were serious ethnic, religious and social fissures. The Hausa-Fulani grouping accounted for no more than 60 per cent of the region's population; at least two in five belonged to minorities. The North was not wholly Muslim: in the early 1950s, about one-quarter of the region's population was classified as Animists and about 3–4 per cent were Christians. These minorities were heavily concentrated in the Middle Belt provinces, where pagans were subjected to a campaign of coerced conversion during the run-up to independence. Islamic society in the emirate North was not divided on sectarian lines, but there were tensions within it between the 'puritan' equality of all believers and the steep social hierarchy, between those militating for an Islamic state ruled by *shari'a* law and secularists wanting the state insulated from religion. The authoritarianism of the NPC regional government, and its blatantly undemocratic approach to electoral politics, stemmed from its inability to act as an 'umbrella' party; rather than articulating the pluralism of the North, it repressed it behind a façade of moral and social solidarity. The main opposition came, not from southern nationalists, but from a regional party claiming to represent the interests of the 'commoners' against the feudal order: the Northern Elements Progressive Union (NEPU) led by Aminu Kano.

The festering contradiction in the modern democratic state inaugurated in 1960 arose from the northern elite's political pre-eminence and the meagre inroads of western modernity into Northern society and culture. At every level of education, the proportion of the relevant age group being educated was far below that in the South. In 1959, only 2 per cent of the children in Sokoto province were in primary schools; only nine of the 944 students enrolled at Ibadan University were Hausa-Fulani, as compared with 408 Yoruba and 333 Ibo (Lloyd, 1970, p. 5; Bevan *et al.*, 1999, p. 22). Regional disparities in educational attainment meant that (with rare exceptions) only southerners possessed the skills and qualifications for responsible jobs in modern commerce, industry and, most cherished of all, public administration, where a new graduate entrant could expect an annual salary 20 times the annual earnings of the average farmer (Diamond, 1987, p. 576). In the North, the mines, commercial firms, dispensaries and even the Native Authorities were obliged to rely on southern immigrants for their clerks and technicians.

The NPC-led federal government, formed after the 1959 general election, depended on a coalition of expediency with the NCNC. Apart from their differences in outlook and ethos, the two were at odds over creating more states: the NPC refused to contemplate dividing up the Northern Region; the NCNC favoured creating new states and a stronger federal government. The mutual mistrust within the coalition became quite open with the publication of the 1962–8 development plan, which proposed concentrating the bulk of federal capital expenditure in the North. Meanwhile, less qualified northerners were being 'jobbed' into high office and commissioned into the army ahead of their southern rivals. In the view of the NCNC, the implicit rules of distributive politics were being flouted. On paper, its more ideologically compatible partner was Awolowo's Action Group, but ideology (and class) counted for little in determining partisan allegiance and party alignments. The bitter rivalry between the NCNC and the AG in the Western Region outweighed their common antipathy towards the North's aristocratic and conservative leadership.

Political contestation was so antagonistic that politicians could not be trusted to count the people accurately. The 1962 census was conducted in an outrageously partisan way because the distribution of power and resources between the regions hung on the outcome. The initial results indicated that the southern population had increased more rapidly than the northern since the last census of 1952, and that the Northern Region no longer had a majority of the population. However, demographic tests showed that the Eastern Region's numbers had been grossly inflated. The Northern government then ordered a 'verification check', from which it claimed to have discovered an additional 8 million people (so preserving the region's majority). The ensuing furore compelled the federal premier to cancel the result and order a new census for 1963. By then census-taking was so politicised, and so fraught with mutual suspicion, that fraud was commonplace. The results indicated that the national population had increased by an altogether incredible 83 per cent in ten years. The North retained its majority (53.7 per cent), though the reliability of that figure is dubious. The NPC exercised its parliamentary muscle to have the results officially endorsed, though they were flatly rejected by the Eastern regional government. The census crisis drove a deeper wedge between the NPC and the NCNC and, without breaking up their federal government coalition, both prepared for the elections due in 1964 by forming electoral alliances with other parties.

Political polarisation between North and South had been accelerated by the destruction of the Action Group in the West, where civil strife amongst Yoruba politicians echoed and revived the internecine conflicts in nineteenth-century Yorubaland (Joseph, 1987, p. 110). The AG split into two factions following its 1962 congress: Awolowo, who had resigned the regional premiership to become leader of the opposition in the federal parliament, sought to transform the AG into a radical, pan-Nigerian socialist movement, in imitation of Nkrumah's CPP. He was bidding to recast himself as a national politician appealing to the poor and underprivileged across regional and ethnic boundaries, and proposed breaking up the country's regional structure. The premier in the Western Region, Chief Akintola, would have none of this: his faction sought a way of rejoining the federal coalition because Yoruba elites were being excluded from government patronage, and were losing their pre-eminent position in the bureaucracy and academia to Ibo rivals.

Both the NCNC and NPC sought to profit from the AG's implosion: the former by carving out a fourth region in the mid-west, where it had considerable support, which would tilt the balance of federal power in its favour; the latter by striking an alliance with a new party formed out of the wreckage of the AG. Awolowo's faction persuaded the governor of the West to depose Akintola, whose supporters provoked a fracas in the House of Assembly when it met to nominate a successor. The federal government then declared a state of emergency and installed a puppet administration. It instituted an enquiry into political corruption during Action Group rule in the West, which as we have noted censured Awolowo in the strongest terms but exonerated Akintola (a farcically one-sided conclusion which destroyed the commission's claim to impartiality). But the most extraordinary turn of events was the laying of charges of treasonable felony against Awolowo and his closest associates, who were alleged to have sent activists for military training in Ghana, and to have smuggled arms into Nigeria, in preparation for a coup. After an eight-month trial (November 1962– June 1963) they were convicted, after former Action Group militants turned Queen's evidence, and sentenced to ten years' imprisonment. Most observers considered Awolowo guilty of arming his followers with smuggled weapons for fear of escalating political violence but that the charge of plotting a coup was unproven and highly implausible (Diamond, 1988a, pp. 111–12). Whatever the truth, the verdict outraged both Awolowo's Yoruba following and young Nigerians in other regions attracted by his political radicalism.

Meanwhile, the federal government had established the Mid-West Region. After six months of emergency rule, Akintola, who had formed a new party from AG defectors, was reinstated as premier of a coalition government with the Western Regional NCNC. For both sides this was a marriage of convenience. The NCNC hoped to dominate the regional government, and looked on Akintola as an expendable ally. He was playing for time to establish his party and seek an arrangement with the NPC; for him, the NCNC was an Ibo party, and he was not going to subordinate the Yoruba to the Ibo (Dudley, 1970, p. 96).

The NPC was alarmed by the prospect of the NCNC replacing the AG as the dominant party in the West, and so made overtures to Akintola, promising him a share of the spoils following a realignment of the federal coalition. The flow of oil revenues, though as yet a modest stream, was alerting all political parties to the enormous financial resources that would spill into the lap of the federal government. Strengthened by support from the federal centre, Akintola issued an ultimatum to the NCNC members of the regional assembly to join his newly formed Nigerian National Democratic Party (NNDP) or be excluded from his government. Most promptly did.

The outcome of these Byzantine machinations was political bipolarisation between two electoral alliances: the NCNC joined with the remnants of the AG and the NEPU to form the United Progressive Grand Alliance; the NPC united with the NNDP and some minor allies in the Nigerian National Alliance, built on their common determination to control federal power, and their common hostility to the Ibo. This realignment was taking place against a background of mounting social turbulence which expressed widespread disgust with political life as such. The hitherto fragmented trade union movement launched a concerted challenge to the country's political class in the spring of 1964. Real wages were declining, so to force a revision of the officially regulated wage structure, the unions called a general strike in June 1964, which brought economic life to a standstill. The 13-day strike was overwhelmingly supported by organised and unorganised wage-earners, and enjoyed widespread public sympathy outside the working class, especially in the cities. It was clearly directed against the federal government – the largest employer of organised labour – and the fact that the politicians made significant concessions under duress weakened their authority, not only over the deeply disgruntled popular classes, but also over the senior civil servants charged with administering the economy. The Lagos bureaucracy now spoke quite openly of the responsibility for saving Nigeria from the politicians; the outcome of the strike was, according to Kirk-Greene, 'another nail in the coffin of the First Republic' (Kirk-Greene, 1971, vol. 1, p. 18).

The opening of the general election campaign in late 1964 provided abundant evidence that the democratic process was, if not quite moribund, then a charade masking the seizure of elective office by intimidation and fraud. The electorate was wooed with vituperative rhetoric and blatant appeals to tribalism. From the start of the campaign, it was clear that many politicians considered the essential issue to be simply whether the federal government would be dominated by the 'South' or the 'North' – or, as it was more often put, by the 'Ibos' or the 'Hausas'. In protest against the licensed thuggery and administrative coercion, the UPGA called an electoral boycott, but it was fully observed only in the East, where the NCNC-controlled regional government instructed the returning officers not to be present at the polls. Where the boycott was observed in the West, its effect was to give a free run to Akintola's NNDP. President Azikiwe, who was still universally identified with the NCNC though his office placed him 'above politics', refused to recognise the results or to reappoint the NPC's Abubakar Balewa as federal prime minister. A tense deadlock ensued when it seemed the Federation might break up. Azikiwe relented after spokesmen for the army and the police, who had taken judicial advice, said they would not support him. Balewa was reappointed at the head of a coalition spanning the NPC, NCNC and NNDP, with the number of ministerial offices increased to 76 so that Akintola's party could reap its reward. The North's political dominance had been unambiguously asserted, though in a face-saving compromise the boycotted contests were held in the East, which enabled the NCNC to recover its seats in the region.

The fate of the civilian regime was sealed with the regional election in the West in October 1965, a vicious contest between the remnants of the AG and the NNDP. It was an election in name only: the results were rigged on a massive scale and Akintola's victory was met with total disbelief. His regime had become deeply unpopular because of its corruption, extravagance and its collaboration with the 'oppressors' of the Yoruba people (Diamond, 1988b, p. 42). The fact that the NPC had intervened on behalf of its coalition partner made the sense of outrage all the greater. The announcement, soon after the poll, that the Marketing Board's cocoa price would fall by nearly half triggered a rural jacquerie, which gradually spread to the towns: by December, a journey by car from Ibadan, the regional capital, to Lagos, the federal capital had become almost too risky (Dudley, 1970, p. 98).

It was in these circumstances that the seven young majors (six of whom were Ibos) carried out their coup. Their heartfelt motive was utter patriotic contempt for the Republic's political class. In the words of their ring-leader, Major Nzeogwu, their enemies were:

> the political profiteers, the swindlers, the men in high and low places that seek bribes and demand 10 per cent, those that seek to keep the country divided permanently so that they can remain ministers and VIPs of waste, the tribalists, the nepotists.

What gave them moral authority to act was that 'Only in the army do you get true Nigerianism' (quoted in Luckham, 1971, p. 33).

The idea of the army as the premier national institution was, it must be said, something of an illusion: like the political parties, the trade unions and even the civil service, the army was poorly institutionalised. More than four out of five officers had been commissioned since independence and their corporate discipline and solidarity were weakened by rapid promotion, an imbalanced age structure and strong horizontal ties which undercut the hierarchy of command. Because few educated Yoruba pursued a military career, the army was generally seen as an alien force in the West. As subsequent events showed, by killing seven of its most senior officers, the majors fatally wounded the army's ability to remain 'above society'.

In the eyes of the literate 'civic' public, the majors were national saviours. The Nigerian press overwhelmingly endorsed the coup. The National Students Union issued a statement of support and students paraded around Lagos with placards reading 'To Hell with Tribalism' and 'This is the Birth of Real Nigerian Freedom'. Even in the North, there was concealed delight (Kirk-Greene, 1971, vol. 1, pp. 38–9). Notwithstanding this jubilant reaction, the conspirators had, in fact, failed to take over the federal government. In Lagos, they lost control of the insurrection to the commander-in-chief, Major-General Ironsi (also an Ibo), who was given a mandate by the remnants of the Federal Cabinet to form a military government. Nzeogwu secured a guarantee of safe conduct for the rebels from Ironsi and what proved to be immunity from prosecution, for none ever faced charges.

The universal approbation that greeted the formation of the Supreme Military Council – even the political parties effusively endorsed it – and the nomination of four military governors for the regions lasted through to May. Ironsi represented a familiar type in post-colonial African politics: the apolitical 'man on horseback', pledged to cleanse the public stables. His overriding objectives were curbing corruption and, in his own words, sweeping away 'loyalties and activities which promote tribal consciousness and sectional interests' (quoted in *ibid.*, p. 42). Tribal associations were proscribed. The salaries of national political office holders were stopped; they were ordered to repay their outstanding loans; and tribunals were set up to enquire into maladministration. The number of ministries, which had been inflated far beyond real need, was reduced. A Commission was appointed to consider how a united Nigeria might be administratively organised. However, the Military Council's drive towards a unitary form of state provoked a backlash against Ironsi and led to his downfall. Considerable disquiet had already been aroused in the North by the promotion of Ibo officers and Ironsi's preference for Ibo advisers, as well as by the failure to charge anyone with the *Sardauna's* murder and the insensitivity with which this was celebrated in some quarters, when, in a radio broadcast of 24 May, Ironsi abolished the regions and dissolved all political parties. The reaction was a pogrom directed against Ibo migrants in the North: hundreds were lynched by mobs yelling 'Let us secede' and 'Down with Ironsi'. The Military Council appeared to have restored its authority in the North, when Ironsi, some senior colleagues and about 200 Ibo officers and men were assassinated by Northern troops on 29 July.

The origins and anticipated outcome of this second coup are not wholly clear, though simple revenge was one motive: sardonic commentators called it the Hausas' 'return match' against the 'January boys'. In the East, the mutiny was repressed by the Military Governor, Lt-Colonel Ojukwu, whose administration was all the stronger because of the power vacuum elsewhere. On 1 August, the rebels asked Lt-Colonel Gowon, a Christian from a small ethnic group in the North whom they had briefly apprehended, to take command, seemingly in the expectation that he would lead the region into secession. He may have been dissuaded from this by strong representations from the British High Commissioner and the American Ambassador shortly before addressing the nation on the radio; both urged that the secession of any area would be a major political and economic disaster for the Nigerian people and a severe setback for independent Africa. If their advice was crucial, it was a rare instance of effective foreign intervention in the long-running crisis. In his address, Gowon hinted strongly at the dismantling of 'our unitary system of government' by negotiation. The regional governors of the West, the Mid-West and the North rallied to the new regime, but Ojukwu was much more ambivalent. He took the view that his legitimacy stemmed from the mandate given to Ironsi by the Federal Cabinet in January, while Gowon was the ad hoc choice of a group of mutineers to head the Military Council and take supreme command of the army. There were, in point of fact, several officers senior to Gowon, who had indeed been fortuitously hoisted into power. Ojukwu regarded him, not as his commander-in-chief, but as a diplomatic partner in the renegotiation of the country's constitution and future. The Oxford-educated Ojukwu's immense self-confidence, which is so evident in the interviews he gave to television journalists, stemmed from an exceptionally privileged background. Like Tshombe, he was the son of a wealthy businessman.

In the coming months, the choice before Nigerians lay, principally, between a loose confederation of four autonomous states and a more closely integrated federation of many smaller states. The first tended to be favoured by the opinion leaders of the three largest 'internal nations', the second by representatives of the minorities. With Ironsi and so many senior officers killed, the unitary state they had championed was now chimerical. The army was evidently infested with ethnic distrust and no longer an integrative force; it broke into chunks after the July coup because troops stationed outside their native regions feared for their lives and returned home. All Eastern officers fled to the East where they began assembling what became Biafra's army. Since the unitary state was no longer an option, Northern leaders drew back from secession. Ojukwu gave a categorical assurance to a meeting of oil executives in August that the East did not wish to secede either. Whatever Gowon's views before the July coup, he soon became committed to maintaining Nigerian unity on the basis of a new, consensually agreed constitution. With considerable political skill, he cut across the North–South division by releasing Awolowo and the other AG leaders from prison and drawing them into the constitutional negotiations between regional delegates. With hindsight, we can see that secession of the West, which foreign observers anticipated when Biafra declared its independence, had been shrewdly deflected. Gowon's disposition was conciliatory, not authoritarian; rather than dictate Nigeria's future, he tried to return the problem to a conference of politicians in September, after an impressive consultation exercise in the regions. The key development during this conference was a shift in the Northern delegation's position with respect to the creation of new states: the Northern minorities and Northern minority troops in particular, were now wielding more influence. Moreover, Northern officers, officials and academics had become acutely aware of the economic disadvantages of secession; they recognised that only by creating new states could an effective central government, with the power to redistribute oil revenue throughout Nigeria, be retained (Williams and Turner, 1978, p. 145).

What wrecked the chances of introducing a new constitution by negotiation was the ethnic violence that erupted in the North on Independence weekend (29 September–1 October). Kirk-Greene alleges that the pogrom was preceded by widespread attacks on Hausas living in the East; others – usually, it must be said, partisans of Biafra – have strongly disputed this (Kirk-Greene, 1971, vol. 1, p. 64; Cronje, 1972, p. 18). In response to inflammatory radio reports of these alleged atrocities, Northern mobs slaughtered resident Ibos with the connivance of the army and police. According to Easterners, the carnage was planned and coordinated; Northern spokesmen sincerely believed it was spontaneous. How many were killed has never been established. In the proclamation of the Republic of Biafra, Ojukwu claimed that 30,000 Easterners had been massacred in the North. Other estimates were much lower, but two leading scholars recently put the death toll of Easterners between May and October at 'between 80,000 and 100,000' (Falola and Heaton, 2008, p. 174). Whatever the true figure, it sufficed to lend credence to the notion that the Ibos were threatened with genocide. In the wake of these massacres, between 1 and 1.5 million refugees returned to the Eastern Region. The influx created mounting pressure to secede and, since the refugees were mainly Ibos, made the region more ethnically homogeneous. There were retaliatory attacks on non-Easterners resident in the East and, in October, Ojukwu expelled them all on the grounds that he could no longer assure their safety. He withdrew the Eastern delegates from the constitutional talks and severed rail links with the North.

The last chance to dissolve the federal structure amicably came with the meeting of the Supreme Military Council at Aburi, in Ghana, on 4 and 5 January 1967, the first Ojukwu attended since the July coup. There can be no doubt about what was said: the verbatim record (including a gramophone recording) of the soldiers' discussions was soon made public. But the interpretation of what was concluded was a different matter. Ojukwu, the most intellectually forceful of the participants, later claimed that Gowon reneged on a 'confederal' agreement that secured the East's essential interests. No civilian advisers were present and it seems Gowon made verbal concessions on the vital issue of regional consent to federal legislation which the Federal Permanent Secretaries and Law Officers considered unworkable when they went through the draft minutes. When it became clear that agreement had not, in fact, been reached, Ojukwu accused Gowon of acting in bad faith. In the following months, the Eastern Regional government prepared for independence by drawing up a national budget, importing arms, arranging for diplomatic representation abroad and sequestering federal taxes levied in the region. It had, in practice, become a sovereign state some months before the formal declaration of independence.

What remained in doubt, until late in the day, was whether Gowon could persuade the rest of the Federation to take military action. The Aburi conference had resolved to settle the crisis without resort to force, a position the military governors of the West and the Mid-West, as well as the Army Chief of Staff, were still holding in early May. The expectation that the West would secede if the East were invaded was aroused by Awolowo's forceful public statements and his withdrawal from the ongoing constitutional talks. He called on Northern troops to leave the West and Lagos, and denounced the army as 'an army of occupation' which reduced the region to the 'status of a protectorate'. Gowon held the wobbling federal alliance together by agreeing to evacuate all non-Yoruba troops from the West and decreeing the division of the Federation into 12 states. The North was split into six states, which broke up the monolith hanging over the South and met the demands of the Middle Belt minorities for autonomy, while the East was broken into three states, in a calculated effort to woo the non-Ibo minorities away from Ojukwu's regime. The area around Lagos became a separate state, but the Western Region otherwise maintained its integrity, which helped secure its reluctant support for military action against Biafra. Gowon broadened his government by recruiting civilian politicians, including Awolowo, to the Federal Executive Council and won round educated opinion outside the East with his patience and flexibility; Ojukwu was increasingly regarded as an intransigent demagogue.

New states meant many more political and administrative offices, and so job opportunities for the educated and ambitious, and more rewards to local communities in the form of scholarships and public projects. The six new states of the North required 42 ministries to replace the 16 of the old regional government. Employment in the North Central civil service alone rose by 80 per cent between 1968 and 1974 (Smith, 1981, p. 359). Bureaucratic expansion was funded by increased allocations from the Distributable Pool Account, into which the oil revenues flowed and from which they were disbursed amongst the states according to federally prescribed formulae.

The federal side waited a month before launching what it called a 'surgical police action' on 6 July, in the expectation that hostilities would last a few days. In the event, the war dragged on for 30 months. Its demographic toll cannot be confidently assessed: deaths from disease, starvation and hostilities in Biafra have been variously estimated at between 1 million and 3 million (Falola and Heaton, 2008, p. 180). The war was unlike any previous conflict in sub-Saharan Africa: it was the first large-scale war fought with modern weapons in which the armies were manned, trained, led and sustained by Africans, and white mercenaries played a minor role (Saint Jorre, 1972, p. 273). African political actors determined its objectives, Biafran tenacity its duration. Biafra was blockaded from early July, entirely cut off from the sea by May 1968 and reduced to an enclave one-quarter the size of the former Eastern Region. Its forces were outnumbered and outgunned. Nevertheless, the Federal Military Government had to expend considerable military resources reconquering the territory. Its army was expanded from 10,000 men in January 1966 to 270,000 by the war's end, and allegedly fired off more small arms ammunition than the entire British forces in the course of the Second World War (Wilson, 1971, p. 630). In addition to waging a war of attrition against the Biafrans, the federal government had to quell serious unrest within its 'home front' in 1968–9 when Yoruba cocoa farmers rebelled against the emergency levies imposed to finance the war, which came after a decade of falling cocoa prices. The unrest compelled the government to reduce taxes and raise the cocoa price.

The war was also unprecedented in Africa in that both combatants claimed to be authentic nation-states, asserting their sovereign prerogatives. For the Federal Military Government, the conflict was an internal matter in which it would brook no mediation, whether by the UN, the OAU, Britain or the Commonwealth. Biafra's publicists adeptly asserted the state's moral right to exist in terms that echoed the Zionist case for the state of Israel: Biafrans were a culturally homogeneous people threatened with genocide; Biafra was their homeland; they were entitled to take up arms in self-defence. The merit of their argument is not at issue here; what needs emphasising is that a significant number of independent African states accepted its validity. Although there was always a consensus in the OAU against secession in *any* member state, Tanzania granted official recognition to Biafra on 13 April 1968; in the following month, Zambia, Côte d'Ivoire and Gabon followed suit. Comparisons with Katanga were inevitable, but Julius Nyerere rejected them as 'superficial'. The crucial distinction, according to the

Tanzanian president, was that, unlike in Katanga, there was no vested neo-colonial or foreign economic interest in secession: 'the Ibos are simply fighting for their own survival and therefore have no strong supporter. That is their strength and weakness: it is the major difference between Katanga and Biafra' (quoted in Cronje, 1972, pp. 283–4).

While the war demonstrated African sovereign autonomy, it also confirmed the continent's age-old dependency on imported military hardware. It could not have been fought without a vast inflow of *matériel* from the industrialised countries and Britain was the chief supplier of infantry munitions, light artillery and armoured cars to the Federal Military Government. The Labour Government gave the Federal Military Government strong diplomatic and moral support, but out of deference to its backbenchers' moral scruples refused to provide combat aircraft or weapons of mass destruction. The Soviet Union made good some of this deficiency by supplying Nigeria with MiG fighters, transport aircraft and bombs, though in insufficient quantities to alter the character of what was essentially an infantryman's war. The USA joined most western governments in embargoing arms sales to both sides. The war cut across Cold War alignments – witness the jarring spectacle of both Britain and the Soviet Union arming the Federal Military Government – which gave the Nigerians considerable latitude in their dealings with the industrialised powers. In November 1968, Gowon signed an agreement with Russia for the construction of Nigeria's first iron and steel mill, which panicky Whitehall officials saw as a prelude to a Soviet sphere of influence in West Africa. The Wilson government's resolve to stick by Gowon – extolled as 'Nigeria's Lincoln' – was if anything strengthened. Biafra's support abroad came predominantly from heterogeneous groups in European 'civil society'; no western government recognised the breakaway state, though Gaullist France came close to doing so. From August 1968, clandestine shipments of French arms enabled the Biafrans to continue a military struggle that had seemed lost, but the quantities provided could not affect the final outcome.

The civil war irrevocably enhanced the federal government's powers vis à vis the states and, unsurprisingly, raised the political salience of the army. Since military officers were rarely competent to formulate economic and fiscal policy, they relied heavily on the Permanent Secretaries in the key ministries. Civilians were strongly represented in the Federal Executive Council (i.e., the Cabinet) between 1966 and 1979, when central governments were essentially national coalitions, with political leaders from all states and many ethnic groups serving

Map 5.3 Nigerian states, 1967–76

under military supervision. Military-bureaucratic rule was almost certainly more prolonged than it would have been had peace been preserved: on 1 October 1970, ten months after hostilities ceased, Gowon announced that the military would remain in power for another six years while it pursued a nine-point programme of reconstruction. Gowon's finest service to Nigeria's peoples was to oversee a peace of reconciliation: he ensured that Ibo civilians were not treated as defeated enemies and that there was no wholesale purge of Biafran public officials. A number who had actively abetted secession were dismissed, but a clear distinction was made between them and those who had simply carried out their duties. Ojukwu fled into exile as Biafra fell and efforts to have him extradited failed, which fortuitously aided reconciliation by focusing culpability on the absent leader. The new East Central State, comprising the Ibo heartland, was placed in the charge of an Ibo official, who had remained loyal to the federal government during the war, but his all-Ibo cabinet included members who had served under the secessionist regime. Federal grants aided the repair of war-damaged infrastructure and the fairly speedy recovery of local industry. The war itself did not break up the alignments of region, ethnicity and party that had so de-stabilised the First Republic: the crucial step had been taken with the creation of more states. Nevertheless, the experience of civil war was so traumatic as to banish secession beyond the 'horizon' of serious politics for a generation.

Conclusions

Comparing the sequence of events in the post-colonial Congo and Nigeria gives us a counter-factual check on the explanations customarily proffered for them, which are not so much wrong, as incomplete. Lumumba's cri de coeur – 'We received our sovereignty without any transition. From being one hundred per cent a colony, we were suddenly one hundred per cent independent' (quoted in Kyle, 2002, p. 595) – was fully justified. The Belgians were reprehensible in not promoting Congolese political autonomy before being rushed to independence. Parliamentary institutions were devised before Congolese politicians had any experience of cooperating in a national arena and while political parties were proliferating and fragmenting. But this explanation will not do for Nigeria, whose politicians had several years' experience of responsible self-government before the final transfer of power, which was of little significance for the structure of domestic politics. And because the explanation will not do for Nigeria, it will not *suffice* for the Congo. To the specific factors which contributed to the catastrophe that overwhelmed the Congo, we have to add the more general preconditions which made all independence settlements in Africa's giant states unstable and conflict-ridden. The Congolese, like Nigerians, were localised peoples with many histories, who lived in oral cultures and depended on extended kinship for social support. Their aggregation into a supposedly national community was an inherently traumatic process made more difficult by neo-colonialism.

6
Nigeria and Congo-Zaire from the 1970s to the Late 1990s: Regional Giants, Giant Failures?

In the early 1970s, Nigeria and Zaire were vying for the leadership of 'Black' Africa. Their large populations, mineral wealth and abundant land, coupled with nuclei of modern industry, rapid improvements in the quality of the labour force and strong state institutions promised a far brighter future than that awaiting newly independent Bangladesh. Inflation had been halted in Zaire and the currency's international value stabilised; there was negligible debt and ample foreign exchange reserves; it was attracting new foreign investors. In Nigeria, the civil war's economic consequences could be shrugged off because its end coincided with the onset of the great oil boom. The state transformed the country's 'public face' by enormous investment in physical infrastructure, national institutions (such as universities) and prestigious events, most notably the great Festival of Black Arts and Culture, held in Lagos in 1977. However, by the later 1990s, Zairians were far poorer on average than Bangladeshis and Nigerians no wealthier. Zaire had virtually ceased to function as a state and the Nigerian Federal Government was unable to suppress armed dissidence in the Niger Delta. Nigerians had so little confidence in their own country as a site of economic opportunity that they were holding about $107 billion of their wealth abroad, or three times as much as the private domestic capital stock (Collier, 2003). Apart from crude oil, Nigeria's 'foreign trade sector' consisted of international fraud and the re-export of narcotics. State decline cannot be represented as a linear narrative, for there were several occasions when the political class in Nigeria and Zaire appeared to be resisting it by reforming institutions and governance, but incipient decay is the inevitable focus of this chapter.

African absolutism: Mobutu in his pomp

When he seized power, there was little to distinguish Mobutu from other military strongmen but over time his regime consolidated a distinctive ensemble of power and authority that has been illuminatingly compared with early modern absolutism (Callaghy, 1984). The structural similarities lay in the absence of any clear distinction between the state as a public entity and the ruler's personal property; the religious aura surrounding his person and the pontifical status of his pronouncements; and the social character of the class through which he ruled.

Mobutu's ascendancy differed from the brutal and arbitrary tyranny of Jean-Bedel Bokassa or Idi Amin in being institutionalised and resting on a broad measure of consent. The new constitution of April 1967 – overwhelmingly ratified by referendum in June – centralised power in the presidency and reduced parliament to a cipher. The office of prime minister had already been abolished, and the practice of promulgating legislative decisions by decree was well established. The political fragmentation into 21 provincettes had been reversed in 1966 by reducing the number of provinces to 12 and transforming them into purely administrative entities, with officials directly answerable to the central government and merely consultative assemblies. A National Police Force was created, with Belgian and American assistance, in July 1966. These measures were tantamount to the restitution of the 'Bula Matari' bureaucratic state, but combined with an autocracy alien to the Belgian mode of government. Huge resources were placed at Mobutu's personal disposal because the presidency services controlled about 50 per cent of state capital expenditure. In May 1967, the Mouvement populaire de la révolution (MPR) was established to mobilise the people behind the president. According to its manifesto, the MPR was nationalist, authentically Congolese and opposed to the 'borrowed theories and doctrines' of both capitalism and communism. *De facto*, Congo-Zaire was henceforth a one-party state, though it did not become so *de jure* until May 1970, when the MPR was declared the supreme institution of the state.

Buoyed up by high international prices for its mineral exports, the Mobutu regime commissioned foreign consortia to undertake several grandiose industrial projects on a 'turnkey' basis. All were financed by foreign loans and all proved to be crushing economic liabilities. Like many African leaders, Mobutu regarded a domestic steel industry as the hallmark of economic independence and, in late 1966, pledged to develop one to exploit the Congo's large iron ore reserves. The state bore the entire cost of the Maluku steel mill built by an Italian–German consortium between 1972 and 1975. Unfortunately, the immense sums needed to open up the reserves were not forthcoming, and the mill operated entirely with imported scrap, with a unit cost up to eight times that of imported steel; 90 per cent of its capacity was never utilised. The project to supply the Katangan industrial belt with electricity generated 1800 km away, at the Inga dam on the lower Zaire River, was an even greater drain on resources. Work began in 1972, at the high tide of the regime's fortunes, for completion in 1977. The project was not, in fact, finished until 1982 – at an estimated cost of $2 billion in current prices – by when all projections of demand for electricity in Katanga, and its unit cost in relation to the price of copper, proved hopelessly ill-founded. The power line was transmitting only half its capacity in the 1980s and the electricity was so expensive that the state had to subsidise its consumption by Gécamines.

After the presidential constitution was adopted the regime sought either to suppress all autonomous civil society institutions or to incorporate them within its own apparatus. The right to strike was indefinitely suspended and independent trade unions abolished, as were ethnic and women's associations. The national union of university students, which had originally welcomed Mobutu's regime, was banned in February 1968, following demonstrations against Vice-president Hubert Humphrey, who had the gall to lay flowers at the Lumumba monument during his official visit to Léopoldville. Henceforth, students could only organise legally through the youth branch of the MPR. In June 1969, a peaceful and apolitical demonstration on the Lovanium campus was suppressed by the army with the loss of 60 student lives. Two years later, when Lovanium students attempted to commemorate the massacre, the regime conscripted them in the army, and then moved to nationalise the three universities.

In December 1971, the regime took control of the country's vibrant religious life with a law allowing the state to dissolve 'any church or sect that compromises or threatens to compromise public order'. Only three churches were officially recognised: the Protestant Church of Christ in Zaire, the Kimbanguist Church and the Catholic Church, while scores of unrecognised religious sects were dissolved and their leaders gaoled. Kimbanguism was an 'Ethiopian' church inspired by a Congolese prophet imprisoned for life by the Belgians; Protestantism was highly Africanised. Both could accommodate themselves to the regime's ambitious bid to master society ideologically and institutionally. Not so Catholicism, which looked abroad for its spiritual leadership and represented an alternative authority structure. Catholic teaching and practice were the main obstacles to propagating the ideology of 'authenticity' – and the cult of Mobutu's personality – which began in earnest in late 1971. As part of the symbolic reclamation of the country, its cities, rivers and citizens for Africa, the regime banned all Christian or 'foreign' names, along with western dress. The theology faculties in the nationalised universities were abolished and enrolment in the MPR youth movement became compulsory for all seminarians. Religious broadcasting and the religious press were banned, while the regime took over the denominational schools and forbad religious instruction. The leader of the Church in Zaire, Cardinal Malula, was forced into temporary exile. The denigration of Catholicism continued until 1975 when, after considerable pressure from the Vatican, the regime abated its hostility and restored some control of the school system to the Church.

As 'authenticity' transmuted into the state religion of Mobutuism, the President strove for the awesome style of political leadership that had so impressed him on a state visit to Kim Il Sung's North Korea in 1974. When the new official doctrine was promulgated in 1974, the Political Commissioner for the Interior announced that 'henceforth the MPR must be considered as a Church and its Founder as a Messiah'. Mobutu's photograph adorned every public office and even replaced the crucifix in places of worship; all places where he had lived and worked were designated national pilgrimage points. The apotheosis of the monolithic and omnipotent state was reached with the 1974 constitution, which gave juridical blessing to the aggregation of Mobutu's personal power: the President headed the MPR, which was defined as 'the nation politically organised'; the state was an appendage of the party. The President presided over the Council of Ministers, the legislature and the Supreme Judicial Council, as well as the party Political Bureau. He effectively nominated the members of all these bodies, and his pronouncements cumulatively constituted the official doctrine of the country (Mobutuism) and had the force of law. Deviationism was declared a constitutional crime.

Unquestionably, the regime's totalitarian surface belied its substance: one-party dictatorships in industrialised and relatively homogenised societies did not achieve the total subjection of society posited by theorists of totalitarianism; the distance between ideological pretension and social reality was vastly greater in Central Africa, where symbolic and physical communication with a dispersed population lacking a common language was more difficult. Although the villages were rapidly emptying, Zairians remained localised peoples in terms of their social identities and loyalties. Behind the corporatist façade of an all embracing single party, Mobutu and his ruling elite had to contend with a fissured and unstable realm. His authoritarianism, with its factitious trappings of traditional African kingship, was a cultivated aura that scarcely disguised the patchy and inefficient functioning of governing institutions even in the regime's best years. Though he claimed to incarnate the state, Mobutu was a ruler of men rather than a head of government who maintained his power by the patrimonial distribution of resources and the Machiavellian manipulation of key office holders.

Although the state owned most of the modern economy by 1970, the basis of ruling-class domination was administrative and coercive power, not control of economic production and exchange. Zaire's rulers were tribute-takers, rather than a bourgeoisie performing essential economic functions. They were, of course, highly dependent on external economic and political support, but at the same time exercised considerable autonomy from foreign governments, foreign investors, transnational corporations operating in Zaire and international financial institutions. To characterise Zaire's rulers as 'the domestic branch of the international bourgeoisie' (Nzongola-Ntalaja, 2002, p. 148) is wildly implausible. Foreign business firms cannot have relished operating in Zaire's politico-legal environment; had they been able to nominate the ruling elite, they would surely have chosen a more compliant set of interlocutors. Thomas Callaghy's characterisation of the ruling group as a political aristocracy is altogether more persuasive. He identified three groups in the ruling hierarchy: an inner circle, revealingly known as the 'presidential family', which consisted of the top level administrative, political and military officials, together with the highest-ranking figures in the territorial bureaucracy, senior managers in the parastatal sector and members of the 'royal' councils (such as the MPR Political Bureau). Loyalty to Mobutu was essential for membership of this inner circle, which included several of the president's relatives and cronies from his native Equateur province. Beyond the presidential family was a second group made up of middle-ranking administrative and military officers based in Kinshasa. An outer, 'provincial' circle included the rest of the territorial prefects and military officers in the regions, together with the middle- and high-level officials in the regional state services (Callaghy, 1984, 1989). The hierarchy was rooted in the wider society by patron–client networks, sometimes based on ethnicity, though chains of connection were often intended to bridge ethnic divisions. Public office was sought because of the opportunities it gave for personal profit, and those closest to Mobutu had almost unlimited licence to plunder. Their insecure hold on office was an incentive to exploit bureaucratic power before the loss of Mobutu's favour threw them into the social abyss of clerical employment. Corruption was not a symptom of state decay: it prevailed at every level of the bureaucratic apparatus at the apogee of the regime. In 1971, an estimated 60 per cent of the state's ordinary revenue was lost through malfeasance (Peemans, 1975, p. 162). When addressing the MPR congress in November 1977, Mobutu offered an astonishingly frank diagnosis of what had become known as 'Le mal zairois':

> [E]verything is for sale, everything is bought in our country. And in this traffic, holding any slice of public power constitutes a veritable exchange instrument, convertible into illicit acquisition of money or other goods ... Worse, even the use by an individual, of his most legitimate right is subjected to an invisible tax, openly pocketed by individuals. Thus, an audience with an official, enrolling children in school, obtaining school certificates, access to medical care, a seat on the plane, an import licence, a diploma ... all are subject to this tax, which is invisible, yet known to the whole world. Accordingly, our society risks losing its political character, to become one vast market place, ruled by the basest laws of traffic and exploitation. (Quoted in Young, 1978, p. 172)

Military rule and the Nigerian oil boom

Oil has been the making – and unmaking – of modern Nigeria. Before the early 1970s, it was not a 'resource-rich' country: the ratio of natural resource rents to gross national income was less than 10 per cent, which was below the average for developing countries. After the 1973 oil shock, the ratio rose to 30 per cent and during the second boom of 1979 to nearly 50 per cent. Since then it has fluctuated with the international price of oil, but there has been no downward trend, which is contrary to the experience of most developing countries. In other words, Nigeria has remained *exceptionally* dependent on oil rents (Iyoha and Oriakhi, 2008, pp. 631–2).

The oil boom unleashed a dynamic chaos in the economy and society. Output rose from 0.54 million barrels per day in 1969 to 2.25 million barrels per day in 1974. There was a sharp check in production in 1975, because of the recession in the world economy, and again in 1978, but the boom continued through to the end of 1980. By then, the price of a barrel of crude oil on the world market was nearly 20 times what it had been in 1970. The value of Nigerian oil exports rose exponentially, from less than US$1 billion in 1970 to nearly $25 billion in 1980. Oil exports accounted for nine-tenths of all exports after 1973; they became the main propellant of economic growth and the taxes raised on them the principal source of federal government revenue. The ratio of exports to gross domestic product rose from about 15 per cent in 1970 to 35 per cent by 1980, an increase entirely attributable to oil. Because of the high export ratio, the distribution of export proceeds powerfully affected the distribution of the entire gross domestic product.

In terms of their average incomes, Nigerians gained no permanent benefit from their country's oil wealth. Real per capita GDP rose by about a quarter between 1970 and 1977, but fell by the same proportion when the second oil boom turned to bust in 1982. In 2000, real per capita GDP was the same as in 1970, though Nigeria had earned about $300 billion from oil exports since the mid-1970s (see Table 6.1). Of course, the true measure of greater material well-being is rising consumption, not income. By this measure, we might wonder whether ordinary Nigerians experienced a boom at all: per capita consumption rose by a meagre 0.3 per cent a year between 1970 and 1977 (Teal, 1988, p. 74).

So what happened to the oil windfall? And how did it impact on the wider economy and society? The industry's earnings were localised

Table 6.1 Per capita GDP in Nigeria and Congo-Zaire, 1970–2000 (expressed (a) in constant US$2000 and (b) in purchasing power parity)

| | Nigeria | | Congo-Zaire | |
	(a)	(b)	(a)	(b)
1970	368	–	327	–
1973	425	–	342	–
1977	462	–	283	–
1982	363	1434	240	720
1987	317	1254	240	720
1990	370	1464	202	605
1993	374	1479	128	384
1997	368	1453	103	310
2000	369	1456	85	255

Source: World Bank, *Africa Development Indicators*, 2009. Unfortunately, the key series for making cross-comparisons, which shows the purchasing power parities of per capita GDP, only begins in 1980.

mainly by taxation and public ownership, and the extra resources were distributed socially by huge increases in public expenditure and public employment. When production took off, the foreign-owned oil corporations determined market prices. During the boom, control over pricing shifted to the governments of the exporting countries, acting through the producers' cartel, OPEC, which Nigeria joined in 1971. At the same time, a state corporation was established to engage in all phases of the industry from exploration to marketing. (It was later amalgamated with the Ministry of Petroleum to form the Nigerian National Petroleum Corporation, NNPC.) By 1974, the Corporation had purchased a 55 per cent share in the major producing companies; by the end of the decade, the Nigerian public share in Shell-BP – the largest producer – was 80 per cent. Through the NNPC, the Nigerian state owned about 70 per cent of all the output.

The huge growth in public revenues allowed the federal government to embark on a developmental spending spree. Federal spending increased nine-fold in current prices between 1970 and 1977, and about three and a half-fold in real terms. As a proportion of GDP it rose from 9.9 per cent in 1973 to 25.2 per cent in 1976 (Bevan *et al.*, 1999, Table 8.1, p. 152). *Total* public spending (i.e., including the states') accounted for well over a third of GDP in the later 1970s. According to Forrest, it was as much as 55 per cent of GDP in 1979 (Forrest, 1986, p. 5). The composition of federal spending changed dramatically: capital expenditure accounted for less than one-quarter of federal spending in 1970–1 and nearly two-thirds on average between 1975 and 1978. The normal inhibitions on public spending were absent because oil revenues did not require the taxation of personal incomes and government was incoherent. National planning documents were effectively worthless: the federal ministries jealously guarded their own share of the spending stream and their separate projects were never coordinated, nor assessed by a calculation of future returns. They were embarked on because the finance was there and interest groups demanded them. The principal culprit was the Ministry of Economic Development which, amidst the euphoria of the 1974 oil boom, approved numerous capital projects for other ministries without properly appraising their technical feasibility, costs and benefits, or the arrangements required to operate them. Senior civil servants in the Ministry of Steel and Industries pressed for a second steel mill, despite (or because of) delays in completing the first at Ajaokuta and in face of the mounting evidence that unit costs greatly exceeded world prices (Bevan *et al.*, 1999, pp. 62–4).

The spending boom can be credited with some solid social achievements, especially the great boost given to public education, the most widely debated topic throughout the 1970s. At the beginning of the decade, only 37 per cent of children of school age were enrolled at primary schools, and the secondary school enrolment ratio was only 4 per cent. By 1980, thanks to a massive school-building programme and the extension of free education, the primary enrolment ratio had risen to 94 per cent and the secondary ratio to 34 per cent. The states took over the schools from private and voluntary agencies. At the primary level, the regional disparity in educational provision largely disappeared, since the share of the northern states in primary school enrolment rose from 19 per cent to 47 per cent during the 1970s. At the secondary level, the disparity remained very marked, with the northern share rising only slightly, from 12 per cent to 18 per cent. The federal government assumed responsibility for funding the universities and created seven new ones (bringing the total to 20 by 1980). Access to health care improved due to a four-fold increase in the number of medical personnel per 100,000 people. The infant mortality rate fell by more than a quarter over the decade.

These achievements were masked and vitiated by the disastrous mismanagement of the spending boom. Financial controls and accounting procedures were grossly deficient, so corruption flourished as expenditure rose. Of the many scandals involving the colossal misappropriation of public funds, the most infamous was the purchase abroad of construction materials by state agents at prices well above market values. Senior public officials, Nigerian private contractors and foreign companies colluded in 'raking off' the public purse. A surreal level of corrupt mismanagement was reached when Lagos harbour was clogged by hundreds of cargo ships laden with cement, waiting up to 15 months to unload (at a huge cost in demurrage charges). The Ministry of Defence, and other departments, had ordered cement in quantities that far exceeded the total cargo capacity of Nigerian ports. To add a final twist to this awful farce, when the cement came to be used in public building projects much of it was spoiled or of inferior quality.

The fiscal relationship with the states added a further element of financial irresponsibility. The oil industry was concentrated in just two states that, up to 1970, monopolised the bounty from the revenues, which the other states found intolerable. A new formula enlarged the common pool of distributed revenue: half was dispensed in equal shares to all states and half according to their populations, as recorded in the 1963 census. By the later 1970s, over 80 per cent of the states' revenues came from federal sources. This was a strong fiscal inducement to campaign for more states: seven were created in 1976, bringing the total to 19, plus the new federal capital of Abuja. It also licensed the states, which had considerable political autonomy, to spend money they did not raise in unaccountable ways, for budgetary control was extremely weak and public auditing either long delayed or non-existent.

The affluence generated by the oil boom diffused through society in a highly unequal fashion, with those closest to the spigot of federal rents lapping up the largest gains. Civil service salaries and pensions were nearly doubled on the recommendation of the Udoji Commission in October 1974. Presumably not by coincidence, the government backdated the award and paid it in a lump sum in the same week as Gowon announced an indefinite postponement in restoring civilian rule. Private formal-sector workers immediately agitated for their 'Udoji', which most employers conceded because they could pass on wage increments in rising prices. This further increased the already swollen money supply and led to a sharpening of the distributional conflicts typical of periods of high inflation: teachers, university lecturers, doctors, bank employees and other professional groups struck for higher wages (in defiance of a 1969 decree banning strikes). The military government began using public employment and the civil service salary scale to conciliate the aggrieved middle classes. The numbers of civil servants rose from 0.5 million in 1973 to 1.5 million in 1981, partly with the expansion of state activity but also because of the reclassification of teachers and other groups as civil servants.

Outside the pool of state largesse, many ordinary Nigerians had to suffer the rising cost of living without a compensatory increase in income. Food prices rose by 273 per cent between 1973 and 1981, compared to a 111 per cent rise for manufactures. Ostensibly, this should have benefited the nation's farmers, and therefore the great majority. Yet, rather puzzlingly, they did not respond to this price signal with commensurate increases in food output. This was partly because the rapid rise in the exchange value of the naira (which appreciated by 87 per cent between 1970 and 1981), combined with reduced import tariffs, led to a shift in consumption from domestically produced to imported foodstuffs (such as white bread, rice, sugar, tinned milk and fish). Furthermore, entrepreneurial farmers turned from agriculture to trade after export-cropping collapsed because of the over-valuation of the naira. The quantity of agricultural exports fell by 78 per cent between 1970 and 1981. By then, Nigeria was spending more on agricultural imports than it earned from agricultural exports (Iyoha and Oriakhi, 2008, p. 643). All too often the farmers who left agriculture to set up small businesses in transport and other services dissipated their energies and savings in what has been called 'a syndrome of unproductive competition' that resulted in uncertainty, tension and turmoil (Berry, 1985, p. 193).

The boom stimulated large increases in manufacturing: output grew by an annual average of 13 per cent during the 1970s and manufacturing employment roughly trebled. The fastest growth occurred in textiles, vehicle assembly, soap and detergents, soft drinks, pharmaceuticals, beer, paints and building materials (Forrest, 1993, pp. 138–41). Manufacturing accounted for 4 per cent of GDP at factor cost in 1970 and 12 per cent in 1982 (World Bank, *World Tables*, 1991, p. 436). Public investment in infrastructure lowered businesses' external costs and facilitated market penetration. The federal government also invested directly in certain industries, such as cement and vehicle assembly, usually by entering joint ventures with a commercial partner to whom it offered funds and a protected market. Private industrial investment increased markedly in the later 1970s and there is no evidence that middle-class Nigerians were unwilling to invest in productive enterprises (Forrest, 1993, p. 160; Forrest, 1994). Nevertheless, manufacturing was less solidly based than the bare figures suggest: on balance, it was no longer 'import substituting' because many expanding lines of production required large inputs of imported raw materials or semi-manufactures. Manufacturing thus became a net user of foreign exchange and a burden on the balance of payments. Moreover, the favourable exchange rate and domestic demand provided such strong incentives to import that firms set up so-called manufacturing operations primarily to increase the flow of imports from parent companies abroad, rather than to produce for the Nigerian market.

By the time Gowon fell from power in late July 1975, he had forfeited public confidence by being too weak or obtuse to deal with the scandalous venality of the state military governors, the most corrupt and dysfunctional rulers yet seen in Nigeria. When plausible accusations of gross malfeasance were made against the governor of Benue-Plateau state, Gowon exonerated him without a public enquiry and permitted his accuser to be detained without trial. After his fall, the state governors were immediately dismissed and arraigned for corruption and maladministration; all but two were convicted – and one was executed. Gowon was overthrown by middle-ranking military officers in a bloodless coup after he had been exposed in the act of suppressing a report that revealed gross misuse of the oil windfall (Bevan *et al.*, 1999, p. 4).

Gowon's successor was the 38-year-old Brigadier Murtala Mohammed, a civil war hero, scion of the northern aristocracy, and reputedly the key instigator of the July 1966 coup. Brigadier Olesugun Obasanjo, a southern Christian and also a distinguished wartime commander, was appointed chief of staff, Supreme Command. All officers above the rank of brigadier were promptly retired. Mohammed had exceptional energy and force of character, and immediately signalled his determination to curb corruption by instituting a Corrupt Practices Investigation Bureau and retiring 10,000 public employees, some with and some without their pensions. The military took its revenge on the civil service mandarins: proportionally, the axe fell hardest on permanent secretaries in the state and federal governments. A disciplinary purge on this scale was unprecedented in Africa; it delighted ordinary Nigerians. Mohammed had no ideological differences with his predecessor: he was a pragmatic economic nationalist who wanted to stimulate private Nigerian capital while expanding the role of the state, but he had no deep-rooted objection to cooperating with multi-national corporations. His originality lay in a passionate concern with the ethics of national life and efficient administration, and in this he reflected the influence of a coterie of northern civil servants and intellectuals misleadingly dubbed the 'Kaduna mafia'. Their mission was to reform and moralise public service in the interests of good government (Othman, 1989, pp. 122–5).

The Mohammed-Obasanjo years (1975–9) marked a high point of reformist authoritarian nationalism, centred on ambitious military officers and civilian technocrats. The federal government took over the operation of the country's two largest newspapers, made broadcasting a federal monopoly, and brought those universities that remained state-run under federal control. Mohammed initiated a comprehensive review of the third development plan, with the intention of controlling inflation by reducing the money supply that had been swollen by spending on public works. Whether he could have imposed greater financial discipline in the medium term, we cannot know, since he was assassinated in February 1976 after only seven months in power. He was a victim of disaffected officers in the Supreme Military Council who resented being passed over for promotion and the large reductions in the army's establishment he had ordered. Forty conspirators were publicly executed after a secret trial before a military tribunal.

Indigenising the economy: Zairianisation and Nigerianisation compared

The indigenisation of expatriate business enterprises was one of the most remarked upon developments in the political economy of post-colonial Africa in the 1970s, and one in which Nigeria and Zaire were to the fore. By comparing how the Federal Military Government and the Mobutu regime implemented the process we can learn much about the relations between political power and the accumulation of capital and wealth in the two states.

In Nigeria, political leaders had envisaged bringing the modern economy under indigenous control since the 1940s. For some, it meant nurturing an autonomous national bourgeoisie: all major parties included wealthy businessmen with a strong self-interest in using public power to improve their position by – for example, reserving import–export trades for Nigerian nationals. Others argued that, because Nigerian private investors were so few, ending foreign control of the modern economy would come only through public ownership. The civil war, and rising oil revenues, made a hitherto distant goal a realisable ambition. The Federal Military Government's deep suspicion that foreign firms were colluding in Biafra's bid for independence gave a fillip to economic nationalism. Oil wealth lifted the fear of capital flight and emboldened bureaucrats to impose tighter controls on foreign companies operating in Nigeria. From 1968, all had to be locally incorporated as entities separate from their 'parent', and it became illegal for a Nigerian-registered company to help anyone purchase its shares.

With the ending of the war, the senior civil servants charged with formulating policy made Nigerianisation the centrepiece of the Second National Development Plan of 1970–4, but emphasised *public-sector* participation in the capital goods industries. By contrast, the Nigerian Enterprises Promotion Decree of 1972 was intended to encourage *private* Nigerian participation in modern business. Why this 'major and radical departure from the initial policy and the basic philosophy of public sector leadership' occurred is not entirely clear (Ezeife, 1981, p. 167). It probably reflected the growing intimacy between businessmen and the military elite, and the desire to foster a truly Nigerian (as opposed to Yoruba or Ibo) entrepreneurial class. But we may also surmise that military and civilian officials saw promoting the private sector as a way of feathering their own nests: their privileged access to information and credit and their interest in acquiring shares made them eager supporters of the business groups. A top bureaucrat told one academic researcher that 'some public officials' had 'an enormous personal interest to go along with any form of programme that was in support of economic nationalism regardless of its consequences on the nation's economy' (quoted in Ogbuagu, 1983, p. 258).

The decree established two schedules of business enterprises: on the first were industries and trades henceforth exclusively reserved for Nigerians in which firms were small scale, the technology was simple and the capital threshold low (for example, garment-making and retail trading). The businesses most affected were owned by Lebanese, Indians and Greeks, who were legally obliged either to find Nigerian buyers for their assets or accept the valuation of the Nigerian Enterprises Promotion Board. They were given a liberal deadline, and the process little resembled the blatant expropriation seen elsewhere in Africa, but the compensation was patently low (Rood, 1976, p. 439). On the second schedule were listed industries and trades in which foreigners could not be owners or part owners, unless the paid-up capital exceeded naira 400,000 and the turn-over naira 1 million. These larger firms were expected to sell 40 per cent of their equity to Nigerians. This schedule covered most of the medium- to large-scale import-substituting sector (bicycle and motorcycle tyres, cement, soap and detergents, brewing etc.) commercial activities (department stores and supermarkets, distributing and servicing motor vehicles) and commercial transport. The policy was designed, not just to reserve certain business activities for Nigerians, but to engineer a shift of foreign investment from consumer manufactures and services to intermediate and capital goods production.

The decree was supposed to be implemented by 1974, but a government white paper revealed that only about one-third of enterprises in the scheduled sectors had actually complied with its provisions. Foreign businessmen frequently retained ownership of their firms by colluding with Nigerian 'fronts'. The decree was amended in 1977 to block such loopholes and in response to the representations of Nigerian business organisations, which wanted nearly all commercial services 'reserved', and opposed the public sector competing with private businessmen in acquiring foreign enterprises. According to the President of the Lagos Chambers of Commerce and Industry:

The Government [was] becoming more and more responsive to the constructive suggestions which the organised private sector of the economy [was] privileged to make from time to time. For the first time, the sector [became] deliberately and meaningfully involved with the development planning process. (Quoted in Ogbuagu, 1983, p. 259)

The amended decree reflected these 'constructive suggestions' by covering all foreign enterprises. In principle, only single non-renewable projects were exempted. Businesses were reclassified into three schedules: Schedule One was as before. For businesses in Schedule Two, the level of Nigerian participation was raised to 60 per cent. A newly created Schedule Three covered all enterprises not listed in the other two schedules in which the minimum Nigerian equity participation was fixed at 40 per cent. Stiffer penalties were prescribed for contravening the decree: all defaulting enterprises were to be sealed up and sold as 'going concerns' to Nigerian buyers, who were expected to retain the employees.

The indigenisation decrees effectively excluded foreigners (mainly Lebanese) from small-scale enterprise and sharply increased the number of Nigerian entrepreneurs, but their major social consequence was to strengthen numerically and financially a rentier class of bureaucrats, professionals and commercial middle-men. By 1979, assets valued at more than $700 million had been transferred from foreign to Nigerian owners, mostly in the form of shares in listed companies which were compulsorily made available for purchase by Nigerians at very attractive prices (and would quickly appreciate in value). At least half the finance to purchase these shares came from low-interest bank loans from the recently nationalised banks. All the share offers were over-subscribed, and the scramble for shares became a regular feature of life for middle-class Nigerians, who procured guaranteed income and substantial financial assets with negligible risk and effort (Joseph, 1978; Sklar, 1979). According to the Nigerian *Business Times* (10 August 1976, cited in Ogbuagu, 1983, p. 265), they were passive investors who 'bought their shares and sat back to wait for the expatriate managers to make a profit for them'. By greatly increasing the numbers of Nigerian shareholders, indigenisation made the nationalisation of the multinationals more unlikely and facilitated their domestication within Nigerian society.

Nigerian indigenisation and related policies only partially achieved their ostensible objective of strengthening domestic capitalism. Investment was choked off in certain 'reserved' industries – such as garment-making – and domestic output failed to keep pace with demand. With the over-valuation of the naira, it was cheaper to import many consumer goods than to produce them domestically. The Shagari government amended the indigenisation decree in 1981 to permit greater foreign participation in garment-making and revive foreign investment. Nigerian businessmen tightened their grip on commerce and the public authorities substantially increased their control of the financial sector. Middle and senior managers found promotion to the highest levels in the private sector easier (Biersteker, 1987, pp. 245–50). Though the political class took a large stake in the corporate economy, and widened its business opportunities, managerial control remained substantially with expatriates. Nigerian shareholders not infrequently pressed for foreign management to be retained and the quota of expatriate executives to be increased. There were more expatriates involved in Nigerian enterprises five years after the indigenisation decrees than before; indigenous private investment still had a small role in developing the modern sector. Nevertheless, Nigerianisation was a relatively orderly process that did no irreversible damage to the economy.

Zairianisation, by contrast, was a disaster from which the Mobutu regime never recovered. The policy originated with Mobutu's abrupt announcement to the National Legislative Council on 30 November 1973 that, to put an end to foreign exploitation: 'farms, ranches, plantations, concessions, commerce, and real estate agencies will be turned over to sons of the country'. The former owners were to receive 'equitable compensation' out of profits over a ten-year period. Given Mobutu's now absolute command of the state, his words had the force of law: the wisdom and practicality of the measure were simply not discussed. Nigerianisation had been a potent example: Mobutu was grasping for continental leadership, and disliked being up-staged by the other giant of tropical sub-Saharan Africa (Young and Turner, 1985, p. 327). The targets were immigrant entrepreneurs running family businesses, from small palm oil plantations to shops and transport firms; in western Zaire, these were mainly Portuguese, while in the east, Greeks, Italians and, more latterly, Pakistanis predominated. Foreign enterprises established under the 1969 investment code were exempted, as were about 120 Belgian colonial companies operating large-scale enterprises, such as railways and breweries, though few had made recent investments.

On 26 December, a plenary session of the top political elite decided that the large plantations, ranches and commercial businesses would go to members of the 'presidential family'. Mobutu was assigned a huge 'royal' domain of plantations, as was his Interior Minister. Choice assets were then distributed in patrimonial fashion to the political aristocracy: leading *acquéreurs* ('acquirers') were, in the main, deputies, political commissioners, regional administrators, high-ranking army officers and party functionaries who ruthlessly milked the confiscated assets. Despite the universal outcry at the political elite's egregious self-interest, what followed was 'a tumultuous, disorderly, and profoundly demeaning scramble for the loot' (*ibid.*, p. 337).

In February and March 1974, approximately 2000 businesses were distributed to rank-and-file 'acquirers', mostly full-time state employees, who were supposed to provide provincial administrators with evidence of their political militancy, personal probity and commercial experience. As a teacher in Lisala complained to an American political scientist, 'The real merchants got nothing' (Schatzberg, 1980, p. 242). By June, the commercial and distributive networks were almost completely disrupted. Employees of the immigrant entrepreneurs were dismissed by 'acquirers' to make way for relatives and co-ethnics; state revenue declined because the new owners refused to pay taxes; prices soared; businesses were abandoned after their assets had been stripped. 'Acquirer' became a term of contempt and the normally docile press became openly critical of the governing class's parasitic greed. In late December, in response to the mounting chaos and social polarisation, the MRP political bureau announced the 'radicalisation of the revolution', a programme of measures designed to fasten the regime's ideological and institutional grip on society. (Some, such as the cult of Mobutu and the takeover of Catholic schools by the state, have already been mentioned.) Certain social scourges were identified and remedies for them proposed. For the scourge of social injustice, the programme proposed combating 'the private appropriation of national riches and large means of production' which conferred unjust advantages on their owners. It was decided that, as of 1 January 1975, the state would take over all construction firms, large units of production and distribution, businesses producing construction materials and large transportation companies. Foreign enterprises established under the investment code were again exempted, so as not to discourage inward investment. To combat the scourge of individualism, members of the political bureau and all MPR cadres would relinquish to the state businesses acquired through Zairianisation; only agricultural activities would be permitted alongside their party-state functions (Schatzberg, 1980).

Economic radicalisation was an admission that Zairianisation had failed. In a major address explaining the new departure, Mobutu proclaimed that he worked for the people, not for the cadres, and was declaring war on the bourgeoisie. Unsurprisingly, this caused immense confusion and panic amongst 'acquirers', some of whom rushed to liquidate their assets before the state expropriated them. Mobutu did something to allay the panic by later announcing that the state would only take over businesses with an annual gross turnover of $2 million. In the event, the radicalisation measures did nothing to repair the chaos wrought by Zairianisation, or much to disgorge the 'acquirers'' recent gains. In March, the regime's fire was turned from the so-called bourgeoisie to the Belgian colonial companies, which were summarily informed that they had been placed under state managerial control. No compensation scheme was announced. A clique of notables was put in charge of the newly radicalised enterprises; though not strictly the owners, they were empowered to divert corporate resources to private ends. The henchman Mobutu installed to head the railways transferred substantial operating funds to his own bank account and fired many Belgian managers. The railways were soon such a shambles that Mobutu had to dismiss him and reinstate a Belgian manager, at a salary exceeding $200,000 (Young and Turner, 1985, p. 356).

The international repercussions of radicalisation added to the regime's appalling problems, for even the best-managed economy would have been in grave difficulties with the fall in the copper price and the soaring price of oil. The owners of Zairianised businesses had received no support from their national states, but Belgium took immediate steps to defend the interests of its expatriate companies by suspending insurance guarantees on exports to Zaire. Parent companies in Brussels cut off all credit and supplies to their 'radicalised' subsidiaries. By the spring of 1975, it was evident that Zaire would be unable to meet its payments on the debts run up with international banks since 1970, which gave Belgium some leverage over compensation for its nationals and the retrocession of expropriated property. In negotiations with international creditors and the IMF in November, a formula was agreed for a return of 40 per cent of the equity in the foreign property that had been confiscated. Zaire now became liable for a very large compensation bill, although the precise amount was never calculated and it is difficult to establish how much was actually paid. In September 1976, a second agreement was reached by which former owners regained up to 60 per cent of their equity, with an obligation to find a Zairian buyer for the remaining 40 per cent over several years. In effect, the regime was offering to restore the whole property, since the 40 per cent proviso was quickly seen as a dead letter. This revised scheme did permit a large-scale restitution of enterprises to former owners; how many actually returned to Zaire to pursue their businesses is unclear. The agreement reached with the Belgian government to compensate Belgians who did not wish to return was a humiliating retreat from the anti-colonialist nationalism with which Mobutu had launched Zairianisation. Belgium agreed to pay the compensation to its aggrieved nationals over a ten-year period, while Zaire would reimburse Belgium, in Belgian francs, over a 20-year period.

Mobutu had initiated the most sweeping, comprehensive and economically destructive set of nationalising measures undertaken in independent Africa, which reflected and reinforced the patrimonial nature of the regime and the tribute-taking character of its ruling class. Private-sector confidence both at home and abroad was forfeited; transport and marketing links were severely disrupted; much productive capacity and infrastructure was neglected. The regime's decay can be traced to the devastation wrought on commercial networks and the legitimisation of a political economy of predation. The adverse consequences of Zairianisation/radicalisation were amplified by a drastic and sustained deterioration in the terms of trade. The international price of copper fell by half in 1975; taking 1970 as 100, the price index was 80.8 in 1974 and 42 in 1975. The impact on Zaire's barter terms of trade was catastrophic: in 1975, twice the quantity of exports was required to maintain the 1970 level of imports. In fact, import volumes fell by half. Foreign trade taxes, which provided 60 per cent of budgetary revenues before the crisis, were sharply reduced. Debt service obligations could not be met, and arrears accumulated; by 1978, external sources of finance had virtually dried up. Food prices escalated because of the rising cost of imports and the shortfall in domestic supply: by 1978, the monthly cost of feeding a family of six in Kinshasa was three times the wage of a semi-skilled worker (World Bank, 1980, pp. 1–21).

The decay and persistence of the Mobutist state

The decay of the Mobutist state was registered in many ways, but the most spectacular was the failure to repel unaided the invasions of southwest Shaba (as Katanga was now called) of March–April 1977 and May 1978, launched by the Front National pour la Libération du Congo from bases in Angola and Zambia. On both occasions, the Force Armée Zaïroise offered almost no resistance. Moroccan units, flown in by French aircraft, repulsed the first, small-scale intrusion. The second was altogether bloodier and more consequential: unemployed young men in the mining centre of Kolwezi greeted the guerrillas as liberators, and vented their anger on the sizeable expatriate community. At least

130 Europeans were killed; the rest fled. The brief occupation was ended when French and Belgian paratroopers were airlifted into Shaba, with American logistical support. The CIA insisted, on slight evidence, that Cubans based in Angola were behind the invasion and that it had Moscow's approval, which persuaded the Carter administration to support the Franco-Belgian airlift. Thousands perished in the recapture of Kolwezi and the region's subsequent 'pacification' by the Zairian army, which proved little more than a uniformed mob. Perhaps 200,000 villagers sought refuge in Angola. The local mining industry, which produced about four-fifths of the copper belt's output, was crippled for months. Soon after the event, Crawford Young wrote:

> Shaba II laid bare the deeper aspects of what appears to be a permanent crisis confronting Zaire. What had once seemed a powerful and reasonably effective regime is overwhelmed by a deepening social crisis provoked by the pauperization of the mass of the populace, evaporating internal legitimacy and external credibility, a crushing debt burden, and the transparent unreliability of its numerous armed forces. (Young, 1978, p. 169)

What Young could not know was that the Mobutist state, whose decay was regularly diagnosed as 'terminal' throughout the 1980s, would survive until 1990, when Mobutu was compelled under internal and external pressure to dismantle the MPR's political monopoly, nor that the dictator would out-manoeuvre his opponents and cling to power until May 1997. The hindsight not available to contemporary analysts imposes on us the duty of explaining the persistence of Mobutu's regime, as well as its decadence.

The factor which immediately stands out from the Shaba crisis is its internationalisation: given the inadequacies of its armed forces, it seems almost certain that Mobutu's regime would have lost its richest province without foreign military aid and might have been overthrown (though the failure of the invasions to detonate uprisings elsewhere makes this doubtful). Foreign assistance was crucially important for the regime's survival, just as it had been for its emergence and consolidation. The array of foreign backers prepared to give Mobutu diplomatic, logistical and military support in the late 1970s and 80s was truly impressive: the USA, France, Belgium and Morocco, even Communist China and North Korea. The underlying reason for this unlikely coalition of support was the deep anxiety created by the large-scale intrusion of Soviet and Cuban military power into Africa following the collapse of Portuguese rule in Angola and the fall of Haile-Selassie in Ethiopia. Zaire was an important player in the Angolan debacle of 1975. During the war against the Portuguese, Mobutu had been the political patron of the anti-Marxist Front for the National Liberation of Angola (FNLA) whose exiled leadership had been based in Kinshasa. When the civil war between the rival Angolan liberation movements broke out in July 1975, the Marxist MPLA solicited Soviet and Cuban aid in the struggle against its rivals while Mobutu committed several battalions on the FNLA's behalf with the encouragement of the USA. Zaire's forces disintegrated before the Cubans in November–December 1975, which was a serious reversal for Mobutu's regime. But more damaging in the long run was the closing of the Benguela railway, which provided the shortest and cheapest route for Shaba's mineral exports, by the MPLA's victory in the Angolan war.

The Carter, Reagan and Bush administrations supported Mobutu because it was in their geo-strategic interests to do so: his anti-communist credentials were impeccable and without him 'there would be chaos', with all that implied in terms of opportunities for communist insurgency and further Soviet advances (Schatzberg, 1991, p. 71). Had economic interests determined their stance towards Zaire, they would surely have cold-shouldered the regime. Its glaring defects could scarcely be overlooked, but the dominant perception of American foreign policy officials was that, while Mobutu may have been a corrupt and brutal leader, he was 'their' corrupt and brutal leader (Schatzberg, 1991, p. 71; see also Kelly, 1993). The fact that his opponents were weak and divided reinforced their conviction that there were no credible political alternatives. French perceptions were rather different: in Gaullist and post-Gaullist eyes, Africa was a region in which France could assert its status as a major political and military power outside Europe, one which refused to submerge its historic national and cultural identity in the American-dominated 'West' (Chipman, 1989). French policy-makers considered that Zaire, as the largest Francophone African state, had a community of interest with the rest of Francophone Africa and therefore with France. In 1975, President Giscard d'Estaing brokered a series of cooperation agreements which led to Zaire's inclusion in the Franco-African 'sphere'. France became the main supplier of military hardware to Mobutu's regime, and its principal diplomatic patron.

Foreign support was all the more functional for Mobutu's survival because he manipulated the complex relationships with external agencies so adroitly. From the later 1970s, his regime came under two sorts of pressure: soaring debt led the International Monetary Fund to press for reform of Zaire's public finances and a restructuring of the relationship between the state and the economy. Simultaneously, the Carter administration – which came into office pledged to an ethical dimension in its foreign policy – tried to make assistance for Mobutu conditional upon meaningful political reforms. He bowed to American pressure to liberalise the regime by permitting relatively free parliamentary elections in 1977: candidates did not have to be hand-picked by the MPR politburo and many independently minded deputies were elected. Although the exercise of presidential power was not significantly constrained, the assembly used parliamentary question time to call cabinet ministers and leading officials to account. This relatively liberal interlude ended in late 1980, when Mobutu cracked down on his parliamentary critics: 13 were gaoled, tortured and banished to remote detention centres (Nzongola-Ntalaja, 2002, pp. 184–5). The deepening of the 'Second Cold War', following the Soviet invasion of Afghanistan and the Iran hostage crisis, meant that Mobutu could crush his domestic opponents without serious admonition from abroad.

Potentially, the international financial institutions had greater leverage over the regime because they could restrict the supply of foreign exchange needed to maintain the political aristocracy's sumptuous lifestyle. In June 1978, the USA, France and Belgium approved a plan to shore up the economy through emergency loans administered by foreign experts under IMF supervision. By then, debt service payments were equivalent to more than two-fifths of export earnings and half the total state revenue. A German banker, Erwin Blumenthal, was appointed to manage Zaire's central bank, while French and Belgian experts were entrusted with running the Finance Ministry and the Customs Agency. In December 1978, Blumenthal cut off credit and exchange facilities to key members of the 'presidential family', and imposed strict foreign exchange quotas. Mobutu and his cronies evaded this restriction by acquiring foreign exchange through the parastatal minerals marketing agency, Sozacom. They also systematically harassed and wore down the foreign experts. At the end of his year's sojourn in Zaire, Blumenthal reported that the 'corruptive system', with its mismanagement and fraud, and the lack of any effective control over the financial transactions of the presidency, would destroy all endeavours towards rehabilitation of the economy. There was, he said, no prospect of Zaire's creditors getting their money back in any foreseeable future (Callaghy, 1986, p. 322). Yet the ultimate sanction, state bankruptcy, was scarcely in their interests, or of the governments which had guaranteed much of the private lending. Through the 'Paris Club' mechanism, the creditor countries rescheduled Zaire's debts five times between 1976 and 1983.

Zairians survived the regime's wanton economic mismanagement by participating in the informal economy, where transactions were not taxed or regulated and often involved barter and criminality. They ranged from unlicensed food marketing to the large-scale smuggling of coffee, gold and diamonds to neighbouring countries, which recouped hundreds of thousands of dollars. Zaire was not, of course, unusual in having a large informal sector, but gross shortages of goods and wages far below subsistence level made it exceptionally pervasive. In the late 1970s, more than half urban wage-earning households were supplementing their incomes by trade (MacGaffey, 1983, p. 361). The informal economy was inextricable from the Leviathan state: the burgeoning of the parastatal sector and the price controls on food, fuel and other items, gave entrepreneurs a strong incentive to evade the formal, highly regulated economy. At the same time, their most profitable connections were often with officials in the parastatal companies, such as Air Zaire or Sozacom. Public employees did not participate in the informal economy out of some innate moral delinquency; like their fellow citizens they had little choice in the matter. Before their banishment in late 1980, the 13 parliamentarians wrote Mobutu an open letter pointing out that not even a junior minister just below cabinet rank could feed a family of six on his monthly salary at current food prices. The salary of a civil servant in charge of a government department was less than half the minister's, and a clerk's less than one-eighth. Yet, men in such positions not only managed to feed, clothe and house their families, they met school fees and even acquired imported luxuries. As Zairians would say, they fended for themselves ('on se débrouille') by illegal trading and selling their services to entrepreneurs.

The Second Nigerian Republic and its aftermath (1979–85)

While Zaire was exhibiting symptoms of advanced decay, Nigeria was undergoing political renewal. The protracted process of restoring civilian rule began in October 1975, when Murtala Mohammed appointed a constitutional drafting committee, drawn from civil society leaders and prominent politicians (though significantly, Awolowo, the spokesman for the left, was excluded). At its first meeting, Mohammed roundly condemned the political parties as 'little more than armies organised for fighting elections' for whom 'winning elections became a life and death struggle which justified all means – fair and foul' (Joseph, 1987, p. 39). The drafting committee ignored this strong hint that political parties be proscribed under the constitution, but accepted the need to break the link between party, region and ethnicity. Despite the crackdown following Mohammed's assassination, public debate during the months preceding the presentation of the committee's draft proposals in December 1976 was free, exceptionally creative and allowed for widespread participation. Political discourse became more rancorous when the constituent assembly was drawing up the new constitution in 1978 because of a quarrel between Christian and Muslim delegates over the place of *shari'a* in the judicial system. At one stage all the Muslim members walked out, and the impasse in the constitutional negotiations was resolved only because the military were still in power. Nevertheless, the Second Republic was conceived in a matrix of popular legitimacy which ought to have ensured its durability.

In its final form, the constitution reflected disillusionment with the First Republic's unstable parliamentarianism and the powerful attractions of America's federalism and – notwithstanding Muslim objections – secularism. A bicameral National Assembly was instituted, with a Supreme Court and State High Courts having judicial and constitutional functions analogous to their American counterparts. The president, vice-president and the governors of the 19 states were to be directly elected by universal suffrage for a maximum of two four-year terms. To forestall ethnic polarisation at the polls, the successful presidential candidate had to win at least a quarter of the vote in at least two-thirds of all states. To avoid ethnic predominance in the federal administration, the president had to appoint at least one federal minister from each state, who had to be an indigene of the state in question. While America provided one political model, the constitution endorsed the 'mixed economy' by requiring the state to bring about greater social justice through the planning, partial ownership and management of the economy, and to avoid the concentration of wealth (Forrest, 1993, p. 64). To combat corruption, an austere Code of Conduct for public officials was incorporated into the document.

The political parties were allowed to rehabilitate themselves but within strict conditions intended to preclude the identification of party with ethnicity: under the 1977 Electoral Decree, all parties contesting the 1979 elections had to eschew any ethnic, religious or regional affiliation, to be registered in every state and to campaign throughout the nation. To reassure the propertied classes that their interests were secure, organised labour was barred by the military from participating in or funding party politics. Only five parties – out of 150 or so – satisfied the conditions laid down in the Decree. Two, the Great Nigeria People's Party and the People's Redemption Party, were essentially new formations, though the latter was headed by Aminu Kano, the veteran northern radical, and gained most of its support in Kano and Kaduna, just as the NEPU had done. But three could trace a clear line of descent, in terms of their leading personalities and principal constituencies, to the great regional parties of the First Republic. The dominant party in the states which had formed the Western Region, the Unity Party of Nigeria, was led by Awolowo and re-created the old Action Group. In what had been the Eastern Region, the Nigerian People's Party stepped into the shoes of the NCNC; although founded by a northern businessman, the NPP was taken over by Azikiwe, who became its presidential candidate. In what had been the Northern Region, the National Party of Nigeria was the successor to the old Northern People's Congress. In 1979, voting preferences in the southwestern and southeastern states were actually more influenced by regional and ethnic loyalties than they had been in the First Republic: while the AG had never polled more than 54 per cent of the vote in the old Western Region, the UPN took 80 per cent of the vote in the states making up that region. The NPP polled over 80 per cent of the vote in the southeastern states, whereas the NCNC had garnered 66 per cent in the old Eastern Region. For all the care taken to minimise the force of ethnicity in political life, most Yoruba and Ibo electors voted out of a sense of ethnic commitment (Dudley, 1981, p. 290).

The situation with respect to the NPN was significantly different: ultimate power within the party lay with 'the northern caucus', through which the Hausa-Fulani 'establishment' still exercised great influence, but it was more ethnically inclusive than any other party in Nigeria's electoral history and had a country-wide constituency. It incorporated regional and cultural differences by a policy of 'zoning', or distributing party offices amongst ethnic groups. The NPN won less than 50 per cent of the vote in what used to be the Northern Region, whereas the NPC had polled over 60 per cent of the vote. The party failed to gain control of the Kano state legislature and the state governorships of Kano and Kaduna. These had once been bastions of the 'emirate north' but were now hotly contested by a new generation of radical intellectuals and professionals in the left-wing PRP who sought to mobilise the peasantry and the urban poor in a struggle to dismantle the traditional power structure (Diamond, 1988b, p. 51).

In the presidential campaign, the NPN was more successful than its rivals in its endeavour to be a truly national party: its winning candidate in 1979, Shehu Shagari, secured over half his votes outside the northern states and attracted considerable support from minorities throughout the nation. He won well over 25 per cent of the total vote in a five-cornered contest, but just failed to meet the condition of securing at least a quarter of the vote in a minimum of two-thirds of the states. Nonetheless, the Supreme Court upheld his election after it was challenged by Awolowo, his main rival; in the circumstances, no other judgement would have been practicable, but it cast a shadow of illegitimacy over Shagari's presidency. No less problematic, from the point of view of the credibility of democratic institutions, was a turn-out of just over a third in the presidential poll – the lowest in Nigeria's electoral history – which meant that Shagari triumphed with the support of about one elector in ten. Voter fatigue lay behind this apathy: the presidential election was the last of five elections held between July and August 1979.

In the federal legislature, the outcome of the 1979 elections bore an uncanny resemblance to the situation 20 years before: the NPN won the largest number of seats and entered a formal agreement with the NPP, which received a share of ministerial offices in return for its cooperation in the legislature. Awolowo's UPN led the opposition. Coalition politics proved no more stable than in the 1960s: as a party, the NPP withdrew from the coalition in mid-1981, because it felt excluded from the most lucrative opportunities for dispensing government patronage, though some NPP ministers ignored party discipline and refused to resign. However, though the structure of politics at the federal centre resembled that of the First Republic, its cultural content had been modified by the diminishing salience of ethnicity and region in party conflict, and the factional quarrels within the parties. The system of 19 states created in 1976 generated a more fluid pattern of alignments than was the case in the 1960s. Nine of the governors elected in 1979 were from the UPN, the GNPP and the PRP, and set themselves up as a political check on the NPN-dominated federal government.

The cockpit of political conflict, chicanery and violence in the First Republic had been the Western Region; in the Second, that dubious distinction went to Kano and Kaduna. The left-wing PRP governor in Kaduna was soon at loggerheads with the NPN-controlled State Assembly in what was a localised class conflict between 'commoners' and an alliance of businessmen, traditional leaders and professionals. The governor sought to abolish exploitative local taxes, investigate land transactions and start a mass literacy campaign. In June 1981, he was impeached and removed from office by the NPN majority in the State Assembly (with the support of PRP dissidents), which opposition forces throughout Nigeria denounced as undemocratic and unconstitutional. In July, the Kano PRP state governor provoked a spasm of destructive violence when he sent the Emir an offensive letter threatening his removal for acts of disrespect to the state government. Rioters burnt down the state government buildings and the residences of several key officials, including that of the governor's chief political adviser, who was killed in the mayhem. The culprits were probably thuggish retainers of the NPN, and of a rival faction in the PRP, egged on to intimidate the governor from office. The extensive destruction, and the perception that the national governing party was trying to achieve by violence what could not been done by impeachment, given the governor's overwhelming support in the state legislature, had a traumatic and deeply polarising effect on politics (Diamond, 1988b, p. 51). At the same time, there was a growing revulsion with party politics as such: it was both a threat to civil order – for repeated clashes between thugs in the pay of parties, factions and rival politicians left mounting casualties, even when elections were not in progress – and a tawdry spectacle of self-interested men ruthlessly pursing power and wealth. The constant stream of suspensions, expulsions and defections from the various political parties, and the lack of disinterested commitment among the politicians, bred a weary cynicism.

The task of maintaining civil peace in the north was greatly complicated by militant Islamists. Inspired by the Iranian revolution of 1979, the Izala movement and the Muslim Students Society rejected the Constitution and openly advocated an Islamic state which would seamlessly integrate public and scriptural law. Many traditional notables and their clerical allies privately sympathised with this ideal, but recoiled from the advocacy of violence to achieve it, especially by radical clerics appealing to the poor and socially underprivileged. The most dangerous was a preacher known as *Maitatsine* (in Hausa, 'he who curses others'), who attracted a large following amongst the urban 'underclass' and illegal immigrants from Cameroon and Niger. His movement expressed total abhorrence for western modernity and all its accoutrements; he condemned as an infidel anyone wearing a watch, or riding a bicycle, or driving a car, or sending their child to the normal state schools. When the police tried to suppress the *Maitatsine*'s vitriolic preaching in December 1980, clashes with his followers escalated into a horrific uprising in Kano, during which he and some 5,000 people were killed after the military intervened (Hickey, 1984; Isichei, 1987). Thousands more died in further clashes in Kano in 1981 and in Maiduguri and other northern cities in October 1982. The conflict became many-sided: the Muslim establishment bitterly denounced the *Maitatsine*'s adherents as heretics, while they in turn attacked the conservative imams as traitors to Islam; zealots among the Muslim Students Association led violent protests against the consumption of alcohol on the campus of Ahmadu Bello University, and were to the fore in burning Christian churches in Kano in November 1982. The turmoil lasted way beyond the fall of the Second Republic

The Shagari administration invested huge sums in its domestic security apparatus but soon dissipated its moral authority because of its complicity in the corruption of public office. The head of state was not quite as lacerating as Mobutu in diagnosing the pathological condition over which he presided, but still disarmingly candid. Shagari admitted to a journalist in November 1982 that: '[W]hat worries me more than anything among our problems is ... moral decadence in our country. There is the problem of bribery, corruption, lack of dedication to duty, dishonesty and all such vices' (quoted in Brownsberger, 1983, p. 225). A body he had set up, known as the Presidential Transition Committee, reported that there was a 'general acceptance among most members of the power elite that power is for profit rather than for responsible exercise of its privileges or for service. This philosophy has resulted ... in the privileges of power being used for pillage' (quoted in Othman, 1989, p. 113). The public contract system gained notoriety for systematic fraud which inflated construction costs far above the costs of executing similar projects in other African countries or in Asia. Nigerian middle-men who negotiated the purchase of military aircraft from British Aerospace received £22 million in 'kickbacks' (Othman, 1984, pp. 450–1; Othman, 1989, p. 131). The introduction of import licensing led to the Minister of Commerce 'mishandling' huge sums in licence fees. To cover up fraud and embezzlement in Nigerian External Telecommunications, the public corporation's 37-storey headquarters was burnt down in January 1983. Political corruption flourished because it brought huge rewards with little risk: the National Assembly never passed the enabling legislation needed to activate the supervisory and investigative bodies that were supposed to enforce the Constitution's Code of Conduct for public servants.

Behind the spectacular instances of financial malfeasance lay an intensely competitive political culture in which public office-holders expected to use their office both for personal gain and that of their home communities and supporters. Richard Joseph, the foremost analyst of Nigerian politics in these years, revived the term 'prebendal' to describe this form of political life in which the state was perceived as a congeries of offices susceptible to individual-cum-communal appropriation. What introduced an element of social reciprocity into the competition to control public resources were the chains of connection between patrons and their clients. The less privileged members of a community looked to the more powerful for help in bettering themselves, not as a favour but as a right. Usually, that meant securing a coveted salaried job, and since such positions were concentrated in the civil service and public sector, an effective patron wielded political power. An individual – writes Joseph – would seek 'the support of an oga or a "godfather", while trying to acquire the basic social and material goods – loans, scholarships, licences, plots of urban land, promotion – and the main resource of the patron in meeting these requests [was] a piece of the state' (Joseph, 1987, p. 55). Even private-sector appointments were influenced by political patronage since the business world was hemmed in by bureaucratic regulations. Viewing the public realm as a field for private opportunity was not an atavism but a rational response to how the contemporary Nigerian state intermeshed with the economy and community networks. To paraphrase Claude Ake, Nigeria's leading political scientist, the highly interventionist state appeared to own virtually everything, including access to status and wealth. 'Inevitably a desperate struggle to win control of state power ensues since this control means for all practical purposes being all powerful and owning everything. Politics becomes warfare, a matter of life or death' (quoted in Joseph, 1983, p. 24).

Shagari's civilian government was no more able to cushion the economy against violent fluctuations in the price of oil than its military predecessor. In 1980, it had the temporary good fortune of seeing government revenues rise to a peak which has never again been attained in real terms. Demand for, and output of, oil fell sharply in 1981, and the price per barrel dropped in the following year, with a devastating impact on Nigeria's terms of trade, exports, GDP and government revenue. Production slumped from 2.56 million barrels a day in 1981 to 1.1 million barrels a day in the first half of 1983, when oil was generating about 90 per cent of foreign exchange earnings and 84 per cent of government revenues. In current US dollars, total export values fell from $27.75 billion in 1980 to $10.85 billion in 1983 (World Bank, *World Tables*, 1991, p. 438). The macroeconomic data indicate that the oil recession administered an economic shock to Nigerian society of unique severity, compared with the recession elsewhere in the continent. Per capita private consumption, expressed in 1987 US$, was reckoned to be $360–$350 a year in 1981–2, which was substantially above the figure for the rest of sub-Saharan Africa at that time. It fell to $290 in 1983, and continued falling until 1987, when it reached a nadir of $160, which was well below the figure for the rest of sub-Saharan Africa (World Bank, *World Tables*, 1991, p. 10).

The Economic Stabilisation Act of 1982, which brought import restrictions, higher import duties and austerity measures, failed to alleviate the mounting economic crisis. Industries dependent on imported raw materials and semi-finished products were crippled by the shortage of foreign exchange. Manufacturing output fell sharply in 1983, when a fifth of industrial establishments had to suspend production for between four to eight weeks, while others went out of business. Thousands of industrial workers were laid off. About 2 million illegally resident aliens were expelled in January and February, in an attempt to 'export' rising unemployment. The restriction of food imports accelerated price inflation. State governments had insufficient revenues to pay their teachers and civil servants or to purchase drugs for hospitals, and many services (including schools) were shut down by strikes. By the end of 1983, the budget deficit had grown to 12 per cent of GDP and external debts had reached $10.21 billion.

On 31 December 1983, the Nigerian armed forces ended the country's second attempt at democracy by dismissing Shagari's civilian government. In a broadcast justifying the coup, Brigadier Sani Abacha referred to the 'inept and corrupt leadership ... imposed on our beloved nation for the past four years' and the hopeless mismanagement of the economy. In a later broadcast that day, the new leader, Major-General Buhari, charged the dismissed politicians with 'subverting the Constitution, squandermania, indiscipline, electoral frauds, and abuse of office' – charges which were all too evidently well-founded (quoted in Othman, 1984, p. 441). The national and state gubernatorial elections in August–September had been outrageously rigged to secure an NPN majority and increase its governorships from seven to 13. When the results were declared in the southwest, the explosion of popular anger left more than 100 dead and destroyed $100 million in property. The public reaction to the coup when it finally came was overwhelmingly favourable (as it had been to the January 1966 coup). The elected politicians had placed such an enormous premium on winning political power, and had so comprehensively abused it that they destroyed the legitimacy of the democratic system. Their incompetence in dealing with the economic crisis stripped them of the last remnants of credibility.

To general applause, the new military government immediately detained hundreds of former politicians, froze their bank accounts and seized vast amounts of cash stashed away in their homes. More than 300 senior public servants were summarily dismissed or retired; over the next 12 months, about 50,000 civil servants were weeded out. In March, military tribunals began prosecuting former officials for corruption; the accused had to prove their innocence, and if convicted faced a minimum 21-year sentence. Draconian measures were taken to eliminate black-market currency operations and other frauds. Alongside this punitive backlash against the civilian politicians and bureaucrats, the military elite took energetic steps to bolster its own status and welfare. Buhari quickly promoted himself, his deputy and 14 other officers to the rank of full general. He instituted a review of the armed services' pay, and ordered the purchase of sophisticated weaponry to proceed, despite a general moratorium on public expenditure.

His regime soon forfeited its initial popularity by repressing civil liberties and press freedom. Voluntary organisations, such as the National Students Association and the Nigerian Medical Association were banned. The Nigerian Security Organisation was given arbitrary powers to arrest and detain without trial anyone deemed to be a security risk. In the general suppression of public debate and critical journalism, even discussion of the country's political future was forbidden. The dictatorship's prescription for what it perceived as Nigeria's social malaise reflected the officer corps' authoritarian and patriotic values and, more obliquely, the Kaduna mafia, which provided the regime with a nucleus of civilian expertise and managerial competence. A 'War Against Indiscipline' was declared, with the aim of rooting out dozens of civic and moral misdemeanours, from driving on the wrong side of the road to littering public parks and devoting little or no time to the upbringing of one's children. The virtues of patriotism, hard work, civility and sexual continence were trumpeted (Othman, 1984, p. 460).

The most urgent task facing the junta was reversing economic decline. It imposed drastic deflation on the urban, industrial and service sectors while prioritising state assistance to agriculture. Public expenditure and public subsidies were curtailed. Public-sector jobs were axed, taxes raised, wages frozen and strikes banned. School fees were reintroduced, which gave an added impetus to the decline in primary schooling (the ratio of children enrolled fell from 92 per cent in 1983 to 75 per cent in 1986). Buhari attempted to staunch the fall in export earnings by 'swap' arrangements with new foreign trade partners and reassured foreign creditors by prioritising the servicing of the external debt: 44 per cent of export earnings were earmarked for debt service in 1985. Whether the austerity measures represented the optimal medicine for Nigeria's economic ailments is debatable, since they exacerbated the depression in the urban economy: value added in manufacturing fell by 25 per cent between 1982 and 1986, partly because of prohibitive import restrictions. There was incalculable distress amongst the huge numbers self-employed in urban services, such as street-vending.

From the military's point of view, the prescription was politically unhealthy because it severely strained relations between the junta's different factions. Buhari and his deputy Idiagbon wanted to pursue a deflationary economic strategy without recourse to a loan from the IMF and the conditions that would inevitably be attached to it. Babangida, the Army Chief of Staff and second most powerful man in the junta, favoured seeking an IMF loan and argued that the government's austerity package would not alleviate Nigeria's economic problems without the structural adjustment advocated by the IMF. There were other causes of dissension within the junta, including what to do with the hundreds of political detainees. Babangida took the liberal view that they should either be put on trial or conditionally released; the Buhari faction was unwilling to risk the public outrage that would follow if all those whom the regime could not hope to prosecute successfully were released. When Babangida overthrew Buhari on 27 August 1985, citing his refusal to govern by consensus within the junta, he quickly relaxed the most repressive features of the dictatorship by releasing most of the detainees and lifting the restrictions on the press. The NSO was dismantled in the following year. He promised a regime that would respect human rights, permit widespread public debate and prepare the country for a return to elected civilian rule. Democracy would be reinstated by 1990.

Babangida's consensual pragmatism did not extend to religious matters: in January 1986, he took Nigeria into the Organisation of the Islamic Conference, without consulting the Christian ministers in the government, the foreign affairs ministry or the Armed Forces Ruling Council. While the move consolidated his authority and popularity in the Muslim north, it alienated the secular intelligentsia and was deeply resented by the burgeoning congregations of fundamentalist Christians. The politicisation of religious identity exacerbated communal tensions, particularly in the Middle Belt, where Muslim and

Christian zealots compete for converts and where conflict between 'indigenous' and 'settler' communities often has religious overtones.

Nigeria and Zaire in the 1980s and beyond: lame Leviathans?

From the early-1980s, the epithet 'lame Leviathan' could have been applied with equal justice to Nigeria and Zaire. The following assessment was penned by a Nigerian at the end of the decade, but we could substitute 'Zaire' for 'Nigeria' without any serious factual distortion: 'For all its enormous natural resources, Nigeria is still a poor country, economically backward and fatally dependent on Western capitalist economies for even such basic needs as cooking oil. Corruption, predatory privatisation of public resources, misuse of office, and abuse of the laws, is pandemic and has reached unprecedented proportions' (Othman, 1989, p. 114). As we have seen, in the 20 or so years after independence, the two states exhibited considerable commonality of experience. Of course, Nigerians and Zairians had more than their share of national (and sub-national) 'peculiarities', but the symmetries underlying the post-colonial historical narratives are undeniable: the breakdown of the original constitutional settlement amidst regional fragmentation and secession; civil war and the restoration of central authority; the assertion of economic nationalism; authoritarian rule resting on the prebendal distribution of political office; a minerals-based economic boom and the decline of agriculture; severe economic recession when mineral prices dropped sharply. In both countries, the expansion of the public sector and the government's regulatory powers resulted in the state becoming the focus for all forms of entrepreneurial activity as well as political life: it consumed the attention of traders, contractors, builders, farmers, professionals, teachers, no less than politicians, the military and bureaucrats. In both, the centrality of the state's economic role was inextricable from an endemic corruption which debilitated public institutions. In both, the 'Leviathan' character of the state elicited invasive social pressures which fragmented and privatised public power. During the decade or more following the oil price crash, the convergence of national experiences was even closer: both states were compelled, principally because of the prior economic mismanagement of their governing elites, to embark on structural adjustment programmes; in both the erosion of administrative capacity and rampant corruption hampered economic stabilisation; in both, authoritarian rulers were challenged by pro-democracy movements at the end of the 1980s, a challenge which was seen off by a mixture of force and guile.

However, a key geopolitical difference cut across the states' commonality of experience: with the ending of Soviet–Cuban intervention in Africa in the late 1980s, Mobutu's anti-communist credentials were rendered worthless and he was unable to resist internationally backed calls for democratisation. The US Congress terminated all military aid to Zaire in November 1990, and most economic aid in 1991, out of belated concern for the regime's human rights record. Nigeria's military rulers were relatively insulated from this type of international pressure. Since independence, the country had always been seen as immune from communist insurgency and safely pro-western. Despite its size, population and oil wealth, it had not been accorded the strategic significance attached to Zaire. The Nigerian generals were indifferent to criticisms of their human rights record by organisations such as TransAfrica and unmoved by Nigeria's suspension from the Commonwealth after the execution of Ken Saro-Wiwa and fellow Ogoni activists in November 1995.

Zaire: attempted reform, hyperinflation and the dismemberment of the formal economy

Mobutu began the 1980s with a desperate bid to staunch the haemorrhaging of public revenues by taxing the informal economy. On 27 December 1979, he ordered an immediate currency freeze and called in Zairian banknotes. Private citizens were given three banking days to exchange a maximum of 3000 zaires for new notes, half of which had to be deposited in a bank. The aim was to recover and tax the huge sums salted away by speculators in the informal economy, but the operation completely ignored the social realities of poor communications. Farmers in remote regions did not use banks and may not even have heard of the currency reform, so many lost their savings. The measure failed to improve the public finances: taxes on trade, which once provided three-fifths of government revenues, declined to 14 per cent by 1985. To compensate, the government had to increase the fiscal take from employees' incomes: 34 per cent of government revenues came from this source in the 1970s and 80 per cent in the 1980s. Since the state was the largest employer, its lower- and middle-level officials bore the burden of increased income taxation (Emizet, 1998, pp. 106–10).

In 1982, the government launched another set of liberalisation policies aimed at increasing the costs of informal economic activities. In late March it abandoned the price regulation of foodstuffs and deregulated prospecting for gold and diamonds, which prompted frantic 'rushes' in the mining regions. But the state insisted that gold and diamonds had to be sold to government-owned shops at fixed prices, so smuggling ensued. In Kinshasa, the monopoly shops were run by Mobutu's henchmen and the patrimonial system of rule retained some coherence, but elsewhere the regime's bureaucracy broke up into self-interested factions, who often gained by allowing smuggling to flourish. In 1988, gold and diamonds smuggled from Zaire accounted for almost 94 per cent of Belgian imports from Burundi and 88 per cent of imports from Congo-Brazzaville. The deterioration of the transport network abetted the dissolution of the national economy into regional fragments and the unchecked growth of unofficial economic activities. It was frequently easier to smuggle goods across borders than to transport them within Zaire itself. One estimate is that 40 per cent of coffee from Upper Congo was smuggled through Uganda in exchange for vehicles. Minerals and spare parts stolen from Gécamines in Shaba were smuggled into Zambia and South Africa. Smuggling – usually with official complicity – broke down the cohesion of the ruling class by diverting economic resources from state managers and reducing the political rents from export proceeds.

Zaire had to agree to an IMF structural adjustment programme in late 1983 as a condition for further strategic drawing rights and the rescheduling of existing loans. The terms were dictated by the neo-liberal 'Washington consensus': currency devaluation; a reduction in the money supply; the elimination of the budget deficit; the decontrol of prices; and the placing of public-sector corporations on a commercial basis. The programme was the first serious reform effort since the economic crisis began in 1974. The state reduced its role in the economy by abolishing its marketing agencies, de-controlling prices (except for petroleum products, public utilities and transport) and deregulating interest rates. It liberalised the external trade regime, revised customs duties and regularised debt payments. Expenditure on education and health was reduced, though there was no effective limit on the public monies which continued to flow through the President's Office. The results of greater fiscal discipline, austerity and a smaller state seemed quite positive to the IFFs: the inflation rate fell in 1984–5 and GDP grew by 1.3–2.0 per cent.

The reforms began to unravel in 1986 when the international prices of copper and cobalt touched new lows and export earnings were far below expectations. To make good the revenue shortfall and abide by the restructuring programme, the regime would have had to tax the incomes of the political aristocracy and curb its privileged access to state-controlled resources. Rather than undermine the foundations of patrimonial rule, Mobutu abandoned the structural adjustment programme, while orchestrating a hate campaign against the IMF's 'economic imperialism'. Although budget receipts were stagnant, civil servant salaries were increased to bolster the regime's social base and deficit spending rose dramatically. Despite the reimposition of some economic controls, inflation accelerated and the zaire began its precipitous depreciation. Copper production collapsed at the turn of the decade because Mobutu would not agree to a World Bank proposal to refurbish the industry, on condition the state relinquished control of Gécamines.

By 1990, economic decline had brought the one-party state to disintegration. Its 'ordinary' revenues from taxing trade and incomes were plummeting: between 1989 and 1992, they fell from more than $1000 million to less than $300 million, below the income of a medium-sized American university. To compensate, the regime turned to the 'seignorage' revenue earned by printing money. By wilfully bloating the money supply, it allowed hyperinflation to dismember the formal economy (De Herdt, 2002). Between 1987 and March 1993 the average annual exchange rate for the zaire fell from Z112 per US$1 to Z2.529 million per US$1. Zairians ceased to have a functional medium of exchange, and the banking system collapsed. People lost faith in ordinary economic routines and sought imaginary solutions to their financial woes. Extraordinary numbers fell for scams offering fantastic returns to depositors or participated in fraudulent money games; the total sums involved probably exceeded 160 billion zaires in May 1991 (almost $37 million at the current exchange rate). When the pyramid schemes collapsed in June 1991, the disillusioned furiously rioted in Kinshasa and fatalities ensued.

The informal sector could no longer function as a 'refuge' from the devastation of the official market economy, and the guarded optimism with which western scholars had observed its workings of around 1980 seemed rather misplaced a decade later. It was not simply that the informal sector could do no more than provide the vast majority with a marginal and chronically insecure existence. 'Informality' equated with the absence of both the rule of law and a fairly policed market with enforceable commercial contracts: it invariably imposed heavy overhead costs on petty producers and traders in the form of bribes and protection money, which had become so insupportable as to bring exchange between town and country virtually to a halt. By its very nature, the informal sector could not maintain the social overhead capital essential for any extensive economic activity: only a fraction of the road network in existence at independence was still fit for motor traffic by the early 1990s and the telephone and electrical systems were a shambles; railways that once linked major cities were overgrown by the jungle. Measuring the decline of the economy accurately was impossible, though it is officially reckoned real GDP fell by an average of 5.5 per cent a year between 1991 and 2000 (Democratic Republic of the Congo, 2006, para. 105). Hyperinflation was uncontrollable, even by drastic monetary reform. A new zaire, introduced on 22 October 1993 and equal to 3 million old zaires, initially exchanged at three to the US$; by January 1998, the exchange rate was 115,000 to the US$. At the end of the decade, the World Bank reckoned that average incomes were a third of their 1970 level (World Bank, 2000, p. 277; see Table 6.1). Half the population of Kinshasa was getting by on one meal a day, while the provision of water was so inadequate that a quarter of the capital's population had to walk more than 1 kilometre to fetch it. Except for artisanal gold and diamond mining, industrial mining had collapsed: Gécamine's copper output fell from 465,000 metric tons in 1990 to 19,000 tons in 2002 (Democratic Republic of the Congo, 2006, para. 122). The social indicators pointed to a 'de-modernising' society: the primary school enrolment ratio declined from 92 per cent in 1972 to 64 per cent in 2002, while the school completion rate had also deteriorated. In rural areas, only 17 per cent of the population had access to safe drinking water in 2005 and 1 per cent to electricity, while 64 per cent of the people lived in rammed-earth houses (*ibid.*, paras 107, 137).

Structural adjustment and economic decline in Nigeria

The Nigerian military was genuinely committed to a structural adjustment programme of its own devising. Babangida's most daring initiative was to sponsor a nation-wide debate in the autumn of 1985 on whether to accept the controversial $2.5 billion IMF loan, with its politically unpalatable conditions, over which his predecessors had procrastinated. Predictably, the public spurned the proposal, but the government claimed this outcome as a mandate for an alternative home-grown strategy, and proceeded to impose monetarist policies which were more stringent than those required by the IMF (Othman,

1989, p. 141). Much of industry was gradually deregulated and the naira was allowed to float, which led to damagingly high rates of interest and a drastically devalued currency. The import licensing system was dismantled, along with the commodity marketing boards. Deep cuts were made in state consumer subsidies, agricultural prices were allowed to rise and a number of public enterprises were privatised, while nearly all were henceforth required to operate on a commercial basis. It was not by any means a wholesale economic retreat on the state's part: the bulk of the privatised enterprises were small-scale and economically peripheral, and their total value amounted to less than 2 per cent of the government's portfolio. The majority of their shares appear to have been acquired by military officers (Tangri, 1995, p. 178). In its review of structural adjustment in sub-Saharan Africa, the World Bank listed Nigeria amongst the success stories on the strength of a 7 per cent increase in the annual rate of GDP growth in 1987–91, as compared with 1981–6 (World Bank, 1994, p. 138). Manufacturing revived (though only temporarily), as did exports of the 'colonial' staples, such as cocoa. The large improvement in the relative returns to farming induced a reverse migration of labour to rural areas after 1986. From its nadir in 1987, household consumption rose by a fifth by 1990. Whether the economy was really 'on the mend' is difficult to say because the Babangida government was relieved of the need to persist with austerity by the up-turn in the oil price prior to and during the first Gulf War. This vastly improved public finances and enabled the government to increase hugely the salaries and benefits of the impoverished middle class.

The Gulf War boom was only a brief respite from the most profound and prolonged economic depression in Nigeria's three decades of independence. Despite the efforts to diversify the economy, it was still in thrall to the international oil price: when that fell to a new low in 1992–5, Nigeria plunged into another economic crisis. The purchasing power of the naira, both on international exchanges and at home, fell relentlessly. Although domestic inflation was nothing like the nightmare in Zaire, it impacted severely on urban workers and salaried public employees; those with professional skills emigrated in large numbers. By 1993, about 21,000 Nigerian doctors were practising in the USA alone; by the turn of the century, between a quarter and a half of graduates lived outside the country. The universities were so impoverished that higher education virtually collapsed (Diamond *et al.*, 1997, pp. 7–9; Falola and Heaton, 2008, p. 223). The headcount ratio of poverty rose from 42.8 per cent in 1992 to 65.6 per cent in 1996

(World Bank, 2000, p. 91). The erosion of living standards contrasted painfully with the sheer greed of the military oligarchy and its civilian allies. Babangida perfected the practice of senior officers looking after their own: by 1989 more than 200 generals, many only in their 40s, had been retired on full pay and with allowances for life. Most went into business where their personal ties to the regime guaranteed their recruitment to the boards of private and parastatal companies. One result of the recycling of senior officers as corporate managers was that the Nigerian military produced more millionaires than any other profession. Fearing discontent amongst junior officers, the government allocated $50 million in February 1992 to import 3000 Peugeots for the private use of captains and majors (Herbst, 1996–7, p. 160).

As Babangida prolonged the so-called transition to democracy, his rule became more arbitrary, corrupt and 'praetorian' in its reliance on coercion and intimidation through the State Security Service. $12.2 billion in oil revenues allegedly 'disappeared' on his watch (International Crisis Group, 2006, p. 13). Vast sums were diverted to extra-budgetary accounts and disbursed to cronies and strategic constituents. Endemic corruption bred an anomie in entrepreneurial life and blurred the line between business and criminality. The civil service lost the remnants of its independence and integrity. With the forbearance and possibly participation of senior officials, Nigeria became a major transhipment point for heroin and cocaine and an epicentre of international commercial fraud. A sum equal to 15 per cent of government revenue flowed to smuggling networks and teams of confidence tricksters, many of them operating with the connivance of top elites (Lewis, 1996, p. 80). The manipulation and corruption of the judiciary in the Babangida years enfeebled the prosecution of economic crimes. Scholars who have collaborated on a detailed study of this period in Nigerian history describe it as a protracted 'collapse into praetorianism and economic destitution, into a plundered economy, a nearly worthless currency, and a politics virtually bereft of rules and institutions' – which would also be a fitting summary of the Mobutu regime's final years (Diamond *et al.*, 1997, p. 2).

Heading off democracy in Zaire and Nigeria

From the later 1980s, Mobutu was challenged internally by pro-democracy activists who coalesced in the Union pour la démocratie et le progrès social (UDPS) under the leadership of Etienne Tshisekedi, who had served Mobutu in various ministerial and diplomatic capacities. On 24 April 1990, Mobutu bowed to his internal and external critics and announced the ending of the one-party state and the re-establishment of multi-party politics, though this most Machiavellian of rulers intended no more than cosmetic changes. More than 200 political parties mushroomed with the ending of the MPR's monopoly: one, headed by Antoine Gizenga claimed the mantle of Lumumba; others were ethno-regional parties; some were created and funded by Mobutu in a calculated and successful attempt to divide his enemies. The major opposition parties formed the Union Sacrée and pledged to drive the president from office. His remaining supporters within the political class came together in what was known as the 'presidential tendency'. Mobutu tried to detach Tshisekedi from the opposition by offering him the premiership, which he initially accepted, then declined because the public reaction in Kinshasa was so hostile. The incident sowed discord within the Union Sacrée. Following the example of Benin, a National Sovereign Conference opened on 7 August 1991, but Mobutu flooded the conference with his supporters, and the opposition temporarily walked out. For several weeks, tension festered until the great outburst of 23 September 1991, when unpaid soldiers went on a looting spree in Kinshasa. Disorder spread throughout the country and foreign technicians working in the mining and industrial enclaves had to be repatriated, bringing the entire formal economy to a halt. Though the soldiers' grievances were real enough, there were strong indications the Mobutu regime orchestrated the looting: it took the precaution of securing the gold and diamond in the state-owned shops and ensured the Special Presidential Guard was paid. Members of the ruling group were speedily compensated for any loss or damage to their property; despite arrears in debt services, the regime had paid out $689 million in compensation for damages in Kinshasa by January 1992, mostly to its cronies (Emizet, 1998, pp. 108–9).

After this outburst, the power struggle between Mobutu and the opposition was played out against a backdrop of massive strikes, riots, looting and kidnapping across the country. Mobutu used every means from corruption to violence to shore up his declining power, and his opponents appeared too irresolute and divided to offer a credible alternative. For eight months, the National Sovereign Conference acted as a constitutional assembly and a remarkably open forum for debate and democratic renewal. It elected Tshisekedi Prime Minister in August 1992 but he had no control over the security forces, the state bank or the treasury. In early December 1992, Mobutu carried out the third coup of his career by closing the Conference. In late January 1993, soldiers went on a second looting spree after they received months of back pay in the new Z5 million notes, which merchants refused to accept. Hundreds died in the mayhem, including the French ambassador, most probably killed by a stray bullet though some believe he was murdered by Mobutist troops searching for Tshisekedi (Nzongola-Ntalaja, 2002, p. 201). The anarchy gave Mobutu a pretext for cracking down on the press, the opposition and dissident churchmen. In March, he ignored Tshisekedi's shadow government by setting up a rival, which took control of the institutional remnants of the central state. There followed a protracted conflict between the 'President's Party' and the fatally divided democratic forces from which Mobutu eventually emerged victorious: one of his most trusted lieutenants, Léon Kengo, was sworn in as Prime Minister in July 1994. The transition to democracy had been aborted, much as it had in Nigeria a few months before.

The symmetry of contemporary political events in 1989–93 was as close as we are likely to find in the histories of two states. Simultaneously with the structural adjustment programme, Babangida had launched a protracted transition from authoritarian rule to democracy. The ban on party politics was lifted in mid-1989 but, rather than permit the chaotic proliferation of parties, the military government instituted a mandatory two-party system. The parties – a supposedly left of centre Social Democratic Party and right of centre National Republican Convention – were soon colonised by the political class and partisan conflicts were internalised. They were allowed to contest the local government, state and gubernatorial elections in 1990–1. The transition was violently punctuated, but not derailed, when Babangida narrowly escaped assassination by army officers in April 1990. The attempted coup had distinct echoes of January 1966: the plotters represented aggrieved southern and Middle Belt minorities and their target was the Hausa/Fulani/Muslim 'establishment'; their declared aim was the expulsion of northern states from the Federation. Babangida responded to the failed coup with a drastic purge of the officer corps. More subtly, he sought to placate minority grievances by creating nine new states and dozens of local government authorities in August 1991. This manoeuvre exacerbated the fragmentation and incoherence of government but ensured that the spoils of office could be distributed more widely.

After seemingly endless procrastination, the 'transition' appeared to reach a dénouement with the presidential election of 12 June 1993, which international observers judged the freest and fairest ballot ever held in Nigeria. The winning candidate, Chief Moshood Abiola, was a Yoruba Muslim business millionaire, with close ties to the military oligarchy, and an unlikely democratic champion. Abiola had sought Babangida's approval for his candidacy (and may even have received a large campaign donation from him) but before the final results could be announced, the Association for a Better Nigeria obtained a court order forbidding their publication. The Association was a 'front' for senior officers who wanted Babangida to remain president and presumably acted with his consent (if not at his bidding). Ten days later, Babangida annulled the election, for reasons which remain obscure. The most plausible is that, as a Yoruba, Abiola was unacceptable to the 'strong man' in the military junta, Sani Abacha, a Kanuri who had been raised in Kano. The excuse Babangida later gave to Karl Maier, that Abiola would have divided the nation, was patently absurd, for he had polled heavily in northern and Middle Belt states as well as his native west (Maier, 2001, p. 71). A wave of violent protests followed the annulled election and many migrants retreated to their homelands in expectation of communal pogroms and civil war (Lewis, 1994, p. 327). Babangida resigned as president and commander-in-chief on 26 August and an interim civilian government took over, pledging to hold a fresh election. Abacha remained Defence Minister and consolidated his personal following in the military and the State Security Service. In early November, he forced the civilian president out when Lagos and other cities were paralysed by strikes in protest at the removal of the fuel subsidy.

The five years of his venal dictatorship were the most bleakly repressive and economically regressive in Nigeria's history. Abiola, who had left Nigeria to seek international support for his presidency, was gaoled on treason charges after his return in mid-1994; his senior wife was assassinated when she campaigned for his release. In March 1995, over 400 officers and civilians were arrested after the security services claimed to have thwarted a coup: the detainees included Obasanjo, Shehu Yar'Adua (a candidate in the presidential election), prominent journalists and democracy activists. Forty alleged plotters were convicted on the flimsiest of evidence after secret trials; Yar'Adua was sentenced to death and Obaṣanjo to life imprisonment, though Abacha commuted these sentences under international pressure.

Meanwhile, the public sector was being looted on a gargantuan scale:

By 1999 corruption was practically institutionalised. Government was widely regarded as a provider of large contracts, distributed by officers in power to people wealthy enough to buy their influence. This was particularly so in the case of the oil industry. Over time the judiciary became intimidated as the rich and powerful manipulated laws and regulations to their advantage. (Nigerian National Planning Commission, 2004, p. xiv)

Nigeria had become one of the world's poorest and most unequal societies. While it was urbanising at a phenomenal 5.3 per cent a year, the secondary sector – particularly manufacturing – was stagnating at about 5–7 per cent of GDP, making Nigeria one of Africa's least industrialised countries, with one of the highest rates of urban unemployment (*ibid.*, p. 9). It was also amongst the most heavily indebted; external and domestic debt amounted to about 70 per cent of GDP.

The symmetry broke down with the very different ways in which the despots' careers were ended: Mobutu was forced into exile in May 1997 when it became clear that his troops would not resist the advancing guerrillas of the Alliance des forces démocratiques pour la Libération du Congo, led by Laurent Kabila, a former Lumumbist turned ivory and gold trader. Eight months previously Kabila did not command a credible military organisation: he rose to power as an instrument of Rwandan and Ugandan expansion into eastern Zaire in the aftermath of the Rwandan genocide. The border authorities could not stem the vast flow of refugees into North and South Kivu, who included many of the genocidal *interahamwe* militia. Paul Kagame, who headed the post-genocide government in Rwanda, and Yoweri Museveni, the Ugandan president, led a coalition of central African states determined to oust Mobutu. Kabila's principal fighting force in the seven-month war against Mobutu's unpaid and demoralised army were Rwandan soldiers and Congolese Tutsi who had been trained in Uganda and Rwanda (Nzongola-Ntalaja, 2002, pp. 225–6).

Abacha's demise was altogether more sudden and a wholly domestic affair: that he died in the arms of two Indian prostitutes seems certain; whether this was due to heart failure brought on by an overdose of Viagra or poisoning by his enemies is unclear. The point to underline is that, for all the regional and social dissension the Abacha regime had caused, the territorial integrity of Nigeria was never seriously in question and it had nothing to fear from neighbouring states. Though Congo-Zaire and Nigeria were both cited as 'failed states' in the later 1990s, there was a huge qualitative difference in their state dereliction: Nigeria remained a territorially effective entity; Congo-Zaire did not.

Conclusions

In endeavouring to sum up these troubled national histories it is easy to slip into fatalism. The economist's version of fatalism sees Nigerians and the Congolese afflicted by the natural resource 'curse'. As an empirical generalisation, developing countries in which natural resource revenues provided a large proportion of GDP grew more slowly than 'resource poor' countries after 1970, partly because they were prone to predatory rent-seeking (Sachs and Warner, 2001). Nigeria and Congo-Zaire were spectacular instances of this 'curse', but they were not fated to grow slowly (or in the Congo's case negatively) and rent-seeking is not an ineluctable syndrome: in Botswana, a relatively strong and competent state minimised the adverse consequences of resource wealth while maintaining a multi-party democracy and over-seeing a consistently high rate of economic growth (Maipose and Matsheka, 2008). Nigeria's bounty of petrodollars represented an eco-nomic opportunity, but they were 'misused, misspent and mislaid' because of 'poor leadership and governance, on the one hand, and ineffective macroeconomic policies, on the other' (Iyoha and Oriakhi, 2008, p. 657). The Congo's mineral resources were plundered first by its ruling class, then by foreign predators the state was too decrepit to repel. Its inability to resist external pressures was – and is – mirrored by an inability to provide citizens with such basic services as issuing birth or death certificates without making them a source of corruption. Public administration is awful because civil servants' salaries are paltry, their career management is characterised by clientelism, physical working conditions are depressing and job descriptions and duties are poorly defined (Democratic Republic of the Congo, 2006, para. 91).

In explaining this doleful outcome the temptation is to resort to the historian's version of fatalism which sees Africa 'cursed' by an institu-tional legacy discordant with its cultural traditions (Davidson, 1992). Comparing Nigeria and Congo-Zaire is a useful check on such fatalism because the colonial institutions and economic structures inherited by the nationalists differed significantly, which makes the countries' polit-ical convergence all the more remarkable. Of course, this is not to deny that colonialism's core legacy in Nigeria and Congo-Zaire was the sov-ereign national state, which has been a powerful agent of societal trans-formation, a source of wealth and patronage for the dominant class, and a site of group competition and conflict. Its ubiquitous presence in economic and social life would surely suggest that national histories have been largely determined by the residue of institutions and ideologies deposited by the colonial experience. Yet, in certain respects, this residue was superficial and transient: in both countries, the state was akin to a grand hotel that the new owners comprehensively refurbished soon after taking over. The external shell was retained, but the internal configuration of suites was altered, and the staffing level vastly increased. The parliamentary constitutions which were supposed to provide house rules for running the establishment proved inoperable and the military coup became the means for changing the management.

When given a 'second chance' at democracy in the 1970s, Nigerians preferred a presidential and federal republic, with consociational mechanisms guaranteeing minority representation in government, very different from the Westminster model of 1960. Subsequent constitutional adaptations have virtually obliterated the colonial heritage in terms of the country's internal political structures. By fragmenting the federation into what are now 36 states and 774 local government areas, government has been brought closer, and in a sense made more responsive to local societies. But each wave of state creation has made social life more conflicted by entrenching sectional loyalties and pitting indigenes (or 'sons of the soil') against 'settlers'. A Nigerian's state of origin is an important matter when he or she is looking for a job or promotion in any public agency (or a university or a newspaper) or applying for a permit to buy land. Too often, ethnic parochialism outweighs individual merit and common citizenship (Bach, 2006, p. 84).

It is often argued that, as a Hobbesian solution to civil chaos, the Congolese political class restored the Leviathan state of their Belgian predecessors, with the implication that the Congolese were 'trapped' by an alien institutional legacy. This argument is easily overstated: while Mobutu's state may have mimicked the Belgian bureaucracy's imperious ways, it was with the signal difference that the charismatic, quasi-deified leader became the chief source of power and patronage in a patrimonial system of rule. The structural dissimilarities between Zaire in the 1970s and the 'model' Belgian colony of the 1950s were as striking as the similarities. Within the inherited shell of the territorial state, the dominant class in Zaire – as in Nigeria – was free to impose governing institutions of its own choosing, sometimes after popular consultation, sometimes not. States able to transfer ownership of expatriate property to their nationals – as Zaire and Nigeria did in the 1970s – cannot plausibly be described as 'neo-colonial'.

Finally, we must note the state's indifferent record in securing human flourishing in the most basic sense. The data on life expectancy and infant mortality for African countries (particularly Congo-Zaire) is often conjectural and there are alarming discrepancies between the sources. As we noted in Chapter 4, after comparing electoral registration in 2006 with the 1984 census, Lambert and Lohlé-Tart concluded that expectation of life fell in Congo-Zaire in the late twentieth, early twenty-first century. The figures in Table 6.2 do not bear this out, but they fairly represent the extraordinary demographic divergence in recent decades between the two African countries and Bangladesh. Nobody could object that this is an inappropriate comparator: Bangladesh has the world's most adverse land–labour ratios, a tropical disease environment and is exceptionally prone to natural disasters. In 2005, it was poorer than Nigeria in terms of per capita GDP (Nigeria having boomed after 2000 with global demand for oil). In the early 1960s, Bangladesh was a more dangerous place for babies and young children than either Nigeria or the Congo; even in the early 1980s, its infant mortality rate was worse than Zaire's. Since then, the rate has fallen by more than half, while it has declined only marginally in the two African countries. The prevalence of HIV can only partly explain this divergence: in 2002, the infection rate amongst both sexes aged 15–49 was 5.8 per cent in Nigeria and 4.9 per cent in the DRC (against an average of 10.4 per cent for sub-Saharan Africa) (Tabutin and Schoumaker, 2004, Table A.10). A larger part of the explanation lies in the public realm's poor performance in delivering primary health care, potable water, basic sanitation and in educating girls and young women in ante- and post-natal care.

Table 6.2 Life expectancy and infant mortality in Nigeria, Congo-Zaire and Bangladesh, 1960/5–2000/5

	Life expectancy (both sexes)			Infant mortality rate (per 1000 live births)			GDP per capita (US$, PPP)
	1960–5	1980–5	2000–5	1960–5	1980–5	2000–5	2005
Nigeria	38.5	44.9	46.7	169.4	131.4	113.8	1892
DRCongo	41.9	47.3	47.7	149.9	119.9	112	264
Bangladesh	41.2	49.4	63.0	174	123.7	57.2	1268

Note: PPP = purchasing power parity.

Sources: UN *World Population Prospects*, on-line database; World Bank, *Global Purchasing Power Parities and Real Expenditures*, 2008a.

Postscript

My purpose here was to describe and explain a history of post-colonial convergence from different colonial origins, and not to trespass on current affairs. Nevertheless, I cannot conclude without reflecting briefly on the recent political transitions in the two countries, for if they mark a distinct break with the past that surely merits the historian's notice. After a new constitution was approved by referendum, the Democratic Republic of the Congo held its first free and fair elections in 40 years in July 2006, with the assistance of the world's largest and most expensive peacekeeping operation, MONUC (the UN Mission in the Congo). Nigeria is presently experiencing the longest period of civilian government in its national history; the third elections since the military relinquished power were held in April 2007, the fourth in April 2011. Nobody can be confident that either country has institutionalised democratic procedures, but both exemplify a common pattern of politics in contemporary Africa, where competitive multi-party elections in presidential systems have become the norm.

Judging by the 2007 elections, Nigeria's political class had 'learned nothing and forgotten nothing'. The polls were brazenly rigged, electors intimidated and officials who tried to be impartial were threatened and physically abused. The ruling People's Democratic Party fought in a spirit of 'winner takes all'; its aim was a one-party state. The EU Observation Mission concluded that 'there can be no confidence in the results of these elections' because of 'the lack of transparency and evidence of fraud' (Human Rights Watch, 2007b; International Crisis Group, 2007; Suberu, 2007). Although President Obasanjo had grudgingly abided by the constitution and retired after his second term of office, constitutional norms meant nothing to most candidates. Many sought the endorsement of 'godfathers' who provided funds, thugs for protection and coercion, and demanded in exchange a 'cut' of public revenues and a say in running public institutions. The elections reflected the criminalisation of government, especially at state and local level, and the huge corrupt gains to be made by capturing public office. A damning report by Human Rights Watch bluntly stated that 'the conduct of many [Nigerian] public officials and government institutions is so pervasively marked by violence and corruption as to more resemble criminal activity than democratic governance' (Human Rights Watch, 2007b, p. 1). The social costs of an endemically 'uncivil' political culture are very high; it has been reckoned, for example, that 3 million people were internally displaced by some form of civil strife during Obasanjo's presidency, while more than 14,000 lives were lost (International Crisis Group, 2006). It is too early to say whether the election of President Goodluck Jonathan (a Christian Ijaw) in April 2011 marked a real turning point in the conduct of national elections. Accusations of vote-rigging and fraud were levelled against Jonathan in the north, but this may have been reflex resentment: international observers were generally agreed that, though not flawless, the electoral process was much fairer than in 2007.

In the Niger Delta, oil has polluted the political and moral, as well as the physical environment. The revenues of Rivers state exceeded those of many sovereign African states after 2001, thanks to the escalating oil price, yet its rampantly corrupt elected authorities failed to deliver even the most basic social services: public schools fell apart and rural health clinics were abandoned by their unpaid, demoralised staff. Criminal gangs hired to rig the 2003 state elections subsequently became a law unto themselves, spreading violence and insecurity throughout the state (Human Rights Watch, 2007a). Militias loosely affiliated with the Movement for the Emancipation of the Niger Delta have stolen crude oil, staged bank robberies and street battles in Port Harcourt and kidnapped wealthy Nigerians and expatriate workers for ransom. Federal troops drafted into the Delta under a state of emergency were themselves accused of brutalising local communities and exacerbating disorder.

In the Democratic Republic of the Congo, the peace process was more successful than anybody could have anticipated when Joseph Kabila's government signed the Pretoria accord with the two main rebel groups in April 2003. (He had succeeded his assassinated father in April 2001.) All signatories were offered lucrative positions in the transitional government and impunity for the human rights abuses committed by their forces, which were supposed to be integrated into the national army. The dismemberment of the country was substantially reversed, Rwandan and Ugandan troops withdrew, and relations with Rwanda greatly improved. There was, nevertheless, good reason for fearing a breakdown of the transitional arrangements because Kabila and his chief rival, Jean-Pierre Bemba (the leader of the Movement for the Liberation of the Congo and one of the four vice-presidents) maintained private armies. Bemba also controlled two TV stations, which pumped out vituperative propaganda against the Presidential 'faction'.

The first round of voting for the presidency and national assembly on 30 July 2006 was largely peaceful and well organised by an Independent Electoral Commission, which foreign donors funded to the tune of $500 million. The political campaigning was amongst the most vigorous ever seen in Africa and the turn-out was about 70 per cent. Just before the results were to be announced on 20 August, fighting broke out in Kinshasa between Bemba's militiamen and Kabila's presidential guards when the latter tried to shut down the MLC's TV stations. Behind the attack on Bemba lay the strongly region- alised support for the main presidential contenders. Kabila had polled heavily in the east, where he was genuinely popular for having ended the war and secured the withdrawal of foreign forces, and his entourage expected to secure an absolute majority in the first round. He was denied victory by his negligible support in Kinshasa (where he won only 13 per cent of the vote) and poor showing in the western provinces. The capital voted strongly for Bemba and could only be secured for Kabila by armed force. The second presidential round on 29 October confirmed the east–west split in political alignment. Kabila won 58 per cent of the vote to Bemba's 42 per cent, but his support was heavily concentrated in the eastern provinces where Swahili has become the main vehicular language in the last generation. Bemba's support lay mostly in the west where Lingala is the lingua franca. Two factors seem to lie behind this regional-linguistic divide. First, the Swahili-speaking traders, 'fixers' and middle-men who flocked into Kinshasa on Laurent Kabila's coat tails in 1997 are much resented for their nouveau riche flamboyance; the younger Kabila, who was raised in Tanzania and speaks Swahili and English better than French and Lingala, was tainted by association. Second, in voting against Kabila, the electors in Kinshasa and the western provinces were voting against their rulers since 1997, who had failed to alleviate mass impoverish- ment. In the east, conversely, electors voted against Bemba (and the MLC) because he was perceived as an accomplice of the foreign inter- ests who had inflicted such misery on the country (Weiss, 2007).

After his electoral victory, Kabila sought to build a broad-based coali- tion behind an authoritarian presidency. The veteran Lumumbist, Antoine Gizenga, was appointed premier of an over-sized government designed to accommodate the disparate elements in the Alliance for the Presidential Majority. His ministerial colleagues included Nzanga Mobutu, the late dictator's son. The opposition was marginalised and harassed, and its leader, Bemba, forced into exile; hundreds of sup- porters were killed following a brutal crackdown by the security forces in early 2007. Kabila dissipated much of his democratic legitimacy by the corrupt means with which he extends his power. Under the new constitution, the provincial assemblies elect provincial governors, who dispose of substantial fiscal resources. Despite the opposition coalition dominating the Lower Congo, Kinshasa and Kasai Occidental assemblies, the Presidential Alliance won the governorships by blatantly bribing assembly members. Many questioned the sustainability of Kabila's regime: Richard Dowden a leading commentator on Africa, warned: 'The ridiculously weak foundations of this state can still collapse overnight' (Dowden, 2008, p. 378). It would be rash to claim the sheer passage of time has belied this warning: Kabila is vulnerable to military coups and escaped an assassination attempt in early 2011. Nevertheless, his regime is proving unexpectedly durable and he is expected to win the presidential election in late 2011. He gains political credit from keeping the peace and the economic revival, thanks to Chinese investment in mining and infrastructure. However appalling the living standards of the great majority, they have improved on the recent past. Moreover, central government under a strong, democratically elected president is buttressed by a now deeply rooted sense of national identity. Unitary sentiment serves as a safety barrier against dismemberment or secession, though it can also be manipulated into chauvinism and xenophobia.

7
Colonialism, Post-colonialism and Ethnic Violence: The Examples of Rwanda and Burundi

Introduction

Even the least attentive reader will have gathered by now that ethnic consciousness is an inescapable (and irreducible) part of African social life. Yet, despite its apparent pervasiveness, ethnicity is a concept with which many scholars are distinctly uncomfortable. They find it difficult to define in a way which covers all instances of group solidarity and exclusiveness labelled 'ethnic'. They are also unsure as to whether ethnicity is a brute datum which explains political behaviour or whether it is really ethnic identity and discrimination that stand in need of explanation (Hyden, 2006, ch. 9, summarises the academic literature). A further reason for scholarly unease lies in the association, in much public discussion (within Africa and without), of ethnicity with 'tribes' and 'tribalism', and the grossly distorting assumption that post-colonial conflicts are historically rooted in primordial 'tribal' identities and animosities. Anthropologists working in Africa long ago dropped the word 'tribe' from their professional vocabulary because it was irredeemably tarnished with a vulgar social evolutionism: a 'tribe' implied a lower form of social and political life. The notion of a self-sufficient 'tribal society', maintaining its distinctive culture and identity in an ahistorical limbo, was an illusion (Southall, 1970; see also Young, 1976, p. 35). Anthropologists were also embarrassed by their discipline's role as the intellectual handmaiden of colonialism in the 1930s, 40s and 50s, when ethnographies of 'tribal society' endorsed the perception of Africans as peoples 'without history' and without the capacity for national self-determination. Despite the expulsion of 'tribalism' from scholarly discourse, the penumbra of ignorance and prejudice lingers on, over-shadowing the more neutral term 'ethnicity'. We should add that, to the irritation of African intellectuals, their political leaders have themselves repeated long-demolished myths of the essentially 'tribal' character of African society and the African past (Bayart, 1993, p. 53). As Peter Ekeh noted in 1990, although western scholars were shunning the term 'tribalism', it was enjoying an 'unprecedented boom not only in everyday interactions among ordinary Africans, but more especially amongst high-ranking Africans in government and university institutions' (Ekeh, 1990, p. 661).

Few (if any) academics would dissent from the proposition that ethnicity in contemporary Africa is a modern phenomenon that gelled during the colonial period and has since proved very malleable in the hands of political and communal leaders. It is not a stable combination of invariables (such as language and cultural heritage) but a complex and shifting social relationship. There is more room for argument as to whether ethnic identities were in the first instance imposed 'from above' for the purposes of administrative control or formed 'from below' by Africans in response to the exigencies and opportunities of the colonial situation. In Rwanda, administrative control and African initiative complemented each other: the Belgian colonial authorities made social categories immutable by instituting ethnic registration, but Rwandan intellectuals were indispensable collaborators in constructing an ideology of ethnic superiority and segregation (Des Forges, 1995, p. 45). Elsewhere, what we might call ethnic aggregation was the work of western-educated Africans seeking to create broader communities of sentiment by amalgamating local societies with common cultural elements into larger wholes. One of the best-studied examples, to which I alluded in Chapter 4, is the Ijeshas of western Nigeria who came to identify themselves as 'Yoruba' during the colonial period (Peel, 1983).

Since independence, the ethnic segmentation typical of African states has commonly been seen as a background precondition for political rent-seeking, economically malign policies and cut-throat competition to control the state (in other words, the malign group behaviour commonly condemned as 'tribalism'). In 1997, two economists – William Easterley and Ross Levine – sought to demonstrate this statistically by correlating ethnic diversity with growth-retarding policies and political instability. They found that the more ethnically fragmented a society, the more likely it was to experience ethnic conflict in the form of pogroms and civil wars. They concluded that 'ethnic diversity ... helps account for Africa's growth tragedy' (Easterly and Levine, 1997, p. 1205). Using much the same method, Paul Collier and Anke Hoeffler have reached different conclusions. They found that the relationship between ethnic fractionalisation and the likelihood of civil war was non-linear: highly fractionalised societies were no more likely to experience civil war than completely homogeneous ones. Those most at risk were ethnically polarised societies where substantial minorities were identifiable targets for persecution and where they could rebel with a realistic prospect of seceding. In their view, the fact that Africa had experienced many civil wars since 1960 was due not to its societies being factionalised into myriad ethnicities but to its poverty (Collier and Hoeffler, 1998).

Statistical studies such as these are an indispensable check on ill-informed generalisation but have their own methodological pitfalls. Both pairs of authors utilised an index of ethnic fractionalisation constructed by Soviet scholars in 1960, when much of Africa was still under colonial rule. Since then, ethnic identities have been politicised and transformed by urbanisation, the adoption by urban incomers of vehicular languages (such as Portuguese in Luanda, Lingala in Kinshasa), the spread of literacy and exposure to mass communications. Regression analysis based on stale data cannot be a substitute for historical enquiry.

Rwanda and Burundi; Hutu and Tutsi

In focusing this chapter on the small, Central African countries of Rwanda and Burundi, there is a clear danger of saying nothing new, or, what is worse, adding to the pool of public ignorance. Few events in the late twentieth century attracted more public interest than the Rwanda genocide of 1994; though much of the commentary was ill informed, abundant expert analysis is now widely available. Alison Des Forges's full and authoritative report, *Leave None to Tell the Story: Genocide in Rwanda* (1999) is accessible online, as is the report of the International Panel of Eminent Personalities which investigated the genocide for the OAU. Regrettably, however, the decade-long civil war in neighbouring Burundi attracted far less attention in the West, and the interaction of ethnic tension and conflict in the two states since independence is often overlooked, even by Africanists. Until the 1990s, they were locked in a mutual antagonism, unique in world politics, which caused crises in one to redound on the other. It is now too easily forgotten that the first accusations of genocide in the Great Lakes region were levelled against Burundi's Tutsi-led government in 1972, after the more-educated and politicised Hutus were indiscriminately murdered following an abortive attempt to overthrow the regime (Lemarchand and Martin, 1974). If any single event persuaded Rwanda's 'Hutu Power' fanatics that all Tutsi had to be eliminated, it was the assassination by Tutsi soldiers of Burundi's first democratically elected Hutu president, Melchior Ndadaye, in October 1993. One purpose of this chapter is to analyse ethnic conflict in Rwanda and Burundi in parallel; another is to further this book's overall aim by putting post-colonial catastrophes into historical perspective.

I should emphasise that both countries followed the chronological trajectory outlined in Chapter 4 pretty closely: the constitutional arrangements made at the end of the Belgian mandate soon gave way to single-party authoritarianism, followed by the rule of military strong men. In both states, the neo-patrimonial distribution of public goods was used to retain support for the ruling clique and, for much of the time, ethnicity was a 'shadow theatre' (to use Bayart's phrase) masking regional and clan rivalries. As primary exporters (principally of coffee) both states were cruelly exposed to collapsing world market prices in 1980s, which meant that mass impoverishment in a context of land shortage and ecological deterioration was a background pre-condition for civil strife. Around 1990, the democratic wave sweeping through Africa compelled the dominant elite in both countries to dismantle one-party systems and schedule elections. In both, political liberalisation was the prelude to escalating violence, the mass flight of refugees and the regionalisation of conflict. In many respects, therefore, the 'shape' of post-colonial history in Rwanda and Burundi was quite typical for African states.

Before proceeding, it is worth asking whether their societies are ethnically divided at all. Although their populations are conventionally categorised into a Hutu majority (roughly 85 per cent) and a Tutsi minority (roughly 14 per cent), the only *indubitably* ethnic sub-group are the Twa, the pygmoid descendants of the original inhabitants of the Great Lakes region. They are about 1 per cent of the population and have long been the butt of racist prejudice on the part of Hutu and Tutsi alike, who will not eat and drink with them. The origins and nature of the Hutu–Tutsi divide are matters of much scholarly controversy: they have been co-habiting the same ecological and political space for many centuries and the usual markers of ethnic difference are conspicuous by their absence. Hutu and Tutsi live on the same hills, speak the same language, once shared the same traditional cosmology and now worship at the same churches and drink at the same bars. I can see no alternative to the 'ethnic' label, principally because Hutu and Tutsi – or more especially their ideologues – interpret their differences as of racial origin. Although we may well consider them objectively mistaken, these interpretations constitute a dimension of their social reality. That said, the boundaries in everyday life seem 'fuzzier' than we would expect in racially conscious societies. Hutu and Tutsi generally have no moral or religious prohibitions against sleeping with, and marrying, each other, though how frequently that happens is difficult to determine. David Newbury asserts that at least one-quarter of Rwandans are of mixed descent, in that both Hutu and Tutsi figured among their eight great-grandparents (D. Newbury, 1998, p. 84). This seems to be an informed guess – since no evidence is offered – and would be consistent with a high degree of endogamy if three-quarters of Rwandans had only Hutu or only Tutsi great-grandparents. In Burundi, where the Hutu and Tutsi identities were much more fluid three generations ago, the proportion of mixed descent must surely be greater. (According to Lemarchand, 'a striking number of Barundi claim a Hutu father and Tutsi mother': 1994, p. 9.) For this reason, physical appearance is an unreliable guide to contemporary social identity (though it was surely less fallible a century ago). The stereotypes which represent the Tutsi as taller, lankier, lighter-skinned and with more aquiline features than the shorter, stockier Hutu can be dangerously misleading. Hutu and Tutsi are often physically indistinguishable and internally differentiated by economic class, clan and regional loyalties, so what has persuaded them that their group identities and differences are so overwhelmingly important as to be matters of life and death?

To answer that completely we would need to refer to the hate propaganda put out by extremist cliques, the docility of ordinary people when ordered by officials and policemen to kill their neighbours and the material inducements to do so, for victims lost goods, houses and land, as well as their lives. But an essential part of the answer is that Hutu and Tutsi are mentally imprisoned by a mythology of their own past. As Alison Des Forges has remarked: 'Rwandans take history seriously. Hutu killed Tutsi for many reasons, but beneath the individual motivations lay a common fear rooted in firmly held but mistaken ideas about the Rwandan past' (Des Forges, 1999, p. 29). Similarly, Lemarchand observed that 'on both sides of the ethnic fault [in Burundi] summoning the past to explain the present has become part of a discursive practice intended to legitimise ethnic ideologies' (1994, p. xiv).

These ideologies work by projecting imaginary corporate identities back into the ancestral past. They derive a cultural legitimacy from the legends of origin in abundant (though conflicting) oral traditions but more importantly build on the long-discredited 'Hamitic hypothesis'. This pernicious fantasy expressed the compulsive ranking by nineteenth-century Europeans of human cultures in a racial (and racist) hierarchy. It can be traced to the observations of the first English traveller in the Great Lakes region, J.H. Speke, and became widely entertained wherever Europeans were puzzled by finding complex state institutions in the heart of Africa. Since they deemed the Bantu too innately primitive to have developed them autonomously, they concluded that these institutions must have been introduced by racially superior invaders – dubbed the Hamites after one of the sons of Noah – who were allegedly Caucasians and now constituted the ruling class. Charles Seligman, one of the pioneers of academic anthropology in Britain, described 'the Hamites' as 'pastoral "Europeans"', arriving wave after wave, better armed as well as quicker witted than the dark agricultural Negroes'. 'The civilisations of Africa' – he claimed – 'are the civilisations of the Hamites; its history the record of these peoples and of their interactions with two other African stocks, the Negro and the Bushman' (Seligman, 1939, p. 96).

The Hamitic myth flourished in colonial Rwanda and Burundi because it legitimised indirect rule through the kingdoms' ethnically defined 'natural' rulers and was internalised by African intellectuals. In both states, the colonial impact enhanced the political and socio-economic domination of aristocratic elites who, whatever they might have been called at the beginning of the colonial era, were officially designated 'Tutsi' by the 1930s. Not all Tutsi were wealthy and powerful by any means; there were poor Tutsi who cultivated their fields and whose way of life was little different from their Hutu neighbours, just as there were poor whites in South Africa. But the Belgian colonial regime accorded all Tutsi a privileged status by exempting them from public labour on the roads and hillside terraces. By the 1940s, nearly all chiefs were Tutsi. When secondary education was instituted for Africans, Tutsi were accorded a disproportionate number of places and consequently monopolised posts in the native administrations. Most African priests and all senior clergy were Tutsi. Crucially, the 'big men' who controlled access to land and could, with the backing of the colonial authorities, exact labour from Hutu peasants were Tutsi. Whether the colonialists simply rationalised pre-existing structures of inequality or assembled what were essentially new edifices out of remnants of the ancien régime has long been debated. What is not disputed, however, is that colonial officials, missionaries and ethnologists *racialised* ethnic differences and *alienated* the privileged minority from the indigenous majority (Mamdani, 2001; Lemarchand, 1970, remains an excellent guide to the historical background. Chrétien, 2003, ch. 4, is a more up-to-date survey).

The terms 'Tutsi' and 'Hutu' are not European inventions: 'Tutsi' originally described the status of an individual – a person rich in cattle – and only later referred to the elite group as a whole; 'Hutu' meant a subordinate or follower of a more powerful person, and subsequently referred to the mass of ordinary people (Des Forges, 1999, p. 32; D. Newbury, 2001, p. 266). When Europeans first arrived in Rwanda in the 1890s, Tutsi and Hutu were readily distinguishable by physical appearance and social deportment: Tutsi patrons evidently held Hutu clients in a servile relationship, which in the kingdom's territorial core was based on a contract involving the exchange of cattle for work and fealty. (The system of power and authority in pre-colonial Burundi was by no means identical and its distinctive features are outlined below.) The writings of the early visitors exhibit a remarkable consensus on these points; though they may have been misled by their own ideological preconceptions, it is impossible to believe they were wholly mistaken. Moreover, abundant oral traditions purported to show Tutsi superiority over the Hutu; powerful Hutu individuals could acquire Tutsi status in the ancien régime, but as a group the Hutu were destined to remain in an inferior position (Lemarchand, 1970, pp. 43–5).

How the terms acquired their connotations is not known for certain. Some time ago, Roland Oliver argued that two very different agrarian ways of life had been in competition throughout eastern and southern Africa since the Later Iron Age (c. 700CE–1500CE). One was a woodland way, derived from the Bantu occupation of the Early Iron Age, and characterised by compact and relatively permanent settlements. It revolved around agriculture rather than stock-raising, planting rather than sowing, matrilineal rather than patrilineal inheritance. The other was a savanna way, introduced originally by Nilotic immigrants, and characterised by dispersed settlement patterns; it revolved around stock-raising and milking, as well as cereal agriculture, and patrilineal rather than matrilineal inheritance (Oliver, 1982). Pastoralists normally exercised an ascendancy over agriculturalists so, for Oliver, Tutsi domination exemplified in acute form a social pattern widespread in Bantu Africa. It must be said that some Rwandan and Burundian specialists reject this thesis. In David Newbury's view, 'Tutsi' and 'Hutu' are broad classificatory labels with little explanatory value for understanding pre-colonial history: that history's major dynamic was the formation and expansion of indigenous dynastic states, which we have no evidence to believe were imposed by incoming pastoralists. The emergence of Tutsi elites was, he argues, a *consequence* of state formation, not a cause (D. Newbury, 2001, p. 266).

This is not a debate we can pursue here, though we must note that the colonial impact greatly extended these states, as well as consolidating their internal structures of domination. The borders of present-day Rwanda and Burundi are often said to coincide with those of the pre-colonial kingdoms, but this is misleading. When the territories were incorporated into German East Africa in the 1890s, the Nyiginya dynasty controlled roughly half of what is now Rwanda and the Ganwa dynasty about half of modern Burundi. Both royal courts were endeavouring to impose their dominion on peripheral states and chiefdoms, but some remained autonomous until about 1920. We should be under no illusions as to the character of pre-colonial state expansion: the 35-year reign of the Rwanda's last wholly independent *Mwami*, Kigeri Rwabugiri (d. 1895) was one long military campaign and his punitive raids on neighbouring polities were utterly ruthless. Under German protection, both courts roughly doubled the areas under their effective administration and in so doing replaced local power holders with administrative chiefs (*ibid.*, p. 313). Europeans were a token presence up to 1914, when the entire administrative-cum-military staff of Germany's Rwanda Residency consisted of ten German nationals; in Burundi, there were six (Lemarchand, 1970, p. 64). The military effectiveness of their coastal *askaris* was well understood, but the colonialists were probably regarded as no more than useful allies in subduing districts hitherto beyond royal control. In 1905, one German administrator defined 'the ideal' of indirect rule as 'unqualified recognition of the authority of the sultans [i.e., the *mwamis*] from us ... in a way that will seem to them as little a burden as possible; this will link their interests with ours' (quoted in Chrétien, 2003, p. 256). Catholicism (introduced mainly by African missionaries from Buganda) had only influenced marginal minorities: there were about 10,000 converts in Rwanda in 1914 and 3000 in Burundi. They were cut off from their kin and the enclosures where they worshipped were perceived as foreign, even strange (*ibid.*, p. 214).

After acquiring their mandate, the Belgians slowly reversed the relationship with the Rwandan monarchy, which became both the subordinate ally of indirect colonial rule and the ritual apex of a Tutsi ethnocracy. (As we shall see, the Burundian monarchy preserved its supra-ethnic character.) *Mwami* Musinga was deposed in 1931 because of his hostility to colonialism and Christianity, but the monarchy was preserved to lend an aura of legitimacy to an administrative hierarchy, based on the Tutsi chiefs, which was qualitatively new. Under the ancien régime, some chiefs had authority over cattle, others over land and others over military duties: their rival and overlapping jurisdictions had served to protect the Hutu peasantry against undue exactions. In 1929–33, the Belgians reorganised the administration by fusing differentiated powers into a single agency. Tutsi chiefs were put in charge of native tribunals, which became instruments through which Tutsi privileges were retained and abused, and Hutu subjection perpetuated. Educational opportunities were rigorously controlled: the sons of Tutsi dignitaries were taught in French and so imbued with 'civilising' values; if Hutu were taught at all, it was in Swahili, the medium of 'native' instruction. French-educated Tutsis were appointed to vacant chieftaincies, made functionaries in the administration and monopolised recruitment to those professions open to Africans (such as pharmacy). For Hutu, taking holy orders was just about the only avenue of social promotion. As part of the 1933–4 census, the ethnic identity of all Africans was registered at local government offices and passes were introduced which identified their bearers as Tutsi and Hutu. In theory, a Tutsi was defined by owning ten or more cattle but there were many exceptions to this rule whose status had to be settled by information provided by the Catholic clergy.

The Belgians were ably assisted in the 'Hamitisation' of Rwandan history and society by Tutsi informants. While Rwanda was under German administration, the custodians of public memory at the royal court had kept the Europeans at a distance, but in the 1920s and 30s the conversion of Tutsi intellectuals to Catholicism, and their acquisition of literacy, brought them much closer to the colonial rulers. Rwanda's dynastic traditions are exceptionally rich and the memorising of historical narratives has long been part of its oral culture. As Tutsi poets and historians began conveying this store of knowledge to Belgian ethnologists, so Tutsi supremacy and the 'Hamitic' character of the ancien régime became mutually reinforcing myths. The collaboration of Tutsi intellectuals and European scholars produced what was in many ways an impressive body of scholarship, but one which presumed Tutsi and Hutu had always been, and were destined to remain, racially defined, internally coherent blocs of people.

Given that the colonial regime had fixed their ethnic identity for good in the early 1930s, it seems puzzling that more than two decades passed before Hutu spokesmen articulated their own collective consciousness. The delayed emergence of a western-educated counter-elite partly explains this, but more important, I think, was the complete absence of towns where Hutu could shake off their primary loyalties to kin, lineage and clan. In 1956, Kigali, the capital, was no more than a large village. Over 99 per cent of Rwandans lived under customary law on hill slopes where each household stood isolated in its own fields. The countryside was devoid of villages; the hill was a little social universe and there was no broader civic community between the peasants and the central authorities. They were fragmented into family units and closely regimented by government, as well as subservient to Tutsi landlords.

Unsurprisingly, therefore, the first organised expression of Hutu social assertiveness emerged under the aegis of the Catholic Church, rather than from within Hutu society. Access to mission schooling for Hutu widened from the early 1950s and a new generation of socially radical missionaries began to commiserate with the plight of the Hutu masses. A seminary-educated Hutu schoolteacher, Grégoire Kayibanda, was made editor of a Church publication and, with the support of sympathetic churchmen, founded the Mouvement Social Hutu in 1957. With eight other former seminarians, Kayibanda published 'Notes on the social aspect of the racial native problem in Rwanda' for the benefit of the UN Decolonisation Mission which visited the Trust Territories in March. Better known as the *Bahutu Manifesto*, it was a riposte to the demand for a rapid transfer of power to the monarchy made shortly earlier by the *Mwami*'s exclusively Tutsi High Council. The Manifesto demonstrated how deeply the Hamitic myth had penetrated the social psychology of the educated. It claimed that 'the conflict between Hutu and Hamites – i.e., foreign Tutsi' was the heart of the Rwandan problem and called for a double liberation from both the 'Hamites' and 'Bazungu (white) colonization':

The problem is above all a problem of political monopoly which is held by one race, the Tutsi; political monopoly which, given the totality of current structures becomes an economic and social monopoly; political, economic and social monopoly which, given the de facto discrimination in education, ends up being a cultural monopoly, to the great despair of the Hutu who see themselves condemned to remain forever subaltern manual labourers and still worse, in the context of an independence which they will have helped to win without knowing what they are doing. (Quoted in C. Newbury, 1988, p. 191)

To remedy this 'problem' the Manifesto called for equality of opportunity in education and employment, and an end to ethnic discrimination. Despite its reasonableness, the Manifesto provoked an arrogant and dismissive response from a group of royal courtiers who declared there could be no basis for brotherhood and cooperation between Hutu and Tutsi, since many years ago the latter had subjugated the former by force.

As the Belgian administration came under UN pressure to prepare the Trust territories for independence, it had to choose between opposing political demands: either it could quickly concede 'monarchical' independence to the Tutsi elite or back the Hutu call for social emancipation prior to 'republican' independence. At UN insistence, the Belgians scheduled local elections on the basis of universal suffrage for June–July 1960, and the emergence of Rwandan political parties to contest them hastened a reversal of the Belgians' alliance with the monarchy and the Tutsi chiefs. Paradoxically, the most militantly anti-colonial party was the monarchist Union Nationale du Rwanda, founded in August 1959, which denied ethnic divisions were part of Rwanda's royal tradition; it received money and diplomatic backing from the communist countries and courted the support of Lumumba's MNC. The sudden death of the childless *Mwami* Mutara in late July gave Tutsi zealots at court the opportunity to enthrone a puppet sovereign without consulting the colonial administration. The Belgians already had misgivings about transferring power to a 'feudal' ruling class that was flirting with communism; this coup persuaded them to throw their weight behind Parti du Mouvement de l'Emancipation Hutu (PARME-HUTU) formed by Kayibanda in October. In November, violent clashes between rival party militants escalated into a general breakdown of order and a spontaneous social revolution, during which Hutu peasants burnt local Tutsi chiefs out of their homes. Several hundred were killed but it was an assault on power and authority, not an ethnic pogrom; the 'petits Tutsi' were largely unscathed.

The Belgians declared a state of emergency, and gave their assent to the great upheaval by formally deposing the remaining Tutsi chefs and appointing Hutu in their place. This opened the way for PARMEHUTU's sweeping victory in the local elections of June–July 1960, when it won 70 per cent of the seats. Its more moderate ally, the Association pour la Promotion Sociale de la Masse, which sought support across ethnic lines, won only 7 per cent. The Tutsi parties were marginalised, although the abstention of nearly half the electorate suggests many Rwandans had yet to be politicised (or could still be intimidated into passivity). In January 1961, the Belgian governor and his most senior military officer facilitated a Hutu-led coup d'état which overthrew the monarchy and proclaimed a republic. In a remarkable display of insurgent Hutu power, their elected councillors converged on Gitamara, with about 25,000 supporters, and declared themselves a constituent assembly, which proceeded to elect a president and form a provisional government. The UN Trusteeship Commission accused the Belgians of helping bring about 'the racial dictatorship of one party' and replacing 'an oppressive system by another one' (quoted in Prunier, 1997, p. 53). These comments reflected the opprobrium being heaped on the Belgians at the UN at this time – for the Katanga crisis was at full pitch and Lumumba had recently been murdered – and ignored their diminishing capacity to manipulate Rwanda's turbulent politics. To their many vociferous critics, the Belgians appeared to be seeking another neo-colonial settlement that would destroy the radical nationalists in the UNR; a more realistic appraisal is that they were simply acknowledging the electoral logic of majoritarian democracy. PARMEHUTU won 78 per cent of the votes in the legislative elections held in September and, by an equally overwhelming majority, Rwandans ratified the abolition of the monarchy in a referendum. When the republic became independent on 1 July 1962, the ruling party's popular mandate was just about the broadest in Africa.

Independence completed Rwanda's transformation to an egalitarian Hutu republic. The old ruling class was socially decapitated by the redistribution of land and the expulsion of Tutsi cadres from the administration. By early 1962, about 120,000 Tutsi had fled, principally to Burundi but also to Uganda, where there are Rwanda-phone pastoralists with an affinity for the Tutsi. (Kinyarwanda – as it is properly called – is one of the most diffused African languages; Kirundi is basically a variant.) How many were driven out by violence and intimidation, and how many went into voluntary exile is difficult to establish. There was wanton killing during the Hutu revolution, but the fatalities are usually numbered in the hundreds. The abortive Tutsi invasion of late 1963 – launched by monarchist exiles in Burundi – brought a terrible escalation of violence on the part of Hutu who sensed their political and social gains would suddenly be reversed. About 10,000 Tutsi were massacred in late 1963, early 1964. The killings expressed the tremendous psychological insecurities among the Hutu majority and their deep and lasting sense of inferiority. According to Luc De Heusch, who was in Rwanda in October 1963, the Belgian military adviser helped whip up a hate campaign against the Tutsis (Heusch, 1995). The savage reaction swept away Tutsi notables who had sought an accommodation with the new regime: some 20 leading personalities, including members of the government, were arrested and summarily executed. That the invasion originated in Burundi exacerbated the Hutus' sense of insecurity for this had *become* a Tutsi-dominated state during the independence process.

In the aftermath of this crisis, the Rwandan government denounced the Economic and Customs Union with Burundi which the UN had insisted on at independence. This severance defied all commercial logic and exacerbated Rwanda's geographic isolation from the international economy, for the best transport links to the sea lay through Burundi. Scale economies that could have been made in administration, revenue collection and the provision of services and infrastructure were forfeited. Of the many obstacles to Rwanda's (and Burundi's) economic development, the most significant was the small size and poverty of the country's domestic market. Even as a single economic entity, Rwanda and Burundi were disadvantaged by being land-locked and – by African standards – land-hungry; their separation magnified the problems.

Burundi: the emergence of a Tutsi dictatorship

Burundi's traditional social system had been more complex and fluid than Rwanda's and lacked the sharp horizontal split between Tutsi and Hutu. Although these were recognised social categories, there were major fissures within, and considerable cultural continuity between them (Lemarchand and Martin, 1974, pp. 5–6). The Tutsi were divided on caste lines between Hima and Banyaruguru; though the latter were socially superior, the former tended to be politically dominant. Each caste was organised into patrilineages, which were the primary reference groups for Tutsi. The degree of social distance between them was at times more perceptible and socially significant than their sense of ethnic difference (if such it was) from the Hutu. Neither Hutu nor Tutsi held traditional claims to authority. The ruling class in the ancien régime were the princes of the blood or Ganwa who were identified as a separate ethnic group. Below this princely stratum, no single fault line of cleavage could be said to determine the allocation of status, wealth or power. In the bitter feuds between the rival princely clans in the nineteenth century, conflict was seldom if ever activated along ethnic lines, and the monarchy had often allied itself with Hutu chiefs against 'over-mighty princes'. By contrast with Rwanda, the ruling dynasty was not aligned with the Tutsi.

After the Belgians acquired the Mandate, they were soon persuaded that Burundi was a degenerate version of Rwanda, which ought to be ruled by a 'Hamitic' pastoral aristocracy. They saw their duty as restoring an imaginary pristine social order and so adopted policies of ethnic stereotyping and favouritism modelled on the neighbouring administration. The Tutsi were accorded privileged access to studentships and senior positions in the native administration; the Hutu administrative elite was gradually squeezed out of office. In the early 1930s, 27 out of 133 regional administrators were Hutu, 30 were Tutsi and 76 were Ganwa; after 1945, there were no more Hutu administrators (Chrétien, 2003, p. 268). Nevertheless, the system of social stratification continued to be comparatively open and flexible and the monarchy remained an institution all Burundi could revere.

For these reasons, in the run-up to independence the Belgians were confronted by a cohesive Burundian nationalism, led by the king's eldest son, Prince Louis Rwagasore. He did not resemble the stereotypical 'Hamite', and by marrying a Hutu demonstrated his freedom from ethnic prejudice. After briefly attending Antwerp University, he had started a cooperative movement amongst the peasantry which aimed to cut out Greek and Pakistani middle-men. In 1958, he set up the Union pour le progrès national (UPRONA), with a platform of independence and social reform which attracted support from all ethnic and religious groups. Hutu were a majority on the party's central committee. Rwagasore soon fell foul of the Belgians, who assisted the formation of the rival Parti Démocratique Chrétien (PDC), which advocated delaying independence. The political atmosphere became more febrile as the legislative elections scheduled for September 1961 approached, but the main fault line in the emerging political class line lay between rival clans within the extended royal family: the Bezi (led by Rwagasore) and the Batare (led by two cousins, whose political instrument was the PDC). The protagonists mobilised their social following around patron–client relations, not ethnicity. UPRONA won 58 out of 64 seats in legislative elections, when half its successful candidates were Hutu, and Rwagasore was designated prime minister of the interim government. A month later, he was assassinated on the orders of the PDC leadership.

His murder removed a unifying and charismatic personality and exposed UPRONA to factional rivalries that soon took on an ethnic coloration. For Hutu politicians, Rwanda's social revolution was an inspirational example, while the influx of Rwandan Tutsi refugees was a dire warning to the Tutsi of what might happen to them. Hitherto, Burundians had not discerned co-ethnics in the neighbouring population; henceforth, they habitually did so. In fact, ethnic self-perception in both countries was sharpened by having across the border a mirror in which their worst nightmares of ethnic triumphalism and victimhood were reflected. With the king's support, the Tutsi faction in UPRONA effected a conservative transition to independence. A Hutu politician, Pierre Ngendandumwe, was appointed prime minister in June 1963 in acknowledgement of the Hutu majority in the National Assembly. But, using the monarchy's considerable prerogatives as a 'front', Tutsi notables consolidated their power by controlling the police, the military and other government organisations. In acting (as they saw it) to forestall the anarchic dissolution of the social order by a tyrannous majority, they confirmed the worst suspicions of Hutu politicians.

Between the run-up to independence and the later 1960s, an extraordinary 'social metamorphosis' – to use René Lemarchand's expression – occurred in Burundi: it changed into a genuine caste society, in which power was monopolised by a closed ethnic 'establishment' representing around 15 per cent of the population (Lemarchand and Martin, 1974, p. 4). The pattern of dominance extended to virtually all sectors of life, restricting access to material wealth, education, status and power to the Tutsi minority. Given the relative openness of traditional society, it was an astonishing transformation.

Its initial driving force was the paranoia gripping the political establishment in the aftermath of the Rwandan killings and the real fear of armed rebellion being launched from across the border. In March 1964, the *Mwami* dismissed four Hutu ministers whose loyalty was suspect and Ngendandumwe resigned shortly thereafter. The already poor relationship with Rwanda worsened because neither government could (or would) prevent border violations; in August, Burundi's foreign minister warned the UN and OAU that the two countries were on the brink of conflict. In January, after months of ministerial instability, the *Mwami* had to reappoint Ngendandumwe to the premiership, but a week later he was assassinated by a Rwandan Tutsi refugee. Each ethnic camp suspected the other of plotting a coup. In the legislative elections of May 1965, Hutu politicians won a two-thirds majority and selected a new leader, Gervais Nyangoma, who was expected to be offered the premiership. Instead, the *Mwami* appointed Léopold Biha, a Ganwa whom Tutsi conservatives regarded as one of their own. In October,

Nyangoma and other Hutu politicians launched the long-anticipated, but ill-prepared coup. Hutu gendarmes killed the Prime Minister and attacked the royal palace, causing the *Mwami* to flee to the Congo, but they failed to take control of government and administration. In the ensuing power vacuum, Tutsi peasants in Muramvya province were massacred by militants loyal to Nyangoma, with the help of Hutu policemen.

To pre-empt a Rwandan-style social revolution, the Tutsi defence minister, the 25-year-old Captain Michel Micombero, seized power by rallying the army, and ordered the liquidation of every Hutu leader of any significance. Thousands of Hutu were massacred in the reprisals which were condoned, if not organised, by the central authorities. The pogrom made ethnic identity – which had once between fluid and relational – fixed and inescapable. A military junta formally proclaimed a republic in November 1966. Its politics were riven by factional rivalries between Hima and Banyaruguru within the Tutsi elite, but overlain by an ethnic differentiation which made Burundi an apartheid state. Social categories were greatly simplified by the assimilation of the Ganwa into the Tutsi and the separation of the population into mutually antagonistic ethnic aggregates (Lemarchand, 1994, pp. 13–16). A distinctive group of Tutsi politicians emerged who were adept at whipping up paranoia and crystallising ethnic solidarities against Hutu elements. Cross-border raids launched from eastern Congo-Zaire by Hutu insurgents racked up social tensions. The radio and press publicity given to the trials and executions of Hutu accused of treasonable complicity in these raids created an atmosphere of pervasive fear.

The social tensions spiralled into a vortex of ethnic hatred in late April–May 1972, after Micombero dismissed the Cabinet and Hutu insurgents attempted a rebellion. How the uprising was planned and led is unclear, but it was poorly organised and many rebels relied heavily on drugs and magic. They attacked their victims indiscriminately and with senseless cruelties. The government's counter-violence in the following months was more systematic and, in terms of its ruthless destruction of Hutu social leaders, calculatedly 'prophylactic'. Hutu society was decapitated as part of a conscious counter-insurgency strategy. To be educated – albeit only to primary level – or to have a responsible job was a death sentence for a Hutu. Estimates of the total number killed range from 80,000 to 200,000. Perhaps 300,000 Hutu fled to Rwanda, Zaire and Tanzania. In the aftermath, Hutu were excluded from the army, the civil service, the university, secondary schools and the modern economic sector. They were so traumatised by the massive reprisals that, for a decade or more, they opted for sullen quiescence: parents did not send their children to school for fear of making them targets in the next pogrom.

Under the military regime that ruled Burundi from 1966 to 1992, all three presidents were Tutsi-Hima from the same village: Micombero, who became increasingly corrupt and mentally unstable, was overthrown by a distant cousin and clansman, Jean-Baptiste Bagaza, in November 1976, but the regime's repressive brutality was undiminished. What was, in fact, an ethno-regional dictatorship had assumed the mantle of 'Third World' radical nationalism: government-sponsored propaganda portrayed ethnicity as a colonial and neo-colonial fiction, dreamt up to perpetuate 'divide and rule' amongst deluded Africans. Behind the verbiage was a gross instance of dysfunctional redistribution and political rent-seeking: Tutsi from Bururi in the south (Bagaza's home region) cornered a quite disproportionate share of public investment, educational opportunities and senior positions in public companies and the army (Ngaruko and Nkurunziza, 2008). Bagaza was in turn removed by Major Pierre Buyoya in September 1987, a more moderate man with a genuine wish to conciliate the Hutu majority, though foreign donors were also pressing him to do so. In 1988, he promised the restoration of representative civilian government after a four-year transition period, appointed a commission to draw up a new constitution and formed a government of national unity, with equal numbers of Tutsi and Hutu ministers, and a Hutu premier. Buyoya at first refused to put *multi-party* democracy on the reform agenda for fear political parties would become vehicles for mobilising ethnic antagonism; he relented only after the wind of change started blowing through Africa in 1990. The liberalisation of the regime created space for the re-emergence of Hutu politics, but the presidency, the army, the police and judiciary, and the key ministries remained under Tutsi control. Hutu were given access to secondary and higher education, but administrative jobs long remained a Tutsi preserve because the 'pool' of Hutu graduates was so small; for example, in 1994, only 13 out of 241 magistrates were Hutu (Uvin, 1999, p. 257).

The liberalisation of the regime was very nearly derailed by further outbreaks of mass violence: in August 1988, Hutu farmers in two northern communes, angered by the corruption and arrogance of local Tutsi administrators, killed up to 3000 Tutsi. When the Tutsi-dominated army restored order, it killed about 20,000 Hutu and forced tens of thousands to flee over the border. In 1991 and 1992, similar events followed the same pattern: Hutu peasants lashed out blindly at Tutsi power-holders and the army retaliated indiscriminately, killing many more than the victims of popular anger. But Buyoya mixed reconciliation with repression: in the autumn of 1988, he appointed a National Commission to Study the Question of National Unity, which reported in May 1989. Although a tendentious document, which tried to shift all historical responsibility for ethnic consciousness and conflict on to the Belgians, it was the first official recognition of the centrality of the 'Hutu–Tutsi problem', and the first statement of specific solutions for resolving it. It helped create a climate of tolerance and openness unknown in the previous 23 years of dictatorship. Ethnically denominated political parties were forbidden under the new Constitution, adopted by referendum in March 1992, and most politicians followed the spirit of the law as they set about building party organisations.

The presidential and multi-party elections of June 1993 were conducted in a remarkably calm spirit and fair manner, and with a massive turn-out (Reyntjens, 1993). Though a plethora of parties had sprung up, the only serious contenders were the predominantly Tutsi UPRONA and predominantly Hutu FRODEBU (Front Démocratique du Burundi), founded in 1986 as a clandestine movement to protest the authoritarianism and human rights abuses of the Bagaza regime. During the political campaigning, UPRONA had sought to smear its rival's reputation with accusations of fomenting ethnic animosity and associating with the outlawed rebel movement, PALIPEHUTU (Parti de la libération du peuple Hutu). This scare-mongering tended to raise the political salience of ethnicity, especially amongst Tutsi public employees and students. Nevertheless, both FRODEBU and UPRONA sought to appeal across the ethnic divide, partly because the new Constitution gave them little choice in the matter. Under the proportional representation system, all parties had to reflect the population's ethnic and regional mix in their lists of candidates. Though the outcome of the elections was a triumph for the Hutu majority, the new political map was not simply drawn along ethnic lines. In the presidential poll, Buyoya, UPRONA's candidate, was unexpectedly defeated by FRODEBU's, Melchior Ndadaye, a Hutu, who received 65 per cent of the popular vote. A significant minority of Hutu must have voted for Buyoya. FRODEBU won four-fifths of the seats in the National Assembly but eight of its 69 deputies were Tutsi, while 12 of UPRONA's 16 deputies were Hutu, a consequence of the party having to put Hutu candidates on its lists. Rioting Tutsi students in Bujumbura condemned the presidential result as an 'ethnic inventory of Burundi', but Buyoya accepted the popular verdict with good grace and the army chief of staff pledged the military's loyalty to the president elect. René Lemarchand was then concluding the manuscript to *Burundi: Ethnocide as Discourse and Practice*, and sounded a decidedly optimistic note: Burundi had, it seemed, turned its back on its violent past. By the time the book went to the press (1994), he was compelled to revise that judgement. As we shall see, Burundi was on the brink of another catastrophe.

Rwanda: the first and second republics

Under its founding president, the First Rwandan Republic (1962–73) followed a familiar political trajectory in post-colonial Africa: PARME-HUTU was declared the sole legitimate party in 1966 and its inner circle of presidential 'cronies' effectively displaced formal governing institutions. The key positions of power and patronage were held by men from Kayibanda's native Gitamara prefecture, which is in the centre of the country where Tutsi dominance had been most strongly entrenched. Thus, the elite were usually the president's clansmen, and shared his burning resentment of the Hutu's historic subservience. Defence of the 1959 Revolution, the social equality of all Hutu and an inverted version of the 'Hamitic' myth were the regime's ideological cement. A catechistic tract published by PARMEHUTU stated: 'Tutsi domination is the origin of all the evil the Hutu have suffered since the beginning of time. It is comparable to a termite mound teeming with every cruelty known to man' (quoted in Chrétien, 2003, p. 307). The government continued the colonial practice of recording ethnicity on the identity cards all Rwandans had to carry, and which were used to exclude Tutsi from public employment.

The much-vaunted social egalitarianism of the 'Hutu republic' was soon belied by the emergence of a wealthy bureaucratic stratum who ran (and profited from) state-controlled services, in alliance with military officers, private merchants and the technocrats who dealt with the many foreign aid agencies operating in Rwanda. An export boom, and the Africanisation of much of the commercial sector, lay behind the emergence of this new social network. (I hesitate to call it a 'bourgeoisie' because Rwanda remained Africa's most rural society. Only 5 per cent of the population lived in towns in 1990.) After plummeting during the revolution, exports of coffee and tea rose sharply in the later 1960s because of soaring demand in the Common Market. The parastatal monopolies which purchased and exported these crops were a key prize in the competition for wealth and power.

The principal cleavage in the state lay between the governing elite from the geographic centre (Kayibanda's cronies) and the political class of the northern region, which was excluded from the plum public-sector jobs. The social psychology of ethnicity in the north was shaped by its distinctive history: within living memory, autonomous Hutu chiefdoms had withstood the encroachments of the Rwandan monarchy so northerners were less culturally conditioned to think of themselves as a subjugated people. By 1970, Kayibanda had become so remote and autocratic – perhaps in imitation of the former *mwamis* – that a coup was the only way to remove him. It was eventually staged in July 1973 by the head of the army, Juvénal Habyarimana, who had followed one of the few careers open to ambitious northerners in the First Republic. He immediately shifted political power from the centre to the north by installing a governing elite drawn mainly from his native Bushiru district. He also brought the economic nationalism so characteristic of African states at this time into political discourse by promising the progressive 'Rwandisation' of the modern economy: wholesale commerce, importing and exporting, and manufacturing were to be taken into Rwandan hands, as were the subsidiaries of foreign companies registered in Rwanda. A new single party, the Mouvement Révolutionnaire National pour le Développement (MRND), was set up to mobilise Rwandans behind state-led development.

Habyarimana seized power in the aftermath of the Burundian genocide, when the country was flooded with traumatised refugees. Their plight rekindled acute 'racial' tension, especially amongst students and white-collar employees. According to the French anthropologist, Claudine Vidal, who was in Rwanda at this time:

> Young educated Hutu and Tutsi experienced for one another a total aversion which went far beyond rivalry. There were evidently many exceptions, but the general tone of mutual loathing had taken on a racial character; everything about the Other was disparaged, his physique, his way of eating and speaking, his origins. (Quoted in Heusch, 1995)

Tutsi students at the National University were blacklisted by anonymous and self-appointed Committees of Public Safety. Children of mixed marriages were targeted, along with 'cheaters' who had changed their 'racial' affiliation. Lists began to proliferate at places of employment. Henceforth, Tutsi were barred from enrolling at the university; those wishing to continue their education had to go elsewhere.

To its credit, the Habyarimana regime made some effort to reintegrate the Tutsi, and swam against the tide of educated opinion by redesignating them a minority ethnicity, rather than an alien race. The official line was that their 'privileged' position in the Church, the professions and higher education was a historic and still present grievance for Hutu, but could be redressed by state-enforced quotas. Hence, school selection, university admissions and recruitment to public employment were to take strict account of ethnic affiliation. However, the quota system was not effective in the private sector, where Tutsi were well represented in commerce and non-governmental organisations. By and large, discrimination against them, and their negative stereotyping, served more to legitimise the government than to exclude Tutsi from social advancement. Limited Tutsi participation in the political sphere was encouraged by Habyarimana, but it was a token presence. During his regime, there was not a single Tutsi burgomaster or state prefect, only one Tutsi officer in the army, two Tutsi members of parliament out of 70 and usually one Tutsi member of the Cabinet (Prunier, 1997, p. 75). Defence of the 1959 Revolution was a constant theme of state propaganda; since it was an article of faith amongst the military-political elite that the Tutsi were a constant threat to the revolution, they lived amongst the Hutu majority on sufferance. Nevertheless, there was no anti-Tutsi violence until the onset of the war with the Rwandan Patriotic Front (RPF) – a Uganda-based organisation of Tutsi refugees and their children – in October 1990. To justify a crack-down on its opponents (including, but not exclusively alleged Tutsi 'fifth columnists'), the regime 'faked' an attack on Kigali. In a climate of mounting ethnic suspicion, hundreds of Tutsi were killed in early 1991; there were further massacres in March 1992, August 1992, January 1993, March 1993 and February 1994, some in retribution for human rights violations committed by the RPF. The initiative was normally taken by 'private' militias associated with different political parties, though the police, the armed forces and local government officials usually participated.

In the meantime, Habyarimana had bowed to his many domestic critics – and the international donors – and ended the single-party regime. The MRND lost its political monopoly and acquired a D for 'Democratie'. More than a dozen rival parties were formed, including the rabidly anti-Tutsi Coalition for the Defence of the Republic. In early 1992, Habyarimana was compelled to form a coalition government.

It is now difficult to form an objective appraisal of Habyarimana's regime because we know the state apparatus over which he had long presided was the instrument for the calculated and systematic slaughter of about 800,000 people between April and June 1994. Habyarimana was killed in a plane crash before the slaughter began, but the men who executed the genocide had been close colleagues and he must have been aware of their genocidal 'mind-set'. His widow and her circle of intimates were hate propagandists before his death and ferocious advocates of exterminating the Tutsi thereafter. Knowing all this, it is tempting to write off the Habyarimana years as a protracted prelude to state failure and social catastrophe. This would be a mistake: Rwanda was Africa's best-administered country, with a good record in providing infrastructure and using foreign aid effectively. A German missionary later recalled: '[In the early 1980s] we used to compare the nearly idyllic situation in Rwanda with the post-Idi Amin chaos in Uganda, the Tutsi apartheid in Burundi, the "real African socialism" of Tanzania, and Mobutu's kleptocracy in Zaire, and we felt the regime had many positive points' (quoted in International Panel of Eminent Personalities, 4.6). Although the democratic opposition was bitterly denouncing the presidential elite for corruption by the late 1980s, Rwandan officials were generally considered honest and competent. In 1989, Rwanda was held up by the World Bank as a model of successful adaption to population pressure and a deteriorating land–labour ratio (World Bank, 1989, p. 105). The country had the world's fastest rate of population growth and had reached the frontier of cultivation: Malthusian logic indicated it was destined for disaster. Yet, until the RPF invasion and civil war (which hugely disrupted agricultural production) 'good governance' had warded off that fate.

Just how much competition for land influenced ethnic identities is difficult to gauge; some accounts suggest that rural people had only the haziest notions of who was Hutu and who Tutsi until they were drawn into political struggles by educated ethnic entrepreneurs (see, for example, Waters, 1995). But there can be no doubt that, in a biblical lifetime, the rural environment became much more inimical to the peaceful coexistence of differentiated social groups, however they identified themselves. In 1914, Rwanda's population was estimated at less than 1 million and was virtually static because of very high infant mortality. Since there was no land shortage, two types of land utilisation – Tutsi cattle-raising and Hutu hoe cultivation – could coexist without straining natural resources. With sanitary measures and the control of epidemics, the population rose eight-fold within three generations: it reached 3 million by 1960, and between 8 and 8.6 million by 1994. Before 1960, the average farm holding was slightly more than 2 hectares per family; by the early 1990s, when the labour force was still overwhelmingly agricultural, it had fallen to 0.6 hectares. There was little artificial check on population growth because, in deference to Rwanda's Catholic clergy, family planning policies were officially disparaged and contraceptives forbidden (Lemarchand, 1970, pp. 30–4). The average Rwandan woman bore eight children. Most young men were still set on acquiring a few fields before they formed a household, but that customary social pattern was becoming more difficult to sustain.

Until the later 1980s, government and society in Rwanda coped remarkably successfully with the deteriorating land–labour ratio. It was one of the few African countries in which agricultural production increased faster than population and without the inequities which accompanied rural development in, say, Côte d'Ivoire. Food production grew at 4.7 per cent a year in Rwanda between 1962 and 1982, while population grew at 3.4 per cent. The area under cultivation was extended by 3.7 per cent a year between 1966 and 1983, principally by draining fertile marshes and valley bottoms. Farmers shifted production from cereals and legumes to root crops and from cattle-rearing to smaller livestock. The number of cattle fell by a fifth between 1970 and 1981. Two-thirds of the cultivated land was double-cropped. Rwanda's programme of soil and forest conservation was amongst the most effective in Africa. Thanks to a nation-wide community tree-planting programme, Rwanda had more trees in the late 1980s than it had at independence and had attained self-sufficiency in fuel wood. There was a huge increase in the number of farms protected by terracing and anti-erosion ditches during the 1980s. Since the urban population was so small, its social interests did not weigh heavily in determining the government's commodity pricing and exchange-rate policies and fiscal priorities. Indeed, the government won plaudits from the World Bank for remaining attentive to the interests of the farming majority and avoiding the 'urban bias' so evident elsewhere in Africa. According to the Bank, a realistic exchange rate, coupled with an absence of excessive taxation, ensured coffee producers received a high share of the border price (World Bank, 1989, p. 105).

The acute economic crisis at the end of the decade laid bare the underlying precariousness of Rwanda's rural economy. The price of coffee, the ubiquitous cash crop, collapsed in the later 1980s, and the spread of disease in the coffee trees blighted prospects of recovery. Income from coffee exports fell by nearly four-fifths between 1985 and 1993, and per capita national income by at least a third. Famine reappeared in the south and southwest in the late 1980s for the first time since 1943. Government indebtedness compelled it to negotiate a structural adjustment programme with the international financial institutions which required reducing its social programmes and imposing fees for schooling, health care and water services. The economic crisis coincided with the onset of war with the RPF and the diversion of government spending from the civilian to the military budget, which absorbed 1.9 per cent of GDP in 1989 and 7.8 per cent in 1993. 'It was' – writes Mamdani – 'as if Rwanda was plunging free fall into a nightmare' (Mamdani, 2001, pp. 148–9). About a million people fled their homes after the RPF took control of the northern provinces in 1993; they mostly languished in displaced persons camps outside Kigali and represented a huge loss to the rural labour force. While the Habyarimana regime, the RPF and the democratic opposition were locked in their political drama, the rural majority faced deepening poverty and the cumulative problems of land hunger and soil erosion. They impacted on Hutu and Tutsi alike; both were internally differentiated, and on the crowded southern lowlands Tutsi pastoralists were as poor and wretched as Hutu peasants.

We should add that Hutu and Tutsi had always sought respite from a harsh way of life in alcohol. Brewing banana beer in the household for domestic consumption was Rwanda's largest single 'industry'; it had much the same role in everyday culture as cocoa leaves in the Andes (Bézy, 1990, p. 25). It deadened the physical and the moral senses.

Convergent catastrophes: Burundi and Rwanda 1993–4

In the summer of 1993, Burundi's transition from dictatorship to democracy was regarded as an example for the rest of Africa, its political class lauded for its moderation and willingness to compromise. Nobody was so quite sanguine about Rwanda's political prospects because of the regime's fragmentation and volatility. Hutu radicalism had found a seductive voice in the independent radio station (Radio Télévision Libre des Mille Collines), which mixed street slang, obscene jokes and good music with vituperative racism; it was so entertaining that even RPF troops listened to it (Prunier, 1997, p. 189). Under the influence of his formidable wife and her brothers, Habyarimana had vacillated between, on the one hand, Hutu extremism and renewing the war and, on the other, agreeing to a permanent settlement with the RPF, as the opposition parties were demanding. By July, he had clearly decided that peace was the only option: he appointed a new prime minister of a coalition cabinet, with a mandate to conclude an agreement that was extremely favourable to the RPF. Under the Arusha accords signed in August, half the ministries in a transitional government of national unity were to be allocated to the RPF. It was also agreed that, when RPF forces were integrated into the national army, half the officer corps would be RPF men. About 500,000 Tutsi refugees in neighbouring countries were given the right to return and seek restitution of their property. The final goal envisaged by the Arusha accords was a multi-party democracy in which the RPF would be one amongst several electoral players, but the Habyarimana regime had made massive concessions to reach that goal. The president had exposed himself to prosecution for human rights abuses for the accords stipulated no officials would be immune from arraignment. The massacres of hundreds of Tutsis in mid-October 1990, and subsequent atrocities, were amongst the crimes for which he could plausibly be held responsible.

In the following months, both countries slid from political compromise to catastrophe. Burundi's democratic experiment was brutally terminated on 21 October, when Ndadaye was assassinated in a military putsch, along with other political figures. Whether the middle-ranking officers who killed Ndadaye acted with the foreknowledge of their military superiors we do not know. The army was an all-Tutsi institution with a dismal record of ethnically targeted violence, but Tutsi intransigence alone seems an insufficient explanation for the putsch. Ndadaye had done everything in his power to allay Tutsi anxieties: despite FRODEBU's thumping majority in the national assembly, he had formed a government of national unity in which UPRONA had a large place and more than a third of ministerial portfolios were held by Tutsi. By appointing a Tutsi woman prime minister, he had kept his promise that the presidency and premiership would not be held by people from the same ethnic group. What almost certainly provoked the putsch were the government's declared intention to open the officer corps to Hutu cadets and the steps taken to 'colonise' the state apparatus by putting FRODEBU militants into public jobs. The military were lashing out in defence of a system of wealth and privilege of which they had long been part (Reyntjens, 2000a).

The putsch failed to overthrow the government, which took refuge in the French Embassy and called for an international force for protection against its own army. UPRONA and the military high command opposed any form of international invention; though the latter reaffirmed its loyalty to the constitution, it seemed to be pondering which way to jump. UPRONA published a memorandum on the 27th which effectively condoned the murders. For a fortnight or so, there was no effective public authority, which contributed to a wave of anarchic violence. When news of Ndadaye's death seeped out, FRODEBU's Hutu militants attacked UPRONA's supporters (usually, though not always, Tutsi); some of the violence was spontaneous revenge, some orchestrated by party functionaries and local government officials. The population resisted a military take-over by blocking roads and destroying bridges, which prevented the forces of law and order from moving around the countryside. When the army did regain mobility, it behaved with its customary brutality. In all, about 50,000 were killed, with Hutu and Tutsi fatalities being roughly equal. Around 700,000 people (mostly Hutu) fled to neighbouring countries (the majority to Rwanda). For the first time in Burundi's history, the population began to segregate on ethnic lines because internally displaced Tutsi gathered around military and administrative centres for protection, while Hutu peasants dispersed into the bush and swamps for fear of military reprisals.

Recognising the government would not be toppled, the army chief of staff ordered the military back to barracks, while requesting an amnesty for the insurgents. But there was to be no return to the *status quo ante*: in the following months a coalition of army and opposition forces set out to destroy FRODEBU in a 'creeping coup'. Groundless accusations that the party had planned to exterminate the Tutsi undermined its legitimacy; the Constitutional Court was used to paralyse the presidency and the National Assembly; FRODEBU officials and supporters were physically intimidated by, or with the complicity of the armed forces. The running of the state was made increasingly difficult by the non-cooperation of civil servants and the judiciary. In negotiations between the '*mouvance présidentielle*' or 'presidential side' and the opposition in early 1994, Tutsi micro-parties with no real constituency threatened renewed violence to secure for themselves positions in government and the administration. They were able to do so because Bujumbura, where the negotiations took place, had become isolated from the rest of the country and much of the capital was ruled by political thugs. After prolonged wrangling, a cross-party government was formed in February which confirmed the ethnic bi-polarisation of the political system. All the ministers from the opposition parties were Tutsi while those from the 'presidential side' were Hutu. The death of Ndadaye's successor, Cyprien Ntaryamira, in the plane crash which killed Habyarimana on 6 April, and the unleashing of the Rwandan genocide spurred the opposition into completely reversing FRODEBU's electoral victory and overturning the 1992 Constitution. In September 1994, a Government Convention was signed under which executive power passed to the National Security Council, an opposition-dominated body, for a transitional four-year period.

This 'creeping coup' took place against a backdrop of escalating civil war. In June, some despairing FRODEDU leaders – including the then Minister of the Interior – resorted to armed rebellion by creating the Forces pour la défense de la démocratie (FDD) as the armed wing of the Conseil national pour la défense de la démocratie (CNDD). Subsequently, the older rebel movements, PALIPEHUTU and FROLINA (Front pour la libération nationale), which mainly recruited amongst Burundian refugees in neighbouring countries, stepped up their cross-border raids. The Government Convention induced a growing paralysis of state institutions by rendering the presidency and National Assembly impotent and failing to create alternatives that were either legitimate or effective. The cabinet was too divided to formulate a coherent response to the mounting violence. All that united the Tutsi parties was their conviction (understandable, given events in Rwanda) that only the army stood between them and genocide. By early 1995, all remnants of state power had been relinquished to the military; the restoration of Buyoya to the presidency in a coup of July 1996 simply put a formal seal on army rule. Meanwhile, Bujumbura, where the civilian politicians congregated, had become more or less divorced from the rest of the country when Tutsi militias expelled nearly all its Hutu inhabitants. In the countryside, the Hutu majority lived in constant fear of the army and Tutsi militias, who terrorised with impunity. Hutu belonging to the FDD and FNL hit back with increasing brutality. Burundi was locked into 'one of the most brutal and deadly civil wars in modern history, fought along ethnic lines' (Uvin, 1999, pp. 262–3).

Ndadaye's assassination, and the influx of Hutu refugees, fomented a feverish paranoia in Rwanda. The self-styled 'Hutu Power' network, the coalition that would make the genocide possible, was built upon his corpse (Des Forges, 1999, p. 137). Even moderate Hutu politicians needed no persuading that the Tutsi could not be trusted now that the worst stereotypes of their vicious and unrelenting disdain for the Hutu were seemingly confirmed. We must add that, with astonishing insensitivity, the RPF used its influence with the Ugandan government to allow Ndadaye's killers to take refuge in Kampala, where they enjoyed RPF hospitality. The August peace agreement was profoundly discredited. Arms were smuggled to the extremist militias; the Tutsi minority was hysterically denounced as the 'fifth column' of the RPF; and death lists were drawn up. Rwandan Army reservists started training the *Interahamwe* militia, originally the youth wing of the MRND. To the consternation of the UN, which had authorised a mission to oversee the implementation of the Arusha accords, Habyarimana began dragging his feet and insisting on new conditions. The February 1994 deadline for the transfer of power to a broad-based transitional government was postponed when the killing of a leading moderate, Félicien Gatabazi, general-secretary of the second largest opposition party, set off a vicious circle of murders within the Hutu political class. His supporters immediately assumed Hutu extremists were responsible, and killed the president of the CDR (Coalition pour la Défense de la République) in revenge. (There is now strong evidence – given at the International Criminal Tribunal for Rwanda – that Gatabazi was killed by an RPF murder gang in a calculated attempt to 'head off' a negotiated peace.) Nevertheless, the breakdown of the Arusha peace process was not a foregone conclusion when Habyarimana attended a regional summit in Tanzania on 6 April. He came under great pressure from the African leaders present to abide by the agreement; on the trip back to the airport President Museveni solemnly asked him to honour his signature (Prunier, 1997, p. 211). One, not insignificant, provision of the accords had already been fulfilled with the stationing of an RPF battalion in Kigali. The military record of the Rwandan armed forces was poor and renewing the war could not have seemed an attractive option.

There is no dispute that the shooting down of Habyarimana's plane as it returned to Kigali that same evening was the occasion, first, for the liquidation of moderate Hutu politicians by the Presidential Guard, then for unleashing the genocide. The Prime Minister, Agathe Uwilingiyimina, and several other Cabinet officials were amongst the first victims. The wave of targeted killings followed the plane's destruction so closely that it was immediately assumed 'Hutu Power' extremists were responsible for firing the SA-16 missiles. A day later, a representative of the Rwandan Army High Command told a US Embassy official in Kigali that the most likely culprits were a dissident unit of the Presidential Guard; nobody in the High Command blamed the RPF. (The official US papers relating to the Rwandan genocide can be accessed on the George Washington University's National Security Archive.) A motive could easily be surmised: Hutu extremists were staring the reversal of the 1959 Revolution in the face. By killing the president, they would thwart the Arusha peace process and reassert Hutu supremacy. His death would remove the psychological barrier that had hitherto inhibited ethnic extermination. The circumstantial evidence pointing to a 'Hutu Power' assassination appeared so strong, that it quickly became the favoured hypothesis in academic accounts of the genocide (Prunier, 1997, p. 221; Cooper, 2002, p. 7; Nugent, 2004, p. 454).

There are now good reasons for doubting this version of events. A former Rwandan Patriotic Army intelligence officer, Jean-Pierre Mugabe, who had defected, testified to the responsibility of Paul Kagame, the RPF's military leader, for the missile attack in an affidavit of April 2000. Mugabe also alleged that Kagame ordered an RPF hit squad to kill Gatabazi after he had refused to be party to a plot to assassinate Habyarimana (Mugabe, 2000). A subsequent Tutsi defector from the RPA, Abdul Joshua Ruzibiza, described in detail how the assassination was ordered by Kagame. Ruzibiza claimed to have witnessed the meeting at the High Command, chaired by Kagame, when the missile attack was authorised. The weapons were – he alleged – originally provided by Uganda and were smuggled into the RPF troops in Kigali. The men in charge of the specialist unit which fired the missiles were named by Ruzibiza (Ruzibiza, 2005, pp. 248–52). In February 2010, the Ugandan *Daily News* published an account by an RPA defector who claimed to be the sole surviving member of this unit, and named the soldier who fired the shoulder-launched missiles (this is accessible on the *Uganda Record* website). Ruzibiza's account was scrutinised by academic specialists (including the jurist and historian, Filip Reyntjens, and the anthropologist Claudine Vidal) and they did not doubt its substance (Centre de Recherche des Relations Internationales/ Center for Peace and Human Security, 2006). In November 2006, a French anti-terrorist judge, J.-L. Bruguière, issued an international arrest warrant for nine RPF/RPA functionaries for their part in the missile attack. As a head of state, Kagame could not be named in the warrant, but the judge recommended his prosecution by the International Criminal Court. However, when one of the nine accused by Bruguière was arrested in Germany and extradited to France, the case collapsed, largely because Ruzibiza claimed he had been manipulated and partially retracted his allegations. (Shortly before his death from cancer in 2010, he rescinded his retraction.)

To rebut Bruguière's charges, the Rwandan government commissioned a committee of experts, chaired by Jean Mutsinzi, a Rwandan judge (and President of the African Court of Human Rights) to investigate the crash. It pinned responsibility on Hutu extremists in the Force Armée Rwandaise, principally Colonel Théoneste Bagosora, *directeur de cabinet* in the Defence Ministry, who were opposed to the Arusha accords (Mutsinzi, 2010). The committee's impartiality is questionable, since all its members belonged to the RPF, and its methods and findings have been subject to devastating critique by Reyntjens. He concludes that the report's 'many flaws' and the committee's 'deliberate tampering with the evidence ... reinforces the conviction that the RPF committed the attack' (Reyntjens, 2010, p. 28).

It is very unlikely anyone will ever stand trial for murdering the plane's passengers, so the evidence will not be properly tested or rebutted in a court of law. When Bagosora and others appeared before the International Criminal Tribunal for Rwanda, in Arusha, the judges allowed the defence to call Ruzibiza and make the allegation against Kagame and the RPF as background to the case, but since Habyarimana's murder was not part of the indictment they did not deliberate on it. They concluded that the issue was immaterial to the charges facing Bagosora, who was duly convicted of genocide and crimes against humanity, though significantly he was acquitted of conspiracy to commit genocide (International Criminal Tribunal for Rwanda: The Prosecutor v. Bagosora *et al.*, 2008).

Though we cannot be certain, the balance of evidence points to the RPF's and Kagame's responsibility for eliminating Habyarimana. If this were the case, what was the motive? And how does this affect our understanding of the onset of the genocide? According to Ruzibiza, Kagame was uninterested in sharing power and knew the RPF would (like UPRONA in Burundi) be a minority party in the democratic regime which was to follow the transition period (due to end in 2000 under the Arusha accords). He anticipated total victory in the renewed civil war and preferred the military option to entering a coalition with the MRND(D). RPF intelligence knew that the Tutsi minority risked extermination in the event of Habyarimana's death; Kagame allegedly calculated that RPF forces would overrun the country before the slaughter gathered pace, and so took that risk. If this accusation is true, Kagame was not just criminally irresponsible in ordering Habyarimana's assassination, but cold-bloodedly callous. Assuming the revelations are well-founded, they must surely revise our understanding of the *context* in which the genocide was launched. The disintegrating regime in Kigali faced a ruthless antagonist which deliberately precipitated a total breakdown. The still graver charge levelled against the RPF is that it perpetrated its own genocide of the Hutu in 1994. We should reject this; we cannot equate the numerous human rights violations by the RPF with the genocide. Nevertheless, it bears heavy responsibility for the escalation of social violence during the civil war: up to late 1993, the war crimes attributable to the Front included summary executions, pillaging and forced deportations. Between the resumption of the war in April 1994 and September of that year, tens of thousands of civilians were massacred by the RPF. The mission sent by the UN High Commission for Refugees, headed by Robert Gersony, reported in early September that the RPF had 'engaged in clearly systematic murders and persecution of the Hutu population in certain parts of the country'. He concluded that up to 45,000 people (including some Tutsi) were indiscriminately slaughtered after they had been lured by the RPF to special 'peace and reconciliation' meetings (Des Forges, 1999, p. 552; Reyntjens, 2004, p. 194; Prunier, 2009, pp. 15–16). The RPF had also, we should note, blocked the proposal for a second UN force to help halt the genocide; while it had good reason to be cynical about international intervention, its veto indirectly contributed to tens of thousands of deaths.

Divergent paths to recuperating state and society in the 1990s

Since the independent but convergent crises of 1993–4, Rwanda and Burundi have followed divergent paths to restoring the state and creating the political conditions in which ethnically aware citizens could coexist peacefully if not amicably. Rwanda became (and remains at the time of writing) a military dictatorship and Tutsi ethnocracy; the official ideology condemns all mention of ethnicity as 'divisionism' and practises ethnic amnesia. However, this repressive political climate has not reduced the ethnic divide, but rather exacerbated it. Burundi's military and politicians eventually agreed (under international duress) on an elaborate form of consociational democracy in which ethnic divisions are constitutionally recognised and minority representation in government is guaranteed, whatever the outcome of the democratic ballot. The institutional expression of ethnicity has lessened its political divisiveness.

Nothing illustrates these divergent paths more clearly than the elections which formally ended the transitional periods in the two countries. The 2003 elections in Rwanda were a vast masquerade: Kagame was elected president after a campaign marred by arrests, disappearances, intimidation and fraud. The political opposition had already been eliminated, along with a free press and independent Rwandan NGOs. The regime's critics (including former supporters and founding members of the RPF) had fled the country in fear of their lives. De facto, Rwanda was once again a one-party state (Reyntjens, 2004, pp. 186–8). Burundi's elections in 2005, held under the aegis of South African-led UN peacekeepers and international observers, were, on the whole, fairly conducted. The outcome was a handsome victory for the CNDD-FDD, which had abandoned the armed struggle and entered government and state institutions only at the end of 2003. It had refused to join the peace process until the army was drastically reformed and subjected to civilian control, a stance which was immensely popular with the great majority of Burundians. The major political division now lay between the CNDD and FRODEBU; both were loosely characterised as 'Hutu' parties, but this designation had lost much of its ideological force. The CNDD stressed its inter-ethnic and 'democratic' character: about a third of its deputies elected to the National Assembly in July were Tutsi, though I should add this was largely a result of the constitutional requirement that parliamentary lists represent all social groups.

All Burundians – even the despised Twa – voted in the confidence that they would be represented in government and their country's state institutions. Under the post-transition constitution (approved by referendum in February 2005), Hutu and Tutsi must be present in the National Assembly in the ratio of 60:40; if this is not achieved as a result of election, co-optation will ensure it. The constitution also requires the co-optation of two Twa deputies. Ministerial portfolios are to be divided 60:40 amongst Hutu and Tutsi. To ensure the armed forces do not revert to being an ethnic stronghold, no more than half their personnel are to be drawn from one ethnic group. The ministers responsible for the army and the national police must be of different ethnicities. Paradoxically, embedding ethnicity in the constitution diminished its salience in political conflict which was much more frag-mented (or less ethnically bipolarised) in the run-up to the 2005 elections than during the failed transition of the early 1990s. Whether ethnic awareness is any less salient in popular mentalities is another matter; anecdotal evidence suggests that prejudice and stereotypes abound in everyday life, especially in the towns. But by institutional-ising the ethnic factor, Burundians have made its manipulation by political entrepreneurs much more difficult. With the eclipse of politi-cised ethnicity, other issues – corruption, land shortages and rural impoverishment, the restitution of the property of returning refugees, the abuse of ordinary folk by men in uniform – have become more egregious (Reyntjens, 2005a, p. 132).

It is a measure of the distance travelled by Burundi's political class that the CNDD government's most irreconcilable enemy has been the FNL, the armed wing of PALIPEHUTU. Its dominant faction rejected the peace agreement and the new consensus around ethnic coexistence. The movement's obduracy can be traced to its origins in the Burundian refugee camps in Tanzania and the central place of the 1972 genocide in the political memory and anti-Tutsi 'vision' of its founders. The current leaders believe PALIPEHUTU has a prior claim on Hutu loyalties because it was the first to take up the armed struggle. The FNL has occasionally allied with the 'Hutu Power' militias ensconced in the eastern Congo in their war against the RPF. In August 2004, it accepted responsibility for the massacre of Congolese Tutsi refugees at Gatumba, in western Burundi, an outrage which led the African Union to denounce the FNL as a terrorist organisation. Negotiations to include it in the political system broke down in the summer of 2007, when FNL units renewed their attacks on government and military posts. The organisation enjoys some support in western districts and amongst hundreds of thousands of Burundian exiles, who share its ethnic reading of the political landscape, but seems too marginalised to drag the country back into generalised conflict (International Crisis Group, Africa Report No. 131, August 2007 2007).

The RPF swept to power in Rwanda over a society that had totally disintegrated: over a million people had died violently, about 2 million had temporarily fled abroad and 1 million were internally displaced. About half a million Tutsi refugees from earlier pogroms had returned in chaotic circumstances (Reyntjens, 2004, p. 178). We can only guess at the number of psychological casualties. Survivors had suffered and witnessed unspeakable sadism. The economy and infrastructure had been devastated. In these circumstances, the new government's achievements in restoring order, a reasonably efficient bureaucracy and initiating economic recovery were quite extraordinary. The so-called international community had been lamentably supine in preventing the genocide and so gave the RPF immense political and moral credit for ending it. Long after evidence of its authoritarianism, human rights violations and ethnic discrimination had piled up, the regime had doughty defenders in the western democracies (including Britain's erstwhile Secretary of State for Overseas Development, Clare Short).

The RPF abided by the power-sharing arrangements specified in the Arusha accords and set up a multi-party government in July 1994, with a majority of Hutu ministers, but it departed from the accords by creating a strong executive presidency. The first incumbent, Pasteur

Bizimungu, was one of the few Hutu in the RPF leadership; though not a nonentity, real power lay with Kagame, for whom the office of vice-president was created to afford him general oversight and control of the government (Prunier, 1997, p. 300). Internal dissension within the coalition government became glaringly evident in August 1995 with the resignation of the Prime Minister and Justice Minister (both from 'junior' coalition parties) along with the Interior Minister, an RPF Hutu. The first two joined an exodus of high-ranking refugees, which included judges, civil servants, journalists and army officers. Once safely abroad, they alleged that the RPF was concentrating and abusing power, condoning human rights violations by the army and intelligence services, and discriminating against Hutu.

A second wave of departures in early 2000 exposed profound internal rifts within the RPF-dominated power structure and between the government and key social groups. The Speaker of the National Assembly and the Prime Minister fled abroad, while President Bizimungu resigned in protest against the regime's authoritarianism and ethnic favouritism. When he founded a new opposition party, the Party for Democracy and Regeneration (PDR), he was arrested on trumped-up charges, imprisoned and the PDR was banned. The government brought in legislation which enabled the executive to suspend all forms of voluntary association and gave it total control of civil society. Political parties were tolerated only if they agreed not to question the RPF's definition of political life.

Although Hutu continued to serve in the Cabinet, their function was to symbolise national unity, not share power. The RPF had consolidated its grip on government, administration, the judiciary and higher education by ensuring most holders of high office were Tutsi: by 1996, they constituted the majority of MPs, senior civil servants and university teachers, four of the six Supreme Court presiding judges, over 80 per cent of the mayors, and the entire command structure of the army and intelligence services. By mid-2000, over 80 per cent of university students were Tutsi. The former Hutu elites had been harassed, imprisoned, driven into exile and even murdered. The Hutu had no collective voice and seem to have responded to their exclusion from wealth, power and higher education with dumb resentment. More vocal opposition came from Tutsi genocide survivors who challenged the political manipulation of justice and the government's cynical co-optation of Hutu personalities suspected of participation in the genocide. Since they were in constant fear of being arraigned, their docility could be relied on (International Crisis Group, Africa Report No. 53, 2002, p.

12). Survivors also resented the many favours shown to Tutsi returnees, especially from Uganda.

The RPF had plausible reasons for distrusting multi-party politics, for the record of Rwandan politicians as a whole during the multi-party interregnum of 1991 to 1994 had been pretty discreditable. Much of the hate propaganda had come from civil society, from newspapers and a radio station independent of the government and from Hutu ideologues in the liberal and intellectual professions. The RPF considered that the people's mentalities had to be transformed through basic education before full civil and political rights were restored. Moreover, it sought to recast Rwandan political culture by making political leaders accountable for their rhetoric, as well as their deeds. But alongside these domestic reasons for its crushing authoritarianism, the government had external imperatives, for the RPF was running a 'warfare state' until the early twenty-first century. The RPA (Rwandan Patriotic Army) fought an extra-territorial civil war against Hutu opponents based in eastern Zaire, where it massacred tens, if not hundreds of thousands of refugees in the autumn of 1996 (Prunier, 2009, p. 124). At the same time, it intervened militarily in the terminal crisis of the Mobutu regime by providing Laurent Kabila with elite troops, officers and equipment. In August 1998, it launched a second invasion of what was by then the DRC in support of the rebel movement, the Rassemblement Congolais pour la Démocratie. Rwanda did not succeed in toppling Kabila, its erstwhile protégé, but joined other states in plundering Congolese resources. In 1999 and 2000, its troops fought several battles on Congolese soil with Ugandan forces over access to minerals. It has been reckoned that the total value of the resources plundered by the RPA from the DRC amounted to 6.1 per cent of Rwanda's GDP in 2000 and covered 146 per cent of its military expenditure; in other words, the war was highly profitable. The RPA's coltan revenues alone amounted to US$80–100 million (Reyntjens, 2005b, p. 599). Military and civilian officials turned to criminal entrepreneurs to dispose of pillaged commodities on international markets.

Post-colonial Burundi and Rwanda in retrospect

Let me draw together the themes of this chapter and relate them to the over-arching questions motivating this study. It is not an easy task because different parts of the evidence pull us different ways. There were times in the post-independence decades when Jacob Ajayi's dismissive description of colonialism as 'a transient phenomenon' which did not deflect African societies from a trajectory under way around 1880 would have seemed quite apt to observers of Rwanda and Burundi. They had not been 'settled' by Europeans and were the most authentically 'African' of all the sub-continent's states, where indirect colonial rule had conserved indigenous institutions and co-opted hierarchical social relations for its own purposes. In so doing, it gave an impetus to state-building processes already in train. The International Panel of Eminent Personalities which investigated the Rwandan genocide for the OAU (and reached rather conflicted conclusions, I must add) noted that 'the chief characteristics of modern Rwanda were fixed' under *Mwami* Rwabugiri in the later nineteenth century: 'from that point, the powerful head of a centralised state provided firm direction to a series of subordinate structures that were ethnically differentiated under Tutsi domination' (International Panel of Eminent Personalities, 2.7). The Belgians organised the colony 'very much along the lines that Rwabugiri had drawn, though [they] made those lines far more rigid, inflexible and self-serving'. The report added: 'while there was no known violence between the Tutsi and the Hutu during those pre-colonial years the explicit domination of one group and subordination of the other could hardly have failed to create antagonism between the two ... it is clear that Rwandans have, in some way, regarded themselves as members of either one or the other ethnic group for well over a century'. In other words, the report (though caustically critical of the colonial legacy) acknowledged that the historical roots of ethnicity were, in this instance, authentically African.

Now, the assertion that colonialism was 'transient' – even 'superficial' – is not inconsistent with the fact that the traditional kingdoms were abolished amid great political (and in Rwanda social) convulsion in the transition from colonial trusteeship to modern state sovereignty. But it was African political actors who overthrew the ancien régime, not the colonialists. Though the Belgians certainly gave the revolution a helping hand in Rwanda, the initiative was Rwandan. The dictatorship of the Hutu majority, and of the Tutsi minority in Burundi, arose out of struggles within the African political class. In Burundi, modern ethnic identities were defined in the course of those struggles and against the backdrop of the Hutu revolution in neighbouring Rwanda.

Yet, it is incontestable that colonial racist ideology and administrative practice had effected a malign distortion of African social relations and social thinking. Rwandans (and to a lesser extent Burundians) were given the vocabulary and concepts with which to translate their differences into a historical narrative that was authentically European. Along with 'race', that most toxic of all categories for differentiating between humans, European historical concepts – 'aristocracy', 'feudalism', 'serfdom' – were projected onto an African social landscape. Educated Tutsi learnt to think of themselves as 'Hamitic people' of the 'Caucasian race' having at base 'nothing in common with Negroes'. They were assured by their colonial governors that they 'were destined to rule, their mere demeanour lends them considerable prestige over the inferior races that surround them' (see Chrétien, 2003, pp. 282–8; the quoted remarks are from primary sources cited in his discussion). Thus, an imported ideology constructed ethnic-cum-racial differentiation, and was all the more potent because it could be harmonised with dynastic tradition and the public memory preserved by court historians. Young Tutsi graduated from Astrida College in Butare (attended by sons of the elite from Rwanda and Burundi) with an overweening sense of their innate fitness to rule. Those Hutu who acquired secondary education and literacy in French in the late colonial years thereby imbibed a crushing sense of their historic social inferiority. They were characterised by officials and missionary teachers with belittling condescension until the Belgians abruptly abandoned their Tutsi collaborators and discovered hitherto undetected virtues in the Hutu majority.

The mass conversion of the Hutu to Catholicism, the most hierarchical and authoritarian of the Christian traditions, underpinned their habit of deference to social superiors. By the early 1930s, nine out of ten Tutsi chiefs had converted in Rwanda, while only 10 per cent of the population as a whole were Catholic (*ibid.*, p. 272). When the numbers of Hutu children being baptised rose very rapidly in the 1950s, the officiating priest was very likely to be a Tutsi. Catholicism has been virtually a state religion in independent Rwanda – Habyarimana and his wife were notably observant and the Archbishop of Kigali was amongst their closest confidants – but even a generation after independence, Tutsi were disproportionally represented amongst the priesthood.

This is not to imply that the malign ideological legacy of colonialism made massive inter-ethnic violence an inescapable destiny; on the contrary, it was eminently avoidable. Political elites manipulated ethnic tensions for their own purposes and periodically wrecked the prospects for an accommodative civil culture by assassinating political enemies. Ndadaye's murder was an unpredictable calamity for both Burundi and Rwanda, which demonstrates how popular attitudes were shaped by brutal events. We can acknowledge the part played by the colonial experience in politicising ethnicity without subscribing either to a crass historical determinism that negates the very concept of moral agency, or to the shallow notion – more often implied than explicitly stated – that responsibility for the genocide 'really' lay with Belgian colonialism. Responsibility for our present actions cannot be displaced onto the past: there were Hutus who resisted the compelling physical and psychological pressures to join in murdering their Tutsi neighbours, and their courageous example demonstrates that men and women were, in a significant sense, free to choose. Participating in the genocide was the much easier choice, but it was nonetheless a choice.

8
Angola and Mozambique

Introduction

Few states constituted since the 1970s have had such traumatic national histories as Angola and Mozambique. They bore the brunt of the general and prolonged crisis in southern Africa following the collapse of Portuguese colonial power and the armed resistance of the white regimes in Rhodesia and South Africa to the claims of African nationalism. In Angola, there was a seamless continuity from colonial war to civil war and foreign intervention. Mozambique went through a similar syndrome of foreign-inspired intervention, civil war and social destabilisation soon after achieving independence. Mozambique's vicious internal war persisted up to the early 1990s, Angola's to the early 2000s. As well as a dreadful toll in life, limb and displaced persons, these conflicts distorted state expenditures and brought economic development and social amelioration to a halt. In 1998, their social indicators of life expectancy and child mortality were amongst the worst in the world (Agadjanian and Prata, 2001). Mozambique was Africa's most impoverished state and the most dependent on foreign aid. Angola is potentially one of the continent's wealthier countries, yet throughout the 1990s its oil and diamond resources were shamelessly exploited by the MPLA government and its rival, UNITA, in order to continue their appalling conflict. The general population, meanwhile, lived in misery, at permanent risk of being killed or maimed by ubiquitous land mines or press-ganged into military service, and denied access to much of the best agricultural land.

These tragic outcomes have a bitter pathos, especially for those on the left, because of the expectations raised when independence was wrested from the Portuguese in 1975. Elsewhere in Africa, nationalist elites inherited the colonial state, and often profited handsomely from the bequest. In Angola and Mozambique, revolutionary movements could claim to have overthrown the colonial state in 'people's wars' from which they derived a popular legitimacy which required no electoral endorsement (Chabal, 1983). They were in the vanguard of 'Third World' socialism and an inspiration for those who believed a revolutionary transformation was possible in post-colonial Africa. By the late twentieth century, disillusionment with the post-colonial regimes was virtually complete: expatriate intellectuals who had been amongst the foremost western supporters of the FRELIMO state in Mozambique acknowledged that it dug its own grave with coercive agrarian policies and its refusal to seek an electoral mandate (Clarence-Smith, 1989; Saul, 1993). The public stock of the MPLA had fallen even lower: as Bayart cynically observed, 'The MPLA's great and overwhelming trouble is that it has to govern a whole people, when it would much prefer to concentrate on the plunder of oil and diamonds' (Bayart, 2000, p. 235). It is tempting to project this disillusionment back into the past and to write off the socialist 'project' as the vehicle for African Stalinism and self-serving bureaucratic elites. That would be a mistake. However misguided some of their socio-economic policies now appear, the commitment of FRELIMO and the MPLA to constructing modern, supra-ethnic 'welfare states' should not be doubted.

In trying to explain why Angola and Mozambique had such traumatic post-colonial trajectories this chapter addresses discrete questions: was the Portuguese colonial inheritance peculiarly baneful? Were the seeds of civil war and state breakdown sown during the long wars of independence? Or were the crises in Angola and Mozambique primarily determined by decisions taken in Pretoria, Salisbury (as it was), Washington, Moscow and Havana? The chapter's relevance to the critical analysis of the post-colonial condition is, I hope, two-fold. Lusophone southern Africa has political, social and cultural characteristics rooted in the singularities of Portuguese colonialism, which are of considerable interest in themselves. But though its specific features are undeniable, Lusophone Africa went through a historical trajectory that was broadly common to the sub-continent's states in the post-independence generation: the single-party states constructed by FRELIMO and the MPLA proved to be 'lame Leviathans', unable to crush their internal enemies and govern all their territory. Their ambitious projects for socialising production through centralised planning, collectivised agriculture and the state ownership of farms and factories were failures, as they were elsewhere. The obstacles on which socialisation foundered were much the same as in other states: dire shortages of skilled manpower; the intractability of the 'uncaptured' peasantry; the resilience of traditional forms of authority and social allegiance in the countryside.

The frustration of 'top-down' economic development exacerbated a familiar syndrome of neo-patrimonial politics, though this was more evident in Angola than Mozambique. Having been at the forefront of Afro-Marxism in the 1970s, the MPLA and FRELIMO regimes led the retreat from the command economy in the 1980s and embraced neo-liberal economics; in the early 1990s, they grudgingly allowed multi-party politics.

The colonial background and the wars of independence

When the Angolan war broke out in early 1961, Portuguese rule in Africa seemed a particularly oppressive anachronism and was notorious for coercing African labour and neglecting African welfare. The social changes conducive to nationalism elsewhere had scarcely begun in Angola and Mozambique, where African political parties were illegal and a highly effective police apparatus suppressed all forms of dissent. Apart from the most perfunctory of advisory 'representative' councils, the Portuguese took no steps towards instituting democratic government, even at a local level. From an African perspective, the similarities between Portuguese colonialism and other colonialisms were perhaps more striking than the differences. One might argue that its exceptional character lay, not in the colonies, but in the poverty, comparative economic backwardness and political authoritarianism of metropolitan Portugal. All colonial powers had fallen back on imperial preference systems when world trade collapsed after 1929, but an exiguous domestic market – which was constantly drained by emigration – compelled the New State to seek economic recovery in a conservative form of imperial autarky. The African territories were 'ring-fenced' for metropolitan exporters by tariffs and exchange controls and locked into a neo-mercantilist system as primary producers, with the aim of achieving imperial self-sufficiency in grains, sugar, tea, coffee, vegetable oils, cotton and other commodities (Newitt, 1981, p. 220). Foreign investment in the colonies was discouraged and the African populace cajoled into industrious habits by fiscal coercion and forced labour on public works. Under the labour laws in force between 1899 and 1961 all Africans had a 'moral and legal obligation to work'; anyone not cultivating the land or exercising a trade had to contract themselves to an employer. Compulsory cotton cultivation, though restricted in Angola to the central lowlands, became widespread in Mozambique, and so provided Portuguese textile manufacturers with their main input at below world market prices. Contract labour for the coffee plantations of northern Angola was secured by conscripting so-called Bailundu workers from the central highlands.

Significantly, the Angolan war began with two unconnected social rebellions against harsh crop and labour regimes (as well as an urban insurrection mounted by the MPLA in Luanda). In January 1961, farmers in the Kwanza and Kwango basins, driven to despair by the paltry price paid for the cotton they were compelled to cultivate, attacked European stores, burnt the cotton seed and barricaded the roads. In March, contract workers on the Primavera coffee plantation in the north sparked a massive rural conflagration when they asked their bailiff for six months' overdue wages: the planters denounced this reasonable request so violently that fighting ensued, and several hundred white settlers and black contract workers were killed. Much of the violence was black on black: Bakongo, whose land had been expropriated by white settlers, turned some of their anger on migrant wage labourers who had been trucked in from the central highlands. When suppressing these rebellions, the authorities allowed white vigilantes to murder indiscriminately (Birmingham and Ranger, 1983, p. 343; the fullest account remains Marcum, 1969). In the first great displacement of peoples during the Angolan wars, many thousands of Bakongo fled to the Congo.

Until faced by nationalist insurgency, the New State's ideology was 'anti-modernist' and reflected its dependence on African peasants whose 'traditional' virtues were extolled and whose education was grossly neglected. Only 6–7 per cent of Angola's school-age children attended school in 1960; nearly all adults in both colonies were illiterate. The putative objective of Portugal's colonial policy was the assimilation of its African subjects so that their status changed from *indigena* to *civilisado* (after 1954 termed *assimilado*). An *indigena* or 'native' belonged to a community ruled directly by a chief, and was in the first instance subject to customary law and liable to obligatory public work. An *assimilado* was exempt from the labour laws and theoretically an equal member of the Portuguese nation, who could aspire to government office on the same terms as whites or people of mixed-race (*mestiços*). To attain assimilated status, an African had to be educated to a certain level and apply to the public authorities for certification. Even amongst the educationally qualified, few availed themselves of this opportunity: assimilation was costly and laborious and its benefits rarely outweighed the loss of customary rights to land. Notwithstanding the official lip-service paid to racial equality and the legal tolerance of inter-racial sex and marriage, *assimilados* were in practice discriminated against in government employment and everyday urban life. In the capitals – Luanda and Lourenço Marques – assimilated Africans competed for jobs and petty trade with the *mestiços*, whose own status had been much reduced by Portuguese immigration.

Despite its 'decadent' reputation, the Portuguese empire in Africa was not inert in the years before the Angolan uprisings. Largely in response to the rapid industrialisation of the metropolitan economy and its reorientation towards Western Europe in the later 1950s, the New State had begun to dismantle the autarkic barriers insulating the colonies from the wider world. The restrictions on foreign investment and trade were eased and the first steps taken to promote manufacturing and processing in the colonies. With the aid of foreign capital, Angola's mineral resources began to be more systematically exploited after 1955. The Belgian Petrofina company took over oil prospecting and started production near Luanda. Portuguese immigration was encouraged: in Angola the white population rose from nearly 79,000 to 173,000 between 1950 and 1960 and in Mozambique from 48,000 to 72,000.

Like all European domination in Africa, Portuguese rule was underpinned by accentuating and manipulating ethnic and religious divisions, which in turn greatly influenced local attitudes to the nationalist insurgencies. In Angola, the most consequential socio-cultural divide was between the coastal creoles – who were Catholic, Portuguese-speaking and sometimes of mixed-descent – and the Africans of the interior. The creoles' historical roots lay in the Atlantic slave trade: their forebears were the Luso-African merchants, based in Luanda and Benguela, who had financed the raiding-and-trading parties that extracted slaves from the interior, and sold them on to the plantation owners of Brazil and São Tomé. Long after the demise of Atlantic slavery, the creoles remained culturally oriented to the wider Lusophone world and became the colonial regime's 'natural' collaborators when it belatedly moved to occupy the hinterland effectively. Around 1910, the Portuguese directly and regularly controlled only about 10 per cent of Angola's territory and most African societies still retained considerable autonomy (Clarence-Smith, 1983, p. 172). The peoples of the eastern region were not finally subjugated until the 1920s. Foreign Protestant missionaries had preceded Portuguese administrators into unpacified territory, with the result that many Ovimbundu of the central highlands converted to Congregationalism, while Methodism and Baptism made great gains amongst the Mbundu and Bakongo of the north.

These racial, ethnic and confessional fault lines were reflected in the emergence of three Angolan anti-colonial organisations which never coalesced under a single nationalist 'umbrella'. The first African political party was the Union of the Peoples of Northern Angola, set up illegally in 1955 as an avowedly Bakongo movement by the Baptist-educated elite. Its headquarters were in Léopoldville and its leaders originally envisaged a common future with their co-ethnics in the Belgian Congo. In 1958, it dropped 'Northern' from its name to broaden its appeal. In 1961, the party hierarchy co-opted non-Bakongo, including Jonas Savimbi, an Ovimbundu from Huambo who served as the organisation's 'foreign minister' for three years. In 1962, the UPA was relabelled the Front for the National Liberation of Angola (FNLA), but remained a 'northern' movement, strongly identified with its original ethnic base and closely connected with the existing African socio-political order. The Front's president, Holden Roberto, began his career on the pan-African left, but grew increasingly suspicious of the modern, urban intelligentsia and envisaged a post-colonial state rooted in African 'traditions' (Chabal, 2002, p. 7). After Mobutu seized power in the Congo, the party hierarchy became over-dependent on his patronage and mired in his clientelistic political system. It failed to develop a programme of political education and mobilisation within Angola; Roberto never ventured across the Zaire–Angola border between the 1961 uprisings and the Lisbon coup (Marcum, 1978, p. 183).

The MPLA (Popular Movement for the Liberation of Angola) was formed in 1957 out of the merger of several illegal groups and with the assistance of the clandestine Portuguese Communist Party. It was Marxist from its inception and ideologically committed to non-tribalism, though its core support was always found amongst the Mbundu, whose homelands are to the east of Luanda. The leadership came from a younger, better-educated generation, which was urban in outlook, dedicated to fashioning a modern secular nation-state and drawn increasingly to the Soviet bloc (and Soviet model of development) during the independence struggle. Since several of its key figures were *mestiços*, the MPLA's rivals were able to depict it as the political vehicle of the old creole elite and neglectful of 'real' African interests. The movement was not much more than a discussion group until February 1961, when it launched an unsuccessful attack on Luanda's gaol where political prisoners were being held.

The third organisation, UNITA (National Union for the Total Independence of Angola) was formed in 1966 by Savimbi some months after he had broken away from the FNLA; its social base was the

Ovimbundu of the central highlands. Savimbi originally identified his movement with Maoism and claimed to represent the peasantry against the Marxist-Leninist intellectuals in the MPLA. After meeting China's ambassador to Egypt, he and a few followers were invited to Beijing in late 1965 for training in guerrilla techniques and political indoctrination, and supplied with arms and money. He was the first Angolan leader to return from exile to lead his movement from the inside: from late 1966 until the 1974 Lisbon coup, most of his time was spent building political networks in eastern Angola (Marcum, 1978, pp. 165–82). In terms of popular party loyalties, the ideological differences between the organisations were inconsequential, though UNITA benefited from the long-standing suspicion of the 'unassimilated' blacks of the hinterlands for the Portuguese-speaking Angolans of the coastal towns. The three organisations experienced acute internal tensions and splits, and all depended heavily on external patrons for logistical and diplomatic support.

Ostensibly, the obstacles to a unified nationalist movement were even greater in Mozambique than in Angola. The colony was not brought under a single administration until 1948 and, until the insurgency compelled the Portuguese to improve the road system, the territory was poorly integrated. The east–west railways which had been built to link Mozambique's ports to Rhodesia and Witwatersrand had not reduced the geographical isolation of the north from the south and tended to emphasise the population's ethnic and cultural segmentation. The experience of labour migration did something to instil a common Mozambican identity (and bring young men into contact with other nationalist movements), but its influence was most palpable in the south. Portuguese culture was only superficially imprinted on the north, which had been islamised by coastal Swahili speakers in the nineteenth century and ineffectively ruled by the chartered Niassa Company until 1929. There was simmering ethnic hostility between the northern Makonde and their Makua neighbours, and both distrusted the more urbanised and creolised 'southerners'. Yet, despite these unpromising conditions for nationalist unity, the diverse anti-colonial elements in Mozambique were eventually mobilised behind a common nationalist front, FRELIMO, set up in 1962 in Dar es Salaam, under the auspices of Julius Nyerere. The organisation's early years did not augur well: it was torn by bitter internal quarrels which culminated in the assassination of its founder, Eduardo Mondlane, in 1969. But, before his death, he had done much to unify the party by espousing an undogmatic, inclusive nationalism. The skilful leadership of his successor, Samora Machel, and the expulsion of many early supporters completed the process of unifying the movement, which proved remarkably cohesive through all the vicissitudes of the anti-colonial struggle, foreign intervention and civil war. The hierarchy was predominantly southern and included *mestiços*, Goanese and whites, but (unlike the MPLA) FRELIMO was not generally perceived as the political vehicle of a creole elite.

In 1961, it was commonly predicted that Angola would soon follow its northern neighbour – the former Belgian Congo – into hasty decolonisation, for the shock administered to the colonial power structure by the uprisings was more violent than the Léopoldville riots two years earlier. The wholesale decolonisation of French Black Africa had been a potent example to Angolans and a UN resolution had called on the Portuguese to implement self-determination (to their consternation, the USA voted with the large majority). In the event, the Salazar regime crushed the rebellions and rode out the international opprobrium. Its long-term response to nationalist insurgency was to accelerate and liberalise the colonies' economic development and to reform their administration. The Portuguese military was able to contain the Angolan insurgency to the forests to the east of Luanda and sparsely populated border regions; the MPLA and its rivals, the FNLA and UNITA, never seriously contested the colonial regime's hold on the towns and major centres of agrarian production (MacQueen, 1997; Cann, 1997). The Angolan economy boomed during the war, thanks partly to the 'Keynesian' stimulus of deficit-financed public expenditure on roads, social infrastructure and military equipment. The aggregate value of exports of coffee, iron ore, diamonds and oil doubled between 1960 and 1968. Export-led growth was complemented by import-substituting manufacturing, which increased 13 per cent annually during the 1960s. By 1970, Angolan factories were producing tyres, cement, fertiliser, aluminium, some steel products, petrochemicals and numerous consumer items. Large-scale foreign capital was attracted to the Cassinga iron mines and the Cabinda oil-fields on the north of the Zaire estuary (Newitt, 1981, p. 238). The Portuguese calculated that the western states would not endanger investment in Angola on the part of 'their' corporations by advocating independence. Furthermore, new investment would generate the wealth with which to modernise the economy and so facilitate and finance counter-insurgency campaigns.

The Salazar-Caetano regime pursued the conflicting objectives of transforming Angola into a colony of Portuguese settlement while winning African 'hearts and minds'. Portuguese immigration was encouraged by assisted passages and agricultural settlement schemes, though the major enticement was expanding job opportunities in Luanda and other cities. Angola's white population peaked at 335,000 in 1973. In the past, Portuguese immigrants had driven 'assimilated' Africans out of urban jobs, but the modern sector grew sufficiently rapidly to offer wage employment to both black and white. In 1961, all forms of compulsory labour, even for public works, were abolished throughout Portuguese Africa, and the status of *indigena* disappeared for the first time since the nineteenth century. The Portuguese military was determined that African farmers and traders should have easier access to produce markets and so share in the general prosperity. Against the vehement protests of white planters and truckers, agricultural extension services and producer cooperatives were established to support Bakongo coffee farmers near the sensitive northern border. They were even allowed to recruit paid migrant labour from the south (Birmingham and Ranger, 1983, p. 347). Social services were rapidly expanded, with the army frequently building schools and clinics or overseeing their construction within strategic villages. The policy of conciliating African opinion extended to public tolerance of the Protestant sects.

In Mozambique, the nationalist insurgency was rather more effective, especially in the far north – where life became too dangerous for Portuguese planters and FRELIMO set up an alternative administration in liberated areas. They were, however, a small part of the colony's territory and far from the major population centres of the Zambezi valley and coastal lowlands, where FRELIMO made few incursions. After independence, the liberated zones were represented as an 'embryonic state' in which the foundations of a socialist society were laid, but this interpretation owed more to the party's revolutionary mythology than the facts on the ground. By regrouping the rural population in large fortified villages (*aldeamentos*), the Portuguese contained the insurgency. It would seem that the war did little to impede economic development because the annual growth rate was about 5 per cent during the 1960s and early 70s and the economy became less dependent on the export of migrant labour and primary commodities.

Thanks to a 'spurt' of import-substituting industrialisation, independent Mozambique was endowed with a diverse industrial base: it produced cement, bricks, tiles, asbestos sheeting, electric cables, steel castings, insecticides, pharmaceuticals and consumer durables, and refined oil on a substantial scale. There was a growing urban middle class and an increasingly prosperous class of small landowners, both

African and European. In these respects, the colonial legacy was favourable (Newitt, 2002, p. 188). In the Cabora Bassa dam on the Zambezi, Mozambique possessed one of the world's largest sources of hydro-electric power. FRELIMO had vowed to stop the dam's construction, which was partly South African-financed, and its completion on schedule testified to the insurgency's limited impact. The glaring deficits in the colonial legacy were widespread illiteracy and the shortage of modern industrial skills, coupled with complete inexperience of representative institutions and responsible government.

Mozambique's economic decolonisation was accelerated when the EEC granted Portugal associate status in July 1970, for this required ending preferential treatment for Portuguese imports and lifting the remaining restrictions on foreign investment. As a result, Portugal's trade with the colonies, notably Mozambique, declined sharply, and the major Portuguese corporations began to liquidate their investments, usually by selling out to South African business interests. By 1974, South Africa was Mozambique's major trading partner and the principal source of external capital. With the reorientation of the Portuguese economy towards Europe, and Mozambique's towards South Africa, the economic rationale for empire was nullified before the nationalists seized political independence.

Acceding to power

The MPLA and FRELIMO had the common experience of developing their organisations and articulating their ideologies in friendly neighbouring states and both were indebted to and influenced by external patrons. But they came to power in starkly contrasting circumstances. FRELIMO had the inestimable advantage of being the sole nationalist claimant when the military revolt in Lisbon in April 1974 sapped the colonial army's willingness to prolong the war. FRELIMO refused to accept a ceasefire – since the Lisbon junta gave no formal commitment to independence – but the colonial army in Mozambique withdrew to barracks and allowed FRELIMO to infiltrate provinces where it had never operated. The last-ditch attempt by General Spínola, the head of the junta, and the colonial authorities to create a 'moderate' alternative to FRELIMO was a pathetic failure. The movement's racial inclusiveness attracted some white democrats in Mozambique and its indistinct ideology of socialist emancipation won key allies in the Armed Forces Movement. Secret dealings between radical officers and FRELIMO fortified its military and political position prior to the Lusaka negotiations in September, when a formal ceasefire was agreed. FRELIMO's imperious demand for a complete, immediate and unconditional transfer of power without prior elections proved irresistible. A temporary government – dominated by FRELIMO's nominees – was established to oversee the transition to independence, set for June 1975. In the interim, most settlers left for South Africa and Rhodesia, taking what capital they could and wrecking their fixed assets. Many were apprehensive about FRELIMO's economic radicalism, others simply unwilling to be governed by Africans. The transitional government did nothing to persuade them to stay, unwisely as it transpired because their technical and administrative skills were to be sorely missed. The government had not secured the demobilisation of black units who had fought for the Portuguese and fled to Rhodesia after the ceasefire, but at independence FRELIMO's claim to be the sole legitimate representative of the people's nationalist aspirations was not contested, either in southern Africa or the wider world. Although scarcely welcome to the white regimes in Rhodesia and South Africa, FRELIMO's victory was a fait accompli with which they were prepared to live. The South African authorities reached an informal understanding with the new government that neither party should aid the other's opposition. While Mozambique began its independent life facing all sorts of hazards, before 1980 the overt hostility of the South African state was not one of them.

The situation in Angola between the Lisbon military revolt and the accession to independence in November 1975 was quite different. None of the three contestants for power had the undisputed legitimacy enjoyed by FRELIMO and all were rent by internal quarrels when the Portuguese dictatorship collapsed. The MPLA's unity had been severely strained by the frustrations of exile politics, the remoteness of the leaders from the guerrilla cadres, and the apparent futility of the armed struggle. The leadership was crippled by an internal power struggle in 1973–4 which left it almost fatally fragmented on the eve of the Lisbon coup. Two rebellious factions split from the party: one eventually went into alliance with the FNLA; the other formed an autonomous splinter movement. The party's principal patron, the Soviet Union, was so disillusioned by the factional strife that it withdrew its accreditation and logistical support. Soviet patronage was restored only in the aftermath of April 1974, when the 'presidential faction' under Agostinho Neto sought to establish itself in Luanda.

Meanwhile, the FNLA's principal patron, President Mobutu of Zaire, had stepped up his support for that organisation. Until April 1974,

Mobutu had little interest in the military overthrow of the Portuguese colonial regime, with which Zaire had important economic ties. A large community of Bakongo exiles were tolerated in Kinshasa as long as they refrained from serious political or military activity. After April, Mobutu – who was hoping to annex the oil-rich Cabinda enclave – sought to ensure that an anti-Marxist coalition came to power in Luanda. His American patrons shared this aim, but were so chastened by events in Vietnam they baulked at direct involvement; instead, US money was channelled to the FNLA through Zaire. At the time of the military revolt in Lisbon, UNITA was not yet a significant military presence in the south, but Savimbi had already evinced ruthless opportunism in his pursuit of power by secretly communicating to Portuguese intelligence officers his willingness to enter a neo-colonial settlement.

In the jostling for power following April 1974, the Armed Forces Movement favoured the MPLA, but the colonial army did not fraternise with its insurgents as it did with FRELIMO. Despite mounting insecurity and inter-racial violence in Luanda, the army held the ring between the rival nationalist movements until they signed the Alvor accord in January 1975, which was supposed to lead to a transitional coalition government prior to national elections. Who would have won these elections had they been held is not an idly speculative question. An OAU fact-finding mission concluded that UNITA would have secured the most votes: it represented the largest ethnic group, the Ovimbundu (about 40 per cent of the population), and had built cross-ethnic support amongst the Chokwe and Lunda peoples through the Congressionalist network (Heywood, 1989, p. 63). Savimbi had dropped his Maoist rhetoric and was championing the peaceful conciliation of all Angolans (including white settlers). Even his detractors mostly concede the probability that UNITA was denied an electoral victory by the outbreak of civil war.

The MPLA and FNLA were building up their forces in Luanda as they signed the Alvor agreement and fighting erupted in July, when MPLA troops expelled rival units from the city. With its Zairian allies, the FNLA remained in control of the north, but the MPLA advanced rapidly southwards against UNITA, which appeared on the brink of extinction. The Angolans' internecine struggle was already entwined with the Cold War, but the prospect of an MLPA victory led to an escalation in external intervention. The US Secretary of State, Henry Kissinger, covertly organised a motley mercenary force to stiffen the FNLA in the north. The operation was incompetently managed and the mercenaries were soon worsted (Westad, 2007, p. 228). More consequentially, in military and political terms, the South Africans restored Savimbi's fortunes by supplying UNITA with arms and advisers and, in October, invading Angola with two columns of armoured cars (though the scale of their intervention was not immediately evident to the wider world). The South Africans later claimed that Kissinger privately sanctioned their invasion. They pushed back the MPLA but were halted before Luanda, thanks largely to the deployment of Cuban troops. The MPLA had, for some months, been discreetly receiving arms and military instructors from Cuba; South African intervention prompted Castro to commit several hundred combat troops in early October. Though dubbed 'Moscow's Gurkhas', there is persuasive evidence that the decision to send them was Castro's alone, taken out of revolutionary solidarity with the MPLA and abhorrence for apartheid South Africa. Although the financial costs of what became a substantial Cuban expeditionary force were borne by Moscow, Cuba was more than a Soviet proxy in southern Africa (Gleijeses, 2002).

When the Portuguese governor departed on 10 November, he did not – and could not – formally transfer power to an independent Angolan government. The MPLA and its Cuban allies were fighting the FNLA and the Zairians for control of Luanda; the resurgent UNITA, stiffened by South African troops and with some FNLA allies, was entrenched in Huambo, in the central highlands. The MPLA won the battle for Luanda and proclaimed the Popular Republic of Angola; Savimbi set up the Democratic Republic of Angola in Huambo. In the 'war of intervention' that followed, three factors determined the MPLA's victory: the size and quality of the Cuban military contingent; the ineffectuality of American efforts to shore up the FNLA and the Zairians in the north; and South Africa's pariah status in international affairs. The last was decisive in terms of African international politics since the Huambo regime was utterly discredited when it was revealed to be a South African protectorate. Conservative African states, such as Nigeria, which had hitherto been wary of recognising the Marxist MPLA government now hastened to do so. Sensing that the 'Democratic Republic' was a hopeless cause, South Africa withdrew its forces to Namibia; as it did so fighting broke out between the UNITA and FNLA 'allies'. By April 1976, the MPLA had taken control of most of the country, though bands of dissidents roamed unchecked in the southeast. Its victory was made easier by the temporary eclipse of American power: the mid- and later 1970s were propitious years to establish Marxist states in Africa because the USA's global hegemony touched a nadir at this time. The American political class was so scarred by defeat in Vietnam that Congress passed the Clark

Amendment preventing the administration from providing UNITA and the FNLA with military aid. The Carter administration, which took office in January 1977, was, in any event, little inclined towards 'adventurism' abroad and made human rights the key note of its foreign policy rhetoric. The Cubans were allowed a free hand to ship a heavily armed expeditionary force to Angola, which numbered about 20,000 troops by 1980, though about half were deployed in rebuilding the civilian infrastructure. Working alongside them were about 17,000 Eastern bloc technicians and advisers.

Nation-building in one-party Marxist states

The newly independent regimes clearly faced daunting obstacles in the way of creating viable independent nation-states. The wholesale flight of Portuguese settlers and officials deprived them of administrative, professional and industrial skills and, since many whites moved to Rhodesia and South Africa, added to the hostile elements in neighbouring countries. Thousands of commercial farms and businesses were abandoned; the networks of bush traders which linked peasant farmers with external markets disintegrated. As 'front line' states in the ongoing struggle against settler colonialism and white racism, Mozambique and Angola were exceptionally exposed to externally directed subversion. Yet the new regimes possessed certain assets which should have made these obstacles more negotiable: they inherited quite diverse economies by African standards, with largely intact infrastructures, and received significant foreign assistance from socialist states, non-governmental organisations and western sympathisers. Although the populations in their charge were ethnically divided, and some groups (such as the Makua and Makonde in northern Mozambique) were mutually hostile, ethnicity generally had less political salience than in other African countries. Neither the MPLA nor FRELIMO was challenged by a regional secessionist movement. Decades of civil war and economic decline have drawn a veil over the regimes' accomplishments in their early years, especially in broadening access to health care and primary education. School enrolment rates rose impressively in both countries in the later 1970s, and they achieved notable reductions in illiteracy. FRELIMO aimed to bring health services to the rural areas so that either a clinic or a regional hospital would be within reach of all Mozambicans. About nine out ten people were immunised against smallpox, tetanus and measles.

What marked the FRELIMO and MPLA leaders out from most post-colonial African elites was a clear 'vision' of what was needed to transform the colonial inheritance. Unsurprisingly in the historical circumstances, that vision was Marxist. Its intellectual certitudes were in some ways a political asset, since they insulated the parties against ethnic favouritism and clientelism, but they also legitimated single-party rule, intolerance of opposition, dogmatic secularism and wedded both regimes to an elitist, 'top-down' model of social transformation. Marxist functionaries, convinced that history was on their side, slipped easily into the bureaucratic, authoritarian ways of the Portuguese. The Christian churches, Islam and indigenous religion were systematically denigrated and both FRELIMO and the MPLA barred religious believers from party membership. In the MPLA's case, orthodox Soviet Marxism defined its world view before the accession to power, although like FRELIMO it waited until 1977 to designate itself a 'vanguard' Marxist-Leninist party. Soviet Marxism's intellectual attraction for the educated, Portuguese speakers who led the MPLA is easy to comprehend. It was a system of thought which allowed them to embrace modernity and eschew indigenous traditions without self-demeaning complicity in the colonial world's disdain for African culture. Most had attended Lisbon University in the 1940s and 50s when the only effective political opposition to the Salazar dictatorship was the clandestine Portuguese Communist Party. Before coming to power the MPLA leaders had some 15 years to reflect on the experience of independence elsewhere in Africa. They were well aware of the failures of African socialism, the corruptibility of officials and politicians, the debilitating competition between ethnically identified communities to control public resources, and the inadequacy of the post-colonial state as a vehicle for economic development. Soviet Marxism offered a prescription for avoiding such mistakes; it was a proven path to socialist modernisation. It was also a recipe for internal party discipline in a movement that had been torn by bitter internecine quarrels and the defection of leading cadres. Understandably, the MPLA hierarchy found Lenin's notion of the vanguard party's monopoly on theoretical rectitude highly congenial: dogmatic insistence on the 'correct' ideological line was a potent weapon in the factional strife before and after acceding to power.

The MPLA's evolution into a Stalinist monolith was hastened by the internal convulsion of May–June 1977, when the former guerrilla leader Nito Alves attempted a coup. During the euphoria following the victories of 1975–6, Alves had mobilised Luanda's black poor into study groups which debated the revolution's direction, an initiative which the regime endorsed in its enthusiasm for people's power. However, the newly radicalised slum-dwellers were soon lambasting the delay in tackling glaring inequality. Their anger was predictably turned against the party's central committee, who now occupied the most affluent 'colonial' quarter, and was sharpened by racial resentment, directed against white and *mestiço* functionaries. In the expectation of a popular uprising, an army faction attempted to seize power and murdered several members of Neto's cabinet. The regime survived thanks to the intervention of Cuban troops, who occupied Luanda radio station and threw a protective cordon around Neto and his surviving colleagues. In the aftermath of the failed coup, its leaders and sympathisers were indiscriminately liquidated and the party hierarchy became truly Stalinist in its vindictive political paranoia. From aspiring to be a mass movement seeking support throughout the land, the MPLA became a self-selected elite mendaciously calling itself the 'workers' vanguard' (Birmingham, 2002, pp. 151–3).

The MPLA's core political programme attempted to mimic the Soviet experience: centralised economic planning was introduced; the processing and manufacturing industries established by the Portuguese were nationalised; agriculture was, in theory, collectivised and the agricultural surplus directed towards the development of socialised production. The programme was hopelessly discordant with the country's human resources and localised economic routines. The mechanised state farms which were supposed to generate a surplus were white elephants; the trading companies set up to replace the networks of colonial bush traders did not function properly; by the mid-1980s both farms and companies were disintegrating. The post-colonial economy was dominated by the spectacular rise of the western-developed oil industry and the vertiginous decline of the non-oil sector. By taking command of the economy, the party-state acted as the 'gate keeper' between the oil reserves and the multi-national oil corporations. It used oil revenues to sustain its urban base and nourish the political elite. Fortunately for the regime, the off-shore reserves were easily secured for US-based corporations, which in effect paid Cuban soldiers to protect their installations. Even at the height of the second Cold War, the MPLA government never threatened the US companies operating in Angola. The dominance of oil, and the volatility of world market prices, destabilised public revenues and monetary policy, and bred corruption. The government attempted to manage its external trading account by rationing foreign currency and tolerating dual exchange rates, an arrangement which the politically privileged abused by purchasing allotments of hard currency at the over-valued official rate and selling it at considerable profit on the black market. At the 1980 plenary congress, party members railed against embezzlement, illegal trading, inflation, unemployment and a state which had become parasitic (*ibid.*, p. 164). When the second congress was convened in December 1985, the MPLA had little to celebrate beyond survival: agricultural exports, such as coffee, had collapsed and the regime depended on imports for 80 per cent of its commercial food supply. Manufacturing production and employment were down by two-thirds from the levels achieved in the last full year of colonial management. The delegates expressed widespread dissatisfaction with statist economic policies and called for 'an accommodation with all types of enterprise in rural areas, notably family types of enterprise and private initiatives in farming and livestock' (Marcum, 1986, p. 184). The centralised state farms were abandoned after the congress and private trading in agriculture was legalised.

FRELIMO declared itself a Marxist-Leninist party at its February 1977 congress and adopted a far-reaching Soviet-inspired development programme. In ideological terms, this formally acknowledged an accomplished fact: FRELIMO had been using Marxist language for some time and had already asserted a vanguard position in the post-colonial order. The Independence Constitution which the party's Central Committee 'proclaimed by acclamation' on 25 June 1975 identified the 'fundamental aims' of the state with those of the party. In February 1976, all land and buildings were nationalised. FRELIMO is generally credited with greater pragmatism and ideological flexibility than the MPLA and it has been suggested that political prudence, as much as revolutionary solidarity, determined the alignment with the Soviet bloc and the mimicry of Soviet political norms and practices (Chabal, 2002, p. 62). Perhaps. The socialist states provided essential economic aid, skilled personnel and diplomatic support against hostile neighbours. Nevertheless, the imitation of these external patrons was scarcely insincere. The leadership was attracted intellectually to Soviet Marxism for much the same reasons as their Angolan comrades: it legitimated single-party dictatorship and provided an organisational model for mobilising women, organised labour and youth. It made the state elite the driving force of economic modernisation. While FRELIMO lauded 'people's power' and mass participation, its rule exhibited a puritanical and top-down vision of social progress and the hierarchical and centralised means to achieve it (Hall and Young, 1997, p. 74). After a wave of nationalisations in December 1977/January 1978, the state-owned sector became dominant in large-scale trade and production and attracted the lion's share of investment funds. To 'command' the economy, a National Planning Commission was set up, staffed with Soviet bloc advisers, but economic management 'on the ground' was woefully inefficient. State employment mushroomed, but, with so few skilled and educated personnel, the vanguard had set its functionaries tasks far beyond their collective capacity. Lamentably, the regime's Marxist orthodoxy was combined with much ignorance as to how collectivisation had been imposed on the Russian peasantry and how the Soviet economic system worked in practice. Prescriptions were adopted as matters of faith without much thought as to whether they were appropriate for Mozambican realities. As Hall and Young tartly observe, FRELIMO leaders were not, of course, the first political activists who, proclaiming from the housetops their reliance on 'experience', proved to be prisoners of the most implacable abstractions (*ibid.*, p. 68).

The consequences of FRELIMO's Marxism for its relations with the great rural majority were disastrous. Its Marxist 'world view' gave rise to an imaginary social landscape whose internal coherence was guaranteed by party dogma. In the abstract, the peasants were idealised as a social pillar of the regime, though actual country folk were treated with ruthless impatience, if not contempt. The peasants' support for the liberation struggle was taken as evincing revolutionary social consciousness, even if the party had to articulate it. This was a deep misunderstanding; all the evidence indicates that, while the peasants overwhelmingly welcomed FRELIMO's victory over the Portuguese, very few wanted to revolutionise agrarian production. Nevertheless, the party believed the peasants had tacitly consented to drastic changes in their ways of living and that it had an implicit mandate to ride roughshod over rural institutions, practices and beliefs, whatever their origin. As well as instituting education and health services, its social programme aimed to reform customary law, revamp the judicial process and establish women's equality, which required replacing traditional rural leaders with party officials. With a certain rough justice, FRELIMO despised the tribal chiefs as colonial 'lackeys'. The so-called *regulos* and *cabos* had raised taxes and enforced compulsory cropping on behalf of the Portuguese, and their proscription in FRELIMO's new order is politically comprehensible. But FRELIMO extended this exclusion from public office to lineage heads and notables who had not been incorporated into the colonial administration; they were banned from standing for the people's assemblies elected in 1977. In the district of Erati (where the anthropologist Christian Geffray undertook research into the social impact of FRELIMO's agrarian policies), the party administrator annulled the assembly elections after villagers had voted overwhelmingly for their lineage chiefs. Thus rebuffed, the villagers defiantly gave their votes to illiterate simpletons, who did not grasp that they been returned as deputies (Geffray, 1990). FRELIMO's posture of democratic accountability was demonstrably a sham, which had marginalised and humiliated the lineage leaders.

State farms and 'villagisation' were the twin tracks of agrarian modernisation. The farms were set up on estates abandoned by settlers and intended as beacons of mechanised agriculture. They absorbed 70 per cent of agricultural investment between 1978 and 1982, but, with few skilled workers able to maintain machinery, their productivity was poor. Though they had privileged access to urban markets, not one was profitable in 1981. The 'villagisation' policy was much influenced by the *ujaama* villages in Nyerere's Tanzania: rural folk were to be concentrated into large communities so that cultivation and animal husbandry could be collectivised, services provided, and new political and administrative structures installed. The policy was rationalised in economic terms, but its ulterior purpose was political: to 'capture' the peasantry for the state and impose bureaucratic control on land use and cattle ownership. The party assumed that rural folk had no social organisation of their own and became fixated on 'organising the peasantry'. The country was soon covered by a hierarchical network of party-state officials, based on the communal village administration. Whatever their customary practices and beliefs, all rural inhabitants were supposed to relinquish their fields, dwellings and prerogatives, and regroup themselves in villages where they could labour collectively on communal fields. Any protest was deemed 'obscurantism', 'superstition' and 'feudalism'. Although the proportion of country dwellers corralled in communal villages never exceeded 15 per cent, 'villagisation' did more than anything else to sap FRELIMO's prestige, authority and power. It drove rural people into a clandestine existence in their own country and created a political environment ripe for exploitation by FRELIMO's opponents, of which the most formidable was the Mozambique National Resistance Movement (RENAMO).

RENAMO and UNITA

RENAMO and UNITA were amongst the most destructive guerrilla organisations in post-colonial Africa. Though neither succeeded in displacing FRELIMO and the MPLA as governing parties, they brought the socialist state and command economy to their knees and were major factors in forcing regime change. At its fifth party congress in 1989, FRELIMO formally relinquished the leadership of the Marxist-Leninist state, while signalling its reconstitution to secure the full panoply of human rights and multi-party democracy. Similarly, in 1990–1 the MPLA formally rejected Marxism-Leninism and instituted multi-party elections. It is arguable that the regimes would have been compelled to transform themselves in any event: the command economies were manifestly failing by the early 1980s and were already partially dismantled when FRELIMO and the MPLA abandoned Marxist-Leninism. After the Reykjavik summit of October 1986, where Mikhail Gorbachev announced the Soviet Union's imminent disengagement from southern Africa, Marxist Angola and Mozambique could no longer rely on 'superpower' patronage and were under increasing pressure to negotiate with their domestic enemies. With the ending of the Cold War and the disintegration of the Soviet bloc, 'soviet-aligned' regimes in southern Africa clearly faced an uncertain future. But the wars waged by RENAMO and UNITA determined how and when the party-state collapsed. The most difficult issue for any analyst is deciding the extent to which these conflicts were driven by indigenous agency. Incontrovertibly, both organisations were much indebted to the South African Defence Forces for matériel and logistical support, but whether they should been seen primarily as 'Apartheid's contras' (to cite the title of William Minter's well-known study) is surely debatable (Minter, 1994). Both were able to continue waging war (and widen their operations) long after South African logistical support had been much reduced. Our historical understanding of UNITA and RENAMO must register the fact that, despite inflicting gratuitous violence and displacing millions, in free and fair elections in the 1990s they won impressive minorities of the popular vote.

In their origins, UNITA and RENAMO were quite different: the former had a legitimate pedigree in anti-colonial nationalism; the latter was the bastard offspring of the Rhodesian Central Intelligence Organisation which, in late 1976, began recruiting a terrorist organisation from the exiled remnants of black units who had fought for the Portuguese. At first, they helped pursue nationalist guerrillas across the Mozambique border but, within a year or so, RENAMO was permanently encamped in Sofala province and launching joint operations with the Rhodesians against strategic Mozambican targets, such as the Beira oil tanks. The Rhodesians had every reason to destabilise the

FRELIMO government, which was providing the Zimbabwean National Liberation Army (ZANLA) with secure bases and orchestrating the enforcement of United Nations sanctions. With the Lancaster House settlement of the Rhodesian conflict in December 1979, RENAMO seemed destined to wither away. The tutelage of the South African Defence Forces brought a renewed lease of life: South African helicopters flew RENAMO guerrillas to a new base camp at Garagua, near the Save River, from which they launched attacks on communal villages, and subsequently on the social and transport infrastructure.

South African intervention was largely due to the domestic political realignment following P.W. Botha's accession to the premiership in 1978, and the formulation of a 'Total National Strategy' for defending the white laager. The stance towards the front-line states shifted from détente to confrontation. The appointment of General Magnus Malan, a hawk, as Minister of Defence, raised the profile of the Military Intelligence Directorate (MID) in government circles. Pretoria now aimed at coercing the FRELIMO government into neighbourly compliance by making the cost of giving sanctuary to ANC guerrillas and activists unbearably high. RENAMO was an instrument of this 'Total National Strategy': its fighters and Rhodesian instructors were incorporated into the South African Special Forces, the operational arm of MID. Documents captured in 1985 confirmed that RENAMO had been coordinating its strategy with South African intelligence officers.

RENAMO initially had negligible popular support and its banditry seemed to pose no serious military threat to the FRELIMO state. The organisation had no political programme and only tenuous roots in Mozambique's local societies. Ethnic background was a factor in the early leadership, which was drawn mostly from the Ndau group of Shona speakers. Afonso Dhlakama, who took command after its first leader was killed in battle, was the son of an Ndau chief. But RENAMO was not ethnically exclusive and its operations did not depend on, nor were they constrained by, this ethnic context. One must add that, since Mozambique was not a Cold War cockpit, RENAMO did not find favour with the Reagan administration (unlike UNITA in Angola). Apart from South Africa, RENAMO's external patrons were an eclectic mix of Portuguese who had fled Mozambique, right-wing religious fundamentalists in the United States and West Germany, and – reportedly – wealthy Arab Muslims angered by FRELIMO's hostility to Islam. Yet, from unpromising beginnings, RENAMO was able to wreck the state structures created by FRELIMO across broad swathes of the country. By 1982, the organisation had destroyed 840 schools, 12 health clinics, 24 maternity clinics, 174 health posts, two centres for the handicapped and 900 shops, while kidnapping 52 foreign technicians and killing 12 (Hall and Young, 1997, p. 129). Its attacks on roads, railways and oil installations severed the export routes to the sea and dismembered the national economy. Gross national product fell by 30 per cent between 1981 and 1986, per capita income halved and exports dropped by 60 per cent. Two-fifths of the national budget was being spent on defence by the later 1980s. FRELIMO's administrative officials were priority targets: their deaths isolated rural communities and disarticulated the state. By 1984, government had collapsed outside the larger towns and trade between town and country had ceased. About a third of basic food requirements had to be met by imports, mostly of food aid. Huge numbers had either taken refuge across international borders or decamped to the cities for safety. Floods and famine added to the misery and societal breakdown. Paradoxically, RENAMO was able to extend its operations into nearly every province, and implant itself in rural communities, despite resorting to fearsome violence. Victims had limbs, sexual organs and facial features lopped off; teenagers were forced to kill their parents and then pressed into service as soldiers and head porters. Yet RENAMO did not recruit solely by terror: it also capitalised on villagers' alienation from the state, whose officials were openly contemptuous of their traditions and who intruded so arrogantly into rural life: in the Erati district, lineage leaders went over to RENAMO en bloc after its guerrillas appeared in the vicinity because the Mozambique Armed Forces had – like the colonial army before them – driven dispersed populations into fortified villages and burnt all their old huts (Geffray, 1990).

By 1983, Dhlakama and his closest lieutenants were seeking to distance RENAMO from its South African sponsors. The leadership outside Mozambique was bitterly factionalised, with black militants resenting the presence of white Mozambicans in key positions and the organisation's dependence on apartheid South Africa. Its first General Secretary, Orlando Christina, a former Portuguese intelligence agent, was murdered by a black faction leader, who was in turn eliminated by Evo Fernandes, a Goanese who was RENAMO's European Representative. The destructive incoherence revealed by these squalid episodes was an incentive to establish greater autonomy for RENAMO and adopt something resembling a political programme. The South African elite were for their part increasingly divided over what policy to follow towards the FRELIMO government: while the military intelligence sought to escalate the violence, Botha and his closest advisers were looking for a modus vivendi. They were being pressed to find one by the Americans, who were concerned that FRELIMO would seek Soviet and Cuban military assistance to repulse RENAMO. Discreet talks between South African and FRELIMO officials led eventually the Nkomati Accord on Non-aggression and Good Neighbourliness of March 1984. This was a bitter pill for FRELIMO to swallow, for it agreed to expel ANC guerrillas from Mozambique and deny them logistical support. South Africa pledged to stop supplying RENAMO with arms and equipment, though there is clear evidence that its military intelligence continued to do so. Immediately after the agreement, huge quantities of arms were covertly airlifted to RENAMO bases inside Mozambique. South African agents – probably acting without Botha's authorisation – advised the rebels on new insurgency tactics that would enable them to conserve resources and operate independently of external backing.

Nkomati was followed by fruitless peace negotiations between FRELIMO and RENAMO. In May, their representatives met for the first time in Frankfurt: speaking for the latter, Fernandes demanded a government of national reconciliation, a multi-party system and cabinet posts in return for peace. In July, he called for 'democratic government based on free enterprise' when he met with two FRELIMO ministers in Pretoria. South Africa was now attempting a genuine mediation between the two sides. In October, after further talks, RENAMO and FRELIMO delegates issued a four-point declaration on ending armed conflict though it was soon evident they interpreted its terms very differently. The South Africans were pressing RENAMO to compromise and, in an ironic reversal, Fernandes accused Botha of bias in favour of Mozambique's communist regime. Henceforth, RENAMO was less and less subject to South African control. From its 'external' and dependent origins as an instrument of regional stabilisation it had evolved into an indigenous war machine which encompassed elements of both authentic peasant revolt and a mindless onslaught on modernity (Hall, 1990, p. 59). Its weaponry had to be imported, but funding came increasingly from right-wing groups in Portugal and West Germany and American religious fundamentalists. One must add that RENAMO was relatively immune to manipulation from outside because, exceptionally amongst African guerrilla movements, it learnt to operate without rear bases in neighbouring countries.

UNITA had come close to destruction after being pushed out of Huambo by the MPLA and Cuban forces in February 1976. Savimbi led his followers on a gruelling four-month march through the bush during which their numbers declined from about 3000 to 67. The movement survived thanks to Savimbi's tenacity and the international alarm at the Shaba invasion launched by Katangan exiles in March 1977. Without any hard evidence, this was interpreted in western capitals as a part of a general Soviet offensive in central southern Africa. France, Saudi Arabia, Morocco and Zaire began channelling arms to the UNITA remnants who had taken refuge in Zambia, while Communist China subsequently sent arms via South Africa. With South African logistical backing, UNITA set up its headquarters in Jamba in southeast Angola, close to the Namibian border. South African air cover prevented the town's recapture by government forces and proximity to the border meant it could be easily supplied. Jamba became a showpiece 'Potemkin village' where the multi-lingual Savimbi would show credulous journalists around the schools and field hospital and expound a democratic credo totally at variance with the murderous dictatorship he exercised over his followers and their families. After the debacle of the Democratic Republic, the South Africans had a cynically instrumental view of UNITA and Savimbi; their primary concern was to insulate the trust territory of South West Africa, which they had administered since 1918 and were now illegally occupying, from the Marxist nationalism of the South West African People's Organisation (SWAPO). From August 1981, the SADF escalated the 'Total National Strategy' with a series of devastating incursions deep into Angola, ostensibly to destroy SWAPO's guerrilla bases, though southern towns and civilian infrastructure were also ruthlessly attacked. The South Africans turned over to UNITA large quantities of Soviet weaponry captured during these raids. The SADF armed, trained and directed UNITA, building the guerrilla band into an army able to sustain conventional warfare.

South African tutelage revived UNITA as a useful auxiliary to its 'Total National Strategy' but the inauguration of the Reagan administration in early 1981 gave it the potential to displace the MPLA state. Thanks to American patronage, an armed force became an alternative regime in waiting. Reagan's presidency was a catastrophe for southern Africa: the administration entered into 'constructive engagement' with South Africa which it regarded as an indispensable ally in the renewed Cold War. The USA's global interests became fused with South Africa's regional interests. Faced by a wave of revolutionary regimes in the 'Third World', the Reagan administration decided to subvert them by sponsoring right-wing insurgents. It vetoed attempts by the UN to restrain South African incursions into neighbouring states, soft-pedalled on apartheid and looked sympathetically on the policy of creating Bantustans. Most significantly, from 1982 the administration 'linked' Cuban withdrawal from Angola into the negotiations for Namibia's independence, which tied Angola's fate with Namibia's for nearly a decade. In contravention of the Clark Amendment, the Reagan administration covertly funnelled arms to UNITA. After his re-election, the administration obtained the repeal of the Clark Amendment in July 1985 and immediately stepped up the flow of weaponry to UNITA: $10 millions' worth of military aid was shipped in 1986 and $30 million annually in 1987 and 1988. Under President George Bush senior, military aid to UNITA reportedly reached $80 million a year (Westad, 2007, p. 391). The flow of US military aid allowed UNITA to refocus its operations from its southern bailiwick to northern Angola, where it was supplied from the Kamina air base in Zaire.

Within the United States, UNITA representatives launched a media campaign, headed by a public relations firm close to the Republicans, to raise Savimbi's profile and prestige. A veil was drawn over his Maoist past and military training in China; his commitment to democratic elections, religious freedom and respect for tribal customs and languages was trumpeted. The high point of Savimbi's apotheosis in the eyes of the American right was his reception by Reagan and Secretary of State George Shulz in the White House in February 1986. He spoke to millions on television and to foreign policy elites at the Council on Foreign Relations and the Center for Strategic and International Studies. His supporters agitated for a consumer boycott of the Chevron oil company, whose operations in 'Cuban-occupied Angola' were generating the taxes and royalties that sustained the Marxist regime. In the middle of Savimbi's visit, the Reagan administration announced that it would be supplying UNITA with anti-aircraft and anti-tank missiles. The administration claimed to be seeking a peaceful outcome to the conflict which would involve South African withdrawal from Namibia as a quid pro quo for Cuban withdrawal from Angola, and the MPLA negotiating a power-sharing agreement with UNITA.

By 1988, the level of US commitment enabled UNITA to shrug off what would have been a body blow at the beginning of the decade: the South Africans' retreat from southern Angola after their defeat by a joint Angolan-Cuban force in the protracted battle for Cuito Cuanavale, the largest conventional engagement ever fought in sub-Saharan Africa. The capability of the South Africans' combat aircraft had deteriorated with the international arms embargo and they had lost air superiority to the Soviet-trained Angolan air force. The white electorate's revulsion at white deaths in the remote savannah had brought mounting pressure to withdraw, which was coupled with the decision to relinquish political control over Namibia. In August, Angola, Cuba and South Africa signed the Geneva protocol, leading to a ceasefire and the complete evacuation of South African forces. This was surely the moment for the MPLA and the Cubans – now numbering 50,000 – to rout UNITA, which was not a party to the protocol. But Soviet military aid had ceased; the MPLA state was debilitated; and UNITA had a stranglehold on much of the national territory and was clearly capable of sustaining the war for months, if not years, without external backing. The MPLA had to contemplate a negotiated settlement because the war's social costs were ruinous: by the end of the decade, over 1 million rural people had taken refuge either in displacement camps within Angola or in neighbouring states, and huge numbers were destitute. More than a quarter of gross national product was being spent on the military: the government's arms imports from the Soviet Union ran to $1 billion annually in the later 1980s and accounted for up to four-fifths of total imports. It was only because of oil production in relatively secure enclaves that the country could pay the high cost of defence and ward off total economic ruin.

Like RENAMO, UNITA had attracted those disaffected by the Marxist state's atheism, agrarian policies and contempt for 'tribal' authority. But unlike RENAMO, UNITA had a pre-history in the religious, ethnic and local allegiances of central southern Angola. The organisation's strength 'on the ground' can be traced to the network of churches, schools and clinics built up by Congregational missionaries amongst the Ovimbundu in the early twentieth century. Savimbi skilfully cultivated these socio-religious roots by creating an evangelical 'Church of Christ in the Bush' within the UNITA-controlled 'Terras Libres de Angola' and integrating leading ministers into the decision-making hierarchy. He was greatly assisted in this by the MPLA's exclusion of all religious believers from party membership and its failure to co-opt any Ovimbundu on to the politburo or to correct their under-representation on the Central Committee. Like RENAMO, UNITA forcibly recruited men, women and children into its ranks and brutalised whole communities. Savimbi also terrorised his own followers into abject obedience by barbarous displays of absolute power, including condemning dissidents as 'witches' and burning them alive in Jamba stadium (Brittain, 1998). But unlike RENAMO, UNITA was able to move beyond a reign of violence and construct stable institutions in the so-called Terras Libres. At the end of 1988, it claimed to be running 975 primary schools and eight secondary schools in the bush and to be funding 300 university students abroad. Savimbi was reportedly heading a new government, self-funded through timber and diamonds exports and serving 3 million people, with ministries of health, education and natural resources (Heywood, 1989, p. 60). These claims must be taken with some scepticism, for Savimbi was a master at manipulating gullible western journalists, but the contrast between UNITA's administration of its territory and RENAMO's predatory nihilism has some substance.

Towards the elections of 1992 and 1994, and after

In the late 1980s, the warring parties in Mozambique and Angola moved with painful caution towards settling their conflicts through the ballot box. The peace processes had completely different outcomes: in Mozambique, against all expectations, RENAMO successfully transformed itself from a war machine to a political party; it accepted its defeat in the elections and assumed a new status as the legitimate opposition within a multi-party political system. In Angola, UNITA evolved in the opposite direction, from political movement to relentless war machine. Savimbi denounced the elections as fraudulent and renewed the civil war. The fighting was the most intense and destructive ever seen in Angola; in 1993, according to UN estimates, over 1000 people were dying every day.

Why the sequence of events was so different in each country is not easy to explain. The fruitless talks between FRELIMO and RENAMO in October 1984 were followed by an increasingly debilitating stalemate. RENAMO lacked the capacity to take the cities or retain captured towns against conventional military assault; FRELIMO was unable to secure the countryside, despite repairing its relations with the Christian denominations, Islam and indigenous religion, and moderating its hostility to the traditional rural leadership. After the Fourth Party Congress in 1983, the government embarked on a series of economic reforms which were intended to reverse the neglect of peasant farmers and increase the production of consumer goods. The reform programme led eventually to decoupling from the Soviet bloc, applying to join the IMF and embracing liberal market economics. None of this brought peace any closer; indeed, FRELIMO was locked in a vicious circle, since the implementation of reforms which were supposed to mend the rift between town and country depended on a peace it could not secure. Yet the party remained astonishingly cohesive, notwithstanding its ideological about-turn and Machel's death in a plane crash in 1986, when Joaquim Chissano took over the leadership without any dissension.

In the summer of 1988, RENAMO came close to cutting the country in two with an offensive along the Zambezi valley. Had it succeeded, the rebels would have been able to set up an alternative government in the north, where they undoubtedly enjoyed wide support. However, with the aid of Tanzanian and Zimbabwean forces, the Mozambican army launched a successful counter-offensive which marked an important turning point in the conflict. Neither side saw any prospect of ultimate military victory; both were under increasing external pressure to enter peace negotiations. In September 1988, Chissano met Botha at Songo in Tete province and secured a pledge to abide by the Nkomati accord, which this time was honoured. He also gave permission to senior church leaders to open direct contacts with RENAMO. They returned from talks in Kenya in February with a clear message that RENAMO was tired of war and open to negotiations. At its Fifth Party Congress in 1989, FRELIMO introduced multi-party democracy: it remained only to recognise RENAMO as a legitimate participant in democratic contest and for RENAMO to transform itself into a political party. The revolution in southern Africa's regional politics begun in February 1990, when F.W. De Klerk unbanned the ANC and unconditionally released Nelson Mandela, increased the international pressure on both parties to negotiate an end to the war.

However, what ultimately pushed them into talks was famine, following the great drought of 1990: it undermined RENAMO's ability to live off the land and reduced combatants from both sides to exhaustion. Through the Vatican and Italian intermediaries, FRELIMO consented in July to direct negotiations in Rome, which resulted in a partial – and fragile – ceasefire in December. RENAMO agreed to halt its attacks on the transport corridor to Beira in return for the confinement of Zimbabwean troops to barracks (though they did not at this point withdraw from Mozambique). Despite serious violations by both sides, the ceasefire held sufficiently to enable contacts through intermediaries to continue. Negotiations stalled for most of 1991–2 for want of a formula that would recognise the government's 'sovereignty' while guaranteeing RENAMO's recognition as a political party of equal standing to FRELIMO. Each side was desperately worried the other would renege on any agreement. RENAMO feared it would be at the mercy of FRELIMO on the outbreak of peace and wanted a power-sharing arrangement in the run-up to elections supervised by the international community; FRELIMO was determined to exclude power-sharing and sought to keep the peace process in Mozambican hands. After seven more tortuous rounds of dialogue, a General Peace

Agreement (GPA) was finally signed on 4 October 1992, which provided for multi-party elections, demobilisation and the formation of a new national army, while RENAMO retained a security role in the areas it controlled. FRELIMO was formally recognised as Mozambique's legitimate government, and RENAMO formally acknowledged as a legitimate political party. Both sides had reluctantly compromised and the accord seemed seriously flawed at the time. It did not augur well that RENAMO had been quite literally bribed into compliance with funds to finance its transformation into a political party. In retrospect, it is evident that the crucial step to securing peace was taken a week later, when the UN Security Council approved the establishment of the United Nations Operation in Mozambique (ONUMOZ) to monitor and verify the agreement's implementation. After some delay, the UN decided to pour resources into Mozambique to prevent the peace process coming unstuck, which was in marked contrast to the niggardly UN operation in Angola. RENAMO received over $17 million from a UN Trust Fund to help transform itself into a political party.

The tasks awaiting the 6800-strong UN force were formidable: apart from supervising the demobilisation and disarmament of about 110,000 soldiers from both sides, it had to oversee the resettlement of more than 5 million refugees and displaced people, and organise elections. Originally scheduled for October 1993, they were delayed for a year by the slow deployment of ONUMOZ and persisting distrust between the government and RENAMO (a distrust deepened by events in Angola, where UNITA resumed the war after losing the elections). Neither side wished to concede an iota of strategic advantage to the other. As Dhlakama made ever more strident demands for the formation of a bipartisan 'government of national unity' after the polls, it seemed increasingly likely that RENAMO would reject an adverse electoral verdict. To forestall a walkout and resumption of hostilities, the churches and several western countries sought to arrange a pre-election 'deal' on forming a RENAMO/FRELIMO coalition. This Chissano publicly rejected, though he offered Dhlakama the status of 'leader of the opposition', complete with salary, benefits and a diplomatic passport. Privately, he reserved the right to negotiate a deal, but only in the event of unfavourable election results.

The elections held on 27–9 October were remarkable for an 85 per cent turn-out on the part of 5.2 million registered voters and for being generally peaceful. They were monitored by 3000 UN observers in an operation costing external donors about $64 million. Not unexpectedly, FRELIMO secured the largest share of the votes (44.33 per cent) and 129 seats in the elections for the 250-seat National Assembly, while RENAMO received 37.78 per cent and 112 seats, with a rightist coalition party winning the remaining nine seats. In the presidential elections, Chissano was re-elected with 53.3 per cent of the votes, while Dhlakama received 33.7 per cent. The polls revealed a sharp north–south divide in partisan support: in the southern provinces, FRELIMO took 57 seats to RENAMO's five, but in the northern and central provinces, RENAMO took 80 seats to FRELIMO's 65. In some areas, election outcomes were influenced by calls for tactical voting from community and church leaders. Reflecting a widespread desire for reconciliation, many heeded this call, voting for Chissano as president, while backing RENAMO for the National Assembly. On 14 November, some days after the United Nations certified the elections 'free and fair', Dhlakama formally conceded defeat. A new, all FRELIMO government was installed in late December.

The Angolan sequence was tragically different, though the internal and external pressures towards a peaceful resolution of the civil war were broadly similar. There was the same impulse in the later 1980s towards a market economy and a multi-party political system, with constitutional guarantees of basic freedoms, though formal abandonment of Marxist-Leninism by the MPLA came slightly later. Famine, following prolonged drought, exhausted combatants on both sides and made the general desire for peace more urgent. The revolution begun by De Klerk meant that South Africa became a more benign regional presence. But there was a signal difference. Soviet disengagement from southern Africa was much more consequential for Marxist Angola than it was for Mozambique: several western governments – including Mrs Thatcher's – were well disposed to FRELIMO, but the MPLA was 'orphaned' by the end of the Cold War. Apart from Cuba, the regime was friendless. The USA's refusal to recognise it until May 1993 was a constant encouragement to Savimbi to remain intransigent.

President Mobutu appeared to have initiated a peace process when he orchestrated a meeting between his protégé, Savimbi, and President dos Santos (at Gdabolite) in June 1989, during a summit of African heads of state. Accords were signed which provided for a ceasefire and the reintegration of UNITA soldiers and partisans into Angolan society, but it was soon flouted by both sides. The MPLA suffered major military reversals after an unsuccessful attempt to relieve Mavinga, in the southeast, and UNITA launched an offensive in the north. Luanda was briefly surrounded, but lack of air power precluded UNITA pushing home its advantage. The MPLA recovered much of its territory and the military stalemate ensued, amid widespread famine. The international pressures on both sides to resume talks increased after US and Soviet representatives agreed their own terms for disengaging from southern Africa when they met at the Namibian independence ceremony at Windhoek in March 1990. Desultory negotiations between the warring parties reopened in April in Lisbon. The Americans had some leverage over the MPLA because they were blocking Angola's application to join the IMF and World Bank and so preventing access to much needed western finance. In return for a promise to support the application, the MPLA's central committee was nudged into announcing sweeping political and economic liberalisation in July. The principle of evolution towards a multi-party state was accepted along with constitutional guarantees of basic freedoms and the need for a market-based economy. The party abandoned Marxism-Leninism for democratic socialism. Angola was formally admitted to the IMF in September. UNITA and the MPLA finally ratified the Bicesse accords of May 1991, under which they agreed to the cantonment of their forces in preparation for presidential and parliamentary elections scheduled for September 1992. All foreign troops were to leave the country and weapons imports were banned. The accords provided for the incorporation of a limited number of MPLA and UNITA troops into a new national army and the demobilisation of the majority after they had handed in their weapons. At the UN, the USA and Soviet Union cooperated on setting up a mission (UNAVEM) to monitor the ceasefire and verify the results of the elections. It was headed by Margaret Anstee, a long-serving UN official, who took up her appointment in February 1992. The responsibility for staging and overseeing the elections was left to a joint UNITA–MPLA political and military commission, assisted by observers from 30 countries. Unfortunately, no mechanism was put in place to ensure that demobilisation actually occurred before elections were held; with the result that UNITA was able to keep its military option open.

The 18 months between the Bicesse accords and Angola's first national elections were – according to David Birmingham – 'the most spectacular period of optimism and freedom the country had ever witnessed' (Birmingham, 2002, p. 171). Thousands of rural refugees in the coastal cities returned to their villages and sought out their surviving relatives. In the towns, people took to the democratic process with relish: enthusiastic crowds attended the rallies addressed by political leaders and followed the television coverage of the political campaigning in bars. Yet, notwithstanding the optimism, the elections were held in an atmosphere of feverish distrust. Both sides saw them as a surrogate for civil war which would enable the victor to 'take all'. Most international observers expected UNITA to win, as did Savimbi. In July, he issued a dire warning that the MPLA would not accept its defeat at the polls; at that moment, he warned, his forces would infiltrate the cities held by the MPLA and destroy the usurpers (Marcum, 1993, p. 219). The MPLA was equally confident of victory, equally persuaded that the only explanation for defeat would be fraud. The elections when they came on 12 September were well attended and considered by UNAVEM observers to have been fairly administered and relatively peaceful. The result was a conclusive victory for the MPLA: it won 53.7 per cent of the popular vote and 129 seats in the parliamentary elections to UNITA's 34.1 per cent of the vote and 70 seats. Third parties took only 12 per cent of the vote. In the first round of the presidential poll, dos Santos won 49.56 per cent of the vote to Savimbi's 40 per cent. Under the electoral law, a candidate had to receive at least 50 per cent of the votes to be declared president. Before the result of the first round could be announced, Savimbi flew to Huambo, where he denounced the poll as fraudulent and issued a barrage of vitriolic threats. The legislative results were not formally endorsed by UNAVEM until 17 October, when Anstee declared them to have been 'generally free and fair'. The USA and the EC publicly concurred. Savimbi responded by heaping personal abuse on Anstee over UNITA radio, and removed all his troops from the new national army. In violation of the Bicesse accords, UNITA had kept most of its units intact and stockpiled arms smuggled through Zaire. Having failed to come to power via the ballot box, Savimbi was all too evidently preparing to resume the war.

The election results should not have surprised impartial observers, since each party scored heavily in its core area. The MPLA took 73 per cent of the vote in the Mbundu-dominated provinces to the east of Luanda; UNITA took 57 per cent of the vote in its core support region around Huambo, which was predominantly Ovimbundu. What determined the outcome at a national level was the fact that, outside their respective cores, the MPLA out-polled UNITA by a margin of about 20 per cent, except for the Bakongo-dominated province of Zaire where the veteran FNLA leader, Holden Roberto, gained a slim plurality. The basic factors determining how people voted were ethno-regional loyalties and the rural–urban divide. Accelerating urbanisation, as a result of huge numbers of internal displacements, diluted the force of ethnic nationalism. Even Ovimbundu migrants voted for the MPLA in the cities, where oil revenues had been used to import food and sustain the population and – for all its corrupt oppressiveness – the governing party represented some sort of security. In the countryside, many non-Ovimbundu voted for UNITA in protest at years of neglect, impoverishment and collapsing infrastructure.

The war that broke out on 12 November was quite different from previous conflicts. They had all been rural in character and heavily influenced by external actors; indeed, with some qualification, one could say they were 'externally driven' up to the later 1980s. The civil war of 1992–4 was 'internally driven' by Angolan actors and focused on the cities, for Savimbi knew he could win power only by destroying the MPLA's urban base. The government was scarcely blameless for the renewed war: after Savimbi flew to Huambo, MPLA militias were allowed to expel UNITA officials from the capital and lynch suspected sympathisers; but the prime cause was the man's megalomania. There were no longer any ideological or programmatic differences between UNITA and the MPLA. If Savimbi had a deeper motive than lust for power, then it was a resentment of the coastal creoles rooted in his black nativism. Hitherto, his unbending determination to eliminate the MPLA had stemmed, at least partly, from the fact that the MPLA had seized power illegitimately (and with outside help) at independence. Many westerners sympathised with this stance. After the elections had been verified, the legitimacy of the MPLA government was not seriously in question abroad; Savimbi's intransigence appeared – indeed was – devoid of all principle. In early December, a government of national unity was set up, still dominated by the MPLA, but with Ovimbundu taking the premiership and the ministries of finance, agriculture and justice. Four junior posts were offered to UNITA deputies who had defied Savimbi's call to leave Luanda. As a sop to black nativism, prominent *mestiço* politicians were removed from high office. The gesture towards political reconciliation was doubtless perfunctory but it would have been difficult for the MPLA to do more since its own militants were pressing for a final settlement with UNITA. The Clinton administration formally recognised the Angolan government in May 1993 and condemned UNITA for rejecting the electorate's verdict and restarting the war. The delay was reprehensible, for non-recognition had implied that both parties were equally responsible for the turn of events. With the best of intentions, Anstee had still sought to negotiate with Savimbi after he resumed the war, which inadvertently lent some legitimacy to his position.

The MPLA's conscripts had demobilised themselves in the run-up to the elections and the government had been unable to circumvent the ban on weapons imports. Consequently, UNITA was much better prepared for the resumption of hostilities; by January 1993, it controlled 75 per cent of the national territory. But UNITA was soon over-extended and vulnerable to the Angolan government's air power: combined offensives drove its forces out of every captured city, but they hit back by seizing the oil-town of Soyo on the northern coast and laying siege to Huambo. A savage battle ensued, probably costing both sides 15,000 casualties, before the city fell to UNITA in early March. Fortified by this success, Savimbi upped UNITA's preconditions for resuming peace talks, which included Anstee's departure. The UN Secretary General, Boutros Boutros-Ghali came close to recommending to the Security Council that UNAVEM be withdrawn and that the protagonists be left to fight on in isolation. What eventually brought a truce was the exhaustion of UNITA's military resources after its early successes and Savimbi's reluctant recognition that victory was not immediately in sight. After protracted negotiations, a new UN peacemaker, Alioune Beye, eventually secured an agreement on a ceasefire in Lusaka in late 1994. It brought peace in name only. UNITA maintained its own 'capital', Bailundu, and controlled extensive territory in the interior with a considerable standing army. In the diamond-producing Kwango valley, up to 100,000 workers were forced to sift the mud for the precious stones which financed arms imports. Land mines were sown over vast areas to defend 'political space'. The rival parties were intensely suspicious of each other and military hardliners on both sides urged that 'one last push' would finish off the enemy. This was the reality underlying the shadow play of political reconciliation. In September 1997, UNITA became part of a power-sharing arrangement in the Government of National Unity (GURN). UNITA's 70 deputies took their seats in the National Assembly and Savimbi was accorded special status as leader of the main opposition party. The National Assembly passed a law guaranteeing him special protection, giving him various privileges and providing him with a salary and perks. But neither party renounced the military option: the essential precondition for permanent peace was the complete demobilisation of UNITA's army, to which Savimbi would not agree. Though formally installed, the Government of National Unity was a political fiction. The ceasefire was never punctiliously observed and broke down completely in June 1998, after some 12 months' preparation for all-out war on both sides.

To say the civil war was 'internally driven' is not to deny that Angolan actors depended on external agencies in many ways: UNITA was supplied with cheap weaponry by the post-Soviet Ukraine and international diamond traders connived at the illegal sale of its diamonds in Antwerp. Mobutu's Zaire offered sanctuary to UNITA's forces in the north and also remained an important conduit for imported weaponry. Mobutu's fall in May 1997 deprived Savimbi of a patron and ally, and triggered the cycle of events leading to the resumption of war. On its side, the Angolan government was sustained by oil revenues and a major client of the international arms trade. But external agencies were permissive not determinant: Angolan actors had it in their power to end the calamity and did not do so.

The contrast with Mozambique is striking; what explains it? Personalities were clearly important: the outcome could have been different had Savimbi been less imperious, charismatic and brutally egotistical. A more colourless and less 'driven' man, such as Dhlakama, might have settled for the positions of opposition leader and vice-president, which the Angolan government, under great external pressure, was prepared to concede Savimbi under the Lusaka protocol. Confirmation of the crucial significance of the personal factor came when Savimbi's death in action in February 2002 removed the major obstacle to peace. Patrick Chabal has argued that, over and above differences in personality was a structural difference in the way RENAMO and UNITA related to the states against which they waged war:

> However much RENAMO sought to destroy Mozambique's infrastructure and eliminate FRELIMO cadres, it never seriously entertained the belief that it could itself challenge FRELIMO's historical place in contemporary Mozambique. Indeed, politically RENAMO always defined itself in relation to, as a mirror image of, FRELIMO. Its future acceptance as a legitimate political organisation depended entirely on its eventual recognition by the FRELIMO state.

UNITA, by contrast, always struggled to reverse the MPLA's victory in the war of liberation in 1975–6 and never accepted the legitimacy of its government. 'UNITA wanted to eliminate the MPLA; RENAMO wanted to be given its place in the political order established and dominated by FRELIMO' (Chabal, 2002, p. 119).

Angola and Mozambique in the 1990s

Around 1993, Angola and Mozambique exhibited acute symptoms of what was fashionably described as 'state failure': they were sovereign entities, with seats in the UN and other international bodies, but within their national territory what were supposedly governing institutions failed to perform crucial functions of statehood. They could not enforce a monopoly of legitimate violence and large tracts of national territory were inaccessible to the national government's officials, just as much economic activity was outside the state's fiscal reach. Two commentators remarked of Mozambique that 'in some ways it has ceased to be a state at all as this is commonly understood' (Hall and Young, 1997, p. 217). By the end of the decade, both Angola and Mozambique could be loosely described as 'recovered' states, which had made apparently irreversible transitions to multi-party democracy and a market economy. On the surface of politics, there were obvious parallels: FRELIMO and the MPLA retained their hold on government long after they had relinquished their monopoly of state power and transformed themselves from revolutionary vanguards to mass electoral parties. By African standards they were relatively well institutionalised and enjoyed residual prestige as leaders of the independence struggle. Despite the severing of the links with the state, party membership continued to be expected of public officials. FRELIMO claimed an astonishingly high membership of 1.4 million in 2000 (Carbone, 2005, p. 430). Yet the parties themselves were increasingly marginalised because in both states the presidency became the real centre of political power and largesse, as it did in many African countries in the 1990s. The record of both governments in improving popular welfare was equally dismal. Their under-five mortality rates were more than twice as high as Zimbabwe's in the late 1990s and maternal mortality was five times higher (Agadjanian and Prata, 2001, p. 333).

These parallels aside, the experiences of 'recovery' in Angola and Mozambique were strikingly divergent. Mozambique was more or less colonised by the UN in 1993–4 and, even after the UN operation was wound down, remained a virtual dependency of the international community. From the early 1990s to the end of the century, foreign aid constituted more than half the gross national product and accounted for about three-fifths of government spending (Newitt, 2002, p. 228). Mozambique is poorly endowed with minerals or other resources and vulnerable to natural disasters, as the catastrophic floods of 2000 demonstrated to the wider world. The revenue base is narrow and insecure, which left the FRELIMO government wholly dependent on the international financial institutions for reconstruction capital, while relying heavily on foreign donors to fund welfare services. Relative to its size, Mozambique was the world's most heavily indebted country in the 1990s, with foreign debts equivalent to about five times GDP.

NGOs took over most of the state's welfare functions in the 1990s and recruited many of its qualified officials by offering better salaries and working conditions. Although FRELIMO increased its share of the vote in the legislative elections of 1999 and 2004, voter participation collapsed from 68.1 per cent of the electorate to 36.3 per cent (having been 87.9 per cent in 1994), which indicates the governing party's hold on office depended on a great mass of political indifference. The moral authority of the FRELIMO-dominated political system was 'hollowed out' by the years of international mendicancy. Mounting political and official corruption, much of it associated with the privatisation of public enterprises, added to the disillusionment with politics. Mozambique had been relatively free from corruption before 1990, and the FRELIMO elite were noted for their puritan austerity; by the end of the decade, corruption was widespread and had even tainted the Chissano family (Walle, 2001, p. 180; Newitt, 2002, p. 232).

Having been paragons of Marxist socialism in Africa before the mid-1980s, the FRELIMO elite became the most single-minded champions of liberal capitalism in the 1990s. They undertook the largest privatisation programme in Africa, by the number of transactions: it was the economic equivalent of military demobilisation, involving more than 1400 transfers of public assets to private owners. The policy was advocated by the IMF and the World Bank but implemented with the convert's zeal by the FRELIMO government. Smaller enterprises, such as retail outlets, were sold first, with the larger and more strategic concerns left till later. Mozambique's private sector was too weak to absorb all the assets put on the market so privatisation was an opportunity for foreigners (usually Portuguese or South African, though occasionally British) to reinvest in the economy. Domestic purchasers were almost invariably party members and most had strong ties to state officials. They received what was in effect a massive subsidy from the state to acquire public property because enterprises were sold off too cheaply and buyers were allowed to delay payments or even default on part of the purchase price. The process lacked transparency and was an opportunity for graft. With economic liberalisation, the political class and public officials had changed, not just their ideology, but also their values. Nonetheless, it would be churlish to deny that liberalisation led to a remarkable economic resurgence in the later 1990s. The proportion of the population living in poverty fell from 80 per cent in the early 1990s to 54 per cent in 2003 (Commission for Africa, 2005, p. 223).

Angola's enviable portfolio of natural resources provided a hospitable environment for egregious misgovernment, but its political elite remained in command of the state apparatus and of the political rents which flowed to the sovereign authority. When civil war was renewed in 1998, the central government's superior economic resources eventually proved decisive; put simply, it purchased on the international arms market the fire-power needed to overwhelm UNITA. The oil industry, which is second to Nigeria's in sub-Saharan Africa, was ideally situated to provide economic sanctuary for the self-serving political elite. It generated huge revenues which allowed the government to purchase military security, service the mounting debt and to subsidise the lifestyle of the politically well connected. The industry's forward and backward linkages to the Angolan economy were, to say the least, tenuous: at the end of the 1990s, only 10,000 Angolan nationals were employed in the sector, which included the state-owned oil company, SONANGOL. The one ancillary business which flourished on the oil boom was providing security. In theory, ordinary Angolans stood to benefit from the redistribution of the political rents accruing from the industry; the far from transparent national accounting data indicate that few did so. Public spending was massively concentrated on Luanda to the neglect of the provinces, which received only 13.5 per cent of the executed budget in 1996 though they contained about two-thirds of the population (Le Billon, 2001, p. 63). Some of this discrepancy can be explained by the fact that UNITA controlled much of the national territory, but more important was the preferential treatment of the capital's population. But rather than mitigating the impact of war and consolidating state governance, oil revenues reinforced economic distortions and undermined popular support for the government.

The dismantling of state socialism did not lead to a 'transparent' and efficient market economy but instead to an unregulated 'crony' capitalism in which elite families manipulated residual administrative mechanisms for allocating resources to their private benefit (Hodges, 2001, p. 46). The continuation of dual exchange rates was, for example, an opportunity for those with privileged access to foreign currency at the official rate to make fortunes from arbitrage. A decree of 1992 removed the prohibitions on ministers going into private business while in office. The abandonment of Marxism-Leninism left a moral void; the politically powerful no longer evinced any sense of social obligation or solidarity. Lucio Lara, a veteran of the independence struggle and former minister, told the British journalist, Victoria Brittain:

> I don't have illusions about many things any more. In the Angolan struggle perhaps we didn't have philosophers or sociologists, but we

had these words of Neto's, 'the most important thing is to solve the people's problems'. Once in the Council of Ministers I heard someone say that we should stop using that phrase. I thought then maybe he was right, because no one spoke out against him. In my opinion this was when the Party began to collapse. The leaders felt they all had the right to be rich. That was the beginning of the destruction of our life. (Quoted in Brittain, 1998, p. 95)

Venality in public life became still more pervasive after dos Santos capitalised on his election to move to a presidential regime, with a strong family resemblance to Mobutu's in Zaire, including systemic corruption and an extravagant personality cult, though with the signal difference that the Angolan leader commanded more abundant resources. The presidency received the lion's share of the signature bonuses paid by oil companies for concessions which were used to reward a clientelistic network of politicians, bureaucrats, businessmen and senior military and police officers. In a move to distance the president from the decaying state administration and place him 'above politics', the Eduardo dos Santos Foundation was set up in 1996, with numerous family members on the pay roll. This supposedly philanthropic body quickly became a crucial means to garner political rents and distribute largesse. As well as receiving considerable public funds (for which it was unaccountable), the oil companies were encouraged to make substantial tax-deductible donations. The foundation allowed dos Santos to undertake carefully selected development tasks and deliver services to key constituents in a manner the dilapidated central state could no longer achieve (Walle, 2001, p. 166).

By the late 1990s, Angolan society under dos Santos's rule was grotesquely polarised between an increasingly urbanised and pauperised mass and a politically favoured, fabulously rich elite. Because of the huge internal displacements, more than half the population lived in cities by 2000 (as compared with the 11 per cent living in urban areas in 1970). The resurgence of war in 1998 brought the total of displaced people to more than 4 million, or almost 30 per cent of the population. Rural refugees entered a chaotic world, devoid of collective welfare, where the most basic needs were met through an unregulated market. More than two out five people in Luanda had to buy their water, at exorbitant prices, from private vendors. Displaced people depended on relatives for food, shelter and help finding work in the mushrooming informal sector. Regular jobs in industry virtually disappeared with the end of centralised planning and the privatisation of nationalised companies, and public salaries collapsed. Manufacturing accounted for only 4 per cent of GDP in 2001 as against 16 per cent in 1973 (Hodges, 2001, p. 113). Most city dwellers survived by casual labour, self-employment in street vending and petty crime. The rise in oil prices at the turn of the millennium boosted the growth of per capita GNP but for most Angolans, it was quite illusory. The proportion of the total population living in extreme poverty more than doubled in the later 1990s, rising from 11–25 per cent. Total school enrolments fell by about half a million between 1980/1 and 1995/6, which was part of a pan-African trend, but the fall was especially marked in Angola because of war, displacement, dwindling resources and mounting poverty. A substantial proportion of public expenditure on education was spent on foreign scholarships for the children of elite families.

One of the ironies of Angola's contemporary history is that, a generation after the mass flight of Portuguese settlers, Angolans were more culturally assimilated to the Portuguese-speaking world than they had ever been under colonialism. People displaced to the cities were more or less compelled to acquire a smattering of Portuguese to survive: it is the sole official language, the exclusive medium of educational and military instruction and the language of the Brazilian soap operas which are the staple fare of Angolan television. Football – a national passion – is followed through Portuguese. Twenty-six per cent of Angolans spoke Portuguese as their mother tongue in the later 1990s, when almost half the children were being brought up as Portuguese speakers. Nowhere else in post-colonial Africa has a European language assumed such prominence as a lingua franca among the mass of the population.

It is a paradoxical outcome: the fact that the Portuguese had been ensconced in coastal enclaves for centuries gives a completely illusory sense of their wider impact on the territories they claimed. The total white and *mestiço* population of Angola in 1900 was just over 12,000. In most of Lusophone Africa, colonialism was as fleeting a phenomenon as anywhere in the sub-continent; the poverty of Portuguese administration meant that it could only scratch the surface of indigenous society. It was, to be sure, authoritarian and sought to bend African labour to the discipline of the market, but when the wars of independence began the overwhelming majority were illiterate subsistence farmers and their families, living under customary law exercised by chiefs. In fighting to retain the African territories for Greater Portugal, the military effected their own 'second colonial occupation', building all-weather roads where they had never existed, as well as schools and dispensaries, and relocating villagers to secure *aldeamentos*. The wars of independence were not militarily significant until the Portuguese revolution of April 1974, but their duration was of capital political importance because it determined the ideological alignment of the nationalist movements and allowed the MPLA and FRELIMO to develop the instruments of 'vanguard party government'. Partly as a result, they were more successfully institutionalised than other African political parties. The duration of the wars also meant that when Portuguese power did collapse, Angola and Mozambique were quickly drawn into white South Africa's confrontation with the 'front-line states' and the global Cold War. Had decolonisation taken place in 1961–2, the sequence would surely have been very different. For a few years, the Marxist regimes in Mozambique and Angola seemed to offer their people greater social justice and equity than most other governments in Africa. They made grievous mistakes and it is now intellectually fashionable to criticise them for attempting societal engineering, which treated people as mere instruments of the 'progressive' state (just as it was once intellectually fashionable to laud their ambitious programmes for socialist development). But it was foreign-sponsored terrorism, not these mistakes, which brought the regimes to their knees.

Summary and Conclusions

What conclusions can we draw from the histories of the eight states discussed in the preceding chapters? It is evident that they do not cohere into a single 'grand' narrative: South Asia and Africa became independent in different geopolitical contexts, and followed different sequences from dependency to sovereign state. The British raj was an empire in itself, with a large measure of devolved government: it generated its own coercive capacity, set its own tariffs and, as a founder member of the United Nations, represented itself in the international system. Britain's political will to remain the paramount power was exhausted by 1947 and the coercive capacity it could call on to defend imperial strategic interests was much diminished. The economic relationship between the metropolitan and the colonial government had been reversed: the Government of India was now Britain's largest creditor, thanks to the accumulation of sterling balances that had paid for wartime expenditure on Indian resources and Indian troops deployed overseas. Sovereign power was hurriedly transferred to the political representatives of India and Pakistan *before* they had decided how government was to be constituted and political order maintained. They inherited legal governing instruments but their constitutional choices were made after, not before independence. They also had to solve a problem that was sorely neglected in the independence negotiations, namely the incorporation of the princely states into the new national entities. Fortunately for India, the secular political class was well organised and skilfully led by a hegemonic nationalist movement, and served by a highly competent bureaucracy. Traditional rulers were deserted by Britain and had neither collective unity nor purpose. But the euphoria of secular nationalism was tempered by a sense of, if not defeat, then poignant reversal. Religiously differentiated nationalism was repugnant to Congress's historic ideals and its 'story' of the nation as a reborn political community. Conceding partition to the Muslim League was a noxious pill, made even more poisonous by the unanticipated social disaster that ensued. (We might add that the assassination of Gandhi by a religious fanatic so soon after independence added to the sense of poignancy.) The simultaneous creation of neighbouring states that were deeply antipathetic, and were exchanging huge numbers of people amidst widespread social violence, had no parallels in Africa. Pakistan contested the post-colonial territorial settlement because it considered Kashmir had been illegitimately incorporated into the Indian Union. Again, this has no parallels in Africa, where the inviolability of the inherited colonial borders remained a cardinal principle of the African international system (at least until the secession of Eritrea).

British Africa was an imperial aggregate from which parts could be chipped off piecemeal. Sudan's independence in 1956 was a by-product of Britain's withdrawal from Egypt and strategic realignment in the Middle East. West Africa, East Africa and Central Africa all followed rather different sequences to independence. In Nigeria, more than a decade of constitution-making preceded sovereign state formation. The 1954 Constitution (the third since 1945) laid down the basic pattern of government for the federation when it became independent. It was the handiwork of the three regions' political leaders, and marked the end of the (largely non-violent) nationalist struggle and the onset of the internal conflicts that destroyed the First Republic. British coercive capacity within Nigeria never amounted to much and was never seriously tested. By 1950, British officials had concluded that only elected, indigenous governments would have the authority to carry West Africans with them into modernisation. With the Cold War becoming ever more frigid, the strategic interest in having African states aligned with the West through membership of the 'new' Commonwealth and sterling area overrode defending expatriate economic interests, substantial though they were. Merchant capitalist firms fended for themselves by recruiting Nigerian middle managers, cultivating Nigerian political leaders, and investing in production for the local consumer market. Except for a few key posts, Nigerians had staffed the administration for some years by the time sovereign power was formally transferred.

The expectations of independence on the part of the literate and western-educated were utopian, and sometimes delusional: in 1959, it was seriously suggested at the Ibadan conference on Representative Government and National Progress attended by French- and English-speaking intellectuals, that armies would be redundant in independent Africa. The delegates wanted to throw off the imperialist yoke, assert human dignity, end discrimination and exploitation, but they 'had little conception of the kind of society they were striving to build outside of vague concepts of Europeanisation and modernisation'. Unlike the Indian National Congress, which had given serious attention to national planning before the transfer of power, Africa's western-educated elites had nothing like a blueprint for economic development, which was 'low on their list of priorities, and subsumed under the concept of well-being and national progress'. They assumed the new states would be led by men like themselves, 'who most thoroughly understood the Western cultural models that were to remain the proto-types of the new structures and institutions to be established'. Some wanted to abolish traditional institutions, such as chieftaincy, consid-ered incompatible with democracy and modernity. The problems and difficulties peculiar to coalition politics were simply ignored (Ade Ajayi, 1982, p. 2).

The secular, self-consciously modern 'leaders of thought' represented at Ibadan were soul mates of the Congressmen who drew up India's 1950 Constitution, but nowhere were they organised by a hegemonic movement, and their structural position within Nigeria's emerging political system was comparatively weaker. In India, secular nationalists accommodated traditional elites to a degree but were indisputably masters of the new political order. In Nigeria, especially in the north, traditional elites retained more than their titles and dignity, and exer-cised substantial political power through modern party organisation. Ahmadu Bello, the North's premier, still aspired to be Sultan of Sokoto, a position (established by his great-grandfather) which would have made him caliph or spiritual leader of the Muslim religious commu-nity. There could be no equivalent to him in Pakistan, where the first generation of political (and military) leaders was resolutely secular and where the landowning 'feudal' classes deferred to religious authority but did not seek to fuse it with political power. When Zia sought to transform Pakistan into an Islamic state, the 'model' of political Islam he envisaged was definitely not a caliphate.

In the Belgian Congo, the sequence from constitution-making to independence was the same, but drastically compressed in time, and the Africanisation of administration was scheduled to follow sedately behind. Congolese representatives drew up the constitution in partner-ship with Belgian officials, whose overriding anxiety was securing an amicable political settlement. Contentious issues, such as the colonial regime's portfolio of assets, which ought to have been settled, were not, because of the inexperience and naivety of the Congolese negotiators. Belgian coercive capacity was seriously eroded by the politicisation of the Congolese masses, whose expectations of independence became fervently millennial. The nationalists never cohered behind a hege-monic party and had radically incompatible conceptions of how their new state would function, and how internal, ethnic 'nations' would be represented. The central government formed prior to independence was a coalition, as it was in Nigeria, but with more discordant elements. When the independence settlement imploded, the Congolese central government was virtually powerless to prevent de facto partition by an alliance of ethno-regional nationalism and corporate neo-colonialism.

The Belgian position in Rwanda and Burundi was different because they were both Mandate Territories, over which the United Nations had supervisory rights, and indigenous constitutional monarchies. The political preparations for Rwanda's independence meant 'reforming' the monarchical system until the Belgians acquiesced in a social revolution, which laid down the tracks on which the country evolved up to 1994. Though a parallel can be drawn with the overthrow of the Sultanate of Zanzibar, Rwanda's Hutu revolution under Belgian auspices was really unique: a true equivalent would have been the Hausa underclass ousting the Fulani emirs while the British Resident looked on. In Burundi, the monarchy survived the transition to independence, but with its prestige weakened by the assassination of the one member of the royal family who strove for, and represented, national cohesion. The overthrow of the monarchy in the Tutsi counter-revolution resembled the near contemporaneous destruction of Buganda's monarchy by Milton Obote.

If Nigeria was at the consensual end of the spectrum of state formation in Africa, Angola and Mozambique were at the revolutionary end. The basic reasons for this lay in the repressive authoritarianism of Salazar's 'New State' and the constitutional doctrine that the African territories were integral parts of Greater Portugal; it was an imperial entity that could not be dismantled piecemeal but had to be defended en bloc in the name of Portugal's historic civilising mission. State-sponsored Portuguese immigration was intended to anchor the imperial doctrine in African soil. The fiction of 'assimilation' in the Portuguese nation meant there could be no accommodation with the claims of African nationalism – much though the Lisbon-educated black elite would have welcomed it. But their gravitation to revolutionary Marxism was tribute to an intellectual assimilation of European political theory and values that was uncommon in English-speaking Africa (most notably in Nigeria where Marxism has never had a significant political following). The geopolitical context in which Angolans and Mozambicans waged anti-colonial war differed radically from that in which Nigerians drew up their constitution, because Africa now had its own international order, and the continent its own Cold War between the newly independent states and the white-dominated south.

Mozambique's revolutionary nationalists were (after considerable dissension) able to cohere behind a hegemonic movement that transformed itself into a 'vanguard' monopoly party; Angolans were not, partly because of the influence of ethnicity and religious confession on political identities, partly because Maoism was now an alternative pole of attraction to Leninism. The Portuguese mustered the coercive capacity to contain organised revolutionary violence and were not expelled by it, but the financial and human costs of colonial warfare debilitated the Portuguese dictatorship. Its fall rendered Greater Portugal indefensible.

The economic contexts in which post-colonial states were formed and their economic legacies from colonialism also varied greatly. South Asian macroeconomic growth stalled around 1920 because the vast agrarian sector had reached its productivity limit, given prevailing techniques and minimal agricultural investment. International demand for raw cotton and jute collapsed after 1929, ruining whole districts that had specialised in their cultivation. Many Indian entrepreneurs left the export sector for better opportunities in East African and South East Asian commerce. Output in some industries soared behind tariff barriers, but there was no structural change in the labour force, which left the overwhelming majority no alternative to employment in subsistence agriculture. Consequently, average incomes stagnated at abysmally low levels. The colonial government was not indifferent to the economic stasis, but its industrial policy failed for want of public resources to substitute for the scarcity (and timidity) of private investment. The self-imposed limitations of the colonial state meant that it was not a motor of import-substituting industrialisation, which was well advanced by 1939, but it did protect 'infant industries'. The most serious impediments to productivity growth in agriculture were market failures: beyond the orbit of the major cities, markets for money, land, capital and labour did not mesh in the rural economy. Prices of the principal commodities varied for no discernible reason in contiguous regions and did not function as 'signals' for economic actors. Capital could not be substituted for land, and the capital stock per agricultural worker was utterly inadequate. There was a strong element of non-market rationality at work: peasants grew hardy but unprofitable grains because they represented a famine store. Property relations on the land, for which the colonial state had historic responsibility, exacerbated market failures: too much land was controlled by rentiers who had no incentive to invest in it. But the nationalist critique of the colonial state as dogmatically laissez faire, extracting tribute and shoring up the parasitic classes, was misdirected: it was quite interventionist after the 1900s and devolved substantial economic sovereignty after 1918; its fiscal 'take' was comparatively small; British investment in Indian railways and other infrastructure more than compensated for the export of Indian financial capital to pay for the 'Home Charges'; tenant legislation gave peasants greater security of tenure. Independence came shortly after an economically disruptive war, in which Indians had not chosen to participate, and the 1943 Bengal famine, for which the wretchedly incompetent wartime administration was responsible. Nationalist anger at the way Britain sacrificed Indian well-being to defend its over-stretched empire was entirely warranted. But the peacetime colonial state had been too small and under-resourced to shift a sub-continental economy out of its low-level equilibrium trap.

Colonialism's legacy of economic infrastructure and institutions (a sound currency, banks, the fiscal system, company law, good public 'housekeeping') was certainly not deleterious, but it was insufficient for the purpose of overcoming economic backwardness. The nationalist strategy of accelerating growth by planned public investment in heavy industry bore similarities with state interventionism in East Asia but was flawed in three respects: first, it was conceived in a spirit of 'export pessimism' and autarky, with damaging consequences for the competitiveness and productivity growth of Indian industries; second, the state under-invested in agriculture until spurred into action by subsistence crises, and so delayed the onset of the Green Revolution; third, the inefficient public sector became over-large and the organised economy over-regulated. The unflattering comparisons often made with South Korea indicate that the problems were as much to do with the strategy's execution as with its fundamental design, though the relative size of the two economies should be kept in mind. A medium-sized economy with a culturally homogeneous population is easier to mobilise than a sub-continental civilisation. Until the post-1991 economic reforms, India's growth rate was usually below West Pakistan's, where average incomes were higher than in India until as recently as 2005 (see below). There were several reasons for this, including Pakistan's success in exporting manufactures and food grains to the Middle East, the scale of Pakistani remittances from that region, and a good record in raising agricultural productivity.

The export boom in African primary produce made for a very different economic context during Nigeria's run-up to independence. Peasant farmers were the direct beneficiaries of buoyant world prices for vegetable fats and cocoa. Their incomes rose (despite the exactions of the marketing boards) as did household consumption and private spending on schooling. A local market emerged for the import-substituting industrialisation of consumer goods. The political economy context was also very different. The first constitution came into effect on 1 January 1947, at the precise moment when economic development became the overriding preoccupation of the colonial government and the Colonial Office. Colonial administrations were no longer required to be self-financing; they could borrow more easily; and they received more development aid. As power was devolved to Nigeria's regional governments economic life became highly politicised: to further development, the marking board surpluses were invested in public-sector enterprises and infrastructure. In the process, ethno-regional economic differences were sharply accentuated in the run-up to independence: groundnut farmers around Kano, for example, experienced none of the prosperity evident in Yorubaland's cocoa districts.

The economic impact of colonial rule on Nigeria's peasant farmers had been quite limited. The money economy, an extensive market, and export production of cash crops long pre-dated the imposition of colonial rule. It provided political security for the deepening of the market by European merchant capitalism (assisted by African and Lebanese traders) and for investment in railways and port facilities, but Nigerians retained much economic discretion. They could opt out of cash crop production if prices fell too low, and proportionally few of them had been either lured or compelled into wage labour before 1960. Their relationship with the international capitalist economy has been termed a 'syncretic articulation' of modes of production and exchange: Nigerian peasants with lineage rights in the land produced, alongside their own food, cash crops such as palm oil that were bulked by African and Lebanese traders, exported by the giant United Africa Company and processed into soap by its affiliate, Unilever. Peasants' cash earnings depended on world markets, but their social relations remained, by and large, rooted in local communities, and their ways of living were structured around kinship and custom. By the 1960s, this 'syncretic articulation' was over-lain by rising demand from Nigerian-based producers. From the early 1970s, the legacy of the 'open' colonial economy was obliterated by the hectic development of the oil industry, which drove up the value of the naira and made the colonial staples uncompetitive in international markets. Bringing the industry under national control did nothing to arrest the immiseration of agriculture by oil wealth, a perverse syndrome which had even more disastrous consequences in Angola.

Turning to the colonial legacy in the Belgian Congo and Portuguese Angola and Mozambique, we must distinguish between what was achieved in the 20 years prior to independence and the lingering consequences of a more distant past. In a much cited paper, three development economists take the Belgian Congo to exemplify the 'extractive states' set up by the European powers to pillage the colony for the benefit of the coloniser. (Acemoglu *et al.*, 2001, p. 1370). This is true of Leopold II's Free State, a demographic disaster with consequences that persisted way beyond the state's dissolution in 1908. But it is not true of the 'model' Belgian colony of the 1950s, which was endowed with an excellent transport infrastructure, medical clinics, primary and technical schools, and where the manufacturing sector was proportionally larger, and more diverse than in Nigeria. The colonial economy integrated mining, plantation export agriculture and peasant food production for local markets rather successfully, given its huge size and sparse population. The export schedule was better 'balanced' between agricultural raw materials, foodstuffs and minerals than was to be the case under Mobutu, so the colonial economy was less vulnerable to fluctuations in the world price of a single commodity. What made the colonial legacy so dangerously destabilising was the complete absence of Congolese managers, executives and professionally qualified personnel. The failure to develop human capital beyond a basic level ensured an abject dependence on expatriate managers of the modern, corporate economy at odds with the Africanisation of the post-colonial state. In Portuguese Africa, very high levels of illiteracy made even routine clerical jobs the preserve of European immigrants and *mestiços*. Much of the legacy of import-substituting manufacturing was literally wrecked in the wanton destruction of fixed capital by departing Portuguese in 1974–5.

The political legacy of the colonial era was not solely the work of the colonialists. They imposed territorial sovereignty and administrative order but colonial subjects produced their own political modernity. Even the repressive paternalism of the Belgians and Portuguese could not prevent the emergence of ethnic cultural organisations that acquired political coloration and purpose. Colonialism literally created political space in which Africans could forge new identities. The generous and touching tribute paid by Ndabanangi Sithole, who spent many years in Rhodesian detention, is worth quoting:

[Colonialism] has given to Africa a new vigorous industrial pattern, a new social consciousness, new insights and visions ... It has annihilated many tribal and linguistic barriers and divisions. The European colonial powers are to be praised for the work they have done in helping the emergence of African nationalism ... The twentieth century African nationalism is indeed a child of European colonialism. (Sithole, *African Nationalism*, 1959, cited in Oliver and Atmore, 1972, p. 275)

This expresses the utopianism of a generation of idealists who could not envisage just how conflicted and contested their political legacy would be. Conflict and disorder were the most prominent features of political life in independent Africa, and for much of the time in independent Pakistan and Bangladesh. A good register of a state's political order is the efficacy and durability of its constitution, which defines political rights and obligations and indirectly the conditions for the 'civil' coexistence of conflicting interests. The abrogation or suspension of a constitution by the military is usually a symptom of irresolvable conflicts within the political class, rather than a general's 'Napoleonic' ambition. Jean-Bedel Bokassa had himself crowned emperor in ludicrous and demeaning imitation of Napoleon, but Mobutu's Zaire was the closest Africa came to a Bonapartist regime. A sub-class of military interventions are revolts emanating from the junior ranks of the officer corps that normally express the patriotic outrage of a professionally disciplined body of men at the 'indiscipline' around them; if successful they result in de facto constitutional change. With the signal exception of India, post-colonial states were particularly prone to being 'brought to order' by the specialists in violence. (This is not just a late twentieth-century phenomenon: the default mode of regime change in the nineteenth-century Spanish American republics was a military junta's *pronunciamento*.) In Pakistan, the military have overthrown civilian governments and imposed martial law on four occasions, and the country has effectively had four constitutions. Nigeria has followed a rather different pattern: a junior officers' revolt brought down the First Republic and led to a period of military government (punctuated by a coup that removed the head of state in 1975 and a junior officers' coup in which his successor was assassinated). A military coup overthrew the Second Republic. The Buhari dictatorship was toppled by Babangida's coup; Abacha overthrew an interim civilian government; both survived junior officers' revolts. In between these interventions, and under the supervision of the military, civilian politicians and 'leaders of thought' devised two constitutions with the broad intention of instituting consociational democracy. (One might argue that the adoption of shari'a law in 12 northern states in 2000–2 was tantamount to a further constitutional revision.) The frequency of junior officers' revolts reflects the Nigerian army's poor corporate discipline (by comparison with Pakistan's), sharp 'generational' differences within the officer hierarchy and strong horizontal ties between men who were schooled together and commissioned at the same time.

Officer revolts in countries with small populations and 'deep histories' of social violence led to dictatorial regimes exercising arbitrary power in a constitutional void. Burundi, the Central African Republic and Uganda are examples amongst the landlocked states where earlier social traumas still reverberated through political life. The cultural roots of the notorious Idi Amin lay in the rampant slave raiding in the nineteenth-century southern Sudan; Bokassa's father was an African chief beaten to death in public by the guards of a French concessionary company for refusing to organise a village work roster.

The one generalisation we can safely make as to the exercise of social power in post-colonial states is that power derived from economic production and exchange was diffuse, embodied in families, castes and ethnically defined communities (*not* classes), and always subordinate to the more concentrated, better-organised power emanating from political movements, government, the bureaucracy and the military. The classic Marxist model in which the function of politics and the state is to secure the economic structure of production relations does not fit the cases of Congo-Zaire or Nigeria, where the ruling class of politicians, bureaucrats and military men have leeched on to the productive economy, and exploited public office and military rank as autonomous sources of wealth. Mobuto, Bagangida, Abacha – men entirely devoid of the capitalist 'spirit' – accumulated fabulous fortunes. They were exceptional only in the scale of their depredations. In the words of the Commission for Africa, 'Africa has suffered from governments that have looted the resources of the state; that could or would not deliver services to their people; that in many cases were predatory, corruptly extracting their countries' resources; that maintained control through violence and bribery; and that squandered or stole aid' (Commission for Africa, 2005, p. 106).

The classic Marxist model is not all that helpful in trying to make sense of India's 'permit-licence-quota' raj: politicians and bureaucrats have determined how entrepreneurs should invest, set administrative limits on which firms could produce what, strictly controlled the import of capital goods and the use of foreign exchange. In the endeavour to overcome economic backwardness, the post-colonial state had no choice but to substitute public for private investment and some branches of production would not have taken off, but from the later 1960s the state began accumulating enterprises it was not competent to run. There were, of course, many parallels in Africa, but the Indian example is paradigmatic of a perverse syndrome Partha Dasgupta analysed in his enquiry into well-being and destitution in the world's poor, predominantly agrarian countries: governments have spent time and resources ineptly trying to produce steel and machinery and have not provided collective goods such as primary health care and school education:

> Phrases such 'public ownership of the means of production', 'priority to manufacturing industries for economic development', and 'centralised command and control for the purposes of resource mobilisation' have proved enduring, even while people have remained uneducated, and have visibly gone malnourished and diseased. (Dasgupta, 1993, p. 543)

That our selected states remain poor will be news to nobody, but there are degrees of poverty and different ways in which societies can be poor, so we should conclude by glancing at some aggregate data, both to gauge their relative poverty and wealth and to take a crude measure of their divergent post-colonial histories. Compiling accurate and genuinely comparable statistics on real income levels in different countries is time-consuming and technically complex. We should, therefore, be grateful to the World Bank for coordinating a survey of per capita GDP at purchasing power parity in 146 countries in 2005. There is always a margin of error in such data, but they are unquestionably more robust than previous estimates. One striking finding is that the impact of over a decade's rapid economic growth on average income in India had been much exaggerated. Indians were, on average, poorer than Pakistanis. Many will find this counter-intuitive: the Indian software industry employed 600,000 people in 2004 and exported more than $13 billion worth of services. But well over three-fifths of the Indian labour force still worked in agriculture, which hit a productivity plateau around about 1990, since when agricultural income has grown at a snail's pace while services and, to a lesser extent, manufacturing have boomed. Indian income growth has now (2011) outstripped Pakistan's, but average incomes are much below Chinese and Indonesian levels. And if we disaggregated India into its constituent states we would find some – such as Bihar – with 'African' levels of

Table C.1 Selected economic and demographic data on South Asian and African states

	GDP per cap, 2005 (PPP) US$	Price level index: food and non-alcoholic beverages (World = 100)	Price level index: clothing and footwear (World = 100)	Expectation of life in 1970	Expectation of life in 2005	Child (under-5) mortality per 1000 live births 1970	Child (under-5) mortality per 1000 live births 2005
Bangladesh	1268	59	49	45	63.1	239	73
India	2126	53	39	48	63.7	202	74
Pakistan	2396	63	40	46	64.6	181	91
Angola	3533	175	125	37.9	41.7	300	260
DRC	264	128	64	46	45.8	245	205
Nigeria	1892	135	62	42.8	46.5	265	194
Mozambique	743	88	73	40.3	42.8	278	145
Burundi	–	83	65	44.1	48.5	233	190
Rwanda	813	67	72	44.6	45.2	209	203

Sources: World Bank, *Global Purchasing Power Parities and Real Expenditures*, 2008a; *United Nations Human Development Report*, 2007–8.

income and poverty, while others – such as Karnataka – have achieved South East Asian levels of prosperity. The failure of the poorest states to grow has made them more prone to social conflict and more likely to be criminally misgoverned. Parts of Uttar Pradesh and Bihar have been virtually lawless for a generation (Frankel, 2005, pp. 605–9).

But the dominating fact revealed by the data is the great divergence in South Asian and African human 'life chances' over the last 40 years, which has little correlation with average incomes. Bangladesh drastically reduced child mortality rates at a very low income level; in oil-rich Angola and Nigeria the improvements were marginal. The nature of poverty diverged with the big differential in the price of foodstuffs, the major determinant of destitution and well-being in poor countries. It is astonishing that $1 would buy the same amount of food in Nigeria as it would in France and Germany (where average real incomes were about 16 times higher) and substantially *less* than it would in Angola. The discrepancy between food prices in the Congo and average incomes was staggering. African countries with abundant agricultural land ought to have a comparative advantage in food production. That food prices are so high in Angola and Nigeria is a consequence of the distorting effect of over-dependence on oil exports on domestic price relativities. In much of the DRC, the division of labour between town and country broke down during the Mobutu regime's terminal crisis and has not been restored. High food prices were the principal reason why poverty was 'deepening' in Africa. South Asian food prices were consistently lower and explain why so many were lifted out of 'food poverty'.

Bibliography

Abrahamsen, R., 'African Studies and the Postcolonial Challenge', *African Affairs*, 102, 407, April 2003, pp. 189–210.

Acemoglu, D., S. Johnson and J.A. Robinson, 'The Colonial Origins of Comparative Development: An Empirical Investigation', *American Economic Review*, December 2001, pp. 1369–401.

Achebe, C., *The Trouble with Nigeria*, Heinemann, 1983.

Ade Ajayi, J.F., 'The Continuity of African Institutions under Colonialism', in T.O. Ranger, ed., *Emerging Themes in African History*, Heinemann, 1968.

Ade Ajayi, J.F., 'Colonialism: An Episode in African History', in L.H. Gann and P. Duignan, eds, *Colonialism in Africa, 1870–1960*, Volume 1: *The History and Politics of Colonialism, 1970–1914*, Cambridge University Press, 1969.

Ade Ajayi, J.F., 'Expectations of Independence', *Daedalus*, 111, 2, Spring 1982, pp. 1–11.

Adedeji, A., ed., *Indigenization of African Economies*, Hutchinson, 1981.

Agadjanian, V. and Ndola Prata, 'War and Reproduction: Angola's Fertility in Comparative Perspective', *Journal of Southern African Studies*, 27, 2, 2001, pp. 329–47.

Ahluwalia, Isher J. and J. Williamson, eds, *The South Asian Experience with Growth*, Oxford University Press, 2003.

Ahmad, Kabir Uddin, *Breakup of Pakistan*, Social Science, 1972.

Ahmed, Ishtiaq, *State, Nation and Ethnicity in Contemporary South Asia*, Pinter, 1996.

Ake, Claude, *Development and Democracy in Africa*, Brookings Institution, 1996.

Akindès, F., *The Roots of the Military-Political Crises in Côte d'Ivoire*, Nordiska Afrikainstitutet, 2004.

Alavi, H., 'The State in Post-Colonial Societies: Pakistan and Bangladesh', *New Left Review*, 74, 1972, pp. 59–81.

Alexander, K.C., 'Caste Mobilization and Class Consciousness: The Emergence of Agrarian Movements in Kerala and Tamil Nadu', in Francine R. Frankel and M.S.A. Rao, eds, *Dominance and State Power in Modern India: Decline of a Social Order, 1*, Oxford University Press, 1989.

American Historical Review, 'Forum on Subaltern Studies', xcix, 1994.

Amin, Mohamed and Malcolm Caldwell, eds, *Malaya: The Making of a Neo-Colony*, Spokesman, 1977.

Amselle, J.-L., *Mestizo Logics: An Anthropology of Identity in Africa and Elsewhere*, Stanford University Press, 1998.

Amselle, J.-L. and E. M'Bokolo, eds, *Au coeur de l'ethnie. Ethnies, tribalisme et états en Afrique*, éditions de la découverte, 1985.

Anstee, Margaret, *Orphan of the Cold War: The Inside Story of the Collapse of the Angola Peace Process, 1992–93*, Macmillan, 1996.

Anstey, Roger, *King Leopold's Legacy: The Congo under Belgian Rule 1908–1960*, Oxford University Press, 1966.

Arbache, J., Delfin S. Go and John Page, 'Is Africa's Economy at a Turning Point?', World Bank, Policy Research Working Paper 4519, 2008.

Arrighi, G. and J.S. Saul, *Essays on the Political Economy of Africa*, Monthly Review Press, 1973.

Austen, R.A., *African Economic History*, Heinemann, 1987.

Austin, G., 'Resources, Techniques and Strategies South of the Sahara: Revising the Factor Endowment Perspective on African Economic Development, 1500–2000', *Economic History Review*, 61, 3, 2008, pp. 587–624.

Bach, D.C., 'Inching Towards a Country without a State: Prebendalism, Violence and State Betrayal in Nigeria', in Clapham, Herbst and Mills, eds, *Big African States*, Wits University Press, 2006.

Bardhan, P.K. and T.N. Srinivasan, eds, *Poverty in South Asia*, Columbia University Press, 1988.

Bardhan, Pranab, *The Political Economy of Development in India*, Basil Blackwell, 1984.

Basso, J.-A., 'Les accords de coopération entre la France et les Etats africains: leurs relations et leurs conséquences au regard des indépendances africaines (1960–1970)', in C.-R. Ageron and M. Michel, eds, *L'Afrique noire française: l'heure des indépendances*, CNRS, 1992.

Bates, R.H., 'Agricultural Policy and the Study of Politics in Post-Independence Africa', in Rimmer, ed., *Africa 30 Years On*, James Currey, 1991.

Bates, R.H., *Essays on the Political Economy of Rural Africa*, Cambridge University Press, 1983.

Bates, R.H., *Markets and States in Tropical Africa: The Political Basis of Agricultural Policies*, University of California Press, 1981.

Bates, R.H., *Patterns of Uneven Development: Causes and Consequences in Zambia*, University of Denver, 1974.

Bates, R.H., *When Things Fall Apart: State Failure in Late-century Africa*, Cambridge University Press, 2008.

Bates, R.H., and M.F. Lofchie, eds, *Agricultural Development in Africa: Issues of Public Policy*, Praeger, 1980.

Bayart, J.-F., 'Africa in the World: A History of Extraversion', *African Affairs*, 99, 2000, pp. 217–67.

Bayart, J.-F., *The State in Africa: The Politics of the Belly*, Longman, 1993.

Bayart, J.-F., S. Ellis and B. Hibou, *The Criminalization of the State in Africa*, James Currey/Indiana University Press, 1999.

Bayley, David H., 'The Police and Political Order in India', *Asian Survey*, 23, 4, 1983, pp. 484–96.

Bayly, Susan, *Caste, Society and Politics in India from the Eighteenth Century to the Modern Age* (New Cambridge History of India, IV.3), Cambridge University Press, 1999.

Bayly, Susan, 'The History of Caste in South Asia', *Modern Asian Studies*, 17, 3, 1983, pp. 519–27.

Beissinger, Mark R. and Crawford Young, eds, *Beyond State Crisis: Postcolonial Africa and Post-Soviet Eurasia in Comparative Perspective*, Woodrow Wilson Centre Press, 2002.

Bello, Ahmadu, *My Life*, Cambridge University Press, 1962.

Benie, Marcel Kouadio, 'Explication de la croissance en Côte d'Ivoire', in Benno J. Ndulu *et al.*, *The Political Economy of Economic Growth in Africa, 1960–2000*, CD supplement to vol. 2, Cambridge University Press, 2007.

Berman, B.J., 'Ethnicity, Patronage and the African State: The Politics of an Uncivil Nationalism', *African Affairs*, xcvii, 1998, pp. 305–41.

Berman, B.J. and J. Lonsdale, *Unhappy Valley: Conflict in Kenya and Africa*, two volumes, James Currey, 1992.

Berry, S., 'Coping with Confusion: African Farmers' Response to Economic Instability in the 1970s and 1980s', in T.M. Callaghy and J. Ravenhill, eds, *Hemmed In: Responses to Africa's Economic Decline*, Columbia University Press, 1993a.

Berry, S., *Fathers Work for their Sons: Accumulation, Mobility and Class Formation in an Extended Yoruba Community*, University of California Press, 1985.

Berry, S., *No Condition is Permanent: The Social Dynamics of Agrarian Change in Sub-Saharan Africa*, University of Wisconsin Press, 1993b.

Béteille, A., *Caste, Class and Power: Changing Patterns of Stratification in a Tanjore Village*, University of California Press, 1965.

Béteille, A., *Society and Politics in India*, Athlone Press, 1991.

Béteille, A., *The Idea of Natural Inequality & Other Essays*, Oxford University Press, 1983.

Bevan, D., P. Collier and Jan Willem Gunning, *The Political Economy of Poverty, Equity and Growth: Nigeria and Indonesia*, World Bank/Oxford University Press, 1999.

Bézy, F., 'Rwanda 1962–1989: Bilan socio-économique d'un régime', *Mondes en Développement*, 18, 69, 1990, accessible on line at http://grandslacs.net/doc/0302 pdf.

Bhalla, S.J. and P. Vashistha, 'Income Distribution in India: A Re-examination', in T.N. Srinivasan and P.K. Bardhan, eds, *Rural Poverty in South Asia*, Columbia University Press, 1988.

Bhatt, Anil, 'Dominant Caste and Political Process', in M.N. Srinivas, S. Seshaiah and V.S. Parthasarathy, eds, *Dimensions of Social Change in India*, Allied, 1977.

Biebuyck, D., 'Land Holding and Social Organization', in M.J. Herskovits and M. Harwitz, eds, *Economic Transition in Africa*, Routledge and Kegan Paul, 1964.

Biersteker, T.J., *Multinationals, the State and Control of the Nigerian Economy*, Princeton University Press, 1987.

Birmingham, D. 'Angola', in P. Chabal, *A History of Postcolonial Lusophone Africa*, Hurst, 2002.

Birmingham, D. and P.M. Martin, eds, *History of Central Africa*, vol. 2, Longman, 1983.

Birmingham, D. and P.M. Martin, eds, *History of Central Africa: The Contemporary Years since 1960*, Longman, 1998.

Birmingham, D. and T. Ranger, 'Settlers and liberators in the south, 1953–1980', in Birmingham and Martin, eds, *History of Central Africa*, vol. 2, 1983.

Birmingham, D., *Kwame Nkrumah*, Cardinal, 1990.

Bliss, C.J. and N.H. Stern, *Palanpur: The Economy of an Indian Village*, Clarendon Press, 1982.

Boahen, A. Adu, *African Perspectives on Colonialism*, Johns Hopkins University Press, 1987.

Bogetic, Z., J. Noer and C. Espina, 'Côte d'Ivoire: From Success to Failure: A Story of Growth, Specialisation and the Terms of Trade', World Bank, Policy Research Working Paper 4414, 2007.

Bose, Sugata and Ayesha Jalal, *Modern South Asia: History, Culture, Political Economy*, Routledge, 1998.

Bose, Sugata and Ayesha Jalal, eds, *Nationalism, Democracy and Development: State and Politics in India*, Oxford University Press, 1997.

Bose, Swadesh R., 'The Pakistan Economy since Independence', in D. Kumar with M. Desai, eds, *The Cambridge Economic History of India, Volume 2: c. 1757–c. 1970*, Cambridge University Press, 1983.

Bowen, Merle L., *The State against the Peasantry: Rural Struggles in Colonial and Postcolonial Mozambique*, University of Virginia Press, 2000 .

Brass, Paul R., 'India: Democratic Progress and Problems', in Harrison, Kreisberg and Kux, eds, *India and Pakistan: The First Fifty Years*, Cambridge University Press, 1999.

Brass, Paul R., *Language, Religion and Politics in North India*, Cambridge University Press, 1974.

Brass, Paul R., 'National Power and Local Politics in India: A Twenty Year Perspective', *Modern Asian Studies*, 18, 1, 1984, pp. 89–118 .

Brass, Paul R., *The Politics of India since Independence* (NCHI, IV.1), 2nd edn, Cambridge University Press, 1994.

Brasted, H.V., and C. Bridge, 'The Transfer of Power in South Asia: An Historiographical Review', *South Asia*, 17, 1, 1994, pp. 93–114.

Brennan, Lance, John McDonald and Ralph Shlomowitz, 'Caste, Inequality and the Nation State: The Impact of Reservation Policies in India, c. 1950–2000', *South Asia*, 29, 1, April 2006, pp. 117–62.

Brittain, V., *Death of Dignity: Angola's Civil War*, Pluto, 1998.

Brown, Judith M., *Modern India: The Origins of an Asian Democracy*, 2nd edn, Oxford University Press, 1994 (1st edn was 1985).

Brown, Judith M., *Nehru: A Political Life*, Yale University Press, 2003.

Brown, Judith M., 'The Mahatma and Modern India', *Modern Asian Studies*, 3, 4, 1969, pp. 321–42.

Brownsberger, W.N., 'Development and Governmental Corruption: Materialism and Political Fragmentation in Nigeria', *Journal of Modern African Studies*, 21, 2, June 1983, pp. 215–33.

Burki, S.J., 'Pakistan under Zia: 1977–1988', *Asian Survey*, 28, 10, October 1988, pp. 1082–100.

Callaghy, T.M., 'External Actors and the Relative Autonomy of the Political Aristocracy in Zaire', *Journal of Commonwealth and Comparative Politics*, 21, 1983, pp. 60–83.

Callaghy, T.M., 'The Political Economy of African Debt: The Case of Zaire', in J. Ravenhill, ed., *Africa in Economic Crisis*, Macmillan, 1986.

Callaghy, T.M., 'The State as Lame Leviathan: The Patrimonial Administrative State in Africa', in Zaki Ergas, ed., *The African State in Transition*, Macmillan, 1989.

Callaghy, T.M., *The State–Society Struggle: Zaire in Comparative Perspective*, Columbia University Press, 1984.

Callaghy, T.M. and J. Ravenhill, eds, *Hemmed In: Responses to Africa's Economic Decline*, Columbia University Press, 1993.

Cann, John, *Counterinsurgency in Africa: The Portuguese Way of War, 1961–1974*, Greenwood, 1997.

Carbone, G.M., 'Continuidade na renovação? Ten Years of Multi-party Politics in Mozambique: Roots, Evolution and Stabilisation of the Frelimo-Renamo Party System', *Journal of Modern African Studies*, 43, 3, 2005, pp. 417–42.

Centre de Recherche des Relations Internationales/Center for Peace and Human Security, proceedings of joint conference on the Rwandan genocide, 2006, accessible on http://www.peacecenter.sciences-po.fr/rwanda-cr.htm.

Chabal, P., 'People's War, State Formation and Revolution in Africa: A Comparative Analysis of Mozambique, Guinea-Bissau, Angola', *Journal of Commonwealth and Comparative Politics*, 21, 3, 1983, pp. 104–25.

Chabal, P., ed., *Political Domination in Africa*, Cambridge University Press, 1986.

Chabal, P., *Power in Africa: An Essay in Political Interpretation*, Macmillan, 1992.

Chabal, P. and J.-P. Daloz, *Africa Works: Disorder as Political Instrument*, James Currey/Indiana University Press, 1999 .

Chabal, P. with David Birmingham, Joshua Forrest, Malyn Newitt, Gerhard Seibert, Elisa Silva Andrade, *A History of Postcolonial Lusophone Africa*, Hurst, 2002.

Chakrabarty, Dipesh, Rochona Majumdar and Andrew Sartori, eds, *From the Colonial to the Postcolonial: India and Pakistan in Transition*, Oxford University Press, 2007.

Chandavarkar, A.G., 'Money and Credit', in *Cambridge Economic History of India*, 2, Cambridge University Press, 1983.

Chandavarkar, Raj, 'Customs of Governance: Colonialism and Democracy in Twentieth Century India', *Modern Asian Studies*, 51, 3, 2007, pp. 441–70.

Chandra, Bipan, 'The Colonial Legacy', in Bimal Jalan, ed., *The Indian Economy: Problems and Prospects*, Viking, 1992.

Chandra, Bipan, Mridula Mukherjee and Aditya Mukherjee, *India After Independence 1947–2000*, Penguin, 2000.

Chatterjee, P., *Nationalist Thought and the Colonial World: A Derivative Discourse?*, University of Minnesota Press, 1986.

Chatterjee, P., *The Nation and Its Fragments: Colonial and Postcolonial Histories*, Princeton University Press, 1993.

Chen, S. and Martin Ravallion, 'The Developing World is Poorer than We Thought, But No Less Successful in the Fight Against Poverty', World Bank, Policy Research Working Paper, 4703, 2008.

Chibber, Vivek, 'Bureaucratic Rationality and the Developmental State', *American Journal of Sociology*, 107, 4, January 2002, pp. 951–89.

Chibber, Vivek, *Locked in Place: State Building and Late Industrialization in India*, Princeton University Press, 2003.

Chipman, John, *French Power in Africa*, Blackwell, 1989.

Chrétien, Jean-Pierre, *The Great Lakes of Africa: Two Thousand Years of History*, Zone, 2003.

Christensen, Cheryl and Lawrence Witucki, 'Food Policies in Sub-Saharan Africa', in Commins, Lofchie and Payne, eds, *Africa's Agrarian Crisis: The Roots of Famine*, Lynne Rienner, 1986.

Clapham, C., *Africa and the International System: The Politics of State Survival*, Cambridge University Press, 1996.

Clapham, C., J. Hurst and G. Mills, eds, *Big African States*, Wits University Press, 2006.

Clarence-Smith, G., 'Capital accumulation and class formation in Angola', in Birmingham and Martin, eds, *History of Central Africa,* vol. 2, 1983.

Clarence-Smith, G., 'The Roots of the Mozambican Counter-Revolution', *Southern African Review of Books*, April/May 1989.

Cohen, J., 'Land Tenure and Rural Development in Africa', in Bates and Lofchie, eds, *Agricultural Development in Africa: Issues of Public Policy*, Praeger, 1980.

Collier, P., 'Africa and Globalisation', Centre for the Study of African Economies, Oxford, 2003.

Collier, P., 'Africa's External Economic Relations: 1960–90', *African Affairs*, 90, 1991, pp. 339–56.

Collier, P., *The Bottom Billion*, Oxford University Press, 2007.

Collier, P. and J.W. Gunning, 'Why Has Africa Grown Slowly?', *Journal of Economic Perspectives*, 13, 3, 1999a, pp. 3–22.

Collier, P. and J.W. Gunning, 'Explaining African Economic Performance', *Journal of Economic Literature*, 37, March, 1999b, pp. 64–111.

Collier, P. and A. Hoeffler, 'On economic causes of civil war', *Oxford Economic Papers*, 50, 1998, pp. 563–73.

Collier, P. and Stephen A. O'Connell, 'Opportunities and Choices', in Benno J. Ndulu *et al.*, eds, *The Political Economy of Economic Growth in Africa, 1960–2000*, vol. 1, Cambridge University Press, 2008.

Collier, R.B., *Regimes in Tropical Africa: Changing Forms of Supremacy, 1945–1975*, University of California Press, 1982.

Commander, S., 'The Jajmani System in North India: An Examination of its Logic and Status across Two Centuries', *Modern Asian Studies*, 17, 1983, pp. 283–311.

Commins, S.K., M.F. Lofchie and R. Payne, eds, *Africa's Agrarian Crisis: The Roots of Famine*, Lynne Rienner, 1986.

Commission for Africa, *Our Common Interest*, 2005.

Conlon, F.F., *A Caste in a Changing World: The Chitrapur Saraswat Brahmans, 1700–1935*, University of California Press, 1977 .

Contamin, B. and Y.-A. Fauré, 'State Intervention in the Economy', in A. Kirk-Greene and D. Bach, *State and Society in Francophone Africa since Independence*, St Martins Press, 1995.

Cooper, F., *Africa since 1940: The Past of the Present*, Cambridge University Press, 2002.

Cooper, F., 'Conflict and Connection: Rethinking Colonial African History', *American Historical Review*, 99, 5, 1994, pp. 1516–45.

Copland, I., 'The Imprint of the Past: Reflections on Regime Change with Particular Reference to "Middle India", c. 1947–50', in Chakrabarty *et al.*, eds, *From the Colonial to the Postcolonial: India and Pakistan in Transition*, Oxford University Press, 2007.

Coquery-Vidrovitch, C., 'The Transfer of Economic Power in French-Speaking West Africa', in Prosser Gifford and W.R. Louis, eds, *Decolonization and African Independence: The Transfers of Power, 1960–1980*, Yale University Press, 1988a.

Coquery-Vidrovitch, C., *Africa: Endurance and Change South of the Sahara*, University of California Press, 1988b.

Coussy, J., 'The Franc Zone: Original Logic, Subsequent Evolution and Present Crisis', in Kirk-Greene and Bach, *State and Society in Francophone Africa since Independence*, St Martins Press, 1995.

Cramer, C., 'Privatisation and Adjustment in Mozambique: A 'Hospital Pass'?, *Journal of Southern African Studies*, 27, 1, 2001, pp. 79–103.

Cronje, Suzanne, *The World and Nigeria: The Diplomatic History of the Biafran War 1967–1970*, Sidgwick and Jackson, 1972.

Crook, R.C., 'Decolonization, the Colonial State, and Chieftancy in the Gold Coast', *African Affairs*, 85, 338, 1986, pp. 75–107.

Crook, R.C., 'Patrimonialism, Administrative Effectiveness and Economic Development in Côte d'Ivoire', *African Affairs*, 88, 351, April 1989, pp. 75–105.

Crowder, M., *The Story of Nigeria*, rev. edn, Faber, 1966.

Cumming, G., 'French Development Assistance to Africa: Towards a New Agenda?', *African Affairs*, 94, 1995, pp. 383–98.

Dandekar, V.M. and N. Rath, 'Poverty in India: Dimensions and Trends', *Economic and Political Weekly*, 6, 1, 2 January 1971, pp. 25–48 and 6, 2, 9 January 1971, pp. 104–46.

Darwin, J., *Britain and Decolonisation: The Retreat from Empire in the Post-War World*, Macmillan, 1988.

Dasgupta, P., *An Inquiry into Well-Being and Destitution*, Clarendon Press, 1993.

Davidson, B., *The Black Man's Burden: Africa and the Curse of the Nation State*, James Currey, 1992.

De Herdt, T., 'Democracy and the Money Machine in Zaire', *Review of African Political Economy*, 93/94, 2002, pp. 445–62.

Decalo, S., 'African Personal Dictatorships', *Journal of Modern African Studies*, 23, 2, June 1985, pp. 209–237.

Decalo, S., 'The Process, Prospects and Constraints of Democratization in Africa', *African Affairs*, 91, 1992, pp. 7–35.

Decalo, S., *Psychoses of Power: African Personal Dictatorships*, 2nd edn, Florida Academic Press, 2000.

Democratic Republic of the Congo, *Poverty Reduction and Growth Strategy Paper*, Kinshasa, 2006.

Des Forges, A., 'The Ideology of Genocide', *Issue: A Journal of Opinion*, 23, 2, 1995.

Des Forges, A., *Leave None to Tell the Story: Genocide in Rwanda* [for Human Rights Watch and the Fédération internationale des droits de l'homme, accessible: http://www.grandslacs.net/doc/1317.pdf], 1999.

Desai, S. and K.F. Sreedhar, 'India: Growth and Equity', in Harrison, Kreisberg and Kux, eds, *India and Pakistan: The First Fifty Years*, Cambridge University Press, 1999.

Dev, S. Mahendra, 'Growth, Employment, Poverty and Human Development: An Evaluation of Change in India since Independence', *Review of Development and Change*, 2, 2, 1997, pp. 209–50 .

Diamond, L., *Class, Ethnicity and Democracy in Nigeria: The Failure of the First Republic*, Macmillan, 1988a.

Diamond, L., 'Class, Ethnicity and the Democratic State: Nigeria 1950–1966', *Comparative Studies in Society and History*, 25, 3, July 1983, pp. 457–89.

Diamond, L., 'Class Formation in the Swollen African State', *Journal of Modern African Studies*, 25, 4, 1987, pp. 567–96.

Diamond, L., 'Cleavage, Conflict, and Anxiety in the Second Nigerian Republic', *Journal of Modern African Studies*, 20, 40, December 1982, pp. 629–68.

Diamond, L., 'Nigeria: Pluralism, Statism, and the Struggle for Democracy', in L. Diamond, J.J. Linz and S.M. Lipset, eds, *Democracy in Developing Countries: Volume Two: Africa*, Lynne Rienner/Adamantine Press, 1988b.

Diamond, L., A. Kirk-Greene and Oyeleye Oyediran, *Transition without End: Nigerian Politics and Civil Society under Babangida*, Lynne Rienner, 1997.

Diamond, L., J.J. Linz and S.M. Lipset, eds, *Democracy in Developing Countries: Volume Two: Africa*, Lynne Rienner/Adamantine Press, 1988.

Dinerman, Alice, *Revolution, Counter-Revolution and Revisionism in Postcolonial Africa: The Case of Mozambique, 1975–1994*, Routledge, 2006.

Dirks, N. B., *Castes of Mind: Colonialism and the Making of Modern India*, Princeton University Press, 2001 .

Dirks, N.B., ed., *Colonialism and Culture*, Ann Arbor, 1992.

Dowden, Richard, *Africa: Altered States, Ordinary Miracles*, Portobello Books, 2008.

Drèze, J. and A. Sen, *India: Economic Development and Social Opportunity*, Oxford University Press, 1995 .

Dube, S.C., ed., *India since Independence: Social Report on India 1947–1972*, New Delhi, 1977.

Dudley, B.J., *Politics and Crisis in Nigeria*, University of Ibadan Press, 1973.

Dudley, B.J., 'The Nigerian Elections of 1979: The Voting Decision', *Journal of Commonwealth and Comparative Politics*, 19, 3, 1981, pp. 276–93.

Dudley, B.J., 'Western Nigeria and the Nigerian Crisis', in Panter-Brick, ed., *Nigerian Politics and Military Rule: Prelude to the Civil War*, Athlone Press, 1970.

Dumont, L., *Homo Hierarchicus: The Caste System and its Implications*, Weidenfeld & Nicolson, 1970.

Dunn, John, ed., *West African States: Failure and Promise*, Cambridge University Press, 1978.

East Africa Royal Commission 1953–1955, *Report*, Cmd 9475, Parliamentary Papers, 1955.

Easterly, W., and R.Levine, 'Africa's Growth Tragedy: Policies and Ethnic Divisions', *Quarterly Journal Of Economics*, November 1997, pp. 1203–50.

Eicher, C.K., 'Facing Up to Africa's Food Crisis', in J. Ravenhill, ed., *Africa in Economic Crisis*, Macmillan, 1986.

Ekeh, P., 'Colonialism and the Two Publics in Africa: A Theoretical Statement', *Comparative Studies in Society and History*, 17, 1, 1975, pp. 91–112.

Ekeh, P., 'Social Anthropology and Two Contrasting Uses of Tribalism in Africa', *Comparative Studies in Society and History*, 32, 4, 1990, pp. 660–700.

Ellis, Stephen, 'Liberia 1989–1994: A Study of Ethnic and Spiritual Violence', *African Affairs*, 94, 375, April 1995, pp. 165–97.

Ellis, Stephen, *The Mask of Anarchy: The Destruction of Liberia and the Religious Dimension of an African Civil War*, New York University Press, 1999.

Ellis, Stephen, 'The Roots of African Corruption', *Current History*, May 2006, pp. 203–8.

Ellis, Stephen, 'Writing Histories of Contemporary Africa', *Journal of African History*, 43, 2002, pp.1–26.

Emizet, Kisangani N.F., 'Confronting Leaders at the Apex of the State: The Growth of the Unofficial Economy in Congo', *African Studies Review*, 41, 1, April 1998, pp. 99–137.

Engels, D. and S. Marks, eds, *Contesting Colonial Hegemony: State and Society in Africa and India*, British Academic Press, 1994.

Ergas, Zacki, ed., *The African State in Transition*, Macmillan, 1987.

Ezeife, E., 'Nigeria', in A. Adedeji, ed., *Indigenization of African Economies*, Hutchinson, 1981.

Falola, Toyin, *Development Planning and Decolonization in Nigeria*, University Press of Florida, 1996.

Falola, Toyin and Matthew M. Heaton, *A History of Nigeria*, Cambridge University Press, 2008.

Falola, Toyin and J. Ihonvbere, *The Rise and Fall of Nigeria's Second Republic 1979–1984*, Zed, 1985.

FAOSTAT: statistics of the Food and Agricultural Organization of the United Nations, available on line at http://faostat.fao.org/site/567/default.aspx#ancor.

Ferguson, J., *Global Shadows: Africa in the Neoliberal World Order*, Duke University Press, 2006.

Fieldhouse, D.K., 'The Economic Exploitation of Africa: Some British and French Comparisons', in P. Gifford and W.R. Louis, eds, *France and Britain in Africa: Imperial Rivalry and Colonial Rule*, Yale University Press, 1971.

Fieldhouse, D.K., *Black Africa 1945–80: Economic Decolonization and Arrested Development*, Allen and Unwin, 1986.

Fieldhouse, D.K., *Colonialism 1870–1945: An Introduction*, Weidenfeld & Nicolson, 1981.

Forbes, Geraldine, *Women in Modern India*, Cambridge University Press, 1996.

Foreign Relations of the United States (FRUS), US Government Printing Office, Washington, various years.

Forrest, T., *Politics and Economic Development in Nigeria*, Westview Press, 1993.

Forrest, T., *The Advance of African Capital: The Growth of Nigerian Private Enterprise*, Edinburgh University Press, 1994.

Forrest, T., 'The Political Economy of Civil Rule and the Economic Crisis in Nigeria (1979–84)', *Review of African Political Economy*, 35, May 1986, pp. 4–26.

Fox, R.C., W. de Craemer and J.-M. Ribeaucourt, '"The Second Independence": A Case Study of the Kwilu Rebellion in the Congo', *Comparative Studies in Society and History*, 8, 1, 1965, pp. 78–109.

Frankel, F.R., 'Caste, Land and Dominance in Bihar', in Frankel and Rao, eds, *Dominance and State Power in Modern India: Decline of a Social Order*, 2 vols, Oxford University Press, 1989(a).

Frankel, F.R., 'Conclusion: Decline of a Social Order', in Frankel and Rao, eds, *Dominance and State Power in Modern India: Decline of a Social Order*, 2 vols, Oxford University Press, 1989(b).

Frankel, F.R., *India's Green Revolution: Economic Gains and Political Costs*, Princeton University Press, 1971.

Frankel, F.R., *India's Political Economy, 1947–2004: The Gradual Revolution*, Oxford University Press, 2005. (This is the second enlarged edition of a work first published by Princeton University Press in 1978. The original text is unaltered.)

Frankel, F.R. and M.S.A. Rao, eds, *Dominance and State Power in Modern India: Decline of a Social Order*, 2 vols, Oxford University Press, 1989.

Freund, B., *The Making of Contemporary Africa: The Development of African Society since 1800*, 2nd edn, Macmillan, 1998.

Furedi, F., 'Superpower Rivalries in the Third World', in K.B. Hadjor, ed., *New Perspectives in North–South Dialogue: Essays in Honour of Olof Palme*, I.B.Tauris, 1988.

Gann, L.H. and P. Duignan, eds, *Colonialism in Africa, 1870–1960*, Vol. 4: *The Economics of Colonialism*, Cambridge University Press, 1975.

Gardezi, H. and J. Rashid, eds, *Pakistan: The Roots of Dictatorship*, Zed, 1983.

Geffray, C., *La Cause des Armes: Anthropologie de la Guerre Contemporaine au Mozambique*, Karthala, 1990.

Gérard-Libois, J., *Katanga Secession*, University of Wisconsin Press, 1966.

Geschiere, Peter, *The Modernity of Witchcraft: Politics and the Occult in Post-colonial Africa*, University of Virginia Press, 1997.

Gibbs, D.N., 'Misrepresenting the Congo Crisis', *African Affairs*, 95, 380, 1996, pp. 453–59.

Gifford, Prosser and William Roger Louis, eds, *Decolonization and African Independence: The Transfers of Power, 1960–1980*, Yale University Press, 1988.

Gifford, Prosser and William Roger Louis, eds, *The Transfer of Power in Africa: Decolonization 1940–60*, Yale University Press, 1982.

Glantz, M.H., ed., *Drought and Hunger in Africa: Denying Famine a Future*, Cambridge University Press, 1987.

Gleijeses, P., *Conflicting Missions: Havana, Washington and Africa, 1959–76*, University of North Carolina Press, 2002.

GlobeScan, Research Findings: Africa in Depth, 2011, accessible on http://www.globescan.com/rf_aid_first_01.htm.

Graf, W.D., *The Nigerian State: Political Economy, State Class and Political System in the Post-Colonial Era*, James Currey, 1986.

Gray, J., *Rebellions and Revolutions: China from the 1800s to the 1980s*, Oxford University Press, 1990.

Greenhough, P.R., *Prosperity and Misery in Modern Bengal: The Famine of 1943–1944*, Oxford University Press, 1982.

Gregory, T., *India on the Eve of the Third Five Year Plan*, Associated Chambers of Commerce of India, Calcutta, 1961.

Guha, Ramachandra, *India after Gandhi: The History of the World's Largest Democracy*, Macmillan, 2007.

Gupta, A., *Postcolonial Development: Agriculture in the Making of Modern India*, Duke University Press, 1998.

Gupta, Dipankar, *Interrogating Caste: Understanding Hierarchy and Difference in Indian Society*, Penguin, 2000.

Guyer, J., 'Representation without Taxation: An Essay on Democracy in Rural Nigeral, 1952–1990', *African Studies Review*, 35, 1, April 1992, pp. 41–79.

Hadjor, K.B., ed., *New Perspectives in North–South Dialogue: Essays in Honour of Olof Palme*, I.B.Tauris, 1988.

Hailey, Malcolm, ed., *An African Survey, Revised 1956*, Oxford University Press, 1957.

Hall, M., 'The Mozambican National Resistance Movement (Renamo): A Study in the Destruction of an African Country', *Africa: Journal of the International African Institute*, 60, 1, 1990, pp. 39–60.

Hall, M. and T. Young, *Confronting Leviathan: Mozambique since Independence*, Ohio University Press, 1997.

Hanson, A.H., *The Process of Planning: A Study of India's Five Year Plans 1950–1964*, Oxford University Press, 1966.

Hargreaves, J.D., *Decolonization in Africa*, Longman, 1988.

Harrison, Selig S., P.H. Kreisberg and D. Kux, eds, *India and Pakistan: The First Fifty Years*, Cambridge University Press, 1999.

Harwitz, M., 'Subsaharan Africa as a Growing Economic System', in M.J. Herskovits and M. Harwitz, eds, *Economic Transition in Africa*, Routledge and Kegan Paul, 1964.

Hawkins, T., 'Industrialisation in Africa', in D. Rimmer, ed., *Africa 30 Years On*, James Currey, 1991.

Headrick, Daniel R., *The Tools of Empire: Technology and European Imperialism in The Nineteenth Century*, Oxford University Press, 1981.

Henriksen, T.H., *Revoluntion and Counter-Revolution; Mozambique's War of Independence*, Greenwood, 1983 .

Herbst, J., 'Is Nigeria a Viable State?', *The Washington Quarterly*, 19, 2, 1996, pp. 151–72.

Herbst, J., 'Responding to State Failure in Africa', *International Security*, 21, 3, Winter 1996–7, pp. 120–44.

Herbst, J., 'Review: Political Liberalization in Africa after Ten Years', *Comparative Politics*, 33, 3, April 2001, pp. 357–75.

Herbst, J., *State and Power in Africa*, Princeton University Press, 2000.

Herbst, J., 'The Structural Adjustment of Politics in Africa', *World Development*, 18, 1990, pp. 949–58.

Herbst, J., 'War and the State in Africa', *International Security*, 14, 4, Spring 1990, pp. 117–39.

Herskovits, M.J. and M. Harwitz, eds, *Economic Transition in Africa*, Routledge and Kegan Paul, 1964.

Heston, A., 'National Income', in Dharma Kumar with Meghnad Desai, eds, *The Cambridge Economic History of India, Volume 2: c. 1757–c. 1970*, Cambridge University Press, 1983.

Heusch, Luc De, 'Rwanda: Responsibilities for a Genocide', *Anthropology Today*, 11, 4, August 1995, pp. 3–7.

Heywood, L.M., 'Unita and Ethnic Nationalism in Angola', *Journal of Southern African Studies*, 27, 1, March 1989, pp. 47–66.

Hibou, B., 'The Social Capital of the State as an Agent of Deception', in Bayart, Ellis and Hibou, *The Criminalization of the State in Africa*, James Currey/Indiana University Press, 1999.

Hickey, R., 'The Maitatsine Uprisings in Nigeria: A Note', *African Affairs*, 83, 331, April 1984, pp. 251–6.

Higgott, R., 'Africa and the New International Division of Labour', in J. Ravenhill, ed., *Africa in Economic Crisis*, Macmillan,1986.

Hodges, T., *Angola from Afro-Stalinism to Petro-Diamond Capitalism*, James Currey, 2001.

Hopkins, A.G., *An Economic History of West Africa*, Longman, 1973.

Hugon, P., 'Models and Economic Performance', in Kirk-Greene and Bach, *State and Society in Francophone Africa since Independence*, St Martin's Press, 1995.

Human Development in South Asia: The Crisis of Governance, Mahbub ul Haq Human Development Centre/Oxford University Press, 1999.

Human Rights Watch, *Chop Fine: The Human Rights Impact of Local Government Corruption and Mismanagement in Rivers State, Nigeria*, 2007a.

Human Rights Watch, *Criminal Politics: Violence, 'Godfathers' and Corruption in Nigeria*, 2007b.

Human Rights Watch, *The War Within the War: Sexual Violence against Women and Girls in the Eastern Congo*, 2002.

Hunter, Guy, *The New Societies of Tropical Africa: A Selective Study*, Oxford University Press for the Institute of Race Relations, 1962.

Husain, Ishrat and Rashid Faruqee, eds, *Adjustment in Africa: Lessons from the Country Case Studies*, World Bank, 1994.

Hyden, G., *African Politics in Comparative Perspective*, Cambridge University Press, 2006.

Hyden, G., *Beyond Ujamaa in Tanzania: Underdevelopment and an Uncaptured Peasantry*, Heinemann, 1980.

Hyden, G. and Donald C. Williams, 'A Community Model of African Politics: Illustrations from Nigeria and Tanzania', *Comparative Studies in Society and History*,36, 1, 1994, pp. 68–96.

Iliffe, John, *A Modern History of Tanganyika*, Cambridge University Press, 1979.

Iliffe, John, *Africans: the History of a Continent*, Cambridge University Press, 1995.

Iliffe, John, *The African Poor*, Cambridge University Press, 1987.

International Bank for Reconstruction and Development (IBRD), *The Economic Development of Tanganyika*, Dar es Salaam, 1960.

International Crisis Group, *Burundi: finalising the peace with the FNL*, Africa Report No. 131, August 2007.

International Crisis Group, *Nigeria: Failed Elections, Failing State?*, Africa Report, No. 126, May 2007.

International Crisis Group, *Nigeria: Want in the Midst of Plenty*, Africa Report, No. 113, July 2006.

International Crisis Group, *Rwanda at the End of Transition: A Necessary Political Liberalisation*, Africa Report No 53, November 2002.

International Panel of Eminent Personalities (IPEP), *Rwanda: The Preventable Genocide*, Report for the OAU, n.d., but 2000, accessible on http://africa-union.org/Official_documents/reports/Report_rowanda_genocide.pdf (accessed 4 July 2008).

International Rescue Committee, *Mortality in the Democratic Republic of the Congo: An Ongoing Crisis*, 2008, available at www.theirc.org/resources/2007/2006-7_congo mortalitysurvey.pdf.

Isichei, E., 'The Maitatsine Risings in Nigeria, 1980–85: A Movement of the Dispossessed', *Journal of Religion in Africa*, 17, 3, 1987, pp. 194–208.

Iyoha, Milton A. and Dickson E. Oriakhi, 'Explaining African Economic Growth Performance: The Case of Nigeria', in B.J. Ndulu, Stephen A. O'Connell, R.H. Bates, Paul Collier and Chukwuma C. Soludu, eds, *The Political Economy of Economic Growth in Africa, 1960–2000*, 2 vols, Cambridge University Press, 2008.

Jackson, R.H. and C.G. Rosberg, *Personal Rule in Black Africa: Prince, Autocrat, Prophet and Tyrant*, University of California Press, 1982.

Jackson, R.H. and C.G. Rosberg, 'Sovereignty and Underdevelopment: Juridical Statehood in the African Crisis', *Journal of Modern African Studies*, 24, 1, March 1986, pp. 1–31.

Jaffrelot, Christophe, ed., *A History of Pakistan and its Origins*, Anthem, 2006.

Jaffrelot, Christophe, *India's Silent Revolution: The Rise of the Lower Castes in North India*, Hurst, 2003.

Jaffrelot, Christophe, 'Sanskritization versus Ethnicization in India: Changing Identities and Caste Politics before Mandal', *Asian Survey*, 40, 4, 2000a, pp. 756–66.

Jaffrelot, Christophe, 'The Rise of the Other Backward Classes in the Hindi Belt', *Journal of Asian Studies*, 59, 1, February 2000b, pp. 86–108.

Jalal, Ayesha, *Democracy and Authoritarianism in South Asia: A Comparative Historical Perspective*, Cambridge University Press, 1995.

Jalal, Ayesha, *The Sole Spokesman: Jinnah, the Muslim League and the Demand for Pakistan*, Cambridge University Press, 1985.

Jalal, Ayesha, *The State of Martial Rule: The Origins of Pakistan's Political Economy of Defence*, Cambridge University Press, 1990.

Jefferies, R., 'Ghana: The Political Economy of Personal Rule', in D. O'Brien, B. Cruise, J. Dunn and R. Rathbone, eds, *Contemporary West African States*, Cambridge University Press, 1989.

Jewsiewicki, Bogumil, 'Rural Society and the Belgian Colonial Economy', in David Birmingham and Phyllis M. Martin, eds, *History of Central Africa*, vol. 2, Longman, 1983.

Jha, Prem Shankar, *India: A Political Economy of Stagnation*, Oxford University Press, 1980.

Joseph, R.A., 'Affluence and Underdevelopment: The Nigerian Experience', *Journal of Modern African Studies*, 16, 2, June 1978, pp. 221–39.

Joseph, R.A., 'Class, State and Prebendal Politics in Nigeria', *Journal of Commonwealth and Comparative Politics*, 21, 1983, pp. 21–38.

Joseph, R.A., *Democracy and Prebendal Politics in Nigeria: The Rise and Fall of the Second Republic*, Cambridge University Press, 1987.

Joseph, R.A., ed., *State, Conflict and Democracy in Africa*, Lynne Rienner, 1999.

Joshi, V. and I.M.D. Little, *India: Macroeconomics and Political Economy, 1964–1991*, World Bank, 1994.

Kalb, M.G., *The Congo Cables: The Cold War in Africa From Eisenhower to Kennedy*, Macmillan, 1982.

Kamarck, A., *The Economics of African Development*, Praeger, 1967.

Kapur, D., J.P. Lewis and R. Webb, eds, *The World Bank: Its First Half Century*, 2 vols, Brookings Institution, 1997.

Kaviraj, S., 'The Imaginary Institution of India', *Subaltern Studies*, VII, Oxford University Press, 1992.

Kay, G.B., *Development and Underdevelopment: A Marxist Analysis*, Macmillan, 1975.

Kay, G.B., *The Political Economy of Colonialism in Ghana*, Gregg Revivals, 1972.

Kelgama, S. and K.S. Parikh, 'Political Economy of Growth and Reforms in South Asia', in Ahluwalia and Williamson, eds, *The South Asian Experience with Growth*, Oxford University Press, 2003.

Kelly, S., *America's Tyrant: The CIA and Mobutu of Zaire*, American University Press, 1993.

Kennedy, P., *African Capitalism: The Struggle for Ascendancy*, Cambridge University Press, 1988.

Kennedy, P., 'Political Barriers to African Capitalism', *Journal of Modern African Studies*, 32, 2, 1994, pp. 191–213.

Khan, Yasmin, *The Great Partition: The Making of India and Pakistan*, Yale University Press, 2007.

Kilby, Peter, *Industrialization in an Open Economy: Nigeria, 1945–60*, Cambridge University Press, 1969.

Killick, A., *Development Economics in Action: A Study of Economic Policies in Ghana*, Heineman, 1978.

Killingray, D., 'The Maintenance of Law and Order in British Colonial Africa', *African Affairs*, 85, 340, July 1986, pp. 411–37.

Kirk-Greene, A.H.M., ed., *Crisis and Conflict in Nigeria: A Documentary Sourcebook*, 2 vols, Oxford University Press, 1971.

Kirk-Greene, A.H.M., 'The Thin White Line: The Size of the British Colonial Service in Africa', *African Affairs*, 79, 314, 1980, pp. 25–44.

Kirk-Greene, A.H.M. (with D. Rimmer), *Nigeria since 1970: A Political and Economic Outline*, Hodder & Stoughton, 1981.

Kirk-Greene, A.H.M. and D. Bach, eds, *State and Society in Francophone Africa since Independence*, Macmillan, 1995.

Kochanek, S.A., 'Briefcase Politics in India: The Congress Party and the Business Elite', *Asian Survey*, 27, 12, December 1987, pp. 1278–301.

Kochanek, S.A., *Business and Politics in India*, University of California Press, 1974.

Kochanek, S.A., *Interest Groups and Development: Business and Politics in Pakistan*, Oxford University Press, 1983.

Kohli, Atul, *Democracy and Discontent: India's Growing Crisis of Governability*, Cambridge University Press, 1990.

Kohli, Atul, ed., *India's Democracy: An Analysis of Changing State–Society Relations*, Princeton University Press, 1988.

Kohli, Atul, *The State and Poverty in India*, Cambridge University Press, 1987.

Kothari, R., 'The Congress "System" in India', *Asian Survey*, 4, 12, December 1964, pp. 1161–73.

Kothari, R., 'The Congress System Re-visited: A Decennial Review', *Asian Survey*, 14, 12 December 1974, pp. 1035–54.

Kothari, Rajni and Rushikesh Maru, 'Caste and Secularism in India: A Case Study', *Journal of Asian Studies*, 251, 1, November 1965, pp. 33–50.

Krishnamurty, J., 'The Occupational Structure', in Dharma Kumar with Meghnad Desai, eds, *The Cambridge Economic History of India, Volume 2: c. 1757–c. 1970*, Cambridge University Press, 1983.

Kudaisya, M.M., 'Reforms by Stealth': Indian Economic Policy, Big Business and the Reforms of the Shastri Years', *South Asia: Journal of South Asian Studies*, 25, 2, 2002, pp. 205–29.

Kumar, Dharma, 'Caste and Landlessness in South India', *Comparative Studies in Society and History*, 4, 3, 1962, pp. 337–63.

Kumar, D. (Dharma), 'Changes in Income Distribution and Poverty in India: A Review of the Literature', *World Development*, 2, 1, 1974.

Kumar, Dharma, 'The Affirmative Action Debate in India', *Asian Survey*, 32, 3, March 1992, pp. 290–302.

Kumar, Dharma, 'The Fiscal System', in Dharma Kumar with Meghnad Desai, eds, *The Cambridge Economic History of India, Volume 2: c. 1757–c. 1970*, Cambridge University Press, 1983.

Kyle, K., 'Lumumba', *International Affairs*, 78, 3, July 2002, pp. 595–604.

Lal, Deepak, *The Hindu Equilibrium*, vol. 1, *Cultural Stability and Economic Stagnation: India c. 1500BC–AD1980*, Oxford University Press, 1988.

Lambert, A. and L. Lohlé-Tart, 'La surmotalité au Congo (RDC) durant les troubles de 1998–2004 : une estimation des décès en surnombre, scientifiquement fondée à partir des méthodes de la démographie', *Observatoire de l'Afrique centrale*, 2009, available at http://www.obsac.com./E20090105172451/index.html.

Lancaster, C., 'The World Bank in Africa since 1980: The Politics of Structural Adjustment Lending', in Kapur, Lewis and Webb, eds, *The World Bank: Its First Half Century*, 2 vols, Brookings Institution, 1997.

Le Billon, P., 'Angola's Political Economy of War: The Role of Oil and Diamonds, 1975–2000', *African Affairs*, 100, 2001, pp. 55–80.

Leechor, C., 'Ghana: frontrunner in adjustment', in Husain and Faruquee, eds, *Adjustment in Africa: Lessons from Country Case Studies*, 1994.

Lemarchand, R., *Burundi: Ethnocide as Discourse and Practice*, Woodrow Wilson Centre Press and Cambridge University Press, 1994.

Lemarchand, R., 'Political Clientelism and Ethnicity in Tropical Africa: Competing Solidarities in Nation Building', *American Political Science Review*, 66, 1, 1972, pp. 68–90.

Lemarchand, R., *Rwanda and Burundi*, Pall Mall Press, 1970.

Lemarchand, R., 'The Burundi Genocide', in Samuel Totten *et al.*, eds, *Century of Genocide: Eyewitness Accounts and Critical Views*, Routledge, 1997.

Lemarchand, R. and D. Martin, *Selective Genocide in Burundi*, Minority Rights Group, Report No. 20, 1974 .

Lentz, C., '"Tribalism" and Ethnicity in Africa: A Review of Four Decades of Anglophone Research', *Cahiers des Sciences Humaines*, 31, 1995, pp. 303–28.

Leslie, W.J., *Zaire: Continuity and Political Change in an Oppressive State*, Westview Press, 1993.

Lewis, Peter M., 'Civil Society, Political Society and Democratic Failure in Nigeria', in Marina Ottoway, ed., *Democracy in Africa: The Hard Road Ahead*, Lynne Rienner, 1997.

Lewis, Peter M., 'Endgame in Nigeria? The Politics of a Failed Democratic Transition', *African Affairs*, 93, 1994, pp. 323–40.

Lewis, Peter M., 'From Prebendalism to Predation: The Political Economy of Decline in Nigeria', *Journal of Modern African Studies*, 34, 1, 1996, pp. 79–103.

Leys, Colin, 'African Economic Development in Theory and Practice', *Daedalus*, 111, 2, Spring 1982, pp. 99–124.

Leys, Colin, 'Confronting the African Tragedy', *New Left Review*, 204, 1994, pp. 33–47.

Leys, Colin, *Underdevelopment in Kenya: The Political Economy of Neo-Colonialism*, Heinemann, 1975.

Lloyd, P. C., 'The Rise of New Indigenous Elites', in L.H. Gann and P. Duignan, eds, *Colonialism in Africa, 1870–1960*, Vol. 4: *The Economics of Colonialism*, Cambridge University Press, 1975.

Lloyd, P.C., 'The Ethnic Background to the Nigerian Crisis', in Panter-Brick, ed., *Nigerian Politics and Military Rule: Prelude to the Civil War*, Athlone Press, 1970.

Lofchie, Michael F., 'Africa's Agricultural Crisis: An Overview', in Commins, Lofchie and Payne, eds, *Africa's Agrarian Crisis: The Roots of Famine*, Lynne Rienner, 1986.

Lofchie, Michael F., 'The Decline of African Agriculture: An Internalist Perspective', in Glantz, ed., *Drought and Hunger in Africa: Denying Famine a Future*, Cambridge University Press, 1987.

Lonsdale, John, 'Political Accountability in African History', in Chabal, ed., *Political Domination in Africa*, Cambridge University Press, 1986.

Loomba, Ania, *Colonialism/Postcolonialism*, Routledge, 1998.

Low, D.A., *Buganda in Modern History*, Weidenfeld & Nicolson, 1971.

Low, D.A., *Eclipse of Empire*, Cambridge University Press, 1991a.

Low, D.A., 'Introduction: Digging Deeper: Northern India in the 1940s', *South Asia*, 18, 1995, pp. 1–12.

Low, D.A., *The Egalitarian Moment: Asia and Africa, 1950–1980*, Cambridge University Press, 1996.

Low, D.A., ed., *The Political Inheritance of Pakistan*, Macmillan, 1991b.

Loxley, John and David Seddon, 'Stranglehold on Africa', *Review of African Political Economy*, 21, 62, December 1994, pp. 485–93.

Luckham, R., 'The Military, Militarization and Democratization in Africa: A Survey of the Literature and Issues', *African Studies Review*, 37, 2, September 1994, pp. 13–75.

Luckham, R., *The Nigerian Military: A Sociological Analysis of Authority and Revolt 1960–67*, Cambridge University Press, 1971.

Luckham, R., 'The Nigerian Military: Disintegration or Integration?', in Panter-Brick, ed., *Nigerian Politics and Military Rule: Prelude to the Civil War*, Athlone Press, 1970.

Ludden, David, *An Agrarian History of South Asia: The New Cambridge History of India*, IV.4, Cambridge University Press, 1999.

Ludden, David, 'India's Development Regime', in Dirks, ed., *Colonialism and Culture*, Ann Arbor, 1992.

Lugan, B., *Afrique: bilan de la décolonisation: vérités et légendes*, Perrin, 1991.

Lugan, B., *Afrique: de la colonisation philanthropique à la recolonisation humanitaire*, Christian de Bartillat, 1995.

MacGaffey, J., 'How to Survive and Become Rich amidst Devastation: The Second Economy in Zaire', *African Affairs*, 82, 328, 1983, pp. 351–66.

MacGaffey, Wyatt, *Religion and Society in Central Africa: The BaKongo of Lower Zaire*, University of Chicago Press, 1986.

MacQueen, N., 'Peacekeeping by Attrition: The United Nations in Angola', *The Journal of Modern African Studies*, 36, 3, 1998, pp. 399–422.

MacQueen, Norrie, *The Decolonization of Portuguese Africa: Metropolitan Revolution and the Dissolution of Empire*, Longman, 1997.

Maier, K., *Angola: Promises and Lies*, Serif, 1996.

Maier, K., *This House Has Fallen: Nigeria in Crisis*, Allen Lane, 2001.

Maipose, G.S. and T.C. Matsheka, 'Botswana', in Benno J. Ndulu, et al, eds, *The Political Economy of Economic Growth in Africa, 1960–2000*, volume 2, 2008.

Mair, Lucy, 'New Elites in East and West Africa', in Turner, ed., *Colonialism in Africa*, vol. 3, *Profiles of Change: African Society and Colonial Rule*, Cambridge University Press, 1971.

Makhan, Vijay S., *Economic Recovery in Africa: The Paradox of Financial Flows*, Palgrave Macmillan, 2002.

Mamdani, M., *Citizen and Subject: Contemporary Africa and the Legacy of Late Colonialism*, Princeton University Press, 1996a.

Mamdani, M., 'From Conquest to Consent as the Basis of State Formation: Reflections on Rwanda', *New Left Review*, 1996b, 216, pp. 3–36 .

Mamdani, M., *When Victims Become Killers: Colonialism, Nativism and Genocide in Rwanda*, Princeton University Press, 2001.

Mann, K. and R. Roberts, eds, *Law in Colonial Africa*, Heinemann/James Currey, 1991.

Manning, C., 'Constructing Opposition in Mozambique', *Journal of Southern African Studies*, 24, 1, 1998, pp. 161–89.

Marcum, John, 'Angola: Twenty-five Years of War', *Current History*, 85, 111, May 1986, pp. 193–231.

Marcum, John, 'Angola: War Again', *Current History*, 92, 574, May 1993, pp. 218–33.

Marcum, John, *The Angolan Revolution: The Anatomy of an Explosion (1950–1962)*, MIT Press, 1969.

Marcum, John, *The Angolan Revolution: Volume II Exile Politics and Guerilla Warfare (1962–1976)*, MIT Press, 1978.

Martin, G., 'Continuity and Change in Franco-African Relations', *Journal of Modern African Studies*, 33, 1, March 1995, pp. 1–20.

Martin, G., 'The Historical, Economic and Political Bases of France's African Policy', *Journal of Modern African Studies*, 23, 2, June 1985, pp. 189–208 .

Martin, M., 'Neither Phoenix nor Icarus: Negotiating Economic Reform in Ghana and Zambia, 1983–1992', in Callaghy and Ravenhill, eds, *Hemmed In: Responses to Africa's Economic Decline*, Columbia University Press, 1993.

Martin, M.L., 'Armies and Politics: The 'Life Cycle' of Military Rule in Sub-Saharan Francophone Africa', in Kirk-Greene and Bach, *State and Society in Francophone Africa since Independence*, St Martins Press, 1995.

Marysse, Stefaan and F. Reyntjens, eds, *The Political Economy of the Great Lakes Region in Africa*, Palgrave, 2005.

Mbembe, Achille, *On the Postcolony*, University of California Press, 2001.

McGowan, Patrick J., 'Afican Military Coups d'état, 1956–2001: Frequency, Trends and Distribution', *Journal of Modern African Studies*, 41, 3, 2003, pp. 370–97.

McMahon, R.J., *Cold War on the Periphery: The United States, India and Pakistan*, Columbia University Press, 1994.

Mencher, Joan P., 'The Caste System Upside Down, or The Not-so-mysterious East', *Current Anthropology*, 15, 4, December 1974, pp. 469–93.

Menon, Nivedita and Aditya Nigam, *Power and Contestation: India since 1989*, Zed, 2007.

Meredith, Martin, *The State of Africa*, Free Press, 2005 .

Metcalf, B.D. and T.R. Metcalf, *A Concise History of India*, Cambridge University Press, 2002.

Metcalf, T.R., *Ideologies of the Raj: New Cambridge History of India*, Cambridge University Press, 1997.

Metcalf, T.R., 'Landlords without Land: The UP Zamindars Today', *Pacific Affairs*, 40, 1/2, 1967, pp. 5–18.

Miller, E.J., 'Village Structure in North Kerala', in Srinivas, ed., *India's Villages*, Asia, 1960.

Minter, W., *Apartheid's Contras: An Enquiry into the Roots of War in Angola and Mozambique*, Zed, 1994.

Mongia, Padmini, ed., *Contemporary Postcolonial Theory: A Reader*, Arnold, 1996.

Moore, R.J., 'Jinnah and the Pakistan Demand', *Modern Asian Studies*, 17, 4, 1983, pp. 529–61.

Morgan, G., 'Violence in Mozambique: Towards an Understanding of Renamo', *Journal of Modern African Studies*, 28, 4, 1990, pp. 603–19.

Morris, M.D., 'The Growth of Large-scale Industry to 1947', in Dharma Kumar with Meghnad Desai, eds, *The Cambridge Economic History of India, Volume 2: c. 1757–c. 1970*, Cambridge University Press, 1983.

Morris-Jones, W.H., 'Parliament and Dominant Party: Indian Experience', *Parliamentary Affairs*, 17, 1963, pp. 296–307.

Morris-Jones, W.H., *The Government and Politics of India*, 2nd edn, Hutchinson, 1967.

Mosley, P., 'Kenya in the 1970s: A Review Article', *African Affairs*, 81, 323, April 1982, pp. 217–77.

Mudimbe, V.Y., *The Invention of Africa: Gnosis, Philosophy and the Order of Knowledge*, James Currey, 1989.

Mugabe, Paul, affidavit for the Centre of Research on Globalisation: 'The Shooting Down of the Aircraft carrying Rwandan President', 2000, available at http://www.globalresearch.ca/articles/MUG109A.html.

Munro, J.Forbes, *Britain in Tropical Africa 1880–1960: Economic Relationships and Impact*, Macmillan, 1984.

Mutsinzi: Report of the Investigation into the Causes and Circumstances of and Responsibility for the attack of 6/04/1994 against the Falcon 50 Rwanda Presidential aeroplane, 2010, available at http://www.mutsinzireport.com.

Mwega, Francis M. and N.S. Ndung'u, 'Explaining African Economic Growth Performance: The Case of Kenya', in Ndulu *et al.*, eds, *The Political Economy of Economic Growth in Africa, 1960–2000*, vol. 2, Cambridge University Press, 2008.

Myrdal, G., *Asian Drama: An Inquiry into the Poverty of Nations*, 3 vols, Allen Lane, 1968.

Nandy, A. (Ashis), *The Intimate Enemy: Loss and Recovery of Self Under Colonialism*, Oxford University Press, 1983.

Nayar, Baldev Raj, 'Business Attitudes towards Economic Planning in India', *Asian Survey*, 11, 9, 1971, pp. 850–65.

Nayar, Baldev Raj, 'Political Structure and India's Economic Reforms of the 1990s', *Pacific Affairs*, 71, 3, 1998, pp. 335–58.

Nayyar, Deepak, 'Economic Development and Political Democracy: Interaction of Economics and Politics in Independent India', *Economic and Political Weekly*, 5 December 1998, pp. 3121–31.

Nayyar, Deepak, 'India's Unfinished Journey: Transforming Growth into Development', *Modern Asian Studies*, 40, 3, 2006, pp. 797–832.

Ndulu, Benno J., Stephen A. O'Connell, R.H. Bates, Paul Collier and Chukwuma C. Soludu, eds, *The Political Economy of Economic Growth in Africa, 1960–2000*, two volumes, Cambridge University Press, 2008.

Neale, W.C., *Economic Change in Rural India: Land Tenure and Reform in Uttar Pradesh, 1800–1955*, Yale University Press, 1962.

Nehru, Jawaharlal, *An Autobiography*, Bodley Head, 1936.

Nest, Michael, ed., *Democratic Republic of the Congo: Economic Dimensions of War and Peace*, Lynne Rienner, 2006.

Newbury, C., 'Ethnicity and the Politics of History in Rwanda', *Africa Today*, 45, 1, January–March 1998, pp. 7–24.

Newbury, C., 'States at War: Confronting Conflict in Africa', *African Studies Review*, 45, 2002, pp. 1–20.

Newbury, C., *The Cohesion of Oppression: Clientship and Ethnicity in Rwanda, 1860–1960*, Columbia University Press, 1988 .

Newbury, D., 'Precolonial Burundi and Rwanda: Local Loyalties, Regional Royalties', *International Journal of African Historical Studies*, 34, 2, 2001, pp. 255–314.

Newbury, D., 'Understanding Genocide', *African Studies Review*, 41, 1, 1998, pp. 73–97.

Newitt, Malyn, 'Mozambique', in Chabal *et al.*, *A History of Postcolonial Lusophone Africa*, 2002.

Newitt, Malyn, *Portugal in Africa*, Hurst, 1981.

Ngaruko, F., and J.D. Nkurunziza, 'An Economic Interpretation of Conflict in Burundi', *Journal of African Economies*, 9, 3, 2000, pp. 370–409.

Ngaruko, F. and J.D. Nkurunziza, 'Why has Burundi Grown So Slowly? The Political Economy of Redistribution', in Ndulu *et al.*, eds, *The Political Economy of Economic Growth in Africa, 1960–2000*, vol. 2, Cambridge University Press, 2008.

Nigerian National Planning Commission, *Meeting Everyone's Needs: National Economic Empowerment and Development Strategy*, Abuja, 2004.

Nkrumah, K., *Africa Must Unite*, International, 1963.

Noman, O., *The Political Economy of Pakistan, 1947–85*, Routledge and Kegan Paul, 1988.

Nugent, Paul, *Africa since Independence*, Palgrave/Macmillan, 2004.

Nugent, Paul, 'States and Social Contracts in Africa', *New Left Review*, 63, May–June 2010, pp. 35–68.

Nzongola-Ntalaja, Georges, *The Congo from Leopold to Kabila: A People's History*, Zed, 2002.

O'Brien, D., B. Cruise, J. Dunn and R. Rathbone, eds, *Contemporary West African States*, Cambridge University Press, 1989.

Ogbuagu, Chibuzo S.A., 'The Nigerian Indigenization Policy: Nationalism or Pragmatism?', *African Affairs*, 82, 327, April 1983, pp. 241–66.

Okonta, Ike, 'Nigeria: Chronicle of a Dying State', *Current History*, May 2005, pp. 203–8.

Oliver, R., 'The Nilotic Contribution to Bantu Africa', *Journal of African History*, 23, 4, 1982, pp. 433–42.

Oliver, R. and A. Atmore, *Africa since 1800*, 2nd edn, Cambridge University Press, 1972.

Osaghae, E.E., *Crippled Giant: Nigeria since Independence*, Hurst, 1998.

Othman, S. (Shehu Othman), 'Classes, Crises and Coup: The Demise of Shagari's Regime', *African Affairs*, 83, 333, October 1984, pp. 441–61.

Othman, S. (Shehu Othman), 'Nigeria: Power for Profit: Class, Corporatism, and Factionalism in the Military', in D. O'Brien, B. Cruise, J. Dunn and R. Rathbone, eds, *Contemporary West African States*, Cambridge University Press, 1989.

Ottoway, M., *Africa's New Leaders: Democracy or State Reconstruction?*, Carnegie Endowment for International Peace, 1999.

Palmer, N.D., 'Elections and the Political System in India: The State Assembly Elections and After', *Pacific Affairs*, 45, 4, Winter 1972–3, pp. 535–55.

Palmer, N.D., 'India in 1976: The Politics of Depoliticization', *Asian Survey*, 17, 2, February 1977a, pp. 160–80.

Palmer, N.D., 'The Two Elections: A Comparative Analysis' , *Asian Survey*, 17, 7, July 1977b, pp. 648–66.

Palmer, R., 'The Agricultural History of Rhodesia', in R. Palmer and N. Parsons, eds, *The Roots of Rural Poverty in Central and Southern Africa*, Heinemann, 1977.

Palmer, R. and N. Parsons, eds, *The Roots of Rural Poverty in Central and Southern Africa*, Heinemann, 1977.

Panter-Brick, K., ed., *Nigerian Politics and Military Rule: Prelude to the Civil War*, Athlone Press, 1970.

Panter-Brick, K., ed., *Soldiers and Oil: The Political Transformation of Nigeria*, Frank Cass, 1978.

Parekh, Bhiku, 'Caste Wars', *Times Higher Educational Supplement*, 1991,15, 2.

Park, R.L., 'Political Crisis in India', *Asian Survey*, xv, 11, November 1975, pp. 916–1013.

Park, R.L. and R.S. Wheeler, 'East Bengal under Governor's Rule', *Far Eastern Survey*, 29, 3, 1954, pp. 129–34.

Patel, I.G., 'On Taking India into the Twenty-first Century (New Economic Policy in India)', *Modern Asian Studies*, 21, 2, 1987, pp. 209–31.

Peel, J.D.Y., *Ijeshas and Nigerians: The Incorporation of a Yoruba Kingdom, 1890s–1970s*, Cambridge University Press, 1983.

Peel, J.D.Y., 'The Cultural Work of Yoruba Ethnogenesis', in Tonkin, McDonald and Chapman, eds, *History and Ethnicity*, Routledge, 1989.

Peemans, J. Ph., 'The Social and Economic Development of Zaire since Independence', *African Affairs*, 74, 295, 1975, pp. 148–79.

Phillips, Anne, *The Enigma of Colonialism: British Policy in West Africa*, James Currey, 1989.

Prakash, G., 'Subaltern Studies as Postcolonial Criticism', *American Historical Review*, 99, 5, December 1994, pp. 1475–90.

Prakash, G., ed., *After Colonialism: Imperial Histories and Postcolonial Displacements*, Princeton University Press, 1995.

Prunier, Gérard, *From Genocide to Continental War: The 'Congolese' Conflict and the Crisis of Contemporary Africa*, Hurst, 2009.

Prunier, Gérard, *The Rwandan Crisis: History of a Genocide*, extended edn, Hurst, 1997 (originally published 1995).

Rakner, L., *Political and Economic Liberalisation in Zambia*, Nordic Africa Institute, 2003.

Ranger, T., 'The Invention of Tradition in Colonial Africa', in E.J. Hobsbawn and T. Ranger, eds, *The Invention of Tradition*, Cambridge University Press, 1983.

Ranger, T. and O. Vaughan, eds, *Legitimacy and the State in Twentieth-century Africa: Essays in Honour of A.H.M. Kirk-Greene*, Macmillan, 1993.

Rapley, John, *Ivoirien Capitalism: African Entrepreneurs in Côte d'Ivoire*, Lynnne Rienner, 1993.

Rathbone, R., 'Ghana', in Dunn, ed., *West African States: Failure and Promise*, Cambridge University Press, 1978.

Rathbone, R., 'Kwame Nkrumah and the Chiefs: The Fate of 'Natural Rulers' Under Nationalist Governments', *Transactions of the Royal Historical Society*, 2000, pp. 45–63.

Ravenhill, J., ed., *Africa in Economic Crisis*, Macmillan, 1986.

Reno, W., *Warlord Politics and African States*, Lynne Rienner, 1998.

Review of African Political Economy, 45/46 Special Issue on Militarism, Warlords and the Problems of Democracy, 1989.

Reyntjens, F., 'A Fake Enquiry on a Major Event: Analysis of the Mutsinzi Report', University of Antwerp, Institute of Development Policy and Management, Working Paper 7, 2010.

Reyntjens, F., 'Briefing: Burundi: A Peaceful Transition after a Decade of War?', *African Affairs*, 105, 2005a, pp. 117–35.

Reyntjens, F., 'Briefing: The Second Congo War: More than a Remake', *African Affairs*, 98, 1999, pp. 241–50.

Reyntjens, F., *Burundi: Prospects for Peace*, Minority Rights Group International, 2000a.

Reyntjens, F., *L'Afrique des grands lacs en crise: Rwanda, Burundi, 1988–1994*, Karthala, 1994.

Reyntjens, F., 'Rwanda, Ten Years On: From Genocide to Dictatorship', *African Affairs*, 103, 2004, pp. 177–210.

Reyntjens, F., *Small States in an Unstable Region: Rwanda and Burundi, 1999–2000*, Nordiska Afrikainstitutet, 2000b, available at http://www.nai.uu.se/publications.

Reyntjens F., 'The Privatisation and Criminalisation of Public Space in the Geopolitics of the Great Lakes Region', *Journal of Modern African Studies*, 43, 4, 2005b, pp. 587–607.

Reyntjens, F., 'The Proof of the Pudding is in the Eating: The June 1993 Elections in Burundi', *Journal of Modern African Studies*, 31, 4, December 1993, pp. 563–83.

Rimmer, D., 'Adjustment Blues', *African Affairs*, 94, 374, January 1995, pp. 109–13.

Rimmer, D., ed., *Africa 30 Years On*, James Currey, 1991.

Rimmer, D., *Staying Poor: Ghana's Political Economy, 1950–1990*, Pergamon, 1992.

Rimmer, D., *The Economies of West Africa*, Weidenfeld and Nicolson, 1984.

Rimmer, D., 'The Elements of Political Economy', in Panter-Brick, ed., *Soldiers and Oil: The Political Transformation of Nigeria*, Frank Cass, 1978.

Rimmer, D. and A.M. Kirk-Greene, *Nigeria since 1970: A Political and Economic Outline*, Hodder and Stoughton, 1981.

Rood, L.L., 'Nationalisation and Indigenisation in Africa', *Journal of Modern African Studies*, 14, 1976, pp. 427–47.

Rothchild, D. and N. Chazan, eds, *The Precarious Balance: State and Society in Africa*, Westview, 1988.

Roy, Asim, 'The Politics of India's Partition: The Revisionist Perspective', *Modern Asian Studies*, 24, 2, April 1990, pp. 385–415.

Roy, S. (Srirupa), 'Instituting Diversity: Official Nationalism in Post-independence India', *South Asia*, 22, 1, 1999, pp. 79–100.

Roy, Tirthankar, 'A Delayed Revolution: Environment and Economic Change in India', *Oxford Review of Economic Policy*, 23, 2, 2007, pp. 239–50.

Roy, Tirthankar, 'Economic History and Modern India: Redefining the Link', *The Journal of Economic Perspectives*, 16, 3, 2002, pp. 109–30.

Roy, Tirthankar, *Rethinking Economic Change in India: Labour and Livelihood*, Routledge, 2005.

Roy, Tirthankar, *The Economic History of India 1857–1947*, Oxford University Press, 2000.

Rudolph, L.I. and S.H. Rudolph, *In Pursuit of Lakshmi: The Political Economy of the Indian State*, Chicago, 1987.

Rudolph, L.I. and S.H. Rudolph, 'Judicial Review versus Parliamentary Sovereignty: The Struggle over Stateness in India', *Journal of Commonwealth and Comparative Politics*, 19, 3, 1981, pp. 231–56.

Rudolph, L.I. and S.H. Rudolph, *The Modernity of Tradition: Political Development in India*, University of Chicago Press, 1967.

Ruzibiza, Abdul Joshua, *Rwanda: L'Histoire secrète*, éditions du Panama, 2005 (His account of the RPF's preparation of the attack on Habyarimana's plane is on pp. 248–52, which can be accessed on http://www.aidh.org/rwand/lire-ruzibiza1.htm).

Sachs, J.D. and A.M. Warner, 'The Curse of Natural Resources: Natural Resources and Economic Development', *European Economic Review*, 45, 2001, pp .827–38.

Sachs, J.D. and A.M. Warner, 'Sources of Slow Growth in African Economies', *Journal of African Economies*, 6, 3, 1997, pp. 335–76.

Said, Edward, *Orientalism*, Routledge & Kegan Paul, 1978.

Saint Jorre, J. de, *The Nigerian Civil War*, Hodder & Stoughton, 1972.

Samad, Y. (Yunus Samad), *A Nation in Turmoil: Nationalism and Ethnicity in Pakistan, 1937–1958*, Sage, 1995.

Sandbrook, R., *The Politics of Africa's Economic Recovery*, Cambridge University Press, 1993.

Sandbrook, R., *The Politics of Africa's Economic Stagnation*, Cambridge University Press, 1985.

Sarkar, Sunil, *Modern India, 1885–1947*, 2nd edn, Macmillan, 1989.

Saul, J.S., 'Rethinking the Frelimo State', *Socialist Register*, 1993, pp. 193–265.

Saul, J.S., 'Socialism in One Country: Tanzania', in G. Arrighi and J.S. Saul, *Essays on the Political Economy of Africa*, Monthly Review Press, 1973.

Schatz, S.P., 'Pirate Capitalism and the Inert Economy of Nigeria', *Journal of Modern African Studies*, 22, 1, March 1984, pp. 45–57.

Schatz, S.P., *Nigerian Capitalism*, University of California Press, 1977.

Schatzberg, M.G., '"Le mal zairois": Why Policy Fails in Zaire', *African Affairs*, 81, 324, 1982, pp. 337–448.

Schatzberg, M.G., 'Military Intervention and the Myth of Collective Security: The Case of Zaire', *Journal of Modern African Studies*, 2, 1989, pp. 315–40.

Schatzberg, M.G., *Mobutu or Chaos? The United States and Zaire, 1960–1990*, University Press of America, 1991.

Schatzberg, M.G., *The Dialectics of Oppression in Zaire*, Indiana University Press, 1988.

Schatzberg, M.G., 'The State and the Economy: The "Radicalization of the Revolution" in Mobutu's Zaire', *Canadian Journal of African Studies*, 14, 2, 1980, pp. 239–57.

Schendel, Willem van, *A History of Bangladesh*, Cambridge University Press, 2009.

Seal, Anil, *The Emergence of Indian Nationalism: Competition and Collaboration in The Later Nineteenth Century*, Cambridge University Press, 1968 .

Searle-Chatterjee, M. and U. Sharma, eds, *Contextualising Caste: Post Dumontian Approaches*, Blackwell / Sociological Review, 1994 .

Seeley, J.R., *The Expansion of England*, 1883, 2nd edn, Macmillan, 1900.

Seligman, C.G., *Races of Africa*, 2nd edn, Butterworth, 1939 .

Sen, Amartya Kumar and Jean Drèze, *India: Economic Development and Social Opportunity*, Oxford University Press, 1995.

Sen, Amartya Kumar, 'Indian Development: Lessons and Non-Lessons', *Daedalus*, 18, 4, Autumn 1989, pp. 369–92.

Sen, Amartya Kumar, *Poverty and Famines: An Essay on Entitlement and Deprivation*, Oxford University Press, 1981.

Shao, J., 'Politics and the Food Production Crisis in Tanzania', in Commins, Lofchie and Payne, eds, *Africa's Agrarian Crisis: The Roots of Famine*, Lynne Rienner, 1986.

Sherman, T.C., 'The Integration of the Princely State of Hyderabad, and the Making of the Postcolonial State in India, 1948–1956', *Indian Economic and Social History Review*, 44, 4, 2007, pp. 489–516.

Singh, I., *The Great Ascent: The Rural Poor in South Asia*, Johns Hopkins University Press, 1990.

Singh, Y., 'The Changing Pattern of Social Stratification in India', in Srinivas et al, eds, *Dimensions of Social Change in India*, 1977.

Sklar, R.L., 'Democracy in Africa', *African Studies Review*, 26, 3–4, 1983, pp. 11–24.

Sklar, R.L., 'The Nature of Class Domination in Africa', *Journal of Modern African Studies*, 17, 4, 1979, pp. 531–52.

Smith, B., 'Federal-State Relations in Nigeria', *African Affairs*, 80, 320, July 1981, pp. 355–78.

Southall, A., 'The Illusion of Tribe', *Journal of Asian and African Studies*, 5, 1–2, January–April 1970, pp. 28–50.

Soyinka, Wole, *The Open Sore of A Continent: A Personal Narrative of the Nigerian Crisis*, Oxford University Press, 1996.

Spivak, Gayatri, *A Critique of Postcolonial Reason: Towards a History of the Vanishing Present*, Harvard University Press, 1999.

Srinivas, M.N., 'Caste in Modern India', *Journal of Asian Studies*, 16, 4, August 1957, pp. 529–48.

Srinivas, M.N., *Caste in Modern India and Other Essays*, Asia, 1962.

Srinivas, M.N., ed., *India's Villages*, 1955, 2nd edn, Asia, 1960.

Srinivas, M.N., 'A Note on Sankritization and Westernization', *Far Eastern Quarterly*, 15, 4, August 1956, pp. 481–96.

Srinivas, M.N., *Social Change in Modern India*, Longman, 1966.

Srinivas, M.N., 'The Social Structure of a Mysore Village', in Srinivas, ed., *India's Villages*, 1960.

Srinivas, M.N., *The Remembered Village*, University of California Press, 1976.

Srinivas, M.N., S. Seshaiah and V.S. Parthasarathy, eds, *Dimensions of Social Change in India*, Allied, 1977.

Srinivasan, T.N. and P.K. Bardhan, eds, *Poverty and Income Distribution in India*, Statistical, 1974.

Srinivasan, T.N. and P.K. Bardhan, eds, *Rural Poverty in South Asia*, Columbia University Press, 1988.

Stengers, J., *Congo: Mythes et Réalités: cent ans d'histoire*, Duculot, 1989.

Stockwell, A.J., 'Malayasia: The Making of a Neocolony?', *Journal of Imperial and Commonwealth History*, 26, 1998, pp. 138–56.

Stockwell, S.E., 'Political Strategies of British Business during Decolonization: The Case of the Gold Coast/Ghana, 1945–57', , *Journal of Imperial and Commonwealth History*, 23, 1995, 2, pp. 277–300.

Suberu, Rotimi T., 'Nigeria's Muddled Elections', *Journal of Democracy*, 18, 4, 2007, pp. 95–110.

Sundarayya, P., 'Telangana People's Armed Struggle, 1946–51. Part One: Historical Setting', *Social Scientist*, 1, 7, February 1973, pp. 3–19.

Swainson, N., 'State and Economy in Post-Colonial Kenya, 1963–1978', *Canadian Journal of African Studies*, 12, 3, 1978, pp. 357–81.

Tabutin, D. and B. Schoumaker, 'The Demography of Sub-Saharan Africa from the 1950s to the 2000s: A Survey of Changes and a Statistical Assessment', *Population (English Edition, 2002)* 59, 3/4, 2004, pp. 457–556.

Talbot, Ian, *India and Pakistan*, Arnold, 2000.

Talbot, Ian, *Pakistan: A Modern History*, St Martin's Press, 1998.

Tangri, R., 'The Politics of Africa's Public and Private Enterprise', *Journal of Commonwealth and Comparative Politics*, 33, 2, 1995, pp. 169–84.

Teal, Francis, 'Domestic Policies, External Constraints and Economic Development in Nigeria since 1950', *African Affairs*, 87, 345, January 1988, pp. 69–81.

Tendulkar, S.D. and B. Sen, 'Markets and Long-term Economic Growth in South Asia 1950–97', in Ahluwalia and Williamson, eds, *The South Asian Experience with Growth*, Oxford University Press, 2003.

Tignor, R.L., *Capitalism and Nationalism at the End of Empire: State and Business in Decolonizing Egypt, Nigeria, and Kenya, 1943–1963*, Princeton University Press, 1998.

Tignor, R.L., 'Political Corruption in Nigeria before Independence', *Journal of Modern African Studies*, 31, 2, June 1993, pp. 175–202.

Tomlinson, B.R., *The Economy of Modern India 1860–1970* (NCHI, III.3), Cambridge University Press, 1993.

Tomlinson, B.R., 'The Historical Roots of Indian Poverty: Issues in the Economic and Social History of South Asia', *Modern Asian Studies*, 22, 1, 1988, pp. 123–40.

Tomlinson, B.R., *The Political Economy of the Raj: The Economics of Decolonization in India, 1919–1947*, Macmillan, 1979.

Tonkin, E., M. McDonald and M. Chapman, eds, *History and Ethnicity*, Routledge, 1989.

Tull, D.M., 'China's Engagement in Africa: Scope, Significance and Consequences', *Journal of Modern African Studies*, 44, 3, 2006, pp. 459–79.

Turner, Victor, ed., *Colonialism in Africa*, vol. 3, *Profiles of Change: African Society and Colonial Rule*, Cambridge University Press, 1971.

Uganda Record: 'Paul Kagame Ordered the Assassination of Habyarimana', 28 April 2010, accessible on http://freeuganda.com/?p=429.

United Nations Development Programme, *Human Development Report 2007/2008*, Palgrave Macmillan for the UNDP, 2007.

Urquart, B., review of Ludo De Witte's *Assassination of Lumumba*, *New York Review of Books*, 48, 15, 4 October 2001.

Uvin, Peter, 'Ethnicity and Power in Burundi and Rwanda: Different Paths to Mass Violence', *Comparative Politics*, 31, 3, April 1999, pp. 253–71.

Vaidyanathan, A., 'The Indian Economy since Independence (1947–70)', in Dharma Kumar with Meghnad Desai, eds, *The Cambridge Economic History of India, Volume 2: c. 1757–c. 1970*, Cambridge University Press, 1983.

Vail, L., ed., *The Creation of Tribalism in Southern Africa*, James Currey, 1989.

Vansina, Jan, *Paths in the Rainforest: Toward a History of Political Tradition in Equatorial Africa*, University of Wisonsin Press, 1990.

Vaughan, Olufemi, 'Decolonisation and Legitimation in Nigeria', in Ranger and Vaughan, eds, *Legitimacy and the State in Twentieth-Century Africa: Essays in Honour of A.H.M. Kirk-Greene*, Macmillan, 1993.

Vaughan, O. and T. Ranger, eds, *Legitimacy and the State in Twentieth-Century Africa: Essays in Honour of A.H.M. Kirk-Greene*, Macmillan, 1993.

Veen, Roel van der, *What Went Wrong with Africa? A Contemporary History*, KIT, 2004.

Velkoff, V.A. and P.R. Kowal, *Population Aging in Sub-Saharan Africa: Demographic Dimensions 2006*, U.S. Census Bureau, Current Population Reports, P95/07-1, Government Printing Office, Washington, 2007.

Vidal, C., 'Situations ethniques au Rwanda', in Amselle and M'bokolo, eds, *Au coeur de l'ethnie. Ethnies, tribalisme et états en Afrique*, éditions de la découverte, 1985.

Vines, A., *Remano: Terrorism in Mozambique*, James Currey, 1991.

Visaria, Leela and Pravin Visaria, 'Population', in Dharma Kumar with Meghnad Desai, eds, *The Cambridge Economic History of India, Volume 2: c. 1757–c. 1970*, Cambridge University Press, 1983.

Wade, Robert, 'The Market for Public Office: Why the Indian State Is Not Better at Development', *World Development*, 13, 4, April 1985, pp. 467–97.

Walle, N. van de, *African Economies and the Politics of Permanent Crisis, 1979–1999*, Cambridge University Press, 2001.

Walle, N. van de, 'The Decline of the Franc Zone; Monetary Politics in Francophone Africa', *African Affairs*, 90, 1991, pp. 383–405.

Wallerstein, Immanuel, *The Modern World-system*, 3 vols, Academic Press, 1974, 1979, 1988.

Washbrook, D.A., 'Caste, Class and Dominance in Modern Tamil Nadu: Non-Brahmanism, Dravidianism and Tamil Nationalism', in F.R. Frankel and M.S.A. Rao, eds, *Dominance and State Power in Modern India: Decline of a Social Order*, vol. 1, Oxford University Press, 1989.

Washbrook, D.A., 'Law, State and Agrarian Society in Colonial India', *Modern Asian Studies*, 15, 1981, pp. 649–721.

Waters, T., 'Tutsi Social Identity in Contempory Africa', *Journal of Modern African Studies*, 33, 2, 1995, pp. 343–47.

Weinbaum, M.G., 'Pakistan: misplaced priorities, missed opportunities', in Harrison, Kreisberg and Kux, eds, *India and Pakistan: The First Fifty Years*, Cambridge University Press, 1999.

Weinbaum, M.G., 'The March 1977 Elections in Pakistan: Where Everyone Lost', *Asian Survey*, 17, 7, July 1977, pp. 599–618.

Weiner, Myron, 'The Parliamentary Elections in India', *Asian Survey*, 17, 7, July 1977, pp. 619–26.

Weiner, Myron, *Party Building in a New Nation: The Indian National Congress*, University of Chicago Press, 1967.

Weiss, Herbert F., 'Voting for Change in the DRC', *Journal of Democracy*, 18, 2, 2007, pp. 138–51.

Werbner, R. and Terence Ranger, eds, *Postcolonial Identities in Africa*, Zed, 1996.

Westad, Odd Arne, *The Global Cold War: Third World Interventions and the Making of Our Times*, Cambridge University Press, 2007.

Wheeler, Richard S., 'Governor General's Rule in Pakistan', *Far Eastern Survey*, 24, 1, 1955, p. 5.

Whitaker, C.S., *The Politics of Tradition: Continuity and Change in Northern Nigeria, 1946–1966*, Princeton University Press, 1970.

White, N.J., 'The Beginnings of Crony Capitalism: Business, Politics and Economic Development in Malaysia, c. 1955–70', *Modern Asian Studies*, 38, 2, 2004, pp. 389–417.

White, N.J., 'The Business and Politics of Decolonization: The British Experience in the Twentieth Century', *Economic History Review*, 53, 3, 2000, pp. 544–64.

Wilcox, Wayne A., 'The Pakistan Coup of 1958', *Pacific Affairs*, 38, 2, 1965, pp. 142–63.

Williams, Gavin and Terisa Turner, 'Nigeria', in Dunn, ed., *West African States: Failure and Promise*, Cambridge University Press, 1978.

Willink Report, *Nigeria: Report of the Commission appointed to enquire into the fears of Minorities and the means of allaying them*, Cmnd. 505, PP 1957–8, vol. IX.

Wilson, H., *The Labour Government, 1964–70: A Personal Record*, Weidenfeld & Nicolson, 1971.

Wilson, K.B., 'Cults of Violence and Counter-violence in Mozambique', *Journal of Southern African Studies*, 18, 3, September 1992, pp. 527–82.

Witte, Ludo de, *The Assassination of Lumumba*, Verso, 2001.

Wood, J.R., 'Extra-parliamentary Opposition in India: An Analysis of Populist Agitations in Gujarat and Bihar', *Pacific Affairs*, 48, 3, 1975, pp. 313–34.

World Bank, *Accelerated Development in Sub-Saharan Africa: An Agenda for Action* ['The Berg Report'], World Bank, 1981.

World Bank, *Adjustment in Africa: Reform, Results and the Road Ahead*, Oxford University Press, 1994.

World Bank, *Africa Development Indicators*, World Bank, 2009.

World Bank, *Can Africa Claim the 21st Century?* World Bank, 2000.

World Bank, *Global Purchasing Power and Real Expenditures: 2005 International Comparison Program*, World Bank, 2008a.

World Bank, *Social Indicators of Development*, World Bank, 1995.

World Bank, *Sub-Saharan Africa: From Crisis to Sustainable Growth*, World Bank, 1989.

World Bank, *The World Bank's Commitment to HIV/Aids in Africa*, World Bank, 2008b.

World Bank, *World Development Indicators*, various years. (This data bank is regularly updated and can be accessed online.)

World Bank, *World Development Report*, World Bank, 1983 onwards.

World Bank, *World Tables*, Johns Hopkins University Press, various years [publication dates for the volumes I used are 1976 and 1991].

World Bank, *Zaire: Current Economic Situation and Constraints*, World Bank, 1980.

Woronoff, J., *West African Wager : Houphouët versus Nkrumah*, Scarecrow Press, 1972.

Young, Crawford, *Ideology and Development in Africa*, Yale University Press, 1982a.

Young, Crawford, 'Patterns of Social Conflict: State, Class and Ethnicity', *Daedalus*, 111, 2, Spring 1982b, pp. 71–98.

Young, Crawford, *Politics in the Congo: Decolonization and Independence*, Princeton University Press, 1965.

Young, Crawford, 'Post-Independence Politics in the Congo', *Transition*, 26, 1966, pp. 34–41.

Young, Crawford, *The African Colonial state in Comparative Perspective*, Yale University Press, 1994a.

Young, Crawford, 'The End of the Post-colonial State in Africa? Reflections on Changing African Political Dynamics', *African Affairs*, 103, 410, January 2004, pp. 23–50.

Young, Crawford, 'The Northern Republics, 1960–1980', in Birmingham and Martin, eds, *History of Central Africa*, vol. 2, Longman, 1983.

Young, Crawford, *The Politics of Cultural Pluralism*, University of Wisconsin Press, 1976.

Young, Crawford, ed., *The Rising Tide of Cultural Pluralism: The Nation State at Bay?*, Maddison, 1993.

Young, Crawford, 'The Third Wave of Democratization in Africa: Ambiguities and Contradictions', in Joseph, ed., *State, Conflict and Democracy in Africa*, Lynne Rienner, 1999.

Young, Crawford, 'Zaire: The Anatomy of a Failed State', in Birmingham and Martin, eds, *History of Central Africa: The Contemporary Years since 1960*, Longman, 1998.

Young, Crawford, 'Zaire: The Shattered Illusion of the Integral State', *Journal of Modern African Studies*, 32, 2, 1994b, pp. 247–64.

Young, Crawford, 'Zaire: The Unending Crisis', *Foreign Affairs*, 57, 1, 1978, pp. 169–85.

Young, Crawford and Thomas Turner, *The Rise and Decline of the Zairean State*, University of Wisconsin Press, 1985.

Young, R.J.C., *Postcolonialism: A Very Short Introduction*, Oxford University Press, 2003.

Young, R.J.C., *Postcolonialism: An Historical Introduction*, Blackwell, 2001.

Ziring, Lawrence, 'Pakistan: The Campaign before the Storm', *Asian Survey*, 17, 7, July 1977, pp. 581–98.

Ziring, Lawrence, 'From Islamic Republic to Islamic State in Pakistan', *Asian Survey*, 24, 9, September 1984, pp. 931–46.

Ziring, Lawrence, *Pakistan: At the Crosscurrent of History*, One World, 2003.

Zolberg, A.R., *Creating Political Order: The Party-States of West Africa*, Rand McNally, 1966.

Zolberg, A.R., *One-party Government in the Ivory Coast*, Princeton University Press, 1964.

Index

Abacha, General Sani (Nigerian Head
    of State), 227, 300, 312–13, 408
Abdullah, Sheik, 47, 48
Abiola, Chief Moshood, 312
Abuja (Nigerian Federal Capital), 280
Aburi conference (January 1967),
    265–6
*Accelerated Development in Sub-Saharan
    Africa* ('the Berg Report'), 217
Acheampong, Colonel (Ghanaian
    Head of State), 216
Action Group (AG), 231–2, 258–61
    264, 295
Adamtee jute mills, 74
Adivasis (Scheduled Tribes), 152
*Adjustment in Africa: Reform, Results
    and the Road Ahead*, 218
Adoula, Cyrille (Prime Minister of the
    DRC), 238, 246, 249
Afghanistan, 40, 50, 104, 292
Africa, sub-Saharan, 1–6, 9–13, 15–17,
    19–20, 24–33, 35–7, 39–41,
    Chapter 4 *passim*; subsistence
    agriculture in, 3, 10–11,13, 23;
    cash crops in colonial Africa, 11,
    12; European partition ('the
    scramble'), 17; colonial impact
    on, 19–20, 24–9, 212; 'second
    colonial occupation', 20;
    'tribalisation' of African societies
    under colonialism, 28; life
    expectancy and age structure, 5,
    10, 181–2, 316, 411; European
    settlers in, 19, 26; proportion
    living below poverty line in 2005,
    31; literacy, 181; institution of
    'one-party' states, 185–6; military
    coups, 186, 196–7, 214;
    commodity exports in 1960s and
    70s, 187–8; African states and
    African capitalism, 183;
    manufacturing in the 1960s and
    70s, 189; 'second decolonisation'
    of the late 1960s, early 70s, 189;
    installation of Marxist-Leninist
    regimes, 190; public expenditure
    and the public sector, 190–2;
de-industrialisation and economic
    regression in the 1980s, 194;
    falling investment ratios in the
    1980s, 194; proportion of
    population living on less than $1
    a day, 194; falling prices for
    commodity exports, 195; Africa's
    share of world trade and
    investment, 188, 195; impact of
    the Cold War on Africa, 193;
    democratic 'wave' of 1989–94 and
    restoration of multi-party politics,
    196–8, 324; agricultural
    stagnation, declining food
    production and famine, 202–3;
    'crony statism' and 'the politics of
    the belly', 208, 214–15; structural
    adjustment in, 39, 208, 216–22;
    primary school enrolment, 181,
    221; spending on health and
    education in late 1990s, 221–2;
    ethnicity in Africa, 41, 212–4,
    231, 294–5, 297, 321–2, 339–40,
    351, 356; 'tribalism', 321–2
Africa's 'First World War', 199
African Affairs, 223
African Economic Research
    Consortium (AERC), 183–4
African Union, 353
Afro-Marxism, 41, 183, 190, 197, 210,
    248, 361, 371, 373
Ahirs, 161
Ahmadu Bello University, 298
Ahmedabad, 52
Ajaokuta steel mill (Nigeria), 278
Ajayi, Jacob, 25, 355
Akali Dal (Sikh autonomy movement),
    80–2
Ake, Claude, 214, 299
Akintola, Chief Samuel (Regional
    Premier of Western Nigeria),
    259–61
Alavi, Hamza, 50
aldeamentos (fortified villages), 367
All India Congress Committee, 109
Allahabad Court, 126
Allende, President, 126

Alliance des Bakongo (Abako), 237
Alliance des forces démocratiques
pour la Libération du Congo,
313
All-India Muslim League, 43–5, 71, 73,
400; League's 'Pakistan' resolution
of 23 March 1940, 44, 94
Alves, Nito, 373
Alvor accord (1975), 370
Ambedkar, B.R., 148–9
ANC (African National Congress), 379,
381, 386
Andhras, 79
Andropov, Y., 193
Angola, 3, 12, 41, 182, 193, 199, 200,
201, 204, 210, 246, 249, 289–91,
359–75, 378–85, 387–99, 406–7,
410–12; Portuguese colonialism
in, 361–4; school attendance in
colonial Angola, 362; Portuguese
immigration, 363, 366, 403; rival
nationalist movements and the
nationalist insurgency, 364–6;
economic development in the
1960s, early 1970s, 366; fall of the
Portuguese regime and the war of
liberation, 369–72; installation of
a one-party Marxist state,
373–5; oil industry and oil
revenues, 374, 384, 390, 393, 396;
foreign-sponsored terrorism and
civil war, 377–8, 381–4; aborted
peace process and the 1992
elections, 388–91; resumption of
civil war, 391–3; dismantling the
one-party state, 378, 388–9; social
polarisation in the late 1990s,
early 2000s, 397–8
Anstee, Margaret, 389–92
anti-Brahminism/non-Brahminism,
153, 162, 164
Argatala conspiracy case, 94
Armed Forces Movement (Portuguese),
368
Armed Forces Ruling Council
(Nigeria), 302
Armée nationale congolaise (ANC),
245, 248–9
Arusha Accords (1993), 345, 348, 350
Arusha Declaration (1967), 189
Asante, 26, 179
Asians in East Africa, 16–17, 35, 190,
224
Assam, 46, 69

assimilado status (in Portuguese
colonial Africa), 362–3
Association des évolués (Belgian
Congo), 228
Association for a Better Nigeria, 312
Association pour la Promotion Sociale
de la Masse, 331
Astrida College, Butare, 357
Awami Muslim League/Awami League,
73, 94–6
Awolowo, Chief Obafemi (Regional
Premier of Western Nigeria),
231–3, 259, 264, 266, 293, 295–6
Ayub Khan, General (President of
Pakistan), 40, 50, 72, 77–8, 83-6,
89–93, 104; becomes C-in-C of
Pakistan army, 50; chief martial
law administrator, 77; introduces
1962 Constitution and assumes
presidency, 84; fall of his regime,
91–2
Azad ('Free') Kashmir, 48, 97
Azikiwe, Nnamdi (President of
Nigeria), 231–3, 255, 261, 295

Babangida, General Ibrahim (Nigerian
Head of State), 209, 227, 302,
308–9, 311–12
Backward Classes Commissions
(India), (first, 1955), 152, 170;
State Commission in Bihar,
171–2; (second national
Commission, 1979), 175–6;
see also Mandal *and*
'Mandalisation'
Baganda, the, 30, 179, 224
Bagaza, Jean-Baptiste, 337
Bagosora, Colonel Théoneste, 349–50
Bahutu Manifesto, 330–1
Bailundu, 362, 392
Bakongo, the, 179, 237, 239–40,
362–4, 367, 370
Balewa, Sir Abubakar (Nigerian Federal
Prime Minister), 261
Baluba, the, 238, 242, 244, 246
Balubakat, 242
Baluchistan, 51, 77, 92
Bambundu, 247–8
Bangala, the, 238
Bangladesh, 1, 2, 31, 43, 76, 93, 96–7,
101, 104, 271, 316, 408, 411;
secedes from Pakistan, 93–7; life
expectancy and infant mortality
in, 316, 411

banias, 45
Bantustans, 382
Banyaruguru, 333, 336
Bapende, the, 247–8
Baptism in Angola, 363–4
Bates, Robert, 206
Batetela, the, 239
Bayart, Jean-François, 9, 25, 180, 211, 324, 360
Bayly, Susan, 146
Beijing, 61, 365
Beira, 378
Beissinger, Mark, 25
Belgian Africa/Belgian Congo, 28, 228, 233–9, 364, 366, 402, 407; late colonial economy, 233–5; primary school enrolment, 235; adult literacy, 235; social disciplining under colonialism, 235; European presence, 236
Belgian mandate in Rwanda and Burundi, 324, 329, 403; end of mandate, 331–4
Belgian-Congolese Round Table Conference (1960), 236, 238, 252
Belgian-Congolese Treaty of Friendship and Cooperation, 241
Belgium, 228, 234, 236–8, 240–1, 243, 245, 288–90, 292
Bello, Ahmadu (*Sardauna* of Sokoto, Regional Prime Minister of Northern Nigeria) 229, 256, 263, 402
Bemba, Jean-Pierre (Vice-President of the DRC), 318–19
Bengal, 1, 2, 15, 20; Bengal famine (1943), 405 (*see also* East Bengal *and* West Bengal)
Bengali/Bengali language movement, 2, 46, 72–3, 75, 99
Benguela/Benguela railway, 291, 363
Benin, 186, 190, 197, 310; Sovereign National Conference (1990), 197
Benue-Plateau state (Nigeria), 281
Berman, Bruce, 25, 216
Béteille, André, 157–8, 161
Beye, Alioune, 392
Bhumihars, 161, 168–9, 172–4
Bhutto, Zulfikar Ali, (Prime Minister of Pakistan), 40, 91, 94, 96, 98, 101–3; appointed President, 98; and 1977 Elections, 101–3; trial and execution, 103

Biafra, 227, 255, 264–9 (*see also* Eastern Region of Nigeria)
Bicesse accords (1991), 389
'Big man' syndrome in Africa, 211
Biha, Léopold, 335
Bihar, 15, 44, 46, 65, 66, 67, 102, 106, 126, 135, 136, 153, 158, 161, 167–73, 175, 410, 411
Biya, Paul, (President of Cameroon), 198
Bizimungu, Pasteur (President of Rwanda), 354
Blumenthal, Edwin, 292
Bokassa, Jean-Bedel, ('Emperor' of the Central African Empire), 272, 408
Bombay Plan, 107–8
Bombay province, 15, 79–80
Bombay (now Mumbai), 24, 44, 52, 151
Bongo, Omar, (President of Gabon), 198
Botha, P.W., (South African President), 379
Botswana, 181, 188, 224, 314
Boutros-Ghali, Boutros (UN General Secretary), 392
Brahmarishi Sena, 174
Brahmin (priestly archetype)/Brahminism, 146, 150–1, 153, 155, 158, 161–6, 168, 172, 176–7
Brazil, 129, 136, 363
Brazzaville, 248, 305
Brezhnev, L., 193
Britain, 2, 18, 20, 22, 33, 48, 187, 201, 267–8, 326, 400, 405; Labour Government, 1964–70, 268
British Aerospace, 298
British East Africa, 16 (*see also* Kenya, Uganda *and* Tanganyika)
British Raj in India, 21, 22, 43, 54, 57, 59, 106, 139, 142, 154; military costs of, 22
British West Africa, 17, 26 (*see also* Gold Coast, Nigeria *and* Sierra Leone)
Brittain, Victoria, 396
Bruguière, J-L., 349
Brussels, 236, 238, 241, 243, 288
Buganda, 13, 30
Buhari, Major-General Muhammadu, (Nigerian Head of State), 300–2, 408
Bujumbura, 338, 346–7

'Bula matari' ('smasher of rocks'), 28, 272

Burkina Faso, 183, 186,

Burkinabe, 210

Burma, 99

Burundi, 41, 200, 248, 305, 323–8, 332–9, 342, 344–7, 350–3, 355–7, 403; colonial impact on ethnic identities, 328, 334–5; Economic and Customs Union with Rwanda, 333; attempted Hutu coup and overthrow of the monarchy, 1966, 336; installation of Tutsi dictatorship and ethnic apartheid, 336–7; partial genocide of Hutu in 1972, 336–7; liberalisation under Buyoya, 337; new Constitution of 1992, 338; elections of 1993, 338; assassination of Ndadaye and aborted democratic transition, 345–6; 'creeping coup' and overturning of 1992 Constitution, 345–6 ; civil war, 347; 2005 elections, 352

Bush Senior Administration, 291, 383

Buyoya, Major Pierre (President of Burundi), 337–8, 347

Cabinda enclave/oil fields, 367, 370

Cabora Bassa dam, 368

Caisse de Stabilisation (Côte d'Ivoire), 191

Callaghy, Thomas, 215–16, 275

Cameroon, 29, 198, 206, 297

Carter Administration, 290–2, 377

Cassinga iron mines, 366

caste in India, 41, 43, 45, 56, 58, 63–4, 80, 109, 111, 140–1, 143, Chapter 3 *passim*; 'anti-caste' provisions of the Constitution, 56, 145, 147–9, 152, 160, 163; caste and the Congress system, 63–4, 156–8; positive discrimination and reservations policies, 147–9, 152, 163–4, 167, 169–73, 175–6, 178; 'caste wars' in Bihar, 161, 167, 174; anti-Brahminism and Dravidian consciousness in Tamil Nadu, 162–6

caste *senas*, 174

casteism, 41

Castro, Fidel, 371

Catholicism/the Catholic Church in Rwanda, Burundi and Congo-Zaire, 235, 328, 330

Center for Strategic and International Studies (US), 383

Central African Federation, 30

Central African Republic, 183, 200

CFA franc/African franc zone, 187, 189–90, 196, 207, 209, 217; devaluation in1994, 209

Chabal, Patrick, 393

Chad, 182, 199–200, 223

Chandra, Bipan, 21

Chatterjee, Partha, 8, 9

Chevron (oil corporation), 383

Chibber, Vivek, 108

Chiluba, Frederick (President of Zambia), 5, 6

China, Communist, 32, 91, 116, 122, 137–8, 165, 201–2, 246–7, 290, 382–3

Chinese–African trade, 201

Chissano, Joaquim (President of Mozambique), 385–8, 395

Chokwe, the, 370

Christina, Orlando, 380

Church of Christ in the Bush, 384

Clark Amendment, 372

Clinton Administration, 391

Coalition for the Defence of the Republic (Rwanda), 341, 348

Cold War, the, 41, 42, 72, 193, 196, 227, 243, 268, 292, 370, 374, 378–9, 382, 388, 399, 401

College of Commissioners (DRC), 245

Collier, Paul, 322

colonialism, modern, 17–21

'colony', changing meaning of the term in later nineteenth century, 17

Comité special du Katanga (CSK), 234

Commission for Africa, 5, 202, 409

Commissioner of Political Affairs (DRC), 255

Commonwealth, the, 111, 267, 304, 401

Communist Party of India, 60, 61, 126, 128; splits into pro-Soviet and pro-Chinese parties, 64

Confédération des Associations Tribales du Katanga (Conakat), 237–8, 241–2

Congo-Brazzaville, 190, 305

Congolese Rally for Democracy, 200

Congo-Zaire, 15, 41, 182, 186, 188–9, 192, 196, 198–9, 200–1, 207, 226, 238–55, 307, 271, 273–5, 283, 285–93, 303–7, 309, 313–14, 317–18, 355, 411; independence constitution, 238; First Republic, 1960–1967, 240–54; 336; population figures, 226; ethnic divisions, 238, 242, 247; secession of Katanga and South Kasai, 241–2; demand for 'second independence' and civil war, 247–8; Mobutu's coup of 1965, 250; fall in marketed agricultural output, 251; terms of trade for mineral exports, 252; monetary reform, 1967, 252; state ownership of the modern economy, 254; decline of agriculture, 254; 1967 Constitution, 272; 'Mobutuism' and cult of Mobutu's personality, 274; 1974 Constitution, 274; state ownership of the modern economy, 275; 'Zairianisation' and the 'radicalisation of the revolution', 286–91; 1977 elections, 292; informal economy, 293, 303; termination of US aid, 1990–1, 304; structural adjustment under IMF auspices, 305–6; hyperinflation, 304, 306–7; primary school enrolment, 307; end of one-party state, 310; fall of Mobutu, 313; life expectancy and infant mortality in DRC compared with Bangladesh, 316, 411
Congregationalism in Angola, 363, 384
Congress (O), 68, 171
Congress (R), 68–9, 171
Congress Forum for Socialist Action, 122
Congress National Planning Committee, 107
Congress Raj, 22, 59, 62, 139
Conseil national pour la défense de la démocratie (CNDD – Burundi), 347, 352
Convention People's Party (CPP) (Gold Coast/Ghana), 179, 185–6, 259
Corrupt Practices Investigation Bureau (Nigeria), 282

Côte d'Ivoire, 13, 32, 181–3, 185, 187, 189, 191, 193–4, 197, 205–6, 209–11, 221, 267, 343 ; Ivorian 'economic miracle', 184, 191; inward migration, 191, 210; declining investment after 1980, 194; coups of 1999 and 2002, and onset of civil war, 197
Council of Islamic Ideology (Pakistan), 103
Council on Foreign Relations (US), 383
creoles in Angola, 363
Cuba/Cuban intervention in Africa, 193, 290–1, 304, 371–2, 374, 381, 383–4, 388
Cuito Cuanavale, battle of, 383
Curzon, Lord, 1

D'Aspremont Lynden, Harold (Belgian African Affairs Minister), 245
Dahomey, 26
Dalits, 128, 149, 159, 163, 166, 172–3 (*see also* 'untouchables')
Dar es Salaam, 365
Dasgupta, Partha, 410
De Heusch, Luc, 332
De Klerk, F.W., (South African President), 386
Delhi/New Delhi, 42, 47, 60, 69, 83, 102
Democratic Republic of the Congo (DRC), *see* Congo-Zaire
'dependency' school, 21
Depressed Classes Federation, 148
Des Forges, Alison, 323, 325
Desai, Morarji, (Prime Minister of India, 1977–1980) 65, 67, 122, 172, 175
Devanagari script, 78
'development of underdevelopment', 20, 21
Dhaka, 73, 96–7
Dhar, D.P. (Indian Planning Minister), 125
Dhlakama, Alfonso, 379–80, 387–8, 393
Dike, Kenneth, 213
Dirks, Nicholas, 146
Distributable Pool Account (Nigeria), 266
Dos Santos, Eduardo (President of Angola), 388, 390, 397
Dowden, Richard, 320

Dravida Kazagham, 164
Dravida Munetra Kazagham (DMK), 64, 164–6
Dravidian ethnic nationalism/autonomy movement, 162–6
Dravidian south of India, 79, 153–4
Dulles, John Foster (US Secretary of State), 77–8

East Africa Royal Commission, 13–14, 37
East Africa, pre-colonial, 26
East Bengal Assembly, 73–4
East Bengal, 2, 52–4, 72–3, 87, 97 (*see also* East Pakistan *and* Bangladesh)
East Central State (Nigeria), 269
East Pakistan, 2, 43, 46, 50, 72–3, 77, 86–9, 93–5, 125; Hindu minority in, 46 (*see also* East Bengal *and* Bangladesh)
Easterley, William, 322
Eastern Region of Nigeria, 231–3, 255, 258, 265–7
Economic Stabilisation Act (Nigeria, 1982), 300
Eduardo dos Santos Foundation, 397
Eisenhower administration, 243–4
Ekeh, Peter, 213, 322
Elisabethville (Lubumbashi), 241, 243
Emergency in India, 1975–7, 2, 40, 42, 58, 70, 101, 126–8, 172
English language in India, 79–80
Equatorial Guinea, 30
Erati district (Mozambique), 376
Eritrea, 1–2, 199, 223, 401
Ethiopia, 2, 190, 193, 196, 199, 291
ethnicity (*see under* Africa, Congo-Zaire *and* Nigeria)
EU Observation Mission (Nigerian elections of 2007), 317
European Common Market, 253, 339
European Economic Community (EEC), 187, 368
évolués, 9, 228, 236, 247

Fazlul Huq, A.K. (Chief Minister of East Pakistan), 73–4
Federal Germany, 89
Federation of French West Africa, 256
Federation of Indian Chambers of Commerce and Industry, 107
Fernandes, Evo, 380

Festival of Black Arts and Culture (Lagos, 1977), 271
FNLA (Front for the National Liberation of Angola), 291, 364, 366, 369–72, 390
Force Armée Zaïroise, 289
Force Publique (Belgian Congo, DRC), 240
Foreign aid to Mozambique, 394
Foreign Exchange Regulation Act (India), 122
franc zone, 3
France/Overseas France, 3, 12, 55, 186–7, 201, 217, 268, 290–2, 349, 382, 411
Francophone Africa, 3, 9, 19, 186–7, 196–7, 207, 209, 291
Frankel, Francine, 11, 40, 139–40, 172
FRELIMO (Front for the Liberation of Mozambique), 210, 360–1, 365–70, 372–3, 375–81, 385–8, 393–5, 399
French colonial Africa, 28
French Union, 29
Front Démocratique du Burundi (FRODEBU), 338, 345–7, 352
Front for the National Liberation of Angola (FNLA), 291, 364, 366, 370–2, 390
Front National pour la Libération du Congo, 289

Gabon, 32, 198, 267
Gandhi, Mohandas, 12, 109, 148–50, 164, 169, 182, 400
Gandhi, Mrs Indira (Prime Minister of India), 2, 40, 57, 59, 62, 65, 67–70, 83, 97, 101–2, 105, 120, 120–4, 126–8, 132, 135, 143, 171–2; and Congress 'split', 62, 65–8; call to *garibi hatao!* (abolish poverty) and the 1971 Elections, 68–9; imposes state of emergency, 70, 126–8; orders the storming of the Golden Temple, 82; and 1977 Elections, 101–2
Gandhi, Rajiv (Prime Minister of India), 39, 175
Gandhi, Sanjay, 70, 102, 124,
Ganwa dynasty (Burundi), 328, 333, 336; overthrown, 336
Gatabazi, Félicien, 348–9
GATT, 187

Gécamines (Générale Congolaise des Minérais), 253, 273, 305–6
Geffray, Christian, 376
General Motors, 254
General Peace Agreement (Mozambique, 1992), 387
Geneva protocol (1988), 384
genocide, in Burundi (1972), 323, 336–7, 353; in Rwanda (1994), 199, 323,
German East Africa, 328
Gersony, Robert, 351
Ghana, 10, 11, 13, 15, 16, 33–4, 182, 186, 189, 191–2, 204–7, 209, 216, 219–21, 259, 265; economic regression in compared with Malaysia, 33–4; state-led industrialisation under Nkrumah, 182; becomes one-party state, 185–6; structural adjustment under Rawlings, 219–20 (*see also* Gold Coast)
Ghulam Mohammed, (Governor General of Pakistan), 71, 74–5
Giscard d'Estaing, President Valery, 291
Gizenga, Antoine (Prime Minister of the DRC), 244–6, 310, 319
GlobeScan, 5, 6
Goa (Portuguese), 20
Gold Coast, 17, 19, 26–7, 179
Golden Temple, Amritsar, 83
Goldenberg scandal (Kenya), 199
Goodyear, 254
Gorbachev, President Mikhail, 196, 378,
Government of India Act (1935), 51, 55, 148
Government of National Unity (Angola), 391–2
Gowon, General Yakubu, (Head of Nigerian Federal Military Government), 263–6, 268–9, 280–2
Gramsci, Antonio, 7
Great Nigeria People's Party (GNPP), 296
Greater Portugal, 29, 398, 403–4
Green Revolution in South Asia, 15, 84, 87, 124, 135–6, 140, 142, 165, 405
Guinea, 186
Guinea-Bissau, 220, 223
Gujarat, 44, 57, 66, 80, 126, 160, 161

Gulf War (1991), 308
Gurmukhi script, 81

Habyarimana, Juvénal (President of Rwanda), 340–2, 344–6, 348–50, 357
Haile-Selassie (Emperor of Ethiopia), 2, 291
Hall, Margaret, 376
Hamites/Hamitic myth, 326, 329–30, 334, 339, 357
Hammarskjöld, Dag (UN Secretary General), 242–3, 245
Harijans ('children of God'), 149
Harrod–Domar growth model, 111
Haryana, 15–16, 81–2, 102, 135–6,
Hausa/Hausas, 12, 231, 261, 263, 265, 295, 297, 403
Hausa-Fulani, 228–9, 231, 257, 295
Havanna, 360
Herter, Christian (US Secretary of State), 78, 243
Hima, 333, 336
Hindi/Hindi belt, 12, 64, 66, 78–82, 153, 154, 162–5, 176–7; Hindi adopted as India's national language, 78–80; hostility to Hindi in Dravidian south, 164–5
Hindu Code acts, 56
Hindus, Hinduism, 1, 12, 82, 146–9, 151, 163
Hindustani, 12, 78
HIV/Aids, 181, 201, 225, 316
Hoeffler, Anke, 322
Hoomi Sena, 174
Hopkins, A.J., 24
Houphouët-Boigny, Félix (President of Côte d'Ivoire), 3, 182, 197, 210
Huambo, 364, 371, 381, 390–2; Democratic Republic of Angola proclaimed in, 371
Human Rights Watch, 317
Humphrey, Vice-President Hubert, 273
Hutu Power, 324, 347
Hutu revolution of 1959–60, 329–33, 341, 348, 356, 403
Hutu, 199, 323–7, 329–42, 344–58; disputed origins of the Hutu-Tutsi divide, 326; meaning of the term, 327–8; impact of colonialism on Hutu identity, 329, 357; emergence of Hutu political consciousness, 330 (*see also* Rwanda, Burundi *and* genocide)

Hyderabad (Pakistan), 92
Hyderabad, Indian princely state, 49, 59–60

Ibadan conference on Representative Government and Progress (1959), 401–2
Ibadan University, 213, 255, 257
Ibadan, 261
Ibo, 229, 231, 242, 255, 257, 259–60, 262–3, 269–70, 283, 295; massacres of, 1966, 265
Idi Amin, (Uganda Head of State), 190, 216, 224, 272, 342, 409
Idiagbon, Major-General Tunde (deputy leader of Nigerian military junta), 302
Igbo (language), 12
Ijeshas, 212, 322
Ileo, Joseph, 238, 244
India Independence Act (1947), 51
India, 1, 2, 4, 7–8, 10–15, 18–24, 31, 36–7, 40–1, 42–4, 46–9, 53–62, 66–8, 74, 78–82, 86, 94, 97–9, 101–2, Chapter 2 *passim*, Chapter 3 *passim*; 400, 402, 405, 408, 410; state crises of the 1970s, 7–8; British conquest of, 8; private and public investment in colonial India, 23–4; foreign trade sector, 32; institutional legacy of British Raj 54–5, 98; adopts Westminster model of democracy, 55; federalism, 58; linguistic reorganisation of the states, 78–80; growth of manufacturing, 128–9; landownership and landlessness, 140–2; life expectancy, 10, 137; literacy/illiteracy, 10, 137; proportion of the population living below the poverty line, 15–6, 21, 134–6; subsidised US grain imports, 13, 119; public sector, 116, 129–31; share of world trade, 106; political corruption under Mrs Gandhi, 124; 1967 elections, 64, 66, 121, 149, 169; 1971 elections, 68–9; 1977 elections, 101–4; *see also* caste in India; Indian Constitution; Green Revolution in South Asia; emergency in India

Indian Administrative Service, 55
Indian Civil Service, 50, 55,
Indian Constituent Assembly, 45, 55, 58
Indian Constitution, 49, 55–8, 64, 67, 70, 127, 145, 147, 149, 152, 160 ; Directive Principles of, 55, 57, 58, 70, 110, 127 ; People's Fundamental rights under, 55, 57, 127; 1st Amendment, 56; 44th Amendment, 57; 26th Amendment, 59; 25th Amendment, 70; 42nd Amendment, 127; implications of the Constitution for caste, 145, 147–8
Indian Five Year Plans, 105; First Plan, 111–13, 158; Second Plan, 114–17; Third Plan, 117–19; Fourth Plan, 123
Indian National Congress, 8, 22, 38–9, 44–5, 56, 58–60, 62–8,145, 400–1; electoral bases under Nehru, 62–3; 'split' under Mrs Gandhi, 67–8,124
Indian Planning Commission, 110–12, 118, 120, 123, 135, 137
Indian Police Service, 144
Indian Political Service, 50
Indian princes/princely states, 58–9
Indian States Reorganisation Commission, 80
Indian Supreme Court, 70, 127
Indian Union, 11, 15, 45, 46, 58, 60, 79, 156, 157, 401
indigena status (in Portuguese colonial Africa), 362, 367
indigénat (penal code in French colonial Africa), 28
indigenisation of the modern economy in Africa, 9, 35, 41, 190, 205
Indo-Chinese war (1962), 119
Indonesia, 99, 133, 219
Indo-Pakistan wars, (1948), 48–9; (1965), 82, 86, 119; (1971), 97–8
Indo-Soviet treaty, 69
Industrial Credit and Investment Corporation (Pakistan), 89
Industrial Development Bank of Pakistan, 89
Industrial Dispute Act (India), 130
Industrial Policy Resolutions (India, 1948 and 1956), 108, 110, 115

Industrial Policy Statement (India), 108
Industries (Development and Regulation) Act (India), 113, 121
Inga hydroelectric dam (Congo-Zaire), 273
interahamwe militia, 313
International Criminal Tribunal for Rwanda, 348, 350
International financial institutions (IFIs), 39, 194, 217, 219
International Monetary Fund (IMF), 217, 219, 252, 288, 292, 302, 305, 308, 385, 389, 395
International Panel of Eminent Personalities to investigate the Rwandan genocide, 356
International Rescue Committee, 200
Iranian Revolution, 1979, 104, 297
Ironsi, Major-General Johnson (Nigerian Head of State), 262–4
Iskander Mirza (Pakistani Defence Secretary), 71, 74–5, 77–8
Islam (in Mozambique), 373
Islam (in Nigeria), 256, 297–8
Islam/Islamisation (in Pakistan), 2, 42, 43, 45, 72, 85, 103–4, 402
Italian Christian Democracy, 62, 211
Izala movement (Nigeria), 297

Jains, 149
jajmani system, 14, 64, 151
Jama'at-i-Islami, 45, 85, 101,
Jamba, 382
Jammu and Kashmir Liberation Front, 49
Jammu and Kashmir, 47, 49, (*see also* Kashmir)
Jana Sangh, 170
Janata party/Janata government (1977–1980), 83, 102, 172–3, 175
Japan, 37, 89, 99, 106
Japanese Liberal Democrats, 62
jati/jatis, 149–51, 154–6
Jats, 161
Jinnah, Muhammad Ali (Governor General of Pakistan), 44, 45, 48, 51, 103
Johnson Administration, 119–20
Jonathan, Goodluck (President of Nigeria), 318
Joseph, Richard, 299
Justice Party (Madras Presidency), 162–3

Kabila, Joseph (President of the DRC), 318–20
Kabila, Laurent, (President of the DRC), 200, 313, 355
Kaduna mafia, 282, 301
Kaduna, 295
Kagame, Paul (Military Chief of RPF, President of Rwanda), 313, 349–51, 354
Kalenjin, the, 209
Kallas, 161
Kalonji, Albert, 238, 242, 246
Kamaraj, K., 65
Kamarck, Andrew, 15
Kamina air base, 383
Kampala, 347
Kannada (language), 80
Kano, 295, 297–8, 312, 406
Kano, Aminu, 257, 295,
Karachi, 40, 52, 54, 77, 97
Kargil conflict (1999), 99
Karnataka, 80, 411
Kasai, 237–8, 242, 245–6, 320
Kasavubu, Joseph (President of the DRC), 237, 239–40, 242–6, 249–50
Kashmir, 36, 47–9, 51, 91, 92, 97, 99, 168, 401; Kashmir conflict of 1948, 47–9; special status under the Indian Constitution, 49
Katanga, 234, 237–9, 241–6, 253, 267–8, 273, 289, 332 (*see also* Shaba)
Katangan Gendarmerie, 241, 249
Kaunda, Kenneth (President of Zambia), 5, 6, 219
Kayasthas, 168, 172–3
Kayibanda, Grégoire (President of Rwanda), 330–1, 339–40
Keno, Léon (Prime Minister of Congo-Zaire), 311
Kenya, 6, 16, 25, 181, 189–90, 193, 199, 209, 222, 386
Kerala, 15, 64, 66–7, 80, 138, 150, 153, 155, 156
Khalistan movement, 83
Khan, Liaquat Ali (Prime Minister of Pakistan), 47, 48, 71,
Khartoum, 223
Kigali, 200, 330, 344, 348–50
Kigeri Rwabugiri, *Mwami*, 328, 356
Kikuyu, 209
Kilvenmani atrocity, 166
Kimbanguist Church (Congo-Zaire), 273

Kinshasa, 200, 275, 289, 291, 305–7, 310, 319–20
Kinyarwanda (language), 332
Kirk-Greene, Anthony, 256, 261, 265
Kirundi (language), 332
Kissinger, Henry, (US National Security Advisor, later Secretary of State), 97, 370–1
Kivu province (DRC), 248, 313
Kolwezi, 289–90
Koris, 161, 168
Kothari, Rajni, 65
Krishak Sramik party, 73
Krupp, 254
Krushchev, Nikita, 243
Kshatriya (warrior archetype), 146, 150, 158, 160–1, 174
Kuba, 237
Kumar, Dharma, 167
Kunwar Sena, 174
Kurmis, 161, 174
Kwaja Nazimuddin (Prime Minister of Pakistan), 71–2
Kwango basin (Angola), 362
Kwanza basin (Angola), 362

Lagos, 212, 228, 232, 260–2, 266, 271, 279, 284, 312
Lahore, 47, 52, 89, 91
Lal Sena, 174
Lal, Deepak, 111, 141, 136, 142
Lambert, A., 316
Lancaster House settlement (1979), 379
Land Apportionment Act (1930 – Southern Rhodesia), 26
Langley, James (US ambassador to Pakistan), 77
Lara, Lucio, 396
Latin America, 204–5, 216
Laws of Manu, 148–9
Lebanese/Levantines in West Africa, 16, 17, 35, 230, 284–5, 406
Lemarchand, René, 325, 335, 339
Lenin, V.I., 110
Leopold II of the Belgians, 228
Léopoldville, 236, 239–50, 273, 364, 366 (*see also* Kinshasa)
Levine, Ross, 322
Leyland (automobile corporation), 254
life expectancy in Africa, 5, 10, 181, 411; in South Asia, 5, 10, 137, 411; in Nigeria and Congo-Zaire, 316, 411

Lingala (language), 323
Lingayat, 155
Lisbon coup of April 1974, 363, 365, 368
Livingstone, David, 27
Lohlé-Tart, L., 316
Loi cadre ('Framework' Law) of 1956, 3
Lok Sabha (Lower House of Indian Parliament), 55, 63–4, 66, 68, 70, 114, 147, 164
Lonsdale, John, 13, 25
Lorik Sena, 174
Lourenço Marques (now Maputo), 363
Lovanium University (Congo-Zaire), 273
Luanda, 323, 363
Lulua, the, 238, 242
Lumumba, Patrice (Prime Minister of the DRC), 228, 236, 239–45, 248, 270, 273, 310, 332
Lunda, the, 370
Lusaka accord (1974), 369
Lusophone Africa, 179, 190, 360, 363, 398

Machel, Samora, 366, 385
Madagascar, 190
Madhya Pradesh, 58, 66, 69,
Madras High Court, 166
Madras Municipal Corporation, 166
Madras Presidency/Madras State, 44, 56, 79, 80, 151, 153, 161–4, 166–7; anti-Brahminism in, 153, 164–6; *see also* Tamil Nadu
Madras University, 162
Mahalanobis, P.C., 114, 137
Maharashtra, 80, 152, 161
Mahbub ul Haq (Chief Economist of Pakistan Planning Commission), 90
Maiduguri (Nigeria), 298
Maier, Karl, 312
Maitatsine uprising (Kano, Nigeria), 297–8
Makonde, the, 365, 372
Makua, the, 365, 372
Malan, General Magnus (South African Minister of Defence), 379
Malawi, 6, 30, 183, 193
Malaysia, 33–4; growth of manufactured exports, 34
Maliki school of Muslim law, 229
Maluku steel mill (Congo-Zaire), 272

Malula, Cardinal (leader of the Catholic Church in Congo-Zaire), 274
Mamdani, Mahmood, 29, 344
Managing Agency Houses, 16, 122
Mandal, B.P., 148, 175–6, 178
'Mandalisation', 176–7
Mandela, Nelson, 5, 386
Maoism, in India, 173; in Africa, 247, 365, 404
Marwaris, 16, 53,
Matadi, 241
Mauritius, 34, 182
Mayalalam, 80
Mbeki, Thabo, (President of South Africa), 225
Mbembe, Achille, 224
Mbundu, the, 363–4, 390
median age in sub-Saharan Africa, 5
Mengistu Haile Mariam (President of Ethiopia), 196
mestiços (in Lusophone Africa), 362–4, 366, 374, 391, 398, 407
Methodism in Angola, 363
Mexico, 129, 136
Micombero, Michel (President of Burundi), 336–7
Mid-West Region (Nigeria), 260
Military Intelligence Directorate (South African), 379
Ministry of Defence (Nigeria), 279
Ministry of Economic Development (Nigeria), 278
Ministry of Steel and Industries (Nigeria), 278
Mishra, L.N., (Indian Foreign Trade Minister), 124
Mitterand, President François, 196–7
Mizos, 83
Mobutu, Joseph-Désiré, later Sese Seko (President of Congo-Zaire), 2, 196, 198, 201, 227, 244–5, 249–53, 272, 274–6, 283, 286–93, 298, 304–6, 309–11, 313, 315, 342, 355, 364, 369–70, 388, 393, 397, 407–8, 412; absolutist character of his rule, 272; diagnosis of 'Le mal zairois', 276; heads off democracy movement, 309–11; forced into exile, 313
Mobutu, Nzanga, 319
modern colonialism, 17–29
Mohammed Ali Bogra (Prime Minister of Pakistan), 72
Mohammed, Brigadier Murtala (Nigerian Head of State), 282, 293
Moi, Daniel arap (President of Kenya), 198–9, 209
Mondlane, Eduardo, 365
Monopolies and Restrictive Practices Act (India), 122, 133
Morocco, 290, 382
Morris-Jones, W.H., 100
Moscow, 61, 290, 360, 371
Mountbatten, Lord (Governor General of India in 1948), 47–8
Mouvement National Congolais (Kalonji – MNC(K)), 238
Mouvement National Congolais (MNC), 236–7
Mouvement populaire de la révolution (MPR – Congo-Zaire), 272–6
Mouvement Révolutionnaire National pour le Développement (MRND) (Rwanda), 340–1, 350
Mouvement Social Hutu, 330
Movement for the Emancipation of the Niger Delta, 318
Mozambique, 3, 15, 27, 41, 193, 209–10, 223, 359–61, 363, 365–9, 372, 375–81, 385–8, 393–5, 399, 403, 407, 411; compulsory cotton cropping, 361; Portuguese immigration, 363, 366; obstacles to unified nationalist movement, 365; nationalist insurgency, 367; economic development in the 1960s and early 1970s, 367–8; installation of the single-party state, 369; expansion of health and educational services after independence, 372; attractions of Marxism and the Soviet model of development, 373, 375–6; state farms and 'villagisation', 377; onset of civil war, 378–9; destruction of social infrastructure, 380; the peace process and the 1994 elections, 380–1, 385–8; dismantling the one-party state, 378, 394–5; economic liberalisation in the 1990s, 395
MPLA (Popular Movement for the Liberation of Angola), 210, 291, 359–62, 364–6, 368, 370–7, 378, 381–4, 388–91, 393–4, 399

Mugabe, Jean-Pierre, 349
Mugabe, Robert, 27
muhajirs (Muslim refugees in
    Pakistan), 46, 52–4
Mujibur Rahman Sheikh (Prime
    Minister of Bangladesh), 94, 96–7
Mukti Bahini (Bangladeshi freedom
    fighters), 93, 96–7
Mulele, Pierre (Maoist revolutionary
    in the DRC), 247–8
Mulungushi Declaration (1968), 189
Museveni, Yoweri (President of
    Uganda), 224–5, 313, 348
Musinga, *Mwami*, 328
Muslim Students Society (Nigeria),
    297
Muslims in India after 1947, 56, 63,
    149, 151, 162, 169–72
Mutara, *Mwami*, 331
Mutsinzi, Jean, 349
Myrdal, Gunnar, 15
Mysore, 154, 157

Nadars, 165
Nagas, 83
naira (Nigerian unit of currency), 280,
    285, 305, 308, 406
Namibia, 200, 371–2, 383–4 (*see also*
    South West Africa)
Narasimha Rao, P.V. (Prime Minister of
    India), 38, 130
Narayan, 'J.P.', 70–1, 126, 143, 171–2
National Commission to Study the
    Question of National Unity
    (Burundi), 338
National Conference (in Kashmir), 47
National Council of Nigeria and the
    Cameroons/National Council of
    Nigerian Citizens (NCNC), 231,
    233, 258–61, 295
National Party of Nigeria (NPP), 295–6
National Planning Commission
    (Mozambique), 376
National Republican Convention
    (Nigeria), 311
National Resistance Army (Uganda),
    224
National Security Council (Burundi),
    347
National Sovereign Conference
    (Congo-Zaire), 310
natural resource 'curse', 314
Nawaz Sharif (Prime Minister of
    Pakistan), 99

Naxalites, 67, 96, 173–4
Nayars, 156
Ndadaye, Melchior (President of
    Burundi), 324, 338, 345, 347, 357
Ndau, 379
Nehru, Jawaharlal (Prime Minister of
    India), 8, 40, 44, 45, 47–9, 62–4,
    68, 79, 80, 105, 107, 109, 110,
    113, 124, 137, 143, 146; sets up
    and chairs Indian Planning
    Commission, 107–11
Nehruvian socialism, 105, 123, 128,
    129, 132, 137
neo-colonialism/neo-colonial, 180,
    189, 234, 243, 246, 249, 268, 270,
    315, 332, 370, 403,
Neto, Agostinho (President of Angola),
    369, 374, 397
'new' international division of labour,
    34, 182
Newbury, David, 325, 327
Ngendandumwe, Pierre, 335
Nguema, Macias, 30
Niassa Company, 365
Niger Delta, 230, 271, 318
Niger, 297
Nigeria, 6, 10, 12–13, 15, 41, 99, 185,
    192, 194, 204, 209, 212, 216, 221–
    2, 226–35, 237, 242, 255–70, 276–
    86, 293–304, 307–9, 311–18,
    401–3; population figures, 226;
    Nigerianisation of civil service,
    227; colonial legacies, 228, 231;
    Nigerian Federation instituted,
    1954, 230, 231; produce
    marketing boards, 227, 229;
    Nigerian military, 227, 231, 262,
    264; First Republic, 1960–1966,
    255–70; 1962 census, 258; general
    strike (June 1964), 260–1; coups
    of 1966, 262–4; massacres of Ibos
    in 1967, 265; states
    reorganisation, 1967, 266; origins
    and course of the civil war,
    255–70; formation of Supreme
    Military Council, 262; Federal
    Military Government, 1966–1979,
    263, 267–8, 280, 283;
    Mohammed–Obasanjo years,
    1975–9, 282; Second Republic,
    1979–1983, 293–301; oil exports
    and the oil boom, 230, 271, 276–
    8; growth of manufacturing, 230,
    281; ethnicity, political

Nigeria – *continued*
partisanship and ethnic violence,
227, 231, 233, 256, 264, 270, 294;
political corruption and
prebendalism, 232, 298; capital
flight, 271; primary school
enrolment, 279, 301; creation of
new states, 1976, 280; increase in
public employment, 280; food
prices and agriculture, 280–1;
Nigerianisation of the modern
economy, 283–6; 1979
Constitution, 294; 1977 Electoral
decree, 294; oil recession of early
1980s, 299–300; military coup of
December 1983 and re-
installation of military
government, 300–2; joins
Organisation of the Islamic
Conference, 302; structural
adjustment under Babangida,
307–8; proportion of the
population below the poverty
line, 308–9; creation of new
states, 1991, 311; presidential
election of 1993, 311–2; elections
of 2007, 317; criminalisation of
government, 317–18
Nigerian civil war (1968–70), 227,
267–9
Nigerian Enterprises Promotion Board,
284
Nigerian Enterprises Promotion
Decree, 1972, 283; amended
1977, 284–5
Nigerian Federal Executive Council,
266, 268
Nigerian National Alliance, 260
Nigerian National Democratic Party
(NNDP), 260–1
Nigerian National Petroleum
Corporation (NNPC), 278
Nigerian National Students Union, 262
Nigerian People's Party (NPP), 295–6
Nigerian Second National
Development Plan, 1970–4, 283
Nigerian Security Organisation/State
Security Service, 301, 309
Nigerian Supreme Court, 294, 296
Nigerian Supreme Military Council,
262–5, 282
Nixon, President Richard, 97
Nizam-i-Mustafa ('Rule of the
Prophet'), 102

Nkomati Accord (1984), 381
Nkrumah, Kwame (President of
Ghana), 5, 27, 179, 182, 185–6,
191, 239, 259
non-alignment, championed by India,
42, 64, 109, 142
North Korea, 274, 290
North West Frontier Province
(Pakistan), 51
Northern Elements Progressive Union
(NEPU – Northern Nigeria), 257,
260, 295,
Northern Nigeria, Protectorate of, 229
Northern People's Congress (NPC),
231, 257–61, 295
Northern Region of Nigeria, 231,
257–8, 295
Northern Rhodesia, 16, 30 (*see also*
Zambia)
Ntaryamira, Cyprien (President of
Burundi), 346
Nyangoma, Gervais (Hutu political
leader in post-independence
Burundi), 335–6
Nyasaland, 6, 30 (*see also* Malawi)
Nyerere, Julius (President of Tanzania),
186, 267, 365
Nyiginya dynasty (Rwanda), 328
Nzeogwu, Major Chukwuma (leader of
January 1966 coup in Nigeria),
262

Obasanjo, Brigadier Olesugun,
(President of Nigeria), 282, 312,
317
Obote, Milton (President of Uganda),
30, 186, 224, 403
Ogoni, the, 304
Ojukwu, Lieut-Colonel Odumwegwu
(Military Governor of Nigeria's
Eastern Region, Biafran Head of
State), 263–6
Olenga, Nicolas, 248
Oliver, Roland, 327
Onitsha, 232
OPEC (Organisation of Petroleum
Exporting Countries), 205, 278,
Organisation of African Unity (OAU),
179, 249, 267, 323, 335, 356,
370
Organisation of the Islamic
Conference, 302
Orientale province (DRC), 239
Orissa, 15, 66, 126

'Other Backward Classes' or OBCs
(India), 152, 160, 163, 165, 167,
173, 175
Ouku, Robert, 198
Overseas Development Assistance
(ODA), 222
Ovimbundu, the, 363, 370, 384,
390–1
Oyo, 212

Pakistan Constituent Assemblies
(first), 51–2, 72–4; (second), 76
Pakistan Industrial Development
Corporation, 53
Pakistan Muslim League, 85, 90
Pakistan People's Party (PPP), 95,
Pakistan Planning Commission, 84, 89
Pakistan, 1, 2, 4, 10, 31, 36, 40–54, 58,
69, 71–8, 81, 82–104, 122, 133,
134, 143, 221, 400–2, 405,
408–11; war with India over
Kashmir, 1948, 47–9; political
economy of defence and defence
expenditure, 40, 50; development
of manufacturing in, 54; 'guided
democracy' under Ayub Khan,
83–90; industrial boom under
Ayub Khan, 86–7; agriculture and
the Green Revolution in, 87–8;
'functional inequality' under
Ayub Khan, 90; war with India
(1965), 82, 119; war with India
(1971), 97–8; 1977 elections in,
101–14; Islamisation under Zia
ul-Haq, 42, 103–4 (*see also* East
Pakistan *and* West Pakistan)
Pakistani Communist Party, 74
Pakistani Constitutions (1956) 76;
(1962), 84–5; (1973), 101
Pakistani land reform (1959), 90
Pakistani Supreme Court, 75
panchayats/panchayati raj, 111, 140,
158–60
paraiyans, 152–3, 162, 165–6
Parti de la Libération du Peuple Hutu
(PALIPEHUTU) (Burundi), 338,
347, 353
Parti Démocratique Chrétien
(Burundi), 334
Parti du Mouvement de
l'Emancipation Hutu
(PARMEHUTU), 331–2, 339
Parti solidaire africain (PSA – DRC),
248

partition of India (1947)/partition of
Punjab and Bengal, 1, 20, 43, 46–
9, 51, 52, 72, 74, 79, 81, 82, 153,
169, 400
Party for Democracy and Regeneration
(Rwanda), 354
'passive' revolution, concept of, 8–9
Patel, Sardar (Indian States Minister),
45, 58, 79, 110
Patidars, 161
patrimonial rule in post-colonial
Africa, 41, 192, 211
Peel, J.D.Y., 212
People's Democratic Party (Nigeria),
317
People's Redemption Party (PRP –
Nigeria), 295
'permit-licence-subsidy Raj', 108, 143,
147, 409
Pervez Musharaff, General (President
of Pakistan), 99
Petrofina, 363
Pondichéry, 20
Poona Pact, 148–9
Port Harcourt, 232, 318
Portugal/Portuguese New State, 361
Portuguese (language), 323
Portuguese colonialism in Africa, 19,
28–9, 361–3
Portuguese Communist Party, 364,
373
post-colonialism, defined, 29–31
Potti Sriramalu, 80
Presidential Transition Committee
(Nigeria), 298
Pretoria Accord (2002), 318
Pretoria, 360
Primavera cotton plantation, 362
Protestant Church of Zaire, 273
Punjab University, 91
Punjab, Indian, 15–16, 66, 80, 81, 83,
102, 135, 136
Punjab, Pakistani, 48, 76, 85, 87, 88,
Punjab, undivided, 20, 44, 45
Punjabi speakers in India, 80–1
Punjabis in Pakistan, 76

Quit India movement of 1942, 44,
126, 161
Qureshi family in Pakistani Punjab, 85

Radio Télévision Libre des Milles
Collines (Rwanda), 344
Rajasthan, 58, 66, 69, 92, 161,

Rajputs, 160, 168–9, 172–4
Ramachandran, M.G. (MGR), 165–6
Rampura, 154–5
Ranadive, B.T., 60
Rassemblement Congolais pour la
 Démocratie, 355
Rawagasore, Prince Louis, 334
Rawaswami Naicker, E.V., (EVR), 164
Rawlings, Jerry (President of Ghana),
 209, 219–20
Razakars, 60
Reagan Administration, 193, 291, 379,
 382–3
Reconstruction Committee of the
 Council (India), 108
Refugees and displaced persons in
 Africa, 193, 199
RENAMO (Mozambique National
 Resistance Movement), 377–81,
 384–8, 393
Renault, 254
Reserve Bank of India, 133
Review of African Political Economy, 218
Reykjavik summit (1986), 378
Reyntjens, Filip, 349–50
Rhodesia, 27, 359, 365, 369, 372
Rhodesian Central Intelligence
 Organisation, 378
Rhodesian Front Party, 27
Rimmer, Douglas, 211, 232
Rivers State (Nigeria), 318
Roberto, Holden (Leader of the FNLA),
 364, 390
Roman Law in colonial Africa, 28
Rudolph, Lloyd, 153
Rudolph, Susanne, 153
Ruzibiza, Abdul Joshua, 349–50
Rwanda, 2, 41, 199–200, 313, 318,
 322–36, 339–44, 346–53, 355–7,
 403, 411; colonial impact on,
 328–9, 357; registration of ethnic
 identities, 329; overthrow of the
 monarchy and independence,
 332; Economic and Customs
 Union with Burundi, 333; First
 Republic, 1962–73, 339–40; coup
 of 1973 and installation of single-
 party state, 339–40; Second
 Republic, 340–3; population
 growth and land–labour ratio,
 342–3; impact of falling coffee
 prices on incomes, 343; economic
 crisis and structural adjustment,
 344; RPF invasion and civil war,
 341–2; background to and onset
 of the 1994 genocide, 348–50;
 elections of 2003, 351 (*see also*
 Hutu *and* Tutsi)
Rwandan Patriotic Army, 349, 355
Rwandan Patriotic Front (RPF), 199,
 341–2, 344–5, 347–8, 350–1,
 353–5

Said, Edward (author of *Orientalism*),
 7
Saigol industrial dynasty (Pakistan),
 89
Saigol, Rafique, 89
Salazar, Antonio (Prime Minister of
 the Portuguese 'New State'), 366,
 373, 403
Salisbury (Harare), 360
Samyukta Socialist Party, 153
'Sanskritisation', 150, 156, 170
São Tomé, 363
Saraswats, 151
Saro-Wiwa, Ken, 303
Savimbi, Jonas (Leader of UNITA),
 364–5, 370–1, 381–5, 388, 390–3
Scheduled Castes and Scheduled
 Tribes (India), 55–6, 63, 147–8,
 151–2, 163, 165–72, 175–6, 178
Seeley, John (author of *The Expansion
 of England*), 18
Senegal, 189, 204, 217
Shaba, 289–90, 305, 382 (*see also*
 Katanga)
Shagari, Shehu (President of Nigeria),
 286, 296, 298, 299
Shari'a law in Nigeria, 257, 294, 409
Shari'a law in Pakistan, 101
Shastri, Lal (Prime Minister of India),
 65, 120
Shona (language), 379
Short, Clare (UK Minister for Overseas
 Development), 353
Shulz, George (US Secretary of State),
 383
Sierra Leone, 182
Sikhs/Sihkism, 46, 56, 80, 82, 83, 149,
 see also Akali Dal
Simla Peace Agreement (1972), 99
Sindh/Sindhis, 77, 92
Singh, Charan (Indian Finance
 Minister), 172, 175
Singh, Inderjit, 141
Singh, Manmohan (Indian Finance
 Minister), 39

Singh, V.P. (Indian Prime Minister), 175

Sithole, Ndabanangi (leader of Zimbabwe African National Union), 27, 407–8

Sklar, Richard, 215

Smith, Ian (Rhodesian Prime Minister), 27

Social Democratic Party (Nigeria), 311

Société Générale, 234

Sofala province (Mozambique), 378

Sokoto Caliphate, 26, 229, 256

Sokoto Province, 12, 257

Somalia, 182, 190, 223

SONANGOL (Angolan State Oil Corporation), 396

Soumialot, Gaston, 248–9

South African Defence Forces, 378–9

South Asia, 1–4, 10–16, 20, 24, 31–2, 35, 37, 39, 40–1, Chapter 1 *passim*, 43, 96–7, 99, 101, 103, 128, 181, 191, 194, 196, 202–3, 221; proportion of the population living below poverty line in 2005, 31, 202; in the 1980s, 194; spending on health and education in late 1990s, 221

South East Asia, 1, 17, 193, 204, 236

South Korea, 111, 116, 122, 132, 218, 405

South Sudan, 223

South West Africa (Mandate territory), 382 (*see also* Namibia)

South West Africa People's Organisation (SWAPO), 382,

Southern Rhodesia, 10–11, 19, 26, 30 (*see also* Rhodesia)

Soviet Five Year Plans, 107

Soviet Union, 64, 69, 128, 193, 246, 268, 369, 378, 384, 389

Speke, J.H., 326

Spínola, General (Head of Portuguese junta), 368

Spivak, Gayatri, 31

Srinivas, M.N., 154–6

Sripuram, 161

Stalin, Joseph, 60

Stanleyville (Kisangani), 240, 244–9

Subaltern Studies, 7–9

Subramaniam, C. (Indian Food and Agriculture Minister), 119

Sudra (labourer or farmer archetype)/Sudra castes, 138, 150, 160–3, 165, 168–70, 172, 175

Swahili, 319, 329, 365

Taiwan, 122

Talbot, Ian, 45

Tamil Nadu, 57, 80, 161–7

Tamil/Tamils, 79, 80, 153

Tanganyika, 12, 28, 28 (*see also* Tanzania)

Tanzania, 15, 189, 203, 209, 267, 319, 336, 342, 348, 353, 377

Tashkent Declaration (1965), 91, 94

Telangana, communist insurrection in, 59–61

Telugu (language), 79

Thanajavur district, 165–6

Thatcher, Mrs, 388

Togo, 189, 206

Touré, Sekou (President of Guinea), 186

Trade Licensing Act (Kenya), 190

Tripura, 46

Tshisekedi, Etienne (Prime Minister of Congo-Zaire), 309–11

Tshombe, Moise (President of Katanga, subsequently Prime Minister of the DRC), 237–8, 241–2, 245–6, 249–50, 252–3, 264; proclaims Katanga's independence, 241

Tutsi, 313, 323–38, 340–2, 350–2; accorded a privileged status by the Belgians, 326–7, 329; meaning of the term, 327; disputed origins of the Tutsi, 327–8; Tutsi exodus from Rwanda, 1961–2, 332; massacres of 1963–4, 332; Tutsi dictatorship in Burundi, 333, 335–7; Tutsi excluded from public employment in Rwanda and the National University, 339–40; massacres of Tutsi between 1991 and 1994, 341; genocide of Tutsi, 1994, 342, 348; installation of Tutsi ethnocracy under RPF, 351, 354 (*see also* Rwanda, Burundi *and* genocide)

Tutsi, Congolese, 313

Twa, 324, 352

Udoji Commission (Nigeria), 280

Uganda, 349, 355

ujaama villages (Tanzania), 377

Ukraine, 392

UN Decolonisation Mission to Rwanda and Burundi, 330

UN High Commission for Refugees, 351
UN Mission to the Congo (MONUC), 317
UN Operation in Mozambique (ONUMOZ), 387
UNAVEM (United Nations Angola Verification Mission), 389–90, 392
Unilever, 406
Union Councils (India), 159
Union Katangaise, 237
Union Minière du Haut Katanga (UMHK), 234, 237, 241–2, 253
Union Nationale du Rwanda, 331
Union of South Africa, 2, 193, 222, 233, 305, 326, 359, 368–72, 379–82, 384, 388
Union of the Peoples of Northern Angola, 364
Union pour la démocratie et le progrès social (UDPS) (Congo-Zaire), 309
Union pour le progrès national (UPRONA), 334–5, 338, 345–6
Union Sacrée (Congo-Zaire), 310
UNITA (National Union for the Total Independence of Angola), 359, 364–6, 370–2, 377–9, 381–5, 387–93
United Africa Company, 406
United Front (in East Pakistan), 73, 75
United Nations Security Council, 48, 246, 392
United Nations, 2, 48, 242–6, 267, 331–3, 335, 351–2, 387–8, 400, 403
United Progressive Grand Alliance (Nigeria), 260–1
United Provinces (colonial India), 44,
United States of America (USA), 42, 69, 72–3, 76, 89, 91, 97, 115, 119, 201, 243, 246, 249, 253, 268, 290–2, 308, 366, 379, 383, 389–90
Unity Party of Nigeria (UNP), 295
'untouchables'/'untouchability', 62, 99, 128, 146–9, 151, 154, 155, 158, 162, 164–6, 169, 172, 177 (*see also* Harijans *and* Dalits)
Urdu, 12, 52, 72–3, 76, 89; imposed as national language of Pakistan by Jinnah, 52
Urquhart, Brian, 243
US Central Intelligence Agency (CIA), 244, 290
US Congress, 304, 372

US Consul General in Dhaka, 96
Uttar Pradesh, 32, 63, 65, 92, 102, 106, 126, 136, 139, 142, 152–3, 160–1, 176, 411
Uwilingiyimina, Agathe (Prime Minister of Rwanda), 348

Vaishya (merchant archetype), 150
Vanniyars, 165
varna conception of the social order, 149–50
Vatican, the, 274, 386
Vedas/Vedic scriptures, 150
Vellalas, 161
Vidal, Claudine, 340, 349

Walle, Nicholas van de, 222
Washbrook, David, 166
'Washington' consensus, 219, 305
Weiner, Myron, 62
West Africa, 17, 24, 26, 32, 35, 188, 204, 209, 214, 268, 401; pre-colonial West Africa, 26
West Bengal, 1, 46, 64, 66–7, 74, 138, 141, 160, 177
West Pakistan, 46, 50, 54, 65, 72, 73, 75, 76, 86, 87, 88, 89, 90, 93–9, 405; growth of manufacturing in, 54, 86
Western Region of Nigeria, 229, 232, 235, 255, 258–60, 266, 295; House of Assembly, 259; regional elections of October 1965, 261
Willink Commission (Nigeria, 1958), 256
Wilson, Harold (British Prime Minister), 268
Windhoek, 389
Witwatersrand, 365
World Bank, 15, 39, 89, 120, 195–6, 203, 207, 217–20, 306–8, 342–3, 389, 395, 410

Yadav (Sudra caste grouping), 160, 168, 170, 172, 173–4
Yahya Khan, General (Pakistani Head of State), 92–6
Yar'Adua, Major-General Shehu (Vice-President of Nigeria), 312
Yoruba, 12, 212, 229, 231, 258–62, 267, 283, 295, 312, 322, 426
Young, Crawford, 39, 223, 248, 290
Young, Robert, 31
Young, Tom, 376

Zaire (province of Angola), 390
zaire (unit of currency in Congo-
    Zaire), 306–7
Zaire, *see* Congo-Zaire
Zakir Hussain, (President of India),
    68
Zambezi river/Zambezi valley, 11,
    367–8, 386
Zambia, 5, 15, 16, 30, 187–90, 192,
    194, 219, 221, 267, 289, 305, 382

zamindars/zamindari abolition, 23, 45,
    58, 73, 138–9, 142, 158, 169
Zanzibar, Sultanate of, 403
Zia il-Haq, General (President of
    Pakistan), 42, 102–4, 402
Zimbabwe, 1, 2, 179–82, 200, 221, 386
Zimbabwe African National Union
    (ZANU), 27
Zimbabwean National Liberation
    Army (ZANLA), 379